ON THE RAILS
AROUND
EUROPE

A Comprehensive Guide to Europe by Train

Edited by Melissa Shales

A Thomas Cook Touring Handbook

PASSPORT BOOKS
a division of *NTC Publishing Group*

Thomas
Cook

Published by Passport Books,
a division of NTC Publishing Group,
4255 West Touhy Avenue,
Lincolnwood (Chicago),
Illinois 60646-1975 U.S.A.

ISBN 0-8442-9037-8
Library of Congress Catalog Card
   Number: 93: 87202

Published by Passport Books in conjunction with
the Thomas Cook Group Ltd

Project Editor: Giovanna Battiston
Map Editor: Bernard Horton
Rail information verified by the staff of the
   Thomas Cook European Timetable
Additional research: Christopher J. Bane

Cover design by Greene Moore Lowenhoff
London Underground map © London Regional
   Transport. LRT Registered User No. 94/1969
London city centre map: Lovell Johns Ltd, Oxon
Text typeset in Frutiger using Advent 3B2 desk-
   top publishing system
Maps and diagrams created using GST
   Designworks
Output by Riverhead Typesetters Ltd, Grimsby
Printed in Great Britain by Bell & Bain Ltd,
   Glasgow

The Writing Team

Edited by Melissa Shales
Written and researched by:
Carol Sykes
Stephen Blyth
Louise Rosen

Additional material by:
Paul Duncan
Robin Gauldie
Jim Keeble
Nicholas Parsons
Martin Rosser

Acknowledgments

Thomas Cook Publishing would like to thank the
following people for all their hard work and co-
operation during the research for this book:
Marielle Albers, The Netherlands Board of
Tourism, London; Elvira Balčiunaite, Lithuania;
Monica Brenchley, German Rail Passenger
Services, UK; Adam Campbell, British Rail;
Tonia Chassapladakis, Thomas Cook Greece;
Amadeo Confessore; The Danish Tourist Board,
UK; Jurate and Liuda Daugiliene, Lithuania;
Explore Worldwide, Aldershot, UK; The Finnish
Tourist Board, UK; Anita Gajdecki; Frank Green;
Ben Haines, London; Lotte Henrikson, Copenha-
gen Tourist Office; Saul Hudson; Andrew
Janczak, Orbis Travel, Warsaw, Poland; Fiona
Kelly, Thomas Cook Travel Archive, UK; Len
Krusegaard, Maersk Travel, Copenhagen, De
mark; Dr Eric Le Fevre, Thomas Cook UK; M
Lunn; John and Eleanor Moe, Norway;
Mills, SNCF; Nomad Safari, Budapest, Hu
The Norwegian Tourist Board, UK; Lucy
Latvia; Andy Parsons; Jeffrey A. Penni
Bucharest; Martha Peterson, Denmark; (
Piciorea; Kate Rew; Dominic Shales;
Symington; The Swedish Tourist Boar
Kashka Szuba, Poland; Danail Todorof
Travel, Slovakia; Conchitta Vamonde,
Tourist Office, London; Frank and Rosi Ve
Davis, IYHF London, UK.

CONTENTS

Introduction	4
How to Use This Book	4
Route Map	6
Route Finders	8
Recommended Routes	8
Through Routes	9
Travel Essentials	10
Travelling by Train	22
Country by Country	30
Sample Itineraries	79
ROUTES AND CITIES	84

*To find a route quickly, use the Route
Map on p. 6 or the Route Finder on p. 8.
To find a town or city quickly, look in the
index, pp. 416–418.*

Special Trains	413
Steam Trains and Little Railways	413
Luxury and Cruise Trains	414
Conversion Tables	415
Index of Places and Subjects	416
Reader Survey	419

INTRODUCTION

Even if the politicians are determined to ignore them, people like trains. Some are completely obsessive on the subject, others merely enjoy the freedom and the buzz that comes from looking at an international departures board.

Setting aside the vast army of commuters and business travellers, European train travellers fall into two main categories. Some choose to dash across the continent, then stop and explore a smaller area in detail. Then there are the hardened travellers – the mainly young and penniless Inter-Railers, and the Eurail pass holders, who are determined to cram as many places as possible into one trip. These superb passes have introduced generations of travellers to Europe, and have given many thousands of people an affordable chance to spread their wings, have an adventure and see foreign places. Most have become confirmed rail addicts.

We hope that *On the Rails Around Europe* will prove useful and entertaining to all rail travellers. However, it would be impossible to cover 25 countries in exhaustive detail and we do realise that there are gaps. Because of the situation in the former Yugoslavia, we have not included the area in this edition. Nor have we dealt with Russia. Britain and Ireland will have their own book in this series, and so we include only London in this volume, because it is the starting point for so many journeys. Much of the information may seem to relate mainly to the young and hard-up. This is not to exclude those with a bit more cash, who will see on second glance that most of the book is just as relevant to them, but merely reflects the fact that those on a really tight budget need more help to survive.

To make your journey smoother, we advise that you also take a copy of the latest, monthly *Thomas Cook European Timetable* (*ETT*), which has much more detailed timetabling (see p. 21). If you plan to make any longer stops, consider buying individual guidebooks, such as the *Thomas Cook Traveller* guides (see p. 21). If you want to keep the weight down, however, we have listed local information points, including stations and tourist offices. Remember always to check station timetables, because there are many more short-distance trains available than the *ETT* has room for.

Finally, we have done exhaustive research to try and make this book as accurate as possible, but things do change. We apologise in advance if you find any errors, and would be very grateful if you could write in with alterations, additions and suggestions to help us improve the next edition.

HOW TO USE THIS BOOK

ROUTES AND CITIES

In these days of the rail pass and the European Union (EU), people tend not to restrict their journeys to one country. The format of this book reflects the way they actually travel, with detailed descriptions of 27 **key cities**, right across Europe, linked by 48 **recommended routes**. These are arranged in alphabetical order – each city chapter is followed by the routes which begin there. **Smaller cities** and **towns** are described along the line of the route on which they lie. In all, the book describes well over 200 cities and towns, and many other smaller places. There are clear cross-references throughout the text and on the route diagrams.

To avoid repetition, each route is described only once, but they are all designed to be used in either direction, e.g. Athens–Istanbul can be easily read and followed by those travelling Istanbul–Athens. We have tried to choose the most logical direction and most routes fan out across Europe from the north-west (i.e. ex-London, Amsterdam and Paris).

WITHIN EACH ROUTE

→ Fast Track

This describes the quickest and most direct journey between the key cities at the beginning and end of each route.

⤳ On Track

This introduces the full route, with times and other train details along the series of recommended stops. Train frequencies, approximate schedules and journey times are given for each segment. Details are deliberately general, so they will not date too fast, but they should give you a clear idea of how convenient any section of the journey will be. The On Track routing does not necessarily follow the shortest line between the key cities. Occasionally, the corresponding Fast Track may go in an entirely different direction (as an example, see Frankfurt–Zurich, on p. 184).

Obviously you do not have to stop at every town we mention and you can often find faster trains to take you from town A to town C without stopping in town B. There simply isn't space to give every combination of these, but local information and the *ETT* will fill in the gaps.

Route Diagrams

These show, in visual form, the line of the route; the various stops; the fastest time between the two end points; journey times between stops; inter-connecting routes (marked by a black arrow); side-tracks (marked by a white arrow); border crossings; and where you need to catch a ferry.

Recommended Stops

Train details are followed by a series of descriptions, of varying length and detail, of recommended stops. These highlight the best options available, but do not cover Europe, or even the routes, comprehensively. Ask the local tourist office for more detail on surrounding options.

◠ Side Tracks from . . .

You will frequently find this heading at the end of a stop. It is used to describe the very best sights, towns and even regions off the main route. Some side tracks are given a full description; others (usually for reasons of space) are merely mentioned as a way of drawing your attention to a place you may like to visit.

THE REST OF THE BOOK

Travel Essentials is a brief alphabetical section of general advice for the traveller, such as what to take, and how to stay safe. **Travel by Train** takes a more detailed look at how the European rail network works, with information and advice on everything from sleeper cars to rail passes and where to buy them. **Country by Country** is designed to provide a brief and basic run-down on each of the 25 countries covered in the book. To avoid repetition, anything common to many destinations within the country has been included here, so always look at this section together with any city or town description. On pp. 79–83 is a selection of **Sample Itineraries**, designed to show the potential of rail travel for fast, snappy tours, involving many countries or tracking a particular theme.

The quickest way to find information on any place, large or small, and on general topics, is to look it up in the **Index** on pp. 416–418. The easiest way to look up a route is to consult the **Master Route Map** overleaf or the **Route Finder** on p. 8. People who wish to reach their destination in a hurry, but don't want to fly, should turn to **Through Routes** on p. 9, which details additional direct long-distance routes.

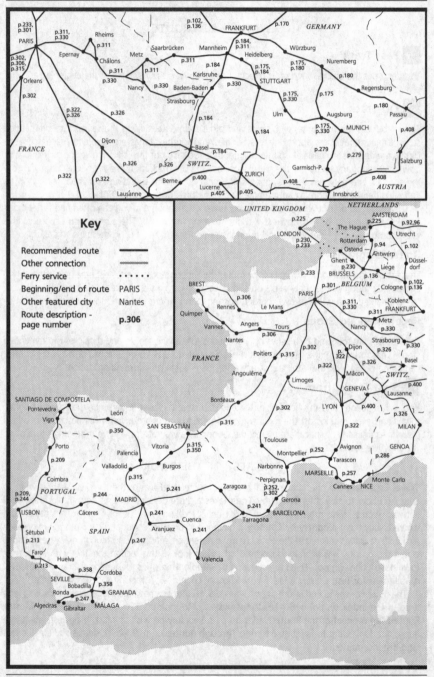

Key

Recommended route	———
Other connection	~~~~~
Ferry service	· · · · ·
Beginning/end of route	PARIS
Other featured city	Nantes
Route description - page number	**p.306**

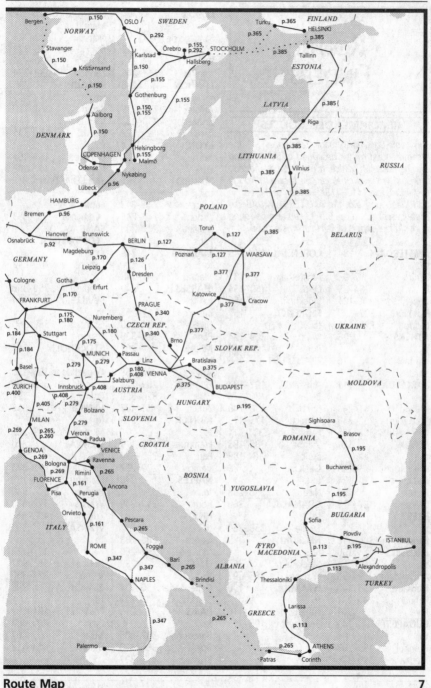

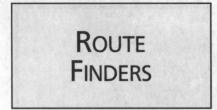

ROUTE FINDERS

RECOMMENDED ROUTES

This table lists, with page references, all the recommended routes described in the text and the key cities in which routes begin and end (other towns and cities can be located through the Index, pp. 416–418). Routes are listed in both directions, e.g. the AMSTERDAM to Berlin route described on pp. 92–93 can also be found in this table under 'BERLIN to Amsterdam'.

AMSTERDAM	84
to . . .	
Berlin	92–93
Brussels	94–95
Copenhagen	96–101
Frankfurt	102–107
London	225–229
ATHENS	108
to . . .	
Istanbul	112–116
Milan	265–268
BARCELONA	117
to . . .	
Madrid	241–243
Marseille	252–256
Paris	302–305
BERLIN	121
to . . .	
Amsterdam	92-93
Frankfurt	170–174
Prague	126
Warsaw	127–129
BREST	308
to . . .	
Paris	306–310
BRUSSELS	130
to . . .	
Amsterdam	94–95
Frankfurt	136–140
London	230–232
Paris	301
BUDAPEST	141
to . . .	
Istanbul	195–203
Vienna	375–376

COPENHAGEN	146
to . . .	
Amsterdam	96–101
Oslo	150–154
Stockholm	155–156
FLORENCE	157
to . . .	
Milan	269–274
Rome	161–165
FRANKFURT	166
to . . .	
Amsterdam	102–107
Berlin	170–174
Brussels	136–140
Munich	175–179
Paris	311–314
Vienna	180–183
Zurich	184–189
GENOA	288
to . . .	
Nice	286–288
GRANADA	360
to . . .	
Seville	358–360
HELSINKI	395
to . . .	
Stockholm	365
Warsaw	385–397
ISTANBUL	190
to . . .	
Athens	113–116
Budapest	195–203

LISBON	204
to . . .	
Santiago de	
Compostela	209–212
Seville	213–215
Madrid	244–246
LONDON	216
to . . .	
Amsterdam	225–229
Brussels	230–232
Paris	233
LYON	324
to . . .	
Zurich	400–404
MADRID	235
to . . .	
Barcelona	241–243
Lisbon	244–246
Malaga	247–248
Paris	315–321
MALAGA	248
to . . .	
Madrid	247–248
MARSEILLE	249
to . . .	
Barcelona	252–256
Nice	257-260
Paris	322–329
MILAN	261
to . . .	
Athens	265–268
Florence	269–274
Paris	326–329
Zurich	405-407
MUNICH	275
to . . .	
Frankfurt	175–179
Paris	330–334
Venice	279–282
NAPLES	348
to . . .	
Rome	347–349
NICE	283
to . . .	
Genoa	286–288
Marseille	257–260
OSLO	289
to . . .	
Copenhagen	150–154
Stockholm	292
PARIS	293
to . . .	
Barcelona	302–305
Brest	306–310
Brussels	301

Frankfurt	311–314
Madrid	315–321
Marseille	322–325
Milan	326–329
Munich	330–334
London	233–234
PRAGUE	335
to . . .	
Berlin	126
Vienna	340
ROME	341
to . . .	
Florence	161–165
Naples	347–349
SAN SEBASTIAN	319
to . . .	
Santiago de	
Compostela	350–353
SANTIAGO DE	
COMPOSTELA	350
to . . .	
Lisbon	209–212
San	
Sebastian	350–353
SEVILLE	354
to . . .	
Granada	358–360
Lisbon	213–215
STOCKHOLM	361
to . . .	
Copenhagen	155–156
Helsinki	365–366
Oslo	292
VENICE	366
to . . .	
Munich	279–282
VIENNA	370
to . . .	
Budapest	375–376
Frankfurt	180–183
Prague	340
Warsaw	377–380
Zurich	408–412
WARSAW	381
to . . .	
Berlin	127–129
Helsinki	385–397
Vienna	377–380
ZURICH	398
to . . .	
Frankfurt	184–189
Lyon	400–404
Milan	405–407
Vienna	408–412

THROUGH ROUTES

Some travellers wish to make their way as quickly as possible to a chosen city to begin their more leisurely travel from that point. This will often mean going through two or more consecutive routes in this book without stopping.

The following table shows a selection of possible longer 'through routes', as an aid to journey planning, with approximate summer frequencies and journey times. All these through routes may also be taken in the reverse direction to that shown but number of trains per day may differ. Some of the trains require payment of supplements and many involve overnight travel. Not all services are daily. Always consult the International Section in the latest issue of the Thomas Cook European Timetable (ETT), which gives up-to-date schedules for these and many other international long-distance trains.

Note: Services shown from London will alter considerably with the introduction of services from London to Brussels via the Channel Tunnel from late 1994 onwards.

Through route	ETT table number	Approx journey time	Trains per day	Notes
Amsterdam–Venice	39	17 hrs	1	Change at Milan
Amsterdam–Milan	39	14 hrs	1	Direct
Amsterdam–Naples	39	21 hrs	1	Change at Milan
Amsterdam–Rome	39	19 hrs	1	Change at Milan
Amsterdam–Vienna	35	14 hrs	1	Direct
Barcelona–Lyon	81	8 hrs	1	Change at Valence
Brussels–Milan	43	12 hrs	2	Direct
Brussels–Rome	43	17–18 hrs	3	Direct or change at Milan
Brussels–Zurich	40	8 hrs	3	Direct or change at Basel
Cologne–Milan	73	10–11 hrs	3	Direct
Cologne–Rome	73	15–16 hrs	2	Direct or change at Milan
Frankfurt–Warsaw	55	19 hrs	1	Direct
London–Berlin	23	21-22 hrs	1	Via ferry Ramsgate–Ostend
London–Cologne	20	9–10 hrs	5	All via ferry Ramsgate–Ostend
London–Copenhagen	21	23 hrs	1	Via ferry Ramsgate–Ostend; alternative route, ferry Harwich–Esbjerg, 27 hrs
London–Hamburg	21	17 hrs	1	Via ferry Ramsgate–Ostend; alternative route, ferry Harwich–Hamburg, 24 hrs
London–Rome	43	17 hrs	1	Via ferry Dover–Calais
London–Warsaw	24	25 hrs	1	Via ferry Ramsgate–Ostend, and change at Brussels
London–Zurich	40	20 hrs	1	Via ferry Ramsgate–Ostend
Paris–Barcelona	47	11–13 hrs	4	Direct or change at Port Bou or Montpellier
Paris–Berlin	25	12 hrs	3	Direct or change at Cologne
Paris–Prague	30	15–16 hrs	2	Direct or change at Frankfurt
Paris–Vienna	32	13–16 hrs	4	Direct or change at Munich; one of these services is the Orient Express
Paris–Zurich	41	6 hrs	6	Direct or change at Basel
Stockholm–Berlin	52	15–17 hrs	2	Change at Malmö

TRAVEL ESSENTIALS

The following is an alphabetical listing of helpful tips for those planning a European holiday by rail.

Accommodation

Europe offers an excellent choice of accommodation, from five-star hotels to cheap bed and breakfasts. Your main problem may be in finding something to suit your budget, especially in high season. The quality of cheaper hotels in Eastern Europe may still be less than inspiring and you will do better with private rooms.

Unless stated otherwise in the text, the city's tourist office will help you find, and often reserve, hotel or other accommodation. This is almost always your best starting point if you haven't prebooked. Don't be afraid to make clear to them your price horizons.

If you prefer to reserve some or all of your hotel rooms in advance, this can usually be done by Thomas Cook or another good travel agent (best done at the same time as you buy your air ticket, if you are coming from outside Europe.)

For those travellers who like to stay in hotels belonging to one of the branded international or national chains, we have indicated in the text which chains are represented in a city, by means of initials immediately under the 'Accommodation' heading: e.g. *BW, Hn, HI* means that the city has Best Western, Hilton and Holiday Inn properties (the initials used are explained in the box opposite). Further details can then be obtained from the chain's central reservation phone number in your own country, or through your travel agent. Chains which operate only in a particular country or region are noted in the Country by Country section, pp. 30–78. In this book we have concentrated on providing details of cheap accommodation, as this is often less easy to find, especially in some larger cities.

Hostelling International (IYHF)

The best bet, for those on a tight budget, is to join HI (Hostelling International), the new name for the IYHF (International Youth Hostel Federation). There is no age limit, membership of a national association will entitle you to use over 5,000 IYHF (International Youth Hostel Federation) member association hostels in 60 different countries, and, besides camping, they are often the cheapest form of accommodation available. Sleeping arrangements are usually in dormitory-style rooms, although some hostels also have smaller one- to two-bedded rooms. Many also have excellent-value dining, cooking and, in some cases, laundry facilities. Membership for those over/under 18 is currently: A$40/12 (Australia); C$25/12 (Canada); NZ$24 plus $10 joining fee (New Zealand); £9/3 (UK); $25/10 (USA). A directory *Budget Accommodation You Can Trust* (£5.95) is also available, which lists addresses, contact numbers, locations and facilities of all IYHF member associations. Buy this upon joining, or from bookshops. Hostels are graded according to their standard of comfort and facilities. Some, especially those in large cities, are open 24 hours daily, while others have lock-out times. You are usually allowed to stay in a hostel for as long as you require but in peak

Hotel Chains

The following abbreviations have been used, throughout the book, to denote the particular chain to which a hotel belongs.

Best Western *BW*	Mercure *Me*
Choice *Ch*	Meridian *Md*
Excelsior *Ex*	Metropole *Mp*
Forte *Ft*	Moat House *MH*
Forum *Fo*	Novotel *Nv*
Golden Tulip *GT*	Parador *Pr*
Hilton *Hn*	Penta *Pe*
Holiday Inn *HI*	Pullman *Pu*
Hyatt *Hy*	Radisson *Rd*
Ibis *Ib*	Ramada *Ra*
Intercontinental *Ic*	Ritz Carlton *RC*
InterHotel *Ih*	SAS *SA*
Kempinski *Ke*	Scandic Crown *SC*
Marriott *Ma*	Sheraton *Sh*
Melia *Ml*	Sofitel *Sf*

periods, if you have not already booked to stay for more than three days, you may be asked to vacate your bed to make way for newcomers.

Although it is not usually compulsory to reserve accommodation, the hostels are often full in summer and you should book as far ahead as possible. In winter (except around Christmas) bookings can be slow and it's worth asking if they have any special price deals. For information, to join, and to book accommodation in advance: Australia *tel: (02) 261 1111*; Canada *tel: (0800) 663 5777*; New Zealand *tel: (09) 379 4224*; UK *tel: (071) 836 1036*; USA *tel: (0202) 783 6161*.

Wherever we have given accommodation details, we have included hostels (represented by the initials **IYHF**). There may also be hostels in towns we have covered in less detail, so always check.

Camping

This is obviously the very cheapest form of accommodation available, if you are prepared to carry your own equipment. There are good campsites right across Europe, with facilities ranging from basic (clean toilets and showers) to luxury sites with dining rooms and swimming pools and even vast complexes of permanent tents, aimed at package tourists with children. The one drawback is that in most of the large cities, campsites can be miles from the centre.

There is no really good pan-European guide to campsites, but most tourist offices can provide a directory of those in their country. Either contact them before you leave home, or trust to luck, make sure you always arrive in a new town with plenty of daylight to spare and ask at the tourist information office when you get there.

Bicycles

In many of the European countries, cycling is popular and the best way to explore locally. You can often hire a bike at one train station and leave it at another. This can even be cheaper than going to bike-hire shops. In many countries it is possible, for a small fee, to carry bikes on some trains, but advance notice may be required. If you think you may be interested in doing some cycling, contact the relevant national tourist

office before you leave for information (addresses of all national tourist offices can be found under the individual headings in the Country by Country section).

Borders

All border formalities between the Scandinavian countries (Denmark, Finland, Norway and Sweden) have been abolished. The European Union (EU) has technically agreed to tighten up controls at the external borders with non-member states and open those between member states. Britain, Denmark and Ireland disagree about this and are going to maintain them. For the meantime, most borders still remain in place, although checks are perfunctory at most. Most former Eastern bloc countries still go through the full routine.

Children

Travelling by train with children is easier than you might think – as long as you have someone to help you haul bags and push-chairs up the steps. Most children even find train travel a great novelty, and thoroughly enjoy themselves. However, they can get bored on long journeys and become a menace to themselves, you and your fellow passengers, so make sure you are not short of ideas to keep them amused and have plenty of food and drink at hand.

If the children are old enough, ask them to keep a detailed travel diary. This will focus their attention on what they see and do, make them think about the whole experience (and remember it afterwards), and collecting and displaying anything from tickets and postcards to dried flowers can become a whole new game.

Most tourist destinations in Europe are reasonably well adapted for children, with hygienic facilities, plenty of baby food and nappies. Baby-sitters are not hard to find if you ask at the local tourist office or church, and many hotels will offer family rooms or provide a cot in a normal double. If you can't find suitable restaurants, you will always be able to find a coffee shop or fast food place with a children's menu or, at the very least, the sort of food they won't spit out. The biggest problem you will face is keeping some sort of familiar routine going if local restaurants don't open until 2200, or the children are simply suffering from a surfeit of museums. Many sights, hotels and forms of transport will accept babies for free, and those under 12 for half-price.

For useful reading try: Maureen Wheeler, *Travel with Children*, (Lonely Planet, £5.95/$10.95).

Climate

The climate in Europe is affected by three main factors: latitude (Scandinavia is colder than Spain); altitude (the Alps are colder than Belgium); and distance from the sea (the central European countries, such as the Czech Republic, can suffer surprisingly harsh winters and unexpectedly hot summers). That having been said, most of Europe has a relatively gentle climate. Rain is common throughout the year, except along some stretches of the Mediterranean. The summer temperature rarely exceeds 28°C (see the climate conversion chart giving centigrade and fahrenheit equivalents on p. 415), except again in the far south (the Mediterranean area), where it can be agonisingly hot (occasionally even 40°C) in high summer. Winter tends to be grey and wet, with temperatures hovering around -5/+5°C, and relatively little snow, except in Scandinavia, the high mountains and parts of central Europe. In the far north, midsummer is the best time to travel, to take advantage of the ultra-long days.

Almost everywhere else, May and September are the best months, and have the added advantage of avoiding school holiday crowds.

Clothing

Most of Europe is very informal these days and, unless you are planning to take society by storm, you will rarely need evening clothes, or even a suit. You should make sure you have some smart casual clothes (not jeans and trainers) for evening wear. People wearing shorts or sleeveless tops may be excluded from some churches, the most traditional of which still expect you to cover your head, so pack a long-sleeved shirt or blouse and a shawl or large scarf. You can encounter rain or cool weather no matter where you go, so at least one sweater or jacket and some sort of rainwear are essential.

In addition, take at least two pairs of trousers, or skirts; a pair of shorts; three to four shirts or blouses and three sets of underwear and non-synthetic socks (one on, one in the wash, one spare). For women, a huge t-shirt is useful for a beach cover-up and sleeping in, as well as during the day. Shoes should be comfortable but light and well broken-in before you set out, and a pair of flip-flops is useful for unhygienic showers and overnight travel. Other than that, look for comfortable, easily washable clothes that pack small and do not need ironing.

For hot weather, clothes should be kept loose

	BERLIN	BUDAPEST	LONDON	MADRID	ROME	STOCKHOLM
JANUARY						
Highest	2°C/36°F	0°C/32°F	6°C/43°F	8°C/46°F	12°C/54°F	2°C/36°F
Lowest	-1°C/30°F	-5°C/23°F	1°C/34°F	4°C/39°F	4°C/39°F	-4°C/25°F
Rain days	14	8	15	6	8	7
APRIL						
Highest	13°C/55°F	7°C/45°F	13°C/55°F	18°C/64°F	20°C/68°F	17°C/63°F
Lowest	8°C/46°F	0°C/32°F	4°C/39°F	12°C/54°F	8°C/46°F	6°C/43°F
Rain days	11	6	13	5	6	8
JULY						
Highest	23°C/73°F	21°C/70°F	22°C/72°F	31°C/88°F	31°C/88°F	28°C/82°F
Lowest	17°C/63°F	13°C/55°F	12°C/54°F	21°C/70°F	18°C/64°F	16°C/61°F
Rain days	9	9	13	2	3	7
OCTOBER						
Highest	13°C/55°F	9°C/48°F	14°C/57°F	19°C/66°F	23°C/73°F	16°C/61°F
Lowest	9°C/48°F	4°C/39°F	6°C/43°F	14°C/57°F	11°C/52°F	7°C/45°F
Rain days	13	9	16	5	9	8

and made of cotton or cotton-mix. For cool weather, the best way to keep warm is by a series of layers. In midwinter, you will need a warm coat or cold-weather jacket, a scarf, hat and gloves, and sensible, non-slip footwear. Pack a tube of Travel Wash (available from most camping shops or chemists) and a piece of string, to serve as a washing line, so you can wash clothes through as you travel and save on the expense and inconvenience of using a launderette.

Currency

Most European countries place no limit on the import/export of currencies. However, almost all in former Eastern bloc countries state that the amount taken out must not exceed the amount taken in, making allowance for the amount spent while there. Some such countries check the amounts on both arrival and departure, others simply query the amount taken out if they feel it is larger than they would expect. The restrictions usually refer only to banknotes/coins – if you are carrying large sums of cash, therefore, you should declare it on arrival in order to avoid problems when you leave.

That said, it is never advisable to carry more cash than necessary and it is sensible to take most of your money in the form of Eurocheques, travellers' cheques and credit cards. Although technically illegal, many travellers find it useful to carry German small notes and coins in Bulgaria, and Romania. There is no black market in currency in Western Europe, and while you may find people eager to trade in some Eastern European countries, you could face heavy penalties if caught. You may also be ripped off by those making the exchange, or lay yourself open to muggers working with them.

The Thomas Cook offices listed throughout this book will cash any type of Eurocheque/travellers' cheque and will replace Thomas Cook travellers' cheques if yours are lost/stolen.

Customs

Importing narcotics and offensive weapons is banned throughout Europe – and penalties for carrying them can be very severe; so, in your own interests, do not be tempted, and do not carry

things for anyone else, especially when you are crossing borders. Professional crooks are very good at passing themselves off as harmless and in need of help and some people are languishing in jail today because they believed a hard-luck story or did someone a 'small' favour. Pornography is also banned in many countries and, since it is notoriously difficult to define, it is better to avoid carrying anything that might offend. If you have to take a prescribed drug on a regular basis, carry something (such as a doctor's letter) that will prove it is legitimate.

There are often restrictions on the import and export of plants and fresh foodstuffs (particularly meat and meat products) and you might be asked to abandon them at borders, so be careful about stocking up just before leaving a country. Before buying souvenirs, check which items are likely to be prohibited, such as those made of ivory or tortoiseshell.

Customs Allowances in the EU

EU member states (Belgium, Denmark, France, Germany, Greece, Ireland, Italy, Luxembourg, the Netherlands, Portugal, Spain, and the UK) have set the purchase of tobacco, alcohol and perfume at the same basic allowance for each country (for the few exceptions, see the Country by Country section), and these apply to anyone aged 17 or over. Estonia is not a member state, but applies EU customs allowances.

To all intents and purposes, there are no restrictions between the EU countries for goods bought in ordinary shops and including local taxes, but you may be questioned if you have excessive amounts. Allowances are:
800 cigarettes, 200 cigars, 400 cigarillos and 1 kg tobacco.
+ 90 litres wine (max. 60 litres sparkling).
+ 10 litres alcohol over 22% volume (e.g. most spirits).
+ 20 litres alcohol under 22% volume (e.g. port and sherry).
+ 110 litres beer.
The allowances for goods bought outside the EU and/or in EU duty-free shops are:
200 cigarettes, 50 cigars, 100 cigarillos, and 250 g tobacco*.
+ 2 litres still table wine.

+ 1 litre spirits or 2 litres sparkling wine.
+ 8 litres Luxembourg wine if imported via the Luxembourg frontier.
+ 50 g/60 ml perfume.
+ 0.5 l/250 ml toilet water.

*Where tobacco is concerned, Denmark, Germany, Italy, the Netherlands, and Spain have more generous allowances for non-Europeans arriving from outside Europe: 400 cigarettes, 100 cigars, 200 cigarillos, and 500 g tobacco.

Customs allowances for coffee and tea are also limited by France and Italy to:
500 g coffee or 200 g coffee extract
+ 100 g tea or 40 g tea extract.

Allowances for those returning home:

Australia: goods to the value of A$400 (half for those under 18) plus 250 cigarettes or 250 g tobacco and 1 litre alcohol.

Canada: goods to the value of C$300, provided you have been away for over a week and have not already used up part of your allowance that year. You are also allowed 50 cigars plus 200 cigarettes and 1 kg tobacco (if over 16) and 40 oz/1 litre alcohol.

New Zealand: goods to the value of NZ$700. Anyone over 17 may also take 200 cigarettes or 250 g tobacco or 50 cigars or a combination of tobacco products not exceeding 250 g in all plus 4½ litres of beer or wine and 1.125 litres spirits.

UK: standard EU regulations apply (see notes on p. 13 and above).

USA: goods to the value of US$400 as long as you have been out of the country for at least 48 hrs and only use your allowance once every 30 days. Anyone over 21 is also allowed 1 litre alcohol plus 100 (non-Cuban) cigars and 100 cigarettes.

Disabled Travellers

Europe, in theory, provides more facilities for the disabled than many other parts of the world. In practice, however, those facilities that do exist often fall short of real needs and expectations, and there is a shortage of helpful bystanders to make up the difference. Travel is feasible, but it will almost inevitably be more expensive, as it is usually only the modern trains, and the more

upmarket hotels which are able to cater for the disabled. You will also have to throw out any thought of spontaneity and make meticulous plans, always writing and phoning ahead to make sure you have a reservation and that there is someone on hand to help you. The amount of advance warning required by the railways varies dramatically, from Austrian State Railways, who ask for three days notice, to the ever-efficient Swiss who only need one day.

There are two main problems to face with the trains – how to get onto them, and whether there is space for you once on board. Although modern rolling stock tends not to have wide gaps between train and platform, in many continental European stations the platforms are quite low and passengers have to climb steps to board trains. Once aboard, only the more modern carriages provide space for a wheelchair; otherwise, space will be provided in the baggage car. The new express services, such as the French TGV and the Spanish AVE, do provide proper facilities for the disabled, while the Norwegian InterCity and night trains have adapted hydraulic lifts, accessible toilets and spacious compartments.

Some national railway offices and tourist offices have leaflets about rail travel for the disabled, while the Dutch also have a telephone information line *(tel: (030) 35 55 55)*. A few national networks offer discount passes for the disabled.

The best routes to travel include the main lines in Scandinavia, Switzerland, Germany, Netherlands, and France. The worst facilities are in Turkey, Spain, Hungary, Greece, Bulgaria and the Czech Republic and Slovakia.

UK information: RADAR, *25 Mortimer Street, London W1N 8AB; tel: (071) 637 5400* publish a useful annual guide called *Holidays and Travel Abroad* (£3.50), which gives details of facilities for the disabled in different countries, including their railways.

US information: SATH (Society for the Advancement of Travel for the Handicapped), *347 5th Ave, Suite 610, New York NY 10016; tel: (212) 447 7284*.

For useful reading try: Susan Abbott and Mary Ann Tyrrell, *The World Wheelchair Traveller*

(AA Publishing, £3.95; Alison Walsh, *Nothing Ventured: A Rough Guide Special* (Penguin, £7.99).

Discounts

In many countries reductions are available on public transport and on entrance fees for senior citizens, students and the young. Some proof of your eligibility is usually required, so always carry something that will provide evidence of your status, e.g. an official document that shows your age or a student card. If a student, get an International Student Identity Card (ISIC) from your union, as this is recognised everywhere and offers a wider range of discounts than the national union card. Some destinations also offer, for a small fee, a book of discount vouchers for anything from museums to restaurants, available to anyone who will pay. In many cases, discount passes for tourists, including some national rail passes, must be purchased before you leave home and are not available in the country itself. Contact the tourist office of any country you intend to visit for full details.

Driving

If you think you might want to hire a motor vehicle while you are away, check requirements with the AA/RAC, or your own national motoring organisation, well before you leave, so that you have time to get any additional licences or insurance cover.

To hire a vehicle (with the exception of a moped), you usually have to be over 21 with two years driving experience. In most European countries your national licence is valid for up to six months, but some require you to have a translation as well, and it can be easier to get an international licence before you leave. Always check that the car is in good condition before you set out.

Most road signs are standardised throughout Europe, but the quality of the signposting varies dramatically, as do the speed limits. Check on any local peculiarities before you set out. Everyone except the British and the Irish drives on the right.

There is a wide network of motor-rail services across Europe, for those who wish to avoid the hassle of long-distance driving but have their own car available during their holiday. Contact your national railway for details.

Electricity

With a few exceptions (notably the UK, which uses 240V), the European countries use 220V. The shape of plugs varies so, if you are taking any sort of electrical gadget, you should take a travel adapter. It is unlikely that you will face power cuts, but a small torch (flashlight) is a useful back-up and essential if camping.

Health

Before you go

Europe, on the whole, is clean and hygienic and there are no compulsory vaccination requirements. However, it is always advisable to keep your tetanus and polio protection up to date and vaccination against typhoid and hepatitis A is also a good idea. You must be able to produce a certificate against yellow fever if you have been in a yellow fever endemic zone in the six days before entering Europe. It's also a good idea to visit your dentist for a check-up before you leave home.

If you are a UK citizen, you should fill in Form E111 before you go (available from your local health authority/doctor/post office). This form entitles you to treatment under the reciprocal health arrangements that exist across most of Europe. However, treatment will not automatically be free: you will be treated as a citizen of the country, which may mean that you have to pay up-front and then reclaim the cost when you return home, or that you have to pay for part of your treatment. If you happen to feel unwell while you are away, try visiting the pharmacy first before you make an appointment with the doctor, as European pharmacists tend to be well trained and may be able to advise you and prescribe treatment on the spot.

Dangers

We all tend to think of Europe as cool and soggy, but there is a severe risk of sunburn in the south and in the high mountain areas. Don't spend hours outdoors without using a high-factor sunblock.

Holiday romances are all very well, but don't get so carried away that you forget all about AIDS – and all the other unpleasant sexually-transmitted diseases. If casual sex is your scene, fine, but do take precautions – one glorious night is not worth a (short) lifetime of regret. Take your own condoms if travelling in Eastern Europe.

Rabies exists across much of continental Europe and, while the risk is very small, you should be wary of stray animals.

Food and water

Most of the tap water in Western Europe is safe. There is a cautionary note advising you of any places where it is not drinkable in the Country by Country section (see pp. 30–78). If in doubt, buy tinned or bottled drinks and water and do not use ice cubes. You should boil or sterilise all tap water (including the water you use to brush your teeth) if you think there may be cause for concern.

Other common sources of infection include unboiled or unpasteurised milk. Also, avoid salads and fruit unless you can wash or peel it yourself. In areas where the sea is polluted, be very wary of fresh seafood. Furthermore, avoid any food which is obviously dirty or which has been left lying around for a long time, and wash your hands regularly, especially when you have been travelling for a long time, or you could transmit germs yourself.

Hitchhiking

If you are on a budget, you may want to try hitchhiking around local towns rather than use public transport. This can be fun and a good way to meet the locals, but it can also be dangerous. To avoid trouble, don't hitch alone, or take any ride when you are outnumbered or clearly physically weaker than the people in the car. In a few countries, such as Poland, there are official schemes for getting drivers and hitchers together, so that both can feel safe. Ask for details at the relevant tourist offices, either before you set off, or once you arrive in the country itself.

Insurance

You must take out travel insurance that covers your health as well as your belongings. It should also give cover in case of cancellation and include an emergency flight home if something goes really wrong (the hospitals in some countries are not places where you would want to linger). If you are likely to do something that might be classified as risky (e.g. ski, drive a moped, dive), make sure that your insurance covers you for the activity concerned. The Thomas Cook Independent Traveller Insurance Package offers comprehensive medical insurance and is available from all Thomas Cook retail travel shops in the UK.

Language

You might arm yourself with a copy of the *Thomas Cook European Rail Traveller's Phrasebook* if you are visiting countries where language is likely to be a problem. It contains over three hundred phrases, each translated into the following nine European languages with their phonetic spellings: French, German, Italian, Czech, Polish, Bulgarian, Spanish, Greek and Turkish. Phrases cover the everyday needs of a rail traveller, from arriving in a European train station to booking accommodation, eating out, changing money, meeting people and coping in an emergency.

In the UK, the phrasebook costs £3.95 and is available from any branch of Thomas Cook, many UK bookshops or phone *(0733) 268943*.

Before you go, learn one or two very basic phrases in a multiplicity of languages, such as: 'Hello. I'm sorry, but I don't speak. . . . Does anyone here speak English?' If it's a language like Greek that uses a non-Latin alphabet, also learn the appearance of a few essential words.

Your chief asset, if you have no language in common with the people you meet, will be your willingness to use sign-language. It is amazing what you can do with gestures and body language, as long as you are prepared to have a go. If you want to know where the post office is, for example, showing someone an addressed envelope may get the message across. Smiles also go a long way towards breaking the ice and encouraging people to be helpful, although be careful that your friendliness is not misinterpreted.

It's sensible to have a pen and paper handy at

all times, so that you can ask people to write down figures like times and prices. Similarly, if they don't understand your pronunciation, you can write down what you are trying to say and let them read it or vice versa.

Luggage

The amount of space available to store luggage on trains varies considerably from country to country but it is always sensible to travel as light as possible.

Soft-sided bags may not be as secure, but are light, easy to carry and can be squeezed into cramped spaces. Backpacks are the best option if you will have to do a lot of carrying; otherwise, go for a large, zippable canvas or plastic bag, with a shoulder strap to leave your hands free. If you've never used a backpack before, shop carefully before making your choice. It is worth spending a bit more money to ensure comfort and durability (the best have a lifetime guarantee). Essential features are a strong internal frame, padded shoulder straps and a hip strap, to lift the bulk of the weight away from your neck. These days, there are also specially adapted frames for women. Don't be too ambitious about how much you can carry – 50 litres for women and 60 for men is about right. For advice on what to pack, see p. 21.

Most major stations have left luggage offices and many will also let you register your bags and send them on ahead to your destination.

Opening Hours

A rough guide to opening hours of banks, shops and museums is given in the Country by Country section, but even then, there is a lot of variation. Don't, for instance, assume that every bank will be open during the banking hours listed – and you may find some that actually stay open longer. Similarly, Sunday is the usual closing day for shops and businesses, while many tourist attractions remain open on Sunday, but will close on Monday or Tuesday. Timings are also subject to huge seasonal variations, with many places closing altogether in winter.

Passports and Visas

Although EU citizens can, in theory, travel to most other EU countries on a National Identity Card or British Visitor's Passport, there are variations and you would do well to use a full passport, which should have at least six months validity left. The individual requirements for European travellers are given in the Country by Country section. As for non-European travellers, this book concentrates on requirements for citizens of Australia, Canada, New Zealand and the USA; others should check with their nearest embassy before they travel. *Anyone* planning to stay more than 90 days in a single country may need a visa and should check.

Some countries will refuse entry to anyone who does not have an onward/return ticket and visible means of support. How this is defined can vary, but in essence it means having sufficient money to cover the cost of food, accommodation and other expenses during your stay. A credit card is a practical way of avoiding precise cash requirements.

In many cases visa requirements have more to do with residence than with nationality, e.g. the visa requirements for an Indian living in India and an Indian living in the UK may be different. People who live abroad should check which regulations apply to them.

Where a country is not mentioned specifically, nationals of that country should assume that they need both a full passport and a visa. Even if you can theoretically obtain a visa at the border, it is probably easier to get it in advance. Allow plenty of time, especially if you need to get several, as it can be a long process. Bear in mind that most visa departments have short, and often eccentric, opening hours. You will also need a whole stack of passport photos and will find that many countries ask you to pay in cash or by postal order and will not accept cheques or credit cards.

In the UK, **Thomas Cook,** *45 Berkeley St, London W1A 1EB; tel: (071) 499 4000* operates a visa service which will order and collect your documents for you.

Public Holidays

These have been listed under the individual headings in the Country by Country section. Many are religious holidays, whose dates vary from year to year; these are given by name rather than date, in chronological order. The principal ones are Good Friday and Easter Monday (March/April); Ascension Day (the 6th Thursday after Easter); Whitsun/Pentecost (on Monday, 11 days after Ascension); Corpus Christi (early June) and Midsummer Day (late June). If an official holiday falls on a weekend, the following Monday or Tuesday often becomes a holiday as well.

There are many local festivals (e.g. saints' days) which are celebrated only in one town but which can disrupt everything in the area. Some are noisy, colourful and great fun, others nothing more than an interruption to normal service. If time is important to you, check in advance to see if your visit will coincide with any sort of holiday. Whatever the case, do bear in mind that train services are liable to considerable alteration on holiday dates; it is a good idea to reserve a seat before you travel and you should recheck timings locally.

Sales Tax

Value Added Tax (known as VAT in the UK) is automatically added to most goods in all the West European countries, but not, as yet, to those in the East. The level varies, but is usually 10–20% (in Spain and Switzerland it can be as low as 6% and in France as high as 23% on some items). It may, or may not, be shown separately on the price of the item.

In most places (except Greece), non-residents can reclaim the tax on *major* spending. This often applies to receipts over £30, but every country sets a different limit on how much you must spend. The refund is also intended to apply to only one article, but if you buy several things in the same shop on the same day, the authorities seldom argue.

In order to reclaim your Value Added Tax, ask the shop assistant to fill in a tax refund form for you. Show the form, the receipt and the goods to Customs on leaving the country and they will give you an official export certificate. This can sometimes be exchanged on the spot (you *must* do so in Scandinavia, where limits are also much lower); alternatively, post the certificate back to the shop (within a month) and (in due

course) they will send the refund. It is sometimes poss-ible to avoid paying the tax in the first place, by asking the shop to send the goods directly to your home address. Anything you save in paper-work at the time, however, is likely to be offset by customs formalities in your own country.

Security

The best way to avoid becoming a victim of theft is to try and give the impression that you are not worth robbing (e.g. do not flash expensive jewellery or rolls of banknotes). Use a hidden money-belt for your valuables, travel documents and spare cash. Never carry a wallet in a back pocket or leave your handbag open and use a 'bag with a shoulder strap slung horizontally. In all public places, take precautions with anything that is obviously worth stealing – wind the strap of your camera case round the arm of your chair or place your handbag firmly between your feet under the table while you eat. Never leave luggage unattended – even if it isn't stolen, many European countries are very terrorist-conscious these days, and chances are it will be reported as a possible bomb. Use left luggage offices and lockers if you arrive at a place one morning and intend to leave that same day. If using computerised lockers, be careful that nobody else sees your re-entry code.

When sleeping rough, in any sort of dormitory or on trains, the safest place for your small valuables is at the bottom of your sleeping-bag. In sleeping cars, padlock your luggage to the seat. In both sleepers and couchettes ask the attendant to show you how to lock the door at night. There is a tendency for backpackers to trust each other, but don't take this too far. Like other groups in society, some are the good guys and others are not. Be particularly safety conscious in areas around stations, especially in large cities.

Mugging is a problem in some areas, but as a rule it is not rife in European city centres, although pickpockets are a real danger there. If you are attacked, it is safer to let go of your bag or hand over the small amount of obvious money – as you are more likely to be attacked physically if the thief meets with resistance. If you do run into trouble, you must report it to the local

Solo Travellers

You, and only you, decide where to go, when and for how long. The excitement and sense of adventure in this freedom inspires many to go it alone, but there are drawbacks. You have no one to help plan the trip, or share the experiences and memories. Responsibilities of finding accommodation, deciphering timetables, buying tickets and looking after bags are all yours. Naturally it's lonely at times, especially if you don't speak the local language. However, it is possible to enjoy solo travel without sacrificing companionship. It's easier to meet fellow travellers and locals than it is in a group, as they are more likely to approach you. Travellers abound in trains, ferries and youth hostels, and just asking where they have come from usually starts conversations. Locals chat, and may even invite you home for a meal, opening up whole new facets of a country. Many experienced solo travellers start alone, but keep flexible schedules, so they can spend time with people they meet en route.

Survival is harder alone so plan carefully. Double-check that you have all the essentials when you set out – there is no one else to rely on. Nor will anyone help carry your bags, so pack lightly. You are more vulnerable to theft, so always carry valuables with you, in a money belt or pouch. And be cautious with new acquaintances: most travellers are honest, but don't hand your bags over to someone you have just met. Keep in touch with home, in case of emergencies. It is becoming easier to make international calls from all over Europe, but you should also send postcards, and, to help stave off loneliness, tell people to write to you poste restante. Finally, remember that the left luggage office can be your best friend. Never mind sightseeing or the weight of your rucksack as you drag it round town – what will really tax your brain is what to do with your bags while you have a shower.

police, even if it is only to get a copy of their report for your insurance company.

Finally, take half a dozen passport photos (useful for all sorts of purposes) and photocopy the important pages and any visa stamps in your passport. Store these safely, together with a note of the numbers of your travellers' cheques, credit cards and insurance documents (keep them away from the documents themselves). If you are unfortunate enough to be robbed, you will at least have some identification, and replacing the documents will be much easier.

Smoking

Throughout Europe smoking is banned in many public places and on public transport and, even where it is allowed, there may be a special area for smokers. In some countries, such as France, Italy and Spain, it seems that these rules are very much ignored and people tend to smoke wherever they are, whenever they want to. Nevertheless, there is a growing dislike of the habit and you should ask before lighting a cigarette.

Telephones

You should have few problems finding a phone in European towns and everywhere is on direct-dial. Useful telephone numbers are provided throughout the book and in the Country by Country section (pp. 30–78) you will find advice on how to make calls.

Time

There are several time zones within Europe. The following list includes only the countries covered by this book.

The United Kingdom uses Greenwich Mean Time in winter, but is GMT + 1 hr in summer. Countries which are **GMT+1** hr in winter, **GMT+2** hrs in summer: Austria, Belgium, the Czech Republic, Denmark, France, Germany, Hungary, Italy, the Netherlands, Norway, Poland, Portugal, Slovakia, Spain, Sweden and Switzerland. Countries which are **GMT+2** hrs in winter, **GMT+3** hrs in summer: Bulgaria, Estonia, Finland, Greece, Latvia, Lithuania, Romania and Turkey. *Thomas Cook European Timetable* (see p. 20) also has a time-zone guide.

Toilets/WCs

There is nothing worse than not being able to find one! Although not a universal concept, pictures representing a male and a female are commonly used in Western Europe. The term 'WC' is also quite widespread and if you see words beginning 'toilet' or 'lava' you are probably (though not necessarily) on the right track.

In some countries (e.g. France) you may come across places where both sexes use the same facilities, even if there are separate entrances, so don't assume automatically that you are in the wrong place. The quality varies considerably. Many are modern, clean and well-equipped, others (even in Western Europe) are of the hole-in-the-ground variety and not very well maintained. So be prepared for anything. This includes always carrying some paper, as you will be very lucky if you never find it missing.

Unfortunately not all countries recognise the need for public facilities and they can be difficult to find, so make use of anything the station has to offer before you set out to explore. You can often get away with using the facilities in hotels if you look as if you might be staying there. If not, service stations or eating/drinking places are the best bet – but be prepared to buy something as, understandably, many reserve the use of their facilities for their clients.

Useful Reading

Thomas Cook Publications

The *Thomas Cook European Timetable (ETT)*, published monthly at £7.90, has up-to-date details of most rail services and many shipping services throughout Europe. It is essential both for pre-planning and for making on-the-spot decisions about independent rail travel around Europe. A useful companion to it is the *Thomas Cook New Rail Map of Europe* (£4.95). Both of these publications are obtainable from some stations, any UK branch of Thomas Cook or by phoning (0733) 268943. In North America, contact the Forsyth Travel Library Inc. *9154 West 57th St, PO Box 2975, Shawnee Mission, Kansas 66201; tel: (800) 367 7984* (toll-free).

Thomas Cook Travellers (£6.99), published in the USA as *Passport's Illustrated Travel Guides* ($12.95), cover the following major European destinations: the Algarve, Amsterdam, Belgium, Cyprus, Florence and Tuscany, Ireland, London, Malta, Munich and Bavaria, Paris, Prague, Turkey and Vienna. Scheduled for publication in 1995 are: Berlin, Budapest, Greek Mainland, Mallorca, Normandy, Provence, Rome and Venice. Both these guides and the *Thomas Cook European Rail Traveller's Phrasebook* are available from any UK branch of Thomas Cook, most UK bookshops, or by phoning (0733) 268943. In the USA, they are available from bookstores and published by Passport Books, Chicago.

Other useful books

The best series' guides are: *Lonely Planet* and *Rough Guides* – in particular, Danford and Buckley, *Rough Guide to Europe* (Penguin, £12.99), for budget travellers; the *Michelin Green Guides* for cultural sightseeing and the *AA Essential Guides* as excellent pocket guides for short stops. If you want to work for a while, buy *Work Your*

> ### 'Where is it?'
>
> A question all of us have asked at some time – and nothing's worse than being unable to find out! In some countries, finding the WC can be a real IQ test.
>
> **Czech and Slovak Republics**: some are marked 'WC', but not all: *muži* or *páni* indicates men, *ženy* or *dámy* indicates women.
>
> **Estonia, Latvia and Lithuania**: there is a triangle on the door of WCs, the direction of the point indicating whether it is for men or women – point down is men; point up is women.
>
> **Finland**: men's doors have an 'M' and women's doors an 'N'.
>
> **Hungary**: WCs are shown as WC or *mosdó* (*férfi* is for men, *nói* for women).
>
> **Poland**: public WCs are often identified simply by a triangle for men and a circle for women.
>
> **Portugal**: look closely at the words: *Senhores* is men, *Senhoras* women.

Way Around the World (Vacation Work, £9.95). The *Travellers Handbook* (Wexas) is also extremely useful for pre-travel planning (currently £11.95, but a new edition will be published on 1 October 1994, costing £14.95).

What to Take

A few things that really are useful are: water-bottle, muesli-type bars, Swiss Army pocket knife, torch (flashlight), sewing kit, padlock and bicycle chain (for anchoring your luggage), small first-aid kit (including insect repellent and antihistamine cream, sun-screen cream, after-sun lotion, water sterilising tablets, something for headaches and tummy troubles, antiseptic spray or cream, medicated wet wipes, plasters for blisters, bandages), contraceptives and tampons (especially if visiting Eastern Europe, where they are difficult to get hold of – try the luxury shop in the city's biggest hotel), safety matches, mug and basic cutlery, small towel, soap, tooth-brush, some detergent, string (for a washing-line), travel adapter, universal plug (often missing from wash-basins), dental floss, sunglasses, alarm clock, note pad and pen, pocket calculator (to convert money), a money-belt and a good book (for long waits at stations and train journeys). For clothing, see the clothing section on p. 12. If you wear spectacles, take a spare pair and a copy of your prescription.

If you're not sure what you're doing about accommodation, take a lightweight sleeping bag, a sheet liner, inflatable travel pillow and eye-mask (invaluable for comfort on long train journeys, even if you look a total idiot).

Finally, pack a large supply of plastic bags, which weigh virtually nothing, take up very little room and are useful for all sorts of things (from storing dirty/wet clothes to keeping your lunch fresh), plus one or two rubber bands to seal them. Strong plastic containers could also come in handy and are far safer than glass ones.

Women Travellers

Some women still feel a little apprehensive about setting off alone, but most of the hazards or hassles they may face have nothing to do with their sex. Sexual innuendo and regular chat-up lines are little more than aggravating. Remember however that many societies are still formal and unliberated, and if you bare all in skimpy clothes, you will invite more than your fair share of hassle. To avoid irritation, dress on the conservative side, walk purposefully and confidently, and avoid direct eye contact with problematic men. Be careful whom you speak to, and while you can be perfectly friendly, keep it cool and off-limits. A short courteous answer is often more fruitful than turning your back, while a firm but polite 'no' is understood in most languages. If in doubt, invent a large boyfriend or protective father, nearby and due back soon. If you feel the need, carry a rape alarm, and if you think you may want to say yes, make sure you have your own supply of condoms. If you don't want to eat alone at night, have your main meal at lunchtime, or take a book for company.

Exercise the usual rules of caution when abroad. Don't go off with people who have been drinking or get into cars with strangers. Avoid dark alleys and lonely, or red-light areas, make sure you have a clear view all round you and, if in doubt, scream first and think later. If you feel threatened, head for the nearest hotel, explain the situation and ask for help. If you need to go to the police, try to find a friendly witness to take with you, as many policemen are far from saintly and you could end up in a still nastier situation.

Most of all, remember that few of the people you meet have designs on your body. Most are nice, friendly, and just want to talk or help you with heavy luggage. If you are too scared to talk to anyone, you will miss out on the best possible parts of your holiday.

Useful Reading–What to Take–Women Travellers

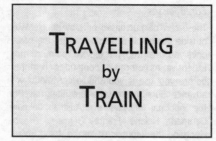

TRAVELLING by TRAIN

This chapter is packed with hints and tips on organising an excursion around Europe by rail.

Information and Booking

In the UK

There are several sources of international rail tickets, passes and information: the **International Rail Centre**, *Victoria Station, London SW1V 1JY; tel: (071) 834 2345.* **Wasteels Travel**, *Victoria Station, London SW1V 1JY; tel: (071) 834 7066.* **Campus Travel (Eurotrain)**, *52 Grosvenor Gardens, London SW1W 0AG; tel: (071) 730 3402.* There is also a 24-hour recorded service (min. £0.36 per minute) for timetable information on trains to Amsterdam, Brussels, Cologne and Paris (*tel: (0891) 888 731*).

In the USA

The Forsyth Travel Library Inc., *9154 West 57th St, PO Box 2975, Shawnee Mission, Kansas 66201; tel: (800) 367 7984* (toll-free). **Rail Europe**, *226 Westchester Ave, White Plains NY 10604; tel: (800) 682 2999* (toll-free). **DER Tours**, *tel: (800) 782 2424.* Several national rail networks have offices in the USA; information is listed under the individual country headings in the Country by Country section (see pp. 30–78).

Elsewhere

Australia/Canada/Hong Kong/New Zealand: obtainable from Thomas Cook branches (and branches of Marlin Travel in Canada) in most major cities. **South Africa**: available from branches of Rennies Travel (Thomas Cook network member) in cities throughout the country.

European Rail Passes

Many countries have rail passes valid only for domestic travel. Those most likely to be of interest are detailed in the Country by Country section and can usually be purchased from any branch of the national railway and its appointed agents.

In order to buy rail passes, you will often have to supply one or two passport-size photos and show your passport or other relevant identification. The passes generally cover all the ordinary services of the national rail companies and can be used on most of the special services provided you pay a supplement. A few, such as Eurail, cover the supplement. In addition, many give free or discounted travel on private railways (such as steam trains and cog railways), buses and/or ferries. A few even give free entrance to transport museums. You will get full details of the 'extras' when you buy the pass. If planning a long journey, look first at the following international passes common to most of Europe.

Inter-Rail Pass

The Inter-Rail Pass has launched generations of young people into the travelling life. A well-established scheme, it provides a practical and ultra-cheap way of seeing most of Europe by train. It can be bought by anyone who will be under 26 on the first day for which it is valid, provided that they can prove that they have lived for at least six months in one of the European countries where the pass is valid (see list below), or are a national of that country, and that they hold a valid passport. It can be purchased up to two months before travel begins. The current cost is £249 for a month and you can buy two consecutive passes for longer journeys. You will not get free travel in the country where you buy the pass, but you may get some discount.

At present, an Inter-Rail pass gives you unlimited second-class rail travel for a month on the national railways of: Austria, Belgium, Bulgaria, Croatia, the Czech Republic, Denmark, Finland, France, Germany, Greece, Hungary, the Republic of Ireland, Italy, Luxembourg, Macedonia, Morocco, the Netherlands, Norway, Poland, Portugal, Romania, Slovakia, Slovenia, Spain,

Sweden, Switzerland and Turkey. It also includes a free crossing on the Hellenic Mediterranean/ Adriatica di Navigazione shipping lines between Brindisi in Italy and Patras in Greece (you will have to pay port tax of approximately L.10000 from Italy to Greece or Dr. 1500 from Greece to Italy). It also gives free or discounted crossings on many other ferries, so check before you travel.

In the UK, Inter-Rail provides a discount of 34% on rail travel in Great Britain and Northern Ireland, plus a discount on the rail portion of tickets between London and the Continental ports, plus 30% or 50% discount (depending on the company) on most of the ferries to Ireland and Europe.

Zonal Inter-Rail Passes

These regional variations on the Inter-Rail Pass are for those under 26. The same rules about eligibility apply (see p. 22). For zonal passes, Europe has been divided into seven geographical zones:
1) United Kingdom and the Republic of Ireland
2) Sweden, Norway and Finland.
3) Denmark, Switzerland, Germany and Austria
4) Poland, the Czech Republic, Slovakia, Hungary, Bulgaria, Romania and Croatia
5) France, Belgium, the Netherlands and Luxembourg
6) Spain, Portugal and Morocco
7) Italy, Slovenia, Greece, Turkey (including shipping lines between Brindisi and Patras)

Passes are available for 1 zone (15 days only; £179); 2 zones (1 month; £209); and 3 zones (1 month; £229). If you have a definite route in mind, these can offer savings over the standard Europe-wide pass. For instance, if you bought a 2-zone pass for zones 5 and 7, you could travel through France into Italy and on to Greece and Turkey for only £209, with a side trip through the Benelux countries on the way home.

Inter-Rail 26+ Pass

This is the same as the Inter-Rail Pass, except that it is for people over 26 and does not cover travel in Belgium, France, Italy, Portugal, Spain or Switzerland. The current cost is £269 for a month or £209 for 15 days.

Eurail Passes

These can be purchased only by people living outside Europe. It is possible to get the passes once you've arrived, but they will be much more expensive. As you can buy one up to six months before you use it you should try and buy in advance. Eurail passes offer unlimited travel on the national railways of: Austria, Belgium, Denmark, Finland, France, Germany, Greece, Hungary, the Republic of Ireland, Italy, Luxembourg, the Netherlands, Norway, Portugal, Spain, Sweden and Switzerland. They also cover most private railways and selected ferries such as the Hellenic Mediterranean/Adriatica di Navigazione shipping lines between Brindisi in Italy and Patras in Greece (although, as with the Inter-Rail pass, you will have to pay a port tax of approximately L.10000 from Italy to Greece or Dr. 1500 from Greece to Italy. In addition to this, Eurail pass holders must pay a high-season (June to October) supplement of L.15000 from Italy to Greece or Dr. 2500 from Greece to Italy). A complete list of bonuses is included on the complimentary map issued with your tickets.

The basic **Eurail Pass** has no age limit. It provides first-class travel on all services and even covers most of the supplements for travelling on express and de luxe trains. It also gives free or reduced travel on many lake steamers, ferries and buses. There are several versions, valid for 15 days, 21 days, 1 month, 2 months or 3 months. Current prices range from US$498 for 15 days to US$1398 for 3 months.

The **Eurail Youth Pass** is much the same, but cheaper, as it is designed for those under 26 and is based on second-class travel. There are versions valid for either 15 days (US$398) or up to two months (US$768).

The **Eurail Flexipass** is similar to the basic Eurail pass, but allows you to travel for any 5 days (US$348), any 10 days (US$560) or any 15 days (US$740) within a two-month period.

The **Eurail Youth Flexipass** allows second-class travel for those under 26 within a two-month period for 5 days (US$255), 10 days (US$398) and 15 days (US$540).

The **Eurail Saverpass** is designed for groups of 3–5 people travelling together at all times (between 1 Oct and 31 Mar two people travelling together is accepted) and offers first-class rail travel over a 15-day period at US$430, 21 days at US$550 and 1 month at US$678.

Euro-Domino Freedom Pass

This is a catch-all title for a whole series of passes allowing unlimited travel on the national railway of an individual country (including most high-speed train supplements). They are not valid for travel in your own country. Conditions of use are the same everywhere and the options available are for any 3, 5 or 10 days within a period of one month. The passes can be purchased by non-Europeans but only upon reaching a country for which the pass applies.

There is no age limit, but the price varies according to age. Those under 26 pay less but are restricted to second-class, while those over 26 can opt for either first or second class. Children pay half (the age at which they qualify for the reduction varies in different countries). The price also varies according to the size of the railway network in the country chosen. The cheapest options (of the countries covered here) are for Luxembourg: from £11 (£14 for those over 26) for 3 days second-class travel to £44 for 10 days first-class travel. The most expensive is for Spain: £378 for 10 days first-class travel.

Passes can be purchased up to two months before travel begins. Countries currently offering them are: Austria, Belgium, Bulgaria, Croatia, the Czech Republic, Denmark, Finland, France, Germany, Greece, Hungary, the Republic of Ireland, Italy, Luxembourg, Morocco, the Netherlands, Norway, Poland, Portugal, Slovakia, Spain, Sweden, Switzerland and Turkey.

In the UK, holders of any Euro-Domino Freedom pass can get up to 50% discount off the rail/ferry ticket from London to a continental port. Other ferry discounts are available, details are supplied with the ticket.

Europass

Available in the USA only, this pass allows flexible first-class rail travel for those over 26, in France, Germany, Italy and Switzerland. If you purchase a 5-day pass (the minimum), you receive unlimited rail travel in your choice of three of the above countries. The more travel days you purchase,

the more countries you can visit. The maximum number of rail-travel days you can choose is 15, and however many you choose, you must travel within a 2-month period. Countries must border each other and travel days may be used consecutively or non-consecutively.

A special second-class Europass Youth is available for those under 26. Prices range from US$280 for 5 days (Europass Youth: US$198) to US$660 for 15 days (US$478). Various bonuses are available and listed on the map which accompanies the rail pass.

Rail Europe-Senior Card

This card is for women over 60 and men over 60 or 65 (depending on the age at which they are classed as a senior citizen in their own country). It offers a discount of 30% (sometimes more) off the cost of rail travel (excluding supplements) in: Austria, Belgium, Croatia, the Czech Republic, Denmark, Finland, France, Germany, Greece, Hungary, the Republic of Ireland, Italy, Luxembourg, the Netherlands, Norway, Poland, Portugal, Romania, Slovakia, Slovenia, Spain, Sweden, Switzerland, and the UK. The card is not available to US citizens.

Most countries have a rail card for their senior citizens, which is needed to buy the Rail Europe-Senior Card. In the UK the Senior Railcard is available to people over 60 (costs £16 p.a.) The Rail Europe-Senior Card, available from British Rail International, costs an extra £5. It becomes valid on the day of purchase and expires on the same date as the domestic card.

Carte Vermeil Plein Temps

This is a French-run rail pass for those over 60. In France it offers a 50% discount on all journeys beginning in the blue period (see **Rail Travel Within France** in the Country by Country section), except the Paris RER and the metro. It also gives a 30% reduction on the national rail networks of Austria, the Czech Republic, Denmark, Finland, Germany, Greece, Hungary, the Republic of Ireland, Luxembourg, the Netherlands, Norway, Portugal, Slovakia and Sweden. Although it gives no reduction on domestic travel in Belgium, Italy, Spain, Switzerland and the UK, it does give a 30% reduction on the cross-border journey from France. It is valid for one year from the date of issue. The current cost is £29.40.

There is a similar, but more limited, version (the *Quatre Temps*), which is primarily for use in France. Both passes are available only from the offices and agents of SNCF.

Regional European Rail Passes

Baltic Pass

Available to holders of ISIC cards (see p. 15), full-time academic staff, and people of any nationality under the age of 26, this allows unlimited rail travel in Estonia, Latvia and Lithuania for 7 days (£13), 14 days (£18) or 21 days (£25). It can be purchased from Campus Travel (see p. 22). Once you arrive in the Baltic states, there can be occasional hassles getting the pass validated (which must be done before you board trains) and it's not as cheap as individual tickets, but still preferable unless you enjoy queuing.

Scanrail Pass

This is available in both the UK and the USA (but not within Scandinavia) and gives unlimited first- or second-class travel on the national rail networks of Denmark, Finland, Norway and Sweden and on some ferries.

In the **UK** it is available from NSB (Norwegian Railways, *tel: (071) 930 6666*, for any 5 days within a 15-day period, any 10 days within the period of 1 month or for 1 whole month. Current prices: 5 days, £125 second class (£151 first class); 10 days, £170 (£208); 1 month, £245 (£306). Prices are different for under 26 year olds: 5 days, £94 (£113); 10 days £128 (£156); 1 month £184 (£231).

In the **USA** it is available for any 4 days in a 15-day period, any 9 days in a 21-day period or any 14 days in a 1-month period Current prices: 4 days, US$159 second class (US$199 first class); 9 days, US$275 (US$339); 14 days, US$399 (US$499). Children (4–12) pay 50%.

Benelux Tourrail Pass

This is available in the UK and the USA and provides unlimited rail travel throughout Belgium, Luxembourg and the Netherlands for any 5 days in a 17-day period. For those over 26, prices are £120/US$205 in first class and £80/US$137 in second class. If you are under 26, you will only be able to purchase a pass in second class, at a cost of £60/US$102.

European East Pass

This is available in the USA only and provides unlimited rail travel throughout Austria, the Czech Republic, Hungary, Poland and Slovakia for any 5 days within a 15-day period or any 10 days within the period of one month. The pass is available for first-class travel only and costs US$185 for 5 days and US$299 for 10 days.

Youth Passes

If you are under 26, there are many other discounted tickets and passes available. Some are to single destinations or for travel in single countries, others (like the examples above) to whole groups of countries. Passes come under many different names such as Euro-Youth, Explorer Pass and BIJ (Billets International de Jeunesse).

If the Inter-Rail/Eurail passes are too general for your needs, contact an organisation that specialises in youth travel such as **Campus** or **Wasteels** (see p. 22).

Tickets

Always buy your ticket before travelling, unless you board at an unstaffed station, or you could face heavy penalties or even criminal prosecution. Throughout Europe, tickets are easily available from many travel agents as well as at stations. Eastern Europe is a little more complicated, as rail transport systems are changing as rapidly as many other aspects of life, and finding accurate information can be difficult. On the plus side, domestic tickets bought there are often cheaper than a ticket for exactly the same route bought outside the country.

Never buy a standard ticket without asking what discounts are available, especially if you are prepared to travel outside peak periods, such as rush hour and the weekend.

Most countries have discounts for children, but there is no set definition of what constitutes a child. They are generally classed as adults at 11/12 years, but the age at which they change from infants (who travel free) to children can range from 2 to 5 years inclusive. Quite a few countries also offer domestic rail cards which give substantial discounts to the disabled, elderly or students although, in most cases, the international passes already mentioned are better value.

Advance Reservations

Seats on many trains cannot be booked but, when they can, it is usually worthwhile, especially in high season and around public holidays (such as Christmas and Easter), when popular routes can fill up a long way ahead and you could spend hours standing in a crowded corridor. For a quiet journey, with a chance to sleep, choose a seat in a compartment. For a lively journey, with conversation and panoramic views all round, choose an open carriage. In both cases, window seats are less disturbed than corridor seats. Solo travellers (particularly women) should always stick with the crowds, for security. If you are travelling during the busy summer period and have no reservation, board your train as early as possible.

Some of the major express trains (usually marked in timetables by an 'R' in a box) are restricted to passengers with reservations. However, you can usually make a reservation up to two months in advance. In all cases, booking is essential if you want sleeping accommodation. This can usually be made by contacting the national railway representatives of the country through which you intend to travel. In the USA, advance reservations and sleeping cars can be booked from Forsyth Travel Library Inc; *tel: (800) 367 7984* (toll-free).

Supplements

If you hold a rail pass, you should be able to use it on all services, but you may have to pay a supplement for some trains, so check carefully if there are restrictions.

You may have to pay a supplement if you travel by Express train and high-speed services such as the French TGV, the German ICE and the Italian ETR 450 Pendolino also have higher-than-normal fares for ordinary tickets. Holders of a first-class Eurail Pass can use most of the special services without a supplement. Other rail pass holders are sometimes exempt from the routine surcharges for express travel, but they have to

pay more for the special high-speed services. If you are happy to put up with a slightly longer and less opulent journey, you will usually be able to find a slower train that will still get you there but without any extra payments.

There's usually a fee for reserving seats but it is seldom large and is normally included in the supplementary payments for the faster trains. Sleeping accommodation (see p. 28) always attracts charges of some sort. Sort out the extras before you start your journey – and make sure you know exactly what you are paying for. You may be able to pay the supplements on the train, but it will almost always cost more.

Types of Train

Many of the best daytime international trains are now branded EuroCity (or **EC**). To qualify, trains have to be fast and offer a certain standard of service, such as food and drink during the journey. All have names, and the EuroCity network continues to expand, now including countries such as the Czech Republic and Poland. During summer 1994, the Eurostar trains linking London with Paris and Brussels through the Channel Tunnel will also be introduced (see p. 29).

Many overnight trains carry names as well as numbers, some, such as the Nord Express and Train Bleu, having long histories. Most are just ordinary trains, but there is a new breed of high-quality night service known as EuroNight (**EN**) which has air-conditioned coaches and extras such as evening drinks and breakfast, which are even available to couchette passengers.

The **IC** or InterCity label is applied by many countries to its fast long-distance trains, although there are slight variations in what they provide. The **ICE** (InterCity Express) designation also crops up in several countries, but is mostly applied to the latest high-speed trains in Germany. **IR** is a new classification for inter-regional express services making more stops than InterCity services, and is used particularly in Germany, where it means 'Inter-Regio', and in Italy, where it means 'Interregionale'. These names are all used to distinguish the faster long-distance trains from local or stopping trains. Types of train unique to a specific country are described in the Country by Country section.

Most longer distance trains in Europe offer both first- and second-class travel, but second class is the norm for local stopping services. Where overnight trains offer seating accommodation, this is usually second class only. As a rule, in Western Europe, second class is perfectly OK for all but the most ardent comfort-seeker. A few Eastern European services still leave a lot to be desired, but tickets are very cheap, and it's worth paying a little more to upgrade to first class.

Finding Your Train

You should have little problem with this and stations are usually easy to cope with. In small stations, you are faced with a limited choice of platforms and can usually find a friendly soul to point you in the right direction.

Most large stations have electronic departure boards or large paper timetables (often yellow) which list the routes, the times of departure and the relevant platforms. They are usually kept reasonably up to date, but watch out for nasty surprises, such as the seemingly ideal train which only runs on the third Sunday in August. In some stations, the platforms are also labelled with details of regular trains or the next departure and may even give the location of special carriages and the facilities on board.

Finally, the trains themselves often have boards on the carriages, stating the principal stops and ultimate destination. Be a little careful, because quite a few long-distance trains have a habit of splitting, with only part of the train going the full distance. If this could be a possibility, check the number of the coach with that on your reservation (if you have one), or ask an official for assistance. Even if they do not speak English, a sight of your ticket will be enough for them to put you in the right portion of the train. Numbers are found on small cards fixed to the side of the coach at the doors or near the destination boards.

First-class coaches usually have a yellow stripe along the top of the windows and large number '1's on the side of the coach, on the door or on the windows. No-smoking coaches are distinguished by signs, usually of a cigarette with a red cross, or one red band, over it.

A sign near the compartment door will indicate seat numbers and which are reserved. In non-compartment trains, reserved seats usually have labels attached to their head-rests (or above the seat or the edge of the luggage racks). In some countries (notably Sweden), however, reserved seats are not marked – so be prepared to move when the passenger who has booked boards the train.

Station announcements are often unintelligible, even if they are in your own language, but are sometimes important. If you hear one that you don't understand shortly before your train is due to leave, ask someone nearby whether the announcement concerned your train. The ideal is to find an official, but other travellers are often helpful. If a lot of people near you start to move away hurriedly, there has probably been a change of platform and, if you ask enough of them, you might actually find the new platform before the train pulls out.

Overnight Trains

A night on the train, being rocked to sleep by the clatter of the wheels, is not to be missed. Sleeping cars can cost about the same as a hotel but have the advantage of covering large distances as you rest and you won't waste precious holiday time in transit. You can also save quite a bit of money, if you are prepared to use couchettes or to curl up on the ordinary seats. Don't do this too often without a break, however, or you will end up totally exhausted. The chatter of other passengers, the coming and going at stations and even the regular checks to make sure you still have all your bags can lead to a disturbed night. Take earplugs and an eyemask and, as there are often no refreshment facilities, take plenty of water and a supply of biscuits with you. If you have a rail card, and your night train arrives at your destination too early in the morning, it may be a good idea to stay asleep on board, travel an hour or more beyond your destination, then take a second train to double back on your tracks. On the second train you can wash, and sometimes take breakfast.

In Eastern Europe, you may be woken for customs and immigration checks, which can involve a search of luggage or the compartment/berth. In Western Europe, the attendant will usually take your passport and ticket and this should prevent you being disturbed. If you would like him to wake you in the morning, specify a stop, rather than a time. That way, if the train runs late, you can sleep longer. If you have entered your compartment and want to sleep, but other passengers have yet to arrive, switch on their small berth lights, and switch off the main light. Before boarding, pack things you will need for the evening and put them into a separate bag, as busy compartments don't allow much room for searching through luggage.

Sleepers and couchettes can usually be reserved up to three months in advance; early booking is recommended as space is limited. If you don't have a booking, it's still worth asking the conductor once on board. Keep some local currency handy.

Sleeping Accommodation

Sleeping cars have bedroom-style compartments with limited washing facilities (usually just a wash-basin) and full bedding. WCs are located at one or both ends of the coach. An attendant travels with each car, or pair of cars, and serves drinks and continental breakfast at an extra charge.

First-class sleeping compartments usually have one or two berths and second-class compartments have three berths. However, there are some special sleeping cars (described as 'T2') which have only one berth in first class and two in second class. An exception to the norm is Spain: their T2 cars are first class and their Talgo trains have four berths in second class. Unless your group takes up all the berths, compartments are allocated to a single sex and small unaccompanied children are placed in female compartments. In Estonia, Latvia and Lithuania berths are allocated on a first-come, first-served basis without regard to sex. You should claim your berth within 15 minutes of boarding the train or it may be reallocated.

Couchettes are more basic – and much cheaper. They consist of simple bunk beds with a sheet, blanket and pillow. They are converted from the ordinary seats at night-time and there are usually four berths in first class and six in second class with washing facilities and WCs at the end of each coach. Males and females are booked into the same compartment and expected to sleep in their daytime clothes.

In a few cases, (notably Italy) overnight trains have airline-style **reclining seats**, which are allocated automatically when you make a seat reservation. These can be free to pass holders.

Washing

The only European sleeping cars with full washing facilities (WC, shower and washbasin) are 'Gran Clase' cars on the overnight Spanish Talgos and the Swedish WL5s, but the Germans and Austrians are planning to introduce new 'hotel' trains which will have showers in some compartments. Some main railway stations have showers for public use.

Eating

Most long-distance trains in Europe have restaurant cars serving full meals and/or buffet cars selling drinks and snacks. There is an increasing tendency for refreshments to be served aircraft-style from a trolley wheeled through the train. Dining cars sometimes have a red band above the windows and doors. Quite a few services offer full meals only to first-class passengers, while others, such as some Spanish services, offer nothing but a full-scale, four-course production. Restaurant cars normally have set times for meals. Buffets are usually open to both classes and serve for longer periods, but even they may not be open for the whole journey.

Always take emergency rations, including a full water bottle and a packet of biscuits. Food and drink are usually expensive on trains so, if you need to save money, take a picnic. Long stops at East European frontiers may allow time to get out and buy food and drink. This is risky: get permission from the control officers, check that you have the right currency and that you have enough time.

The Channel Tunnel

The idea of a cross-Channel tunnel was first proposed as long ago as 1802, but it was 1881 before anybody made a serious attempt to build one. The British stopped this, and later efforts, for fear of military invasion, and the project only got the green light in 1985, once the UK, France and Germany were all members of the EEC. This extraordinary feat of engineering actually consists of three tunnels (one in each direction for trains, and one in the centre for services and safety), each one 50 km long. Opened by Queen Elizabeth II and President Mitterand on 6 May 1994, at the time of going to press the start of actual services had been delayed, and although timetables and the price of the shuttle had been announced, ticket prices for passenger trains were not yet published.

Le Shuttle

Running from Cheriton, near Folkestone, to Coquelles, at Calais, this is the car transporter service, with trains leaving every 15 mins. Operators are aiming at a maximum journey time of 1 hr, from terminal to terminal, including waiting, loading and unloading. Both UK and French customs and immigration are passed before boarding. There are well-lit cars with toilet facilities and room to stretch your legs, but no refreshments or seats. Passengers remain in or near their car for the duration of the crossing. Book in advance or on arrival.

Passenger services

Eurostar day trains concentrate on two routes. **London (Waterloo)–Paris (Nord)**: one per hour in each direction, taking 3 hrs (2 hrs 30 mins by the year 2000). **London (Waterloo)– Lille (Europe)–Brussels (Midi/Zuid)**: one per hour in each direction, taking 3 hrs 15 mins (2 hrs 40 mins after the completion of the new Belgian high-speed link; 2 hrs 10 mins by 2000). Additional trains will run at peak demand periods. Connections can be made at Brussels for trains to Amsterdam, Germany etc. and at Lille for TGV's to the rest of France.

 The service will be on new trains with first- and standard-class accommodation. All seats will have personal foot rests, reading lights and magazine racks. All first-class seats recline. There are also family compartments with foldaway tables and baby-changing facilities. First-class tickets will include a full meal (served in your seat), and in the rest of the train, there will be two bar-buffet coaches and a trolley service. Passengers will clear customs before boarding and immigration checks will be on board. There will be no duty-free sales.

Beyond London and Overnight

These services are not due to come on stream until late 1995. Until then, there will be special connecting services between the various UK regions and London Waterloo, as well as the usual Inter-City trains to other London stations. **Beyond London day services** will run south from Edinburgh, via Newcastle and York (amongst other stops); and from Manchester, via Birmingham (and several other stops) to Brussels, Lille and Paris. **Overnight services from London** will include trains to Amsterdam (via Rotterdam, The Hague); Dortmund (via Cologne, Dusseldorf); and Frankfurt (via Bonn, Koblenz). **Beyond London overnight services** will include trains from Glasgow to Paris and Brussels; Swansea to Paris; and Plymouth to Brussels (the last two interconnecting in Bristol).

 Overnight trains will be made up of reclining seats, deluxe sleepers with en-suite shower and toilet, and standard sleepers, with en-suite toilet. All cabins will have a private basin, tea and coffee-making facilities. There will be a light refreshment service.

 A new international tickets and reservation system, based at Lille Europe, will be connected by computer to allow ticketing through many travel agents and most UK stations, for the Eurostar and most other major European routes.

COUNTRY
by
COUNTRY

AUSTRIA

Capital: Vienna (*Wien*). **Language**: German; English is widely spoken in tourist areas. **Currency**: Schilling (S.); 1 Schilling = 100 Groschen.

Passports and Visas

A British Visitor's Passport is sufficient, as are National Identity Cards of Belgium, France, Germany, Greece, Italy, Luxembourg, Malta, the Netherlands, Portugal, Spain, and Switzerland. Visas are not needed by nationals of the EU, Australia, Canada, New Zealand or the USA. Others should check.

Customs

Import allowances for those arriving from Europe aged 17 or more: 200 cigarettes or 50 cigars or 250g tobacco, 1 litre spirits and 2.25 litres wine, or 3 litres beer and 1 litre spirits. Allowances are doubled for non-Europeans arriving from outside Europe.

Useful Addresses in the UK

Embassy, *18 Belgrave Mews West, London SW1X 8HU; tel: (071) 235 3731*. **National Tourist Office and Railways**, *30 St George St, London W1R 0AL; tel: (071) 629 0461*.

Useful Addresses in the USA

Embassy, *3524 International Court NW, Washington DC 20008; tel: (202) 895 6700*. **National Tourist Office**, *500 Fifth Ave (Suite 2009-2022), New York, NY 10110; tel: (212) 944 6880*.

Living in Austria

Accommodation

The Austrian National Tourist Office can supply information about all types of accommodation, including camping. Hotels are graded on the usual five-star system, but even one-star establishments are pricey. *Gasthaus/Gasthof* indicates an inn and *Fruhstuckspension* a bed-and-breakfast place. The best value is usually a private room (look for a sign saying *zimmer frei*), but many of them require you to stay several nights and some charge a supplement for short stays. *Jugendherberge* is the word for a youth hostel. In summer some universities let rooms and it's always worth asking when you're in a university town.

Camping is popular and there are lots of sites. The general standard is high, with cleanliness and efficiency the keynotes, and hot water available almost everywhere; the down-side is the high prices. For camping information *tel: (0222) 89 12 12 22*. Many sites open summer only, but some open year round. In Alpine areas, use the numerous refuge huts.

Food and Drink

The Austrian pattern is: continental breakfast, lunch (1200–1400), coffee and cake (notably the famous *Sachertorte*) in mid-afternoon and dinner (1800–2200). Lunch is usually more expensive in cafés than in restaurants. Drinks in bars and clubs cost more than in eating places. A filling snack, sold by most butchers, is *Wurstsemmel*: slices of sausage with a bread roll. Tea and coffee are widely available. Beer is the most popular drink, but Austrian wine is good and schnapps comes in many varieties.

Opening Hours

Banks: in Vienna – Mon, Tue, Wed, Fri 0800–1230 and 1330–1500, Thur 0800–1230 and 1330–1730 (some do stay open through the lunch hour). Elsewhere, the norm is – Mon–Fri 0800–1230 and 1430–1600. **Shops**: Mon–Fri 0800–1830 and Sat 0800–1300 (many stay open until 1700 on the first Saturday of the month or close for an hour or two at lunch-time). **Museums**: there is no real pattern to opening times and several of the smaller ones open only a few days a week, so check locally.

Postage

Post offices can be recognised by a golden

trumpet symbol and are often located close to the station or main square. They all handle poste restante (*Postlagernde Briefe*). Nationwide hours are Mon–Fri 0800–1200 and 1400–1800, but offices in major towns tend to stay open during lunch and open on Saturdays. The main ones in cities frequently open 24 hours a day. Stamps (*briefmarke*) can also be purchased at *Tabak/ Trafik* stands.

Public Holidays

1, 6 Jan; Easter Monday; 1 May; Ascension Day; Whit Monday; Corpus Christi; 1, 15 Aug; 26 Oct; 1 Nov; 8, 25, 26 Dec. Many people take unofficial holidays on Good Friday, Easter Sunday, Whit Sunday, 2 Nov, 24 Dec and 31 Dec.

Public Transport

The efficient Austrian long-distance bus system consists of orange **Bundesbahn** buses, run by ÖBB and generally based by rail stations, and yellow **Post-buses**, run by the postal system, which usually leave from beside post offices. Both serve mountainous areas and other places inaccessible to trains, rather than duplicating inter-city rail routes.

All cities have excellent bus and/or tram systems. It is possible to buy tickets on board, but is cheaper to get them in advance from *Tabak/ Trafic* booths. They are validated in a little machine on board, often marked with an 'E' (*Entwerter*).

Telephones

The system is efficient and it is quite easy to use ordinary pay-phones if you're somewhere without a telephone centre. Most boxes have instructions in English and most of the international operators speak it. Even remote places have booths that will take telephone cards, (*Wertkarten*), available from post offices, stations and some shops.

To call abroad from Austria: *tel: 00*. To call Austria from abroad: *tel: 43*. To call international enquiries and operator: *tel: 08*. To call national enquiries and operator: *tel: 16 11*. **Emergencies**: Police: 133; Fire: 122; Am-bulance: 144

Rail Travel Within Austria

The national rail company is *Österreichische Bundesbahnen (ÖBB)*. Most lines are electrified and the railway system is fast and reliable, with *IC* trains every 1–2 hours and regional trains timed to connect with *IC* services. Other fast trains are: *D* (ordinary express trains often only with second-class seating); *E* (semi-fast or local trains which are usually second class); *EC*; *EN*; and *SC* (*Super-City*, with stops only in larger cities).

Major services have both first- and second-class seating and most overnight trains have sleeping-cars (up to three berths) and couchettes (four or six berths). Some ordinary seating compartments are allocated exclusively for people wishing to sleep through the night.

A single supplement, payable in Austria, covers first-class travel on all *EC* and *SC* trains and also (on request) the cost of seat reservations. Reservations are usually possible and are recommended at peak times. They can be made up to three months in advance for sleeping-cars and two months in advance for couchettes.

Fares and Passes

The main domestic passes are: **Bundesnetzkarte**, valid for first- or second-class travel for one month on all ÖBB lines, including the Schneebergbahn and Puchbergbahn mountain railways and the four **Österreich-Puzzles** (Austrian Puzzles) Ost, West, Nord and Süd, which cover geographical boundaries and give unlimited rail travel for any 4 days within a 10-day period. The Österreich-Puzzles cost S.1485 in first class and S.900 in second class (there is a reduction for those under 26).

BELGIUM

Capital: Brussels (*Bruxelles/Brussel*). **Language**: French, Flemish, Dutch and German are all official languages, in different areas. Most people speak both French and Flemish, and English is also widely spoken. **Currency**: Belgian Francs (BFr.); 1 Franc = 100 Centimes.

Customs

Standard EU regulations apply (see pp. 13–14),

but there is an extra allowance of 8 litres of Luxembourg wines, provided they are imported directly across the Luxembourg border.

Passports and Visas

A British Visitor's Passport is sufficient, as are EU National Identity Cards. All other travellers need a full passport. Visas are not needed by the above, nor by nationals of the EU, Australia, Canada, New Zealand and the USA (provided they hold passports valid for at least three months beyond the end of their stay). Others should check.

Useful Addresses in the UK

Consulate, *103 Eaton Square, Victoria, London SW1W 9AB; tel: (071) 235 5422.* **National Tourist Office**, *Premier House, 2 Gayton Rd, Harrow, Middlesex, HA1 2XU; tel: (081) 861 3300.* **Belgian National Railways**, *439 Premier House, 10 Greycoat Place, London SW1P 1SB; tel: (071) 233 0360* (answerphone out of office hours).

Useful Addresses in the USA

Embassy, *3330 Garfield Street NW, Washington DC 20008; tel: (202) 333 6900.* **National Tourist Office and Railroad Representatives**, *745 Fifth Ave (Suite 714), New York, NY 10151; tel: (212) 758 8130.*

Living in Belgium

Accommodation

Accommodation in Belgium tends to be pricey and you're unlikely to get anything for less than BFr.1,000 (BFr.600 single) in even a one-star hotel in a small place (at least twice/three times that in major towns and tourist areas). If money is tight, therefore, aim for private rooms or hostels (of which there are plenty).

The Benelux countries (Belgium, the Netherlands and Luxembourg) have a common hotel-rating system and all hotels must display, beside the entrance, a blue plaque giving the rating. The lowest category is 'O', meaning that only accommodation is offered, although that must meet minimum requirements of hygiene and comfort; next is 'H', indicating moderate comfort and at least one bathroom per ten rooms. After that, you move onto the more usual star system,

---

> **Belgium**
> - Belgium offers a wide range of discounts for the old and the young, so it's always worth your while to ask before you purchase tickets for anything.
> - A weekly English-language publication called *The Bulletin* is available from news-stands for BFr.75 and lists everything from films in English to job opportunities.

---

the one-star places being obliged (as a minimum) to have a wash-stand in every room and to serve breakfast. Hotel rates displayed include VAT and service charges; breakfast may, or may not, be included. During summer, hotel accommodation can be hard to find and it's best to pre-book, especially in Bruges and on the coast. **Central Booking Service**; *tel: (02) 513 7484.*

Rough camping is not permitted – you must use official campsites. It's often possible to camp on farms, but only with permission. Each provincial tourist office produces a list of campsites in its area and most also list bed and breakfast establishments, including private homes. Get full details of campsites from **Royal Camping and Caravanning Club of Belgium**, *rue Madeleine 31, B-1000 Brussels; tel: (02) 513 12 87.*

Food and Drink

Most restaurants have fixed-price menus (*menu du jour*) which are much cheaper than à la carte. Menus, with prices, are displayed outside most eating-places, so you can check what is on offer before you enter. You should try the waffles (*gaufres*) and chocolates, for both of which Belgium is justly famed. Belgium produces over 300 beers (both dark and light) and they are by far the most popular local drink.

Opening Hours

Banks: Mon–Fri 0900–1600 (some close for lunch). **Shops**: Mon–Sat 0900/1000–1800 (often later on Sat), but some close 1200–1400. Some food shops open on Sun. **Museums**: open six days a week 1000–1700. The closing day varies but it's usually Mon or Tues (check locally).

Postage

Major post offices (**Le Post/De Post**) are open Mon–Fri 0900–1700 and some also open Friday evening and Saturday morning. Smaller ones usually close 1200–1400. Post boxes are red and attached to walls or poles.

Public Holidays

1 Jan; Easter Monday; 1 May; Ascension Day; Whit Mon; 21 July; 15 Aug; 1, 11 Nov; 25 Dec.

Public Transport

Main rail and bus stations are usually close together, so transfers are easy. All cities have a good local transport network, offering a choice between individual tickets or multiple-trip tickets. These are better value. You can buy tickets from drivers but it's cheaper to get them in advance at the station. The best value is usually a tourist ticket, valid for all the city transport for 24 hours. Tickets are validated in a box on boarding.

Although it's legal to hail taxis in the street, drivers tend to ignore signals and it's better to find a taxi rank – or to telephone.

Telephones

There are both coin boxes and Telecard booths. Telecards can be purchased at rail stations, post offices and news-stands.

To call abroad from Belgium: *tel: 00*. To call Belgium from abroad: *tel: 32*. For the local operator: *tel: 997*. For the national operator: *tel: 1307 (1207* in Flemish areas). For the European operator: *tel: 1304 (1204* in Flemish areas). For the international operator: *tel: 1322 (1222* in Flemish areas). **Emergencies**: Police: 101; Fire: 100; Ambulance: 100.

Rail Travel Within Belgium

The Belgian national railway system is operated by *Société des Chemins de fer Belges (SNCB)*; also known in Flemish as *Nationale Maatschappij der Belgische Spoorwegen (NMBS)*. The rail network is comprehensive and reliable, with fast and frequent services linking all the major cities.

IC trains stop only at main stations. *IR* trains are also fast, but stop at some intermediate stations. *L (local)* trains stop at all stations en route. All three operate at regular intervals and timetables are co-ordinated to avoid long waits when a change of train is necessary. Seat reservations are possible only for international journeys. Every main station has a railway information counter and an international reservations desk.

Fares and Passes

For those aged 12–25, **Go Pass** provides eight trips within Belgium, the only restriction being that you may not travel before 0800 on weekdays. The **Half-fare Card** enables the holder to travel through Belgium for a month, paying only 50% of the normal first- and second-class fares. The **Tourrail** pass gives unlimited train travel for any 5 days in a 17-day period.

Train tickets should be bought in advance but, if necessary, you can get them on the train provided you pay an extra BFr.50 and tell the conductor you intend to do so *before* you board. If you board without clearing it first, you are liable for a fine of BFr.1,000.

Tickets can be purchased up to five days in advance, but you must tell the ticket office what day you intend to travel since the tickets are valid only for that day. Ordinary return tickets cost twice as much as singles and you have to return the same day, but there are weekend tickets. You can upgrade your class of travel once on board.

BULGARIA

Capital: Sofia (*Sofija*). **Language**: Bulgarian, which is a Slavic tongue and uses the Cyrillic alphabet. Some English, German and French is spoken in larger hotels, restaurants and shops in main cities and resorts. Russian is more widely understood, but is unpopular. Nodding the head up and down indicates 'no' (*ne*) and shaking it from side to side means 'yes' (*da*). **Currency**: Leva (Lv.). 1 Leva = 100 Stotinki. The import/export of local currency is prohibited and, on leaving, you must re-convert Leva into hard currency before you go through passport control. Receipts (*bordereaux*) will be given for every exchange transaction and when you pay for accommodation. These must be retained as they will be needed when you leave. Major credit cards are accepted in larger hotels, restaurants and shops and their use is spreading.

Passports and Visas

A full passport is required by all travellers. Nationals of Australia and the USA do not require visas. Nationals of most other countries are exempt from carrying a visa if travelling in groups of at least six or can provide proof of two or more nights' prepaid accommodation in Bulgaria.

When you arrive you will be given a *carte statistique*. Take good care of this. It has to be date-stamped every time you check into, and out of, any form of accommodation. When you leave Bulgaria, the stamps will be checked.

Customs

The allowances are: 250 cigarettes or 250g tobacco products, 1 litre spirits, 2 litres wine, and 100g perfume.

Useful Addresses in the UK

Republic of Bulgaria Consular Section, *186/188 Queen's Gate, London SW7 5HL; tel: (071) 584 9400.* **National Tourist Office (Balkan Holidays)**, *Sofia House, 19 Conduit Street, London W1R 9TD; tel: (071) 491 4499.*

Useful Addresses in the USA

Embassy of Bulgaria, *1621 22nd Street NW, Washington DC 20008-1921; tel: (202) 387 7969.* **National Tourist Office (Balkan Holidays)**, *161 East 86th Street, New York, NY 10028; tel: (212) 573 5530 or 722 1110.*

Living in Bulgaria

Accommodation

In Sofia, Balkantourist remains a useful source, but private agencies now offer accommodation booking, information and exchange facilities. The better hotels have information desks which can be of considerable help to travellers.

Food and Drink

Bulgaria produces vegetables of all kinds, which you will find in dishes such as: *bop* (lentil soup), *gjuvetch* (vegetable stew), and *kiopolou* (aubergines/eggplants). Lamb and pork are also popular.

Tea is usually green and served without milk; coffee is of the Turkish type (black, strong and

---

Bulgaria

- Protection against hepatitis A is recommended.
- Balkantourist was the official tourist agency and has offices all over the place. It is still the best place to go for information, to change money and to book accommodation.
- Many street names are being changed, so make sure you get up-to-date city maps.
- There are some restrictions on photography and you should not use your camera at airports, railways, military installations, bridges or tunnels. Some border zones have restricted access.
- Many consumer goods are hard to find, so take with you all you think you will need in the way of films, cosmetics, toilet paper, tea-bags, and medicines.

---

with sediment), although espresso can be found in a few hotel bars. Bottled fruit juices are cheap and readily available. *Slivova* is a hangover-producing plum brandy, so take care. The aniseed-flavoured *mastika* and *raki* are also potent. The local beer is cheap, but an acquired taste. Bulgarian wine is cheap and good. The tap water is safe to drink except in the rare places where a sign indicates otherwise.

Opening Hours

Banks: Mon–Fri 0800–1230 and 1300–1500, Sat 0800–1400. **Shops**: Mon–Fri 0800–1700/1900, Sat 0800–1400. **Museums**: vary widely, but the norm is 0800–1830, closing on either Mon or Tue. A 'Non-Stop' sign indicates that the establishment stays open 24 hours a day.

Postage

Stamps (*marki*) can be bought only from post offices (*poshta*), usually open Mon–Sat 0830–1730.

Public Holidays

1 Jan; 3 Mar; a few days around Easter; 1, 24 May; a few days around Christmas.

Public Transport

There are good rail and long-distance bus networks. Unusually, buses are slightly more expensive than trains, but both are very cheap by Western standards. At small stops, you can only buy your bus ticket once the bus is in and they can see how many spaces are available.

Local city transport is very cheap and runs frequently. However, the hardware is often decrepit and there are packed crowds at rush hour.

Telephones

Coin boxes are fine for local calls, but go to the central telephone office (not necessarily in the post office) in major towns if you want to phone anywhere further afield.

To call abroad from Bulgaria: *tel: 00*. To call Bulgaria from abroad: *tel: 359*. To call the international operator: *tel: 0123*. To call the local operator: *tel: 121*. **Emergencies**: Police: 166; Fire: 160; Ambulance: 150.

Rail Travel Within Bulgaria

The national rail company is *Bulgarian State Railways* (BDŽ). Station indicator boards can be confusing. One platform may serve two tracks and platforms and tracks are both numbered.

The rail system is fairly comprehensive and there are three types of train: express, fast and slow. Journeys on the electrified lines between Sofia and the other major cities are fast. Elsewhere, electrification is not complete and you should be prepared to travel slowly.

Trains are very busy and seat reservations are recommended (obligatory for express trains). All medium- and long-distance trains have first- and second-class carriages and a limited buffet service. Overnight trains between Sofia and the Black Sea resorts have first- and second-class sleeping-cars and second-class couchettes.

Notices and signs at stations are in Cyrillic; learn what the name of your destination looks like and ask what time the train is due to arrive there, so you don't have to rely on spotting a sign (not very numerous). A good route map can be helpful to work out where you are.

Fares and Passes

With the exception of Sofia Central Railway Station, which has an international ticket counter, only domestic tickets are available from stations. Rila Travel, with offices in all cities, handle international travel. Even for local journeys, it's better to buy your ticket in advance, as there are usually long queues at stations. You can buy tickets on the trains but that costs twice as much.

THE CZECH REPUBLIC

Capital: Prague (*Praha*). **Language**: Czech is the official language of the Czech Republic. Czech and Slovak are closely related Slavic tongues, mutually intelligible by natives of both the Czech and the Slovak Republics. Some English, Russian and German is also understood, although Russian is less popular now than it was. Shops where the staff are linguists usually have a sign saying so. **Currency**: Czech Korunas or Crowns (K.); 1 Koruna = 100 Hellers. Non-residents may import/export up to 100 Crowns and there are no restrictions on foreign currencies. Credit cards are widely accepted in tourist areas.

Passports and Visas

Full passports are required by everyone. Visas are not needed by EU nationals, nor by citizens of Canada or the USA. Nationals of Australia and New Zealand need visas and must have passports valid for at least six months. Others should check.

Customs

The following allowances apply only to those who are aged 18 or over. They are: 250 cigarettes or equivalent in tobacco, 1 litre spirits, and 2 litres wine (halve these quantities if your stay is to be for two days or less).

Useful Addresses in the UK

Embassy, *28 Kensington Palace Gardens, London W8 4QY; tel: (071) 243 1115.* **Čedoc (Czech Tourist Office)**, *49 Southwark Street, London SE1 1RU; tel: (071) 378 6009.*

Useful Addresses in the USA

Embassy, *3900 Linnean Ave NW, Washington DC 20008-3897; tel: (202) 363 6315.* **Čedok (Czech Tourist Office)**, *10 East 40th Street, New York, NY 10016; tel: (212) 689 9720.*

Living in the Czech Republic

Accommodation

You should have a choice of one–five-star hotels, private rooms and pensions, and, at a much more basic level, old-style tourist hotels (effectively dormitory-type barracks), hostels and inns with a few spartan rooms. However, the quality (once outside the five-star range) can leave a lot to be desired. Although people are trying to upgrade as fast as possible, it is still probably safer to look at private rooms than cheap hotels. Some places may still insist on payment in hard currency.

This is the most popular of the former Eastern bloc countries and the deluge of tourists has resulted in a real shortage of beds. Always book ahead. The state tourist organisation, Cedok, runs booking offices across the country, as well as in London and New York; while CKM in Prague will advise on youth hostels (both for a commission).

There are plenty of campsites (usually May–October only), most of which cater for caravans as well. Rough camping is forbidden.

Food and Drink

Lunch is around 1130–1400/1500 and dinner 1800–2130/2200. The cuisine is rich and meat-based, but vegetarian restaurants are beginning to appear. Schnitzel and dumplings (*knedliky*) are on virtually every menu, as is *gulaš*, a spicy meat dish in which wine is a major ingredient.

Eating and drinking are cheap, especially in *bufet* (where you stand while eating), and *samoobsluha* (self-service). *Kavarny* and *cukrárny* serve coffee (often Turkish-style) and delightful pastries. Beer halls (*pivnice*) and wine bars (*vinárna*) are good places to eat. Czech beer and Slovak wine are excellent. Budweiser originated here, but the original (*Budvar*) is better.

Opening Hours

Banks: Mon–Fri 0830–1715. **Shops**: Mon–Fri 0900–1200 and 1400–1800, Sat 0900–1200. Food shops usually open much earlier. Food and souvenir shops often open on Sun. **Museums**: (usually) Tue–Sun 1000–1700. Most castles close on national holidays and from Nov to March.

Postage

There is a full postage service (including post restante), but it is slow and erratic. It is also cheap. Usual post office opening hours are 0800–1900. Stamps are also available from newsagents and tobacconists.

Public Holidays

1 Jan; Easter Monday; 1, 9 May; 5–6 July; 28 Oct; 24–26 Dec.

Public Transport

The rail network here is good, but there is also a comprehensive long-distance bus network, run by CSAD. Bus stations are well-organised, with platforms, ticket offices and amazingly complicated schedule boards. Officially, you should book in advance, but you can buy tickets from the conductor, although he will give priority to those with reservations.

Telephones

To call abroad from the Czech Republic: *tel: 00*. To call the Czech Republic from abroad: *tel: 42*. **Emergencies**: Police: 158; Fire: 150; Ambulance: 333

Rail Travel Within the Czech Republic

The national rail company is *Českých Drah (ČD)*. The rail network is cheap and extensive, but always crowded. The fastest trains are *expresný*. The *rychlík* cost as much as the express. The few *spešný* (semi-fast) trains cost less. *Osobný* (slow) trains should be avoided.

All trains offer both first- and second-class travel. Most long-distance trains have dining-cars and overnight services between cities have sleeping-cars. Seat reservations are recommended for express trains but cannot be made on the day of travel. Bookings can be made at the counter marked 'R' at stations. To reserve sleepers, you must go to an office of the Czech Travel Bureau (Čedok), located in most towns.

Fares and Passes

A **Czech-Slovak Flexipass**, available in the USA only (from the Forsyth Travel Library, see p. 22), covers 5 days unlimited travel within a 15-day period throughout both the republics. There is also an **Explorer Pass**, valid for 7 consecutive days (or multiples thereof) which covers first- or second-class rail travel. It is available to anyone under 26 and to any holder of an ISIC card. It must be purchased (from Campus Travel – see p. 22) before you go.

DENMARK

Capital: Copenhagen (*København*). **Language**: Danish; the Danish alphabet has three extra letters: æ, ø and aa/å. In alphabetical lists, all three come after the z. Almost everywhere English is spoken and understood. German and French are also widely spoken. 'Ikke' means 'not' and is used on signs to indicate that something is not allowed. **Currency**: Danish Kroner (DKr.); 1 Krone = 100 Øre.

Passports and Visas

A British Visitor's Passport is sufficient, as are EU National Identity Cards. EU nationals, Scandinavians and nationals of Australia, Canada, New Zealand and the USA do not need visas. Others should check.

Customs

Standard EU regulations apply (see pp. 13–14).

Useful Addresses in the UK

Embassy, *55 Sloane St, London SW1X 9SR; tel: (071) 333 0266.* **Tourist Board**, *Sceptre House, 169/173 Regent Street, London W1R 8PY; tel: (071) 734 2637.* **Danish State Railways**, *c/o DFDS Seaways, Scandinavia House, Parkeston Quay, Harwich, Essex, CO12 4QG; tel: (0255) 554681.*

Useful Addresses in the USA

Embassy, *3200 White Haven Street NW, Washington DC 20008-3683; tel: (202) 234 4300.* **Scandinavian Tourist Board**, *655 Third Ave (18th Floor), New York, NY 10017; tel: (212) 949 2333.*

Living in Denmark

Accommodation

Standards are good and the choice is wide.

However, the Danish Tourist Board neither runs an official grading system nor makes hotel bookings. Prices in some hotels are reduced during school holidays.

There are several different hotel passes/ cheques which can be bought in advance and offer discounts in some chains. For example, savings of up to 50% are offered with the **Scandinavian Bonus Pass** and the **PreSkandinavia Hotel Check System**. For a hotel room in Copenhagen, expect to pay about DKr. 350. Prices are generally lower elsewhere.

There are about 100 hostels and over 500 campsites. Hostels don't impose age restrictions and offer family rooms. Beds cost about DKr. 55–85 (sleeping bags are not allowed). If you don't have IYHF or national YHA membership, guest membership is available for one night, at a price.

Campers need a camping pass – either an international Camping Carnet or a Danish carnet (available from campsites and tourist offices). There are fines for illegal camping. For more information, contact **Campingrådet**, *Hesseløgade 16, DK-2100 Copenhagen Ø.*

Food and Drink

Danish cuisine is simple and based on the excellent local produce: fish, meat, dairy products and vegetables. *Smorrebrød* are simple but often stunning open sandwiches of rye bread. *Frikadeller* are pork meat balls. Try the *weinerbrod* (*real* Danish pastries) and ice cream cones. Food is quite expensive, but almost invariably of good quality and attractively presented. Portions tend to be large. Self-service places are cheapest for eating out (besides takeaways) and the system is to have several small helpings, rather than one large one.

All tap water is drinkable. Tea and coffee are widely available. There are many excellent local lagers (including Carlsberg and Tuborg). Most wines and spirits are imported. The local spirit is *akvavit*, a potato-based schnapps consumed in a single gulp. All alcohol is expensive, as is chocolate.

Opening Hours

Banks: (in Copenhagen) Mon-Fri 0930-1500/ 1600 (Thur 0930–1800). Hours vary elsewhere.

Shops: Mon–Thur 0900/1000–1730, Fri 0900–1900/2000, Sat 0900–1300/1400 (until 1600/1700 on the first Saturday of each month). **Museums**: (mostly) Tue–Sun 1000–1500 or 1100–1600. In winter, hours are shorter and some museums don't open at all.

Postage

Postboxes are red, with a yellow horn and crown.

Public Holidays

1 Jan; Maundy Thursday to Easter Monday; Great Prayer Day (the fourth Friday after Good Friday); Ascension Day; Whit Sunday–Monday; the afternoon of Constitution Day (5 June); 25, 26 Dec.

Public Transport

Long-distance travel is best done by trains, as the inter-regional bus service is fairly sparse. There are excellent regional and city bus services however, many of whose timetables are designed to connect with trains. All cities also have taxis and there is an extensive ferry service connecting up all the islands.

Telephones

To call abroad from Denmark: *tel: 009*. To call Denmark from abroad: *tel: 45*. **Emergencies**: Police: 112; Fire: 112; Ambulance: 112.

Rail Travel Within Denmark

The state railway system is *Danske Statsbaner (DSB)*, but there are also some private lines. *IC* trains are comfortable long-distance expresses which link major cities and can reach speeds of around 124 mph. Classes of travel: *Salon* (first class), *IC-Pladser* (double seats with a table between them), *Hvilepladser* (seats recline) and *Familiepladser* (for family groups). Other trains are classified *IR* or *RE (Regional)*, and have frequent services on most lines.

Sleepers on domestic services have one berth in first class and two berths in second class. Couchettes have six berths and are second class only. Seat reservations are compulsory on some trains, including the plush *IC* trains and any that board ferries to cross the Great Belt (Store Baelt) between Funen and Zealand.

Fares and Passes

Most European rail passes (see pp. 22–26) include discounts on some ferries, which are an integral part of the transport system and are automatically covered by the cost of any other through train or bus ticket. An efficient bus network links station stops with local towns.

ESTONIA

Capital: Tallinn. **Language**: Estonian (a member of the tiny Finno-Ugric language group, which also includes Finnish and Hungarian). Some Finnish could be useful and Russian is more widely understood but not popular. It can be very difficult to communicate without a dictionary or phrasebook. **Currency**: Kroons or Crowns (EEK); 1 Kroon = 100 Sents. There are no restrictions on the import/export of any currency, but you must change some money into Kroons when you enter Estonia. Travellers' cheques can be changed at banks (and occasionally post offices) but it's easy to get caught out so always carry some cash. Credit cards are gaining recognition, but are still only accepted in a few places.

Passports and Visas

Full passports are required by all categories of travellers. Visas are not needed by holders of full British passports, nationals of Australia, Canada, New Zealand and the USA. Almost everyone else does require a visa and should check. Estonian visas are also valid for Latvia and Lithuania.

Customs

Although it is not a member state, Estonia applies the standard EU regulations (see pp. 13–14).

Useful Addresses in the UK

Embassy of Estonia, *16 Hyde Park Gate, London SW7 5DG; tel: (071) 589 3428.*

Useful Addresses in the USA

Embassy of Estonia, *1030 15th Street (Suite 1000), Washington, DC 20005; tel: (202) 789 0320.* **Estonian Consulate General and National Tourist Office**, *630 Fifth Ave (Suite 2415), New York, NY 10111; tel: (212) 247 7634.*

Living in Estonia

Accommodation

Hotels are still fairly thin on the ground. Home stays offer accommodation in farmhouses, summer cottages, homes and small boarding houses. Try to be back at your lodgings/hotel by 2200 (usual lock-out time), unless you've checked that it's all right to be later.

Food and Drink

There are some good cafés and restaurants in all large towns, but the dishes on offer depend more on the availability of basic supplies than on the menu. Ask the waiter to recommend something if you are not sure what to have. The pattern of eating is to have a large helping of *hors d'oeuvres* and modest helpings thereafter. Fish is a common ingredient. Many restaurants are open noon to midnight, with a break of a couple of hours: usually 1700–1900 (reservations are advisable, especially in the big hotels).

Tap water is not safe to drink anywhere, buy bottled water instead. Tea and coffee are widely available. The most popular drink is beer (*olu*). Vodka and brandy are better value and some bars serve mulled wine. Vana Toomas is the Estonian liqueur.

Opening Hours

Banks: Mon–Fri 0930–1730. **Shops**: Mon–Fri 0900/1000–1700/1800, Sat 0900/1000–1500/1700. Shops often close for an hour or two between 1200 and 1500. In Tallinn some open on Sunday afternoons. **Museums**: The days of opening vary enormously and many museums open for only a few days every week, so you need to check locally. On the days they are open, this is usually from 1100 to 1600.

Postage

Stamps are sold by large hotels and post offices, but the service is erratic and you could arrive home before your postcards.

Public Holidays

1 Jan; 24 Feb (Independence Day); Good Friday; Easter Monday (unofficial); 1, 2 May; 23, 24 June; 18 Nov; 25, 26, 31 Dec.

The Baltic states

When travelling through any of the Baltic states (Estonia, Latvia or Lithuania) make sure you have a sufficient supply of any routine medicines you may need, from the humble aspirin onwards.

Public Transport

Buses travel to more destinations than trains and can be considerably quicker. Buy tickets before boarding from the ticketing windows. Don't expect staff to speak English.

Telephones

The change in currency from roubles to Kroons has meant public phones have been abandoned until they can be replaced with card phones although you can still make local calls for free. To make international calls try the post office, or for convenience the large hotels which charge a premium. The recent modernisation of the telephone lines means calls no longer travel via Moscow and you might actually get through. It still pays to be patient however as the long-distance lines can be overcrowded and to book a call can take up to an hour.

To call abroad from Estonia: *tel: 10*. To call Estonia from abroad: *tel: 37*. For local directory assistance: *tel: 09* (from offices and establishments); *tel: 065* (from private homes). To book a call: *tel: 007* (English spoken). **Emergencies**: Police: 02; Fire: 01; Ambulance: 03.

Rail Travel Within Estonia

Estonian Railways (*EVR*) is the national operator. Trains fan out from Tallinn to the rest of the country (and into Latvia, Lithuania and Russia), but the suburban services are the most frequent and the others tend to get very crowded. Domestic services are slow, but very cheap.

There are two classes: 'soft' has fully upholstered seats and 'hard' has plastic/leather seats. Both convert to berths for overnight journeys. Soft is a couchette with four berths; hard may be either four-berth couchettes or an open-plan sleeping compartment. In both, there is a charge for all bedding, including mattresses. Some trains have normal two- or four-berth

European sleeping-cars and some trains have only hard class, but there is no advance information about which, so ask locally.

When travelling between the Baltic States, book for soft (first) class. Through sleepers to West/Central Europe are of Western (*Inter-City*) type with one or two berths in first class and three berths in second class (all with full bedding included). Trains that run only by day are second class. Advance reservations are necessary (except for purely local trains) if you want to be sure of a seat. Timetables run horizontally instead of vertically. Travel to Riga is best done overnight on one of the sleeper trains. Berths are four to a cabin and bedding is provided for a small charge. For information on trains *tel: 007*.

FINLAND

Capital: Helsinki (*Helsingfors*). **Language**: Finnish and, in the north, Lapp (or Saame). Finnish is a truly complicated tongue, which defies the efforts of most foreigners. Among other things, place names are not always written in the same way, so you need to concentrate when working out your schedule. Swedish is the second language, but not very widely spoken. English is spoken and understood to a large extent, especially in the south and amongst the young and those in the tourist trade. **Currency** Markka (Mk.); 1 Markka = 100 Pennies.

Passports and Visas

A British Visitor's Passport is sufficient, as are EU National Identity Cards. Visas are not needed by nationals of Scandinavia, the EU, Australia, Canada, New Zealand or the USA. Others should check.

Customs

Any European resident aged 16 or more is entitled to an allowance of 200 cigarettes or 250g tobacco. The allowance is twice as much for those from outside Europe. Anyone aged 20 or more may also import: 2 litres beer, 1 litre alcohol under 22% volume, and 1 litre spirits. Those aged 18/19 are allowed 2 litres beer, and 2 litres alcohol under 22% volume.

Useful Addresses in the UK

Embassy, *38 Chesham Place, London SW1X 8HW; tel: (071) 838 6200*. **Tourist Board**, *66/68 Haymarket, London SW1Y 4RF; tel: (071) 839 4048*. **Finlandia Travel Agency** (sells Finnrail pass), *227 Regent St, London W1R 7DB; tel: (071) 409 7334/5*. **NSR Travel** (sells Scanrail pass), *Norway House, 21/24 Cockspur Street, London SW1Y 5DA; tel: (071) 930 6666*.

Useful Addresses in the USA

Embassy, *3216 New Mexico Ave NW, Washington, DC 20016-2782; tel: (202) 363 2430*. **Scandinavian Tourist Board and Railroad Representatives**, *655 Third Ave, New York, NY 10017; tel: (212) 949-2333*.

Living in Finland

Accommodation

Whatever your taste or budget, Finland can offer accommodation to suit. At the top end of the market, there are international hotels, beautiful spas and health resorts. Slightly cheaper accommodation can be found in the *gasthaus* (small family hotels with full restaurant service); farmhouses; summer hotels (budget hotels that operate from 1 June–31 August; the rest of the year, they house students); finhostels and youth hostels. Self-catering options include apartments (suitable for a stay of a few days or more), cottages, holiday villages (there are many in the Lakeland area) and campsites (350 across the country). The main camping season is May–Sept.

Most of the major hotel chains have bookig centres in Helsinki, where you can make reservations for the rest of your trip. It is increasingly common for hotels to offer reduced rates – especially in summer – so always ask. Alternatively, use the Hotel Booking Centre in Helsinki Railway Station, for accommodation of all varieties. There are other hotel booking centres across the country. Ask for the nearest at the tourist office; if there isn't one close, they will supply you with names and addresses for you to call yourself.

Food and Drink

The Finns have four meals per day: breakfast

0630–1000; lunch 1100–1300; dinner 1600–1900; and supper 1900–2400. In restaurants, there is often a fixed-price menu which represents a considerable saving on à la carte.

Restaurants are expensive, but you can get good-value breakfasts at many of the large hotels, without being a resident. Buffet lunches of the eat-as-much-as-you-like variety are common and good value. It is also possible to eat for a reasonable price at fast-food stands (grillit), snack-bars (baari) and cafeterias (kahvila). They are often self-service and seldom offer alcohol, other than mild beer. The more upmarket ravintola are restaurants that sometimes have dancing.

Especially in the south, Finnish cuisine is very cosmopolitan and you have to make a special request for local dishes. Fish is a major ingredient and you might like to try reindeer stew (at its best in Lappland). Milk is very popular and coffee is consumed in vast quan-tities. Liqueurs are made from every conceivable type of fruit and alcohol is readily available in restaurants and bars, but only to people over 18 – and at a price. Beer (olut is priced according to strength, the strongest and most expensive category being olut IV).

Opening Hours

Banks: Mon–Fri 0915–1615. **Shops**: Mon–Fri 0900–1800 (stores 0900–2000) and Sat 0900–1500 (stores 0900–1800). **Museums**: opening hours vary considerably so check locally. The usual closing day is Monday. Many, especially in the country, are closed in winter.

Postage

Most post offices are open Mon–Fri 0900–1700; some have extended opening hours. Post boxes are yellow.

Public Holidays

1, 6 Jan; Good Friday; Easter Monday; May Day Eve and May Day; Ascension Day; Whitsun; Midsummer Eve; Midsummer Day; 1 Nov; 6 (Independence Day), 25, 26 Dec.

Public Transport

The fastest way of getting around is to fly. Finnair offers a comprehensive range of domestic flights

---

> ### Finland
>
> Protection against polio is recommended. In summer mosquitoes are a real problem, particularly in the north, so take a strong repellent.

and there are a number of discounts available, so explore the options. The Finnish coach service operates on 90% of public roads and is hailed as the busiest in the world. Coach travel is relatively cheap and there are specially reduced fares available if you buy tickets from coach stations or travel agents, rather than on the bus. With a YIEE card (which costs Mk.35, if you are under 26) you are eligible for a 30% reduction on journeys over 80 km, and 50% if you pay in advance. Coach timetables conveniently fit in with rail, air and boat services. A copy of Suomen Kulkernavot (the most complete collection of timetables available; bought from a kiosk or coach station) will allow you to plan your trip. Express services provide fast connections between main towns but cost slightly more than stopping services.

Inside most Finnish cities and towns, local passenger transport is good. Buses depart as frequently as every 3 mins. In Helsinki you also have the option of trams or the underground. In most local transport systems, you are responsible for stamping your own tickets – the stamp machines are usually orange and near the centre.

Telephones

To call abroad from Finland: tel: 990. To call Finland from abroad: tel: 358 + area code, omitting the first 9. To call national directory enquiries: tel: 118. To call international directory enquiries: tel: 92020. To call the operator: tel: 92022. **Emergencies**: Police: 112; Fire: 112; Ambulance: 112.

Rail Travel Within Finland

The national rail company is Finnish Railways (VR). The railway network is extensive, clean and comfortable. It covers 6,000 km (of which 1,445 km are electrified) and links all the major towns; trains reaching a maximum speed of 87 mph. Trains include IC and EP: special fast trains on which reservations are compulsory.

There are no couchettes. Sleeping-cars have one berth in first class and two or three berths in second class. Sleeping accommodation costs less Mon–Thur than at weekends.

Fares and Passes

The **Finnrail** pass gives unlimited first- or second-class travel on *VR* for 8, 15 or 22 days. It can be purchased either before you go or once you have arrived inside Finland. Some rail passes are valid on buses that have replaced trains on old routes, so it's always worth asking if yours is acceptable.

FRANCE

Capital: Paris. **Language**: French; quite a few people can speak and understand a little English, particularly in Paris. **Currency**: French Francs (Ffr.); 1 Franc = 100 Centimes.

Passports and Visas

A British Visitor's Passport is sufficient, as are EU National Identity Cards. Visas are not needed by nationals of EU countries, Canada, New Zealand or the USA. Australians do need visas. Others should check.

Customs

Standard EU regulations apply (see p. 13–14).

Useful Addresses in the UK

Consulate General, *21 Cromwell Road, London SW7 2DQ; tel: (071) 838 2000.* **Maison de la France (Tourist Office)**, *178 Piccadilly London W1V 0AL; tel: (0891) 244 123.* **French Railways Ltd (SNCF)**, *French Railways House, 178/9 Piccadilly, London W1V 0BA; tel: (071) 495 4433.*

Useful Addresses in the USA

Embassy, *4101 Reservoir Road NW, Washington DC 20007; tel: (202) 944 6000.* **French Government Tourist Office**, *610 Fifth Ave, New York, NY 10020-2452; tel: (212) 757 1125.* **Railroad enquiries** *tel: (914) 682 7920.*

Living in France

Accommodation

Tourist offices supply free lists of most types of accommodation in their area, but it's usual for them to charge a fee (about FFr.10) if you want them to do your booking. Advance reservations are recommended for the larger towns and resort areas in summer.

Paris is expensive. Elsewhere, prices for double rooms (without en suite facilities or breakfast) in one-star hotels begin at about FFr.200. Singles are often the same, but may be a few francs cheaper. Some places offer a continental breakfast within the price of rooms, irrespective of whether or not you choose to eat it. When you have a choice, you will probably find that the hotel breakfast is overpriced and you will do better to go to the nearest café. All hotels and campsites are graded, using the star system, and this is usually fairly accurate.

Relais et Châteaux, *av. Marceau 9, 75116 Paris; tel: 47 23 41 42* is an upmarket association consisting of some 150 hotels that were originally châteaux or manor houses and will supply leaflets about them. They are usually places of some character, set in large grounds. They invariably pride themselves on the standard of cuisine. **Logis** are small, fairly cheap, family-run hotels (in small towns and rural areas) that are comfortable and serve local cuisine. They almost invariably have a lot of character, are excellent value and can be identified by a distinctive yellow and green sign. A paperback guide called *Logis de France* is on sale from tourist offices and from most bookshops in France – and some in the UK. Another chain of friendly, budget hotels is **France-Accueil**, *rue Dessous-des-Berges 85, 75013 Paris; tel: 45 83 04 22,* who supply free listings of their establishments. **Gîtes Ruraux** are furnished cottages, etc., which can be hired by families (or other groups of people) for a week/month at a time. Bed and breakfast places are **Chambres d'hôte** and local tourist offices will supply lists for their area.

Youth hostels are known as **Auberges de Jeunesse (AJ)** and are usually of high standard, but not breathtakingly cheap. Some are IYHF and some are run by similar, but purely French, companies. Since most of the hostels are on the outskirts of towns and local buses tend to stop running early, many people opt for more central budget hotels – there's often very little difference in the cost.

Camping is popular throughout France and campsites are numerous: **Michelin** produce a guide to the best ones. You can also get a guide from the **Federation Française de Camping et de Caravanning**, *rue de Rivoli 78, 75004 Paris; tel: (1) 42 72 84 08*. Some are de luxe and no cheaper than hotels, others rough. The cheapest ones with good facilities are usually **Camping Municipal**. Many sites are fully booked well in advance and (especially in July and August) it is unwise to assume that you will find space available if you just turn up. It is very often possible to camp on private farms, but on no account do so without the farmer's permission: they are usually armed and do not hesitate to shoot at trespassers. Local tourist offices usually have lists of farms where camping is possible and of farmhouses offering accommodation.

In mountain areas there is a chain of refuge huts run by **Club Alpin Français**, *av. de Laumière 24, 75019 Paris; tel: (1) 42 02 68 64*.

Food and Drink

For the French, breakfast normally consists simply of coffee and croissants, although you can get a variety of other things in cafés and bars if you ask. Lunch and dinner are taken seriously and not hurried. Lunch begins at 1230/1300 and dinner (the main meal) at around 2000. There is a seating charge at tables: if you want to save money, stand at the bar. In restaurants, *à la carte* can be expensive, but most have a fixed menu (the *menu du jour*) that can be superb value. Baguettes (French bread sticks) with a variety of fillings (*un sandwich*) are cheap and satisfying – most cafés sell them, or you can save even more by making your own.

Wine is freely available everywhere, but in bars most people drink beer or spirits. All alcohol in bars is expensive these days and exorbitant in Paris.

Opening Hours

Banks: Mon–Fri 0900–1200 and 1400–1600.

Shops: Mon–Sat 0900–1200 and 1430–1830. A few open through the midday break. Bakeries are open before all meals; other food shops frequently open on Sunday mornings and some may remain open during the evening. **Museums**: 0900–1800 (with many variations). Closed one day a week (usually Monday or Tuesday) and on public holidays. Many offer free entrance on Sunday, except when there is a special exhibition.

Postage

Most post offices (*bureaux de poste* or *PTT)* open Mon–Fri 0800–1200 and 1430–1900; Sat 0800–1200, and most offer a poste restante facility. Stamps (*timbres)* can also be purchased from any café or shop with a red *Tabac* sign.

Public Holidays

1 Jan; Easter; 1, 8 May; Ascension Day; Whit Sunday–Monday; 14 July; 15 Aug; 1, 11 Nov; 25 Dec.

Public Transport

In almost all large towns the train and bus stations are close together, so it's easy to get into the centre of town even if the railway drops you on the outskirts. Any bus service for which the timetable shows *Autocar* is run by SNCF and will accept rail passes/tickets. If you haven't seen the timetable, it's always worth asking if your pass/ticket is valid.

City **bus** services are good during the day, but often provide only a skeleton service in the evenings (after around 2030) and on Sundays. Licensed **taxis** (avoid others) display white lights on the roof if they are free, orange ones if they are not. They are metered but there are usually surcharges for luggage, extra passengers, animals and journeys beyond the city centre. Public transport in rural areas is very poor and you will need to make your own arrangements.

Telephones

The system is efficient, so international calls can be made from phone boxes, which are plentiful. Alternatively, many post offices have metered phones and you can pay when you have finished. Some phone boxes take coins, but there is an increasing trend for only phone cards (*télécartes)* to be accepted. These are available from post offices, train stations and some newsagents.

To call abroad from France: *tel: 19*. To call France from abroad: *tel: 33*. The number for the international operator is *19 33 11*, but the service can be very slow. To call the Paris region from elsewhere in France prefix the number with *161*. No prefix is needed for other French regions unless you are calling from Paris, in which case you should prefix the number with *16*. To call the national/local operator and directory enquiries: *tel: 12*. To call international directory enquiries: *tel: 19 33 12 + the country code*. **Emergencies**: Police: 17; Fire: 18; Ambulance: 15.

Rail Travel Within France

The national rail company is *Société Nationale des Chemins de Fer Français (SNCF)*. Except in the Paris region, the network of local lines is not very extensive, but on main routes and those branch lines still in operation, trains are fast, reliable and comfortable, though not always frequent. The French are proud of the *TGV* (*Train à Grande-Vitesse*), one of the fastest trains in the world, with speeds of up to 186 mph

The overnight trains offer a choice between sleeping-cars (*wagons-lits*) and the much cheaper couchettes (six berths in a compartment, sheet and pillow provided). On a few routes, there are *Cabine 8* cars: second-class carriages fitted with eight semi-reclined bunks per compartment. They are treated as seats for reservation purposes and no supplement is payable.

Restaurant cars offer a full service at meal times, either in a dining-car or delivered to first-class seats (order in advance on seat-only services). At other times there's a buffet or trolley service.

Fares and Passes

Supplements, which also include the seat reservation fee, are payable for all *TGV* trains, and some other trains running at peak times. France has three fare periods, dependent on the day and time of travel. Basically, blue is for off-peak (quiet) periods, white is for busier times (usually weekends) and red for some peak holiday dates.

The **Carrissimo** is a pass for those aged 12–25. It is valid for either four or eight journeys and gives 50% discount on travel in the blue period and 20% discount on travel in the white period for up to four people travelling together, but the number of journeys is divided by the number of passengers.

Carte Vermeil Quatre Temps is for travellers over 60. It gives a 50% discount on four single (or two return) rail journeys in France but they must begin in the blue period. It also gives a 30% reduction on cross-border journeys to about a dozen countries (including the UK). **Carte Vermeil Plein Temps** gives greater scope (see p. 24). There is no age limit on the **Carte Couple**, which allows two people to travel for the price of one. Reservations are compulsory for sleeping-cars and the *TGV*. They are recommended for international travel and any travel during red periods. All tickets must be date-stamped before boarding, by using the machines (*composteurs*) at the platform entrance.

GERMANY

Capital: Bonn/Berlin (the functions of the capital are gradually being transferred to Berlin). **Language**: German; English and French are widely spoken in the west, especially by young people, less so in the east. In German it is customary to roll several words into one and the polysyllabic result can be daunting. You will find it less confusing if you split the words into their component parts. *Hauptbahnhof*, for example, is an amalgam of haupt/chief, bahn/railway and hof/yard. **Currency**: Deutsche Marks (DM). 1 Mark = 100 Pfennig.

Customs

Standard EU regulations apply, but the Danes must spend at least 24 hours in Germany before they are entitled to the allowances.

Passports and Visas

A British Visitor's Passport is sufficient, as are EU National Identity Cards. Visas are not needed by nationals of EU countries, Australia, Canada, New Zealand or the USA. Others should check.

Useful Addresses in the UK

Embassy, *23 Belgrave Square, London SW1X*

8PZ; tel: (071) 235 5033. **National Tourist Office**, *Nightingale House, 65 Curzon St, London W1Y 7PE; tel: (071) 495 3990.* **German Rail Sales**, *The Sanctuary, 23 Oakhill Grove, Surbiton, Surrey, KT6 6DU; tel: (081) 390 0066.*

Useful Addresses in the USA

Embassy of the Federal Republic of Germany *4645 Reservoir Road NW, Washington DC 20007-1998; tel: (202) 298 8140.* **German National Tourist Office**, *Chanin Building, 122 East 42nd Street (52nd Floor), New York, NY 10168-0072; tel: (212) 308 3300.* **German Federal Railroad (DB)**, *747 Third av. (33rd Floor), New York, NY 10017; tel: (212) 371 2609.*

Living in Germany

Accommodation

The general standard of accommodation in the West is high, but so are prices and you will be doing well if you find a room for less than DM15 in really remote areas, or DM50 in cities. Standards in the East are far lower but prices are rising rapidly. All over Germany the prices vary enormously according to demand and you should make a point of avoiding *messen* (trade fairs) and other special events, unless you are prepared to pay over the odds. Prices are also inflated in the tourist season (Christmas to mid-March in ski resorts, May to October elsewhere), with prices really soaring in July and August.

Hotels and boarding houses (**gasthof/gasthaus**) can be booked in advance through a department of DZT: **Allgemeine Deutsche Zimmerreservierung** (ADZ), *Corneliusstrasse 34, Frankfurt/Main; tel: (069) 74 07 67.* Advance booking is essential in high season and always advisable. **Pensionen** or **fremdenheime** are pensions and *zimmer* means 'room' (generally in a private home). These are usually cheap but expect you to stay for at least two nights. Look for signs in the windows (*zimmer frei* and *zu vermieten* indicate availability; *besetzt* means they are full) or book through the local tourist office. You must be prepared to pay for this type of accommodation in German cash, as credit cards and cheques are seldom accepted by small establishments.

Jugendherberge (DJH) are youth hostels and there are around 600 in Germany (mostly affiliated with the IYHF/HI). In Bavaria there is an age limit of 27, elsewhere there is no limit but preference is usually given to the young. It is necessary to book well ahead in peak season and in the east (where they are the best form of accommodation unless you can afford the top hotels). In Germany they really are youth hostels and often used by school parties, which has resulted in the introduction of a new category of accommodation, **Jugendgastehaus**, which is aimed more at young adults.

Camping is the cheapest form of accommodation. **Deutscher Camping-Club (DCC)**, *Mandlstr.28, Munich*, publishes an annual list of over 1,500 sites and there are at least 1,000 more in the West, almost always with good facilities. There are fewer in the east, but you can get a list from **Camping and Caravanverband**, *Postfach 105, Berlin*. DZT also publish an annual list of the best 700 or so, including a map. Most sites open only May–Oct and it is advisable to book a few days in advance. A few are open all year and usually have space out of season.

Food and Drink

Breakfast is any time from 0630 to 1000. Lunch is around 1200–1400 (from 1130 in rural areas) and dinner 1800–2130 (earlier in rural areas).

German cuisine is fairly rich and served in large portions, with pork and potatoes the staple ingredients, but it's easy to find lighter things, such as salads. Breakfast is often substantial, consisting of a variety of bread, cheese and cold meat. Germans eat their main meal at midday, with a light supper in the evening, but restaurants and pubs also offer light lunches and cooked evening meals. The cheapest way to eat is to patronise *imbisse*: roadside stalls serving a variety of snacks. For lunch, the best value is the daily menu (*tageskarte*). There are simple restaurants (*gaststätten* and *gasthöfe*) which include regional dishes. A visit to a *biergarten* or *bierkeller* is a 'must' and Germany also produces a range of fine wines.

Opening Hours

These vary from place to place and are not stand-

Germany   **45**

ard even within one city. As a rule of thumb: **Banks**: Mon–Fri 0830–1300 and 1430–1600 (until 1730 Thur). Hours have been shorter in the east, but are changing. **Shops**: Mon–Fri 0900–1830 (until 2030 Thur) and Sat 0900–1400. On the first Saturday of the month, larger stores open until 1800. **Museums**: Tue–Sun 0900–1700 (many until 2100 on Thursday). Some open Monday and some close for an hour or more at lunch.

Postage

The usual post office hours are Mon–Sat 0800–1800 and the main post office in each town has a poste restante facility. Address letters to the *postlagernde*. All postal codes in Germany are in the process of being changed, so check that any you have are still current.

Public Holidays

1, 6 Jan; Good Friday; Easter Sunday–Monday; 1 May, Ascension Day; Whit Sunday–Monday; Corpus Christi*; 15 Aug*; 3 Oct; 1 Nov*; Day of Prayer (third Wednesday in November); 24, 25 Dec; 26 Dec (afternoon).
   *Catholic feasts, celebrated only in south.

Public Transport

All inter-city travel is by train, with buses used just for travel to remote areas. Most major bus routes are run by the railways, so you can get information about them at the rail stations.
   Many big cities have a U-bahn (U) underground railway and an S-bahn (S) urban rail service. City travel passes cover both, as well as other public transport. International passes usually cover the S, but not the U. Where ferries are an integral part of the city's transport, they are often included in the city transport pass.
   Domestic fares are expensive in the west and are fast catching up in the east. A day card (*Tagesnetzkarte*) or multi-ride ticket (*Mehrfahrkarte*) usually pays its way if you take more than three rides. If there's no machine at the stop, get your ticket from the bus driver. The usual system is to get tickets from automatic machines and then validate them in little boxes in the station or on board the vehicle.

Telephones

In theory the eastern and western systems have been integrated but, in practice, the technology in the east still leaves a lot to be desired and it's advisable to arrange things so that any important calls are made while you are in the west, where the system is very efficient. Black telephone boxes have instructions in English and most operators speak it. Phonecards are obtainable from any post office and (largely because the coin system is cumbersome and expensive) their use is increasing rapidly. **Kartentelefon** boxes take only cards.
   To call abroad from Germany: *tel: 00*. There are a few exceptions, but the kiosks all give full information. To call Germany from abroad: *tel: 49*. To call the international operator: *tel: 0010*. To call the national operator: *tel: 010*. To call international directory enquiries: *tel: 001188*. To call national directory enquiries: *tel: 01188*. **Emergencies**: Police: 110; Fire: 112; Ambulance: 112.

Rail Travel Within Germany

The West German *DB* (*Deutsche Bundesbahn*) and East German *DR* (*Deutsche Reichsbahn*) have joined to form *Deutsche Bahn* (*DB*). There are also some privately owned railways. The main station in each town is Hauptbahnhof (Hbf) and any sizable station will be able to supply a computer print-out showing the connections along the route in which you are interested. Train tickets must be purchased before you board, unless you are prepared to pay a hefty supplement.
   Long-distance trains are: *ICE* (an ultra-modern service which cruises at up to 174 mph), *IC* and *IR* plus *EC* and *EN*. The *RB* and *RSB* are modern, comfortable regional services linking up with the long-distance network. There are also reasonably fast *Eilzug* (*E*) and *D* trains. Ordinary commuter trains – *City-Bahn* (*CB*), *S-Bahn* and *Nahverkehrszug* (*N*) – are all slow services.
   Most German trains offer both first and second class, but some are only second class. Overnight services often have second-class seating and sleeping accommodation (sleeping-cars with up to three berths and/or couchettes with four or six berths). Seat reservations are possible for most fast trains, but not local trains.
   In the west most long-distance trains have

dining-cars. In the east they may have either dining-cars or a buffet service.

Passes

German **Regional Passes** are only available in the UK. There is no age limit and they are available for first- and second-class unlimited travel within one of 15 designated German regions for any 5 or 10 days in a 21-day period. They can be used on any *DB* trains (including *IC* and *EC)* and on the *S-Bahn*, but not on the *ICE* unless you are prepared to pay a supplement. **Tramper-Monats** tickets (available to anyone under 23 and to students under 27) give second-class travel for a month on all *DB* trains (except the *ICE*, for which a supplement is payable) as well as on railway-run buses (*Bahnbusse*) and the *S-Bahn*.

GREECE

Capital: Athens (*Athinai*). **Language**: Greek; English is quite widely spoken in tourist areas, but you could have problems in rural areas. Italian, French and German are also spoken to some extent. Greece uses a Cyrillic alphabet, but street signs are usually in both Greek and English. There is no definitive way of transliterating from Cyrillic to Roman script, so be aware that Greek names can appear in a number of ways in Roman script: for example, *Sindagma* or *Syntagma*. Language and body language can be misleading. The head nodding up and down can mean 'no', while '*ne*' (pronounced 'nay') means 'yes'. People often stand closer together than is common elsewhere in Europe. No offence is intended. **Currency**: Drachmae (Dr.). Credit cards are accepted by the larger places in Athens, but their use is not widespread.

Customs

Standard EU regulations apply (see p. 13–14), but Greece imposes a minimum age limit of 18.

Passports and Visas

Turkish nationals are not permitted to enter Greece at all if their passports indicate that they have visited, or intend to visit, the Turkish-occupied part of Cyprus. A British Visitor's Passport is sufficient, as are the National Identity Cards issued by Austria, Belgium, France, Germany, Italy and Luxembourg.

Portuguese nationals need a visa for a stay of more than two months. Unless they stay longer than three months, visas are not needed by other EU nationals, nor by the nationals of Australia, Canada, New Zealand or the USA. Others should check.

Useful Addresses in the UK

Consulate General, *1A Holland Park, London W11 3TP; tel: (071) 221 6467*. **National Tourist Organisation and Railway Representatives**, *4 Conduit St, London W1R 0DJ; tel: (071) 734 5997*.

Useful Addresses in the USA

Embassy, *2221 Massachusetts Ave NW, Washington DC 20008-2873; tel: (202) 667 3169/ 939 5800*. **National Tourist Organiza-tion**, *Olympic Tower, 645 Fifth Ave (5th Floor), New York, NY 10022; tel: (212) 421 5777*.

Living in Greece

Accommodation

As befits one of the most popular tourist countries in the world, there is a huge array of accommodation from luxury five-star hotels in Athens to beach resorts, pensions, village rooms, self-catering apartments and youth hostels. You should have no problems, except in high summer and over Easter, when you should book ahead. Out of season, you can sometimes negotiate discounts, particularly if you want to stay for several nights. At the lower end of the scale check the room before paying. On the whole, private rooms cost no more than the youth hostels and are infinitely more pleasant.

There are plentiful campsites, particularly on the coast, or at major sights, such as Delphi. Many of them are well-equipped, shady and pleasant and may even have restaurants, swimming pools, and basic shops. The tourist office has a full list.

Food and Drink

Breakfast is light; lunch and dinner are full meals. You can choose from the menu (almost all are

---

Greece

The Greek penal system is harsh and it is a crime to sell your belongings while you are there. Electrical items, in particular, may be noted in your passport, when you arrive in the country. Should you have anything of value stolen, therefore, it is essential to report the fact to the authorities immediately.

printed in Greek and English) or just point at anything you fancy in the display cabinet. Lunch is usually 1230–1500 and dinner in tourist areas is generally 1930–2130. The Greeks themselves eat much later (not before 2100).

Greece is not noted for its cuisine, but it is possible to eat quite well without spending a fortune, especially if you avoid meat and fish (as it's easy to do). If fish is not very expensive, you can be sure that it's not fresh.

Coffee is the usual drink and tea is hard to find. The Greeks do not drink coffee to finish the meal and many eating-places will not serve it, so head off to a bar after dinner. Somewhat confusingly, bars serve coffee while alcohol is far cheaper in restaurants than in bars. The tap water is safe, but generally so heavily chlorinated that many people prefer to buy the universally available bottled mineral water. *Ouzo* is an aperitif and, unless you are extremely hard-headed, you should treat it with caution. For the evening's drinking, try *retsina*, a resin-flavoured white wine, or beer; chilled draught lager, both good and cheap, is readily available. Greek brandy is rather rough.

Opening Hours

Banks: (usually) Mon–Fri 0800–1400, but in tourist areas they tend to close later and sometimes open at weekends. **Shops**: these set their own hours and there is a lot of variation, so you should check at your hotel for what is commonest in that area. The normal pattern is: Mon, Wed 0900–1700, Tue, Thur, Fri 0900–1900 and Sat 0830–1530. **Museums**: most are open Tue–Sat 0830–1500/1730, but small ones tend to close earlier. Most also open on Sunday, but for a shorter time. Some of the major places

open daily in summer. No two archaeological sites open at precisely the same time, but the usual pattern is roughly 0830–1500 in winter (closing at sunset in summer). Most museums and sites close on major public holidays and open for only half the day on minor ones.

Postage

There are plentiful post offices in all towns and even in larger villages, recognised by a yellow circle on the sign. They normally open Mon–Fri 0800–1300, although those in larger towns may open Sat morning also. You can often exchange money in post offices, while stamps are also on sale in kiosks and card shops.

Public Holidays

1, 6 Jan; Shrove Monday (the day before Shrove Tuesday: Feb/March); 25 Mar; Easter; Labour Day (early May); Whit Monday; 15 Aug; 28 Oct; 25, 26 Dec. The big holiday is Orthodox Easter and virtually everything closes, usually from Good Friday to Easter Monday inclusive.

Public Transport

The rail network in Greece is rather skeletal and much long-distance travel is done on buses, usually operated by KTEL. Most towns have well-organised bus stations, with clear details of services, and buses generally keep to schedule.

The islands are connected by a web of ferries and hydrofoils. The biggest base on the mainland is Piraeus, but there are also local services from several other cities. Ask for details at the tourist offices or take a copy of *The Thomas Cook Guide to Greek Island Hopping* (£9.95).

Local transport is usually by bus. Only in Athens are there trolley-buses and metro. Services are usually well-run and efficient, but you should check whether you can buy your ticket from the conductor or must get it before boarding (the situation changes). Taxis are allowed to pick up two separate fares on each trip and, if you don't want this to happen, you must insist they put the flag down. If you don't mind sharing, try hailing a cab that's already occupied.

Telephones

To call Greece from abroad: *tel: 30*. To call

abroad from Greece: *tel: 00.* **Emergencies**: Police: 100; Fire: 199; Ambulance: 150/166 (which you use varies across the country, if in doubt, try both). You may have language problems with all of them, however, so you would do better to call the Tourist Police in Athens on 171 (manned 24 hours a day by an English speaker). Ask them for the equivalent number in any other place you intend to visit.

Rail Travel Within Mainland Greece

Most Greek trains are run by *Organismos Sidirodromon Ellados (OSE).* Sleepers/couchettes are of standard European type. Reservations are possible (and recommended) on most express trains.

Fares and Passes

Many European rail passes (see pp. 22–26) offer discounts on ferry services between Greece and Italy. There are discount cards for rail travel over 10, 20 or 30 days, but with the exclusion of the main Athens to Thessaloniki route where some IC trains operate (advance reservation and a hefty supplement required), the network is limited and most services are both slow and infrequent. Even if you have a rail pass, therefore, it may well be worth your while to travel by bus. All fares within Greece are cheap, but inflation is high and this could change.

HUNGARY

Capital: Budapest. **Language**: Hungarian (Magyar); a fair amount of English is spoken in tourist areas. German is more widely understood, though certainly not universally. Bear in mind that there is a Hungarian word that sounds like 'bus' and is rude. When asking about buses, make sure you pronounce the word 'booss'. **Currency**: Forints (Ft.); 1 Forint = 100 Fillers (Fillers are seldom seen). Officially: when you leave Hungary you may re-convert half your Forints (not exceeding US$100) back into hard currencies. Unofficially: you may find that little hard currency is available. Change a little at a time and keep all receipts. Acceptance of credit cards is spreading rapidly, but they are not yet universal: American Express seems to be the

---

Hungary

- Tap water is safe, but wash fruit and raw vegetables carefully before eating.
- Anyone staying in Hungary for more than a month must register at a police station within 48 hours of arrival. This is done automatically by the proprietor if you are staying at a hotel or campsite.
- Crime is increasing with westernisation, hard currency being the main target, so keep an eye on your possessions.
- IBUSZ is the national travel bureau, with offices all over the country. Much of the literature it produces is written in English. Touriform is another extremely helpful company with English-speaking staff. There is an office in central Budapest. For information in English, *tel: 361 1172 200.*
- Now they are independent again, the Hungarians are changing street names to get rid of the Russian influence. To avoid confusion, get an up-to-date street map on arrival in each city.

---

most widely recognised. Eurocheques and travellers' cheques are accepted in small denominations.

Customs

The allowances are: 250 cigarettes or 50 cigars or 250g tobacco, 2 litres wine, and 1 litre spirits.

Passports and Visas

All visitors require full passports. Visas are not needed by EU nationals, Canadians or citizens of the USA. Nationals of Australia and New Zealand must get visas in advance. Others should check.

Useful Addresses in the UK

Embassy: *35B Eaton Place, London SW1X 8BY; tel: (071) 235 2664.* **Hungarian Tourist Office (IBUSZ)**: *c/o Danube Travel; 6 Conduit St, London W1R 9TG; tel: (071) 493 0263.*

Useful Addresses in the USA

Embassy: *3910 Shoemaker Street NW, Washington DC 20008-3811; tel: (202) 362 6730.*

Greece–Hungary

Hungarian Travel North American Division (IBUSZ): *1 Parker Plaza (Suite 1104), Fort Lee, NJ 07024; tel: (201) 592 8585.*

Living in Hungary

Accommodation

There is a wide range of accommodation of reasonable quality, but the prices are higher than many elsewhere in Eastern Europe. Amongst the new tourist ventures in the country is a huge plan to turn some 2,000 of Hungary's castles into hotels! If you are not in the luxury price-bracket, the best bet will probably be a private room or pension, in preference to the youth hostels or old Soviet-style tourist hotels. There is a reasonable network of campsites, particularly in resort areas, some of which also have cabins to rent. Rough camping is forbidden.

Food and Drink

Hungary's cuisine has been influenced by its neighbouring countries and is very varied. Pork lard, smoked sausages, sour cream, flour and paprika are all basic ingredients. Lunch is the main meal and is served 1200–1400. Dinner is early and you should aim to begin eating well before 2100. Most restaurants have a very cheap fixed-price lunch (called a *menü*: usually soup or salad, a main course and a pudding.

Önkiszolgáló and *ételbár* are self-service snack bars. They and *bisztro* are fairly cheap. *Csárda* offer a limited menu but often have folk music. *Vendéglő* are moderately priced restaurants which tend to offer home-cooking and *étterem* are restaurants with a larger selection. Don't expect unordered items brought to your table to be free: refuse anything you don't want and check the bill before you pay. There are many spas in Hungary – try some of the bottled mineral waters. The number of beer cellars is growing and you can get both bottled and draught beers. Wine bars are popular and many local wines are very good. Most bars offer a range of fruit schnapps (*pálinka*).

Opening Hours

These vary considerably and are growing longer as Western influence increases. The following is just a rule of thumb: **Banks**: Mon–Fri 0800/1000–1400/1800 and Sat 0900–1200/1400. Some also close early on Friday. **Shops**: Mon–Fri 0900/1000–1800/1900 (until 2000 Thur) and Sat 0900/1000–1300/1400. Shops sometimes close for lunch but department stores often stay open on Saturday afternoon. Food shops open Mon–Fri 0600/0700–1900/2000, but many open later and at weekends. **Museums**: the norm is: Tue–Sun 1000–1800. The smaller ones have shorter hours and many open only in the summer months. There's usually one day when entry is free (often Wednesday or Saturday). They close on public holidays.

Postage

The postal service is slow but reasonably reliable. Post boxes are red.

Public Holidays

1 Jan; 15 Mar; Easter Monday; 1 May; Whit Monday; 20 Aug; 23 Oct; 25, 26 Dec.

Public Transport

Rail offers the best way of getting around the country, however there are also buses – local and long-distance – and, along the Danube or on Lake Balaton, you might like to take to one of the (very slow) ferries for a change. Within towns (outside Budapest), all public transport is by bus, or trolley-bus. Taxis can be cheap, but make sure that the meter is running or that you agree a price ahead of time.

Telephones

To call Hungary from abroad: *tel: 36*. To call abroad from Hungary: *tel: 00*. **Emergencies**: Police: 07; Fire: 05; Ambulance: 04.

Rail Travel Within Hungary

The national rail company is *Hungarian State Railways (MÁV)*. Every town in the country is linked to the railway system, but most trains are very slow, some using four-wheel diesel cars. However, there are efficient express services linking Budapest to the major provincial towns and to Lake Balaton. The slow trains are called *személyvonat*, the expresses *gyorsvonat*. The best services to the provincial towns are the blue expresses: *sebesvonat* or *expressz*. Sleepers/ couchettes are the standard European type. All seats and sleepers for international travel need to be booked well in advance.

Snacks are theoretically available on all express trains, but demand often exceeds supply, so it's better to take your own. You can sometimes find an English version of the timetable, which includes a good map of the network.

Fares and Passes

The **Explorer Pass** is for those under 26 and for any holder of an ISIC card. It gives unlimited first- or second-class rail travel in Hungary for 7 days (or multiples thereof), but must be purchased before you go (from Campus Travel – see p. 22). **Rail cards** which give unlimited travel for seven or ten days are among the other concessions available. All international fares must be paid in hard currencies. Domestic fares are very cheap, but rising. At the moment first-class travel is cheap enough to be worthwhile.

ITALY

Capital: Rome (*Roma*). **Language**: Italian is the only official language but there are strong dialectal differences. In the cities and tourist areas many people speak some English, but it's seldom spoken at all off the beaten track. **Currency**: Lira (L.).

Customs

Standard EU regulations apply (see p. 13–14).

Passports and Visas

A British Visitor's Passport is sufficient, as are EU National Identity Cards. Visas are not needed by EU nationals, Commonwealth citizens or nationals of the USA. Others should check.

Useful Addresses in the UK

Consulate, *38 Eaton Place, London SW1X 8AN; Visa tel: (071) 259 6322.* **Italian State Tourist Board**, *1 Princes St, London W1R 8AY; tel: (071) 408 1254.* **Italian Rail Travel**, *Wasteels, adjacent to Platform 2, Victoria Station, London SW1V 1JT; tel: (071) 834 7066.*

Useful Addresses in the USA

Embassy, *1601 Fuller Street NW, Washington, DC 20009; tel: (202) 328 5500.* **Italian Government Travel Office (ENIT)**, *630 Fifth Ave (Suite 1565), Rockefeller Center, New York, NY 10111; tel: (212) 245 4822 or 2324.* **Italian Rail Travel**, *CIT Tours Corporation, 594 Broadway (Suite 307), New York, NY 10012; tel: (212) 697-2100.*

Living in Italy

Accommodation

All hotels are classified according to a 5-star system and inspectors set a maximum (seasonal) rate which must be displayed in each room. It does not necessarily include showers or breakfast, but extras must be listed separately, so complain (to the tourist office if all else fails) if your bill does not agree with the rates listed. You must, by law, obtain a receipt from all hotels.

Most establishments now term themselves **hotel** or **albergo**, but some are still called **pension** (one-, two-, or three-star) or **locande** (one-star). There are many private rooms, unofficial and otherwise. You can find the unofficial ones by looking for signs saying *affitta camere*, often in shop windows. It's worth trying to bargain, but you will usually pay about the same as for a one-star hotel. **Alberghi diurni**, near stations or in the centre, are essentially day rooms: you can have a wash without taking a room for the night.

There is no shortage of **youth hostels**, but relatively few belong to the IYHF and the standard varies considerably. It is often just as cheap and more convenient to stay at a one-star hotel.

Camping is popular and there are over 2,000 sites (all tourist offices have information about their area), but they are often fairly expensive and/or difficult to reach without a car. There are few places where you can rough camp without asking permission. **Touring Club Italiano (TCI)**, *Corso Italia 10, Milano; tel: (02) 85 261 or 852 6245*, publish an annual guide. Alternatively, you can get a list from **Federcampeggio**, *Casella Postale 23, 50041 Calenzano (Firenze); tel: (055) 88 215 918*, who can also make bookings. These two organisations produce a detailed directory of campsites, *Campeggi e Villagi Turistici in Italia*, available from bookshops in Italy (L.30,000).

Agriturismo, *Corso V Emanuele 101, 00186 Roma; tel: (06) 852 342*, has information about staying in rural cottages and farmhouses. **Club Alpino Italiano**, *Via Fonseca Pimental 7, 20122 Milano; tel: (02) 26 141 378*, can supply details of mountain refuge huts.

Food and Drink

Italians enjoy eating and there's a wide variety of food available everywhere, with pasta as just one of many options. A full meal will consist of antipasta (cold meats etc.), pasta, a main course, and fruit or cheese. Italian ice-cream (*gelato*) is among the world's best.

Trattorie are simple establishments which are cheaper than *ristoranti*. Most *osterie* are trendy and expensive. *Alimentari* stores often prepare excellent and interesting sandwiches. *Rosticerrie* sell good hot take-aways, while *tavole calde* are cheap sit-down places. Smaller establishments seldom have menus: just ask for the dish of the day if you want something reasonably priced. Menus are displayed by the entrance. Look for cover charges (*coperto*) and service (*servizio*), both of which will be added to your bill. Prices on *Menu Turistico* include taxes and service charges.

Coffee comes in many forms, from espresso to liqueur. There are various types of Italian beer and many fine wines. Bars are good places to get a snack, such as a roll or toasted sandwich as well as to sample the local 'fire-waters' such as *grappa*.

Opening Hours

Banks: Mon–Fri 0830–1300 and usually for an additional hour in the afternoon (exactly when varies). **Shops**: (usually) Mon–Sat 0830/0900–1230/1300 and 1530/1600–1900/1930. In July/August many close on Monday morning or Saturday afternoon. A few stay open all day, every day. **Museums**: national museums and archaeological sites usually open Tue–Sun 0930–1300/1400 and some re-open 1600–1900, but there is no real pattern and smaller ones please themselves. Although Monday is the usual closing day, it is not uncommon for this to be Sunday or Tuesday or for them to stay open all week. Most

---

Italy

- Women are often hassled in Italy. The most effective response is a look of disgust.
- Pickpockets are numerous in major cities, so be wary. A particularly Italian crime is for bag-snatchers to ride motor scooters – so walk with your bag on the side away from the road.

---

sites and museums refuse entry within an hour or two of closing time.

Postage

Usual post office hours are Mon–Sat 0800–1830, but there's no Saturday opening in many small places. The postal service is slow and it's worth paying for anything urgent to be sent express. Stamps (*francobolli*) are available from post offices, tobacconists (*tabacchi*) and some gift shops in resorts. Poste restante (*Fermo posta*) is possible at most post offices, but you have to pay a small amount when you collect.

Public Holidays

All over the country: 1, 6 Jan; Easter Monday; 1 May; 15 Aug (virtually nothing opens); 1 Nov; 8, 25, 26 Dec.

Regional saints' days: 25 Apr in Venice; 24 June in Florence, Genoa and Turin; 29 June in Rome; 15 July in Palermo; 19 Sept in Naples; 4 Oct in Bologna; 6 Dec in Bari; 7 Dec in Milan.

Public Transport

Buses are often crowded but serve many areas inaccessible by rail and tend to be punctual. Services are drastically reduced at weekends and timetables do not always reflect this fact. Tickets for long-distance and local buses are usually obtained before boarding (some local ones are bought on board). Long-distance tickets are usually available from train stations or CIT offices, while local tickets are from machines, newsstands or tobacconists.

Taxis are metered, but can be expensive, with a substantial flat fare to start with and extra charges for baggage, journeys out of town and travel on holidays or late at night. You can hail

---

taxis on the street, but steer clear of unofficial ones.

Telephones

The phone system is in a constant state of overhaul, with frequently changing numbers ranging from two to eight digits. Directories may list two numbers – try both. If they're of different lengths, the longer is likely to be the new version.

Most public phones have instructions in English and take coins, phonecards (*carte telefoniche/scheda*), or both. Cards are available from automatic machines near the phones, tobacconists and news-stands. You can make international calls by using a phonecard, but in some small towns you must go to an office of the state phone company, **SIP**, or (occasionally) **ASST**. They often have branches in the stations; if not, you should find one near the main post office. You may also come across the old phones that take only tokens (*gettoni*). If so, you should be able to get the tokens from whoever owns the phone, or find an automatic dispenser nearby. *Gettoni* are often accepted as small change, so don't be surprised if you are given some instead of small denomination coins.

Scatti phones are quite common – these are metered and you pay the operator/owner when you have finished, but they are normally in places like bars and the 'operator' may well add a service charge, so check before you commit yourself. Hotels invariably charge over the odds.

To call abroad from Italy: *tel: 00*. To call Italy from abroad: *tel: 39*. For English information and assistance for intercontinental calls: *tel: 170*. For English information on calling Europe and the Mediterranean area: *tel: 176*. For local operator assistance: *tel: 15*. For local directory enquiries: *tel: 12*. **Emergencies**: Fire: 115; Police, Ambulance and other services: 113.

Rail Travel Within Italy

The national rail company is *Ferrovie dello Stato* (*FS*). There are plans to introduce a new supertrain in 1994. Currently known as the *ETR 500*, the prototype can reach speeds of up to 186 mph

The *Pendolino* (*ETR 450*) trains reach up to 155 mph These are luxury express services between major cities. Reservations are necessary and there is the usual basic supplement to use the trains plus another (usually £10–£20) before you board (which, in first class, covers such extras as hostess service, newspapers and food).

Reservations are also obligatory for *IC* and *EC* services. *IR* trains are semi-fast expresses. The *espresso* are long-distance domestic trains, with both first and second class, which stop only at main stations. The *diretto* stop frequently and are very slow, while the *locale* stop almost everywhere. The rail network is extensive and the service reasonably punctual. Some long-distance trains won't carry passengers for short distances. Sleepers have single or double berths in first class, three berths (occasionally doubles) in second class; couchettes have four berths in first class and six in second class.

Most long-distance trains have refreshment facilities. Dining-cars offer a full service at meal times and snacks the rest of the day. Buffet cars are self-service, catering coaches or bar cars. Don't drink the tap water on trains. Queues at stations are often long and it's better to buy tickets and make reservations at travel agencies (look for the *FS* symbol).

Fares and Passes

Biglietto Chilometrico can be used by up to 5 people, but the allowance is divided by the number of travellers. It is valid for 3,000 km, in the course of which you can have 19 different stops over a period of 2 months. The **Italian Flexicard** allows travel for any 4 days out of 9, any 8 days out of 21 or any 12 days out of 30. It should be purchased in the UK as it is available in very few other places. The **Travel-at-will** tickets allow non-Italian residents to travel on any Italian train for 8, 15, 21 or 30 days. All three domestic passes give a choice of first- or second-class travel. If you board without a ticket there is an automatic fine of up to 20% of the fare. Buy tickets for short journeys (up to 100 km) from any tobacconist.

LATVIA

Capital: Riga. **Language**: Latvian is the national language, but is spoken by only about half the population. Russian is more widely understood, but unpopular with native Latvians. Of the three

Baltic countries, Latvia has the smallest indigenous population and the language, almost wiped out by Russian (as happened in Estonia and Lithuania), is on the endangered list. Latvian is an Indo-European, non-Slavic and non-Germanic language and is similar only to Lithuanian. English and German are increasingly widely spoken. **Currency**: The new Latvian currency, the Lat, was fully introduced in October 1993; 1 Lat = 100 Santims. Currency exchange outfits are numerous but changing travellers' cheques isn't so easy. Credit card recognition is growing, but is far from universal.

Customs

The following allowances are for people aged 16 or over: 200 cigarettes or 200g tobacco products, and 1 litre alcohol.

Passports and Visas

Full passports are required by all travellers. Visas are required universally except by nationals of Estonia, Lithuania, Hungary, UK, the Czech Republic and Slovakia. They can be obtained at the airport and the sea passenger ports by US and most European nationals but it is advisable to get them in advance. A Latvian visa is valid for the other Baltic countries. However, the situation is liable to change so check at the nearest embassy at least three weeks before travelling.

Useful Addresses in the UK

Embassy, *72 Queensborough Terrace, London W2 3SP; tel: (071) 727 1698.* (This address may change in 1994; so check.) The **Latvian Bookshop**, which sells maps and guidebooks is based at the embassy; *tel: (071) 229 1652.*

Useful Addresses in the USA

Embassy, *4325 17th Street NW, Washington, DC 20011; tel: (202) 726 8213/4.*

Living in Latvia

Accommodation

The more sophisticated accommodation tends to cluster around Riga and the seaside resort Jurmala, once colonised by Russian holiday-makers, including Boris Yeltsin.

For bed and breakfast, farmhouse and self-catering accommodation (and fishing and mushroom picking) contact **Lauku celotajs** (Country Traveller) *Republikas Sq. 2 1119, Riga, LV 1981; tel: 327 629.* Most camping facilities are in the area of Jurmala.
Latvian Youth Tourism Centre, *2 Kr. Barona str., Riga LV 1050; tel: 225 307.* The **Association of Latvian Travel Agents** (ALTA) *PO Box 59, Riga, LV 1012; tel: 213 627.*

Food and Drink

What restaurants offer depends largely on the availability of supplies. Latvian cuisine features richly-seasoned gravy and fish is more common than meat. The brown granary bread and sweet pastries are excellent. There are lots of different berries in season and they are often used in delicious ice cream sundaes. Don't drink the tap water. Tea and coffee are both widely available. Latvian beer (*alus*) is cheap, strong and quite good. *Kvass* is a mildly alcoholic rye drink which is often sold on the streets in summer.

You should book a table if you want to dine in a major hotel. Many restaurants close in the late afternoon (usually 1700–1900).

Opening Hours

Banks: open mainly Mon–Fri 0900–1600. Some open Sat 0900–1230. **Shops**: Mon–Fri 0900/1000–1800/1900 and Sat 0900/1000–1500/1700 (often closed 1400–1500). Many close on Mondays, as well as Sundays. Food shops usually open earlier and close later. **Museums**: days of opening vary enormously and many open on only a few days every week, most commonly from Tuesday or Wednesday to Sunday, 1100–1700.

Postage

Post offices (*pasts*) are open Mon–Fri 0900–1800 and Sat 0900–1300. Post boxes are yellow.

Public Holidays

1 Jan; Good Friday; Easter Monday (unofficial); 1 May; Mothers' Day (second Sunday in May); Midsummer Eve; Midsummer Day; 18 Nov; 25, 26, 31 Dec.

Public Transport

Public transport is still extremely cheap for Westerners and taxis are usually an affordable option. Try and avoid bumped-up taxi fares by negotiating a price before you get in. Buses and trams are often spilling over with passengers and can be a hotbed for pick-pockets.

The long-distance bus network is a popular alternative to the often slow domestic train service. Buses travel to most destinations on a relatively frequent basis.

Telephones

Special telephone tokens (bought from the kiosks and post offices) are needed to use the public telephones which can only make local connections. International calls are difficult and extreme patience is needed.

To call abroad from Latvia: *tel: 8 194* (calls must be booked in advance). For urgent connections *tel: 8 15* and pay US$1.30 per minute. To call Latvia from abroad: *tel: 371.* To call Directory enquiries: *tel: 09.* **Emergencies**: Police: 02; Fire: 01; Ambulance: 03.

Rail Travel Within Latvia

The national rail company is *Latvian Railways (LVD).* Domestic services can be unbearably slow although the network appears to be improving. Toilets on board are often without running water and are sometimes even closed. Timetables run horizontally rather than vertically.

There are two classes: 'soft' (first) has fully upholstered seats and 'hard' (second) has plastic/leather seats. Prices are relatively low, so it is worth booking soft class for extra comfort. Both classes convert to berths for overnight journeys. Soft is couchette-style, with four berths. In hard there may be either four-berth couchettes or an open-plan sleeping compartment. In both, there is a charge for all bedding (including mattresses – local currency required). Some trains have normal two or four berth European-style sleeping-cars and some have only hard class, but there is no advance information about which you will be on, so ask locally.

Through sleepers to West/Central Europe have one or two berths in first class and three berths in second class. All include full bedding.

All day trains are hard class. Reservations are necessary except for purely local journeys.

Fares and Passes

Kiosks line the streets and gather round the stations. From here buy either individual or, more sensibly, several tickets which are validated on board the buses or trams. The same tickets apply for both. For longer stays a monthly transport ticket can prove convenient and, if you have student ID, an even cheaper solution. On the spot fines are charged for unauthorised travel.

LITHUANIA

Capital: Vilnius. **Language**: Lithuanian. Lithuanian and Latvian belong to the same language group and are Indo-European in origin. Russian is still common on signs around the traditional lines of communication, the railways and the telephones. However while Russian may be helpful, this reminder of the years of Soviet occupation would be unpopular and a phrasebook is indispensable. **Currency**: Lithuanian Litai; 1 Litas = 100 Cents. There are no restrictions on the import/export of foreign currencies. Travellers' cheques can be cashed at some banks and at major tourist hotels: US$ or Deutschmarks are best. Recognition for credit cards (especially Visa) is limited, but growing.

Customs

The following allowances are constantly changing, so you will need to check just before travelling. The present allowance is: 200 cigarettes or 50 cigars or 250g tobacco and 1 litre spirits, or 2 litres wine.

Passports and Visas

All visitors require full passports. Visas are required for those who are not nationals of the UK, Iceland, Denmark, Poland, the Czech Republic or Slovakia. They can be obtained at the borders and, for Westerners, are also valid in Latvia and Estonia.

Useful Addresses in the UK

Embassy, *17 Essex Villas, London W8 7BP; tel: (071) 938 2481 or 937 1588.*

Useful Addresses in the USA

Lithuanian Consulate-General and National Tourist Office
41 West 82nd Street, New York, NY 10024; tel: (212) 582 1345 or 247 1169.

Living in Lithuania

Accommodation

Builders are moving fast to meet the demand, but hotel accommodation – especially at the more comfortable end of the market – can still be very hard to come by. Booking in advance is strongly recommended. Prices are often listed in DM or US$, suggestive of the fact that they bear little relation to local costs. Hotels do exist, but are rare and often hard to find. A better bet is to go to the agencies who arrange accommodation with local families. If looking away from the capital, book ahead or at least have some names, addresses and phone numbers. Check out any accommodation before you part with your money.

Food and Drink

Despite the fact that menus often have a long list of dishes, the actual choice is very small. Things most likely to be available are: *cepelinai* (the national dish – meat balls in potato), *blynai* (mini-pancakes) and *kotletas* (pork cutlets). Fish and dairy products are common ingredients of all dishes.

Lithuanians eat their evening meal early and you should aim to order by 2000, even in places which are theoretically open much later. Many restaurants close for an hour at lunch-time!

Do not drink tap water, opt for bottled water instead. Tea and coffee are widely available. Vodka (the best is *Kvietine*) and very sweet liqueurs are the main spirits. Lithuanian beer is becoming increasingly hard to find (the best is *Utenos alus*) as the drinking-places prefer to sell Western brands. The beer bars in Vilnius are worth a visit if you want to see 'the other side' of Lithuania. They are usually large rooms where snacks and watered-down beer are sold to sometimes belligerent hard drinkers.

Lithuania

It isn't really worth taking cigarettes because they are not taxed in Lithuania, which makes them very cheap, and western brands are widely available.

Opening Hours

Banks: opening hours vary, but you can be reasonably sure banks will be open Mon–Fri 0930–1230. Some open earlier and/or close later; some also open on Saturday. **Shops**: (large shops) Mon–Fri 1000/1100–1900; many also open Saturday until 1600. Some close for lunch (1400–1500) and some close both Sunday and Monday. The local shops have their own systems and there is no pattern to this at all. Food shops have longer hours: Mon–Sat 0900-1400 and 1500–2000, Sun 0800–1400. **Museums**: these open on different days and at different times. Most are closed Monday and open at least Wednesday and Friday (entrance to many is free on Wednesday). Most are open at least 1100–1700, but a few open only in the morning or the afternoon, so you must check locally.

Postage

All towns have a post office with an international telephone service.

Public Holidays

1 Jan; 16 Feb; Easter Sun and Mon; the first Sun in May; 6 July; 1 Nov; 25, 26 Dec.

Telephones

To call Lithuania from abroad: *tel: 370*. To call abroad from Lithuania: *tel: 8 10 + country code*. To call the international operator: *tel: 8 194* (English spoken). **Emergencies**: Police: 02; Fire: 01; Ambulance: 03.

Rail Travel Within Lithuania

The Lithuanian railway company is *LG*. There is a reasonable rail network linking Vilnius with the other Lithuanian towns. Domestic services are both very slow and very cheap.

There are two classes: 'soft' (first) has fully upholstered seats and 'hard' has plastic/leather seats. When travelling between the Baltic States, it is worth spending a little extra on soft class. Both classes convert to berths for overnight journeys. Soft is couchette-style, with four berths. In hard there may be either four-berth couchettes or an open-plan sleeping compartment. In both, there is a charge for all bedding, including mattresses (local currency required). Some trains have normal two- or four-berth European-style sleeping-cars, some have only hard class, and there is no advance information about which will arrive, so ask locally. Through sleepers to West/Central Europe have one or two berths in first class and three berths in second class (all include full bedding). Day trains are single class. Reservations are necessary, except for local trains.

THE NETHERLANDS

Capital: The Netherlands has two capitals: one (Amsterdam) is administrative and the other (The Hague – Den Haag) is legislative. **Language**: Dutch is the official language. English is widespread and almost universal in Amsterdam; German is also widely spoken and French to a lesser degree. The universal greeting at any time is 'Dag' (which is repeated on parting). If you say this in a friendly manner then continue in English, etiquette is observed and you need not feel awkward about speaking no Dutch. **Currency**: Guilders (F.); 1 Guilder = 100 Cents. Guilders are also known as Florins and price tags usually show 'f', but 'fl', 'Dfl', 'Hfl' and 'Gld' are also common. Changing money on the street is illegal and notes which are torn or defaced are often refused in shops and banks. US dollars and German marks are the easiest currencies to change.

Passports and Visas

A British Visitor's Passport is sufficient, as are EU National Identity Cards. Visas are not needed by nationals of the EU, Australia, Canada, New Zealand or the USA. Others should check.

Customs

Standard EU regulations apply (see p. 13–14).

Useful Addresses in the UK

Embassy, *38 Hyde Park Gate, London SW7 5DP; tel: (071) 584 5040.* **Netherlands Board of Tourism**, *Egginton House, 25/28 Buckingham Gate, London SW1E 6LD; tel: (0891) 200 277* (premium-rate calls). Or: *PO Box 523, London SW1E 6NT.* **Netherlands Railways**, *c/o Board of Tourism; tel: (071) 630 1735.*

Useful Addresses in the USA

Embassy, *4200 Linnean Ave NW, Washington, DC 20008-1848; tel: (202) 244 5304.* **Netherlands Board of Tourism**, *355 Lexington Ave (21st Floor), New York, NY 10017; tel: (212) 370 7367.*

Living in the Netherlands

Accommodation

The Netherlands is a participant in the Benelux hotel-classification scheme (see Belgium, p. 32). The tourist board produces full-colour brochures listing all the hotels in the country.

Standards are high and even the cheapest places are usually clean and comfortable – low prices reflect limited facilities rather than poor quality. Room rates start at about F. 65 for a double, so you make a considerable saving by using hostels or camping. In many towns, *VVV* (*Vereniging voor Vreemdelingenverkeer*) can supply a list of private homes in which rooms are available, so it's always worth asking about this. Advance booking is advisable, often necessary, and there's a central (free) booking service: **Netherlands Reservation Centre**, *PO Box 404, 2260 AK Leidschendam; tel: (070) 17 54 54* (English language). Mon–Fri 0800–2000 and Sat 0800–1400.

The HQ of the **Dutch Youth Hostels Association (NJHC)** is *Prof. Tulpplein 4, 1018 GX Amsterdam; tel: (020) 551 3155. VVV* have listings for bed and breakfast accommodation. You can book through **Bed and Breakfast Holland**, *Warmondstraat 129 1e; tel: (020) 615 7527.*

The tourist board also produce a full-colour brochure in English which gives full details (including pictures) of all the official campsites in the country. There are plenty of them and some have cabins as well as facilities for tents.

Food and Drink

Dutch food is simple and substantial, with emphasis on its excellent dairy products. Try the traditional pancakes (*pannekoeken*). A popular snack is thick-cut chips with mayonnaise. There are many Indonesian restaurants for those who like spicy food.

Most eating-places are open 1100–1430/1500 and 1730–2200/2300. Many offer a good-value day-special *dagschotel* or tourist menu. There's usually a selection of tasty snacks at the traditional 'Brown cafés'. Both tea and coffee are readily available. The Dutch beers and liqueurs are excellent. The ubiquitous *jenever* is a strong, slightly oily gin made from juniper berries.

Mensas are subsidised student canteens which are very cheap and not restricted to students. They are to be found in all university towns, but are open only during term-time.

Opening Hours

Banks: Mon–Fri 0900–1600/1700, closing an hour or two later on Thursdays. **Shops**: Mon–Sat 0900/0930–1730/1800 (until 2100 on either Thur or Fri) and Sat 0900/0930–1600/1700. Many close on Monday morning and for one other half-day each week. **Museums**: these vary but usually open Tue–Sun (or Mon–Sat) 1000–1700. In winter many have shorter hours. They also open on most public holidays, although for shorter hours.

Postage

The post office logo is *ptt post* in white on a red background. Most post offices open Mon–Fri 0830–1700, but the larger ones may also open Sat 0830–1200. Parcels can be sent only from major post offices. There's a freephone information number about the postal services and charges: *tel: 06 0417*. Stamps (*postzegels)* can be purchased from tobacconists.

Public Holidays

1 Jan; Good Friday; Easter Sunday–Monday; 30 Apr; 5 May (Liberation Day); Ascension Day; Whit Sunday–Monday; 25, 26 Dec.

Public Transport

You cannot call individual stations for informa-

The Netherlands

- The Netherlands has a big hard-drugs problem and the police are very alert, so make a fast exit if a street dealer tries to engage your attention.
- April/May is tulip time and the whole country becomes rather crowded. If you're not interested in the tulips, it is a good idea to time your visit for June/September.
- The national tourist office within Holland is **Vereniging voor Vreemdelingenverkeer**, known simply as *VVV*. They have offices in every city, which are marked by blue triangular signs. Most of them have English-speaking staff, supply English-language literature and provide a comprehensive service, but they do charge a small fee for making bookings. The minimum opening times are: Mon–Fri 0900–1700 and Sat 1000–1200, but many branches open longer and, especially in summer, you may find they are open quite late seven days a week.
- Anyone under 26 can ask for a **CJP (Cultureel Jongeren Paspoort)**, which costs F. 15 and provides discounts on museums (and similar establishments) as well as some cultural events. The **Museumjaarkaart** (from *VVV* and all participating museums for F.40 (less if you are 65 or more, a student, or under 18) is valid for a year and provides free or reduced entry to about 400 museums.

---

tion, but there are centralised numbers covering all transport enquiries. For national rail and bus enquiries *tel: 06 9292*, for all international journeys *tel: 06 92963*. You just tell them where and when you want to go and they will check all the connections. The system is run by computers, so is both fast and accurate, but the calls are at premium rates (F.50 per unit).

All taxis have a 'taxi' sign on the roof (lighted when they are free) and it is customary to board them at ranks or to phone (most bars etc. will do

---

this for you). Although it is not actually illegal to hail taxis in the street, it is not the custom and you will be lucky if one stops.

Strippenkaart is a strip ticket (available from GVB, stations and newsagents) that is valid on any city train, metro, bus or tram in Holland. The whole country is divided into travel zones and for each journey you use one section to board plus one for each zone in which you travel. In cities, the strip is validated by a yellow box on board buses and trams and at the entrance to metros; in smaller places, the driver stamps them. Once stamped, that section of the strip is valid for the following hour, even if you change from one vehicle or form of transport to another (so long as you don't increase the number of zones). The most common strip is one with 15 sections that costs F. 10.25.

Individual tickets are also valid for an hour's travel on all the public transport and can be purchased from bus and tram drivers on boarding, as can short strips, but this is much more expensive than buying them in advance.

Another alternative is the **Dagkaart**, which covers all urban buses and trams. Combined tickets (**Dagtochtkaartjes**) cover boats, trains and buses. Both can be valid for as many days as you need. There are many other discounted fares, but the structure is complex and most are of more interest to residents than international travellers. Credit cards can be used to purchase international tickets, but not for local tickets. Inspectors (usually in uniform) operate frequent checks and can impose hefty on-the-spot fines if you cannot produce a valid ticket. They are unimpressed by foreigners' pleas of ignorance.

Telephones

Telephone booths have a white *ptt telecom* logo. Cash booths are green, blue booths take only telecards. You can get telecards at post offices, stations and tobacconists. If you dial a popular number (e.g. a theatre) and get a recorded message in Dutch, it is almost certainly saying that you are in a queue, so hold on until somebody takes over.

To call abroad from the Netherlands: *tel: 09*, then pause until you get the dialling tone again. To call the Netherlands from abroad: *tel: 31*. For

the operator: *tel: 06 0410*. For international directory enquiries: *tel:* 06 0418. For national directory enquiries: *tel: 008*. **Emergencies**: Police: 0611; Fire: 0611; Ambulance: 0611.

There is an increasing tendency for ordinary enquiry/booking numbers to be replaced by centralised 06-prefixed numbers. When the system started these were free (some still are) but most of the new ones charge at the premium rate (F.50 per unit) and there is no real way of knowing which is which, so be prepared to pay.

Rail Travel Within The Netherlands

The national rail company is *Nederlandse Spoorwegen (NS)*. NS operates an efficient system and there are fast, comfortable trains everywhere. Most *IC* (*Inter-City*) services run every half-hour. *Sneltreins* take the most direct line and *stoptreins* serve all stations en route. Most *EC* trains have restaurant facilities. Most *IC* trains have a trolley service. Seat reservations are only possible for international journeys.

Fares and Passes

The **Netherlands Rail Rover** is valid for one day or seven consecutive days of unlimited rail travel on all trains, first or second class. It can be extended to cover all buses and trams, plus the metros in Amsterdam and Rotterdam.

NORWAY

Capital: Oslo. **Language**: Bokmål and Nynorsk are both variants of Norwegian. Danish is almost universally spoken, as is English. Norwegian has three additional vowels: æ, ø and å, all of which come after z in alphabetical listings. **Currency**: Norwegian Kroner (NKr.); 1 Krone = 100 Ore.

Customs

People aged 16 or more who are resident in Europe are entitled to an allowance of 200 cigarettes or 250g tobacco and 200 cigarette papers. The following allowances are doubled for anyone over 16 who lives outside Europe.

People aged 20 or more are entitled to an allowance of 2 litres wine not exceeding 22% volume or 1 litre spirits not exceeding 60% volume, and 1 litre wine not exceeding 22% volume. Residents of non-European countries are also entitled to 2 litres beer.

Passports and Visas

A British Visitor's Passport is sufficient, as are EU National Identity Cards. Visas are not needed by Scandinavians, nationals of the EU, Australia, Canada, New Zealand or the USA. Others should check.

Useful Addresses in the UK

Embassy, *25 Belgrave Square, London SW1X 8QD; tel: (071) 235 7151.* **Norwegian Tourist Board**, *Charles House, 5/11 Lower Regent Street, London SW1Y 4LR; tel: (071) 839 6255.* **NSR (Norwegian State Railways) Travel Bureau**, *21/24 Cockspur St, London SW1Y 5DA; tel: (071) 930 6666.*

Useful Addresses in the USA

Embassy, *2720 34th Street NW, Washington, DC 20008-2799; tel: (202) 333 6000.* **Scandinavian Tourist Board**, *655 Third Ave, New York, NY 10017; tel: (212) 949 2333.*

Living in Norway

Accommodation

Hotels are expensive, but Norwegian law permits camping anywhere that is over 150m from buildings and fences, as long as you leave no traces of your stay. DNT (the Norwegian Mountain Touring Association) provides information for campers and has huts throughout Norway (open at Easter, then from late June to early September). Many are staffed and serve hot meals; keys are available for the ones which are unmanned.

Food and Drink

Eating and drinking in Norway is extremely expensive and you will save a lot by stocking up in supermarkets (*Rema 1000* and *Netto* are nationwide supermarket chains). *Konditori* are bakeries, which often serve sandwiches and pastries relatively cheaply. There are also cheap street kiosks for things like hamburgers and hot dogs. Restaurants sometimes have *dagens rett*, which are relatively cheap full meals, and self-service *kafeterias* are usually reasonable.

Breakfast is normally a substantial buffet-style meal including things like goat's cheese and pickled herring, with tea, coffee or milk. Lunch, either similar to breakfast, or an open sandwich, is normally eaten 1200–1500. Dinner is usually a three-course hot meal. Fresh fish is popular, delicious and cheaper than meat. Dinner is traditionally 1600–1900, but habits are changing and the larger places are now more likely to serve it 1800–2200.

Norwegian tap water is exceptionally pure. Alcohol (even beer) can raise the cost of eating from expensive to exorbitant and is served in restaurants only to people over 18, only after 1500 and never on Sundays. *Gløgg* is a mulled wine drink that is popular in winter.

Opening Hours

Banks: Mon–Fri 0815/0830–1500/1530 (Thur–1700). A few banks in Oslo are open later and some rural banks have shorter hours. **Shops**: Mon–Fri 0900–1600/1700 (Thur 0900–1800/2000) and Sat 0900–1300/1500. Many stalls, supermarkets and shopping malls are open later. **Museums**: (usually) Tue–Sun 1000–1500/1600. Some also open on Monday.

Postage

Post offices are generally open from Mon–Fri 0800/0830–1600/1700 and Sat 0830–1300. Post boxes can be identified by the trumpet and crown on yellow boxes (for local mail) and red boxes (for all other destinations).

Public Holidays

1 Jan; Maundy Thursday–Good Friday; Easter Sunday–Monday; 1, 17 May; Ascension Day; Whit Sunday–Monday; 25, 26 Dec.

Public Transport

Norway has a thorough and complex transport system with trains, boats, buses and planes, many of which link up together, so that your fjord ferry will connect with the train, which will connect with the local bus into the village. Local transport is nearly always by bus (except for ferry connections between small islands and across fjords). There are also taxis in every town. Don't hail them in the street. Find a rank or phone.

Telephones

To call Norway from abroad: *tel: 47*. To call abroad from Norway: *tel: 095*. To call directory enquiries: *tel: 0181; 0180* (within the Nordic countries). **Emergencies**: Police: 002; Fire: 001; Ambulance: 003.

Rail Travel Within Norway

The Norwegian state railway is *Norges Statsbaner (NSB)*. Norwegian trains are punctual, modern and comfortable, but they do not cover the whole country: most routes converge on Oslo and they run north only as far as Bodø. After that you must use buses. Fast trains are *ICE, IC, IN (Inter-Nord*: daytime international services) and *ET* (Express Trains). Second-class seating on long-distance trains is very comfortable.

Sleepers on internal services have one berth in first class and two or three in second. Couchettes are all second class and have six berths. Reservations are necessary on all express (*ekspresstog*) and many other fast (*hurtigtog*) trains and you may be refused permission to board if you do not have one. Most routes are scenic, particularly the Oslo–Bergen line, and some express trains have observation cars.

POLAND

Capital: Warsaw (*Warszawa*). **Language**: Polish; many Poles, especially the older ones, speak German or French. The younger ones (particularly students) are more likely to speak English, but not fluently and only in tourist areas. Russian is widely understood, but not popular. **Currency**: Złoty (Zł.). You will be asked to fill in a currency declaration form on arrival. Any you have left can be re-converted when you leave, but it's not worth changing a lot as many people are very happy to be paid in hard currencies. They are not restricted and the US$ is accepted so universally that it is almost a second currency.

You are unlikely to be able to change travellers' cheques or Eurocheques anywhere other than at a large bank or Kantor exchange office. Kantor sometimes give better rates than banks and their opening hours are longer. The following branch of **Thomas Cook** will also be able to change your travellers' cheques, free of charge in the case of Thomas Cook travellers' cheques: *Orbis Travel, Marszalkowka Str. 142, Warsaw*. Credit cards are widely accepted in large establishments and their use is increasing elsewhere, but they are still far from universal.

Customs

The following allowances are for people aged 17 or over: 250 cigarettes or 50 cigars or 250g tobacco, 1 litre wine, and 1 litre any other alcoholic beverage.

Passports and Visas

All visitors require full passports. British passport holders do not require visas, nor do nationals of the USA. Nationals of Australia, Canada and New Zealand do need visas. Others should check.

Useful Addresses in the UK

Embassy, *73 New Cavendish St, London W1N 7RB; tel: (071) 580 0476*. **Polish National Tourist Office (Orbis)**, *246 King St, London W6 0RF; tel: (081) 741 5541*. **Polish State Railways** *c/o Orbis; tel: (071) 637 4971*.

Useful Addresses in the USA

Embassy, *2640 16th Street NW, Washington, DC 20009-4202; tel: (202) 234 3800*. **Polish National Tourist Office (Orbis)**, *500 Fifth Ave, New York, NY 10110; tel: (212) 867 5011*.

Living in Poland

Accommodation

Orbis runs a chain of international hotels across the country, and some slightly less expensive motels. Otherwise, your best bet will probably be a pension or private room. In popular holiday areas, you may be able to hire a holiday cottage for a longer stay. In high summer there are also youth hostels and university rooms available. With everything changing from day to day and rampant inflation, accommodation of a decent quality can be hard to find outside the major centres and you cannot rely on the tourist offices to help. Try and find a good, up-to-date hotel listing and be prepared to make your own arrangements.

Food and Drink

You can get fast food from street stalls. Other places include milk bars (*bary mleczne*), which serve cheap vegetarian dishes; *Zajazdy* which are reasonably priced roadside inns and cafés that serve delicious pastries and cream. Many restaurants close around 2100 but those in hotels stay open later, often serving until around 2300.

Potato pancakes, sweet dumplings and a sort of large-scale ravioli are among the national dishes. Freshwater fish, pork and cream are very common ingredients. The best thing is usually the soup, on which the Poles place a heavy emphasis. The Poles drink mineral water in preference to tap water, which is not safe. Tea is served black and in glasses, but you can ask for milk to be brought separately. Most wines are imported and expensive, so are sold by the glass. Polish beer has a very distinctive taste, and the vodka is excellent.

Opening Hours

Banks: Mon–Fri 0800–1500/1800. **Shops**: Mon–Fri 0800/1100–1900 and Sat 0900–1300. **Food shops**: Mon–Fri 0600–1900 and Sat 0600–1300. **Museums**: these vary greatly, but are usually open Tue–Sun 1000–1600. They seldom open on public holidays and are often closed the following day as well.

Postage

Post offices (*Poczta*) open Mon–Sat 0700/0800–1800/2000 (main offices). Note that the word *Przerwa* on the glass windows means break and the booth is closed between the times shown. In each city, the post offices are numbered (the main office is always 1) and the number should be included in the post restante address. Post boxes are green (local mail), blue (air-mail), or red (long-distance mail).

Public Holidays

1 Jan; Easter Sunday–Monday; 1, 3 May; Corpus Christi; 15 Aug; 1, 11 Nov; 24, 25, 26 Dec.

Public Transport

PKS buses are cheap and more practical than trains for short trips or off-beat destinations. Tickets include seat reservations (the seat number is on the back) and can be purchased in advance from the bus station. In rural areas, bus drivers will often halt away from official stops if you wave them down.

Telephones

Until recently public telephones were operated exclusively by the telephone coins on sale at post offices and ruch kiosks. Newer telephones operate on telephone cards and if you can find one, these are much more efficient.

To call Poland from abroad: *tel: 48*. To call abroad from Poland: *tel: 901*. To call an English speaking operator: *tel: 903*. **Emergencies**: Police: 997; Fire: 998; Ambulance: 999.

Rail Travel Within Poland

The Polish national rail service is operated by *Polskie Koleje Panstwowe* (*PKP*), with some minor lines run by *Lubusz Koleje Regionalna* (*LKR*). The rail network is extensive, cheap and punctual, but services can be slow and infrequent. At the time of writing, trains were liable to cancellation without notice, due to the dire economic condition of the country.

At stations, departures (*odjazdy*) are on yellow paper and arrivals (*przyjazdy*) on white. The express trains (*ekspres* – prefixed '*EX*') and direct trains (*pospieszny*) that are almost as fast are printed in red. The black *osobowy* are the slowest.

Trains usually have both first- and second-class seating and most Westerners feel first class is worth the extra cost (about 50% more, but still cheap by Western standards). Overnight trains usually have first- and second-class sleepers, as well as second-class couchettes. Reservations are needed on all express and some direct services. Most long-distance trains have buffet services and the WARS (buffet) carriages can be a good place for a cup of tea. The food is definitely not recommended.

Fares and Passes

There is a **Polrail Pass**, which allows an unlimited number of rail trips on some routes for 8, 15 or 21 days, but normal fares are very cheap and it's usually more economical to buy ordinary single and return tickets.

PORTUGAL

Capital: Lisbon (*Lisboa)*. **Language**: Portuguese, which is difficult to understand when it is spoken but, if you speak any other Latin languages, you will probably understand enough of the written form to get by. English, French and German are spoken to some extent, but mostly in tourist areas. **Currency**: Escudos ($). 1 Escudo = 100 Centavos. In written form, the $ sign comes between the Escudos and the Centavos, where there would normally be a decimal point.

Customs

Standard EU regulations apply (see p. 13–14).

Passports and Visas

A British Visitor's Passport is sufficient, as are EU National Identity Cards. Visas are not required by nationals of the EU, Australia or New Zealand. Nationals of Canada and the USA may stay for up to two months without a visa.

Useful Addresses in the UK

Consulate-General, *3rd Floor, Silver City House, 62 Brompton Rd, London SW3 1BJ; tel: (071) 581 8722/4.* **Embassy**, *11 Belgrave Square, SW1X 8PP; tel: (071) 235 5331.* **Portuguese National Tourist Office**, *22/25A Sackville St, London W1X 1DE; tel: (071) 494 1441.* **Portuguese Railways**, *Address as Tourist Office; tel: (071) 839 4741.*

Useful Addresses in the USA

Embassy, *2125 Kalorama Road NW, Washington, DC 20008-1619; tel: (202) 328 8610.* **Portuguese National Tourist Office**, *590 Fifth Ave (4th Floor), New York, NY 10036-4704; tel: (212) 354 4403.*

Living in Portugal

Accommodation

The possibilities for accommodation in Portugal are almost endless: you name it, they've got it. You can choose anything from a five-star hotel to a campsite, from a private home to a hostel. Information about all forms of accommodation (including private homes, which range from manor houses to farms) is available from government tourist offices or the **Direccao-General do Turismo**, *Avenida Antonio Augusto de Aguish 86, 1004 Lisbon; tel: (1) 57 50 86/57 51 45.*

There are many campsites throughout the country. Information from the **Portuguese Camping and Caravan Association** *Avenida 5 de Outubro 15-3, 1000 Lisbon; tel: (1) 52 33 08/52 27 15.* *Pousadas* are state-run establishments in three categories. Some are converted national historic monuments, others are modern buildings in historic locations: both these types are four- to five-star standard. The third category is composed of comfortable modern inns or lodges, built in locations chosen for their wild remoteness and fabulous views: these are three- to four-star. Advance reservations are essential. *Estalagens* are small inns that usually provide only bed and breakfast.

Food and Drink

The Portuguese pattern of eating is to have a fairly frugal breakfast and two big main meals: lunch (1200–1500) and dinner (2000–2300). Places that have evening entertainment may stay open until around midnight and, if so, tend to offer a late supper. The cafés and pastry shops usually stay open all day, so you can have a snack at any time. There is a wide choice of eating-places. Most of the bars, restaurants and cafés serve alcohol. Eating is not expensive but, if your budget is strained, go for the meal of the day *prato do día* or *menú*.

Eating is taken seriously, the cuisine flavoured with herbs rather than spices and rather heavy on olive oil. There is lots of delicious seafood and you should try some of the varieties of *caldeirada* (fish stew). Other local dishes are *bacalhau* (dried salted cod in various guises) and *leitão* (roasted suckling pig). The most popular pudding is a sweet egg custard. There are lots of spas and bottled mineral water is available everywhere. The country is, of course, the home of port, but there are also several excellent (and often cheap) wines, such as *vinho verde*. Do not be surprised if you are charged for pre-dinner bread, olives, or other nibbles that are brought to your table unordered. If you don't want them, say so.

Opening Hours

Banks: Mon–Fri 0830–1145, 1300–1445/1500.
Shops: Mon–Fri 0900/1000–1300, 1500–1800/1900 and Sat 0900–1300. Shopping centres in cities often open daily 1000–2359. **Museums**: Tue–Sun 1000–1700/1800. Some close for lunch and some are free on Sundays. Palaces and castles usually close on Wednesdays.

Postage

Correio indicates both post-boxes and post offices. Most post offices open Mon–Fri 0900–1800 and Sat 0900–1300, although the smaller ones close for lunch and are not open on Saturdays. Most large post offices have a *poste restante* facility.

Stamps (*selos*) can be purchased from anywhere with a sign depicting a red horse or a white circle on a green background.

Public Holidays

1 Jan; Shrove Tuesday; Good Friday; 25 Apr; 1 May; 10 June; Corpus Christi; 15 Aug; 5 Oct; 1 Nov; 1, 8, 25 Dec.

In addition, there are a number of local holidays for the days of the patron saints, for example, 13 June in Lisbon and 24 June in Oporto.

Public Transport

Maps and details of the public transport system in each town are obtainable from the local tourist office.

The long-distance nationalised bus company is **Rodaviaria Nacional**, *Avenida Casal Ribeiro 18, Lisbon; tel: (01) 57 77 15*. Bus stops are marked *paragem*. You must extend your arm or the buses won't stop. Taxis are black with green roofs and illuminated signs. They are plentiful and cheap. Within cities they are metered but elsewhere fares are negotiable and drivers are entitled to ask you to pay for their return journey. Luggage over 30 kg adds 50% to the fare and there is a 20% night surcharge (2200–0600). Tips of 10% are expected.

Each city has Tourist Passes which are valid for either four or seven days and can be used on all public transport services within that city. You can buy single tickets as you board buses and trams, but you save money by buying books of tickets in

---

Portugal

- Portugal has a multi-lingual telephone information service for tourists, based in Lisbon, *tel: (01) 70 63 41*. The police (dark-blue uniforms in towns and brown in rural areas) are also helpful and have red arm bands if they are bi-lingual.
- Some grocers and small post offices offer a laundry service (*lavandarias*). They can be hard on clothes but are very efficient.
- It's not unusual for places of worship to be locked outside the hours when services are being held, but there is usually a key-holder living close by who is happy to open up on demand. Ask around.

---

advance. When you board a bus, you insert one, two or three tickets in the machine behind the driver. On trams the conductor punches the tickets you give him. How many you use depends on the length of the journey.

Telephones

Coin-operated kiosks are the most common, but the number that take phonecards (available from post offices and some tobacconists) is increasing rapidly. There's a surcharge (often hefty) for using phones in hotels etc. If you want to make an international call, the easiest way is to go to a post office: the clerk assigns a booth (you may have to queue) and times the call. Pay at the end. The phone system is being upgraded and you may find some numbers have changed.

To call abroad from Portugal; *tel: 00*. To call Portugal from abroad; *tel 351*. For the operator; *tel: 118*. This is a general number for local/overseas calls and other enquiries. Ask for the service you want. **Emergencies**: Police: 115; Fire: 115; Ambulance: 115

Rail Travel Within Portugal

The national rail company is *Caminhos de Ferro Portugueses* (*CP*). The *CP* network is fairly comprehensive, clean, punctual and cheap, but domestic services are a little slow. All long-distance trains have first- and second-class seating, but the local trains are usually second class only.

CP has four categories of train: *Regional* (local and slow, stopping everywhere), *IR*, *IC* and *Servico-Alfa* (modern and fast with few stops, mainly on Lisbon-Oporto route; supplement payable).

Long-distance trains usually have dining cars and many others have mini-bars. Seat reservations are compulsory on international and express trains (and some others) and recommended for all long-distance travel.

Train timetables are available from information desks at main stations and tourist offices. *CP* also operate a general information service, based in Lisbon; *tel: (1) 87 60 25/87 70 92.*

Fares and Passes

Special **Tourist Tickets** are available (from *CP* in Portugal) for first- or second-class travel for 7, 14 or 21 days. The one restriction is that they can be used only on blue days, which (roughly speaking) are all except Fridays, Sunday afternoons, Monday mornings, the eves of public holidays and the holidays themselves. There are very heavy fines if you board a train without buying a ticket in advance. Tickets are available from any travel agency and most main stations.

ROMANIA

Capital: Bucharest (*Bucuresti*). **Language**: Romanian, which can sound a little like French, a language which is widely spoken in the cities, especially amongst older people. In its written form, many words of Romanian will be understood by anyone with a knowledge of Latin languages. Some German and Hungarian is also spoken. In tourist areas there is some knowledge of English, but not elsewhere. **Currency**: Lei. The import/export of local currency is prohibited. There are no restrictions on the import/export of foreign currencies and there is no longer an obligatory currency exchange. Credit cards are accepted in major hotels, but seldom elsewhere.

Customs

The allowances for adults are: 200 cigarettes or 300g tobacco, 2 litres alcoholic beverages, and 4 litres wine or beer.

Romania

- Gypsies are a problem in Romania and (with some justification) blamed for most thefts, so be especially wary when they are around.
- Many things which are readily available in the West are hard (if not impossible) to get in Romania and you should take your own supply of routine medicaments and toiletries. Don't expect to find paper, soap and towels in public facilities.
- Street names are being widely changed in Romania. Be prepared for discrepancies between street signs and maps.
- Protection against hepatitis A is recommended.

Passports and Visas

All visitors require full passports and visas.

Useful Addresses in the UK

Embassy, *Arundel House, 4 Palace Green, London W8 4QD; tel: (071) 937 9667.* **Romanian National Tourist Office**, *Currently: 17 Nottingham St, London W1M 3RD; tel: (071) 224 3692.* However, they are hoping to move to Marylebone High Street during 1994, so check.

Useful Addresses in the USA

Embassy, *1607 23rd Street NW, Washington, DC 20008-2809; tel: (202) 232 4747.* **Romanian National Tourist Office**, *573 Third Ave, New York, NY 10016; tel: (212) 697 6971.*

Living in Romania

Accommodation

Hotels vary enormously in quality, even within the same category, and prices can be high, as foreign rates are much higher than those charged to Romanians. Rooms in both hotels and private apartments are bookable through local tourist offices. You will often have to pay a hefty commission, but should get some guarantee of quality. Individuals, particularly in stations or near major hotels, may offer unofficial private rooms. These will invariably be cheaper, but may be ghastly. Look up the area on a map to make sure you won't be stuck out in the suburbs, and always check the room before handling over any money. Campsites in Romania have a reputation for being both grim and expensive.

Food and Drink

The better restaurants offer a reasonable choice, but food supplies are limited and in most places you're likely to get pork or beef with tinned or pickled vegetables. Most eating-places open at around noon (although some open for breakfast at around 0700) and close around midnight, but many take a break 1600–1900.

Tap water is safe to drink, but heavily chlorinated. Water in drinking-fountains is usually straight from springs and more palatable. Wines from the Black Sea region are excellent and the plum brandy (tuica) is good. Coffee shops (cofetarie) serve both real coffee (complete with grounds) and instant (nes), but milk is in short supply and seldom offered. Cakes, where available, are usually mouth-watering.

Opening Hours

Banks: Mon–Fri 0900–1200/1300. **Shops**: Mon–Sat 0900/1000–1300 and 1500–1800/2000. Some food shops open at around 0600. Very few shops are open on Sundays. **Museums**: (usually) Tue–Sun 1000–1800, but they can vary and it's best to check locally.

Postage

Post offices usually open Mon–Sat 0800–2000, Sun 0800–1200. Post boxes are yellow and marked Posta. Try not to use the facilities here, however, as the system is very unreliable and there is no viable poste restante service.

Public Holidays

1, 2 Jan; Orthodox Easter (a week later than the Catholic Easter); 1, 2 May; 1, 25, 26 Dec.

Saturdays and Sundays are official public holidays and all government agencies shut at weekends. Some places close from 25 December to 3 January inclusive and most take more than the official holiday.

Public Transport

Trains are the best option for long-distance transport. Buses are slow, crowded and uncomfortable. There are passenger ferries and hydrofoils along the Danube.

Local transport is cheap and convenient, though often very crowded. There are usually stalls or kiosks at major bus or tram stops selling tickets. Taxis, especially in Bucharest, are somewhat of a lottery – with semi/unofficial drivers on the roads.

Telephones

To call Romania from abroad: tel: 40. To call abroad from Romania: tel: 00. It's possible to phone abroad from the newer call boxes. **Emergencies**: Police: 955; Fire: 981; Ambulance: 961.

Rail Travel Within Romania

The national rail company is Căile Ferate Romane (CFR) and the ticket agents display signs with either 'CFR' or 'SNCFR'. Express trains are accelerat and rapide. The persoane are very slow and should be avoided. Trains are, on the whole, a bit dilapidated and it is worth paying the extra to travel first class (although even that is not particularly comfortable).

On long-distance journeys you can usually get sleepers (vagons de dormit) or couchettes (cuseta). Reservations are obligatory on most services (except local) and passengers without reservations have to pay a surcharge. It is advisable to book, anyway, since trains are often crowded. Reservations and ticket purchases can be made at the CFR agencies in town. Queues are long but not as bad as a few years ago.

Fares and Passes

Tickets for domestic journeys can be purchased only an hour or so before departure, but reservations can be made without tickets.

SLOVAKIA

Capital: Bratislava. **Language**: Slovak is a Slavic tongue closely related to Czech. Some Russian and German, and a little English is also understood. Shops where the staff are linguists tend to have signs saying so. **Currency**: Slovak Korunas or Crowns (K.); 1 Koruna = 100 Hellers. Non-residents may now import/export up to 100 Crowns in local money and there are no restrictions on foreign currencies.

Customs

The following allowances apply to people who are aged 18 or over. They are: 250 cigarettes or equivalent in tobacco, 1 litre spirits, and 2 litres wine (half these amounts if your stay is to be for 2 days or less).

Passports and Visas

Full passports are required. Visas are not needed by nationals of the EU, Canada or the USA. Nationals of Australia and New Zealand need visas and passports valid for at least six months. Others should check.

Useful Addresses in the UK

Embassy, *25 Kensington Palace Gardens, London W8 4QY; tel: (071) 243 0803.* **Čedok (Slovak Tourist Office)**, *49 Southwark Street, London SE1 1RU; tel: (071) 378 6009.*

Useful Addresses in the USA

Embassy, *3900 Linnean Ave NW, Washington DC 20008-3897; tel: (202) 363 6315.* **Čedok**, *10 East 40th Street, New York, NY 10016; tel: (212) 689 9720.*

Living in Slovakia

Accommodation

You should have a choice of one- to five- star hotels, private rooms and pensions, and, at a much more basic leve, old-style tourist hotels (effectively dormitory-type barracks), hostels and inns with a few spartan rooms. However, the quality (once outside the five-star range) can leave a lot to be desired. It is probably safer to look at private rooms than cheap hotels. Some places may still insist on payment in hard currency.

Private rooms, youth hostel beds and hotel rooms can be booked through a variety of agencies, including the Slovak versions of Cedok and CKM (the student travel bureau). Local

---

> ### Slovakia
> - The old Czechoslovakian organisations, Cedok, the national tourist agency, and CKM, the student travel bureau, have now been reincarnated as Cedok-SCK Slovakia and CKM-Slovakia respectively.
> - There have been numerous changes of street names in Slovakia over the past few years so ask for an up-to-date map or list of changes.

tourist information offices can also help with the search for accommodation. Local individuals are beginning to offer rooms to arriving travellers.

Food and Drink

Lunch is around 1130–1400/1500 and dinner 1800–2130/2200. The cuisine tends to be rich and meat-based, but vegetarian restaurants are beginning to appear.

Slovak food is very similar to Hungarian and Schnitzel and dumplings (*knedliky*) are on virtually every menu, so is *gulaš*, a spicy meat dish in which wine is a major ingredient. Eating and drinking are cheap, especially in *bufet* (where you stand while eating), and *samoobsluha* (self-service). *Kavarny* and *cukrárny* serve coffee (often Turkish-style) and delightful pastries. Beer halls (*pivnice*) and wine bars (*vinárna*) are good places to eat. Czech beer and Slovak wine are both excellent.

Opening Hours

Banks: Mon–Fri 0830–1715. **Shops**: Mon–Fri 0900–1200 and 1400–1800, Sat 0900–1200. Food shops usually open much earlier. They, and souvenir shops often open on Sundays. **Museums**: (usually) Tue–Sun 1000–1700. Most châteaux close on national holidays and from November to March.

Postage

There is a full postal service (including post restante), but it is slow and erratic. It is also cheap. Usual post office opening hours are 0800–1900. Stamps are also available from newsagents and tobacconists.

Slovakia

Public Holidays

1 Jan; Easter Monday; 1, 9 May; 5 July; 28 Oct; 1 Nov; 24–26 Dec.

Public holidays are to be changed by the independent government. 29 Aug and 19 Sept have been proposed as new holidays, and it is unlikely that 9 May, 28 Oct and 1 Nov will remain public holidays. However, the final decision has not been made.

Public Transport

The long-distance public transport system is still integrated, to some extent, with that of the Czech Republic. There could be changes as they disentangle the two countries. The rail network here is good, but there is also a comprehensive long-distance bus network. Bus stations are well-organised. Officially, you should book in advance, but you can buy tickets from the conductor, although he will give priority to those with reservations.

Telephones

To call Slovakia from abroad: *tel: 42*. To call abroad from Slovakia: *tel: 00*. **Emergencies**: Police: 158; Fire: 150; Ambulance: 155.

Rail Travel Within Slovakia

The national rail company is *Železnice Slovenskej Republiky (ŽSR)*. The rail network is cheap and extensive, but the trains are always crowded. The fastest trains are *expresný* , but *rychlík* cost as much as the express. The few *spešný* (semi-fast) trains cost less. *Osobný* (slow) should be avoided.

All trains offer both first- and second-class travel. Most long-distance trains have dining cars and overnight services between cities have sleeping cars. Sleepers/couchettes are of standard European type. Seat reservations are recommended for travel by express train, bookings can be made at the station counters marked 'R'. To reserve sleepers, you must go to an office of the official tourist board. It is now possible to make couchette reservations at the main Bratislava station.

Fares and Passes

A **Czech-Slovak Flexipass** covers 5 days unlimited travel within a 15-day period through-

out both the Republics. There is an **Explorer Pass** for 7 consecutive days (or multiples thereof) which covers first- or second-class rail travel. It is available to anyone under 26 and to any holder of an ISIC card, but must be purchased (from Campus Travel – see p. 22) before you go.

SPAIN

Capital: Madrid. **Language**: Castilian Spanish is the most widely spoken language. The three other official languages are: Catalan, spoken in the east; Galego, spoken in Galicia (in the northwest), and Basque, which is common in the Basque country, Navarra, Cantabria and even across the Pyrenees into France. English is fairly widely spoken by people in tourist-related industries in major cities and coastal areas. Bear in mind, when con-sulting dictionaries or directories, that in Spanish listings 'CH' comes at the end of the 'C' section and 'LL' at the end of the 'L' section. **Currency**: Pesetas (Ptas); 1 Peseta = 100 Centimos.

Customs

Standard EU regulations apply (see pp. 13–14).

Passports and Visas

A British Visitor's Passport is sufficient, as are EU National Identity Cards and those issued to nationals of Andorra, Austria, Liechtenstein, Malta, Monaco and Switzerland. Visas are not needed by nationals of the above countries, Australia, Canada, New Zealand or the USA. Others should check. Non-EU nationals must hold onward or return tickets plus a minimum of £25 (sterling) per day of their intended stay, or a minimum of Ptas 50,000.

Useful Addresses in the UK

Consulate-General, *20 Draycott Place, London SW3 2RZ; Visa tel: (071) 581 5921/6.*
Spanish National Tourist Office, *57 St James's St, London SW1A 1LD; tel: (071) 499 0901.*

Useful Addresses in the USA

Embassy, *2700 15th Street NW, Washington, DC 20009; tel: (202) 265 0190.* **Consulate**, *150 East 58th Street (16th Floor), New York, NY*

10155; tel: (212) 355 4080. **Spanish National Tourist Office**, *665 Fifth Ave, New York, NY 10022; tel: (212) 759 8822.*

Living in Spain

Accommodation

It is worth remembering that while tourist offices will give you information about accommodation, they are not allowed to make hotel reservations. In major cities there are often hotel booking agencies at the airports and railway stations.

Except when there's a fiesta, or it's peak season in tourist areas, accommodation is easy to find. Prices away from major resorts start at about Ptas 1,500 for a double room (around Ptas 1,200 for a single). Double beds are rare (double rooms usually have twin beds) and there's usually a higher charge if you do want a double (*matrimonio*) room. The standard of rooms within any given lodging-place can vary quite a lot, so always ask to see the room *before* you commit yourself to that establishment. If you want en suite facilities, it's worth saying whether you prefer a shower or bath, as there's often a choice (baths are sometimes more expensive).

By law, places that officially provide accommodation must place a notice (updated every year) in every bedroom stating the maximum amount payable for that room. The price includes all taxes and service charges (but seldom breakfast), and you should pay no more than the stated amount (which is for the room, not per person).

Every type of accommodation is officially graded, which ensures that standards are usually good and, on the whole, you pay for what you get. However, there can be an overlap between different types of accommodation, e.g. the best *Hostales Residencias* are often better value than the low-grade (one- to two-star) hotels.

All hotels and hostels are listed in the **Guia de Hoteles**, an annual publication available from tourist offices. There are blue plaques beside doorways that state the category of accommodation: **'H'** indicates Hotel, **'HS'** Hostales, **'HR'** Hostales Residencias, **'P'** Pension and **'F'** Fonda etc. If there is also an **'R'** on the plaque, do not expect a full dining service. **Paradores**

Nacionales are three- to five-star state-owned establishments and can be very expensive, but usually worth it. There are around 90 in Spain and the vast majority either occupy historical buildings or are in places of outstanding natural beauty. There's a central booking service in Madrid for Paradores throughout the whole country (*tel: (1) 435 97 00* or *(1) 435 97 44*). **Private homes** which offer rooms are known as *Casas Particulares.* They seldom have much in the way of facilities but are usually central and almost invariably very cheap. *Casas Rusticas* are farmhouses and *Refugios* are mountain huts. **Cheap boarding-houses/pensions** are variously known as *Fondas, Pensiones, Posadas, Ventas* and *Casas de Huespedes.* Slightly higher up the scale in terms of both price and facilities are *Hostales* and *Hostales Residencias.* These tend to cluster together in specific areas, often either around the station or around the main square.

There are dozens of **IYHF** hostels around the country and some universities offer accommodation in student dormitories (*Colegios Mayores*) when students are not in residence. There are over 500 **campsites** (some open all year, others just in summer) and the Tourist Office issues a list of the approved ones (*Guia de Campings* – Ptas 400), which are classified as luxury, first, second and third class. Book locally or through the **Federación Española de Empresarios de Campings**, *Principe de Vergara 85, Madrid; tel: (1) 562 99 94.* You can 'rough camp' in most suitable places, but not on tourist beaches.

Food and Drink

In Spain, the pattern is to have a light breakfast: coffee or hot chocolate with rolls or fritters (*churros*). The main meal is lunch (1330–1500 – nearer 1500 on Sunday). Dinner is a little lighter, but can still consist of three courses, and is eaten late, at around 2200.

Restaurants are open only for lunch and dinner, so go to caféterias (usually open 0800–2400) for breakfast and light meals/snacks. They serve tea, coffee and alcohol. Bars offer snacks (*tapas*), as well as wine and beer.

There's not a great deal of variety in Spanish cuisine and the quality if often poor, but you can eat reasonably cheaply. *Platos combinados* and

Menú del día are both good value. If you want an inexpensive light meal, ask for *raciones*, a larger portion of *tapas*. The best-known Spanish dish is *paella*, which originated in Valencia; it is at its best when made to order – which takes about half an hour. Another famous dish is *gazpacho* (cold tomato soup), which originated in Andalusia and is found mainly in the south. An enjoyable tradition is to go *tascas*-hopping, the equivalent of the English pub-crawl, e.g. you move from bar to bar having *tapas* (little more than nibbles, intended as aperitifs) or *raciones* (rather more substantial snacks) and a beer (or glass of wine) at each.

In Spain you have to choose a drinking-place according to what you want to consume. For beer, you need a *bar* or *cerveceria*, for wine a *taberna* or *bodega*. For cider (in the north), you need a *cidreria*. The custom is to pay for all your drinks at the end of the evening, although this is changing in some resort areas. Many drinking-places have a dining-room (*comedor*) at the rear if you want a full meal, or you can go to a proper restaurant (*mesón*). Water is safe to drink, but tastes better in some places than in others. The Spaniards like mineral water, which is available everywhere. Coffee tends to be strong. There are some excellent wines (notably from the Rioja and Penedés regions) and Jerez is, of course, the home of sherry. Sangria is a very palatable drink based on wine and fruit juice. Beer is popular.

Opening Hours

Banks: Winter: Mon–Thur 0830–1630; Fri 0830–1400; Sat 0830–1300. Summer: Mon–Fri 0830–1400. **Shops**: Mon–Sat 0930/1000–1400 and 1700–2000/2030, but major stores do not close for lunch and food shops often open on Sunday. **Museums**: these vary enormously, but most open 0900/1000 and close any time from 1400 to 2030 – the ones that stay open late usually close for siesta. Few are open Monday and some also close (or open for only half a day) on Sunday. A long lunch-hour is normal, especially in the south, and you can expect to find many things closed 1300–1500.

Postage

Most post offices (*correos*) open 0800–1400 and 1700–1930. The larger ones offer a poste restante (*lista de correos*) facility. Stamps (*sellos*) can also be purchased from tobacconists (*estancos*). Mail boxes are yellow with red stripes and overseas mail should be put in the slot marked *extranjero*. The Spanish postal system is notoriously slow but you can pay extra for urgent (*urgente*) delivery, to speed up your overseas mail.

Public Holidays

1, 6 Jan; several days at Easter; 1 May; Corpus Christi; 24 June; 25 July; 15 Aug; 12 Oct; 1 Nov; 6, 8 Dec and several days at Christmas. Not of all of these are official holidays, but many places close anyway. In addition to the national holidays, each region has at least four more, usually the local saints' days.

Public Transport

The city bus services are very efficient and taxis are easily available.

When they are free, taxis display a green light on the roof at night and a '*Libre*' sign against the windscreen by day. They are metered and cheap. There are surcharges for travel on Sundays or late at night, luggage placed in the boot and travel outside the town (including to airports and stations).

There is no nationwide bus company but there are numerous regional companies (*empresas*) which, between them, provide a reasonably comprehensive (if confusing) network, so buses (which are cheap) can be used to fill most of the many gaps in the railway system.

Telephones

The state telephone company is *Telefonica* and every large town has at least one office, where you can use a booth to make a call and pay the clerk afterwards.

Most of the ordinary public telephone booths (marked *telefono publico* or *locutorio*) take cash and have instructions in English. Some booths take phonecards, which are obtainable from tobacconists. Most bars also have pay telephones, but they are usually more expensive than the ordinary booths.

To call abroad from Spain: *tel: 07*. To call Spain from abroad: *tel: 34*. The number for the international operator depends both on where you are calling from and where you are calling to. If you are in Madrid, the number is 008 for Europe and 005 for all other continents. If you are elsewhere in Spain, the number is 9198 for Europe and 9191 for the other continents. To call the national operator: *tel: 009*. To call the local operator: *tel: 003*. **Emergencies**: Police: 091 everywhere; Fire: 080 in most towns, but can vary; Ambulance: numbers vary from place to place, so check locally.

Rail Travel Within Spain

The main rail company, *Red Nacional de Ferrocariles Españoles (RENFE)*, controls all the major routes on broad-gauge lines and the standard gauge *AVE* line. Some coastal lines and suburban services, however, are narrow-gauge and run by *FEVE* and other locally owned companies. In the cities, the two often operate from different stations and the station staff will provide information only about their own network. *AVE* are high-speed, luxurious trains which have just come into service between Madrid and Seville. There are three classes: *Turista*, *Preferente* and *Club*. The *Talgo* trains are international express trains which are very comfortable and fast.

The *electro* trains are comfortable and quick, but have a fair number of stops, while *expresos* and *rápidos* are the ordinary trains, which are relatively slow. *Estrellas* are night trains with first- and second-class seating and sleeping compartments. Some carry a refreshment service. Stopping trains are known as *cercanías*, which are much slower and (unlike most of the expresses) seldom air-conditioned. Other types of trains are slow and should be used only if you have plenty of time to spare, although many *FEVE* services have scenic routes. Most overnight trains have first- and second-class sleeping cars (*coche-cama*) and second-class couchettes (*literas*). The luxury sleepers (*Gran Clase*) have showers and separate WCs. Most long-distance trains have a refreshment service of some kind.

Seat reservations are compulsory (in practice as well as in theory) for all express and international trains and these should be made as far ahead as possible. If you have not booked,

you may be unable to board. The booking number (*Numero Ordenador*) designated to each train for reservation purposes is not the same as the number of the train itself – so make sure there is no confusion when you book.

Fares and Passes

For most services (but not all) *RENFE* accepts the European rail passes (see pp. 22–26). *FEVE* does not. Domestic rail fares depend on the colour of the day (RENFE can give you details of which is which). Basic fares apply to white days, you pay 10% more to travel on red days and get a reduction if you travel on blue days. Some days are split; then the colour depends on the time and direction of travel. Domestic tickets are valid for two months from the date of issue and can be issued up to two months in advance.

SWEDEN

Capital: Stockholm. **Language**: Swedish is the official language; English is widely spoken in most areas. Finnish, German and Lapp are also spoken. **Currency**: Kronor or Crowns (Skr.); 1 Krona = 100 Öre.

Customs

The tobacco allowances given below are for people aged 15 or over and the alcohol allowances for people aged 20 or over.

Residents of European countries may take into Sweden: 200 cigarettes or 100 cigarillos or 250g tobacco and 200 cigarette papers, 2 litres beer and either 2 litres wine and no spirits, or 1 litre spirits and 1 litre wine. Non-residents of Europe are allowed the same amount of alcohol but double the quantity of tobacco products.

Passports and Visas

A British Visitor's Passport is sufficient, as are EU National Identity Cards. Visas are not needed by Scandinavians, nationals of the EU, Australia, Canada, New Zealand or the USA. Others should check.

Useful Addresses in the UK

Embassy, *11 Montagu Place, London W1H 2AL; tel: (071) 724 2101.* **Swedish Travel and**

Tourism Council, *73 Welbeck St, London W1M 8AN; tel: (071) 935 9784.* **Swedish State Railways**, *c/o Norwegian State Railways, 21/24 Cockspur St, London SW1Y 5DA; tel: (071) 930 6666.*

Useful Addresses in the USA

Embassy, *600 New Hampshire Ave NW (Suite 1200), Washington, DC 20037-2462; tel: (202) 944 5600.* **Scandinavian Tourist Board** *655 Third Ave (18th Floor), New York, NY 10017; tel: (212) 949 2333.*

Living in Sweden

Accommodation

The familiar big hotel names appear in Sweden's largest towns, but are outnumbered by the more modest Swedish hotels. Unusually, prices are much lower during the summer (July–early August) and at weekends, when expense accounts freeze up. There is no star rating system, but for an indication of facilities/standards, check the annual guide, *Hotels in Sweden.* *Rum* accommodation is cheaper, literally a room without breakfast. Ask the tourist offices for details. They also have information on Sweden's 250 self-catering chalet villages. For farm accommodation, contact **LFR**, *Vasagatan 12, S-105 33 Stockholm; tel: (08) 787 5100.* For details of the country's 750 campsites, contact the Swedish Camping Owners Association, **SCR**, *PO Box 255, S-45117 Vadevalla; tel: (0522) 39345.*

Youth hostels, which are generally of a very high standard, are known as *vandrarhjern.* A full list is available from **STF**, *PO Box Drottninggatan 31, S-101 20 Stockholm; tel: (08) 790 3100.*

Food and Drink

The Swedes eat early and, in the smaller towns, lunch is served around 1100–1400 and dinner around 1800–2100. In cities, meals are generally served a bit later. Breakfast often consists of *smörgåsbord* and features several varieties of fish, ham and cheese as well as bread, jam and cereal. For lunch, the best value is the *dagens rätt* (dish of the day). Cafeteria-style places are cheaper than most and you won't come away hungry. If you want something typically Swedish, ask for *Husmanskost*: it means 'home cooking' and is likely to be a traditional recipe. Taxation of alcohol is designed to discourage drinking and even low-alcohol beer is expensive. Alcohol is sold only to people over 20.

Opening Hours

Banks: Mon–Fri 0930–1500. Some city branches have longer hours. Shops: Mon–Fri 0900–1800; Sat 0900–1400. **Museums**: vary widely, some opening for only a few hours, a few days each week, others opening daily and all day. In winter hours are shorter and most open-air museums close altogether. Monday is the most usual closing day.

Postage

The postal service is efficient. Post offices in larger towns open Mon–Fri 0830–1800/1830; Sat 0800–1300. You can also buy stamps at branches of Pressbyrån. Post boxes are yellow for international and blue for local mail.

Public Holidays

1, 6 Jan; Good Friday; Easter Monday; 1 May; Ascension Day; Whit Monday; Midsummer Day; 1 Nov (All Saints Day); 25, 26 Dec. Places often close early the day before.

Public Transport

The transport system is highly efficient and keeps going through all seasons and weathers. It's worth booking ahead on both trains and buses in summer. There is a good network of local and long-distance buses, and the main bus stations are usually right next door to the train stations. There are also some very good standby flight fares for those under 26. All tourist offices and travel agents have copies of the full integrated timetable, *Tidtabellan.*

Telephones

To call abroad from Sweden: *tel: 009.* To call Sweden from abroad: *tel: 46.* For domestic enquiries: *tel: 0013.* For international enquiries: *tel: 0019.* Phone cards are cheapest for long-distance calls. **Emergencies**: Police: 90 000; Fire: 90 000; Ambulance: 90 000.

Rail Travel Within Sweden

The national rail company is *Statens Järnvägar* (*SJ*), but some local lines are run by regional authorities. There is one central rail information line for the whole country, always charged at a local rate, *tel: 020 75 75 75*.

There is a new high-speed *X2000* train (up to 124 mph) which, at the time of writing, operates principally between Stockholm and Gothenburg. Most lines are electrified and the *IC* trains are fast, efficient, frequent, comfortable, and expensive.

Sleeping-cars have one or two berths in first class and three berths in second class. Couch-ettes are second class and have six berths. Special first-class *IC Natt* sleeping cars (with shower and WC in each compartment) are available on many overnight services. Virtually all long-distance trains have a refreshment service of some kind. Seat reservations are always advisable and are compulsory for all trains that are marked 'R' or 'IC' in the timetables. Reserved seats are not labelled and are claimed by presenting the seat ticket on the train. Swedish trains have children's play areas.

Fares and Passes

A special supplement is payable for travel on *X2000* trains, but in first class this includes a meal tray, beverages and a newspaper.

SWITZERLAND

Capital: Berne. **Language**: German, French, Italian and Romansh are all official languages of Switzerland. Most Swiss people speak more than one of these languages fluently and knowledge of English is fairly widespread. **Currency**: Swiss Francs (SFr.); 1 Franc = 100 Centimes or Rappen.

Customs

The following allowances are for people aged over 17 or over: 200 cigarettes or 50 cigars or 250g tobacco, 2 litres alcohol up to 15% volume, and 1 litre over 15% volume. People who live outside Europe are entitled to twice the tobacco allowance.

Passports and Visas

A British Visitor's Passport is sufficient, as are EU National Identity Cards. All other travellers require a valid passport. Visas are not needed by nationals of the EU, Australia, Canada, New Zealand or the USA. Others should check.

Useful Addresses in the UK

Embassy, *16/18 Montagu Place, London W1H 2BQ; tel: (071) 723 0701*. **Swiss National Tourist Office (SNTO) and Railway Representatives**, *Swiss Centre, Swiss Court, London W1V 8EE; tel: (071) 734 1921*.

Useful Addresses in the USA

Embassy, *2900 Cathedral Ave NW, Washington, DC 20008-3499; tel: (202) 745 7900*. **Swiss National Tourist Office (SNTO)**, *Swiss Center, 608 Fifth Ave, New York, NY 10020; tel: (212) 757 5944*. **Railroad Representatives**, *Rail Europe Inc., 226/230 Westchester Ave, White Plains, NY 10604; tel: (800) 682 2999 (toll-free)*

Living in Switzerland

Accommodation

Swiss hotels have high standards, but are expensive and you'll be very lucky to get anything for less than SwFr.50 single or SwFr.80 double. In rural areas it is often possible to get rooms in private houses, but these are few and far between in cities and budget travellers (unless they are camping) rely heavily on youth hostels – so book these as far ahead as possible. Every major town and major station has a hotel-finding service, sometimes free and seldom expensive. If you don't want twin beds, you must ask for a 'matrimonial' or 'French' bed.

The **Swiss National Tourist Office** (SNTO) may be able to provide leaflets on accommodation (they sometimes charge for these and do not make bookings). If not, you can get them direct from the national associations. They publish a *Swiss Hotel Guide for the Disabled*, which distinguishes between those places suitable for people with walking impediments and those suitable for wheelchairs. The **Swiss Hotel Association**, Schweizer Hotelier-Verein (SHV), *Monbijoustr.130, Postfach, 3001 Bern; tel: (031) 370*

41 11 publish an annual hotel guide in four languages. This is free and, as well as giving full information about hotels (including an explanation of the rating system), contains information about such things as postal rates.

There are hundreds of **campsites** in Switzerland (most open summer only). They are graded on a five-star system; guides are available from **Schweizer Camping und Caravanning Verband**, *Habsburgerstr.35, 6004 Luzern; tel: (041) 23 48 22* or **Verband Schweizer Camp-ings**, *Seestr.119, 3800 Interlaken; tel: (036) 23 35 23.* 'Rough' camping is not permitted.

Food and Drink

There is a wide range of both food and eating-places. The cheapest are *migros* (supermarket cafeterias). Lunch is the main meal and most restaurants have a fixed-price lunch menu (*tagesteller*) that is good value.

Swiss cheese is often an ingredient in local dishes; Swiss *fondue*, for instance, is bread dipped into a pot containing melted cheese, garlic and kirsch. Other regional dishes are strips of veal in cream sauce (*zürcher geschnetzeltes*) and fried potatoes with onion (*rösti*).

Opening Hours

Banks: Mon–Fri 0830–1200 and 1400–1630. **Shops**: Mon–Fri 0800–1200 and 1330–1830, Sat 0800–1200 and 1330–1600. Many close on Monday morning. **Museums**: the usual closing day is Monday, but this is not always the case. Opening hours vary, so check locally.

Postage

Post office opening times are usually Mon–Fri 0730–1200 and 1345–1830; Sat 0730–1100. In cities, however, major branches usually stay open for much longer. Poste restante (*Postlagernd*) facilities are available at most post offices.

Public Holidays

1, 2 Jan; Good Friday; Easter Sunday–Monday; Ascension Day; Whit Sunday; 25, 26 Dec. 1 May and 1 Aug are public holidays in some areas.

Public Transport

Swiss buses, both long-distance and local, are punctual to the second. The yellow Postbuses fill gaps in the railway network and the terminal is usually by a post office. Free timetables are available from post offices and the Swiss Pass is valid, but there is a surcharge (SwFr.5) for scenic routes. If you don't have a Swiss Pass, it may be worth buying a regional 7-day pass (from any post office in that region). It's seldom worth getting the city transport passes as the easiest way to get around the centres is on foot.

Telephones

The national network is **PTT** and all their offices (usually, but not always, located in post offices) sell phonecards. Phonecards are also available from most rail stations. In the PTT offices you can pay for international calls when you have finished. All telephone boxes have instructions in English and all telephone operators can speak it. The pink pages at the front of directories list local and international codes.

To call abroad from Switzerland: *tel: 00*. To call Switzerland from abroad: *tel: 41*. To call international enquiries and operators: *tel: 191*. To call national enquiries and operators: *tel: 111*. **Emergencies**: Police: 117; Fire: 118; Ambulance: 144.

Rail Travel Within Switzerland

The principal rail carrier is *Swiss Federal Railways* (*SBB*), known in French as *CFF* and in Italian as *FFS*; but there are many other small, private lines. The train service is fast, clean and as punctual as one would expect in a country noted for producing high-quality clocks and watches. The fastest trains are the various types of *IC*. All express trains stop only at major cities. The *Regionalzug* are local trains and much slower, but they often follow very scenic routes.

Some international trains have sleepers with three berths and/or couchettes for up to six people. Reservations are compulsory on special observation/sightseeing trains (i.e. the *Panoramic*, and *Bernina* expresses). Sleeping cars can be booked up to three months in advance, couchettes and seats up to two months ahead. If connecting by air, you can check in and book your luggage through from any station in the country.

Fares and Passes

European rail passes (see pp. 22–26) are valid on some private railways in Switzerland. Two discount tickets are the **Swiss Pass** (valid for 4, 8, 15 days or for 1 month) and the **Flexipass** (valid for any 3 days in a 15-day period). Both are available for first- or second-class travel on *SBB* services and also cover most other Swiss transport.

TURKEY

Capital: Ankara. **Language**: Turkish; French, English and German are also spoken to some extent in tourist areas. **Currency**: Turkish Lira (TL.). On departure you can reconvert Lira into hard currencies only up to the value of US$100, so don't change more than necessary and keep exchange receipts.

Customs

The allowances are: 5 (100 cc) or 7 (70 cc) bottles of wine and/or spirits and 200 cigarettes and 50 cigars, or 200g tobacco and 200 cigarette papers, or 50g chewing tobacco, or 200g pipe tobacco, or 50g snuff. Additionally, you may purchase: 400 cigarettes, 100 cigars and 500g pipe tobacco from a Turkish duty-free shop on entering the country. In addition to the usual prohibitions, there are some surprising restrictions on things like films, so get full details from the Turkish tourist office before you go. UK Customs are knowledgeable about the value of Turkish carpets, so be prepared to pay duty for them on your return.

Passports and Visas

All travellers require a passport; a British Visitor's Passport is sufficient. Nationals of Ireland, Italy and the UK can purchase visas at the border. They are not need-ed by nationals of the other EU countries, Australia, Canada, New Zealand or the US. Others should check.

Useful Addresses in the UK

Consulate-General, *Rutland Lodge, Rutland Gardens, London SW7 1BW; tel: (071) 589 0360*. **Turkish Tourist Office**, *1st Floor, 170/173 Piccadilly, London W1V 9DD; tel: (071) 734 8681/2*.

Turkey

- Protection against hepatitis A, polio and typhoid is recommended and also against malaria if you plan to visit Asian Turkey. Be wary of drinking tap water and milk.
- Drug laws are so stringent that you can get into trouble for just being in the company of a user – and Turkish jails are not pleasant – so steer well clear.
- Turkey is an Islamic country (albeit liberal) and you must be careful not to offend. Use your right hand (or both hands) to pass and receive things – never the left hand alone. Women should always dress modestly and take especial care when visiting mosques. Also remember to remove your shoes. Never forget mosques are places of worship and it is a privilege for non-Muslims to enter at all; few Islamic states permit such visits.
- Bargaining is the norm, and to be enjoyed. You are likely to be offered tea during the course of the haggling – this is a courtesy and payment is not expected, nor does accepting it put you under obligation to buy.

Useful Addresses in the USA

Embassy, *1606 23rd Street NW, Washington, DC 20008; tel: (202) 387 3200*. **Turkish Tourist Office**, *821 UN Plaza, New York, NY 10017; tel: (212) 687 2194/6*.

Living in Turkey

Accommodation

There is a huge concentration of hotels in the major cities and around the coast, which is virtually lined by resorts these days. Prices and types range from the luxurious and ultra-expensive to dirt-cheap and cockroach-ridden, although the quality doesn't always match the price. Top range hotels are wonderful. On the whole, the others tend to be reasonably clean and comfortable, even if they might not match your notions of interior design. At the lower end of the scale, in the many small pensions, guest houses and private rooms, always check out the room and the plumbing before you agree to take it. In high summer, look for somewhere with air-conditioning or a fan, and always take your own plug (they are rarely provided). Eager touts often hang around bus and train stations and can prove good value.

Food and Drink

Both eating and drinking are very cheap in Turkey, if you stick to local-style food – and there's really no reason not to, as the Turkish cuisine is excellent. Very similar to Greek food, but better cooked and without the grease, it tends to be fairly plain and based on whatever vegetables and fruit are in season, with fresh seafood, lamb and chicken (other meats are found, but less often). Puddings are usually very sweet, many featuring semolina, honey and/or nuts. Coffee (black and very strong) tends to be (relatively) expensive but tea (black, sweet, often herbal and very cheap) is easily available. You will have to specify if you want your drink unsweetened. You may be given milk with your tea at breakfast, but seldom at any other time. There is a wide choice of local wines, some of them very good. *Raki* (a grape and aniseed drink taken with water) is popular. The local beers are palatable. Most spirits are imported. Be wary of drinking tap water and milk.

In cities, eating-places are open most of the day. In smaller places the normal eating hours are 1200–1500 and 1900–2200. In most restaurants there is a counter where you can see what's on offer, and it's customary to have a good look. If you don't speak Turkish, just point at whatever appeals to you.

Opening Hours

Banks: Mon–Fri 0830–1200 and 1330–1700. **Shops**: Mon–Sat 0930–1300 and 1400–1900. Shops in tourist areas often open until 2100 and also on Sunday. The covered bazaar in Istanbul is open Mon–Sat 0800–1900. **Museums**: (generally) Tue–Sun 0900/0930–1630/1700. Palaces keep much the same hours, but tend to close on Tuesday or Thursday rather than Monday.

Postage

Post offices have yellow PTT signs. The main offices in Istanbul and Ankara open 24 hrs daily, smaller offices across the country open Mon–Fri 0830–1230, 1330–1730.

Public Holidays

1 Jan; 23 Apr; 19 May; 30 Aug; 29 Oct. There are also two three-day Islamic holidays (at the end of Ramadan and Kurban Bayrami), but the dates for these depend on the lunar calendar and vary considerably from year to year.

Public Transport

The rail network covers only the major cities and goes nowhere near many of the most popular tourist area. Otherwise, look to the buses, of which there are many, with services to absolutely everywhere. There are also luxury long-distance coaches, which come with lace at the windows and videos upfront. Reserve in advance to choose a good seat (well worth it, given the quality of some of the roads and driving). For local transport, the best option is to use the dolmus (shared taxis) which run on standard routes and leave as soon as they have a full load. The only slight problem is that the Turkish notion of a full load means people hanging out of the window.

Telephones

To call Turkey from abroad: *tel: 90.* To call abroad from Turkey: *tel: 99.* **Emergencies**: Police: 055; Fire: 000; Medical and general emergencies: 077.

Rail Travel Within Turkey

The national rail company in Turkey is *Türkiye Čumhuryeti Devlet Demiryollan* (*TČDD*). Rail services in Turkey are not very fast but the system is extensive. The fastest express trains are the *mototren, ekspres* and *mavi tren*. Overnight services usually have sleeping cars and couchettes, both of which should be booked in advance. You should reserve seats on the better trains. The food in dining-cars is both good and cheap.

Fares and Passes

European rail passes (see pp. 22–26) are valid in European Turkey (i.e. as far as Istanbul).

UNITED KINGDOM

Capital: London. **Language**: English and, in a very small way Welsh, and Gaelic. **Currency**: Pounds Sterling (£). 1 Pound = 100 Pence.

Customs

Standard EU regulations apply (see pp. 13–14).

Passports and Visas

Full passports are not needed by people holding National Identity Cards, nor do they need visas. No visas are needed by citizens of Australia, Canada, New Zealand or the USA (unless they want to work). Others should check.

Useful Addresses in the USA

Embassy, *3100 Massachusetts Ave NW, Washington, DC 20008; tel: (202) 462 1340.* **British Tourist Authority (BTA)**, *551 Fifth Ave (7th Floor), New York, NY 10176 tel: (212) 986 2200.* **BritRail Travel International Inc**, *1500 Broadway, New York, NY 10036; tel: (212) 575 2667.*

Living in the United Kingdom

Accommodation

There's a huge array on offer from major chains at all prices in the big cities and business areas, to luxury hotels both in town and in many stately homes and country houses. Lower down the scale are cheaper country homes, old coaching inns, farm house accommodation, bed and breakfast, hotels etc. The list goes on and on. The BTA (British Tourist Authority), the AA (Automobile Association), the RAC (Royal Automobile Club) and numerous other organisations all run ratings systems and publish listings guides. Head for the nearest tourist office or bookshop and take your pick.

Food and Drink

Usual eating hours are: breakfast 0730–0900, lunch 1200–1400, afternoon tea (an institution rather than a regular meal) 1600–1700 and dinner 1930–2130.

With the exception of spirits, which are expensive (due to prohibitive taxation), how much you spend on eating and drinking depends

---

United Kingdom

Driving is on the left, so look right before crossing roads (unless there's a sign saying otherwise). The British are notorious for jay-walking and you should not assume that it is safe to cross when someone else steps into the road.

---

entirely on you, because there is a wide range of choice in every price bracket. British cuisine is plain and based on a wide variety of excellent produce, local and otherwise. Traditional dishes include rare roast beef with Yorkshire pudding (a form of batter), fish and chips (the fish coated in batter and the french fries large-cut); and ploughman's lunch (bread and cheese with a pickle sauce).

The ubiquitous cup of tea is usually served with milk, but you can ask for black (or lemon in some places). With coffee, you should specify whether you want it black or white. The British are fond of their beer, which is heavier and more bitter than lager and not chilled. There are now almost as many wine bars as pubs in the town centres and there are also specialist cock-tail bars. Many drinking-places have a 'happy hour', during which prices are halved.

Opening Hours

Banks: Mon–Fri 0930–1530. Some also open Saturday morning. **Shops**: Mon–Sat 0900–1730. Some have an early closing day and/or a late-closing day and some (particularly small food shops) open on Sundays and stay open until late evening every day). **Museums**: there are variations, but the norm is Mon–Sat 0900/1000–1730/1800 and Sunday morning or afternoon (occasionally the whole day).

Sunday is the usual closing day for shops and banks, but most tourist attractions are open.

Postage

There's an excellent postal service with a wide network of post offices and sub-post offices (which mainly double-up as the local newsagent or convenience store). Opening hours are usually Mon–Fri 0930–1730, and Sat 0930–1300. Smaller offices shut for lunch and on Wednes-

---

United Kingdom

day afternoon. Stamps are also sold in some shops and hotels. Post boxes are red.

Public Holidays

In England and Wales: 1 Jan; Good Friday; Easter Monday; May Day (first Monday in May): Spring Bank Holiday (last Monday in May); Summer Bank Holiday (last Monday in August); 25, 26 Dec. There are variations in Scotland and Ireland.

Public Transport

The main rail network is good, but expensive. There is an excellent network of inter-city coaches, run mainly by National Express. Bus networks within most towns are good, but once out in the country, local buses are very few and far between and when they do arrive, take forever to get anywhere. If you want to see the countryside, arrange your own transport.

Telephones

British telephone boxes are traditionally red, but the silvery grey type have now replaced them in most towns and cities. There are plentiful public phone boxes which run on a mix of coins, phone cards (on sale at newsagents) and credit cards.

To call abroad from the UK: *tel: 010*. To call the UK from abroad: *tel: 44*. For domestic enquiries: *tel: 192*. For international enquiries: *tel: 153*. **Emergencies**: Police, Fire, Ambulance, or Coastguard: *tel: 999*.

From 16 April 1995 National and International dialling codes will change. The number 1 will be inserted after the initial 0 in UK area codes and new area codes will be introduced for 5 major cities. The international access code will change from 010 to 00.

Rail Travel in the UK

The overland rail network is run by *British Rail* (*BR*), but government policy is to privatise the whole network within the next few years. *BR* should not be confused with *London Transport* (*LT*), which runs the tubes (subway) and most of the other public transport services in the capital.

IC trains are fast, comfortable and reliable. Most other services also work well, though commuter trains (particularly around London) stop frequently and are more prone to delays and cancellations.

Sleeping-cars have one berth in first class and two berths in second class. Dining-cars usually operate Mon–Fri on major services, but are mostly only for first-class passengers. *Pullman* (*P*) services offer full meals to passengers in their seats and should be reserved in advance. On most long journeys, there is either a catering-car or a refreshment trolley. There may, or may not, be dining facilities on Sat–Sun, even if they are scheduled. Similarly, they may be available for only part of the journey.

Advance reservations are always essential for sleepers and are recommended for long-distance travel at busy times. British trains do not have numbers, so you just quote the departure time and destination.

Fares and Passes

European rail passes (see pp. 22–26) do not provide free travel in the UK, just some discounts.

All-Line Rail Rovers give unlimited first or second-class travel on all BR trains for 7 or 14 days. They also give discounts on several private railways. There are much cheaper **Rail Rovers** for travel in specified areas. If you can book at least seven days in advance, there are cheap **Apex** fares on many IC trains. It is *much* more expensive to travel during rush hour, and there is a wide variety of fares at very different prices. After 0930, it is often cheaper to buy a return ticket.

SAMPLE ITINERARIES

Here are ten themed tours using many of the recommended routes, with a few digressions and short-cuts added. You can adapt them to your own tastes or just use the general idea to plan your own itineraries.

PLANNING AN ITINERARY

Practicable trips are easy and fun to plan if you remember a few golden rules:

1. Work out train times with an up-to-date copy of the *Thomas Cook European Timetable*, and always read the footnotes to the tables, which give exceptions or further information. When travelling, re-check the timings at the station – not only because train schedules can change, but also because there may be convenient local trains which the Thomas Cook timetable doesn't have space to include. A copy of the *Thomas Cook New Rail Map of Europe* isn't essential but increases your planning potential. (For details of both publications see p. 21).
2. Don't plan quick change-overs – leave plenty of time between train. It's better to spend an unexpected wait of hour or two viewing the town than miss your connection through unforeseen delays.
3. Unless you have accommodation pre-booked, plan to arrive in your overnight stop with enough time to find the accommodation you want. Make the tourist information office your first call on arrival.
4. Build in plenty of time towards the end of your trip to return to your home base – try not to plan on a 24-hr dash back across Europe to reach your plane or ferry on time.
5. Build in as many routes as possible using *frequent* train services.
6. Don't plan in great detail - fill in the detail as you travel. This gives you more flexibility (to stay another day in an unexpected gem of a town, or take an interesting detour on the spur of the moment) and helps you cope with the unexpected, such as alterations to rail schedules. It is also more fun – after all, if you wanted a totally planned trip you wouldn't be travelling this way.

The following tours start from Amsterdam or Paris, but you can also begin any of them in Brussels, or in London (add on the appropriate cross-Channel route, pp. 225–234). They will work equally well if you plan on flying into any of the en-route cities they include. The suggested overnight stop is always in **bold type**.

1. THE CLASSIC EUROPEAN CITIES (28 days)

For those who want to 'do' Europe in one trip, this takes in as many of the famous sights as possible.

Day 1: Paris–Milan (p. 326), change at Milan, Milan–**Florence** (p. 269). Days 2, 3: **Florence**. Day 4: Florence–**Rome** (p. 161). Days 5, 6: **Rome.** Day 7: Rome–Florence–Bologna–**Venice** (Rome–Florence, then Florence–Milan, routes to Bologna; change there for frequent connections to Venice). Days 8, 9: **Venice**. Day 10: Venice–Verona–Innsbruck (Munich–Venice route, p. 279). Stay overnight in either **Verona** or **Innsbruck**, which will allow time for a half-day stop in the other. Day 11: Verona or Innsbruck–**Salzburg** (from Innsbruck follow the Zurich-Vienna route, p. 408). Day 12: **Salzburg**. Day 13: Salzburg–**Vienna** (Zurich–Vienna route). Days 14, 15: **Vienna**. Day 16: Vienna–**Prague** (p. 340). Days 17, 18: **Prague**. Day 19: Jump between routes, from Prague to **Nuremberg** (several direct trains). Day 20: Nuremberg–Frankfurt (Frankfurt–Vienna route, p. 180)–**Cologne** (Amsterdam–Frankfurt route, p. 102). Day 21: **Cologne** and the Rhine valley. Day 22: Cologne–**Amsterdam** (Frankfurt–Amsterdam route, p. 102). Days 23, 24: **Amsterdam**. Day

25: Amsterdam–**Brussels** (p. 94). Day 26: **Brussels**. Day 27: Brussels–**Paris** (p. 301). Day 28 onwards: **Paris** (your rail pass has probably now expired but you can enjoy Paris without it.)

2. WINE-TASTER'S EUROPE (28 days)

Sample the great vineyards of western Europe without worrying about drink-driving laws!

Note: the Spanish stops may be eliminated if you wish to give more time to the classic French and German areas, or you can construct a variant of this itinerary which turns from France to Chianti and other Italian wine-growing regions – see the routes on pp. 161, 269 and 279 especially.

Day 1: Paris–**Tours** (Paris–Madrid route, p. 315). Days 2, 3: **Tours** and the wines of the Loire. Day 4: Tours–**Bordeaux** (Paris–Madrid route). To visit the Cognac region, make an overnight stop at Poitiers. Otherwise, go straight from Tours to Bordeaux. Days 5, 6: **Bordeaux**. If you want to eliminate the Spanish stage, take a direct train from Bordeaux to Marseilles and continue as from Day 14. Day 7: Bordeaux–**Burgos** (Paris–Madrid route). Day 8: **Burgos** for a trip to the Rioja region. Day 9: Burgos–Miranda de Ebro (change)–**Zaragoza**. Day 10: Zaragoza–**Barcelona** (Madrid–Barcelona route, p. 241). Day 11: **Barcelona** (sample the *Cava*). Days 12–13: a leisurely Barcelona–**Marseille** (p. 252), breaking your journey overnight in the Languedoc region at **Perpignan** or **Montpellier**. Days 14–15: **Marseille**, a great base for getting to know Provence and its wines. Day 16: Marseille–**Lyon** (Marseille–Paris route, p. 322). Days 17, 18: **Lyon** for trips to Dijon and other centres of Burgundy. Day 19: Lyon–Zurich (p. 400)–**Stuttgart** (Zurich–Frankfurt, p. 184). Day 20: **Stuttgart**, for the wine areas of Baden. Day 21: Stuttgart–**Heidelberg** (Zurich–Frankfurt route). Day 22: **Heidelberg** and its student taverns. Day 23: Heidelberg–**Frankfurt** (Zurich–Frankfurt route). Day 24: after a night in the Frankfurt cider taverns, Frankfurt–**Cologne** (Amsterdam–Frankfurt route, p. 102). Days 25, 26: **Cologne** for exploring the Rhine and Moselle. Day 27: Cologne–Brussels (Brussels–Frankfurt, p. 136)–**Paris** (Brussels–Paris connection, p. 301). Day 28

onwards: Relax with a glass of wine in **Paris**.

3. CASTLE MANIA (14 days)

If castles, palaces and lesser mansions are your thing, try this whirlwind tour. (On a longer journey you could plan to include the castles of southern France, Spain or the Czech Republic).

Day 1: Amsterdam–Cologne–**Koblenz** (Amsterdam-Frankfurt route, p. 102). Day 2: From **Koblenz** take rail or boat to see the castles of the Rhine. Day 3: Koblenz–Frankfurt (Amsterdam–Frankfurt, p. 102); Frankfurt–Würzburg (Frankfurt–Munich, p. 175). You can stop here for half the day to see the Residenz and the Marienburg fortress. Continue Würzburg–**Munich**. Day 4: From **Munich** a trip to Neuschwanstein, see p. 179. Day 5: Munich–Stuttgart (Paris–Munich, p. 330); Stuttgart–**Heidelberg** (Frankfurt–Zurich, p. 184). Day 6: Explore **Heidelberg** and its castle. Day 7: Heidelberg–Mannheim–**Paris** (Frankfurt–Zurich route to Mannheim, then a direct connection to Paris, see Paris–Frankfurt route, p. 311). Days 8, 9: **Paris**. Trips to the palaces of Versailles and Fontainebleau. Day 10: Paris–Orléans–**Tours** (Paris–Barcelona route, p. 302). Take a train from Orléans to Tours that stops at the château towns of Blois and Amboise. Day 11: **Tours**. Buses or trains to one or two of the great Loire valley châteaux. Day 12: Tours–Paris (Paris–Madrid route, p. 315); Paris–**Brussels** (p. 301). Day 13: **Brussels**. Take a one-day trip to Ghent and Bruges, using part of the London–Brussels route (p. 230). Or view the palaces of Brussels. Day 14: Brussels–**Amsterdam** (p. 94)

4. THE NEW EUROPE (14–28 days)

Visit the emerging nations of eastern Europe in this variable-length trip. For the Baltic states, see the 'Northern Lights' itinerary.

Central Europe only (14 days)

Day 1: Amsterdam–**Berlin** (p. 92). Day 2: Berlin–Dresden–**Prague** (Berlin–Prague, p. 126). Days 3, 4: **Prague**. Day 5: Prague–Vienna (Prague–Vienna, p. 340)–**Budapest** (Vienna–Budapest, p. 375). Days 6, 7: **Budapest**. Day 8: Budapest–**Vienna** (p. 375). Day 9: **Vienna**. Day 10: Vienna–**Warsaw** (p. 377). Day 11: **Warsaw**. Day 12: Warsaw–**Berlin** (p. 127). Day 13: **Berlin**. Day 14: Berlin–**Amsterdam** (p. 92).

Balkan Extension (21 days)

As far as Prague, then:

Day 5: Prague–Vienna–**Bratislava** (Prague–Vienna, p. 340); Vienna–Budapest, p. 375). Day 6: **Bratislava**. Day 7: Bratislava–**Budapest** (Vienna–Budapest, p. 375). Days 8, 9: **Budapest**. Day 10: Budapest–**Bucharest** (Istanbul–Budapest, p. 195). Day 11: **Bucharest**. Day 12: Bucharest–**Sofia** (Istanbul–Budapest route). Day 13: **Sofia**. Day 14: Sofia–Budapest–**Vienna** (Istanbul–Budapest route). Day 15 : **Vienna**. Day 16: Vienna–**Warsaw** (p. 377). Days 17, 18: **Warsaw**. Day 19: Warsaw–**Berlin** (p. 127). Day 20: **Berlin**. Day 21: Berlin–**Amsterdam** (p. 92).

5. ART-LOVERS' PARADISE (21 days)

A whistle-stop tour for culture vultures, taking in some of the world's greatest art collections and buildings. If overnight travel doesn't appeal, lengthen it to 28 days. The long haul between Spain and Italy contains no major galleries but a host of lesser treasures – check out the route descriptions. Don't forget the galleries and museums in London, if you begin the trip from the UK, and check each city description for other great museums.

Days 1, 2: **Paris** (Louvre and many others). Day 2 evening: Paris–Madrid (p. 315). Days 3, 4: **Madrid** (Prado, El Escorial). Day 4 evening: Madrid–Barcelona using the Fast Track (p. 241). Days 5, 6: **Barcelona** (Picasso, Miró, Gaudí, and Dali at Figueres). Day 6 evening: Barcelona–Marseille (p. 252). Day 7: **Marseille**. Day 8: Marseille – Nice – Ventimiglia – Genoa – Pisa – Florence (Marseille–Nice, p. 257; Nice–Genoa, p. 286; from Genoa the Milan–Florence route, p. 269; an all-day journey with changes at Ventimiglia and Pisa.). Days 9, 10: **Florence** (Uffizi – and the whole city). Day 11: Florence–**Rome** (p. 161). Days 12, 13: **Rome** (Vatican, and the many museums and churches). Day 14: Rome–**Venice** via Bologna (using Florence–Rome p. 161 and Milan–Florence p. 269 as far as Bologna, although there are also some direct

Rome–Bologna trains). Day 15: **Venice**. Day 16: Venice–**Vienna** (See through route, p. 9). Day 17: **Vienna** (Kunsthistorisches Museum and Hofburg). Day 18: Vienna–Salzburg–**Munich** (Frequent direct trains – with time to break your journey for a few hours in Salzburg). Day 19: **Munich** (Alte & Neue Pinakothek). Day 20: Munich–Frankfurt–**Amsterdam** (Frankfurt–Munich route, p. 175; Amsterdam–Frankfurt route, p. 102). Day 21 onwards: **Amsterdam** (Rijksmuseum and Van Gogh Museum).

6. SUN-SEEKING ROUTES

If sun, sea and sand appeal more than culture, follow our routes to the Mediterranean. Circular tours are impractical, so be prepared to return the way you went out. Allow 2–3 days outwards and return, unless you are happy with a succession of connections at unsocial hours, in which case 2 days may be sufficient. From Paris, try:

Spain

Paris–Madrid (p. 315, with possibilities for sampling the Bay of Biscay at Bordeaux or Biarritz), then Madrid–Malaga for the Costa del Sol. Or Paris–Barcelona (p. 302) for the Costa Brava.

Portugal

Paris–Madrid again, then Madrid–Lisbon (p. 244), where the coastal resorts begin, and finally Lisbon–Seville route (p. 213) as far as Faro and the Algarve.

French and Italian Rivieras

Paris–Marseilles (p. 322), Marseilles–Nice (p. 257), Nice–Genoa (p. 286): a wide choice of resorts along this stretch.

Neapolitan Riviera

Paris–Milan (p. 326), Milan–Florence (p. 269), Florence–Rome (p. 161) and Rome–Naples (p. 347) for Sorrento, Amalfi, etc.

Greece

The classic Inter-railer's marathon is rewarded by possible weeks of Aegean island-hopping (with a copy of the *Thomas Cook Guide to Greek Island Hopping*): Paris–Milan (p. 326), Milan–Brindisi–

Athens (p. 265). Don't overlook the possibilities of the Adriatic Riviera at Rimini.

7. NORTHERN LIGHTS (21–28 days)

A journey of discovery in the seaports, forests and fjords of Scandinavia, or in the other direction to include northern Germany, Warsaw and the Baltic states.

Scandinavia (21 days)

Day 1: Amsterdam–**Copenhagen** (p. 96). Days 2, 3: **Copenhagen**. Day 4: **Copenhagen**–Odense–Aarhus and return (Side-trip, see p. 150). Day 5: Copenhagen–**Oslo** by Fast Track (p. 150). Days 6, 7: **Oslo**. Day 8: Oslo–**Bergen** (p. 150, On Track route). Day 9: **Bergen**. Day 10: Bergen–**Oslo**. Day 11: Oslo–**Stockholm** (p. 292). Days 12, 13 **Stockholm**. Day 14: Stockholm–**Helsinki** (p. 365). Days 15, 16: **Helsinki**. Day 17: Helsinki–**Stockholm**. Day 18: Stockholm–**Copenhagen** (p. 155). Day 19: **Copenhagen**. Day 20: Copenhagen–**Hamburg** (Amsterdam–Copenhagen route, p. 96). Day 21: Hamburg–**Amsterdam** (continue Amsterdam–Copenhagen route; time for sightseeing in Hamburg in the morning).

Baltic extension (28 days)

Day 1: Amsterdam–**Hanover** (Amsterdam–Berlin, p 92). Day 2: Hanover–**Berlin** (Amsterdam–Berlin). Days 3, 4: **Berlin.** Day 5: Berlin–**Warsaw** (p. 127). Days 6, 7: **Warsaw**. Day 8: Warsaw–**Vilnius** (Warsaw–Helsinki route, p. 385). Day 9: **Vilnius**. Day 10: Vilnius–**Riga** (Warsaw–Helsinki route). Day 11: **Riga**. Day 12: Riga–**Tallinn** (Warsaw–Helsinki route). Day 13: **Tallinn**. Day 14: Tallinn–**Helsinki**. Days 15, 16: **Helsinki**. Day 17: Helsinki–**Stockholm** (p. 365). Days 18, 19: **Stockholm**. Day 20: Stockholm–Oslo (p. 292). Days 21, 22: **Oslo**. Day 23: Oslo–Copenhagen (p. 150). Days 24, 25: **Copenhagen**. Day 26: Copenhagen–**Hamburg** (Amsterdam–Copenhagen route, p. 96). Day 27: **Hamburg**. Day 28: Hamburg–**Amsterdam** (Amsterdam–Copenhagen route).

8. IBERIAN PILGRIMAGE (21 days)

As well as taking you to some of the continent's most impressive and beautiful cathedrals, this tour will uncover a wealth of other churches, chapels, monasteries and convents. Spain is only one example: you can adapt this idea to France, Italy, Germany – in fact virtually any country or region of Europe is a treasure-house of church architecture.

Day 1: Paris–**Burgos** (Paris–Madrid, p. 315). Day 2: **Burgos** (Cathedral, Las Huelgas Réales). Days 3, 4: Burgos–**Santiago de Compostela** (San Sebastián–Santiago, p. 350 – the pilgrim's route: see route description for possible overnight stops). Day 5: **Santiago de Compostela** (Cathedral). Day 6: Santiago–**Lisbon** (p. 209). Day 7: **Lisbon** (Cathedral, S. Jeronimos Monastery, Fatima). Day 8: Lisbon–**Seville** (p. 213). Days 9, 10: **Seville** (world's largest Gothic cathedral). Day 11: Seville–Cordoba–**Madrid** (Seville–Granada, p. 358 to Cordoba, then Madrid–Málaga route, p. 247). Day 12: **Madrid** (Many convents and churches). Day 13: Madrid–**Barcelona** (p. 241). Days 14, 15: **Barcelona** (Sagrada Familia, Cathedral, S. Maria del Mar; a two-day rail excursion to Lourdes via Toulouse would be possible – a short rail trip to the monastery of Monserrat is easier). Day 16: Barcelona–Marseille–**Avignon** (Marseille–Barcelona route, p. 252; Paris–Marseille routes, p. 322). Day 17: **Avignon** (Palais des Papes). Day 18: Avignon–**Paris** (Marseille–Paris). Days 19, 20, 21: **Paris** (Notre-Dame, Ste-Chapelle). Rewarding one-day excursions would be Paris–Chartres (Paris–Brest route, p. 306) to see Chartres' Gothic masterpiece for its renowned stained glass. and Paris–Rheims (Paris–Frankfurt route, p. 311) to see the French kings' former coronation cathedral.

9. ANCIENT EUROPE (28 days)

The great civilisations of the past still live in the treasures of museums and the fascinating sites scattered across Europe. This tour brings together the best of the ancient world. London-based tourists can add the British Museum to this list. If you go as far as Istanbul, the practical return is by air, unless you can face several days of non-stop train travel.

Days 1, 2: **Paris** (the ancient treasures of the Louvre). Day 3: Paris–Brest–**Quimper**–Carnac and its prehistoric menhirs (Paris–Brest route, p. 306). Day 4: Quimper–Brest–**Paris**. Day 5: Paris–**Marseille** (p. 322). Days 6, 7: **Marseille** (the Roman remains at Nîmes, Arles and Orange). Day 8: Marseille–Nice–Ventimiglia–Genoa–Pisa–**Florence** (Marseille–Nice, p. 257; Nice–Genoa, p. 286; from Genoa the Milan–Florence route, p. 269; this is an all-day journey with changes at Ventimiglia and Pisa.). Day 9: **Florence**. Day 10: Florence–**Rome** (p. 161). Days 11, 12, 13, 14: **Rome** (the Forum and countless other ancient buildings). Day 15: Rome–**Naples** (p. 347). Day 16: **Naples** (excursion to Pompeii and Herculaneum). Days 17, 18: Naples–Foggia–Brindisi–Patras–**Athens** (Naples–Foggia connection, p. 349; Milan–Athens route, p. 265). Days 19, 20, 21, 22: **Athens** (The Acropolis and other sites, plus the museums. Take at least one trip to an Aegean island if time allows, and to the Peloponnese.). Days 23, 24: Athens–Levadia (Delphi)–Litohoro (Mt Olympus)–**Thessaloniki** (Roman remains) (Athens–Istanbul route, p. 113, with an overnight stop of your choice between Athens and Thessaloniki). Day 25: Thessaloniki–**Istanbul**. Days 26, 27, 28: **Istanbul** (Byzantium and the Ottoman Empire, with possible excursions to Ephesus, Troy and Halicarnassus if you have time).

10. MOUNTAINS, LAKES AND RIVERS (14–21 days)

In contrast to the others, this itinerary is more concerned with scenic beauty than towns and cities. We have chosen central Europe and the Alps, but you can devise equally attractive tours in many other regions. Scenic lines are listed in the Thomas Cook European Timetable and highlighted on the New Rail Map of Europe (see p. 21). The basic itinerary lasts 14 days, but you can lengthen it by stopping over in some of the delightful areas to which it takes you.

Day 1: Amsterdam–**Cologne** (Amsterdam–Frankfurt route, p.102). Day 2: Cologne–**Frankfurt** (Amsterdam–Frankfurt route), down the Rhine valley, with a chance to make some of the journey by river cruiser. Day 3: Frankfurt–Zurich (p. 184), side-tracking to stay overnight in **Konstanz**. Day 4: Konstanz to Zurich (Frankfurt–Zurich route), changing to Zurich–Vienna (p. 408) through the Vorarlberg and Tirol as far as **Innsbruck**. Day 5: A day in **Innsbruck**, perhaps visiting one of the surrounding mountain villages. Day 6: Innsbruck to **Verona** (Munich–Venice route, p. 279), through the Dolomites. Day 7: Take one of the frequent trains from Verona to **Milan**, perhaps stopping off at Peschiera to view Lake Garda. Day 8: From Milan on the Zurich–Milan route (p. 405) to **Lucerne**; the line passes Lakes Como and Lugano and through the Alps in some spectacular loops. Day 9: Zurich–Milan route back to **Zurich**. Day 10: Use Zurich as a base for exploring west into Switzerland for at least a day (see Zurich–Lyon route, p. 400). Day 11: Frankfurt–Zurich route Fast Track (p. 184) will lead you through the Black Forest and back to **Frankfurt**. Day 12: Frankfurt–**Brussels**, p. 136; up the Rhine and then from Cologne westwards through the Meuse valley. Day 13: **Brussels**. Either catch up with city life or take the Side-Track through the scenic Ardennes to Luxembourg (p. 135). Day 14: Brussels–**Amsterdam** (p. 94).

AMSTERDAM

The city's name derives from a 13th-century dam on the River Amstel: the square known as 'Dam' marks the spot. It was in the 17th century that the town achieved international status (as a trading centre) and assumed its present shape, with the building of three new canals: Herengracht, Keizersgracht and Prinsengracht. Although small in sightseeing terms (unless you're heavily into museums and art galleries), Amsterdam is a delightful city in which to linger; an attractive, laid-back place full of tree-lined canals, decorative architecture, flower-filled window boxes and a lively street life, which includes alfresco barrel organ performances. You should allow several days just to enjoy it.

Tourist Information

VVV's (see pp. 58) main office is opposite Centraal: *Stationsplein 10; tel: 34 03 40 66.* Open daily: Easter–Sept 0900–2300; Oct–Easter 0900–1800. It's very busy and you should be prepared to queue. There's a branch (with shorter hours) at *Leidsestraat 106.*

Get the *Tourist Guide to Public Transport*, which shows all the city transport (except boats), plus the major attractions and how to get to them. VVV sell a useful biweekly listings guide, *What's On in Amsterdam*, for which they charge, but you can often get it free from restaurants, hotels and similar places.

AUB Uitburo, *Leidseplein 26; tel: 621 1211* (Mon–Sat 1000–1800), also distributes information about the city's entertainments and makes bookings for a small fee.

Arriving and Departing

Airport

Schiphol, *tel: 474 7747* or *517 9111*, is about 14 km south-west of town. The single terminal is large but user-friendly. The extensive duty-free shops have really low prices and the tourist office dispenses free lists (in English) of useful telephone numbers.

Transfers by train are easily the cheapest option, with services every 15 minutes 0500–0100 (hourly 0100–0500). The journey between Schiphol station and Amsterdam Centraal takes about 20 minutes.

Stations

Centraal/CS, *tel: 620 2266*, is the terminal for all the city's trains and only five minutes walk to Dam. Virtually all buses and trams begin at Centraal, but buy a ticket from the GVB office in *Stationsplein* before you board.

Amsterdam has half a dozen other stations. All are outside the centre and (with the possible exception of **Amstel**, to the south) they are of little interest to visitors, so be careful not to get off the train until you reach Centraal.

Getting Around

The city centre is horseshoe-shaped, due to the curving canals, and it can be confusing when you first arrive, but it doesn't take long to get the hang of things (bear in mind that *gracht* means 'canal'). Most tourist leaflets include maps of **Centrum**, the central zone, where virtually everything of interest is located.

Centrum is fairly large and, although it is possible to walk everywhere, the best way to see the city is to concentrate on one area at a time: get there by public transport and then explore on foot. The tram system is extensive and efficient. The water transport is fun and uses conveniently positioned quays.

Amsterdam is a city made for strolling and there are numerous people who arrange walking tours. One of the most interesting and unusual is **Mee in Mokum**, *Hartenstraat 16, tel: 625 1390*. Book in advance and ask for an English commentary.

Travel Information and Tickets

GVB, *Stationsplein 15; tel: 627 2727*, is the public transport company. Information, passes and maps of the system (including the travel zones) are available from them and every bus/tram stop gives details of the lines which use it.

The *strippenkaart* is the most common form of multiple ticket. You seldom need more than two sections at a time as virtually everything of interest is in Centrum. GVB also offer a wide variety of passes for unlimited city travel over differing periods, some of which include boats and/or museums, so tell them exactly how long you're staying and what you'd like to include.

The Metro

The **metro** is designed for commuters and is of little use to visitors.

Trams and Buses

The **trams** start Mon–Fri 0600, Sat 0630 and Sun 0730. They stop around midnight. It is usual to board by the rear door, although you can use the others if you are in danger of missing the tram – pressure on the lowest step keeps the door open.

Buses are boarded by the front door (showing your ticket to the driver). They are usually less convenient than the trams, but do operate limited night services: look for a black square on the bus-stop.

Taxis

For **taxis**, *tel: 677 7777*. The main ranks are at *Centraal Station*, *Dam*, *Rembrandtsplein* and *Leidseplein*.

Canal Journeys

The canals are an integral part of Amsterdam, and an excellent way to appreciate the city, so take at least one boat-trip. **Water-taxis** are available (*tel: 675 0909*), but not cheap. There are **canal cruises** with multi-lingual commentaries, but it's more to the point to use **canalbuses** (*Nieuwe Keizersgracht 8; tel: 623 9886*), so you can get on and off at will. The quays where they stop are indicated at street-level.

Museumboats (*Stationsplein 8; tel: 622 2181*) leave Centraal quay at 30-minute intervals from 1000 to 1515 and make five stops, all in places convenient for museums. Get a ticket valid for the day – preferably one that includes entrance to some museums.

For individual exploration, you can hire **canal-bikes** (*Amstel 57; tel: 626 5574*) by the hour. These are pedal-boats for two or four people. There are four different moorings in summer (just Centraal in winter) and you can start at one and finish at another. Alternatively, there are **aquarents**, which can be hired by the hour or half-day from **Rederij Noord-Zuid** (*tel: 679 1370*). These are virtually noiseless self-drive motor-boats that take up to six people. You can get a map and suggested routes when you hire your boat. Remember to 'drive' on the right.

Disabled Travellers

Places like museums, churches and cinemas usually have good facilities for disabled people and there's a special taxi service, but the trams are totally unsuitable for anyone with mobility problems and the older buildings often have steep steps and narrow doorways. Details of facilities can be obtained from your nearest Dutch tourist office.

Living in Amsterdam

Accommodation

Amsterdam offers a wide range of accommodation, but it also has a great many visitors and for most hotels you should book at least a week in advance (more if you're going in peak season) and be prepared to pay a deposit. If you just turn up on the day, you might be lucky – or you might find yourself commuting from somewhere like Haarlem.

Hotel chains in Amsterdam include *Ch, Fo, Ft, GT, HI, Hn, Ic, Ma, Me, No, Ra, SA, SC*.

The cheap places are not in any particular area. One of the best ways to find them is through the omnipresent touts at Centraal. The legitimate ones will have a printed card with the name, address and prices of the place they represent and you should avoid anyone who cannot produce such a card. Insist on seeing your room before you hand over any money and, if you don't like the look of it, ask to be taken somewhere else.

IYHF hostels: **Vondelpark**, *Zandpad 5; tel: 683 1744* (tram nos. 1/2/5 to *Leidseplein*) and **Stadsdoelen**, *Klonveniersburgwal 97; tel: 624 6832* (tram nos. 4/9/16/24/25 to *Muntplein*).

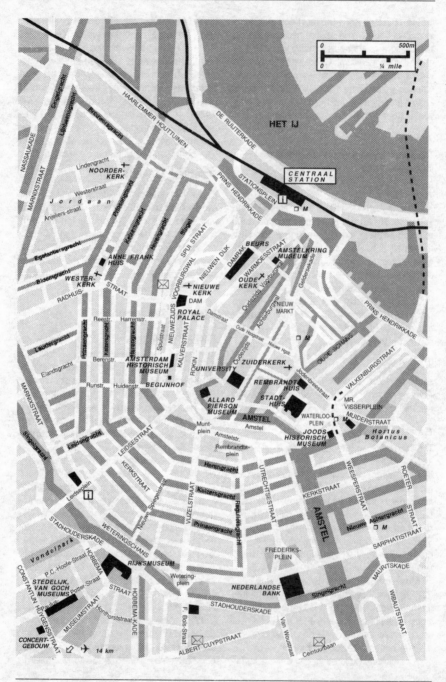

The cheapest place in town is **Eben Haezer Christian Youth Hostel**, *Bloemstraat 179; tel: 624 4717* (tram nos. 13/17 to *Marnixstraat*). **Amstel**, *Steiger 5 (Pier 5), De Ruijterkade; tel: 626 4247* (behind Centraal), is the last of the traditional barge hotels.

Amsterdam's **campsites** are: **Vliegenbos**, *Meeuwenlaan 138; tel: 636 8855* (bus 32; 10 mins from Centraal) and **Het Amsterdamse Bos**, *Kleine Noordijk 1, Aalsmeer; tel: 641 6868* (buses 171/172; 30 mins from Centraal).

Communications

The main **post office** is at *Singel 250; tel: 556 3311*. Mon–Fri 0830–1800 (Thur–2000) and Sat 0900–1500. It offers a *poste restante* facility.

Two places which are open 24 hours a day and let you pay for calls after you have finished are: **Telehouse**, *Raadhuisstraat 48/50* and **Tele Talk Centre**, *Leidsestraat 101*. The city code for dialling into Amsterdam is 20.

Eating and Drinking

Amsterdam is a good place to eat, with many unpretentious restaurants in every price range and a wide choice of cuisine, with most parts of the world represented. Throughout the centre, there are plenty of food stalls and also *Eetcafés* and bars which sell local food at reasonable prices.

Around the *Spui* you will find some of the city's trendiest cafés, while the areas around *Nieuwmarkt*, *Dam* and *De Pijp* (especially along *Albert Cuypstraat*) are the best for Eastern cuisine – Indonesian is particularly popular.

For those on a tight budget, try one of the *mensas* (student canteens) at *O.Z. Voorburgwal 237* (Mon–Fri 1200–1400 and 1700–1900) and *Weesperstraat 5* (Mon–Fri 1700–1925).

Embassies

Most embassies are in The Hague (Den Haag), less than 30 mins away by train (see p. 225). **Australia** *Carnegielaan 14, The Hague; tel: 070 310 8200*. **Canada** *Sophialaan 7, The Hague; tel: 070 361 4111*. **New Zealand** *Mauritskade 25, The Hague; tel: 070 346 9324*.

UK *Koningslaan 44, Amsterdam; tel: 676 4343*. **USA** *Museumplein 19, Amsterdam; tel: 664 5661*.

Laundry

Look for a sign saying *Wasserette*. One chain, **The Clean Brothers**, has branches at *Jakob Van Lennepkade 179*; *Westerstraat 26*; *Kerkstraat 56* and *Rozengracht 59*.

Money

Thomas Cook bureaux de change are at: *Dam 23–25*; *Scandic Crown Hotel, Damrak 1–5*; *Leidseplein 31a*. Outside banking hours, the GWK exchanges at Centraal and Schiphol are the best bet. They are open 24 hours a day.

Security

Amsterdam is safe by large-city standards, but there are some street thieves who specialise in vulnerable pockets and shoulder bags. Mugging is a problem only at night and almost exclusively in areas where junkies hang out, so you're unlikely to have problems if you avoid shadowed and deserted side-streets.

Centraal Station is an extraordinarily ornate 19th-century structure and *Stationsplein* a hive of activity, so new arrivals tend to get distracted by their surroundings and become vulnerable to the opportunistic thieves that hang around there. Exercise more than usual caution in looking after your belongings and leave nothing unattended.

The red light district is a den of thieves, so take as little with you as possible and be careful how you use your camera. Many of the habitués do not appreciate being photographed and your last sight of your camera might well be as it sinks into the nearest canal.

Police phone no: *622 2222*.

Entertainment

Nightlife

There's excellent nightlife, both varied and affordable. Few places have a dress policy and many establishments stay open until 0400. Although there are many bars, clubs, discos and casinos, it is around the cafés that the crowds gather: many offer various kinds of live music, especially South American, rock and jazz. Entrance fees (where they exist) are low, but prices for drinks tend to be inflated.

Leidseplein (very touristy) and **Rembrandts-plein** (popular with locals as well as visitors) are lively, noisy centres of evening activity. The **Jordaan** area (west of *Prinsengracht*) is pleasant for an evening in a non-touristy environment.

Theatres, Cinemas and Concerts

The **Stalhouderij**, *Bloemdwarstraat 4; tel: 626 2282*, stages English-language plays and there are other theatres which frequently perform works in English.

Most films are shown undubbed (the exceptions state *Nederlands gesproken* (Dutch spoken) on the listings) and most non-English films have English subtitles. There are several multi-screen cinemas in the area of *Leidseplein*.

Classical music can be found at the **Concertgebouw**, *Van Baerlestraat 98; tel: 671 8345*, and dance/opera at the decorative **Muziektheater**, *Amstel 3; tel: 625 5455*, where backstage tours are possible (except in July). Both frequently offer free lunch-time concerts.

De Ijsbreker, *Weesperzijde 23; tel: 668 1805*, is the venue for international modern and experimental music.

South of *Leidseplein* is **Vondelpark**, a pleasant park which contains some architectural oddities and the **Openluchttheater** (*tel: 673 1499*), where alfresco performances are staged on summer weekends. These are extremely varied, but both jazz and folk feature prominently. The park also contains the **Nederlandse Filmmuseum**, which often shows silent films.

The Fringe

Among other things, Amsterdam is noted for its enlightened views about marijuana and homosexuality.

There is a nationwide gay and lesbian organisation which is based in Amsterdam: **COC**, *Rozenstraat 8; tel: 623 1192*. They have their own disco and will provide full information about other gay venues, both in Amsterdam and elsewhere in Holland.

The city has many 'smoking' coffee-shops where hash and pot can be purchased and smoked (usually to the accompaniment of ear-shattering music). This is not legal, but the police usually turn a blind eye. One reason for this tolerance is that it contains the problem, so do not assume that what is tolerated in one place will be permitted in another.

Shopping

The city's **flea market** is on *Waterlooplein* and the famous **flower market** is on *Singel*. VVV produce a leaflet called *Markstad* which gives details of these and the many other regular street markets. They have other leaflets on shopping which are useful if you are actually planning to buy.

Kalverstraat is the main shopping street, a pedestrian (and usually overcrowded) place that runs from *Dam* to *Muntplein*. Another pedestrian precinct is *Nieuwendijk*, parallel to *Damrak*. For fun shopping, try the alleys off *Keizersgracht*, on the stretch between *Leidse-gracht* and *Nieuwe Spiegelstraat*.

The top store in Amsterdam is **De Bijenkorf**, on *Damrak*. If you go for designer labels, there's an upmarket shopping area south-east of *Vondelpark*, especially along *Pieter Cornelisz Hooftstraat* and *Van Baelestraat*.

Sightseeing

Amsterdam has over 40 museums (covering such diverse subjects as trams and sex) and around 150 art galleries, so the ones mentioned below barely scratch the surface and you should get a full list from VVV.

The Centre: Centraal to Singelgracht

Amstelkring, *O. Z. Voorburgwal 40* (opposite Centraal), was a wealthy merchant's house and the bottom of the building is still furnished in period style. Above that, three lofts were knocked into one to provide a place of worship for Catholics during the Reformation (17th–18th centuries), a time when they were forbidden to practice their faith in public. The attic is now an atmospheric museum devoted to that era.

From Centraal, Damrak leads directly south to the city centre, **Dam**, where there's a distinctive war memorial which is a favoured meeting-place for tourists. On the west side of the square is **Koninklijk Paleis**. This was the 17th-century town hall and the interior reflects the glory of that age. It acquired its present name (which means 'royal palace') in the early 19th century, when Louis Bonaparte moved in, and much of his Empire furniture remains. Also in Dam is the much-rebuilt Gothic **Nieuwekerk**, used for state functions and special exhibitions. It contains a very ornate organ, on which there are sometimes recitals.

South of Dam is the **Amsterdam Historical Museum**, *Kalverstraat 92* (boat: *Herengracht*; tram: *Spui*), which covers the city's history, the 17th-century section being the most impressive. At the top of the building is a carillon where you can try your hand at bell-ringing.

Not far away (off *Sint Luciensteeg*) is the **Begijnhof**, once home to a community of upper-class religious women and still a peaceful spot, consisting of a group of 17th- and 18th-century buildings around a courtyard. Across the way is the 15th-century church where they worshipped, the only church in the city that retains its medieval tower.

West of Dam

The **Anne Frank Huis**, *Prinsengracht 263* (boat: *Prinsengracht*; tram: *Westermarkt*), was where a Jewish family hid from the Nazis for two years. They were betrayed in 1944 and only the father survived the concentration camps. The 13–14 year-old Anne recorded the family's lifestyle in a moving diary that was discovered after the war and became an international best-seller. You can see all the rooms she described and there are numerous documents from the period which illustrate vividly the horrors of being a Jew at that time.

For a complete change of mood, try two nearby museums. The **Theatre Museum** at *Herengracht 168* has changing displays that usually feature hands-on exhibits. **Spaarpotten**, *Raadhuisstraat 12*, contains over 2,000 money boxes of wildly differing designs.

The 17th-century **Westerkerk**, *Westermarkt*, with Amsterdam's highest tower (85m) gives one of the few bird's-eye views of the city.

The Old City: east of Damrak

De Walletjes (Little Walls) – the Red Light District is (roughly) the area between *Warmoestraat* and *Gelderskade* and is one of the city's top tourist attractions, visited as much by women as by men. Although there are plenty of ladies offering their traditional skills, most visitors to this area are more interested in attending a sex theatre. One of the more reputable is **Theatre Casa Rosso**, at *O. Z. Achterburgwal 106*, a street which also contains brothels and sex shops.

The **Oude Kerk**, *Oudekerksplein, Warmoesstraat*, is a place with a long history. Little of what remains is pre-16th century, but it's still worth a visit.

The Museum Quarter: south-west of centre

The Rijksmuseum, *Stadhouderskade 42* (boat: *Singelgracht*; tram: *Museumplein*), is one of the world's great museums and not to be missed. Among the major exhibits are thousands of examples of Asiatic art, an outstanding collection of Meissen and what is acknowledged as the world's best collection of 17th-century Dutch paintings. These include numerous Rembrandt masterpieces, notably *The Night Watch*, and four superb Vermeers.

The old **Heineken Brewery**, *Stadhouderskade 78* (a few blocks east), is now a museum and tours include a drink or two. Incidentally, the entrance fees go to charity.

The **Vincent Van Gogh Museum**, *Paulus Potterstraat 7* (boat: Singelgracht; tram: Museumplein/Van Baerlestraat), contains some 200 paintings and 500 drawings (not all on display at the same time). They cover his whole artistic life and were collected by his art-dealer brother, Theo. There are also some everyday items connected with him and works by his friends.

Amsterdam has been important in the diamond trade since the 16th century and is still a world centre, so prices are comparatively low and many diamond merchants lay on tours. You can watch the stones being cut and polished without obligation and, if you want to buy, it's worth shopping around. One of the largest companies is **Coster Diamonds** (who cut the Koh-I-Noor), *Paulus Potterstraat 2–4*.

At *Paulus Potterstraat 13* is the excellent **Stedelijk Museum**. The exhibits are continually changed, but what's on display should range from Manet and Toulouse-Lautrec to Picasso and Warhol. Don't miss the applied art on the ground floor.

Hollandse Menage, *Vondelstraat 140* (south-west of *Leidseplein*, a continuation of *Leidsestraat*), is a must for horse-lovers. You can have a drink while you watch the animals at work in the arena and the decor has an equine motif.

Jewish Quarter: south-east of Dam

Although there was discrimination in some areas of life, the Jews played a very important part in the development of Amsterdam. By the time World War II broke out, they formed 10% of the population, concentrated in **Jodenhoek**, but fewer than a quarter of them survived the Nazis.

Jodenbreestraat was the main street of the quarter and no. 6 was where Rembrandt lived for over twenty years. **Rembrandthuis** (boat: *Amstel*; tram: *Visserplein*) isn't very evocative, but does contain 245 of his engravings and there's a regular slide-show about his life. Further down the street is a gateway with a motif of skulls which leads to the early 17th-century **Zuiderkerk**, the first Protestant church built after the Reformation. It has a splendid spire that was said to have inspired Christopher Wren's rebuilding of London churches.

The nearby **Joods Historisch Museum**, *Jonas Daniel Meijerplein 2*, is housed in what was a complex of late 17th-century Ashkenazi synagogues. It has been rebuilt since the war and is imaginatively arranged to present (primarily) the happier aspects of Judaism. Along the street is the 17th-century **Portuguese-Israelite Synagogue**, which was once the largest in the world, built by Sephardic Jews partly to snub the less powerful, but far more numerous, Ashkenazim.

Amstel: south-east of Jodenhoek

The **Herengracht Canal** was the city's grandest and one stretch (between *Vijzelstraat* and *Leidsestraat*) is known as the 'Golden Bend'. This typifies the old city's architecture, when buildings were tall and thin (to minimise taxes based on width) and protruding gables were needed to winch up furniture that was too big to be manoeuvred up the narrow staircases.

This is an excellent place for a canal-side stroll and the **Willet-Holthuysen Museum**, *Herengracht 605*, enables you to see what life inside was like. Another good example of a canal house is a couple of blocks south-west, the atmospheric **Museum Van Loon**, *Keizersgracht 672*.

Artis: east of the centre

'Artis' is the common name for the **zoo**, which is home to around 6,000 animals (kept in natural surroundings), but the zoo is part of a complex and the ticket also covers an aquarium, a planetarium, a zoological museum and beautiful gardens. There is a special boat from Centraal: **Artis Express**, *tel: 622 2181*.

Across the street, **Hortus Botanicus**, *Plantage Middenlaan 2*, is a small botanical garden with around 6,000 species.

The Docklands: north of Artis

The **Kromhout Shipyard Museum**, *Hoogte Kadijk 147*, is a place devoted to restoring historic vessels and you can watch the artisans at work. The **Scheepvart Maritime Museum**, *Kattenburgerplein 1*, is housed in a 17th-century arsenal so vast that it contains several whole ships. You can board the *Amsterdam*, a replica of an 18th-century East Indiaman with costumed personnel.

Tropenmuseum (Tropical Museum), *Linnaeusstraat 2* (tram: *Mauritskade*), has diverse exhibits connected with Third World problems, from Indian slums to South American rain forests. Allow plenty of time.

Amsterdamse Bos (bus no. 170/171/172; from April to October there are also special trips by antique trams) is an 80-hectare park on the southern fringe of the city which is an excellent place to relax, especially if you have children who are becoming a bit restless. Inspired by the Bois de Boulogne, the park contains thousands of trees, many picnic glades, a rowing lake and facilities for swimming, canoeing, cycling and walking (200 km of tracks). The **Bosmuseum** is devoted to the construction of the park and to its flora and fauna.

🌀 Side Tracks from Amsterdam

The **Bloemenveiling** (Flower Auction) takes place in **Aalsmeer** (a little under an hour by bus no. 172) Apr–Sept Mon–Fri 0730–1100, but it's usually over by 1000, so go early. This is the world's largest flower market and there's a visitors' gallery which gives a bird's eye view, with a multi-lingual commentary explaining the proceedings. On the first Sunday in September there's a parade, with flower-covered vehicles, from Aalsmeer to the centre of Amsterdam (around 12 km).

Zaanse Schanz (15 mins by train) is a typical (if touristy) restored 17th/18th-century village, complete with five working windmills and traditional handicrafts. Take the train to Koog-Zaandijk.

Alkmaar (about 35 mins by train) is famous for the large and colourful open-air cheese market that is held from mid-April to mid-September. It takes place on Fridays, from 1000 to 1200, but you need to arrive well before 1000 for a good view. The market dates from the early 14th century, but nowadays it's primarily for tourists. The town is worth visiting anyway, as it's a picturesque place with several interesting buildings: the **Waag** houses a cheese museum, the **Biermuseum** is devoted to beer and has a bar with numerous varieties and **St Laurenskerk** is a Gothic 15th-century church with a huge pipe organ.

The ancient town of **Hoorn** (40 mins by train) was an important port until the damming of the Zuider Zee cut it off from the sea. It maintains a harbour on **Ijsselmeer**, a freshwater lake, and the well-preserved 17th-century mansions and warehouses make it an excellent place for a stroll. The extraordinarily eclectic **Westfries Museum**, *Rode Steen 1*, is crammed with items evoking the 17th-century days of glory. From mid-June to mid-August, Hoorn is renowned for its lively **Wednesday Market**, a traditional affair where medieval costumes are worn and such ancient crafts as clog-making, basket-weaving and net-mending can be seen.

To the north of Hoorn (on the same train; another 20 mins or so) is **Enkhuizen**. The **Zuider Zee Museum** tells the story of the reclamation of this area – Enkhuizen was one of the ports that found itself cut off from the sea. There's an indoor section, **Binnen Museum**, containing such things as historic fishing craft, and a well-labelled open-air section (reached by boat) with over 130 buildings reproducing streets rescued from 19th-century fishing villages that were destroyed. You can watch old-style craftsmen at work. The open-air section is open only from mid-April to mid-October.

Volendam (30 mins by bus) is great fun, particularly for children. It's a former fishing village, with picturesque wooden buildings, where the people have turned to tourism. They are very friendly, dress in traditional costume and are happy to pose.

Not far away (and linked by a frequent express boat Mar–Oct) is **Marken**, more to the point if you want a genuine taste of the past. This quiet village was cut off from the mainland in the 13th century and remained an island until 1957, when a 2.5 km causeway was constructed. The constant danger of floods caused stilted houses to be built and the architecture is extremely picturesque. The people are a close-knit Protestant community who follow the old lifestyle and many still wear traditional dress, so the whole place is literally a living museum.

At **Kaatsheuvel** is **Efteling**, a fairy-tale theme park, usually enjoyed as much by adults as by children. Among the attractions are goblins and wizards, roller coasters and land-scaped grounds, the Fairy Tale Forest, the Forbidden City, the Tales of 1001 Nights and the Dream Flight (from the centre of the earth to outer space). NS arrange day-trips: details from Centraal or VVV. If you prefer to make your own way, take a train to **'s Hertogenbosch** (every half-hour, taking about an hour), then a bus to Efteling. If you are going to Utrecht, you may prefer to make it a Side Track from there as it's about halfway between Amsterdam and Kaatsheuvel.

AMSTERDAM
to
BERLIN

A fairly direct journey between the Netherlands and eastern Germany via Hanover, where there are exceptionally lovely palace gardens.

TRAINS

ETT tables: 22, 231, 701, 700.

→ Fast Track

The journey between Amsterdam (Centraal) and Berlin (Zoo) takes about 8 hrs 30 mins. There are at least three direct trains each day, one (with sleepers and couchettes) overnight.

∿ On Track

Amsterdam–Apeldoorn

There are trains at hourly intervals throughout the day and the journey takes a little over 1 hr.

Apeldoorn–Border–Osnabrück

The journey between Apeldoorn and Osnabrück can be made about seven times a day, of which four are through trains (on the others a change is necessary at Hengelo on the Dutch side of the border). All journeys take about 2 hrs.

If you're not interested in Apeldoorn, you can travel to Osnabrück without changing; see the Amsterdam–Copenhagen route, p. 96.

Osnabrück–Hanover (Hannover)

Trains operate approx. every hour and the journey takes about 1 hr 20 mins.

Hanover–Brunswick (Braunschweig)

There are trains every half-hour or so and the journey takes 30–40 mins.

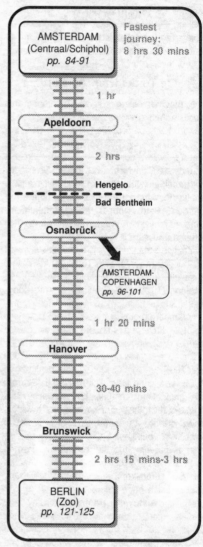

AMSTERDAM (Centraal/Schiphol) *pp. 84-91*

Fastest journey: 8 hrs 30 mins

1 hr

Apeldoorn

2 hrs

Hengelo
Bad Bentheim

Osnabrück

AMSTERDAM-COPENHAGEN *pp. 96-101*

1 hr 20 mins

Hanover

30-40 mins

Brunswick

2 hrs 15 mins-3 hrs

BERLIN (Zoo) *pp. 121-125*

Brunswick–Berlin

Services are frequent, but the journey between Brunswick and Berlin (Zoo – add 30 mins for Hbf) can range from 2 hrs 15 mins to over 3 hrs, so it's worth checking the schedules. Most of the trains have a refreshment service.

APELDOORN

Stop here for the **Paleis Het Loo**, a beautifully restored 17th-century palace, furnished in period style, with a variety of royal possessions on display in the old stables and formal gardens.

By contrast, at **Apenheul**, 350 monkeys and apes roam free in a protected woodland and there's an island with a gorilla colony.

OSNABRÜCK

Dominated by the **Neumarkt** shopping complex, Osnabrück is worth a short stop just to stroll through the **Altstadt** and have a look at the rather lopsided **St Petrus Dom**, the pretty **Marienkirche** and the 17th-century **Friedensaal (Rathaus)**. The **Diözesanmuseum** is worth a brief visit.

HANOVER (HANNOVER)

Station: *tel: (0511) 19419*. This is central. Follow the red line to the information office, open Mon–Sat 0900–1800.
Tourist Office: *Ernst-August-Platz 2; tel: (0511) 168 3002*. Mon–Fri 0830–1800; Sat 0830–1400.

Accommodation

Chain hotels include *Fo, HI, Ic*. For cheap accommodation, try along *Joachimstr*. The **IYHF** (reservations advisable) is at *Ferdinand-Wilhelm-Fricke-Weg 1; tel: (0511) 131 7674* (U: 3/7 to *Fischerhof*).

Getting Around

The tourist office supply free plans of the garden complex and the *Red Thread Guide* (DM3). The red line painted in the street will lead you to the places of major interest . The walk takes roughly 2 hrs.

Sightseeing

Hanover, ancestral home of the first four King Georges of England, is a pleasantly green place which is worth visiting for its museums and gardens. The centre is a pedestrian zone.

The most popular rendezvous is the famous **Kropcke Clock**, connected to Hbf by *Bahnhofstr*.

The high-gabled, carefully restored **Altes Rathaus** is a splendid edifice with elaborate brickwork. Alongside is **Marktkirche**, with some 14th–15th-century stained glass and a bulky tower that is the city's emblem. Kramerstrasse, which gives a taste of the old city, leads towards the **Historical Museum**, *Pferdestr. 6*, with such exhibits as state coaches, reconstructed farm interiors and old maps .

Across *Friedrichswall*, the high-domed **Neues Rathaus**, which includes models of the 17th-century city, is adjacent to the **Kestner Museum** is of decorative arts.

The wide-ranging **Landesmuseum**, *Am Maschseepark 5*, includes natural history, a fascinating archaeological section (with Bronze Age jewellery), while the paintings include works by Holbein, Botticelli and Raphael. The **Sprengel Museum** next door is devoted to modern art, covering such forms as photography and graphics as well as paintings.

Grosser Garten Herrenhausen, 10 mins from Kropcke (U: *Herrenhausergarten*) consists of four once-royal gardens, two of which are the English-style landscaped **Georgengarten** and the formal **Grosser Garten**, the scene of spectacular fountain displays in summer. Frequent musical and theatrical performances are staged in the palace and gardens.

BRUNSWICK (BRAUNSCHWEIG)

Station: *tel: (0531) 19419*. 15 mins south-east of the centre (tram no. 1 to the Rathaus).
Tourist Office: By the station (*tel: (0531) 79 237*. Mon–Fri 0800–1800; Sat 0900–1200.

Brunswick blossomed in 1166 when an influential prince, Henry the Lion, settled here. An ancient bronze lion still guards the cobble-stoned **Burgplatz**, while **Dankwarderode**, Henry's fortress, now forms part of the excellent **Herzog–Anton–Ulrich–Museum** (the rest is on *Museumstr.*). Part of the **Braunschweig Landesmuseum**, at *Hinter Agidien*, is devoted to Jewish culture.

Other notable buildings include the awe-inspiring 12th-century **St Blasius Dom** (where Henry is buried), with its twisted columns, candelabra and Byzantine crucifix; the 11th-century **Magnikirch** and the 13th–15th-century **Rathaus**.

AMSTERDAM to BRUSSELS

This route is essentially a quick journey from the Netherlands to Belgium, but makes provision for a stop in Antwerp en route.

TRAINS

ETT tables: 18, 220, 205.

→ Fast Track

There are regular services daily between Amsterdam (Centraal) and Brussels (Nord or Midi/Zuid). The usual journey time is about 3 hrs. Refreshments are available on most services.

⟿ On Track

Amsterdam–Rotterdam

Trains run regularly during the day between Amsterdam (Centraal and Schiphol) and Rotterdam (Centraal), journey time about 1 hr.

Rotterdam–(Border)–Antwerp (Antwerpen)

There are regular services daily between Rotterdam (Centraal) and Antwerp (Centraal). The journey takes about 1 hr 20 mins.

Antwerp–Brussels (Bruxelles/Brussel)

There are frequent trains throughout the day between Antwerp and Brussels (all stations) and you shouldn't have to wait more than half an hour. The journey takes 40 mins.

All these trains stop at Mechelen (about halfway); see Side Tracks from Brussels, p.134.

ROTTERDAM

For information about Rotterdam, see p. 226.

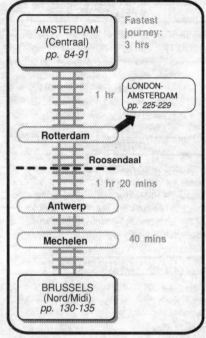

ANTWERP (ANTWERPEN)

Stations: Centraal, *Koningin Astridplein*, tel: *(3) 233 7015*, is 2 km east of the centre but linked by tram (nos 2/15) to Groenplaats. The marble-decorated station is worth a visit in its own right and there is a tourist information bureau just outside. There is a **Thomas Cook** bureau de change in the square. The other station, **Berchem**, is on the south-eastern edge of town; some international trains stop here and not at Centraal.

Tourist Office: Dienst Voor Toerisme, *Grote Markt 15; tel: (3) 232 0103*. Open Mon–Sat 0900–1800 and Sun 0900–1700.

Getting Around

Centraal is the hub of the city's transport system and maps can be obtained from the metro stop there (Diamant): Mon–Fri 0800–1200 and 1300–1600. Tickets cost BFr.35 but you can get a block of eight for BFr.154. There are also tourist cards (BFr.140) valid for 24 hours.

The zoo and diamond museum are near Centraal. Most of the other major sights are within easy walking distance of Grote Markt/ Groenplaats and the tourist office produces a booklet recommending town walks (which are signposted).

There are buses but the tram system provides the best way of getting around. Some lines (which are marked M) run underground. The tourist office arranges multilingual bus tours.

Flandria, *Haverstraat 1; tel: (3) 231 3100*, arranges river and harbour cruises.

Accommodation

The tourist office provides lists of hotels. Chains with properties in the city are: *Hl, Hn, Nv, Pu, SC*. There are some cheap hotels near Centraal, but be wary because some are the kind that rent by the hour rather than the night.

The **IYHF**, *Eric Sasselaan 2; tel: (3) 238 0273*, is about 3 km south of the centre (tram no 2). You can often stay free in return for doing a few hours work. Not far east of the hostel is the **campsite**, *Vogelzanglaan; tel: (3) 238 5717*.

Sightseeing

Antwerp, the chief Flemish city, stands on the Scheldt River and is Europe's second largest port. It has a rich legacy of art and architecture and two other major attractions. The **Dieren-tuin (Zoo)** (by Centraal) is renowned for its work with endangered species (the complex includes two natural history museums and a planetarium). The **Diamantmuseum**, *Lange Herental-sestraat 31* (halfway between Centraal and Grote Markt), covers all aspects of the diamond trade (which is far larger than Amsterdam's) and you can watch the cutters at work.

The main square is **Grote Markt**, home to the Brabo fountain (which depicts the legend of the city's founding), guild houses topped by golden figures and the Renaissance **Stadhuis (Town Hall)**. Not far away is another major square, **Groenplaats**, which is dominated by the 123 m spire of **Onze-Lieve Vrouwekathedral**, inside which are three masterpieces by Rubens.

The medieval **Steen** (Castle), *Steenplein*, is a 13th-century structure with 16th-century embellishments that houses the **Maritime Museum**, where you can board real ships.

The artist Rubens spent the last 30 years of his life in **Rubenshuis**, *Wapper 9* (about halfway between Centraal and Grote Markt; metro: *Meir*). It is an evocative place although it contains only minor examples of his work. Rubens was the major influence in the design of **Sint-Carolus Borromeuskerk**, *Hendrik Conscienceplein*, and he is buried in **Sint-Jacobskerk**, *Lange Nieuwstraat*, a 15th-century Gothic structure with 17th-century Baroque ornamentation.

The **Plantin-Moretus Museum**, *Vrijdag-markt*, is a well-preserved 16th-century printing works which is now a museum of printing. Straight out of a fairytale, the old butcher's hall, **Vleeshuis**, *Vleeshouwerstraat*, is now an applied arts museum with exhibits that include some excellent woodcarvings.

Museum Voor Schone Kunsten (Royal Art Gallery), *Leopold de Waelplaats*, south of the centre (bus no 8), is a neo-Classical building housing over 2,500 paintings, including the world's best collection of works by Rubens and an almost unrivalled collection of Flemish art from the 14th to the 17th century.

Antwerp's 16th-century **Beguinage**, *Rodes-traat 39* (metro: *Opera*), is a restful area of cobbled streets and small houses. Beguinages were Flemish institutions somewhat like convents, but the vows were less strict than those taken by nuns and, instead of being in a closed order, the women devoted their lives to serving the community.

The **Openluchtmuseum Voor Beeld-houwkunst**, *Middelheim Park*, is dotted with sculptures by Rodin and Moore (among others).

On Sunday mornings, the **Vogelmarkt (Bird Market)**, *Oude Vaartplaats*, on the south side of the city, does sell birds — and almost everything else.

Cogels-Osylei, south-east of town, near Berchem station, is a residential avenue that is full of extraordinary (often over the top) modern architecture (of which there are further examples in surrounding streets).

For other Belgian cities, see the London–Brussels route (p. 230).

AMSTERDAM
to
COPENHAGEN

This itinerary, between the Netherlands and Denmark, makes several stops in northern Germany. The varied attractions en route range from Viking ships to Hanseatic mansions, from the Pied Piper legend to the reality of the notorious Reeperbahn.

TRAINS

ETT tables: 22, 650, 665, 50, 460.

→ Fast Track

The one direct service between Amsterdam (Centraal) and Copenhagen, in summer only, is overnight and takes about 12 hrs. Second-class couchettes are available, but there's no refreshment service.

⌇⌇ On Track

Amsterdam–(Border)–Osnabrück

There are four trains every day, taking about 3 hrs and with a refreshment service. The border is crossed at Hengelo, but you don't need to leave the train. Border officials may, or may not, come on board.

If you want to visit Apeldoorn and Osnabrück, see the Amsterdam–Berlin route (p. 92).

Osnabrück–Bremen

Trains are hourly, the journey is about 55 mins.

Bremen–Hamburg

Trains operate at hourly intervals and the journey takes a little under an hour.

Hamburg–Lübeck

There are frequent trains throughout the day and

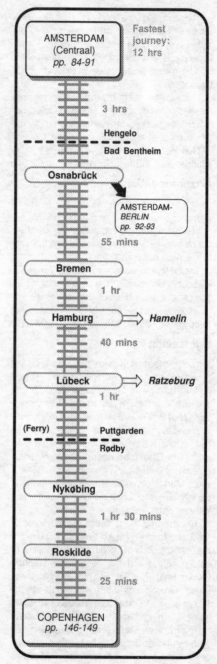

AMSTERDAM (Centraal) pp. 84-91

Fastest journey: 12 hrs

3 hrs

Hengelo
Bad Bentheim

Osnabrück

AMSTERDAM–BERLIN pp. 92-93

55 mins

Bremen

1 hr

Hamburg ⇒ *Hamelin*

40 mins

Lübeck ⇒ *Ratzeburg*

1 hr

(Ferry) Puttgarden
Rødby

Nykøbing

1 hr 30 mins

Roskilde

25 mins

COPENHAGEN pp. 146-149

the longest gap is an hour. The journey takes about 40 mins.

Lübeck–(Puttgarden–Border–Rødby)–Nykøbing

There are half a dozen EC trains a day at reasonable hours, plus a few ordinary trains at anti-social times, so it's probably worth paying the supplement although it makes little difference to the journey time. The leg between Lübeck and Puttgarden takes roughly an hour.

On arrival at Puttgarden (or Rødby in the other direction), the whole train is loaded onto a ferry and the crossing takes a further hour. Then the whole train just drives off the ferry and continues its journey. This is the main rail link between Germany and Denmark and the cost is included in rail tickets/passes. There are refreshment services and good-value duty-free shops on board. Border formalities are minimal, sometimes non-existent. The rail leg between Rødby and Nykøbing takes about 25 mins.

There's not much to detain you in Nykøbing, but you shouldn't have to wait long for a connection. If you're not interested in visiting Nykøbing or Roskilde, you can simply stay on the boat-train (the train journey between Rødby and Copenhagen takes just over 2 hrs).

Nykøbing–Roskilde

Services are fairly frequent (not more than 2 hrs apart), the journey taking about 1 hr 30 mins.

Roskilde–Copenhagen

Trains run throughout the day, about four per hour, and the journey takes about 25 mins.

BREMEN

Station: Hbf, *tel: (0421) 19419*. This is fairly central, to the north of the main area of interest. **Tourist Office**: *Hillmannplatz 6; tel: (0421) 308 0038*. Close to the station. Mon–Fri 0930–1830 (Thur–2030), Sat 0930–1400 (longer on the first Sat of the month) and Sun 0930–1530.

Accommodation and Food

Hotels in Bremen include *Me, Nv, Pu* and *Sf*. The **IYHF**, *Kalkstr.6; tel: (0421) 17 13 69*, is on the western side of *Altstadt*: bus no. 26/tram no. 6 to *Brill*.

The **Ratskeller** (in the Rathaus) has been a bar since the early 15th century and offers 600 different wines. Cheap eating-places can be found on and around *Ostertorsteinweg*.

Getting Around

The **Bremer Kärtchen** gives two days unlimited travel on all the city's buses and trams, but (with the exception of some museums) the things of interest cluster around *Marktplatz*.

Sightseeing

Altstadt, on the north-east bank of the River Weser, is the main area of historical interest, having survived largely because an RAF bomber pilot could not bring himself to destroy it.

Marktplatz is dominated by the **Rathaus**, a 15th-century structure overlaid with a Renaissance façade. It's worth joining a tour to see the splendid interior. Among the Hanseatic houses lining the square is **Schutting**, a Flemish-inspired guild of merchants' mansion. **Liebfrauenkirchhof** is a lovely 13th-century hall church with medieval murals and beautiful stained glass.

In *Marktplatz* are two notable statues. One is a 15th-century, 10m-high portrait of Roland (Charlemagne's nephew), which is a symbol of the town's independence. Legend has it that Bremen will remain free as long as he is standing. The other (modern) illustrates the Grimm Brothers' fairy-tale about the *Four Musicians of Bremen*: a donkey, dog, cat and rooster.

The 11th-century twin-spired **St Petri Dom**, *Sandstr. 10–12*, is beautiful in a sombre way, with mosaic arches, a 16th-century organ gallery and a 13th-century bronze font. In the **Bleikeller** (basement: open May–Oct) are some perfectly-preserved corpses, believed to be of men who fell from the roof during construction and were saved from corruption by the lack of air.

To the south side of *Marktplatz* is **Bottcherstr.**, a street that is a neo-Gothic fantasy from the 1920s. It houses craft workshops, restaurants, a casino and a musical clock that chimes three times a day: at 1200, 1500 and 1800. The 16th-century **Roselius Haus** is a museum of medieval art and furniture.

The **Schnoorviertel** area (between the Dom and the river) consists of well-preserved 16th–18th-century buildings, many of which are now craft shops. Just to the east is **Kunsthalle**, *Am Wall 207*, which has an eclectic collection of works from the Renaissance to the present day.

The **Übersee Museum**, *Bahnhofplatz 13*, is devoted to items gathered from around the world, while the **Landes/Focke-Museum**, *Schwachhauser Heerstr.240*, to the north-east of town, is the place to visit if you are interested in local history.

HAMBURG

Ferries: Landungsbrücken, *Brücke 9; tel: (040) 38 90 71* (2 km along the shore from St Pauli), is the terminal for ferries from the UK and Scandinavia. There's a tourist kiosk between piers 4 and 5, open daily 0900–1600.

Stations: **Hauptbahnhof (Hbf)** handles most long-distance trains. It's central and on the U-Bahn. The tourist office (*tel: (040) 30 05 12 30*) is open daily 0700–2300. Hbf also houses the main post office (international phones on the second floor), which is open very long hours. The station's main exit is on *Kirchenallee*. **Altona**, in the west of the city, is the terminal for most trains serving Schleswig-Holstein. **Dammtor**, north of the centre, is unlikely to be of interest to visitors. All rail information: *tel: (040) 19419*. Frequent S-Bahns link the three stations.

Tourist Offices: The **main office**, *Bieberhaus, Hachmannplatz; tel: (040) 30 05 12 44*, (close to Hbf) opens Mon–Fri 0730–1800 and Sat 0800–1500. Get the free *City map and tips from A–Z*, which includes a map of the city rail system, full details of the *Hamburg CARD* and an outline guide to the city's attractions.

Thomas Cook bureau de change: *Ballinndamm 39.*

Budget Travel: SSR Reiseladen, *Rothenbaumchaussee 61; tel: (040) 410 2081*. Mon–Fri 0900–1800 and Sat 0900–1200.

Accommodation and Food

As one of Europe's busiest commercial centres, Hamburg offers a wide range of hotels, including representatives of the following chains: *Ft, Ma,* *Hl, Ic, Ra, SA*. For cheaper accommodation it's safest to pre-book at the IYHF or one of the three **Mitwohnzentralen**: *Lobuschstr.22; tel: (040) 39 13 73, Rutschbahn 3; tel: (040) 41 80 18,* and *Haubachstr.8; tel: (040) 398 5118.* The two **IYHFs** are: *Alfred-Wegener-Weg 5; tel: (040) 31 34 88,* central (U/S: *Landungsbrücken*) and *Rennbahnstr.100; tel: (040) 651 1671,* in the eastern suburbs (S: *Horner Rennbahn*).

Good fish restaurants line the bank of the Elbe. Prices tend to reflect the areas in which they are located, but the places in *Rathausmarkt* are not exorbitant and it's a good place to watch the world go by. *Kirchenallee, Altona, Univiertel* and *Schanzenviertel* are cheap eating areas.

Getting Around

The main area of interest is small enough to be walkable. **HHV**, *Steinstr. 1; tel: (040) 32 29 11,* run efficient buses, U-Bahn (underground) and S-Bahn (urban trains), as well as a limited night bus service in the central area.

The *Hamburg CARD* is good value and offers a choice of validity. It provides unlimited travel on all public transport (including port ferries), discounts on the Hummelbahn and some tours and free entrance to about a dozen museums.

The **Hummelbahn (Bumblebee)** is a fun run, an air-supported vehicle that 'buzzes' all over town. The city is dominated by water and a boat-trip is part of the experience. **Hadag**, *tel: (040) 56 45 23,* run daily English-language harbour tours Mar–Oct/Nov. **Binnenalster** and **Aussenalster** are artificial lakes, created in the 13th century when the River Alster was dammed. Yachts and rowing boats can be hired from companies on *An der Alster*, by the Hotel Atlantic. In summer there are ferry cruises from the *Jungfernstieg quay; tel: (040) 34 11 41.*

Nightlife

The city is noted for its very varied nightlife. The tourist office can provide details of the possibilities, which range from a lively gay scene to music of all kinds and some of the world's most infamous sex shops.

St Pauli is the quarter ruled by the sex industry (U: *St Pauli*; S: *Reeperbahn*). There's little point in going before 2200 and you should not go

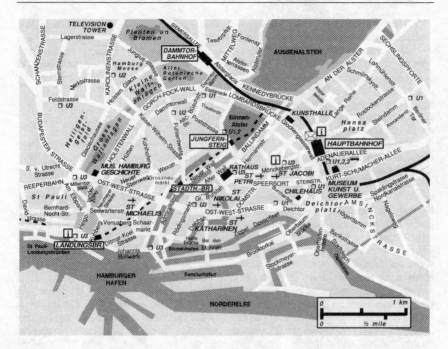

alone. The infamous 600m-long **Reeperbahn** is becoming quite respectable, but *Grosse Freiheit* is notorious for its windows of ladies for sale and three major sex clubs. Males over 18 (entry is forbidden to everyone else) may like to see *Herbertstr.*, a street where little is left to the imagination.

Sightseeing

Hamburg is a semi-autonomous city-state, officially classified as a *Land* (federal state) rather than a town. It was virtually destroyed by a fire in 1842. Lying on the River Elbe, it is Europe's third largest port and a major industrial city, but that's difficult to believe when you are there because enlightened post-war planning has produced a lively place in which two-thirds of the area consists of parks and water.

The oldest surviving area is around the harbour, where two museum ships are moored: the tall ship *Rickmer Rickmers* and *Cap San Diego*, a fairly modern trading vessel known as the 'White Swan of the South Atlantic'.

Speicherstadt, just east of the docks, is a district of 19th-century gabled warehouses, now a customs-free zone which is great for a stroll. **Blankenese**, connected to *St Pauli* by ferry, is a maze of small lanes and stairways that is more like a fishing village than a city suburb. Every Sunday the **Altona Fischmarkt** (U/S: *Landungsbrücken*) takes place. The auction hall opens at 0500 in summer (0700 in winter) and proceedings finish at 1000. Freshly caught fish is sold, but so is almost everything else.

The neo-Renaissance **Rathaus**, *Marktplatz* (U: *Rathaus*), can be toured when government is not in session. It's adorned with countless rich tapestries, chandeliers and paintings. The city's skyline is dominated by six towers, one belonging to the Rathaus and the others to churches: **St Petri**, *Monckebergstr.* (U: *Rathaus*), the oldest building in the city centre; the 14th-century **St Jakobi**, *Steinstr.* (U: *Monckebergstr.*); **St Katharinen**, *Am Zollkanal* (U: *Messberg*), is Gothic with a Baroque tower; **St Nicolai**, *Ost-West-Str.* (U: *Klosterstern*), has the tallest tower. The most impressive belongs to **St Michaelis**, *Krayenkamp 4c* (U/S: *Landungsbrücken*), a

132m-high Baroque structure with a viewing level at 82m which gives panoramic views. This is the city's symbol and a trumpet solo is played from the tower every day.

Chilehaus, *Burchardstr./Pumpen* (U: *Messberg*), is a highly original Expressionist structure symbolising a ship at sea. The **Kunsthalle**, *Glockengiesserwall 1* (U/S: *Hbf*), has a superb art collection stretching back to medieval times. Virtually every important artist from northern Europe is represented, as well as such southern ones as Canaletto, Goya and Tiepolo. The collection is complemented by the modern works in the next-door **Kunstverein**. The **Museum für Kunst und Gewerbe**, *Steintorplatz 1* (U/S: *Hbf*), has an excellent collection of art from ancient Egypt, Greece and Rome, along with newer works (right up to date), including impressive Chinese and Japanese sections. The **Museum für Hamburgische Geschichte**, *Holstenwall 124* (U: *St Pauli*) is the place to go if you want to know about the city's history. On a less elevated plane, the **Holstenbrauerei**, *Holstenstr. 224*, offers regular (free) brewery tours (except in August) that end with a sampling. West from *Aussenalster*, the **Museum für Volkerkunde**, *Rothenbaumchaussee 64* (U: *Hallerstr.*), contains a collection of Third World and folk art. Of particular note are the Javanese shadow-puppets and pre-Columbian jewellery.

A few blocks to the south, and overlooked by the 280m **TV Tower** (U: *Messehallen*; observatory open daily), is **Planten un Blomen** (U: *Stephanplatz*; S: *Dammtor*), a flower-park with illuminated fountain displays and music on summer nights (May–Sept). The **Hagenbeck Zoo** (U: *Hagenbecks Tier-park*) contains around 2,000 animals (over 370 species) in 54 open-air enclosures surrounded by deep ditches. It was one of the first zoos to adopt this style of caging. In May and June there are Saturday evening 'jungle nights' with fireworks. Hamburg's **Dom**, *Heiligengeistfeld* (U: *St Pauli*) is not a cathedral, but a funfair with spring, summer and autumn seasons.

⌁ Side Track from Hamburg

Hamelin (Hameln) lives off the legend of the Pied Piper, which is illustrated everywhere and acted out every Sunday in summer. It's a pleasant, if over-commercialised, old town that was little touched by the war and has plenty of historic buildings. The trains from Hbf are frequent and take about 45 mins.

LÜBECK

Station: *tel: (0451) 19419*. 5 mins walk west of Altstadt.

Tourist Offices: There's a small office in the station, but (apart from hotel bookings) it offers a very limited service and it's better to pick up a (free) town map and head for the **central office**, *Am Markt 1; tel: (0451) 122 8106*. Mon–Fri 0930–1800 and Sat–Sun 1000–1400.

Accommodation

There are several reasonably priced hotels around Hbf. **IYHF**, *Am Gertrudenkirchhof 4; tel: (0451) 33433*, north-east of *Burgtor* (bus nos. 1/3 from Hbf). The **YMCA** run a convenient **Sleep-In**, *Grosse Petersgrube 11; tel: (0451) 78982*, in the old town near *Petrikirche*.

Getting Around

There's an excellent bus network, but most things of interest are in the small (and largely intact) 12th-century inner city.

Sightseeing

Lübeck, the most interesting town in **Schleswig-Holstein**, was the capital of the Hanseatic League (a 14th–16th-century trading association) and it's an attractive place with a wide range of architectural styles. The twin-towered **Holstentor** (between Hbf and Altstadt) is Lübeck's emblem, a 15th-century structure that was one of the four city gates. Inside is a small **Historical Museum** which houses a model of the 17th-century town. Along the waterfront nearby are some lovely gabled buildings.

The historic centre, **Alstadt**, perched on an egg-shaped island is a World Heritage Site. The Gothic **Petrikirche**, now an art gallery, has a lift up the 50m spire: excellent for orientation.

The nearby **Museum für Figurentheater**,

Kleine Petersgrube 4–6, is devoted to theatrical puppets from all over the world. In **Grosse Petersgrube** is a music academy formed by knocking 22 handsome houses together. Both places give regular public performances.

Markt is dominated by the striking L-shaped 13th–16th-century **Rathaus**, the core of *Altstadt* and typical of Lübeck's architectural style of alternating red unglazed and black glazed bricks: a style copied by the Dutch and more common in Holland. Opposite the east wing is **Niederegger Haus**, *Breitestr.*, which is renowned for vast displays of marzipan (the town has been producing it since the Middle Ages). Opposite the north wing is the 13th-century **Marien-kirche**, a brick-built Gothic church with square towers that was the model for many in the area. Later embellishments were damaged in the war and ignored in the process of restoration. It contains a magnificent retable and the world's largest mechanical organ (still in use).

To the north of *Altstadt* is the lovely **Heil-igengeistspital**, *Konigstr.9*, which is very ornate inside and out. **Engelsgrubestr.** is lined by the well-preserved houses of long-ago sea captains. A block away is **Jakobikirche**, a 13th–14th-century sailors' church with square pillars on which there are Gothic paintings. Its Baroque organ is used for short recitals every Saturday afternoon. Across the street are two patricians' houses, **Behnhaus** and **Dragerhaus**, which are now a museum. The former has some excellent paintings and the latter impressive interiors with 19th-century furnishings. The façade of **Kath-arinenkirche**, *Konigstr./Glockengiesser Str.*, a block south, is adorned with life-size statues.

To the south of *Altstadt*, **St-Annen-Museum** has a first-rate collection from the 13th to the 18th century, including a magnificent Memling triptych of *The Passion*, and a statue-adorned courtyard. Nearby is the large brick-built **Dom**, which contains an allegorical triumphal arch and ornate rood screen.

- -
◣ Side Track from Lübeck

Fifteen minutes by train (or boat in summer), **Ratzeburg** is a charming old town, picturesquely located on a lake. It has a 12th-century **Dom** with a three-naved basilica and lovely 15th-century retable. The **Ernst-Barlach Museum** is devoted to a multi-talented 20th-century artist whose bronzes and wood-carvings are particularly fine.

- -

ROSKILDE

Station: *tel: (42) 35 09 00*. Everything of interest is in the centre: about 3.5 km (downhill). **Tourist Office**: *Fondens Bro 3; tel: (42) 35 27 00*. Mon–Fri 0900–1700 and Sat 0900–1300.

Accommodation

IYHF, *Horgaarden, Horhusene 61; tel: (42) 35 21 84*. Bus nos. 601/604 drop you 1.5 km away. From April to September **camping** is possible by the beach at **Vigen Strandpark**, *Baunehojvej 7–9; tel: (46) 75 79 96* (bus no. 602). In early July there's a major open-air rock festival with a special campsite and a shuttle bus from the station.

Sightseeing

Known as the 'Town of Viking Ships and Royal Tombs', Roskilde was Denmark's first capital and its history goes back to the 10th century. By the 12th century, however, the limitations of the harbour had become obvious and the focus of shipping shifted to Copenhagen. The drop in the town's importance meant it was ignored by invaders and much of the old city is intact.

The twin-towered **Cathedral**, *Domkirke-plasden*, dominates the skyline. This brick edifice (circa 1170–1280) replaced a 10th-century limestone one that was Denmark's first Christian church. It is the traditional burial place of Danish royalty and also contains a 500-year-old clock featuring St George and the dragon (whose dying scream marks each hour).

In the **Viking Ship Museum**, *Strandengen*, are five 11th-century vessels that were deliberately scuttled to block the harbour entrance and protect the town from enemy fleets. The ships (of different types) were brought back to the surface in 1962 and are being painstakingly restored.

On Wednesday and Saturday mornings there's a wide-ranging flea market in **Staendertorvet**, the town square.

AMSTERDAM
to
FRANKFURT

This route, between the Netherlands and central Germany, provides an enormous contrast between the industrial Ruhr cities and the wonders of nature in De Hoge Veluwe National Park and the spectacular Rhine Gorge.

TRAINS

ETT tables: 28, 240, 650.

→ Fast Track

No direct trains run between Amsterdam (Centraal) and Frankfurt am Main, but if you change at Cologne there are seven good connections a day changing at Duisburg or Cologne. The total journey takes about 5 hours, but all the fast trains are EC/IC, so a supplement is payable. All have a refreshment service.

∿ On Track

Amsterdam–Utrecht–Arnhem

Frequent trains operate throughout the day and your wait should not exceed half an hour. The total journey takes just under an hour and Utrecht is roughly half-way.

Arnhem–(Border)–Duisburg

There are nine EC trains every day, the journey taking just over an hour. The border is at Emmerich but formalities are minimal and you don't need to leave the train.

Duisburg is a steel town where you change trains to reach Essen and/or Düsseldorf. If you don't want to visit either, just stay on board for another 35 mins or so for Cologne (Köln).

The Brussels–Frankfurt route (pp. 136–140) intersects with this route in Cologne.

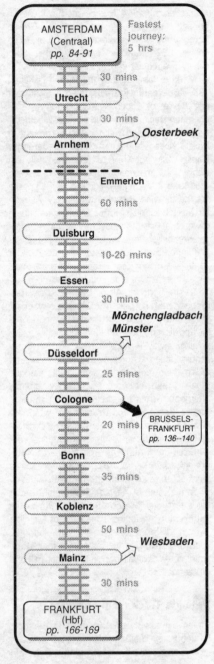

AMSTERDAM (Centraal) pp. 84-91

Fastest journey: 5 hrs

30 mins

Utrecht

30 mins

Arnhem → *Oosterbeek*

Emmerich

60 mins

Duisburg

10-20 mins

Essen

30 mins

Mönchengladbach Münster

Düsseldorf

25 mins

Cologne → BRUSSELS-FRANKFURT pp. 136--140

20 mins

Bonn

35 mins

Koblenz

50 mins → *Wiesbaden*

Mainz

30 mins

FRANKFURT (Hbf) pp. 166-169

Duisburg–Essen

Services are very frequent, and include local S-Bahn trains. The journey takes 10–15 mins.

Essen–Düsseldorf–Cologne–Bonn–Koblenz

Trains operate every 30 mins or so. The journey takes about 30 mins Essen–Düsseldorf; 25 mins Düsseldorf–Cologne; 20 mins Cologne–Bonn; and 35 mins Bonn–Koblenz.

Koblenz–(The Rhine Gorge)–Mainz

Trains operate every 30 mins from early morning to early evening, plus one or two later. The journey takes about 50 mins on express trains, nearly twice as long on local services. With views of the Gorge nearly all the way, however, few people want to rush the journey. Try to get a window seat on the same side as the river.

Mainz–Frankfurt am Main (Hbf)

Fast trains are hourly, taking some 30 mins to central Frankfurt (15 mins to the airport). There are also frequent but slower S-Bahn trains.

UTRECHT

Stations: Centraal Station and the bus station are together, separated from the old quarter by the unappealing Hoog Catharijne business and shopping area. The information booth in the train station distributes free maps. When it's closed, buy one from a slot machine.
Tourist Office: *Vredenburg 90; tel: (06) 34 03 40 85.* 5-mins walk from Centraal.

Accommodation

Chains include *HI* and *SC*. There are no cheap hotels, but VVV can often get a discount. **IYHF**: *Rhijnauwenselaan 14; tel: (03405) 61277,* (Bunnik, 3 km from Centraal.) **Campsite:** *Arienslaan 5; tel: (030) 713 870 (bus no. 57: Veemarkt).*

Sightseeing

Utrecht was a medieval religious centre, although many churches were destroyed by a 17th-century hurricane. **Domkerk**, *Domplein*, is a late-Gothic cathedral with fine stained-glass windows and a 112m tower, **Domtoren**, which gives a marvellous view – if you can face the 450-plus steps. The 14th-century choir and 15th-century cloister survived the hurricane.

The **Rijksmuseum het Catherijneconvent**, *Nieuwe Gracht 63*, contains medieval religious paintings and sculptures. Further south, the **Centraal Museum**, *Agnietenstraat 1*, has an amazing diversity of exhibits, including period rooms and costumes, a fully-furnished 17th-century doll's house and a 9th-century Viking ship. The **Rietveld Schroder House**, *Prins Hendrikiaan 50*, was designed in 1924 and exemplifies what was known simply as *De Stijl* (The Style) – an innovative use of space and primary colours.

Spoorweg Museum, *Oldenbarneveltlaan 6*, housed in a disused 19th-century station, is a must for train buffs, while the **Museum van Speelklok tot Pierement**, *Buurkerkhof 10*, is an enchanting museum of mechanical musical instruments, from music boxes to barrel organs. If you want to hear some of them being played, join a tour.

At the **Oudaen Brewery**, you swig your beer in a genuine steam brewery located in the cellar of a medieval canal-side mansion.

ARNHEM

Stations: Train and bus stations are together on the edge of the centre, next to the tourist office. **Tourist Office:** *Stationsplein 45; tel: (085) 420 330.*

Accommodation

Try **Pension Warnsborn**, *Schelmseweg 1; tel: (085) 425 994.* **IYHF**: *Diepenbrocklaan 27; tel: (085) 420 114,* 5 km north of the station (bus no. 3: Alteveer). Nearest **campsites** are: *Bakenbergseweg 257* (north-west of the centre, bus no. 11) and *Kemperbergerweg 771; tel: (085) 431 600* (bus no. 11 towards *Schaarsbergen*).

Sightseeing

Arnhem has an outdoor museum, an indoor zoo and an annual jazz festival (in June), but the main attraction is 6 km north of the town: the superb **De Hoge Veluwe National Park**.

De Hoge Veluwe National Park

An art-loving heiress named Helene Muller married nature-loving Anton Kroller and the pair established this delightful 13,000-acre estate, which encompasses dunes, fens, moorlands, forests (coniferous and deciduous), a museum and a sculpture park, as well as lots of cafés and children's playgrounds. Among the animals that wander freely in the park are deer, boars, moufflons (wild sheep) and even a few kangaroos.

In the **Kroller-Muller Museum's** modern art collection (one of the best in Europe) are paintings by Van Gogh (276 of them!), Braque, Picasso, Seurat, Mondriaan and Renoir (among others), while the **Sculpture Park** includes works by Rodin, Epstein, Moore and Hepworth.

There's a visitors' centre at the *Hoenderloo Gate; tel: (08382) 1627.* The two other entrances are near Otterlo and at Rijzenburg. There's a regular bus from Arnhem station to Otterlo (4 km from the visitors' centre). From late June to early August, an hourly excursion bus makes several stops within the park.

Once there, buy a map and (unless you're a very keen walker) borrow a bicycle (free) or hire a horse: there's a lot of ground to cover.

The **Burghers' Bush and Desert Zoo** is basically a vast greenhouse enclosing an indoor safari park, desert and tropical rain-forest, with about 70 different animals from around the world and over 1,600 species of plants.

Nederlands Openlucht consists of over 100 reconstructed buildings (with appropriate interiors). These have been transported from all over the country and are grouped to give a picture of Dutch rural life spanning two centuries.

Side Track from Arnhem

At **Oosterbeek** (a 5-min train journey) are a beautifully maintained war cemetery and an **Airborne Museum** with an audio-visual programme (English commentary) about the September 1944 débâcle known as 'Operation Market Garden' and depicted in the film *A Bridge Too Far.*

ESSEN

Station: Hbf, *tel: (0201) 19419*; central, two blocks from Münster.
Tourist Office: *tel: (0201) 23 54 27.* Mon–Fri 0900–1800 and Sat 1000–1230. Inside Hbf look for the *Freiheit* sign.

Sightseeing

The 9th-century **Münster** contains a superb 10th-century gold Madonna, a seven-branched candelabrum (c. AD 1000) and a **Treasury (Schatzkammer)** full of priceless items. Nearby, the small **Johanniskirche** has an interesting double-sided retable. The **Alte Synagogue** is a monument to Jews who perished at the hands of the Nazis.

The mansion of the infamous Alfred Krupp, **Villa Hugel**, to the south of town, is now on view. Further south, the **Folkwang Museum** has a superb collection of 19th- and 20th-century art. In the same building is the **Ruhrland Museum**.

DÜSSELDORF

Station: Hbf, *tel: (0211) 19419*: about 2 km from the east bank of the Rhine, where most things of interest are concentrated.
Main Tourist Office: *Immermannstr. 65B; tel: (0211) 35 05 05* (opposite Hbf). Mon–Sat 0800–2200 and Sun 1600–2200.

Accommodation

It's worth consulting the hotel booking office in Hbf (Mon–Sat 0800–2200 and Sun 1600–2200). Chains include *BW, Hl, Hn, Ic, Ra, SA.* **IYHF:** *Düsseldorferstr.1; tel: (0211) 57 40 41,* in the *Oberkassel* district, just over *Rheinkniebrücke* (bus no. 835). **Campsite:** *Niederkasseler Deich 305; tel: (0211) 59 14 01* (U: Belsenplatz, then bus no. 828 to *Strandbad Lorick*).

Sightseeing

The area of interest is small and walkable. Düsseldorf thrives on commerce and is dominated by three modern monuments to Mammon: the **Thyssen Skyscraper**, **Mannemann Haus** and the **TV Tower**. There's little of historical interest, but the museums are worth visiting and the nightlife is excellent.

Königsallee ('Die Kö') is an almost mandatory place for a stroll, with upmarket shops beside a tree-lined canal. **Altstadt**, marked by **Schlossturm**, the remains of the original castle, is more fun – a pedestrian zone that's a hive of entertainment around the clock.

St Lambertus, beside the river, is noted for its lopsided spire. It contains a Gothic tabernacle and a 15th-century Pieta. In *Grabbeplatz* are the **Kunstsammlung Nordrhein-Westfalen**, a wide-ranging museum of modern art with nearly 100 works by Paul Klee, and **Kunsthalle**, which hosts constantly changing exhibitions. On *Ehrenhof* are the **Kunstmuseum** (an eclectic collection, including Rubens' *Assumption* and a superb glass section), the **Kunstpalast** (contemporary art) and the **Landesmuseum** (all about economics). The **Hetjens Museum**, *Schulstr.*, concentrates exclusively on ceramics. There are also museums devoted to Heine and Goethe.

- - - - - - - - - - - - - - - - - - -

◢ Side Track from Düsseldorf

Düsseldorf's S-bahn is part of an integrated system linking the major Ruhr cities and **Mönchengladbach** is only 20 mins away. It has a **IYHF** which is an alternative if the one in Düsseldorf is full. The 13th-century Roman-esque-Gothic **Münster** has a superb central window. If you have a taste for the avant-garde in art, don't miss the **Museum Abteiberg**.

- - - - - - - - - - - - - - - - - - -

COLOGNE (KÖLN)

For description see pp. 139–140.

BONN

Station: Hbf, *tel: (0228) 19419*, beside the bus terminal and right in the centre, on the edge of the pedestrian precinct.
Tourist Office: *Münsterstr.20; tel: (0228) 77 34 66.* Mon–Sat 0800–2100; Sun 0930–1230. *Bonn from A to Z* has a good map and listings in English.

Consulates

Most embassies are in Berlin, but most countries (not the UK) also have consulates in Bonn.
Australia: *Godesburger Allee 107; tel: (0228) 81030.*
Canada: *Godesburger Allee 119; tel: (0228) 81 00 60.*
New Zealand: *Bundeskanzlerplatz; tel: (0228) 228 0725.*
USA: *Deichman Ave 29; tel: (0228) 339 2053.*

Accommodation

There's a choice of reasonable accommodation in Bad Godesburg, which is also where the best **IYHF** is situated: *Horionstr.60; tel: (0228) 31 75 16* (U 16/23: *Rheinallee*). The **campsite** is in the suburb of Mehlem, south of Bad Godesburg: *Im Frankenkeller 49; tel: (0228) 34 49 49* (U 16/23: *Rheinallee*, then bus no. 613).

Getting Around

The areas of interest are quite widespread, so it's worth investing in a travel pass. There are several, some covering Cologne as well as Bonn (the transport systems are integrated), so ask the tourist office for guidance.

Sightseeing

Bonn mushroomed when it became the post-war capital of West Germany and it is less a city than a series of linked, suburban villages.

In **Altstadt** there are some pedestrianised streets lined with gabled 17th- and 18th-century houses. *Markt* has a much-photographed pink Rococo **Rathaus**, while *Münsterplatz* is dominated by the 12th-century **Münster**, with an interior that features gold-leafed mosaics. **Beethovens Geburtshaus**, *Bonngasse 20*, is a well-arranged museum devoted to the Bonn-born composer.

On the other side of Hbf is the **Landesmuseum**, *Colmantstr.14--16*, which exhibits a skull discovered in 1856 near a village by Düsseldorf. It is around 60,000 years old and a whole class of mankind has been named after the village: Neanderthal.

Heading south, the chestnut-lined *Poppelsdorfer Allee* leads to **Schloss Poppelsdorf**, now part of the university, and the **Botanical Gardens**. A few blocks west is **Robert-Schumann Haus**, *Sebastianstr.182*, devoted to the composer. To the south is **Kreuzberg**, a 17th-century chapel with rich 18th-century embellishments.

Bad Godesburg (across the Rhine, U no. 16) is dominated by **Godesburg**, the most northerly of the Rhine castles. The old keep is intact and provides panoramic views. This suburb is where most of the diplomats reside; interesting if you like seeing how the other half live.

Another east bank village worth visiting is **Schwarzrheindorf** (bus nos. 540/550), home of **Doppelkirche**, a 12th-century church that is actually two separate chapels; one for the nobility and the other for lesser folk.

KOBLENZ

Station: Hbf, *Bahnhofplatz 2; tel: (0261) 19419.* South-west of the centre, 25-mins walk downhill (or bus no. 1) to the riverside area from which cruises **(Rheinfähre)** depart.
Tourist Offices: Opposite Hbf; *tel: (0261) 33134.* Mon–Fri 0830–1300 and 1415–1700. They provide boat schedules and a city map that includes listings. **Branch** by docks, *Konrad-Adenauer-Ufer.* Open only June–Sept, Tue–Sat 1200–1825.

For **regional** information: **Rheinland-Pfalz**, *Lohrstr. 103; tel: (0261) 31079.* Open Mon–Fri 0800–1600.

Accommodation

There are some reasonable hotels around Hbf and in *Ehrenbreitstein*. The **IYHF** is housed in the Festung (*tel: (0261) 73737*) and is popular, so book well ahead. The down-side is that the ferry and chair-lift both stop very early so, after taking a bus (nos. 7/8/9/10) to *Charlottenstr.*, you end the day with a long uphill climb. The **campsite** is at *Lützel*, across the Moselle. There's a ferry

The Rhine Gorge

The Rhine runs from the Alps through Switzerland, Germany and Holland, into the North Sea. The most spectacular stretch is between Koblenz and Mainz, an area of wooded hills, picturesque wine-producing villages and towering castles: some in ruins, others restored. Even today's modern vessels have to negotiate some stretches of the Rhine Gorge with care: there are watch-towers which use radios to steer them through when the water level (which fluctuates unexpectedly) is particularly low. It's not surprising that the Gorge gave birth to the legend of the Lorelei: a beautiful maiden whose singing lured sailors onto the rocks.

The train gives an excellent view (including the Lorelei if you are on the opposite side of the Rhine), but it's more fun (though not cheap) to travel by boat. The area is very touristy in summer, so spring and autumn are more pleasant (most things are closed in winter).

The most comprehensive selection of cruises (with trilingual commentary) is offered by **KD (Köln-Düsseldorfer) Line**, who accept Eurail and German Rail Passes, but not Inter-Rail. Head office is in Cologne, but they also have offices in Koblenz (*tel: (0261) 31030*) and England: **KD German Rhine Line**, *28 South Street, Epsom Surrey, KT18 7PF; tel: (03727) 42033.*

If you can't afford a full cruise, consider a short one. Boppard and Bingen, for example, are both interesting villages at which the trains stop and you could cruise between them, admiring several castles from afar, for (currently) DM28.

across during the day. *Campingplatz Rhein-Mosel; tel: (0261) 82719.*

Sightseeing

Koblenz is at the Rhine/Moselle confluence and **Deutches Eck**, the focal point of the town, is the tip of a peninsula between them. The pleasant gardens along both rivers combine to provide an attractive five-mile stroll. Another good walking area is the pedestrianised **Altstadt**, with a variety of restored buildings – several housing museums or wine cellars.

Koblenz began life under the Romans and some of their remains can be seen in the vaults beneath **Florianskirche** (c. AD 1100), which was re-modelled in Gothic style in the 14th century and further embellished in the 17th century. **Liebfrauenkirche** is a beautiful edifice which incorporates elements of several styles with some fine stained glass in a really elegant fashion, while **St Kastorkirche** contains some rare altar tombs and Gothic murals.

Ehrenbreitstein (across the Rhine, ferries in summer) is dominated by an enormous fortress, the **Festung**, which began life in the 10th century. A cable-car (**Sesselbahn**) operates May–Oct. As well as providing a fantastic view, Festung contains two regional museums, albeit not particularly interesting ones A big firework display (**Rhein in Flammen**) is staged here on the second Saturday in August.

MAINZ

Station: Hbf, *tel: (06131) 19419*, north-west of the centre.
Tourist Office: *Bahnhofstr. 15; tel: (06131) 28 62 10*. Mon–Fri 0900–1800, Sat 0900–1300.
Ferries: KD Line cruises leave from the docks opposite Rathaus.

Accommodation

There are relatively few hotels and advance booking is sensible. **IYHF**, *Otto-Brunfels-Schneise 4; tel: (06131) 85332*: in *Volkspark, Weisenau* (bus no. 1). **Camping Maaraue** (*tel: (06134) 43 83*) is across the river, by Theodor-Heuss bridge (bus no. 13: *Brückenkopf-Kastel*).

Sightseeing

Distances between the places of interest are not great. Streets leading down to the Rhine have red name-plates and the streets running across them have blue name-plates.

It was in Mainz, in the 1450s, that Gutenberg established the first printing-press with moveable type: a system that changed little until this century. The **Gutenberg Museum**, *Liebfrauenplatz*, is a fascinating place containing a replica of the original press and one of the few surviving vellum bibles.

Altstadt is a largely pedestrian zone around *Augustinerstr*. This street is touristy but others are charming, such as the cobbled *Kirschgarten*, with its restored half-timbered houses. **Marktbrunnen**, *Markt*, is the country's oldest Renaissance fountain and is still surrounded by market stalls every Tuesday, Friday and Saturday morning.

Martinsdom escaped serious bomb damage and is one of the most impressive cathedrals in Germany, a massive structure of red sandstone with six towers, surrounded by 18th-century houses. Inside are elaborate archbishops' tombs spanning six centuries and 9th-century murals of New Testament scenes. The adjacent museum houses some superb old sculptures.

St Ignaz, *Gutenbergplatz*, is a rich mixture of Rococo and neo-Classicism, with painted cupolas and a splendid interior. In front of it is the tomb of Hans Backoffen, who designed many of the sarcophagi in the Dom as well as the 16th-century *Crucifixion* that marks his own tomb.

The Gothic **Stefanskirche** (to the east) has a set of deep blue stained-glass windows that were designed by Chagall to symbolise the post-war reconciliation.

North of *Altstadt* is **Landesmuseum**, *Grosse Bleiche 49–51*, which has a room of Roman remains, much better than the displays in the **Römisch-Germanisches Museum**, *Rheinstr.*, once the episcopal palace of the powerful Electors of Mainz.

Side Track from Mainz

Wiesbaden first became a fashionable resort in the 19th century, when the gentry developed a taste for spas. Today it has 26 thermal springs (and a casino). You can have a full therapeutic treatment at the baths, or simply taste the waters in the **Kochbrunnen** fountain. There are frequent trains from Mainz, the journey taking about 10 mins.

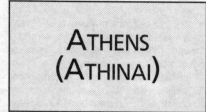

ATHENS
(ATHINAI)

Athens, the birthplace of Western philosophy, democracy, theatre and medicine, has had an indelible effect on the course of Western civilization. Athens was at its height in the 5th century BC, under Pericles, when the city was supreme amongst the Greek city-states. The playwrights Aeschylus, Sophocles and Euripides, historians such as Thucydides, and the founder of Western medical science, Hippocrates, lived and worked here. Later the Athenian philosophers Socrates, Plato and Aristotle were all to have a profound influence on Western thought.

The halcyon days of such an influential city were remarkably short-lived. As power in Greece shifted north to Macedonia and Alexander the Great, Athens steadily declined and by the 2nd century AD the city had become no more than a minor outpost of the Roman Empire. Athens was virtually to vanish from the stage of European history until 1834, when it became capital of the new Kingdom of Greece on the withdrawal of the Turks.

The growth of the city since then has been rapid but undistinguished, producing a capital of uniform concrete suburbs set around the ruins of its glorious past. Modern Athens is noisy and bustling, but many of its 4 million inhabitants live a laid-back, village-style life and the remnants of the ancient city are still compelling.

Tourist Information

The **Greek National Tourist Organization (EOT)** maintains two information kiosks just off *Syntagma Square*: one in the **National Bank of Greece**, *2 Karageorgi Servias St; tel: 322 2545* or *323 4130*, Mon–Fri 0800–1400 and 1530–2000; Sat 0900–1400; the other in the **General Bank**, *1 Ermou St; tel: 325 2267* or *325 2268*, Mon–Fri 0800–1800; Sat 0900–

1300. Both offices do little more than distribute leaflets, but their literature is helpful if you ask for specific information. Their individual fact sheets are more informative than their general brochures. They have details of local and regional transport schedules and up-to-date opening times of sights.

There are also EOT offices in the **East Terminal** of the airport, *tel: 961 2722* and in **Piraeus Zea Marina**, *tel: 413 5730*.

The tourist police in Athens (*tel: 171*) can help with accommodation or information. Their head office is *7 Singrou Ave; tel: 923 9224*.

Arriving and Departing

Airports

Hellinikon airport is 15 km from Athens. International airlines serve the East Terminal; *tel: 96 991*. Bus no. 91 runs between the terminal and *Syntagma Square (Platia Syntagma)* every 30 mins during the day and every hour during the night. Olympic Airways flights, both domestic and international, use the West Terminal; *tel: 926 9111*. Bus no. 90 runs to *Syntagma Square*, also at 30 mins intervals.

Stations

Trains from Thessaloniki, Northern Greece, Bulgaria and Europe use **Larissis Station (Stathmos Larisis)**, *Theodorou Diligiani; tel: 524 0646* or *524 0601*. Trains from Patras and the Peloponnese use the **Peloponnese Station (Stathmos Peloponisou)**; *tel: 513 1601*. Greece's railway system is skeletal and this is reflected in the stations at Athens, both of which are small and unimpressive.

The two stations are only 200 yards apart: the Peloponnese being behind Larissis over the metal footbridge. They are about 2 km northwest of *Syntagma Square* (tram no. 1). The nearest metro stop is currently *Victoria*, about 500m to the east.

International rail tickets can be bought at Larissis station or at the OSE offices in Athens: *1 Karolou St; tel: 522 2491, 6 Sina St; tel: 362 4402*; and *17 Filellinon St ; tel: 522 4302*. For domestic railway timetable information, *tel: 145*; for international services, *tel: 147*.

Ferries

The **Piraeus Port Authority** handles services to the Greek islands, *tel: 451 1311* or *453 7107*. The port itself, 8 km south-west of Athens, is served by train and metro.

Getting Around

The free map of Athens available from the tourist office is excellent. It indicates trolley-bus routes and metro stations and gives details of bus services. Central Athens, from *Syntagma Square* through the *Plaka* to the Acropolis, is walkable. Athens' streets are noisy and busy, but not unbearable – except in a heatwave.

The Metro (Subway)

There is currently only one metro line in Athens, which runs from Piraeus north to the centre of town, where there are stations at *Monastiraki* (for the Acropolis and the Plaka), *Omonia Square* (for the Archaeological Museum) and *Victoria Square* (for the main-line stations). The metro continues north to *Kifissia*.

Tickets are available from station kiosks or self-service machines; validate them in the machines at station entrances.

Construction is under way on another metro line, with stations at *Syntagma Square* and Larissis mainline station. The building work is quite intrusive, although it has thrown up interesting archaeological finds, such as two Roman wells at *Syntagma Square*.

Trolley-buses and Buses

Buy tickets for buses or trolley-buses from blue booths near bus stops or from kiosks throughout Athens. Validate tickets on board. The network is far more comprehensive than the metro; the tourist office map gives clear details. Most routes pass through either *Syntagma Square* or *Omonia Square*.

Taxis

Taxis in Athens are easy to find, except during the rush hour, around lunch-time and early afternoon. Flag down a taxi, state your destination to the driver and, if his existing passengers are going the same way, he will let you in.

Living in Athens

Accommodation

The **Hellenic Chamber of Hotels** provides a booking service for hotels in Athens. They can be contacted before arrival at *24 Stadiou St, Athens; tel: 323 6962*, or after arrival in Athens at *2 Karageorgi Servias St, Syntagma Square; tel: 323 7193*, next door to the tourist office in the National Bank.

Hotel groups represented in Athens include *Ch, Hn, Ic, Ma* and *Nv*. The tourist office itself has a standard list of class A–C hotels. Ask for details of class D and E hotels if you are looking for cheaper options. Athens has a flourishing collection of private hostels catering to budget travellers. Many hostels send out people to distribute leaflets and solicit customers on the trains arriving in Athens from Patras.

Hostels cluster in the *Plaka* area, which is noisy but ideally located for the main sights, or in the area between *Victoria Square* and the stations. Except during the height of summer you should have plenty of options. The **IYHF**, *57 Kypselis St; tel: 822 5860*, 2 km north of *Syntagma Square* (trolley nos. 2/4/9), is further out than most of the private hostels. **Camping** is allowed only at the official sites, all of which are some way from the centre: the tourist office has details.

Communications

The main **post office** is at *100 Eolou St; tel: 321 6063*, Mon–Sat 0730–2030. One branch is in *Syntagma Square; tel: 323 7573*, Mon–Sat 0730–2030 and Sun 0730–1330.

The Greek Telecommunications Organization (OTE) has an office open 24 hrs at *85 Patisson St*. The office at *15 Stadiou St; tel: 322 1002*, is open Mon–Fri 0700–2400 and Sat–Sun 0800–2400. International calls can be made at both offices. You can make local calls from public coin boxes. The dialling code for Athens is (301).

Eating and Drinking

Many restaurants in the centre of town are oriented towards tourists, but eating in Athens is still an enjoyable and satisfying experience. Head to the *Plaka*, between the Acropolis and

Syntagma Square, where countless restaurants put out tables. The atmosphere is hard to beat and prices, although slightly inflated, are still reasonable. *Syntagma Square* is the place for Western fast-food chains and over-priced cafés. Away from the centre, restaurants become less touristy.

Embassies

Australia: *37 D Soutsou St; tel: 644 7303.*
Canada: *1 Ioannou Genedou St; tel: 723 9511.*
New Zealand: No embassy in Athens, but the British Embassy should be able to help in case of emergency.
UK: *1 Ploutarchou St; tel: 723 6211.*
USA: *91 Vassilissis Sofias Ave; tel: 721 2951.*

Entertainment

The English-language daily *Athens News* has listings of entertainments where language will not be a problem.

The cheapest, and possibly the most entertaining, evening pastime in Athens is strolling through the *Plaka* amidst the crowds of other promenaders and diners.

The **Athens Festival** (June–Sept) provides more formal entertainment. Events staged in the **Odeon of Herodes Atticus** include ancient Greek theatre – Aristophanes, Sophocles and so on – plus classical music and ballet, performed by Greek and international companies and orchestras. For information, *tel: 322 1459.* There are plenty of lighter tourist offerings in the summer, including the **Sound and Light** show on *Pnyx Hill; tel: 322 1459* and **Folk Dances** in *Philopappus Theatre; tel: 324 4395.*

Shopping

The **flea market** around *Monastiraki Square* is a lively collection of street stalls selling variable and occasionally dubious merchandise. Many stalls seem to be staffed by Western travellers.

Sightseeing

The Acropolis

To many, the **Acropolis** symbolises Greece. The 'high city' served as Athens' stronghold until it was converted into a religious shrine in the 13th century BC.

Pericles built the **Parthenon** (Home of the Virgin), between 447 and 432 BC. Designed by Iktinus and Phidias, it is the finest example of Doric architecture still in existence. Close examination of the temple reveals irregularities: columns are closer together at the corners, where light can shine between them; columns are of differing widths and bulge one third of the way up; the roof line is curved. The combined effect is one of the finest optical illusions ever devised, giving the impression from afar of perfect symmetry. Today, the temple maintains its grandeur, despite the intrusions of scaffolding and cranes as part of a long-term EU-funded restoration project. Most of the dramatic friezes that adorned the Parthenon's exterior, the controversial Elgin Marbles, are in the British Museum, although the Acropolis Museum has some fragments.

The **Erechtheum**, to the north-west of the Parthenon, is most notable for its six *caryatids* – graceful sculptures of women. Due to the detrimental effects of air pollution, the originals have been removed and replaced by the replicas on display today. Four of the originals are on display in the Acropolis Museum.

The delicate **Temple of Athena Nike** (Victory), with its eight small columns, stands perched on the south-west corner of the Acropolis. Built around 420 BC, during a pause in the Peloponnesian War, the temple was once the only place from where you could look out to the sea over the defensive walls; it is considered one of the finest Ionic buildings left in Greece.

The bulky **Propylaea**, the great gateway to the Acropolis, takes up most of the western end of the hill and today welcomes thousands of visitors. Arrive early if you want any peace or uninterrupted photo opportunities.

The **Acropolis Museum**, to the east of the Parthenon, contains some interesting material, in spite of Lord Elgin's plundering in 1816.

Beyond the Acropolis

From the Acropolis you obtain extensive panoramic views of Athens and beyond. Most of the city suburbs are anonymous concrete swathes, distinguished only by dark green

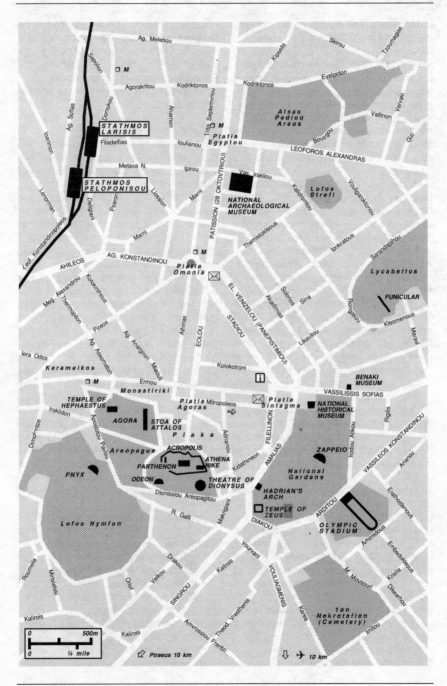

City Centre Map

awnings, but in areas close to the Acropolis you can pick out many other ancient ruins. Just below the Acropolis hill, on the south side, are two ancient theatres. The **Theatre of Dionysus**, built in the 4th century BC, was the oldest in Greece and thus can lay claim to being the first in the Western world. Only bare ruins remain, although the plan of the theatre can be identified easily, especially from above. The Roman **Odeon of Herodes Atticus** has been reconstructed and is, once again, in use as a theatre.

The remains of the **Temple of Olympian Zeus** are also clearly visible, east of the Acropolis. There are only a few surviving columns but it is still possible to absorb the grandeur of what was the largest temple in Greece. Next to it is **Hadrian's Arch**, constructed by the enthusiastic Roman builder-emperor to mark where the ancient Greek city ended and his new city began. Across *Vassilissis Olgas Avenue*, to the north, are the **National Gardens**, which stretch up to *Syntagma Square* and offer a break from Athens' infamous traffic. The **Olympic Stadium**, across *Vassileos Konstandinou Ave* from the National Gardens, stands on the site of an ancient Athenian version and was host to the first modern Olympics in 1896.

To the north-west of the Acropolis lie the extensive ruins of the **Agora**, the central focus for much of Athens' commercial and intellectual life. Here the ideas of democracy were discussed and developed by the great thinkers of the time. In the Agora is one of the best-preserved ancient Greek buildings, the immaculate **Temple of Hephaestus** or **Thesseion**, built in 440 BC and decorated with elaborate friezes. The **Stoa of Attalos**, built by King Attalos II in the 2nd century BC, has now been restored as a museum displaying objects found during excavations of the Agora. There are entrances from *Adrianou St*, *Thissio Square*, just off *Monastiraki Square* and the path on the north side of the Acropolis. The **Areopagus**, below the entrance of the Acropolis, was the open-air meeting place for the Athenian supreme court.

Across the rail lines from the Agora is **Kerameikos Cemetery**, the burial place for influential Athenians of ancient times. The **Kerameikos Museum**, *148 Ermou St*, contains discoveries from the cemetery. Round to the west of the Acropolis is **Pnyx Hill**. Here the *Ecclesia tou Demou*, or public assembly, of the Athenian State met and enacted the Athenian form of democracy.

Museums and Churches

For a comprehensive and incomparable collection of relics from Athens and many other Greek sites, head to the **National Archaeological Museum**, *44 Patision St; tel: 821 7717*. The line-up of exhibits is both exhaustive and exhausting: allow yourself a full day to do the museum justice. Exhibits range through Minoan frescoes, Mycenaean gold, a selection from a phenomenal collection of over 300,000 coins, sculptures, *kouroi* and much more.

Although the National Archaeological is undoubtedly the finest in Greece, there are plenty of other museums offering their own insights into Greek life, both modern and ancient. The **Museum of Cycladic and Ancient Greek Art**, *4 Neofitou Douka St*, concentrates on the simple yet influential art forms from the Cyclades Islands. The **National Gallery and Alexander Soutzos Museum**, *Vassileos Konstantinou Ave*, has a more general and conventional collection of Greek art. The diverse, entertaining collection in the **Benaki Museum**, *Koumpari St and Vassilissis Sofias Ave*, includes everything from ancient Greek relics through to mementoes from the War of Independence. The **Byzantine Museum**, *Varsidissis Sofia 22*, houses icons from this later glory of Greek culture.

Several churches survive in Athens from the 10th–13th century. These include **Agia Kaphikareas**, *Ermou St*, **Agios Eleftherios** (or **Panagia Gorgoepikoos**), near *Mitopoleos Square*, and **Agia Apostolli**, near the *Agora*. The **Byzantine Museum**, *22 Vassilissis Sofias Ave*, shows elements of the Byzantine influence from the 4th century onwards.

From **Lycabettus Hill**, the highest in Athens at 278m, the view surpasses even that from the Acropolis. Take the funicular railway up and the path down for the best round-trip.

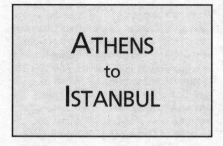

ATHENS
to
ISTANBUL

This route links Greece and Turkey. Between Athens and Thessaloniki the route passes close to Delphi, site of the Oracle of Apollo, and Mt Olympus, mythical home to the Gods. East from Thessaloniki the line runs parallel to the Bulgarian border, through remote and rugged territory, before crossing into Turkey.

TRAINS

ETT tables: 965, 970, 971, 974, 975

 Fast Track

There are no through trains between Athens and Istanbul, the most direct route involving a change in Thessaloniki.

There are nine trains between Athens (Larissis) and Thessaloniki. Six are by day, with a refreshment service. Reservations are required and supplements payable. Most overnight trains have couchettes and sleeping-cars, but no refreshment service. The journey time is 6–8 hrs.

There is only one train a day between Thessaloniki and Istanbul and it carries no sleepers, only seating (second class in through carriages), even though the journey takes about 17 hrs – an average speed of 50 kph. There are refreshments only on the Greek section (between Thessaloniki and Pithion). The border crossing is fairly time-consuming. You have to leave the train and the formalities are slow. Flags painted on the bridge over the River Evros mark the frontier.

It is theoretically possible to do the Athens–Istanbul journey with only one overnight leg, as the daytime express trains between Athens and Thessaloniki should connect with the Istanbul trains. However, delays often occur and it is

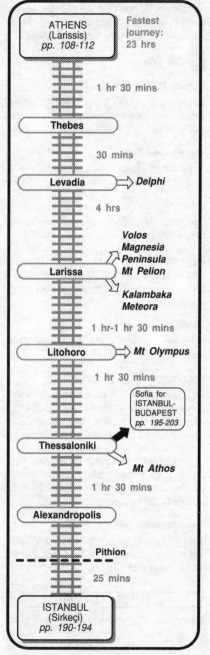

ATHENS (Larissis) pp. 108-112   Fastest journey: 23 hrs

1 hr 30 mins

Thebes

30 mins

Levadia ⇒ *Delphi*

4 hrs

Volos
Magnesia
Peninsula
Larissa   *Mt Pelion*

Kalambaka
Meteora

1 hr-1 hr 30 mins

Litohoro ⇒ *Mt Olympus*

1 hr 30 mins

Sofia for ISTANBUL-BUDAPEST pp. 195-203

Thessaloniki

Mt Athos

1 hr 30 mins

Alexandropolis

Pithion

25 mins

ISTANBUL (Sirkeçi) pp. 190-194

possible you will miss the connection and have to spend a night in Thessaloniki – or take an overnight train between there and Athens.

On Track

Athens–Thebes (Thivai)

There are eight trains a day between Athens and Thebes, but a couple of them are during the early morning hours. They take about 1 hr 30 mins.

Thebes–Levadia

All the Athens–Thebes trains also serve Levadia. Journey time, Thebes–Levadia is about 30 mins.

Levadia–Larissa

Five trains a day operate between Levadia and Larissa, the journey taking about 4 hrs.

Larissa–Litohoro

There are five trains daily, but one of them runs in the middle of the night. The journey takes 1 hr – 1 hr 30 mins.

Litohoro–Thessaloniki

There are five trains a day, the journey taking about 1 hr 30 mins.

Thessaloniki–Alexandropolis

There are five trains a day between Alexandropolis and Thessaloniki. Four are by day, all with a refreshment service. The Evros Express runs overnight, has a refreshment service and carries couchettes. The journey averages about 7 hrs.

There is one train a day between Thessaloniki and Sofia (in Bulgaria), where you can join the Istanbul–Budapest route (see pp. 195–203). The journey takes about 9 hrs.

Alexandropolis–(Border)–Istanbul

There is one train a day between Alexandropolis and Istanbul (as detailed for Fast Track) and the journey takes about 10 hrs.

THEBES (THIVAI)

Station: *tel: (0262) 27 531*, 1 km north of the centre.

Thebes is more interesting for its place in

Greek mythology than for its present offerings. Supposedly founded by the Phoenician king Kadmos, this was the city in which that Oedipus unwittingly married his mother (having killed his father on the way from Corinth). Another claim to fame (according to legend) is that Hercules was born here. Present sights include the **Archaeological Museum**, which contains relics from the area's Mycenean tombs, and the **Fountain of Oedipus (Agii Theodori)** spring.

LEVADIA

Station: *tel: (0261) 28 046*, 3 km from the centre, but taxis are available.
Tourist Police: *tel: (0261) 28 551.*

Levadia is a common stopping point for travellers en route to Delphi. The town fulfilled a similar role in ancient times. Those heading to the Oracle at Delphi could stop at Levadia's **Oracle of Zeus Trofonios** on top of Profiris Ilias, one of the two hills overlooking the town. The remains of a 14th-century **Castle** that was built over the site of the Oracle can still be seen.

Side Track from Levadia

There are regular buses (taking about an hour) between Levadia and **Delphi**, where there's a **Tourist Office:** *44 Pavlou St; tel: (0265) 82 900.* Mon–Sat 0800–2030 and Sun 1000–1500.

Delphi is synonymous with its **Oracle**, the greatest spiritual power in ancient Greece, said to be situated over the centre of the world. This belief was aided by leaking volcanic gases which induced lightheadedness and trance-like stupors. People came from far and wide to seek wisdom; questions were submitted to the Pythia (the priestess of Apollo) and her answers were interpreted by male prophets – so ambiguously that they could never be proved wrong. The most dramatic aspect of the **Temple of Apollo** (the Oracle), however, is its location, perched on the cliffs of Mt Parnassus and reached by the paved, zigzagging **Sacred Way**. Delphi is one of the largest remaining ancient sites in Greece, with a host of other ruins, notably a **Stadium** and an **Amphitheatre** The famous bronze of a *Charioteer* is among the many beautiful artefacts on display in the outstanding **Delphi Museum**.

Thousands of visitors make the modern pilgrimage to Delphi, so come early (or out of season). The plus-side is that there's plenty of cheap accommodation, including a good **IYHF**: *31 Appollonus St; tel: (0265) 82 268.*

LARISSA

Station: *tel: (041) 236 250*, 1 km from the centre.
Tourist Office: EOT, *18 Koumoundourou St; tel: (041) 250 919.* **Tourist Police:** *86 Papanastasiou St; tel: (041) 227 900 or 222 152.*

Archaeological finds date the presence of man in Larissa to around 10,000 BC. Now capital of Thessaly, Larissa is one of the few rail junction towns in Greece. The **Archaeological Museum** houses some ancient relics of the city. Legend has it that the legendary 'Father of Medicine' Hippocrates died here – not a great advertisement for the ancient town's health care.

Side Tracks from Larissa

Volos was an important town in the Mycenean age and is now the main base from which to explore the **Mt Pelion** region to the north-east and the **Magnesia Peninsula** to the south-east. The city itself, from where Jason set sail in the *Argo* in search of the Golden Fleece, has little to offer except a reasonable **Archaeological Museum**. There are fairly frequent trains from Larissa, taking about 1 hr. **Station**: *Papadiamandi St; tel: (0421) 23 712 or 25 759.* **EOT Office**: *Riga Fereou Square; (0421) tel: 36 233.* **Tourist Police**: *217 Alexandras St; tel: (0421) 27 094.*

The major tourist attraction in northern Greece, **Meteora**, is reached by bus from **Kalambaka**, to which there are five trains a day from Larissa, with a change in Paleofarsalos. The full journey takes about 2 hrs 30 mins. Paleofarsalos is 'On Track' between Athens and Thessaloniki, if you want to visit Meteora without going to Larissa.

Kalambaka (meaning beautiful fortress) has an early 14th-century **Cathedral**, which contains some 13th–14th-century paintings and a lovely marble pulpit. **Roman remains** are still visible around the cathedral. **Tourist Police:** *10 Hatzipetrou St; tel: (0432) 22 813.*

The town stands at the foot of **Meteora**, 24 perpendicular rocks which soar to 600m. In the 11th century Byzantine monks began to build monasteries on the summits. Exactly how they managed this is still something of a mystery since the only means of access at that time was by containers hoisted up the cliff face by pulleys – if this sounds familiar, you've probably seen the James Bond film *For Your Eyes Only*. By the 14th century there were 24 monasteries perched on the top, but the number of inhabitants decreased and only 5 are still occupied. Nowadays their function has more to do with showing visitors round than with religion. Females are expected to wear skirts of a reasonable length – no shorts or trousers.

LITOHORO

Station: *tel: (0352) 81 990*, near the coast, 5 km east of town. Buses run between the station and the town.
Tourist Office: *Ag Nickalou 15; tel: (0352) 81 250* (in the Town Hall). Mon–Sat 0900–1400 and 1700–2100, and Sun 0900–1400. The **IYHF** *(2 Enipeos St; tel: (0352) 81 311 or 82 176)* also has information on the various climbs.

Litohoro is the jumping-off point for the 2,917m-high **Mt Olympus**, the home of the ancient gods. A mortal first climbed the mountain in 1913. Now a collection of footpaths offer a variety of short walks (with superb views) and enable experienced hikers to reach the summit. You don't need any special equipment (other than suitable footwear) for the full ascent, but it does demand real fitness and takes two days – ask the Tourist Office to book a place for you in the mountain refuge hut.

THESSALONIKI

Station: *tel: (031) 517 517*, about 1 km west of the town centre. Bus no. 3 runs from the station to the centre, passing *Aristotelous Square.*

Tourist Information: EOT Office, *8 Aristotelous Square; tel: 271 888* or *222 935*. Mon–Fri 0800–2000 and Sat 0830–1400. They are extremely helpful. There is an information desk at the station which can help direct you there. **Tourist Police**: *Dodekanissou St*, near *Dimokratias Square*; *tel: 544 162*.

Getting Around

Thessaloniki is a large city, but many of the interesting sights are within 10–15 mins walk of the tourist office. Buses cover the city comprehensively. Buy tickets from the conductor, who sits at the rear.

Accommodation

As befits a major city, Thessaloniki has a full range of accommodation – ask the tourist office for a list. The cheaper D and E class hotels mostly cluster along *Egnatia St* – the continuation of *Monastiriou St*, east of the station. There's a fairly central **youth hostel**: *44 Al. Svolou St; tel: (031) 225 945*.

Communications

The main **post office** is at *45 Tsimiski St; tel: 264 208* and the main **telephone office** is at *27 Karolou St (Ermou St)*.

Consulates

UK: *8 Venizelou St; tel: (031) 278 006.*
USA: *59 Nikis St; tel (031) 266 121.*

Sightseeing

Thessaloniki, the second largest city in Greece, was founded in 315 BC by Kassandros and named after his wife, Salonika, the sister of Alexander the Great. Situated on the Via Egnatia, the town was an important Roman outpost. During the Byzantine age, it was second in influence only to Byzantium (Istanbul). Unfortunately, much of the old town was destroyed by a fire in 1917 and Thessaloniki today is a modern, busy city, laid out stylishly along the waterfront.

A **Museum of Byzantine Art and History** is housed in the **White Tower**, an unmistakably Venetian structure on the waterfront that once formed part of a more extensive sea wall and provides excellent views of the town. The superb

Archaeological Museum, near the White Tower, contains the contents of *Royal Tombs* discovered at Vergina in 1977. The exceptional gold-trimmed armour, weapons and gold-leaf head-dresses are eclipsed by the charred bones of the buried king, believed to be Philip II of Macedonia, father of Alexander the Great. There's also a very interesting **Ethnological Museum**, *Vassilissis Olgas 68*, the best of its kind in Greece.

Thessaloniki's Roman heritage includes remains of the **Forum**, *Filipou St*, the **Palace of Galerius**, *Navarinu Square*, the **Baths**, next to Agios Dimitrios church, and the distinctive **Arch of Galerius**, which sits off *Egnatia St*, near *Sintrivaniou Square*.

The city also has a fine collection of Byzantine churches, the most notable of which are **Agios Georgios** and the restored 4th-century **Agios Dimitrios** rotunda.

Side Track from Thessaloniki

Mt Athos, the easternmost peninsula of Halkidiki, is home to a community of monks who have followed a Byzantine lifestyle for over 1000 years. There are still 20 functioning monasteries here. Due to an edict issued by Emperor Constantine Monomakis in AD 1060, only men may enter. To obtain the required permit, contact the Ministry of Foreign Affairs, Directorate of Churches, *2 Zalokosta St, Athens; tel: (01) 362 6894*, or the Ministry of Northern Greece, Directorate of Civil Affairs, *Diikitiriou Square, Thessaloniki; tel: (031) 270 092*. You may need to show scientific or religious interest. Buses run from Thessaloniki to Ouranoupolis, whence ferries sail to Dafni, from where you can get a local bus to Karies, the capital of Mt Athos.

ALEXANDROPOLIS

Station: *tel: 26 395 or 26 212*, by the port.

At the eastern extremity of northern Greece, Alexandropolis is little more than a watering hole for travellers heading to or from Turkey. If you want a change of pace from the trains, ferries sail between here and Turkey (tickets from agencies on the waterfront).

BARCELONA

Barcelona, metropolis of the revolutionary and astute Catalan people and once home to Pablo Picasso, Joan Miró, and Antoni Gaudí, is one of Europe's most enduring cities, with Roman remains, a stunning Gothic old quarter, and a mass of superlative Modernist architecture.

Tourist Information

There are four tourist information centres. Two, at **Estació de França**, tel: (93) 319 57 58 and **Estació de Sants**, tel: (93) 490 91 71 offer information only on the city and open 0800–2000 daily. The other two, run by the Catalan state government (the Generalitat), give information on Catalunya and the whole of Spain. Gran Vía de les Corts Catalanes 658; tel: (93) 301 74 43. Mon–Fri 0900–1900, Sat 0900–1400. International terminal, Barcelona Airport; tel: (93) 478 47 04. Mon–Sat 0930–2000, Sun and hols 0930–1500. From 15 Jun–15 Sept, the tourist office runs **street information services**. Look for staff in red and white uniforms.

There are also four **youth information offices** and an excellent tourist office brochure, Barcelona for Young People, aimed at the young and students, although much of the information applies to all budget travellers.

The **Centre d'Informació i Assessorament per a Joves**, 32 Ferran; tel: (93) 402 78 00, gives information and assistance on cultural, sports and leisure facilities in the city. Open weekdays 1000–1400 and 1600–2000. The **Servei d'Informació i Promoció d'Activitats Juvenils**, Rambla Catalunya 5; tel: (93) 301 40 46, organizes adventure sports and international exchanges between young people. Open weekdays 1700–2100. The **Servei d'Informació de la Direcció General de Joventut**, Viladomat 319; tel: (93) 302 28 58, gives information on leisure activities and work for young people and students. It issues the Carnet Jove, which gives

discounts in the city. Open weekdays 0900–1200. The **Oficina de Turisme Juvenil**, Gravina 1; tel: (93) 302 06 82, gives advice on best travel prices for young people and issues International Youth Hostel Cards, amongst other services. Open weekdays 0900–1400.

Arriving and Departing

Airport

Aeroport del Prat is 12 km south-west of the city. Airport information, tel: (93) 478 50 00. **RENFE trains** (tel: (93) 490 02 02) run every 30 mins, between about 0600 and 2230, to and from Estació de Sants (journey time: 18 mins,) and Estació Plaça de Catalunya (journey time: 25 minutes). Cost: Ptas 300.

The aerobus (cost: Ptas 400) runs to and from Plaça de Catalunya every 15 minutes on weekdays and every 30 minutes during the weekend and on holidays (0530–2300). Additional stops are shown on the city map available from tourist offices. For information, tel: (93) 412 00 00.

Stations

There are two main stations: the central **Estació de França**, Av. Marqués de l'Argentera, used by all the main international trains, and **Estació de Sants**, Pl. Països Catalans (about 3.5 km from the old town – along C. de Tarragona or Av. de Roma). RENFE information: tel: (93) 490 02 02.

Ferries

From the port, virtually next door to Estació de França, ferries are available to the Balearics and Sicily. **Barcelona Port Information**; tel: (93) 317 42 62; **Transmediterránea**, tel: (93) 412 25 24.

Getting Around

The main social area of the Ramblas is pedestrianised, while only locals would dare drive through the narrow ways of the Gothic quarter (Barri Gotic). Together, these areas form the core of the city, and are best seen on foot. The Gothic quarter is considered by many as unsafe after dark, and the Barri Xines on the opposite side of the Rambla is definitely so.

Metro (Subway) and Suburban Trains

There are two fast and clean metro-type systems. The **Metro**, run by the city (*Ciutat*), has four colour-coded lines numbered 1, 3, 4, and 5. Line 2 was never built. Trains are designated by the name of the last stop. The **Generalitat**, run by the Catalan State, serves fewer places in the centre, but can take you out into the suburbs and beyond.

The same tickets are valid on Metro and Generalitat lines and there is a flat rate for all journeys, regardless of distance or location. You have to pay again if you transfer between the two lines. There are two types of card, both valid for ten journeys: T1 (Ptas 590) and T2 (Ptas 560). T1 cards are also valid on buses.

Tourist Bus

The **Bus Turistic** runs from 0900–2130 from 12 June–12 Oct and a ticket costs Ptas 1000 per day for adults. There is a maximum wait of 20 mins at any of the 15 stops and a full tour lasts 2 hours. A tourist information officer accompanies every bus, and your ticket includes discounts at several attractions. For more information on city transport, *tel: (93) 412 00 00*.

Taxis

Yellow and black cabs can be hailed in the streets. Make sure you have change as the drivers often seem not to. Taxis for the disabled: *tel: (93) 358 11 11*.

Living in Barcelona

Accommodation

Barcelona has as wide a range of hotels as any major European city, including the following major brands: *Ch, Hn, Md, Ml, Nv* and *RC*. Hotels are graded in stars from one to five and a recent review of the system means that if it calls itself a hotel, it is now obliged to have en-suite bathrooms in all rooms. Prices (excluding VAT) vary with the season from Ptas 12–33000 (five-star) to Ptas 3900 (one-star). If it is not a hotel, it has to be a *pension*, according to the new rules. *Pensiones* come as two- and one-star accommodation, (both priced between Ptas 1500 and Ptas 4000, plus VAT, with shared facilities). Many are located in the old part of the town, and demand is high in peak seasons. Within the *Gothic quarter*, you are less likely to end up inadvertently lodging in a brothel if you stick to the streets between *Carrer del Carme*, *Portaferrissa*, and *Santa Anna*. For further information, try calling the **Barcelona Hotel Association**; *tel: (93) 301 62 40*.

Approximately 15 student's halls of residence become **hostels** for young people in the summer. For details, contact a youth information centre (*see Tourist Information* above). There are also six **youth hostels**, all members of IYHF. It is advisable to book in advance. The most central is **Kabul** in the *Gothic quarter*; *tel: (93) 318 51 90*.

There are 12 **campsites** within easy reach of Barcelona, mostly on the coast to the south of the city. Catalunya has 70% of all Spain's campsites. For details, call the **Associació de Campings de Barcelona**, *tel: (93) 317 44 16*.

Communications

The main **post offices** are at *Pl. Antoni Lopez 1* (weekdays 0800–2200, Sat 0800–2000, Suns and hols 0900–1400); *Ronda Universitat 23* (weekdays 0830–2030); and *Gran de Gràcia 118* (weekdays 0900–2100). Stamps are available at post offices and all tobacconists, from where you can also buy phone cards (Ptas 1000 or 2000), required for most public telephones. **Telephones** are available at *Fontanella 2*, Mon–Sat, 0900–1300 and 1600–1900.

To phone Barcelona from abroad: *tel: 34 (Spain) + 03 (Barcelona) + number*. To phone Barcelona from elsewhere in Spain: *tel: (93) + number*.

Eating and Drinking

Catalan cooking is known as good peasant fare, made from ingredients such as cuttlefish, serrano ham and salt cod. *Crema catalana* is a delicious local dessert, similar to *crème caramel*. Catalunya is also famous for its *champenoise* sparkling wine, *Cava*. **Xampany**, *Carrer de Valencia 200*, sells more than 200 varieties and offers tastings.

In the evenings, many restaurants do not

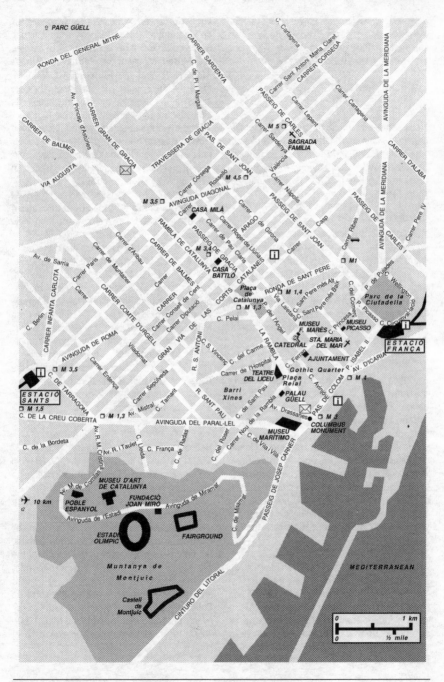

have a set menu, so eating out can be expensive. As an alternative, visit several bars and have a drink and some *tapas*. Try along *Carrer de la Mercè* (be careful at night).

Entertainment

Nightlife

Prepare to sleep through the next day – nightlife proper in Barcelona starts at 0100 and ends with cocktails at 0900. There is a wide range of clubs, bars and discos, catering for all musical tastes from rock to jazz; the busiest nights are Thurs–Sat.

Cinemas and Music

There are 52 **cinemas** in Barcelona, of which only a few show films in their original language (with subtitles) rather than dubbed. They are shown as VO (version original) in the listings. It is traditional in Barcelona to tip the usher about Ptas 25. The **Filmoteca de la Generalitat de Catalunya**, *Travessera de Gràcia 63*, shows less commercial films. Barcelona holds an international film festival in June/July.

Shopping

Barcelona is rapidly gaining ground as one of the great European centres of fashion and design, so clothes and leatherwork are some of the best buys. Souvenir foods, such as hams and olive oil, are also worth a look. The main shopping streets are *Passeig de Gràcia, Rambla de Catalunya*, and *Avinguda Diagonal* (from *Rambla de Catalunya* to *Plaça Francesc Macià*). Wandering off these streets sometimes pays dividends, and if you don't mind not being able to find the shop again the next day, try the streets in the *Gothic quarter*, near the cathedral.

Sightseeing

Art goes hand in hand with architecture in Barcelona. In this deeply style-conscious city, there is always a brave juxtaposition of old and new. The **Picasso Museum**, *Carrer de Montcada*, is formed from two Gothic palaces on a street just 3m wide. Of the city's numerous other museums, the most unmissable are **Fundació Miró**, *Plaça Neptú, Montjüic*; the **Fundació Tàpies**, *Aragó 225*; the **Museu d'Art de Catalunya**, *Palau Nacional, Montjüic*; the **Museu d'Historica de la Ciutat**, *Plaça del Rei*; the **Museu Monestir de Pedralbes**, *Baixada Monestir 9*; and the **Museu d'Art Modern**, *Plaça d'Armes, Parc de la Ciutadella*. They are almost all of value for the buildings alone, let alone the art. Museums are closed on Mondays.

The city also has an enchanting, if confusing **Gothic quarter**, a web of tiny dark streets radiating out from **La Seu Cathedral**, *Plaça de la Seu*, a magnificent Gothic edifice, started in 1298 but only finished in 1892.

The 1992 Olympics were used as an excuse to rescue a desolate warehouse district and 4 km of seafront to create a fascinating new district of fine modern architecture.

Pride of place however must go to the works of the superb Modernist architect, Antoni Gaudí (1852–1926). He used the city as his canvas, leaving such extraordinary, swirling masterpieces as the unfinished cathedral, the **Sagrada Familia**, *Plaça Sagrada Familia*, and the **Casa Milà**, *Paseo de Gracia*. The excellent tourist office listings magazine, *Barcelona Prestige*, details a walking guide to Gaudí's 10 buildings and there is a museum dedicated to him, the **Casa-Museu Gaudí**, in the **Parc Güell**, an area he himself designed as a decidedly eccentric English garden suburb.

Views over Barcelona

Helicopter trips are available (*tel: (93) 209 27 55*). At less cost is the cable car (*tel: (93) 317 55 27*) which climbs 1,292 m from La Barceloneta in the port area to the hill of **Montjüic**, where it connects with another (*tel: (93) 256 64 00*) up to the castle.

You can also get good views of Barcelona by climbing a tower at Gaudí's **Sagrada Familia**, the **Columbus monument** at the bottom of the *Rambla*, or the Aeroplane and Big Dipper rides at the **Montjüic** fairground. If you want architecture as well as a view, try the **Torre de Collserola**, by Norman Foster, or the roof of the Gothic **Basilica of Santa Maria del Mar** (1700–2030), regarded by many as Barcelona's finest church.

BERLIN

Divided for over 40 years, Berliners are today piecing together their fractured city, still scarred with rubble and wasteland where the Wall once stood. A relatively new city, eminent only from the 19th century, Berlin has had an extraordinary history, as capital of Bismarck's newly unified Germany, Hitler's capital and power base, and as the symbol of the Cold War. Long-famed for the avant-garde and the alternative, Berlin is now re-emerging as a focus of youth culture and the intelligentsia.

Tourist Information

The main **Vertebras** (tourist information office) in the Europa Centre, *Budapester Str. 10787; tel: (030) 262 60 31*, opens Mon–Sat 0800–2230, Sun 0900–2100. There are also offices at **Tegel Airport** and the two of the three main railway stations: **Zoo Bahnhof**, *tel: (030) 313 90 63*, open Mon–Sat 0800-2300 and **Hauptbahnhof**, *tel: (030) 279 52 09*, open Mon–Sun 0800–2000. For written enquiries contact the central administration at *Martin-Luther-Str.105, 10825 Berlin*. **Thomas Cook** bureaux de change: *Friedrichstrasse 56*; *Schönefeld Airport*.

Arriving and Departing

Airports

Most flights from the West are to **Tegel Airport**, *tel: (030) 60 91 21 39*, 10 km from the centre of town. Bus nos.109 and 128 connect with the U-bahn; the first to *Jakob-Kaiser-Platz* and the second to *Kurt-Schumacher-Platz*. Allow about an hour. Taxis are not much more expensive.

Schönefeld Airport (19km south-west) served the East in the days of the Berlin Wall and since reunification the destinations haven't changed much. For enquiries *tel: (030) 60 91 21 39*. The S-bahn runs to Hbf (29 mins) and Zoo (48 mins), main-line trains to Lichtenberg (19 mins).

National buses

These are run by **ZOB** (Zentraler Omnibusbahnhof), *tel: (030) 301 80 28*. The main station is at *Kaiserdamm*. Buses run daily to all major cities and smaller towns.

Stations

Berlin has four main-line stations: **Berlin Zoologischer Garten** (shortened to Zoo), *Hardenbergplatz 11*; **Berlin Friedrichstrasse**, *Georgenstr.14–18*; **Berlin Hauptbahnhof** (Hbf), *Am Hauptbahnhof*; and **Berlin Lichtenberg**, *Weitlingerstr.22*. The first two lie in the west and the others in the east, with Zoo and Hauptbahnhof being the main stations for long-distance trains. Most trains stop at both and some at all four. All are central and connect with the U-bahn.

For all rail information ask at the **Bundesbahn Information Office**, *Hardenbergstrasse 20; tel: 19419*. Open Mon–Fri, 0830–1830.

Getting Around

A brief aquaintance with the public transport network is inevitable if you want to see the whole city. Free photocopied street maps can be picked up from the tourist offices. A more comprehensive version costs DM5–DM10 from newsagents. Train maps are easy to find but for bus maps you must go to the **BVG information centre**, outside Zoo Bahnhof, *tel: (030) 256 2462*. Open Mon–Fri 0800–1800, Sat 0700–1400 and Sun 0900–1600. Here you can get the *Region Berlin Linienplan* (DM3) and free smaller transport maps.

Public Transport

The 20 lines of the **U-bahn** (underground) and **S-bahn** (suburban surface trains) offer quick transport to most spots within the 40km diameter of Berlin. The stations are easily recognised by the white U on a blue square or white S on a green circle and lines are colour-coded and numbered. Direction is indicated by the name of the final destination. **Buses** are also convenient and a good way to see the city (the best sightseeing routes are no.12, which runs along an east–west axis through the city, and no. 100). Bus-stops are indicated by a green H on a yellow background.

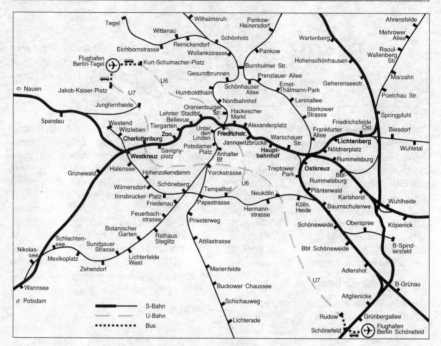

Tickets

Tickets can be bought from automatic machines on station platforms, bus drivers or ticket offices and are validated by punching the ticket once on board or on the platform. A single allows travel on any bus, train or tram for a period of 2 hours. A *Sammelkarte* (the equivalent of four singles) is a cheaper option and a 24-hour ticket (*24-Stunden-Karte*) can be even more economical if you are planning several journeys. Weekly (Mon–Sat) tickets are also available.

Boats

For daily boat trips along the River Spree, go to the restaurant terrace at the **Kongress Halle, Greenwich-Promenade** in Tegel, **Tiergarten** pier or **Wannsee** pier. For information *tel: (030) 394 49 54* or *(030) 810 0040*.

Living in Berlin

Accommodation

Most tourist accommodation is in the west, especially in the environs of Zoo, Ku'damm and Charlottenburg, although in the east it is currently still slightly cheaper. The tourist information offices will make reservations for a small fee and give advice, addresses and telephone numbers. **Thomas Cook** network member **Reisebüro Helios**, *Uhlandstrasse 73; tel: (030) 860 0050* also makes hotel reservations. There is a wide range of top quality, international hotels, including *Ch, Ex, Hn, Ib, Ic, Ke, Mp, Nv, Pe* and *Rd*. For a list of cheap hotels and hostels (including prices) ask for the *Accommodation for young visitors* booklet at the Tourist Office. Prices start at about DM35 for hostels, and cheap hotel rooms (pensions) start at about DM70 for a single and DM90 for a double.

Apartment Sharing Centres (**Mitwohnzentralen**) arrange vacant room and apartment rental for a fee based on the cost of the accommodation. There are several such centres, the one at *Kurfürstendamm 227/228; tel: (030) 88 30 51* is near Zoo.

Campsites in Berlin are usually out of town; for a list ask at the tourist office. A few minutes

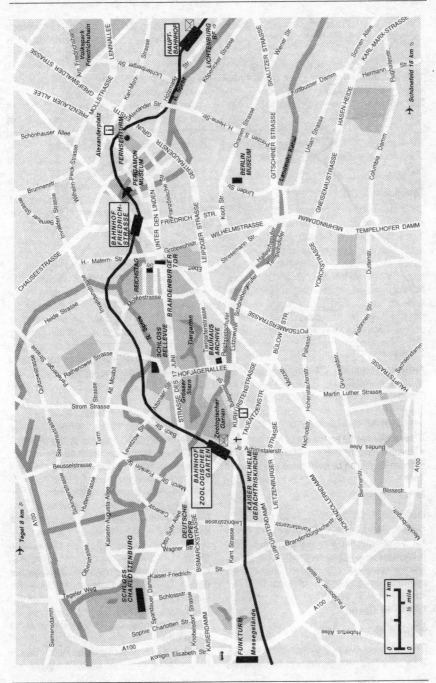

walk from **Tegel** U-bahn, an international **youth-camp** offers places for DM9 a night.

Communications

There is a 24-hour post office at **Zoo Bahnhof** where you can also collect Post Restante mail. Post offices are usually open Mon–Fri 0900–1800; Sat 0900–1200.

To phone Berlin from abroad, tel: 49 (Germany) + 30 (Berlin) + number; to phone Berlin from elsewhere in Germany, tel: 030 + number.

Eating and Drinking

Berlin has a huge array of restaurants, cafés, bars and street stalls, from typically German establishments to kebab houses and pizzerias. In the centre, there are concentrations around Zoo station and Ku'damm. In the east of the city, head for the Nikolai quarter or Gendarmenmarkt. For a treat, try the cakes at coffee shops, while for cheap food and a happy evening's drinking head for the pubs (kneipe) around Savigny Platz, Kreuzberg and Prenzlauer Berg.

Embassies and Consulates

Australia: Kempinski Plaza, Uhlandstr.181–3; tel: (030) 88 00 880

Canada: IHZ Building, Friedrichstr.95; tel: (030) 261 1161

New Zealand: Bundeskanzlerplatz 2–10, Bonn; tel: (030) 228 070

UK: Unter den Linden 32–34; tel: (030) 201 840

USA: Neustädtische Kirchstr; tel: (030) 238 5174

Entertainment

Famed since the 1930s for and because of Cabaret, Berlin has a well-deserved reputation for diverse and non-stop entertainment, from opera, theatre and film to club-land and rock. There are two listings magazines: Zitty and Tip, available from newsagents for about DM4. For listings in English, try the Tourist Office monthly Check Point.

Shopping

Berlin is one of Europe's shopping meccas. The West still has greater variety and hosts Berlin's chief shopping boulevard **Kurfürstendamm**, 3km of boutiques and cafés. **Fasanenstr.** has designer shops, while **Kreuzberg** is considered the centre of alternative Berlin. The main street for records, second-hand clothes and cafés here is Oranien-str.

Away from the centre, each of Berlin's 23 districts has its own shopping areas, such as Schönhauser Allee, in Prenzlauer Berg; and Wilmersdorfer Str. in **Charlottenburg**.

For flea market (**Flohmarkt**) shopping, try the Trodelmarkts at Str. des 17. Juni (Sat and Sun; S-bahn: Tiergarten), and **Charlottenburg**, Ku'-damm-Karree, (daily, except Tues). **Winterfeld-platz** is the central food market (Wed and Sat, 0800–1400; U-Bahn: Zoo).

Sightseeing

Zoo Bahnhof is central for sightseeing in the west. From here the **Charlottenburg Schloss** (U: Sophie Charlotte Platz) lies south-west in the district of the same name. Built by Frederick I (immortalised in the statue in the Court of Honour) for his wife Sophie Charlotte, domed a few years later and more recently restored inside, the palace also boasts landscaped gardens and museums with impressive Egyptian and Antique collections.

Ku'damm

South from the palace, 3km-long **Kurfür-stendamm** is very much the centre of life in the West, lined with trees, shops, restaurants, cafés and cinemas. Following the Ku'damm (as it is known to Berliners) eastwards leads back to Zoo Bhf and the **Gedächtniskirche** (Kaiser Wilhelm Memorial Church), its maimed and gaping tower left unrepaired in memory of World War II.

Budapester Str. leads past the **observation tower** in the Europa Centre, (the shopping mall covered in neon signs) to the **Zoologischer Garten** (zoo) and **Tiergarten**. This was the former Prussian hunting ground and one of the oldest parts of Berlin. In the middle of the wooded parkland stands the **Siegessäule**, a 67m column built after the defeat of the Danish (1864), Austrians (1866) and the French (1870–71). Worth climbing for the view. To the west is

Schloss Bellevue, residence of the Federal President, and to the east the 1960s **Kongresshalle**.

The Great Divide

Check-point Charlie used to be the only point of entry into East Berlin for foreign visitors. It is now marked by the **Check-point Charlie Museum**, which tells the story of the many ingenious, life-risking and only sometimes successful attempts to flee the GDR. In all, 75 died, marked by small crosses where they fell.

Boadicea-like, the goddess Victory crowns the six doric columns of the **Brandenburg Gate**, *Pariser Platz*,, which stands between *Str. den 17 juni* (the date in 1953 when 200–400 anti-Soviet protestors were shot) and *Unter den Linden*. The last of the original 14 city gates of Berlin, erected in 1788, this was a frequent venue for Prussian and Nazi military displays. The current gate, a post-war replica, became a symbol of the divided Germany. It was reopened in Dec 1989.

Unter den Linden

The spine of pre-war Berlin, this is still an impressive broad boulevard flanked by monumental public buildings, almost all of which needed restoration after World War II. During the Cold War, it became the focal point of the Eastern sector. Behind the **Deutsche Staatsoper** (opera house) stands the Catholic **Cathedral of St. Hedwig** (founded in 1809). Further along, **Humboldt University** numbers Einstein, Marx and Engels amongst its more famous alumni.

The Baroque **Zeughaus** (Arsenal), one of the most visually impressive buildings on the street, now houses the **Museum of German History**. In the past three years some sort of objective balance has been restored to what was an inevitably biased display. Also look out for the **Deutsche Staatsbibliothek** (library) and the **Kronprinzen Palais**.

Museuminsel

'Museum Island', within the River Spree, houses several excellent museums, which together have (but do not display) some 1.2 million works of art. The most famous is the **Pergamon**, one of Europe's best collections of antiquities, including Egyptian and Byzantine art and the notable altar of Zeus, dated to 180BC. The **Bode Museum**, *Monbijoubrücke*, in the north-west corner, houses early Christian art, Egyptian works and 15th–18th century paintings. The **Nationalgalerie** is strong on 20th-cen-tury art and particularly the Expressionists, in-cluding work from the *Brucke* and *Blaue Reiter* schools. There is also a 19th-century collection.

From here take the *Rathausbrücke*, past the **Berliner Dom** and the **Palast der Republik** to *Rathausstr*. On the right look out for the restored 13th-century twin-towered **Nikolaikirche**, Berlin's oldest building. The **Rotes Rathaus** (Red Town Hall, so called on account of its bricks), leads to the base of the **Fernsehturm**. This 365m spike, piercing a globe-shaped Tele-café and viewing gallery at 200m, is one of Berlin's most persistent sights.

- - - - - - - - - - - - - - - - - - - -

Side Track from Berlin

POTSDAM

Tourist Office: Touristenzentrale, *Freidrich-Elbert-Str.5; tel: (0331) 21 100*, open Mon–Fri 1000–1800, Sat–Sun 1100–1500.

Potsdam is a purpose-built fantasy of landscaped gardens and palaces, 45km south-west of Berlin (easily reached by S-bahn or rail). The town celebrated its 1000th year in 1993 but really only peaked artistically in the late 17th century, when it became the seat of the Hohenzollern dynasty and a haven for exiled Huguenots. It has now earned a place on the prestigious UNESCO list of the world's cultural heritage.

The best feature is the 12-roomed Rococo **Sanssouci Palace** (1745–47) (*Sanssouci* means literally 'without a care') set amidst the 725 acre **Park Sanssouci**. A leisurely walk through the park will uncover the **Chinese Tea House** (1754-7), the pagoda-like **Drachenhaus** (Dragon house), **Schloss Charlottenhof**, and the **Rö-mische Bäder** (Roman Baths) (both early 19th century). There are many other architectural gems dotted here, in the town and, on the other side of the **Havel River**, in **Babelsberg Park**.

- - - - - - - - - - - - - - - - - - - -

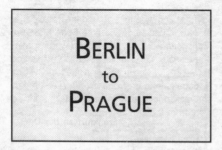

BERLIN
to
PRAGUE

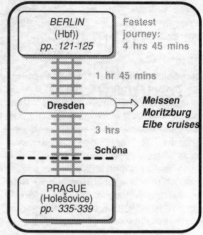

BERLIN
(Hbf))
pp. 121-125

Fastest
journey:
4 hrs 45 mins

1 hr 45 mins

Dresden ⟹ Meissen
Moritzburg
Elbe cruises

3 hrs

Schöna

PRAGUE
(Holešovice)
pp. 335-339

This route connects the German and Czech capitals, meeting the River Elbe at the historic and much-restored city of Dresden.

TRAINS

ETT tables: 60, 680.

 Fast Track

Five or six trains daily (some EC with supplement), with dining-car, taking 4 hrs 45 mins.

⌇⌇ On Track

Berlin Hbf–Dresden Hbf

About eight IC/EC trains daily; time 1 hr 45 mins.

Dresden Hbf–Prague (Praha) Holešovice

Trains about every 2 hrs, taking 3 hrs (EC trains take 2 hrs 30 mins).

DRESDEN

Stations: Hbf; *tel: (0351) 4 71 06 00*; **Neustadt**; *tel: (0351) 5 11 85.*
Tourist Offices: *Prager Str.10; tel: (0351) 4 95 50 25* (near Hbf). Apr–Oct, Mon–Sat 0900–2000 (–1200 Sun); Nov–Mar, Mon–Fri 0900–1800 (–1400 Sat, –1300 Sun). *Neustadter Markt (Fussgängertunnel); tel: (0351) 5 35 39.* Mon–Fri 0900–1800 (–1600 Sat), Sun 1100–1600.
Thomas Cook: Thomas Cook Reisebüro Sachsen Tours, *Münzgasse 10; tel: (0351) 494 8117* provides foreign exchange and travel services to visitors.
Accommodation: Hotel groups in Dresden include *Hn* and *Me*.

Capital of Saxony from the 15th century until 1918, Dresden was one of Europe's most beautiful cities until the Allied air-raid (1945) left little standing and many dead. Reconstruction work has restored much of the architectural damage, particularly the Baroque splendour near the Elbe. From Hbf, take *Prager Str.* to **Altmarkt**, past the **Church of the Holy Cross**, on to **Neumarkt** and **Frauenkirch**, a ruin serving as a war memorial. West are the **Zwinger Palace** (1709-1722) and the **Orangery** (vast porcelain collection). A reconstruction of the **Semper Opera House**, ruined by fire, then bombs, was unveiled in 1985. **Dresden Castle** met similar fates. The **Catholic Court Church** evolved when Augustus the Strong (1694–1733) sought the (Catholic) Polish crown. His heart is in the crypt.

⌒ Side Tracks from Dresden

At **Meissen** (38 mins from Dresden Hbf) is the famous china manufactory with an exhibition hall, demonstration workshop and gift shop: *Talstr. 9; tel: (03521) 541*. **Moritzburg** (a 50-min trip from Dresden Hbf, changing at Radebeul Ost onto a steam train) boasts an immaculate moated castle, one of Europe's best.

The **Weisse Flotte**, authentic coal-fired paddle steamers, sail on the Elbe to and from Dresden: *Terrassenufer 2; tel: (0351) 437 241.*

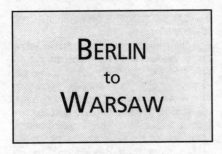

BERLIN to WARSAW

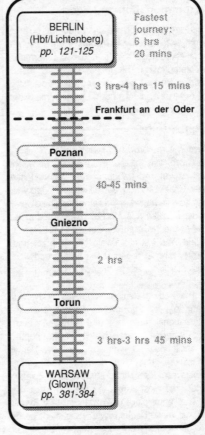

BERLIN (Hbf/Lichtenberg) *pp. 121-125*	Fastest journey: 6 hrs 20 mins

3 hrs-4 hrs 15 mins

Frankfurt an der Oder

Poznan

40-45 mins

Gniezno

2 hrs

Torun

3 hrs-3 hrs 45 mins

WARSAW (Glowny) *pp. 381-384*

This journey, starting in Germany, crosses the vast Central European Plain to link two great but badly battered cities. The scenery is uninspiring but the route follows the Piast Trail, which links some of Poland's most historic towns and tells the saga of the country's birth..

TRAINS

ETT tables: 56, 850.

→ Fast Track

Three trains run daily, two daytime (EC) from Berlin Hbf taking about 6 hrs 30 mins (reserve in advance; dining-car). The overnight train (sleeping car and couchettes but no dining car) departs from Berlin Lichtenberg and takes 9 hrs. All three services have compulsory reservation. If you are starting from Warsaw, all the above trains leave from Centralna.

∿ On Track

Berlin–Border–Poznań

Two EC services run daily, taking 3 hrs 10 mins.

Poznań–Gniezno

There are eight fast services a day, taking 45 mins (40 mins on the twice-daily express train).

Gniezno–Toruń

Two fast trains run daily (one of these is late night or early morning), journey time 1hr 10 mins. The four local trains take about 1 hr 30 mins.

Toruń–Warsaw (Warszawa)

Three trains run daily, taking 3 hrs by day and 4 hrs by night.

POZNAŃ

Tourist Office: the **Provincial and Central Office**, *Stary Rynek 59; tel: (061)52 61 56*, on the old square, is very good, so pick up as much as you can here. There are also offices at *24 Wroniecka street; tel: (061) 52 98 05* and the station.

Station: the main station, **Poznań Głowny**, *tel: (061) 52 72 21* is a short bus ride from the town centre. It has a 24-hr rail information office, *tel: (061) 66 12 12*, tourist information *tel; (061) 66 06 67* and a currency exchange. Most international trains stop here, although some arrive and depart from **Starołeka** station, 5 km south-east.

Accommodation and Food

There are plenty of cafés and restaurants on Stary Rynek, where you will also find *Dom Turysty*, a hotel-come-hostel, with rooms and dormitory accommodation. The city has a large number of hotels. Most are designed for trade fair delegates on expense accounts, but there are some within a lower price range.

Sightseeing

Poznań is the provincial capital of *Wielkopolska* and historically the cradle of the Polish state. The first capital and bishopric were founded here over 1000 years ago, while kings were crowned and now lie buried in the cathedral. The city was under Prussian rule for 125 years, freed at the end of the 18th century, but fell to the Nazis in World War II. It has always been a great trade centre, lying at a geographical crossroads, and this has resulted in a rich legacy of fine architecture.

The trading element continues today, with many of those who visit Poznań attending international trade fairs (the largest in Central and Eastern Europe). The city is also popular amongst violinists who come for the Henryk Wieniawski International Violin Competition. Others come simply to enjoy one of Poland's oldest and most attractive cities.

The centre-piece of Poznań is **Stary Rynek**, the old market square with its gabled, pastel, arcaded burghers' houses topped by sloping roofs. The jewel in the crown is the 16th-century Renaissance **Town Hall**, one of Europe's finest, which should be visited at midday when two mechanical goats emerge from above the clock to lock horns.

The Hall houses the *Historical Museum of the City of Poznań* and the *Chamber of the Renaissance* has a beautiful painted coffered ceiling (1555). In front of the Town Hall stand a copy of the pillory used for 16th-century floggings and a Rococo fountain.

Also on the square, the **Museum of Musical Instruments** is rated as one of the best of its kind, home to about 2000 instruments, with a room dedicated to Chopin. The **Archaeological Museum**, found in the 16th-century Renaissance **Górków Palace** has exhibits from 15,000 BC–7000 BC.

In the partially reconstructed **Przemuysláw Castle**, the **Arts and Crafts Museum** has exhibits from the 12th century. In all Poznań has 15 museums of which the most recently opened is the **Anti-Communist Museum**, *ul.Botaniczna*. The **National Museum**, *ul. Paderewskiego*, has a good fine art collection, including several Dutch, Spanish and Italian masters.

Numerous small churches form an outer ring around the square. One of the best is the typically Baroque **Kościół Frany** (the Poznań Parish Church), dedicated to St. Mary Magdalene. Next door, the **Jesuit Monastery** was once the residence of Napoleon and the venue for Chopin's concerts. In the middle of the River Warta, the oldest part of Poznań sits on the island of **Ostrów Tumski**. Here stands the **Cathedral**, first built in the 9th century, greatly expanded in the 14th century and heavily restored after World War II. Inside, in the 19th-century **Golden Chapel**, lie the tombs of **Miesko I** and **Boleslav the Brave**, the first two kings of Poland.

The greenery is above par, with two zoos and a palm house (part of the largest botanical garden in Poland). For picnics, **Park Chopina** is only 250m from the old market square and there are many more parks, mainly in the west and north about 1 km away. On the edge of the city is the 100sq km **Wielkopolski Park Narodowy** (Great Poland National Park), easily accessible by train.

GNIEZNO

Tourist Office: Gniezno lacks a municipal *Informacja Turystyczna (IT)* office. Instead the sparsely stocked **Orbis** office (*Stary Rynek*) is a stark remnant of the past. However, Gniezno is easy to manage and the cathedral isn't difficult to find (head west from the square). The bookshop next door to Orbis sells town maps and guide books to the cathedral, while Orbis will help you with accommodation. There is one youth hostel at *ul. Pocztowa 11; tel: (0661) 13 23*.

Station: *tel: (0661) 21 11*, within walking distance of the town centre, next to the bus station.

Sightseeing

Gniezno is a small but highly significant city. Excavations have shown that the first settlements date to the early stone Age, and this was the first capital of Poland. The chief sight is the 14th-century **Cathedral**, distinguished by the Romanesque bronze doors (1170) depicting the life of St Adalbertus. Inside, the main attractions are the saint's red marble tomb and silver shrine. West of Lake Jelonek, the **Museum of the Origin of the Polish State** offers information on early Polish history.

TORUŃ

Tourist Office: there is a well-organised **IT** office on the ground floor of the **Ratusz** (Town Hall), *Rynek Staromiejski, 1; tel: (056) 237 46*, in the old town square.
Station: the main one is **Toruń Główny**, *ul. Kujawska 1; tel: (056) 272 22*. Five others share the name Toruń; nearest to the old city is **Toruń Miasto**. From the main station, bus nos. 22 or 24 will take you to the old town centre. Buy your ticket in advance at the tobacco kiosk.

Sightseeing

Don't believe the tourist literature that tells you that Toruń (the capital of Pomerania) hasn't changed since the Middle Ages. Nevertheless, this medieval town is second only to Cracow in terms of its architectural heritage.

The first city to be founded by the Order of the Teutonic knights (1233), it was later part of the Hanseatic League, usefully standing beside the Wista (Vistula) River. After this prosperous era, the 13th–15th centuries, Toruń fell first to the Swedes and then to the Prussians and has been in Polish hands only since 1945.

Over the years, the city's main claims to fame have been its holy lime trees, its excellent gingerbread and sweets, and, of course, its most famous citizen, Copernicus, who discovered that the earth moved around the sun.

A good starting point for sightseeing is the market square, the *Rynek Staromiejski*. Its main building, the **Old Town Hall**, built in the 14th century, is now home to the **Regional Museum**. Nearby is a monument, erected in 1853 and one of many memorials to Copernicus. To appreciate the square properly, get a leaflet from the Tourist Office called *Toruń Rynek Staromiejski*. Look for the burgher's house called **Pod Gwiazda** (literally 'under the star') at no.35, originally 15th-century, but with ornate Baroque additions. Inside it has a 17th-century hanging staircase and the **Museum of Oriental Art**. Not far from the old square, the **Nicholas Copernicus House**, *ul. Kopernik 17*, is where the great scientist was born. The interior has been recreated in line with 15th-century building practices and there is a model of old Toruń as well as a *light and sound* spectacle, and a host of Copernicus memorabilia.

From here, head south-east towards the river for the ruins of the **Ruiny Zamku Krzyackiego** (Teutonic Castle), destroyed in 1454, and the best preserved remnants of the **medieval city walls**.

Toruń also has several fine churches, including the Gothic Franciscan hall church of **St Mary's**, on the old market square. In the new town area, the 14th-century **St James**, off the attractive *Rynek Nowomiejski*, has Gothic flying buttresses outside and Gothic frescoes and Baroque decoration inside. Technically, the oldest is the Gothic **St. Johns**, *ul. Zeglarska*, although most of it dates to the mid 15th century. The Presbytery however goes back another three centuries.

There are several more museums and churches, numerous attractive streets and houses. The **Planetarium** has commentaries in English and there are boat trips from the landing stage on *Bulward Filadelfijski*.

BRUSSELS (BRUXELLES)

Since it is the headquarters of both the EU and NATO, as well as being home to a large number of immigrants from the Mediterranean lands, Brussels is exceptionally cosmopolitan, with a lifestyle to match.

Tourist Information

City, TIB, *Hotel de Ville, Grand-Place; tel: 513 89 40.* June–Sept daily 0900–1800; Oct–May Mon–Sat 1000–1400. **National**, *rue du Marché-aux-Herbes 61; tel: 504 03 90.* Summer daily 0900–1900; Winter, Mon–Sat 0900–1800 and Sun 1300–1700. **Infor-Jeunes**, *rue du Marché-aux-Herbes 27; tel: 512 32 74,* Mon–Fri 1200–1745, is a mine of information.

Arriving and Departing

Airport

National is at *Zaventem; tel: 720 71 67,* 14 km north-east of the centre. There is a tourist information desk, *tel: 722 30 00.* Daily 0600–2200. An express rail link operates until nearly midnight, with trains every 20 mins or so to all three main stations; the journey is 15–25 mins.

Stations

The telephone number for all rail enquiries is *219 26 40.* The three main stations, Nord, Midi and Centrale, are linked by underground tram, as well as rail. Most long-distance trains stop at both Nord and Midi, but only a minority stop at Centrale, which is primarily for commuters. **Nord/Noord**, *pl. Rogier,* is just north of the main ring road (and on the edge of a red light district). **Centrale/Centraal**, *blvd de l'Imperatrice,* is 5 mins walk from Grand-Place. The area outside **Midi/Zuid** is best avoided at night – if arriving or departing late, take a taxi.. The tourist office in Midi (*tel: 522 58 56)* is open March–

October 24 hours a day. There are many other stations, of little interest to tourists.

Buses

The main **STIB bus station** is at *10 r. Brezoianu .*

Getting Around

Brussels is officially bilingual but, in practice, French is far more widely used than Flemish and we use the French version of addresses here.

Most of the places of major interest are in a small area within easy walking distance (in a triangle formed by Grand-Place, the Parc de Bruxelles and the Palais de Justice). Allow a couple of days, more if you want to get the feel of the city. There are plenty of parks in which to relax between bouts of activity. Outside the centre you have a choice of metro, bus and tram, all very efficiently run by **STIB**.

Two useful publications are *BBB Agenda*, which lists events, and *Brussels Guide and Map*, which is BFr.50.

Tickets

Tickets which cover the metro, buses and trams can be purchased individually (BFr.40) or you can get a ten-trip ticket (BFr.250). There's also a tourist pass (BFr.160), which gives unlimited travel on all city transport for 24 hours.

The multi-ride tickets can be purchased from STIB kiosks, tourist offices, some news-stands and metro stations. They are validated by boxes on board buses and trams or by the automatic barriers at metro stations. Individual tickets can be purchased from bus/tram drivers.

Public Transport

You can get free route maps of the city transport system from metro stations, STIB kiosks and tourist offices. Fairly new and efficient, but not very extensive, the **Metro** (subway) operates from 0600 to midnight. Many stations have been beautifully decorated by local artists, but don't hang around to admire them for too long as most stations lock automatically when the last train has gone. There are comprehensive networks of **buses** and **trams**, which are yellow (when not covered in advertisements). Most stop around 2200: the night service is limited and taxis are then the best bet. **Taxis** can be phoned (*tel: 511 22 44* (Green) or *513 62 00* (Orange)) or picked up at strategically positioned ranks, including main squares and stations.

Living in Brussels

Accommodation

The tourist offices make a charge for bookings, but this is actually a deposit as it is deducted from your hotel bill. The range of accommodation is wide, and includes the following chains: *Ch, Fo, Hn, Me, Pu, Ra SA, SC, Sf* and *Sh*.

There are plenty of budget hotels in the areas of *Ixelles* and *pl. Ste-Catherine*, but the areas around Midi and Nord should be avoided. Advance booking is recommended. Brussels offers a number of hostels, IYHF and otherwise. **Maison Internationale**, *chaussée de Wavre 205; tel: 648 85 29* or *648 97 87* (bus nos. 37/38 from Nord or no. 38 from Centrale to the Trone stop or train from either station to Gare du Leopold) is recommended for single travellers – it also permits camping in the garden. **IYHF**: *Heilig Geeststraat, rue du St-Esprit 4; tel: 511 04 36* (behind Notre-Dame-de-la-Chapelle, bus no. 20 from Midi) and **Jacques Brel**, *rue de la Sablonnière 30; tel: 218 01 87* (metro: *Madou*).

Communications

There is a **24-hour post office** at Midi, *av. Fonsny 48*. The main post office in town is Centre Monnaie, *pl. de Brouckere* (2nd floor). Mon–Thur 0900–1800, Fri 0900–1900 and Sat 0900–1200. The city's telephone code is 02.

Eating and Drinking

The Belgians enjoy eating and there's a huge choice of restaurants serving excellent food, but prices tend to be very high: the best value is the *plat du jour* (menu of the day). Many bars sell food and give better value than the restaurants, as well as offering a vast range of Belgium's unmissable beers.

Around *Grand-Place* (especially on *Petite rue des Bouchers*) you will find every imaginable type of eating-place, including fast-food chains. Two local variations are *frites* stalls (for French fries with salt or mayonnaise) and carts (mainly in *pl.*

Ste-Catherine) selling steamed mussels.

Quartier Marolles is an area of cheap restaurants and bars. In *Grand-Sablon*, a square with fairly upmarket cafés and restaurants, is Wittamer – a renowned pastry shop in a city famous for pastries.

Laundry

Salon Lavoir, *rue Haute 5*, Mon–Fri 0800–1800.

Embassies

Australia: *rue Guimard 6; tel: 231 05 16.*
Canada: *av. de Tervuren 2; tel: 735 60 40.*
New Zealand: *blvd du Regent 47; tel: 512 10 40.*
UK: *rue Arlen 85; tel: 287 62 11.*
USA: *blvd du Regent 27; tel: 513 38 30.*

Money

Nord and Midi have exchange facilities that are open daily 0700–2300 (at Centrale daily 0800–2100). They don't charge commission, but their rates are poor and you're usually better off paying the charge made by banks and exchange booths. **Thomas Cook** bureau de change is at *4 Grand-Place*.

Entertainment

There are many clubs and discos. You can often get in free, but have to buy at least one (expensive) drink. Clustered around *Fernand Cocq* and the lower end of *chaussée d'Ixelles* are lots of bars with live music, many of which stay open until the early hours.

Brussels prides itself on its reputation for jazz and there's a wide choice of venues, detailed in a publication called *Jazz Streets*. The operatic productions at the **Théâtre Royale de la Monnaie**, *pl. de la Monnaie*, are of international quality and it's not easy to get seats. **Cirque Royal**, *rue de l'Enseignement*, hosts many touring dance and opera companies, while classical music concerts are held at **Palais des Beaux Arts**, *rue Ravenstein 23*, and pop concerts at **Forest National**, *av. du Globe 36*. Many churches have free Sunday morning concerts.

It is unusual for films to be dubbed, so you should find plenty in English.

Shopping

Most of the lace shops centre on *Grand-Place*, but not everything on offer is the real thing, so ask whether it is Belgian or made in the Far East.

Of the many delicious chocolates, Leonidas and Godiva are the brands most popular with the Belgians themselves and their shops are all over the city.

To the south-east of the centre are upmarket areas for shopping, near *porte de Namur* and *av. Louise*. Around *rue Neuve* (a pedestrianised shopping street) there are many shopping malls that offer a wide range of affordable goods.

Brussels has several markets. The **Crafts Market**, *pl. de l'Agora*, covers jewellery and the like (Sat–Sun 1000–1800). The **Vieux Marché**, *pl. du Jeu de Balle*, sells absolutely everything and is open daily 0700–1400. The **Midi Market** (around Midi Station) resembles an African *souk* and is the place to go for bargains in food and clothes (Sundays 0500–1300).

Sightseeing

Grand-Place is the heart of the city, as it has been for centuries, and the guild houses are detailed enough to merit close inspection. The brewers' house is still owned by the guild and contains a **Brewery Museum**. The square's most imposing building is the Gothic **Hotel de Ville** (Town Hall), in which there are a succession of impressive rooms with gilt mouldings, frescoes and tapestries. The neo-Gothic **Maison du Roi** houses the **Musée de la Ville**, which depicts the city's history and displays the 500 costumes which are often used to clothe the **Manneken-Pis**, *rue du Chêne*, the famous fountain of a little boy urinating that is the city's symbol. Designed by Jerome Duquesnoy in 1619, he is sometimes referred to as 'Brussels' oldest citizen' and there's more than one version of the story he represents.

One of the city's newer attractions is the Art Nouveau **Centre Belge de la Bande Dessinée**, *rue des Sables 20*, housing a museum devoted to Belgian strip cartoons, notably Tintin.

The **Cathédrale St-Michel**, *pl. Ste-Gudule*, is a 13th-century Brabant-Gothic edifice that has just been restored. The particularly fine stained-glass windows were designed by a 16th-century court painter.

The home of the Belgian Parliament is the **Palais de la Nation**, *rue de la Loi* (metro: *Parc*). Facing it is **Parc de Bruxelles**, at the far end of which is the **Palais Royale**, *place des Palais*, which is open to the public in August and full of rich decorations, including some Goya tapestries.

Nearby are the two superb museums that make up the **Musées Royaux des Beaux Arts**. The **Musée d'Art Moderne**, *rue de la Régence 3*, is housed in an interesting modern building which was designed to do full justice to the 19th- and 20th-century paintings on display. The **Musée d'Art Ancien**, *pl. Royale 1*, contains some excellent examples of the Flemish and Dutch schools, including Breughel and Bosch.

Notre-Dame-de-la-Chapelle, *rue Haute*, is Brussels' oldest church, a 13th-century Gothic structure containing the 16th-century marble tomb of Pieter Breughel the Elder.

The 15th-century **Notre-Dame-du-Sablon**, *pl. du Grand-Sablon*, is a much-loved church that once housed a statue of the Virgin said to have miraculous powers. The **place du Petit-Sablon** features a small garden adorned with 48 statues representing the medieval guilds (each figure carries something connected with his trade) and a fountain that tells the story of two 16th-century Belgian counts who opposed Spanish tyranny.

Adolphe Saxe, inventor of the saxophone, was Belgian-born and the **Musée Instrumental**, *rue de la Régence*, has a section devoted to him, as well as over 1000 instruments; some go back to the dawn of time and many are unique.

The neo-Classical **Palais de Justice**, *pl. Poelaert* (metro: *pl. Louise*), is fittingly impressive. The 500-step ascent to the cupola is hard but, on clear days, rewarded by an excellent view of the countryside around the capital.

North-west of the centre

In 1958 Brussels hosted a World Expo. The **Atomium**, *blvd du Centenaire* (metro 1A: *Heysel*), a gigantic model of an iron atom that was constructed for that event, is still there and has become a symbol of the city. It contains a museum about atomic energy, but the main attraction is a ride on the escalators that link the different modules. From the top module there's

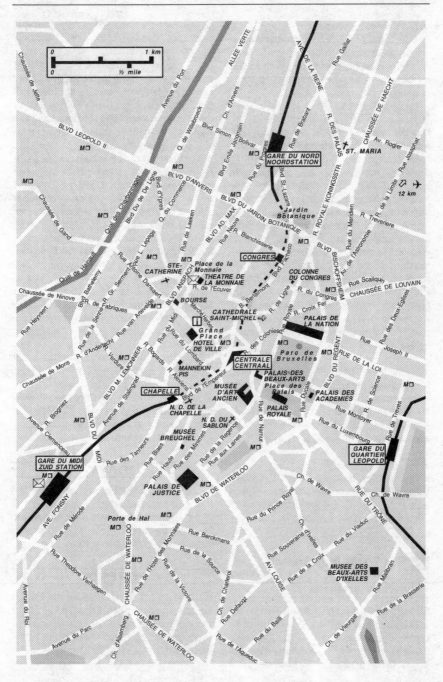

an unparalleled circular view.

Close to the Atomium are a **Planetarium** and the **Bruparck**, an entertainment park which includes a 29-screen cinema, an indoor aquatic complex and miniaturised versions of European landmarks.

East of the centre

Quartier Léopold is marked by wide boulevards and is home to the **Berlaymont Building** (the headquarters of the EC), *rue de la Loi*, (metro 1A: *Schuman*) and the pleasant **parc Léopold** (metro: *Schuman*), in the south of which is the **Institute of Natural Science**. The exhibits range from dinosaurs to deadly insects.

The **parc du Cinquantenaire** (metro: *Schuman/Merode*) was laid out in the late 19th century. The central Cinquantenaire is a monumental arch and the buildings on either side house the **Musées Royaux d'Art et d'Histoire**, where there are whole galleries devoted to the great early cultures (Greek, Egyptian, etc.). **Autoworld** has one of the world's best collections of vintage cars and there is also a military museum.

South-east of the centre

Musée Victor Horta, *rue Americain 25, Ixelles*, was the home of a Belgian Art Nouveau architect and many people think it's worth the trip south-east (tram nos. 81/92) to see the house, as the interior is absolutely typical of his style.

South-west of the centre

If you like beer, it's worth visiting the **Musée Gueuze**, *rue Gheude 56, Anderlecht*, 10 mins walk from Midi. It's a working brewery which offers tours that include a sampling.

- -

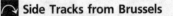 **Side Tracks from Brussels**

MECHELEN

Station: Centraal, *Koning Albert I plein; tel: (015) 41 59 11*. About 10 mins walk south of the centre. There are frequent trains between Brussels and Mechelen, taking about 15 mins. **Tourist Office:** *Stadhuis, Grote Markt; tel: 20 12*

56. Apr–Sept, Mon–Fri 0800–1800 and Sat–Sun 0930–1700; Oct–Mar, Mon–Fri 0800–1700 and Sat 1000–1700.

This old religious centre is now a pleasant town focusing on **Grote Markt**, which is flanked by medieval buildings, including the **Town Hall** (*Stadhuis*). Tapestry has been a Flemish craft for centuries and **Koninklijke Manufactuur Van Wandtapijten** has fine displays and offers tours of a working tapestry mill.

The Cathedral of **St-Rombout** dominates the centre. The interior is largely black and white marble, the light from stained-glass windows illuminating Van Dyck's *Crucifixion* and other works of art. The tower has two carillons, each with 49 bells, where campanologists from all over the world come to learn their art. Among the exhibits in the **Museum Hof van Busleyden** (housed in a splendid 16th-century mansion) is a section on bells.

To glimpse a fairy-tale world, visit the **Speelgoedmuseum**, filled with toys from everybody's childhood. Another magical place is the tiny **Horlogerie** Museum, crammed with ticking antique clocks.

The Church of **St-Jan** has a magnificent altar triptych by Rubens, the *Adoration of the Magi*. Another Rubens triptych, the *Miraculous Draught of Fishes*, is in **Onze-Lieve Vrouw over de Dijle** (across the river). **St Pieter and Paulus** has an oak pulpit carved to depict the work of Jesuit missionaries.

LEUVEN

This is an old university town with many fine buildings, including a High Gothic Town Hall (*Stadhuis*) and the 15th-century **St-Pieterskerk**. There are trains hourly (from all three Brussels stations), the journey taking about 25 minutes.

WATERLOO

Waterloo is a 1 hr 30 mins–2 hr bus ride south of Brussels. There are also trains from Centrale. If you climb to the top of the Lion Mound (226 steps), you get a panoramic view of the battlefield and there are several related museums.

LUXEMBOURG

Station: Centrale Station, Luxembourg Ville, *tel: 49 24 24*, is about 15 mins walk south of the centre and is the hub for taxis and buses. The blue and yellow buses cover the city and some outlying areas: details of these and long-distance services from the information counter in the station, where you can get 10-ride tickets.

Tourist Offices: Municipal, *pl. d'Armes*; *tel: 22 28 09*, is in the old town. Daily 0900–1830/1930 (closed Sunday in winter). They can recommend a walking route. National, in the Luxair office, *pl. de la Gare*; *tel: 48 11 99*. Daily 0900–1800/1900 (closed Sunday in winter).

Arriving and Departing

The Grand Duchy of Luxembourg is south of Brussels, just over the border from the Belgian province of the same name. The journey takes about three hours by train and the service is frequent from all three main stations in Brussels.

You don't need to change money, as Belgian notes are accepted everywhere. Belgian and Luxembourg francs are worth the same and notes are more-or-less interchangeable but you may have problems with coins, so don't get left with too many.

Accommodation

Ib, *Ic* and *Pu* hotels can be found in Luxembourg Ville. For budget accommodation, try the area near the station, or the **IYHF**, *rue du Fort Olisy 2*; *tel: 22 68 89*. Bus nos. 9/16 from the station. The **campsite** is north of the centre, on the edge of Grungewald forest. Bus no. 20 (or 40 mins walk) from the centre.

Sightseeing

Luxembourg is a small, independent country with a population of less than half a million, 25% of whom live in the capital. French and German are both official languages, but a local form of German is the most commonly spoken. Almost everyone can speak some English, including the emergency services (*tel: 012*). **Ville de Luxembourg** was founded in Roman times and is dramatically sited on a gorge cut by the rivers Alzette and Petrusse. It falls naturally into three sections: the old centre is on the north of the Petrusse gorge and home to most of the sights; the modern city and the station are south of the gorge; Grund is the valley settlement.

Walking from the station to the centre, the 19th-century **Passerelle Viaduct** provides a great view of the city perching on the gorge.

Carved out of the rock at **Petrusse** are some 24 km of underground passages that formed part of the original defences. Two of the *Casements* (as they are known) are open to the public. There are similar passageways at Rocher du Bock, the site of the original fortress.

The old city centres on *place d'Armes*, from which everything of interest is within easy walking distance.

The royal residence since the 19th century has been the **Palais-Grand-Ducal** and there are guided tours when no state functions are taking place. In the **place de la Constitution** is a war memorial in the form of a golden woman. The **Cathédrale Notre-Dame** was a 17th-century Jesuit church and retains a Baroque crypt and organ loft. **Maquette** is a small museum that depicts the fortress at various stages of its history, while exhibits in the **Musée de l'Etat** range from the Stone Age to the 20th century.

The 17th-century **Citadelle du St-Esprit** is on the site of a former monastery. From the citadel, you can take a lift down to the **Grund**, to have a look at the settlement in the valley and relax in the pleasant parks.

Out of Town

If you want to see more of the Grand Duchy, you can get a *billet réseau* which provides unlimited (second-class) travel on all the country's trains and buses. The cost is LFr.120 for one day, or you can get a block of five for LFr.480. There are plenty of campsites and hostels scattered around the country. The wonderful scenery of the Ardennes (north from the capital) is particularly worth seeing, with countless verdant valleys interspersed by rocky crags on which ancient castles are perched. You could make the focal point of your visit to this area **Diekirch**, where there are a 7th-century church and traces of Celtic and Roman habitation.

BRUSSELS
to
FRANKFURT

This route takes you from Belgium to Germany and includes the Belgian towns of the scenic Meuse valley.

TRAINS

ETT tables: 33, 210, 215, 200, 700, 650.

➡️ Fast Track

The full journey between Brussels (both Midi and Nord) and Frankfurt am Main (Hbf) takes just over 5 hrs and involves a change at Cologne. There are at least nine connections daily.

A supplement is always payable on the IC trains along the German segments (on which there is a dining car), but can be avoided on the stretch between Brussels and Cologne.

〰️ On Track

Brussels–Namur

Trains are very frequent (at intervals of about half an hour throughout the day) and the journey takes about an hour. Most call at all three main stations in Brussels.

Namur–Liège

Trains between Namur and Liège (Guillemins) are frequent throughout the day and the journey usually takes 40–50 mins.

Liège–(Border)–Aachen

There are about 15 trains a day between Liège (Guillemins) and Aachen (Hbf) and the gap between them is seldom as long as two hours. The journey takes 40–45 mins.

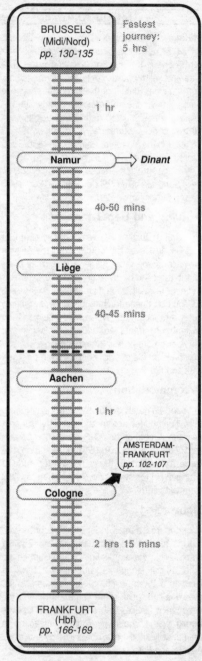

BRUSSELS (Midi/Nord) pp. 130-135

Fastest journey: 5 hrs

1 hr

Namur ⟹ Dinant

40-50 mins

Liège

40-45 mins

Aachen

1 hr

AMSTERDAM-FRANKFURT pp. 102-107

Cologne

2 hrs 15 mins

FRANKFURT (Hbf) pp. 166-169

Aachen–Cologne (Köln)

There are at least 20 trains a day (more if you don't mind paying a supplement) between Aachen (Hbf) and Cologne (Hbf) and there's seldom a gap of much more than an hour between them. The journey averages 1 hr.

Cologne–Frankfurt am Main

There are hourly EC and IC trains between Cologne (Hbf) and Frankfurt (Hbf), the journey taking about 2 hrs 15 mins (or 2 hrs if you want Frankfurt airport). *For the On Track description (along the Rhine Gorge), see the Amsterdam–Frankfurt route, pp. 102–107.*

NAMUR

Station: *tel: (081) 25 21 11.* This is a three-minute walk north of the centre.
Tourist Offices: Municipal *pl. Leopold,* about 300 m from the station; *tel: (081) 22 28 59.* Open Mon–Fri 0900–1200 and 1400–1700 and Sat–Sun 0900–1200 and 1400–1500. You can get multi-attraction tickets, which cover things like river trips and entrance to museums, and are cheaper than paying for each individually. **Provincial** *rue Notre Dame 3; tel: (081) 22 29 98.* Open Mon–Fri 0800–1200 and 1300–1700.

Getting Around

Distances are not vast and walking between the major attractions is quite possible, but the overall area of interest is fairly widespread and you may like to use buses to cover the longer stretches.

Accommodation

The tourist office can provide details of hotels; for travellers on a budget there are a couple of cheap hotels near the station and the tourist office lists private homes that provide accommodation. The **IYHF,** *av. Felicien Rops 8; tel: (081) 22 36 88* (bus nos 4/5 from the station) is definitely above average. The nearest official **campsite** is in *Lives-sur-Meuse,* about 10 km away, but the tourist office can provide a list of farms which permit camping (with prior permission).

Sightseeing

The capital of the French-speaking Belgian province of Wallonia, Namur is a resort set attractively at the confluence of the Meuse and Sambre rivers. You can take a variety of boat excursions on the Meuse.

The town is dominated by a medieval **Citadel** which began life as a Celtic hill fort. It is now a 15th–19th-century complex that has been converted into a tourist area. The 19th-century **Château**, which stands in lovely gardens, now houses a hotel. You can reach the complex by taking a cable-car (from *Pied-du-Château*) and go round it on a miniature train.

The **Cathédrale Saint-Aubin,** *pl. St-Aubin,* is a domed 18th-century structure with rich decorations from the Rubens school. Its treasury, which contains several priceless objects, is the **Musée Diocesan,** *pl. du Chapitre.* One item of particular interest is a golden crown which is a reliquary for what are reputed to be pieces of Christ's crown of thorns.

The **Musée de la Forêt,** *route Merveilleuse 9,* is devoted to the Ardennes flora and fauna and there are over a dozen other museums. Among them are the **Musée Archéologique,** *rue du Pont,* with Roman finds from the Meuse Valley; the **Musée des Arts du Namurois,** *rue de Fer 24,* which has a fine collection of medieval art; and the **Musée de Groesbeeck de Croix,** *rue Joseph Saintraint 5,* which exhibits many 17th- and 18th-century *objets d'art* from the region.

As a complete contrast, the riverside **Casino,** *av. Baron de Moreau,* is one of the town's more modern attractions.

- - - - - - - - - - - - - - - - - -
Side Track from Namur

Dinant is one of the main tourist centres in the picturesque Ardennes and trains from Namur are frequent (at least every hour), the journey taking less than 30 mins. In summer, it is also possible to take a full-day river trip which allows about two hours in Dinant. The **tourist office** (*rue Grande 37; tel: (082) 22 28 70*) is open Mon–Fri 0830–1700 (open daily in high season).

About 500 m from the station, on the left bank of the Meuse, is the **Grotte la**

Merveilleuse, a beautiful complex of caves with white stalactites and waterfalls. The 13th-century church of **Notre-Dame** has been converted, but retains a superb rose window and graceful proportions. The **Citadel** houses arms and war museums. It stands 100 m above the Meuse (reached by cable-car) and gives a tremendous view of the valley. **Mont-Fat** (reached by chair-lift) is a recreational park which incorporates such natural features as a maze of underground passages, prehistoric caves and hanging gardens.

LIÈGE

Station: Guillemins, *tel: (041) 52 98 50*. This is 2 km south of the city centre (bus nos 1/4), with a tourist office: *tel: (041) 52 44 19*.

Tourist Offices: Municipal:, *Féronstrée 92; tel: (041) 22 24 56*. Open Apr–Oct, Mon–Fri 0900–1800 and Sat 1000–1600 and Sun 1000–1400; Nov–Mar, Mon–Fri 0900–1700. Provincial: *blvd de la Sauvinière 77; tel: (041) 22 42 10*. Open Mon–Fri 0830–1800 and Sat 0830–1300.

Getting Around

The centre is small and easily covered on foot: a 3 km walk will take you past all the major sights. There are buses if you wish to go further afield. Boat-trips on the river are available (*tel: (041) 87 43 32*) and there are tours by taxi (*tel: (041) 67 66 00*).

Accommodation

Hotel chains in Liège include *Ft, Hl, Ib* and *Ra*. The cheapest hotels are in the area around the station.

Sightseeing

At first glance, Liège looks fairly unpromising (just a large industrial city at the confluence of the Meuse, Ourthe and Vesdre), but there is much to reward visitors. There are two quite distinct sections, the old and the modern town, the boundary between the two being marked by the *pl. de la République Française*. The city has a rich legacy of art, as reflected in the many churches and museums.

Little is left of the original **Citadel** but, if you can face the climb up *Montagne de Bueren* (374 steps), you will be rewarded with an excellent view.

The city centre is the **pl. St-Lambert**, where you will find the 16th-century **Palais des Prince-Évêques**, which was once a magnificent royal home and now houses the provincial government and Court of Justice. You can visit the two inner courts, one of which has 60 columns, each individually carved. **Le Perron** is an ornate fountain that symbolises the town's history. In the **Hôtel de Ville** the Salle des Pas Perdus contains Delcour sculptures.

In the new town, the **Cathédrale St-Paul**, *rue Bonne-Fortune*, has a fine interior and its treasury includes priceless items of gold, silver and ivory, while the **Église St-Denis**, off *rue de la Cathédrale*, has a notable 16th-century wooden altarpiece.

The octagonal **Église St-Jean**, *pl. Neujean*, has some good sculptures and the Romanesque **Église St-Jacques**, off *pl. St-Jacques*, is built in varying architectural styles and has an interesting interior, including five Renaissance stained-glass windows.

Situated in a square of the same name, the **Église de St-Barthélemy** is a restored Romanesque building which contains a superb 12th-century bronze baptismal font.

The **Musée Curtius**, *quai de Maestricht 13*, is devoted to the decorative arts and has an outstanding collection of glass and porcelain, with over 9,000 pieces. The **Musée d'Armes** (at no 8) houses an extensive collection of firearms, many of them very ornate.

The most interesting of several museums devoted to different aspects of the region is the **Musée de la Vie Wallonne**, *cour des Mineurs*, which is housed in a restored Franciscan monastery and contains craft tools such as those used by coppersmiths and glassblowers. The **Musée d'Art Religieux**, *rue Mère-Dieu*, contains some excellent examples of Mosan (Meuse Valley) craftsmanship, including several jewel-encrusted religious objects.

The **Aquarium**, *quai Van Beneden 22*, has 40 excellently laid-out tanks creating a diversity of underwater habitats and containing over 300 types of sea creature. There is also a **Zoological Museum**.

AACHEN

Station: *Reumontstrasse 1; tel: (241) 143 3422.* This is a 10-minute walk from the centre.
Tourist Offices: (central), *Atrium Eliserbrunnen, Friedrich-Willem Platz; tel: (241) 180 2960.* Open Mon–Fri 0900–1830 and Sat 0900–1300. By the station, *Bahnhofplatz 4; tel: (241) 180 2965.* Open Mon–Fri 0900–1830 and Sat 0900–1300.

Sightseeing

Now of importance only as a frontier town between Belgium and Germany, Aachen was once a great city. Charlemagne enjoyed the thermal springs and made it the capital of his great empire, building an octagonal chapel in his palace. His chapel is now the heart of the **Dom** (Cathedral), hence the French name for the town, Aix-la-Chapelle. Some of the original structure survives and his successors added many embellishments. Charlemagne's gilded tomb is here and the imperial throne, but the latter can be seen only if you join a guided tour.

The **Treasury** (*Schatzkammer*) is one of Europe's richest. Among the other priceless objects it houses are a solid gold bust of Charlemagne and a jewel-encrusted 10th-century cross.

There are statues of 50 former emperors on the facade of the 14th-century **Rathaus**, a building which incorporates two of the original palace towers. Inside are replicas of the crown jewels (the originals are in Vienna).

In the new **Ludwig Forum für Internationales Kunst**, *Julicherstrasse*, is an excellent collection of East European art.

COLOGNE (KÖLN)

Station: *tel: (0221) 19419.* This is very central, just north of the cathedral (*Dom*).
Tourist Office: *Unter Fettenhennen 19; tel: (0221) 3345,* by the Dom. Mon–Sat 0800–2230 and Sun 0900–2230. They dispense a variety of free literature.

Accommodation

Central rooms are almost always at a premium and the cheap hotels are very scattered. The tourist office may be able to help, but it's possible nothing will be available if you don't book ahead. Hotel chains in Cologne include *Ex, HI, Hy, Ic, Pu, Ra,* and *SA.*

The more central of the two **IYHF** hostels is *Siegesstr. 5A; tel: (0221) 081 47 11,* 15-mins walk from Hbf, over the Hohenzollernbrucke, a couple of blocks south of Deutz station.

The most accessible **campsite** is *Weidenweg, Poll; tel: (02210 83 19 66,* south-east of Altstadt (tram 16: *Marienburg*).

Sightseeing

Some sights are scattered round the city, but the major ones are all clustered together near the Dom.

Cologne has several claims to fame. Apart from being home to one of the world's greatest cathedrals and the place where *eau de Cologne* originated, it has more breweries than any other city in the world (24, all producing the distinctive local beer *Kölsch*). It also hosts the **Karneval**, one of Europe's greatest street celebrations. This week-long festival precedes Lent and is enormous fun – but stay away if you don't like crowds.

Over two thousand years old, the city was important in Roman times and as a medieval centre. After a period of decline, the 18th century saw a revival in the town's fortunes when a supposed aphrodisiac made by distilling flower blossoms found fame as a perfume. If you want the genuine **eau de Cologne**, look for labels saying *Echt Kölnisch Wasser* or buy 4711: **Haus 4711**, *Glockengasse*, has been the home of the perfume since 1792. Its *glockenspiel* that chimes every hour 0900–2000.

The Cathedral

The Gothic **Dom** began life as a 12th-century golden shrine housing alleged relics of the Magi, but building was interrupted and it was not completed for over 600 years. The result justifies the wait, with stained glass covering several centuries and a magnificent chancel, but so

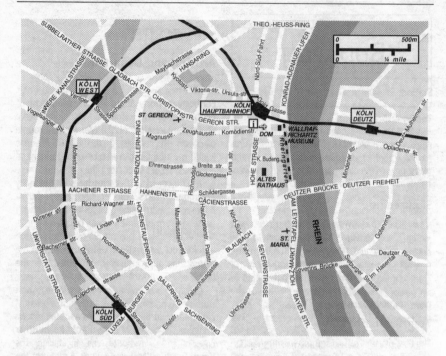

many superlatives apply that it is invidious to pinpoint any particular feature. The 9th-century *Gero Crucifix* in the north chapel and the 15th-century triptych of the *Adoration of the Magi* in the south chapel, for instance, are among the world's best of their kind. Allow plenty of time to absorb the masterpieces in the cathedral itself and also those in the treasury and museum.

Museums

The neighbouring **Römische-Germanisches Museum**, *Roncalliplatz 4*, was built around the *Dionysos Mosaic*, an excellently preserved work of over a million pieces that dates from around AD 200 and was discovered only in 1941. The museum contains other Roman relics, including an officer's tomb and outstanding displays of glass, jewellery and everyday items.

Nearby, on *Bischofsgartenstrasse*, is a modern complex that includes three museums. The smallest, **Agfa-Foto-Historama**, is a must for anyone interested in photography. The 15th–16th-century works are the highlight of the

Wallraf-Richartz-Museum, while the **Museum Ludwig** is home to works by 20th-century masters. The multi-style **Rathaus** has been faithfully reconstructed and features an octagonal Gothic tower and a Renaissance facade, with a *glockenspiel* that rings twice daily, at 1200 and 1700. Behind it, from *Kleine Budengasse*, there is access to the subterranean remains of the Roman **Praetorium**, including the grand vaulted sewer, and **Mikwe**, a 12th-century Jewish ritual bath.

Surrounding the centre is a chain of a dozen well-restored 10th–12th century Romanesque churches, of which **St Gereon** (to the west) is the most interesting, although **St Maria im Kapitol** (to the west) has the finest interior.

The **Museum für Ostasiatische Kunst**, *Universitätstr.100* (tram nos. 1/2) has a cosmopolitan collection, including a Japanese stone garden. Cologne has many other museums, the more unusual devoting themselves to **Carnivals**, the **Secret Police**, **Eating Utensils** and **The Beatles**.

BUDAPEST

Budapest is arguably the finest of all the great cities on the Danube. The city has features found in other European capitals – grand Habsburg architecture similar to that in Vienna, broad boulevards inspired by Paris, even a medieval castle hill like Prague – yet it still maintains a unique Hungarian character.

Budapest has always been one of the most vibrant cities in Eastern Europe and was well placed to capitalise on the lifting of the Iron Curtain. The city now attracts thousands of visitors, who are drawn to its animated streets, spectacular setting, fine array of historical sights and reasonable cost of living.

Tourist Information

The best place to obtain sightseeing information about Budapest is at **Tourinform**, *2 Süto út; tel: 117 9800* (metro: *Deák tér*). The multilingual staff are extremely knowledgeable and can supply free leaflets and maps. Open daily 0800–2000.

Ibusz, the Hungarian tourist organisation, has offices throughout Budapest; although primarily intended for booking rooms and organising tours, they also have useful city information. Ibusz have convenient offices at all three railway stations, open 0800–1800/2000: *Nyugati (tel: 112 3615), Keleti (tel: 122 5429)* and *Déli (tel: 155 2133)*. In addition they have offices at both terminals of FeThis airport (open 0700–2100) and the international pier (open 0700–2100). The most useful Ibusz office in central Budapest is at *3 Petofi tér; tel: 118 5707 or 118 4842* (metro: *Deák tér* or *Ferenciek tére*). This is open 24 hrs for accommodation booking and information. Further important Ibusz offices in Budapest are at *3c Károly körút; tel: 121 1000* and *6 Vigadó út; tel: 118 6466*. The latter, open Mon–Fri 0900–1700, also serves as the **Thomas Cook** office in Budapest. Most major hotels have

Ibusz desks in reception, open Mon–Sat 0800–2000 and Sun 0800–1200.

Arriving and Departing

Airports

Ferihegy airport, about 15 km south-east of Budapest, has two terminals. Most airlines serve Ferihegy 1 (*tel: 157 2122*); Malév and a couple of others use Ferihegy 2 (*tel: 157 7831*). The Ferihegy 2 number can also be used for general enquiries. To get to or from the city centre there is a choice of expensive (and occasionally extortionate) taxis, moderately priced shuttle buses which are widely advertised to arriving passengers, or extremely cheap public transport. For the latter, take bus no. 93 from outside the terminal buildings to *Köbánya–Kispest*, the last stop on the bus route. From there you can take metro line 3 into the centre of Budapest.

Stations

There are three major railway stations in Budapest. These are: **Nyugati Pályaudvar** (West Station), *Nyugati tér; tel: 149 0115;* **Keleti Palyaudvar** (East Station), *Baross tér; tel: 113 6835;* and **Déli Pályaudvar** (South Station), *Magyar Jakobinusok tér; tel: 175 6293*. There are no simple rules for determining which station serves which destination. For example, trains from Romania serve either Nyugati or Keleti. Always check from which station your train leaves. All three are linked by the Budapest metro. Keleti and Déli are on line 2, Nyugati on line 3. All are fairly central, so metro journeys between the centre and the stations are brief.

Getting Around

Budapest is fairly easy to navigate with a reasonably large-scale map; some of the free maps are lacking in detail. Comprehensive street and transport maps of Budapest are displayed in all metro stations; copies of thes or larger-scale central maps can be bought from the ticket kiosks. The Danube (Duna) runs north to south, with Buda on the hills to the west and Pest to the east. The 22 districts of Budapest – 6 in Buda, 15 in Pest and 1 on Csepel Island – are indicated by Roman numerals, and appear in street addresses and on maps. District I contains *Castle Hill* in Buda, district V the *Belváros* in the centre of Pest.

Much of Budapest can be discovered on foot; although distances between sights are not negligible, the public transport system is excellent and whisks you effortlessly across the city.

Metro

The Budapest metro is quick and easy to use. There are three lines, which intersect at *Deák tér*. Tickets are available from kiosks in stations or machines (exact change of a multiple of the ticket price is needed). Tickets must be stamped in the machines at the station entrances for lines M2 and M3 but on board the trains for line M1, which runs just beneath *Andrássy út* (the second-oldest underground railway in the world – after London's Metropolitan Line). A new ticket must be used if you change lines. One- and three-day unlimited travel passes are available, or you can purchase a ten-pack of tickets for the price of nine. Weekly/monthly passes (photo required) are also available.

Buses, Trams and Suburban Trains

Buses, trolley-buses and trams criss-cross Budapest and are useful in areas not served by the metro. The tickets are the same as for the metro: punch them in the machines on board. The suburban network of HÉV overground trains serves more far-flung areas, including Óbuda and the remains of Aquincum. Maps available at metro stations show all the transport routes.

Taxis

There are masses of taxis, so you should have no difficulty hailing one on the street. You may have trouble, though, ensuring that the driver does not overcharge you. Remember to check the meter is switched on when you get in.

Living in Budapest

Accommodation

Budapest's accommodation structure has evolved rapidly over the past few years in an effort to cope with the large growth in visitors. There are now many resources for helping new arrivals find somewhere to stay.

Hotels are generally more expensive than hostels or private rooms. Ask for a list at Tourinform. Familiar brands established in Budapest include *Fo, Hn, Hy, Ic, Ke, Nv, Pe, Ra* and *Rd*. Some of the top hotels have wonderful locations, either on the Pest Danube river bank or up in *Castle Hill*. Pensions, also bookable through Ibusz, offer a compromise between private rooms and hotels.

Private rooms often have more character than rooms in hotels or hostels, and the host can often add local colour to your visit. It is possible to find rooms right in the centre of town; even cheaper ones, deemed to be non-central, are often only two or three metro stops from *Deák tér*. Rates can be fairly high for very short stays. Rooms can be booked at the **Ibusz** offices, **Budapest Tourist**, *(5 Roosevelt tér; tel: 118 1453)*, or at one of the many other tourist agencies. Hustlers occasionally tout unofficial rooms outside the Ibusz office at *3 Petőfi tér*.

Youth and student accommodation in Budapest is also growing. The student travel service **Express**, *16 Szabadság tér; tel: 131 777*, books beds in hostels. More conveniently, hostel organisations advertise widely in the railway stations and can offer free transport to the hostels. The **More Than Ways** university hostel organisation, *152 Dózsa György út; tel: 129 8644*, runs a collection of university dormitories which turn into hostels in July and August and a couple of year-round ex-dorms. The **Hungarian Youth Hostel Federation**, *21 Konkoly Thege; tel: 156 2857*, lists 18 hostels and dormitories in Budapest.

Camping is possible in Budapest. There are a handful of sites accessible by bus, situated in the Buda hills and listed in tourist office handouts.

Communications

The main **telephone office** is at *17–19 Petőfi S ut; tel: 117 5500*. The main **post office** is next door. There are post offices open 24 hrs at *51 Teréz körút* (near Nyugati station) and *11 Baross tér* (near Keleti station). The dialling code for Budapest is 1.

Eating and Drinking

The opening of the Iron Curtain has resulted in a

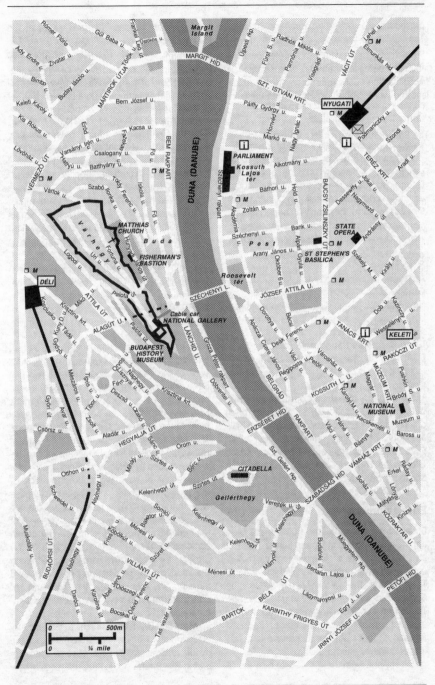

proliferation of western restaurants in Budapest. The standard fast-food chains are all well represented; the remarkable McDonalds at Nyugati station is almost a tourist attraction in its own right.

Traditional Austro-Hungarian food, such as paprika-spiced goulashes or schnitzels, is filling, tasty and widely available, although prices increase dramatically closer to the main tourist areas – especially in the eateries of *Castle Hill*.

The same is true for coffee houses, delicatessens and patisseries, for long a traditional feature of Budapest life. The coffee houses around *Vörösmarty tér* can charge up to five times as much as those only a couple of metro stops away near the stations. Supermarkets are well stocked, so picnics make a good lunch.

Embassies

Australia: *30 Délibáb út.; tel: 153 4233.*
Canada: *32 Budakeszi út.; tel: 176 7711.*
New Zealand: has no diplomatic representation but, in case of emergency, the British Embassy should be able to help.
UK: *6 Harmincad út.; tel: 118 2888.*
USA: *12 Szabadság tér; tel: 112 6450.*

Money

There are plenty of exchange offices in Budapest, but check rates carefully, as they are often different for cash, travellers' cheques and 'small' amounts of money (meaning less than Ft.250,000). Ibusz Hungarian Travel Co., *Vigadó Utca 6*, the **Thomas Cook** network member in Budapest, offers foreign exchange and Thomas Cook travellers' cheques refunds.

Entertainment

Budapest has one of the most diverse and lively entertainment scenes in Eastern Europe. The city also has a gaggle of English-language newspapers, all with some entertainment listings. They include the (weekly) *Daily News*, the *Budapest Sun*, and the *Hungarian Times*. Tourinform also has many details – ask for the excellent monthly listings guide *Budapest Panorama*. The magazine *Grapevine* is a less formal guide to pubs and clubs.

On any one night there is likely to be a choice of top-quality concerts. Opera is staged at the **State Opera House**, *22 Andrássy út; tel: 153 0170*, and the **Erkel Theatre**, *30 Köztársaság tér; tel: 133 0540*. Classical concerts are performed at the **Academy of Music**, *8 Liszt Ferenc tér; tel: 142 0179*, and the **Vigado Concert Hall**, *2 Vigadó tér; tel: 118 9903*. Frequent organ recitals are given in the **Matthias Church**, *Castle Hill*, and **St Stephen's Basilica**. Budapest also has countless cinemas and many films are shown in English.

Club life is colourful and occasionally lewd: the city is fairly well known for its topless bars and the red light area around the VIII district.

Budapest is also renowned for its thermal baths, some of which date back to the Turkish occupation and beyond. There are plenty to choose from: ask at the tourist office for a list. The baths come in varying degrees of price and friendliness, one not always related to the other.

Sightseeing

Buda

Probably the most prominent feature of Budapest is **Castle Hill** (*Várhegy*), on the west bank of the Danube in Buda. The hill was first built upon in the 13th century and has since been occupied by Turks, Habsburgs, Nazis and Soviets; however, the streets still follow their medieval plan. At the south end stands the **Royal Palace**. The first fortifications were built by one of Hungary's medieval kings. A Renaissance palace was succeeded by a Habsburg construction, later occupied by the Nazis and reduced to rubble by the Soviets. The present building is strictly post-war, but foundations and ramparts from the Renaissance palace survive in the lower levels of the **Budapest History Museum**. The **Hungarian National Gallery** contains Hungarian art through the ages (fairly hard going, although the modern art can be exciting). The third museum in the palace, the **Museum of Contemporary History**, has fascinating temporary exhibitions.

Matthias (Mátyás) Church, a 19th-century extension of a 13th-century church, stands in the middle reaches of Castle Hill. Used as a mosque during the Turkish occupation, the church now contains the tomb of King Béla III. Outside is a handsome statue of King St Stephen (István), a key figure in Hungary's history, who brought the Magyar tribes together in the 10th century.

The twee white staircases, ramparts and towers of **Fisherman's Bastion** afford a classic view of the Danube and Pest, although swamped by tourists and street musicians. Allegedly Danube fishermen defended this area in the Middle Ages (a more prosaic explanation of the name is that the local catch was sold here). The neighbouring Hilton Hotel incorporates remains of a Dominican Abbey, surprisingly tastefully restored. The streets to the north and west are full of Baroque houses and Gothic stonework. The western ramparts offer a quiet promenade and fine views. You can walk up to *Castle Hill* from *Déli* or *Moskva tér* metro stations; shuttle buses also run from *Moskva tér* and there is a funicular (the second ever built) from the end of the Chain Bridge.

Gellért Hill (*Gellerthegy*), south of Castle Hill, is, at 130m, a slightly more challenging climb. From the top you look down on the Royal Palace; the views from here are unsurpassed. The **Liberation Monument** commemorates, ironically enough, the Soviet liberators of Budapest. The squat, featureless **Citadella** was built by the Habsburgs after the 1848 revolution to subjugate the city, replacing a wooden Turkish fort.

The **Buda Hills**, to the west, offer a wooded retreat for walking and recreation. It is possible to do a circuit of the woods on novel modes of transport, via a cogwheel railway from *Szilágyi Erzsébet fasor*, the narrow-gauge Children's Railway, and a chair-lift. **Margit Island**, in the Danube offers miles of river promenades. North of *Castle Hill*, in Buda, lies the exclusive suburb of **Roszadomb**. Further north is **Óbuda** (*Old Buda*), the oft-forgotten third constituent of Budapest, but the oldest settlement of the city. The remains of Roman **Aquincum**, a regional capital in the 2nd and 3rd centuries AD, can be visited from the *Aquincum* or *Romai-Furdo* HEV stations.

Pest

Pest, the eastern half of the city, is flat, commercial and busy. The layout is formed by two concentric semicircular avenues, with major avenues radiating out like spokes. The hub of the half-circle is the **Belváros**. Here you'll find **Váci út**, the smartest shopping street in Budapest, and **Vörösmarty tér**, full of street caricaturists and over-priced cafés. The waterfront promenade is largely unremarkable, except for great views of *Castle* and *Gellért Hills*. Pest's posh hotels have taken over most of the best sites here, although the **Vigadó Concert Hall** adds a little bit of style. Liszt, Mahler and Wagner performed here.

Further north along the bank stands the **Parliament** building, an extravagant neo-Gothic construction of 1884–1904, captured in countless photos from across the river. Tours of the building can be arranged through the tourist office.

St Stephen's Basilica, the largest church in Budapest, is another memorial to Budapest's patron saint. Built in the late 19th century, the basilica is currently being restored. It contains the sacred mummified hand of the saint himself.

The **National Museum**, *14--16 Múzeum körút*, contains what is alleged to be the coronation regalia of King St Stephen, as well as exhibitions detailing Hungary's colourful history split into two sections, pre- and post-896, the settlement of Hungary by the Magyars. The **Central Synagogue**, *2--8 Dohány út*, off *Károly körút*, holds 3,000 people and is one of Europe's largest. St Saens and Liszt both played the organ here. A metal weeping willow stands in memory of the victims of the Budapest ghetto.

Andrássy út, Budapest's most famous avenue, runs out north-east from *Bajcsy Zsilinsky ut*. The avenue enjoyed a brief spell as *Népköztársaság útja* (Avenue of the People's Republic) before reverting to its former name. The neo-Renaissance **Opera House**, *22 Andrassy út*, has seen performances by Mahler and Klemperer, amongst others. For information on tours, *tel: 143 1360*. Further along *Andrassy út*, past the Oktagon, is the **Liszt Memorial Museum**, *35 Vörösmarty út*, where the composer lived in the late 19th century.

Andrassy út ends at **Heroes' Square** (*Hösök tere*) where the stark **Millenary Monument** marks 1000 years of Magyar settlement.

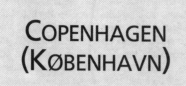

COPENHAGEN (KØBENHAVN)

Proud of its history, home of the oldest kingdom and the oldest 'gagade' (pedestrian street) in the world, Copenhagen nevertheless has a buzzing youth culture. Tivoli's bright lights and fast rides are still the major crowd puller, the antithesis of the 'hygglig' (an untranslatable word that means something a bit like 'cosy') lifestyle found on rainy days in coffee shops.

Tourist Information

Office at *1, Bernstorffsgade*, tel: *(01) 33 11 13 25*, opposite the station by Tivoli's main entrance gate. Open daily 22 Apr–31 May 0900–1800; 1 June–19 Sept 0900–2000; 20 Sept–26 Apr Mon–Fri 0900–1700, Sat 0900–1400. Comprehensive information (including the essential *Copenhagen This Week*), on all of Denmark. **Youth tourist information**: at the excellent **Use It**, *13 Rådhusstraede*, tel: *(01) 33 15 65 18*. Open daily in summer, 0900–1900; mid-Sept–mid-June, Mon–Fri 1000–1600. There is an information desk at the airport. **Thomas Cook's** office in Copenhagen is Maersk Travel, *Marina Park, Sundkrogsgade 12*; tel: *(01) 39 29 34 66*.

Arriving and Departing

Airport

Kastrup Airport, tel: *(01) 31 54 17 01*, can be reached from the city centre by taxi (about DKr.120) or by bus. The SAS bus runs to and from the main railway station (exit *Bernstorffsgade*) every 10–15 mins 0600–2100. Journey time: 20 mins. Bus no. 32 is a longer but slightly cheaper alternative which departs from *Rådhuspladsen* (outside the Town Hall) every 10 mins.

Trains

København Hovedbanegårde (the main station) is at, *Bernstorffsgade*, tel: *(01) 33 14 88 00*

(domestic), *33 14 30 88* (international). In summer, there is an **Inter-Rail Centre** with showers and information. All international and domestic trains travelling west or south also stop at **Høje Taastrup**, *Banestrøget 5*; tel: *(01) 42 52 33 66*.

Regionaltog services (indicated by the letters 'Re') are slower, with more stops, than the main-line trains. The *Inter-city* trains to and from Copenhagen require a reservation (*pladsbillet*) which costs DKr.25 (also usually required for travel in Fyn and Jylland). Buy them at the DSB *Rejsecentres* (travel centres).

Buses

There is no main bus station so enquire at the tourist office for specific destinations.

Getting Around

Maps (with bus routes marked) are free from the tourist office and **Use It** (which provides excellent guides covering the city 'by foot', 'by bike', or 'by bus'). Bicycles are a real alternative to public transport. Hiring is cheaper than a 24-hour bus and train pass and roads are, literally, made for it. Try the *DSB Cykelcenter, Reventlowsgade*; tel: *(01) 33 14 07 17*, at the station.

Public transport is either by bus (pick one up from Rådhuspladsen) or train. The area of greater Copenhagen is best served by the 11 **S-tog** (metro) lines which converge on the centre. From the S-tog you can link up with the main-line service. Within the centre, jump on and off the S-Tog between Østerport and København H.

Tickets

Buses and trains form part of an integrated system and tickets are valid on both. Fares are calculated on the basis of different zones (shown on the many maps on display on the trains and buses, or pick up a leaflet at the station). The cheapest ticket (DKr. 10) covers travel in two zones for one hour and is the equivalent of a single. A 24-hour pass costs DKr.65 and it can be hard to get your money's worth.

A *klippekort* is a multiple ticket validated by the machines on board buses and on station platforms. The *Copenhagen Card* (DKr 120–250), valid for 1, 2 or 3 days, covers public transport in Copenhagen and most of Sealand,

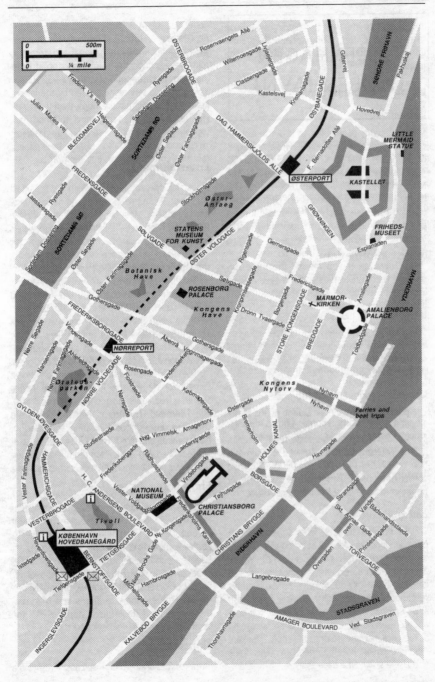

and offers free entrance to most sights. It is on sale at the airport, DSB stations in greater Copenhagen, hotels, travel agents and the tourist office.

Living in Copenhagen

Accommodation

There are many possibilities so it is advisable to contact the *Accommodation Service* at the Tourist Office, *tel: (01) 33 12 28 80*, open daily 22 Apr–19 Sept 0900–2400; 20 Sept–24 Apr, Mon–Fri 0900–1700 and Sat 0900–1400. **Use It** don't charge for reservations. Outside their opening hours (see Tourist Information) there is an external display-board indicating room vacancies in hostels and sleep-ins. Booking ahead is advisable if you have somewhere in mind. However, if you reserve the same day through the tourist office you can save at least 25% on hotel rooms. Hotel groups in the city include *Ch, Ex, SA* and *Sh.*

The sleep-in on *Per Henriks Allé; tel; 35 26 50 59*, open Jul–Aug, offers hostel-style, conveniently located accommodation. The most central **campsite** is **Bellahøj Camping**, *Hvidkildevej; tel: (01) 31 10 11 50*, open Jun–Aug.

Communications

The **post office** at the main station opens Mon–Fri 0800–2200, Sat 0900–1600, and Sun 1000–1700 and will also receive poste restante mail.

The **Telecom Centre**, also at the main station, *tel: (01) 33 14 20 00* (open 0800–2200), is a convenient option. Phone boxes take cash or phone cards, available from the post office.

Eating

Try the polser (sausages) from street stalls, or open sandwiches. As well as being very Danish, fast food such as this is cheaper, in a city where eating out can be expensive. Lunchtime menus can cost about DKr.50. Another option is ethnic restaurants. The (red-light) districts *Halmtorvet* and *Istedgade* have many; *Frederiksberg* is another good area. Chinese food is cheap, and as the price increases so does the choice: Balkan, Japanese, Greek, Italian. *Copenhagen This Week* and Use It's *Playtime* have listings.

Embassies

Australia: *21, Kristianiagade; tel: (01) 35 26 22 44*
Canada: *1, Kristen Bernikowsgade; tel: (01) 33 12 22 29*
New Zealand: None – try Australian or British.
UK: *40, Kastelsvej; tel: (01) 35 26 46 00*
US: *24, Dag Hammerskjolds Alle; tel: (01) 31 42 31 44*

Entertainment

Clubs stay open until 0500, when the breakfast bars open. Films are shown in original language and subtitled. Most cinemas offer half-price tickets on Mondays. The **Palads**, *Axeltorv 9*, is the largest. Many cafés and bars have live music (jazz is very popular); for a list of venues, consult the **Use It** publication, *Playtime*.

Tivoli amusement park is Copenhagen's playground, with everything from fairground rides to ballet, and 29 restaurants. It is best seen at night when the fairy lights are switched on. Three nights a week (ask on arrival), fireworks are let off just before midnight. **Tivoli Billet-bureau**, *Vesterbrogade 3*, for the park and other tickets.

The city's theatrical tradition is long. Amongst some 160 stages, the **Royal Theatre** reigns supreme (red lights outside mean it's sold out). The **Mermaid Theatre** is English. The **Scala** shopping centre, good for eating and dancing, has a cinema and disco. The kiosk/ticket office at *Norreport S-tog* sells same-day discounted tickets. *Copenhagen This Week* carries listings.

Shopping

Prices are comparable with other Western European capitals. Design plays an important part in Danish living and household objects, kettles, candlesticks and clocks are good buys. Streets around *Vesterbro, Nørrebro* and *Studiestraede* have many trendy boutiques and second-hand book, record and clothes' shops. Nevertheless **Strøget** (home to **Illums** and **Magasin**, the two biggest department stores) is still the essential area for serious shoppers.

Sightseeing

Entrance fees are common, so consider buying a

Copenhagen Card. Museums close Mondays or weekends.

At the heart of Copenhagen, **Strøget**, a collective name given to the pedestrian-only zone punctuated with pretty squares, is full of shoppers and strollers. Within the area, **Rundetårn** (The Round Tower), *Købmagergade 52*, is an excellent place for a view of the pitched roofs and parks in the distance.

On the far side of *Gothersgade*, the green-roofed Dutch Renaissance-style palace **Rosenborg Slot** sits majestically in the **Rosenborg Have**, *Østervoldgade* (S-tog: *Nørreport*), adjacent to the **Botanical Gardens**, stocked with exotic and interesting plants. The palace, no longer home to the royals, is now a museum of sumptuous 17th-century interiors and furnishings with thrones, tapestries, and chandeliers. The crown jewels are displayed in the basement. From here, beaver-topped guards march to the current royal domicile, **Amalienborg** (at 1130 and only when the queen is in residence). This quartet of Rococo palaces (mid-18th century) frames an octagonal, cobbled courtyard, overlooked by the equestrian statue of Frederick IV. Adjacent **Ameliehaven** is a narrow strip of densely planted garden; good for picnics.

To the north (S-tog: *Østerport*) **Den Lille Havfrue**, the statue of Hans Christian Andersen's Little Mermaid, sits wistfully staring into the middle-distance. Apparently the most photographed woman in the world and highly overrated. Also much photographed is the small, 300-year-old **Nyhavn** (new harbour), bordered by picturesque, 18th-century town houses, ships' masts and cafés. **Kongens Nytorv** joins the quaint harbour with one end of the Strøget. Grand buildings and trees encircle this city square.

Charlottenborg, a 17th-century Dutch-style Baroque palace built for a royal son now houses the **Royal Academy of Arts**. On the nearby corner of *Kanalgade* is **Det Kongelige Teater**, Denmark's finest theatre.

Walking south (down *Holmens kanal* and over the bridge) leads to **Stotsholmen Island**. History, royalty and politics converge in the 100-year-old **Christiansborg**. Bishop Absalon built the first castle (whose ruins are displayed in the base-ment) here in 1167. Today the palace is used for entertaining heads of state. Also housed in the palace, the **Folketing** (Parliament) has daily (summer) or weekly (winter) tours when the house is not sitting. For **Tivoli**, *see Entertainment*.

Museums

The **Ny Carlsberg Glyptotek**, *Dantes Plads 7*, was founded from beer sales by the famous brewing family and is probably the best museum in Copenhagen. Don't miss the Danish Golden Age painting, Rodin's sculptures, the Roman busts and portraits and the collection of French Impressionist work.

Exhibits in the **Nationalmuseet**, *Ny Vestergade 10*, start with the Stone Age and lead you on a cultural tour of Denmark's history. Bertel Thorvaldsen (1770–1844) scattered his sculptures all over Europe but **Thorvaldsens Museum**, *Posthusgade 2*, is the best round-up of his figures.

The **Statens Museum For Kunst** (Royal Museum of Fine Arts), *Sølvgade 48–50*, houses parts of the royal collection, with Danish paintings from the 17th century, and works by European masters such as Matisse, Picassso and Munch.

Side Tracks from Copenhagen

DSB offer special sight-seeing tickets to **Odense**, **Legoland** (see p. 152), Louisiana, Karen Blixen Museum and **Around the Sound** (a round trip to Malmö) which include train travel, entrance to sights, and sometimes discounts. Not necessarily cheap, but very good value.

Louisiana, doyenne of modern art, is a short walk from Humlebaek station. The harmonious setting, in parkland overlooking the Sound is complimented by sculptures by Henry Moore, Max Ernst and Dubuffet, amongst others. Inside most of the permanent collection is post-1945.

Similarly tranquil, the **Karen Blixen Museum**, *Rungstedlund, Rungs Strandvej 111*, is set in a wood and bird sanctuary where the author lived from 1931 until her death and where she wrote *Out of Africa*. The museum includes her private residence.

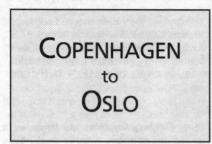

COPENHAGEN to OSLO

This route climbs up through northern Denmark before crossing the water to make a giant loop round southern Norway, using fjord-hugging ferries and the Bergen–Oslo railway, through some of Europe's most spectacular scenery.

TRAINS

ETT tables: 480,450,464,1050,482,1072,481,

⟶ Fast Track

Two trains (reservations required) run daily via Helsingborg and Gothenburg, a completely different line from that of the On Track route. By day there is a dining car and by night sleeping cars and couchettes. The journey takes 10 hrs.

⟿ On Track

Copenhagen–Odense–Aarhus (Århus) –Aalborg

An InterCity service (reservation required) operates every hour Copenhagen–Odense (2 hrs 40 mins), Aarhus (4hrs 20 mins) and Aalborg (6 hrs). Trains have dining-cars, and are carried on the ferry from Korsør to Nyborg.

Aalborg–Hirtshals

There is no direct train. Aalborg–Hjørring services run every hour, taking 40 mins. The line between Hjørring and Hirtshals is private (*tel: 98 92 02 55*) and trains run every 30 mins–1 hr, taking 25 mins.

Hirtshals–Kristiansand

Color Line (*tel: 45 99 56 19 77*; station *tel: 98 94 10 53*) makes three daily crossings (4 hrs 15 mins) to Kristiansand. To be sure of a cabin in

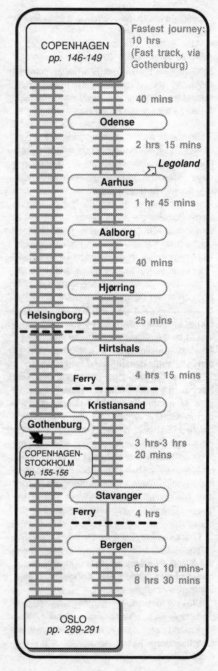

summer it is sometimes necessary to reserve two weeks ahead. Inter-Rail discount 50%.

Kristiansand–Stavanger

This route is dotted with beaches and weather-boarded red and yellow holiday homes nestling in the trees. The journey takes 3 hrs–3 hrs 20 mins by train (three daily).

Stavanger–Bergen

This part of the journey is by ferry (2–3 sailings daily). Journey time is about 4 hrs. Boats hug the coast the whole way, offering some superb views of the southern fjords.

Bergen–Oslo

Four services run daily (3 on Sats) taking 6 hrs 15 mins–7 hrs 55 mins (8 hrs 30 mins overnight – but do this trip in daylight!). Seat reservations (NKr.20) are compulsory for all tickets.

ODENSE

Station: *tel: (066) 12 01 48*. This forms the northern boundary of the city centre. Behind it is a **railway museum**.
Tourist Office: **Rådhuset**, *Jernbanegade; tel: (066) 12 75 20*. June 15–Aug 31, Mon–Sat 0900–1900, and Sun 1100–1900; Sept 1–June 14, Mon–Fri 0900–1700, and Sat 1000–1300.

Sightseeing

Denmark's third largest city and over 1000 years old, Odense is the birthplace of Hans Christian Andersen, the legendary teller of fairy-tales (who spent an unhappy childhood here). The city has museums, a cathedral, some 18th-century houses and many outdoor activities. Most sights lie within a square kilometre south of the station.

There are two shrines for those making the pilgrimage to Hans Christian Andersen's home town. **H.C. Andersen's Barndomshjem** (child-hood home), *Munkemollestraede 3–5*, has a couple of rooms crammed with letters and personal belongings. More noteworthy is the **H.C. Andersen Hus**, *Hans Jensen straede 39–43*.

For art lovers there are at least two places of interest. The **Fyns Kunstmuseum**, *Jernbanegade 13* (free on Weds) houses one of the best collections of Danish art outside Copenhagen. **Brandts Klaedefabrik**, *Brandts Passage, 37*, is a former mill which now houses a cultural centre with temporary exhibitions and modern art.

Sankt Knud's Domkirke (St Knud's Cathedral), *Flakhaven*, houses the 900-year-old remains of the posthumously canonised king, killed by irate taxpayers. From here a stroll down the cobbled *Overgade* leads to **Montergarden**, a couple of well-preserved 18th-century houses containing the **City Museum** with coins, medals and Viking displays.

Den Fynske Landsby, 4 km south (bus nos .21 and 22), is a splendid open-air museum with resurrected 18th- and 19th-century buildings, a school, poorhouse, smithy and water-mill, some thatched, timbered houses, and animals lining the streets. In the summer fairy-tale performances take place.

Museum Hollufgrad, *Hestehaven 201*, on the outskirts of the city (bus no. 81), is an upmarket amusement park, set in and around a 16th-century manor house, offering sculpture workshops, exhibitions, a golf course, and displays of prehistoric and Viking artifacts. Special activities are arranged in summer.

Bus nos.12, 31 and 32 head south-west from the city to **Tivoli**, the amusement park based on the prototype in Copenhagen, while on the other side of the Afarten River lies the **Zoo**. River cruises also make this journey.

AARHUS (ÅRHUS)

Station: *tel: (086) 13 37 77*. Just south of centre.
Tourist Office: In the **Rådhuset**, *Park Allé; tel: (086) 121600*, a good example of Danish architecture in Norwegian marble (guided tours available). Open Jan 2–June 13, Mon–Fri 0930–1630 and Sat 1000–1300; June 14–20, Mon–Sat 0900–1700; June 21–Aug 8, Mon–Sun 0900–2000; Aug 9–Sept 12, Mon–Sun 0900–1900; Sept 13–Dec 31, Mon–Fri 0930–1630 and Sat 1000–1300.

Accommodation

Expect to pay at least DKr.250 for a hotel room, although cheaper alternatives are available. **Aarhus Youth Hostel**, *Marienlundsvej 10; tel:*

(086) 16 72 98, is 4 kms from the centre, a few minutes from the beach and Marselisborg forest. The nearest campsite (open Apr–Sept) is **Blommenhaven Aarhus**, *Ørneredevej 35* (bus nos.19 or 6). Private accommodation can be organised by the tourist office through the *Meet the Danes* programme (closed Dec 15–Jan 15).

Sightseeing

Second city to Copenhagen, Aarhus is a large port, commercial and cultural centre, in many ways Jutland's capital. Only the resurrected, re-constructed old town is pretty, but many activities are laid on for visitors. The large student population makes for some lively entertainment and only 4 km away in both directions beautiful beaches encourage explora-tion.

The biggest attraction in Aarhus is the **Den Gamle By** (Old City), *Viborgvej*, an open-air museum with 70 houses from across Denmark (the oldest are 16th-century) recreating life in an old market town, complete with cobbled streets and craft shops. It is set in the **Botanical Gard-ens**, west of the city centre (bus no. 3: *Hasle*).

Aarhus Domkirke, *Bispetorv*, is the longest church in Denmark, with a 93m nave. The church is mainly late Gothic and inside you will find several restored, pre-Reformation frescoes, once concealed to conform with the new religion.

Just to the west, under the Unibank, a display of Viking remains found during building work for the bank forms the core of the **Vikingemuseet**, *Sankt Clements Torv*. On the other side of the cathedral, at *Domkirkeplads 5*, the **Kvinde-museet** concentrates on the lot of modern woman, and the **Besaettelses-Museet** covers Danish Resistance during World War II.

A short walk from here, **Vor Frue Kirke**, *Frue Kirkeplads*, exhibits the crypt belonging to the original cathedral, dating from about 1060.

The superb **Mosegard Prehistoric Museum**, 5 km south of town, is home in particular to the 2,000-year-old **Grauballe man** found in a bog in 1952. There are good walks nearby.

◢ Side Tracks from Aarhus

Legoland, the only real toy town, made from millions of plastic bricks, is probably one of Denmark's most famous sights, great for children and a real nostalgia trip for many adults.

To get there, either take a bus from Aarhus (about 2 hrs on the Maerska Airline bus to Billund Airport) or take the train to Vejle. From here shuttle buses cover the 27 km to Billund.

AALBORG

Station: *tel: (098) 16 16 66*, a short walk down *Boulevarden* from the town centre.

Tourist Office: **Aalborg Tourist Bureau**, *Østerågade 8; tel: (098) 12 60 22*. June 1–Aug 31, Mon–Fri 0900–1700 and Sat 0900–1600. Otherwise, Mon–Fri 0900–1600 and Sat 0900–1200. This office has a phenomenal collection of brochures for most parts of Jutland.

Sightseeing

Jutland's second largest and voted (1990) Eur-ope's tidiest city, Aalborg sits astride the Lim Fjord. In the 17th century a prosperous herring trade put it on the map, although Vikings were the first settlers here. Today it is chiefly known for the powerful aquavit which shares its name.

Budolfi Domkirke (St Botolphs Cathedral), on the corner of *Algade* and *Østeragåde* is a whitewashed, mainly Gothic church with a Bar-oque steeple. It lies in the very centre of the old town. The **Aalborg Historiske Museum**, *Al-gade 48*, displays finds from the Viking Burial ground, a glass-works collection and period fur-nished rooms.

Behind the museum, the **Monastery of the Holy Ghost** is now an old people's home. Back on *Østeragåde*, there are two well-preserved 17th-century houses (nos.9 and 25).

The **Nordjyllands Kunstmuseum** (Museum of Modern and Contemporary Art), *Kong Christ-ians Allé 50*, is home to 20th-century art and a sculpture garden (free on Tuesdays off season).

Other attractions include the **Zoo Molepark-vej**, one of the most up to date in Europe; **Tivoliland**, with 80 amusements; and the ugly **Aalborgtarnet** (Aalborg Tower) which offers views from 105m.

KRISTIANSAND

Station: *tel: (042) 02 65 00*, the **bus terminal** and **ferry port** (Color Line, *tel: (042) 78800)* are also here, just off *Vestre Strand gate.*
Tourist Office: *Dronningens gt. 2; tel: (042) 22 60 65.* Jun 14–Aug 15 Mon–Fri 0800–1900, Sat 1000–1900, and Sun 1200–1900. The rest of the year it is open Mon–Fri 0800–1600.

Accommodation

Hotel prices usually include breakfast and are reduced in summer. There is a youth hostel, **Kristiansand Vanderhjem** *(Badminton Senteret), Kongsgård Allé 33c; tel: (042) 29 53 69.* **Campsites** are prolific.

Sightseeing

Kristiansand is Norway's fifth largest town and Sorlandet's principal town. For many this is the gateway to Norway. The excellent **Kristiansand Passet** gives free or reduced admission to most sights in the area. It's available from the tourist office, zoo, hotels and campsites. Summer sightseeing **boat trips** around the archipelago (lasting 2–3 hrs) sail from Quay 6.

Surrounded by water on three sides, the city was laid out on a grid pattern in 1641 on the instructions of King Christian IV. *Markensgate* is the town's liveliest street. The old quarter, **Posebyen**, is typified by its little wooden houses. Sights in town include the **Christiansholm Festning**, a circular coastal fortress, built in 1672, and the neo-Gothic **Cathedral**, *Kirkegt.*

Many of the sights lie a short distance out of town. **Gimle Gard** (Gimle Manor), *Gimlevn 23,* 2 km east, is a richly furnished Empire-style mansion, with a botanical garden, animals and a natural history museum. **Kristiansand Dyrepark**, 12 km east, has a zoo with 100 different species, including wolves, a water park, and *Kardemomme By*, a fairytale children's village with trolls and towers. The **Vest-Agder Fylkesmuseum**, *Vigevn, Kongsgard,* is an open-air museum, with reconstructed houses.

STAVANGER

Station: *Jernbaneveien; tel: (051) 52 61 37* is

next to the bus station, about 10 mins walk from the harbour.
Harbour: Color Line has sailings from *Strandkaien; tel: (051) 52 45 45,* to Newcastle and Hirtshals in Northern Denmark (4 hrs).
Tourist Office: *Stavanger Kulturhus, Solveberget; tel: (051) 89 62 00.* Open Mon–Fri, 0900–1700, Sat 0900–1400. In summer, there is an information desk at the harbour.

Locals here are known as *Siddis* from the word *iddis* meaning sardine label, pointing to the historical significance of fishing to the town. Oil now dominates local trade and this has created a large expatriate community, earning the city its epithet 'Oil capital of Norway'. The picturesque harbour is lined with small boats, and the old town is delightful. There's a fine 12th-century **Cathedral**, *Kirkegata*, a **Canning Museum**, *Ovre Srandgate 88A*, and, 5 km west, an **Iron Age Farm**. Also, try the **Maritime Museum**, one of several mansions, and take to the hills or the water for superb views of the fjords (in particular, from **Pulpit Rock**).

BERGEN

Station: *Stromgaten; tel: (05) 96 60 00*, next to the main bus station, 10 mins walk from the centre.
Harbour: Two lines run services to **Stavanger**: **Color Line**, *tel: (005) 54 86 60* run infrequently and **Flaggruten** operate express boats from *Munkebryggen, tel: (05) 23 87 80.* Sailings to Denmark, Scotland, Faroe Islands and Iceland leave from *Skoltegrunnskaien.*
Tourist Office: On the waterfront at *Bryggen; tel: (005) 32 14 80.* Open May 2–Sept 30, Mon–Sat 0830–2100, and Sun 1000–1900. Open the rest of the year, Mon–Sat 0900–1600.

There are many excursions into the fjords. From *Strandkai*, there are day-trips to **Sognefjord**, **Flamby** and **Voss** by boat, bus and train (at NKr.160–470 these are not cheap).

Getting Around

Within the city, you can get almost everywhere on foot, but the 219 days of annual rainfall might encourage use of the yellow buses (a 48-hr pass allows unlimited access to the network). Ferries across the harbour leave Mon–Fri 0700–1615. Cable-car trips to the top of Mount Ulriken allow a view of Bergen, squeezed between the sea and the mountains.

Accommodation

There is a wide array of accommodation, from the plush and expensive, to pensions and several hostels. Try the **Montana Youth Hostel**, *30 Johan Blydtsvei; tel: (005) 29 29 00*. There are several **campsites**, fjord cottages and private rooms. Enquire at the tourist office.

Sightseeing

A Hanseatic port founded in 1070 by King Olav Kyrre, this is the second-largest city in Norway, capital during the 12th and 13th centuries, the gateway to the fjords, and the nearest railway station to Scotland's Shetland Islands. It is surrounded by seven mountains and its setting, the narrow cobbled streets of weatherboard houses and the Hansa-style zigzag roof lines, combine to make it one of the most charming towns in Scandinavia. It is also an excellent base from which to explore the looking-glass fjords and the mountain heights.

At the centre of the old medieval quarter, the wharf area, **Bryggen**, contains a charming row of tidy, medieval houses, now stuffed full of restaurants and craft shops, which are on UNESCO's World Heritage list in spite of the fact that many are post-fire reconstructions. For shabbier, but more genuine houses, try some of the surrounding backstreets.

There are two museums here, the **Hanseatic Museum**, which offers an insight into the life of a 15th-century merchant, in one of Bergen's best preserved old buildings, and the **Bryggens Museum**, which displays archaeological finds, from the 12th century onwards, the result of several digs in the Bryggen area.

Elsewhere, the **Vestlandske Kunstindustri-museum**, *Permanenten, Nordahl Bruns Gate 9*, has a fine display of decorative arts, including superb local silverwork (17th–18th centuries). The **Stenersen Collection**, *Rasmus Meyers alle*, displays post 18th-century art, with works by Ernst, Klee, Munch and other great modern names. There are more Munch paintings in the **Rasmus Meyers Samlinger**, just along the street. There are several other small museums, some fine churches and a couple of towers. On the edge of the city are a large **aquarium**, *Nordnes* (bus no.4), and a **funicular railway** up 320m **Mt Fløien**. A little way further out, **Troldhaugen**, *Nordasvannet*, is the former home of and now a museum dedicated to the great local composer, Edvard Grieg. Nearby is the many times rebuilt **Fantoft Stavkirche** (a typically Norwegian stave church).

BERGEN–OSLO LINE

This is one of the most strikingly beautiful rail journeys in Europe, from the plunging fjords in the west, over the high central mountains to the calmer meadowlands surrounding Oslo. On the way, it passes crystal lakes and waterfalls, prosperous, green farms and desolate mountain wastelands.

The first main stop is **Voss**, a lakeside country town and Alpine sports centre, with a dramatic cable-car, the **Hagursbaren**, covering a height difference of about 600 m in 4 minutes.

The train continues on but many people and organised tours prefer to take the connecting bus to **Vinje** and **Gudvangen**, and catch the ferry along the fabulous *Naeroyfjord* to **Flåm**. Here, you rejoin the train for a truly spectacular 20 km journey to **Myrdal**, climbing 884 m in 40 mins, with 20 tunnels and superb views.

The next section is through the high country, a terrain beloved of summer hikers and winter skiers. **Haugastol** can be a good point of departure for walking tours. At **Hallingskeid**, the track enters a 10 km long tunnel, coming out near **Finse**, a tiny mountain village used by explorers for their Polar training. At 1200m, it is the highest station on the line.

From here, the tracks cross a bleak but magnificent mountainscape of icy lakes and snow-capped peaks to **Geilo**, probably the largest winter sports centre in Northern Europe, teaming with hotels and chair-lifts. After **Gol**, a farming community and winter sports centre within easy reach of Oslo, the train gradually winds its way down through lush green farmland to Oslo.

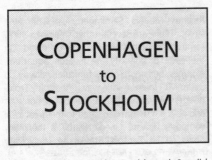

COPENHAGEN
to
STOCKHOLM

This route between the Danish and Swedish capitals runs through gentle lakelands, connecting with Gothenburg, Sweden's second city.

TRAINS

ETT tables: 465, 1213, 1215, 466, 469.

→ Fast Track

This is via Helsingør (supposedly the site of Hamlet's castle) and Helsingborg. Three trains run daily (refreshments available), taking 8 hrs 5 mins–8 hrs 20 mins (longer overnight); reservations required. Overnight trains have couchettes, and first- and second-class sleepers.

~~> On Track

Copenhagen–Malmö

Several ferry sailings daily, taking 45 mins.

Malmö–Helsingborg

Several trains run daily (fewer at weekends), taking 50 mins–1 hr.

Helsingborg–Gothenburg (Göteborg)

There are 7–8 trains daily (fewer at weekends), taking 2 hrs 45 mins–3 hrs 15 mins. Most trains run through from Malmö and have dining cars.

Gothenburg–Stockholm

Several trains daily with dining cars, taking 3 hrs 10 mins–4 hrs 35 mins. The fastest services are X2000 high-speed trains, which require a hefty supplement. The overnight train (second-class couchettes; first- and second-class sleepers) takes 6 hrs–6 hrs 30 mins (no refreshment service).

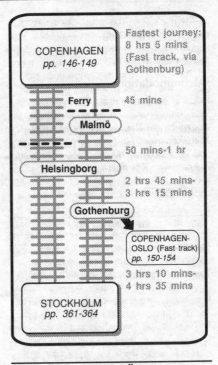

COPENHAGEN-OSLO (Fast track) pp. 150-154

MALMÖ

Station and Harbour: **Centralstationen**, off *Skeppsbron*; for information *tel: (040) 20 20 00*. Ask about local passes, such as the **Öresund Runt** (free travel on local trains, ferries and the hydrofoil for two or three days or a week). Ferry and hydrofoil terminals are on *Skeppsbron*. Boats to Copenhagen: **Flygbåtarna** *tel: 040 10 39 30* and **Pilen** *tel: (040) 23 44 11*.

Tourist Office: *Skeppsbron 2, Borshuset; tel: 040 30 01 50*. In Centralstationen, near the harbour and 2 mins walk from the centre. Open 0900–1700. The tourist office publishes a useful booklet, *Malmö This Month*, and sells the **Malmökort**, a good-value pass for free transport, tours and museum entrance (SKr.90 for one day; there are also two-, three-, and seven-day versions).

Sightseeing

Sweden's third city, this is a lively place which benefits from the influence of Copenhagen (1 hr by ferry/hydrofoil). The central square **Stortorget** and nearby **Lilla Torg** form a core of charming old wooden buildings, while the formidable 16th-century **Malmöhus** used to be the local jail. The state apartments are now open and the fortress also houses Malmö's finest museums, including the **Stadsmuseet** (Town Museum) of local history and art, the **Konsthall**, the **Aquarium** and **Natural History Museum**. The **Tekniskamuseet**, *Turbinbron*, has a maritime and technological collection, including a submarine. The **Kommendanhuset**, *Malmöhusvägen*, has a museum of arms and armaments, and the **Vagnmuseet** has some fine carriages.

HELSINGBORG

Station: Beside the ferry port. *tel: (042) 17 23 00* Mon–Fri; weekends *tel: (020) 75 75 75*.
Tourist Office: *Rådhuset; tel: (042) 120 310*.

Helsingborg, which has an illustrious history, is mentioned in the 10th-century sagas, and was once one of the main centres for Baltic shipping. However, it was totally destroyed by the Danes in 1658. To-day, there are few sights, but it is worth a quick stop. The 13th–14th-century **Kärnan** (Keep), *Kärngränden*, is all that remains of a once-formidable castle, while the **Stadhuset** (Town Hall), *Södrastorgatan 31*, has a small museum of local history and dead animals. Just north of town, the **Frederiksdalsmuseet**, *Oscar Trapps Vag*, is an open-air village museum in the grounds of an 18th-century manor, while the Dutch Renaissance-style **Solfiero Slott**, *Solfierovägen* (5 km on Lärod road), was built in 1865 as a royal summer palace.

GOTHENBURG (GÖTEBORG)

Station: *Nils Ericssonplatsen; tel: (031)175 000.* Central.
Tourist Office: *Kungsportsplatsen 2; tel: (031) 10 07 40.* Sept–Apr: Mon–Fri 0900–1700, Sat 1000–1400; May: Mon–Fri 0900–1800, Sat–Sun 1000–1400; 1–21 Jun and 10–30 Aug: daily 0900–1800; 22 Jun–9 Aug: daily 0900–2000. The **Göteborgskortet** (Gothenburg Card) gives free transport, entry to museums, other attractions, football matches and nightclubs; boat and coach tours and shopping and restaurant discounts. Available from the tourist office, Liseberg, Pressbyrån kiosks, hotels and campsites (SKr.100 for 24 hrs).

Getting Around

Most places are within walking distance. The **bus** and **tram** network is run by *Göteborgs Spårvägar; tel: (031) 80 12 35.* Information and tickets from travel centres at *Brunnsparken, Drottningtorget, Nils Ericssonplatsen* and *Folkungabron*. **Vintage trams** run from Central Station to Liseberg (May–Sept at weekends; daily in July). For details and booking: *Spårvägssällskapet Ringlinen; tel: (031) 80 12 35* (timings). There are guided tours on a miniature train, the **Göteborgtåget** (departs from *Tradsgardsforeningen Park – Södra Vägen* entrance). **Padden** run boat trips round the city canals (May–Sept) leaving from *Kungsportsbron*; boats to **Nya Elfsborg Fortress** (May–Sept) and **Vinga Island** (Jun–Aug) leave from *Stenpiren*.

Sightseeing

Sweden's most important port, this has pretty streets, a wide network of canals and a host of museums and other attractions. The season is short this far north, but there are delightful areas for walking, such as the prettily restored **Haga**, and the **Fish Harbour**; the huge and electric **Liseberg Amusement Park** (open Apr–Sept; tram no.5 from *Brunnsparken*); and great botanical gardens, such as **Trädgårdsföreningen Park, Botaniska Trädgården**, and the **Slottskogen**, home to the Natural History Museum and a children's zoo. Other major attractions include a wide variety of boat and tram tours (see Getting Around). The biggest of the museums is the archaeological, historical and ethnographic **Kulturhistoriska Museet**, in the *Östindiska Huset, Norra Hamngatan 12*. The **Konstmuseet**, *Götaplatsen*, has a large and imposing fine art collection with works by a host of grand masters (Rubens, Rembrandt, Picasso and several of the great Impressionists). The **Maritima Centrum**, *Lilla Bommenshamnen*, is home to a fascinating **Ships Museum**, while the **Sjöfartshistoriskamuseet**, *Karl Johansgatan 1*, near *Stigbergstorget*, covers maritime history.

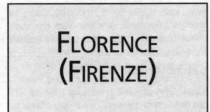

FLORENCE (FIRENZE)

One of the greatest of Italy's old city-states and perhaps still the country's most beautiful city, Florence attracts so many visitors that for much of the year they vastly outnumber locals, at least in the historic centre. There is concern that tourism is beginning to damage the fabric of the medieval buildings. The city, with its extraordinary wealth of art and architecture, can be extremely crowded, and you must be prepared to wait in line to see its most famous exhibits, such as Michelangelo's David.

Tourist Information

The **Azienda Promozione Turistica** (**APT**) has its head office at *Via Manzoni 16, tel: (055) 234 6284/5*, and is open Mon–Sat 0830–1330. The **City of Florence** has tourist information offices at *Chiasso dei Baroncelli 17; tel: (055) 230 2124/230 2033* and at *Piazza della Stazione* (arrival end), *tel: (055) 212245*. There is a combined city and province of Florence office at *Via Cavour 1r; tel: (055) 276 0382*, open 0800–1400 except Sun.

Arriving and Departing

Airports

Amerigo Vespucci Airport, 4km north-west of the city, *tel: (055) .373 498/318 000*, handles mainly domestic and some European services. The **airport bus** is operated by SITA, *Via Santa Caterina da Siena 157, tel: (055) 483 651* (Mon–Fri), *(055) 486 517* (Sun).

Pisa's **Galileo Galilei Airport** (84 km) is the main regional hub for international flights, *tel: (050) 500 707*. Hourly trains run between the airport and Florence's Santa Maria Novella Station, taking about 1 hr. There is a terminal for this airport within the station, *tel: (055) 216 073*.

Stations

Santa Maria Novella (**SMN**), *Piazza della Stazione* is Florence's main rail hub. It is a short walk from the city centre, and the main **bus station** (*tel: (055) 215154*) is next door.. The fast ETR 450 Milan/Florence/Rome express service stops at **Rifredi** station, 3 km north of the city centre. For information on all stations, *tel: (055) 288 785*, 0900–1700.

Getting Around

Most sights are in the compact central zone and the best way to see them all is on foot. You can cover much of the city in two days. You can also rent bicycles from the municipal rental location at *Piazza della Stazione*, next to the SMN station, and at several other outlets around the city. Town maps are available from tourist offices and from ATAF (see below).

Buses

Florence's **Azienda Trasporti Autolinee Fiorentine** (**ATAF**) municipal buses run from 0515 to 0100. There is an ATAF information office opposite the main entrance of SMN rail station, *57 Piazza del Duomo, tel: (055) 580 528*. Buy your tickets singly from machines at main bus stops, in books of five from tobacconists or bars and cancel them in the machine on boarding. Tickets last for one hour from the time the machine stamps them, and you may change buses. You can also buy an all-day *turisticche* (tourist ticket) which costs less than five times the price of a single.

Taxis

Licensed taxis are white with a yellow stripe. Prices are high (flag fall is about six times the cost of a one-hour bus ticket). Avoid unlicensed cabs, which are even more expensive.

Living in Florence

Accommodation

Europe's busiest tourism city as well as a major venue for trade fairs and for business travel, Florence has some magnificent luxury properties such as the exquisite Villa Cora and the elegant

Excelsior. At the other end of the scale, accommodation pickings for the budget traveller are slim. Whichever rung of the accommodation ladder you plan to alight on, try to book well ahead.

The range of hotel chains in the city naturally is wide, and includes: Ch, Ex, HI, Nv, Pu, Sf, Sh.

The cheapest accommodation, though not always the most salubrious, is near the SMN station. Elsewhere, lodgings outside the city centre and south of the Arno are cheaper than those in the city's historic heart. The **Informazione Turistiche Alberghiere (ITA)** booth at the SMN station may be able to find you a room if you arrive without a booking; open 0830–2100.

Florence has three **youth hostels**: advance booking is recommended at all three. They are: **Villa Camerata**, *Viale A. Righi 2/4, tel: (055) 601 451*; **Ostello Santa Monaca**, *Via Santa Monaca 6, tel: (055) 268 338*; **Villa Favard**, *Via Rocca Tedalada* (no tel., open June–Sept only, very basic space for those with sleeping bags). There are **campsites** at: **Italiani e stranieri**, *Viale Michelangelo 80, tel: (055) 681 1977* (Apr–Oct) and in the grounds of the Villa Camerata youth hostel (*see above*). A further list of campsites in and around Florence is available from **Centro Internazionale Prenotazione Federcampeggio**, *Casella Postale 23, 50041 Calenzano, Firenze, tel: (055) 882 391*, which also handles campsite bookings.

Communications

The main **post office** is at *Via Pelliceria 53*, open 0815–1800 (poste restante 0815–1930). There are usually long queues. You can buy stamps from tobacconists and from stationers. National **telephone** service at the *Via Pelliceria* post office is open 0800–2230. You can also make calls from the *Via Pietrapiana* office, open 0800–1745 daily, and at the SMN station office, open 0800–2145, closed Sun and hols.

To phone Florence from abroad: *tel: 39 (Italy) + 55 (Florence) + number*; to phone Florence from elsewhere in Italy: *tel: (055) + number*.

Eating and Drinking

Florence has a good supply of reasonably priced eating-places. You can cut costs by opting for fixed-price (*prezzo fisso*) meals which give you a choice of first courses, a choice of main courses, and fruit or cheese. Since one of the first course choices is always pasta, this makes a filling meal. An even cheaper option is the *tavola calda*, a buffet-style self-service restaurant where you can choose a single dish or a full meal. These are found all over town and cover and service charges are included in the price displayed for each dish.

As in other Italian towns, drinks taken standing or sitting at the bar are a great deal cheaper than those drunk at a table, and restaurants outside the main sightseeing semi-circle are usualy cheaper than those catering to visitors close to the main sights. For picnic ingredients try an *alimentari* (grocery shop) – but remember that they shut for lunch!

Consulates

UK: *Lungarno Corsini 2, tel: (055) 284 133*.
USA: *Lungarno Amerigo Vespucci 38, tel: (055) 239 8276*.

Money

Banks which change money usually display the sign **Cambio** (Exchange). There are also exchange kiosks at SMN station and at numerous city centre locations. Eurocheques are also widely accepted, but credit cards are useful only in the more expensive shops and restaurants.

Thomas Cook bureau de change is located at *Ponte Vecchio, Lungarno Acciaiuoli 6R; tel: (055) 289781*. They will cash Thomas Cook travellers' cheques free of commission charge and can offer emergency assistance in the event of them being lost or stolen.

Entertainment

Florence offers plenty to do and see, especially at street level. On summer evenings, street performers and fortune-tellers take over the *Piazza della Signoria*, the *Piazza del Duomo* and the *Via Calzaiuoli*, which connects them. At the other end of the scale, opera is as popular as anywhere in Italy, though it is an expensive way to spend an evening. The English-language

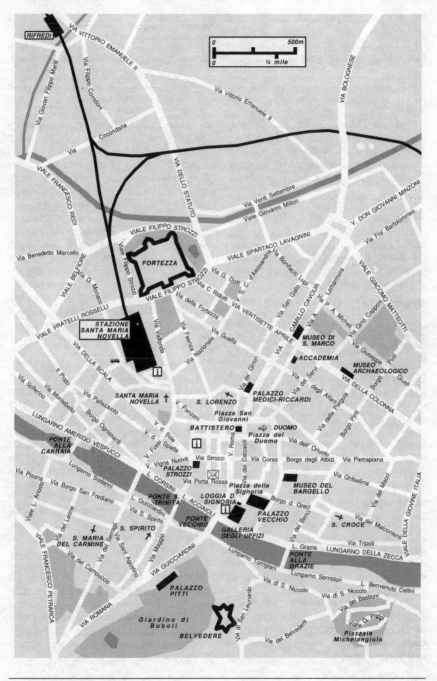

listings guide *Florence: Concierge Information* can be picked up at most hotel desks. If you can read Italian, the monthly *Firenze Spettacolo* can be bought at most bookstalls.

Nightlife

A lively, local youth culture boosted by a large, summer, floating population ensures that there are plenty of clubs and discos, though the in-place to dance changes virtually week to week. There is often an admission fee for the larger discos and drinks are usually very expensive. There are also several rock and reggae venues.

Theatres, cinemas and concerts

Many recent US and US releases come to major city-centre cinemas undubbed. There are numerous theatres, the most important of which is the **Teatro Comunale**, the venue for most opera and classical concerts. Theer is a big music and opera festival in May–July.

Shopping

Florence offers some of the finest quality products in the world, especially in leather-work, linen, and jewellery. It also has some of the most expensive shops in the world. Cheaper buys for souvenir shoppers include hand-made paper and pottery. See where the wealthy shop on *Via Tornabuoni* and *Via della Vigna Nuova*, where, if you have to ask the price you clearly can't afford it. Then visit the *Piazza Ciompi* flea market (open daily, go early), the Mercato Nuovo on *Via Calimala*, or the vast Tuesday-morning market in the *Casine park* for buys within your range.

Sightseeing

You will pay an entrance fee for every building you visit in Florence. However, EU citizens under 18 and over 60 are entitled to free admission to state-owned museums, which include some of the major sights such as the Accademia, the Uffizi and the Palazzo Pitti.

The city is divided by the Arno, with most of its glorious medieval heart on the north bank. Five bridges cross the river. The most central, the **Ponte Vecchio**, built in 1345, is a tourist attraction in its own right.

North of the Arno

Most of the the the important sights lie in a semicircle north of the Arno River, within a 2-km radius of the Galleria Uffizzi. These include Florence's 'musts': the **Uffizi**, *Piazzale degli Uffizi 6*, with its works by Michelangelo, Giotto, Raphael and Botticelli; the **cathedral (*Duomo*)** of Santa Maria del Fiore and the **Baptistry** (*Battisterio di San Giovanni*) – the oldest building in Florence, 5th–8th-century with superb 15th-century bronze doors by Ghiberti; **San Lorenzo** and the neighbouring Medici chapels (*Piazza Madonna degli Aldobrandini)*; the 13th-century **church of Santa Croce**.

Outside the semicircle, 3 km north-east of the centre, lie the **Galleria Accademia** (*V. Ricasoli 60*) and the **Museo di San Marco** (*Pzza di S. Marco 1)*, both essential viewing, the Accademia for Michelangelo's David and the San Marco for Fra Angelico's Annunciation. Close to the Accademia (400m east), at *V. della Colonna 36*, the **Museo Archaeologico** has a good collection of Roman and Etruscan art.

South of the Arno

Cross the Arno by the Ponte Vecchio to reach the main attractions south of the river: the grandiose 15th-century **Palazzo Pitti**, housing the wealth of the Medicis, a fine gallery of modern art, and the huge collection of paintings in the Palatine Gallery. Nearby are Brunelleschi's fine church of **Santo Spirito**, with splendid paintings, which is surrounded every morning by a lively street market, and the church of **Santa Maria del Carmine**, noted for its frescoes by Masaccio. Still further south, behind the Palazzo Pitti, lie the city's landscaped green lung, the **Giardino di Boboli** and beside it a 16th-century fortress, the **Forte di Belvedere**.

Views of Florence

Despite the inevitable crowds, the view of the **old city** from the **Ponte Vecchio** is still one of the most stirring in Europe. A wider view is offered from **San Miniano al Monte**, the church and cemetery atop *Monte alle Croci*, on the south side of the Arno above *Piazzale Michelangelo*.

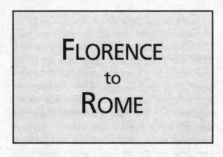

FLORENCE
to
ROME

This route meanders through the hilly heart of Tuscany and Umbria, Italy's most popular and enchanting tourist region.

TRAINS

ETT tables: 370, 386, 385.

→ Fast Track

There are frequent trains every day between Florence (SMN or Rifredi) and Rome (mostly Termini). It is worth being selective, because the journey (via Orvieto, not the On Track route) varies from under 2 hrs to nearly 3 hrs. Supplements are payable for some services.

~~~ On Track

Florence–Arezzo

About a dozen fast trains a day run between Florence (SMN) and Arezzo, the journey usually taking around 40 mins.

Arezzo–Perugia

There are four daily services direct, nine if you change at Terontola-Cortona. The journey averages 1 hr 10 mins.

Perugia–Assisi

There are around 15 trains a day, the journey taking 20–30 mins.

Assisi–Spoleto

Only one convenient direct train, but if you change at Foligno (roughly 15 mins from Assisi, 20 mins from Spoleto) there are about a dozen trains daily on both legs. Some connections are better than others..

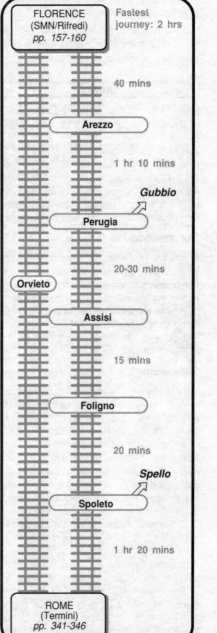

FLORENCE (SMN/Rifredi) pp. 157-160

Fastest journey: 2 hrs

40 mins

Arezzo

1 hr 10 mins

Gubbio

Perugia

20-30 mins

Orvieto

Assisi

15 mins

Foligno

20 mins

Spello

Spoleto

1 hr 20 mins

ROME (Termini) pp. 341-346

Spoleto–Rome

There are at least ten trains a day between Spoleto and Rome (Termini). The journey takes about 1 hr 20 mins by IC or IR trains.

AREZZO

Station: *tel: (0575) 22 663.* In the modern sector, west of the centre: walk up the hill to the old town.

Tourist Office: by station; *tel: (0575) 377 678.* June–Aug only, Mon–Sat 0900–1300 and 1600–1900, and Sun 0900–1300. **EPT:** *Piazza Risorgimento 116; tel: (0575) 23 952,* post the latest information on accommodation outside, so consult that if you arrive out of office hours.

Accommodation

Rooms are very difficult to find over the first weekend of every month, but you should have few problems at other times. There are several budget establishments near the station.

Private Hostels: Piero della Francesca, *Via Borgo Unto 6; tel: (0575) 354 546,* near *Piazza Grande*; and **Villa Severi**, *Via F Redi 13; tel: (0575) 29 047* (bus no. 4).

Sightseeing

The old town is towards the top of a hill, the modern town below it, connected by the pedestrianised *Corso Italia* and the motorised shopping street, *Via Guido Monaco.*

Arezzo was a major settlement in Etruscan, Roman and medieval times. Today its economy rests on jewellers, goldsmiths and antiques, but don't think you'll find a bargain by attending the **Antiques Fair (Fiera Antiquaria)**, in *Piazza Grande* on the first Sunday of every month.

The **Museo Archeologico**, *Via Margaritone 10,* not far east of the station, is the only major sight in the lower town. Within it, the **Anfiteatro Romano** is noted for excellent Etruscan bronzes and 1st-century BC vases.

The city's major attraction is Piero della Francesca's brilliant fresco cycle of the *Legend of the True Cross*, on display in the 14th-century **Basilica di San Francesco**, *Via della Madonna del Prato,* in the centre of the old town.

Santa Maria della Pieve, *Piazza Grande*, is an outstanding Romanesque church with lively 13th-century carvings over the entrance, a multi-windowed square campanile and a tiered Pisan façade. It contains a notable Lorenzetti polyptych from 1320. The square is home to several other architecturally interesting buildings, including the **Palazzetto della Fraternità dei Laci**, which has a Gothic ground floor and Renaissance upper storeys, and the pillared **Loggiata del Vasari**. On the first Sunday of September, the square becomes the setting for a traditional joust, **Giostra del Saracino**, with four knights tilting at a wooden Saracen.

The large **Duomo** overlooks the north of town, but the 16th-century stained glass is rather dark and it's not easy to see the interior paintings clearly. Della Francesca's fresco of *Mary Magdalene* is near the organ, next to a large marble tomb possibly designed by Giotto.

Just inside the western wall of the old town is the mainly 13th-century **Chiesa di San Domenico**, *Piazza Fossombroni*, with a fine rose window over the door. The interior features colourful 15th–16th-century frescos, a fine *Crucifix* by Cimabue and an *Annunciation* by Aretino. Very close (and signposted) are the **Casa di Petrarca**, *Via dell'Orto*, home of the great poet, and the **Casa di Giorgio Vasari**, *Via XX Settembre 55*. Vasari, biographer of the great Renaissance artists, was born in Arezzo and designed his own house, covering the interior with frescos.

PERUGIA

Station: FS (State Railway), *tel: (075) 500 1091* or *71 865.* 4 km south-west of the centre (an uphill walk) or 15 mins by bus (nos. 26/27/36) to *Piazza Italia.* Tickets from a forecourt booth or machine by the entrance. The private **FCU (Ferrovia Centrale Umbria)** railway terminal is **Stazione Sant'Anna**, *tel: (075) 23 947,* from which you can get a *scala mobile* (escalator) to *Piazza Italia.*

Tourist Office: *Palazzo dei Priori, Piazza IV Novembre; tel: (075) 23 327.* Mon–Sat 0830–1330 and 1530/1600–1830/1900, and Sun 0900–1300. Get *Umbria Informazione* and the detailed walking guide. **Digiplan** machines at the station and *Piazza Italia* provide computer print-outs for tourists.

Accommodation

There is plenty of cheap, central accommodation, but advance booking is essential during the international jazz festival (10 days every July). **Hostel**: 2 mins from the Duomo: **IYHF:** *Via Bontempi 13; tel: (075) 22 880.* **Campsite**: **Paradis d'Ete**, *Colle della Trinita; tel: (075) 795 117,* 5 km from town (bus no. 36), or you can rough camp by **Lago Trasimeno**, reached by bus and train.

Sightseeing

Ignore the unattractive modern suburbs and head straight for the almost intact medieval centre, by bus or escalator. From *Piazza Italia* the pedestrianised *Corso Vannucci* runs north to the Duomo and all the major sights are within walking distance. The street itself is the centre of activities for a cosmopolitan crowd, almost around the clock.

The **Duomo**, *Piazza IV Novembre*, is a large, plain medieval building, supposedly home to the Virgin Mary's wedding ring (kept inside 15 locked boxes and almost never seen). In the centre of the square is the 13th-century **Fontana Maggiore**, a triumph of decoration by Nicola and Giovanni Pisano.

The **Palazzo dei Priori**, *Corso Vannucci*, is a somewhat forbidding structure with battlements, a great Gothic portal and long rows of windows. Fan-like steps lead up to the *Sala dei Notari*, which is noted for its frescos – fun rather than masterpieces. The **Galleria Nazionale dell'Umbria**, on the 4th floor, contains mainly Umbrian works (notably by Pinturicchio and Perugino), but has a few Tuscan masterpieces, including della Francesca's *Madonna and Saints with Child* and a triptych by Fra Angelico. The **Collegio della Mercanzia** is covered with magnificent carved panelling, while the **Collegio di Cambio** has restored frescos (including a self-portrait) that are considered to be Perugino's finest works. It is believed he had help from the young Raphael (his greatest pupil).

Sant'Agostino, *Corso Garibaldi*, is rather sad, with a few patches of frescos hinting at previous glories. There is still a beautiful choir and the ceiling of its **Oratory** is absolutely smothered in decorations. Continue along the street, to the extreme north of the centre, to reach **Sant'Angelo**, a lovely, tranquil 5th-century church that incorporates the columns of a circular Roman temple.

The lower section of the massive **Arco di Augusto**, *Piazza Fortebraccio*, is a rare survivor from the Etruscan era because the Romans used it as a base for their 40 BC additions.

San Domenico, to the east, is an enormous church where several outstanding works of art hint at happier days. Authorship of the well-preserved 14th-century *Tomb of Pope Benedict XI* is unknown, but it's superbly crafted and clearly the work of a master sculptor. The **Museo Archeologico Nazionale dell'Umbria**, in the cloister, includes an excellent collection of Etruscan artefacts.

Don't miss the 10th-century basilica of **San Pietro**, south-east from the centre. The decorations, dating from the Renaissance, are unbelievably rich, with scarcely an unadorned patch. The paintings were executed by a host of artists, including Perugino, di Lorenzo, Caravaggio and (disputed, but likely) Raphael. Another highlight is the magnificently carved choir.

⌁ Side Track from Perugia

Apart from a few dire Fascist monuments, **Gubbio** is a typical Umbrian hill-town, largely medieval, with steep narrow streets and red-roofed pinkish houses. *Piazza Grande della Signoria*, home of the turreted **Palazzo dei Consoli**, provides superb views. The **Museo Civico** contains the most complete extant record of the Umbrian language, in seven bronze tablets, *Tavole Eugubine* (300–100 BC). **Tourist Office**: *Piazza Oderisi 6; tel: (075) 922 0693.* Ten buses a day run from Perugia's *Piazza dei Partigiani*, by the FCU station.

ASSISI

Station: *tel: (075) 804 0272.* This is not in Assisi

proper, but in *Santa Maria degli Angeli*, about 5 km south-west and uphill all the way. Buses run to the centre every half hour.

Tourist Office: *Piazza del Comune 12; tel: (075) 812 534.* Mon–Sat 0800/0900–1300/1400 and 1500/1600–1830/1900, and Sun 0900–1300. They provide a good map in English and have lots of information about accommodation, including pilgrim hostels.

Getting Around

The centre is fairly small, full of interest and best seen on foot. If you want to go further afield, take a bus.

Accommodation

There is plenty of accommodation of every grade, but booking is advisable – essential for Easter, the Feast of St Francis's (3–4 Oct) and *Calendimaggio* (a medieval celebration of spring held in early May). **IYHF:** *Via Valecchi; tel: (075) 816 767,* 10-mins walk from *Piazza San Pietro.* **Campsite:** *Fontemaggio; tel: (075) 813 636,* 4 km east of town and uphill. Take a taxi or follow the signs from *Porta Cappuccini.*

Sightseeing

St Francis of Assisi was born in 1182, a truly remarkable man who revolutionised medieval religious thinking, largely by practising what he preached: poverty, chastity and obedience, leading to love of God and appreciation of all living things. He founded the Franciscan order, the world's largest, and his home town became (and remains) a major pilgrimage centre.

The **Basilica di San Francesco**, at the western end of the old town, has a collection of masterpieces that most galleries would envy. Several great artists were employed, inspiring each other into innovative forms of painting that departed from the rigid Byzantine conventions. St Francis expressed the wish to be buried simply, but the news of his death (in 1226) brought a flood of donations from all over Europe and construction of the basilica began in 1228. It consists of two churches: the lower designed for peaceful meditation by his tomb, while the soaring upper church was intended to mollify the faction who wanted a glorious

monument. Despite almost continuous Masses, dim lighting, enforced dress code (modesty is the key), ban on photography and rule of silence (largely ignored), the **lower church** is always packed and far from peaceful. Virtually every available inch of wall is covered by paintings and frescos of outstanding quality; the ones that attract most attention are by Cavallini, Martini and Lorenzetti. Steps by the altar lead to the **Treasury**, which contains a rich and diverse collection of items donated over the centuries. Sadly, most of Cimabue's frescos in the **upper church** are now in extremely poor condition, so the glory goes to his protégé Giotto, whose 28 panels of frescos about St Francis begin to the right of the high altar.

The *Piazza del Comune*, in the centre of the old town, is dominated by the 1st-century AD **Tempio di Minerva**. The restored **Palazzo Comunale** houses the **Pinacoteca**, which contains a small but worthwhile collection of Umbrian Renaissance items, while the **Museo Civico** displays Etruscan and Roman fragments.

To the east of the centre, below the attractive **Duomo**, ist he **Basilica di Santa Chiara**. St Clare was an early friend of St Francis and, with his guidance, established the Order of the Poor Clares, the female equivalent of the Franciscans. The church contains a Byzantine crucifix that is reputed to have started Francis on his religious career by commanding him to 'repair God's church'. He took that to mean **San Damiano** (signposted from Porta Nuova), a peaceful place that would certainly be more pleasing to St Francis than his own basilica.

Rocca Maggiore, the old fortress, towers dramatically above the northern edge of the city, providing panoramic views of the town and surrounding countryside.

Basilica di Santa Maria degli Angeli, near the station, surrounds a chapel used by St Francis and the spot where he died. Much more evocative, if you fancy a 4 km forest walk to the north-east, is **Eremo delle Carceri**, on the slopes of Mt Subasio. It was here, in caves, that the original Franciscans lived. You can see the cell later used by St Francis and the altar where he addressed the birds.

SPOLETO

Station: *tel: (0743) 48 516.* In the lower town, with a long uphill walk south to the medieval town (or orange bus to *Piazza Libertà* – tickets from the station bar). You can get a free city map from the station's news-stand.

Tourist Office: *Piazza Liberta 7; tel: (0743) 220 311.* Daily 0900–1300 and 1530/1600–1830/ 1930.

Accommodation

Book well ahead for the summer arts festival. At other times, look in the lower town. Alternatively, try **Foligno**, 26 km north-east and linked by trains that run until late. The **IYHF** is there: *Piazza San Giacomo 11; tel: (0742) 52 882.*

Campsites: *Camping Monteluco; tel: (0742) 220 358,* 15-mins walk south from *Piazza Libertà,* is very small and opens only in summer. *Il Girasole; tel: (0742) 51 335,* in the village of *Petrognano,* is larger and has a pool (hourly bus from station).

Sightseeing

The main area is fairly small, centred on *Piazza del Mercato.* There are buses for travel further afield. Spoleto's fortunes have fluctuated since it was founded by Umbrians in the 6th century BC. After several centuries of power, it fell into obscurity until being chosen (in 1958) to host Italy's leading arts celebration. The **Festival dei Due Mondi** is now an annual interruption to the town's usual peace – and all the prices soar.

San Salvatore, in the lower town, is located in the cemetery. Built by 5th-century monks, it has changed little since their day. The design of early religious buildings was based on Roman temples and the church looks more pagan than Christian. It's atmospheric at any time, especially so at dusk. About 200m south is the Romanesque **San Ponziano**, which has an interesting 10th-century crypt, but you have to ask the caretaker to let you in.

Part of the small **Roman Amphitheatre**, *Piazza Libertà,* at the southern end of the old centre, has been carefully restored and is now used for festival performances. Another section is occupied by the convent of **Sant'Agata**,

which houses a small collection of Roman artefacts. The **Arco di Druso** (AD 23), 100m north, leads to *Piazza del Mercato,* which was the Roman forum and is still a market and social centre. It's a great place to linger, surrounded by attractive old streets.

Nearby, the small **Pinacoteca Comunale** is housed in the **Palazzo del Municipio** and an escort is compulsory. The decor is magnificent and some of the paintings outstanding, especially in the Umbrian section. **Sant'-Eufemia**, above the Duomo, is a lovely little Romanesque church remarkable for its *matroneum,* a gallery where the women worshipped, segregated from the men below.

A green hill behind the **Duomo** sets off the porticoed façade, with its eight rose windows, Byzantine mosaic and square tower, a perfect blend of Romanesque and Renaissance elements. Although the interior Baroque additions are less happy, nothing can spoil Fra Lippo Lippi's last great frescos. Also of interest are the *Cappelle Erioli,* with a *Madonna and Child* by Pinturicchio, and the Cosmati marble floor.

Rocca, a huge 14th-century castle to the south-east of town, guards one of the finest engineering achievements of medieval times, the **Ponte delle Torri**: a bridge 240m long, supported by ten arches 80m high. It affords fantastic views and, on the other side of the gorge it spans, there's a pleasant 2 km walk (turn right) leading to **San Pietro**, with a façade adorned by some of the region's finest Romanesque sculptures.

Side Track from Spoleto

Spello is 20 mins by train from Spoleto (or Assisi), the station being 200m from the main road. It's a typical little hill-town with tiers of pink houses, cobbled alleys and churches, a picturesque place with some Roman remains. The 13th-century church of **Santa Maria Maggiore** contains a chapel full of brilliantly restored frescos by Pinturicchio and a 15th-century ceramic floor. **Tourist Office:** *Piazza Matteotti 3.* Open only in summer. Telephone enquiries: *(0742) 350 493* or *352 814.*

Spoleto

FRANKFURT AM MAIN

Frankfurt may have the least romantic image of any German city, but as it is one of the country's most important rail junctions you may well have to spend some time here. In fact, Frankfurt is a lot more enticing than its dull reputation would suggest. To balance its shortage of splendid historic buildings it has a host of well-designed modern museums, a bubbly nightlife, and a user-friendly approach to rail travellers.

Tourist Information

Verkehrsamt Stadt Frankfurt am Main (City Tourist Board) offices are at *Kaiserstr. 52; tel: (069) 212 3 88 00*, at the Frankfurt Hauptbahnhof (Hbf) station, opposite track 23, *tel: (069) 212 3 88 49/51* (Mon–Sat 0800–2200 (2100 Nov–Mar), Sun and holidays 0930–2000) and in the city centre at *Römerberg 27, tel: (069) 212 3 87 08/9* (Mon–Fri 0900–1900, Sat, Sun and holidays 0930–1800)

Arriving and Departing

Airport

Flughafen Frankfurt-Main (9 km south-west of the city) is central Europe's busiest. Happily, it is also one of the most modern and best-designed. The airport is divided into three sections. The tourist information desk is in area B, *tel: (069) 690 351*, open 0630–2200. Hotel booking agencies are also in Area B Arrivals Hall. There are restaurants in all three areas. You can change money at banks and bureaux de change in all three areas; Deutsche Verkehrs und Kredit Bank in Area B Arrivals Hall has the longest opening hours, 0600–2300.

    S-Bahn suburban trains (service S15) to Frankfurt Hbf, the city's main station, leave every 10 mins. First train leaves at 0433, last at 0033. Trains to the airport from Hbf start at

0414 and run until 0043. Weekday rush hour (0630–0830 and 1600–1830) fares are 33% higher than off-peak fares. The trip takes 11 minutes. The airport also has its own IC services hourly to Cologne, Dortmund, Hamburg and Nuremberg, *tel: (069) 19419* for information.

Station

Hauptbahnhof (Hbf), has direct connections to nearly every major European city, with more than 2,000 trains a day carrying 250,000 passengers. Last daily departure for InterCity Express, EuroCity and InterCity long-distance trains to German and other cities is at 2000. The station has an assortment of bars and restaurants, none of them first-rate. There is also a tourist information office, opposite track 23 (*see above for opening hours and tel.*), which will find you a room on arrival. **Deutsche Bahn** (German Rail) general enquiries: *tel: (069) 23 05 21*. **Frankfurt Hbf** reservations, *tel: (069) 2 65 38 46* Information, *tel: (069) 19419*

Getting Around

Frankfurt is not a very attractive city for the stroller, but it has its rewards, notably the **Museumsufer** (Museum Row) on the banks of the Main and a plentiful supply of parks to picnic in. The rest of the city is a conglomerate of big corporate offices, apartment blocks and shopping complexes. Fortunately, getting around is easy, with an efficient combination of S-bahn (overground) and U-bahn (underground) trains, trams (streetcars) and buses, all of which are run by the **Frankfurter Verkehrs und Tarifverbund** (**FVV**). You will find directions to the system, in six languages including English, on the blue automatic ticket machines at all bus stops and stations. To spread the city's traffic burden, there is a 33% surcharge on all public transport fares during the morning and evening rush hour (0630–0830 and 1600–1830).

Tickets

Buy tickets at newspaper booths and blue automat machines at S-bahn and U-bahn stations. Tickets are valid for all FVV transportation. A **tageskarte** (one-day ticket) gives unlimited travel in the central zone for just over three times the cost of a single ticket. You can also buy **streifenkarten** (multi-trip ticket strips), good for five trips. Tickets must be stamped in the machine provided on boarding.

FVV fares and travel network information, tel: (069) 26940.

Streetcars, U-bahn and buses

U-bahn trains provide the fastest and most frequent point-to-point services for north/south travel. The hub for the U-bahn network is the **Hauptwache** station, which is linked to the Hbf by S-bahn lines S1, S2, S3, S4, S5, S6 and S14. Streetcars are a better option for short trips in the city centre. For U-bahn, streetcar and bus information call Stadtwerke Frankfurt am Main, tel:(069) 1368 2236/2295/2428.

S-bahn and Deutsche Bahn buses

Overground trains are operated by DB (German Rail) and are the best way to get to the airport and to outlying districts, with services radiating in all directions from Hbf. DB also operates bus services to some outlying areas. For information tel: (069) 23 05 21.

Taxis

Taxis are plentiful and metered. A short city-centre journey will cost you about six times as much as a single FVV ticket.

River journeys

The Main, which flows through the middle of the city, connects with the Rhine and offers a range of one-day cruises and longer excursions. Popular options include the one-day Loreley cruise offered by **Fahrgastschiffahrt Wikinger II**, Adolf-Udrid Nauheimer, Eiserner Steg, 6000 Frankfurt 1, tel: (069) 28 28 86. This cruise departs several days a week (schedules change) at 0830, returning at 2115. The company also operates a range of shorter trips (45 minutes to 2 hours) with several departures a day in summer. Longer cruises are offered by KD Line, whose Frankfurt agent for information and reservations is **KD Agentur Malachi Faughnan**, Am Eisernen Steg, Mainkai 35, 600 Frankfurt/Main 1, tel: (069) 28 57 28.

Living in Frankfurt

Accommodation

The range of accommodation is extensive, from a wide array catering to business travellers and conference-goers through to an assortment of decidedly sleazy cheap pensions near Hbf. Between these extremes, Frankfurt offers fairly plentiful inexpensive accommodation, including a floating hotel and Europe's biggest youth hostel. Mid-range accommodation may be in short supply if you arrive during one of the city's many trade fairs, but there is rarely a problem finding a room at the cheaper end of the range. Chains include BW, Ch, Hl, Ic, Ma, Nv, Pu, Ra, and Sc. The **tourist office** in Hbf, opposite track 23, will book you a room. Accommodation can also be booked on arrival at the airport through **DER Deutsches Reiseburo**, tel: (069) 69 30 71, 0800–2100 daily, or **Flughafen Frankfurt-Main Reiseburo**, tel: (069) 6 90 6 62, 0800–2100, both in area B Arrivals. Europe's biggest **youth hostel**, **Haus der Jugend**, with 500 beds, is at Deutschherrnufer 12, 6000 Frankfurt 70, tel: (069) 61 90 58.

Communications

The Hbf post office is open 24 hours. The main city centre **post office**, Hauptpostamt, Zeil 110, 6000 Frankfurt 1, tel: (069) 2111-0, is open Mon–Fri 0800–1800, Sat 0800–1200. A late counter is open Mon–Fri until 2100, Sat until 1800 and Sun 1200–1600.

To phone Frankfurt from abroad: tel: 49 (Germany) + 69 (Frankfurt) + number. To phone Frankfurt from elsewhere in Germany: tel: (069) + number.

Eating and Drinking

Given Frankfurt's less-than-exciting reputation, you are in for a pleasant surprise when it comes to food and drink. Not only does the city have a representative of virtually every national cuisine, it also has a plentiful choice of neighbourhood bars, cafés and restaurants serving local and regional treats which include (of course) sausages and ham dishes, tasty beers, red and white wines and the city's own beverage, apple

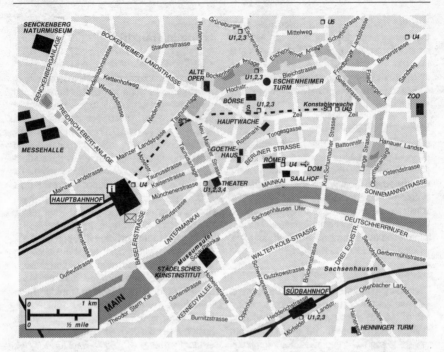

wine. There are plenty of stand-up cafés and street stalls where you can fill up on sausages or a whole assortment of fast foods such as kebab, pizza, and *felafel*. Ethnic restaurants are not normally cheaper than a meal in a simple *lokale* (tavern), where food is usually simple, filling, and of the meat-and-potatoes variety. The *apfelweinlokale* (apple wine tavern) is a Frankfurt institution and a collection of them are to be found along and around *Neuer Wall*, in the *Sachsenhausen* district south of the river. A wreath of pine branches over the door means freshly pressed apple wine is available.

Consulates

Australia: Consulate General, *Gutleitstr.85, 6000 Frankfurt 1, tel: (069) 27 39 090*.
UK: Consulate General, *Bockenheimer Landstr.42, 6000 Frankfurt 1, tel: (069) 17 00 02 0*.
USA: Consulate General, *Siesmayerstr.21, 6000 Frankfurt 1, tel: (069) 75 35 0*.

Money

All banks change money. City centre banks are normally open Mon–Fri 0830–1530 or 1600; suburban branches may close between 1300 and 1430. You can also change money at main post offices in the city and at the airport and in major department stores, which charge a high commission. Deutsche Verkehrs-Kredit Bank at the south side of Hbf has the longest city-centre opening hours, 0630–2200 daily, *tel: (069) 26 48 201*. **Thomas Cook** have bureau de change facilities at *Kaiserstr.11; tel: (069) 134733*.

Entertainment

Frankfurt makes up for much of its commercial greyness by a lively and varied choice of entertainment, which spans everything from the latest in dance music to the best of classical and opera, movies, cabaret and theatre. For lovers of the classics and the opera, this is one of Europe's more affordable cities, with youth and student discounts available at virtually all venues.

Nightlife

Frankfurt has a lively satirical cabaret and

alternative theatre scene, but you need good German and a sharp eye for political background to make much sense of it. More accessible are the city's many music bars, catering to all tastes from rock and blues to jazz and piano favourites and open late. Discos and dance clubs are also plentiful, though they do not compete with some livelier German cities. One feature of Frankfurt nightlife is that it's livelier during the week than at weekends, when many natives head for second homes in the countryside. Tickets and information on all types of event are available from the tourist information offices at the airport and Hbf. The tourist board also publishes the monthly **Frankfurt Programme** (in German only, but easily understood) listing every event each month.

Theatres, cinema and cabaret

Frankfurt boasts several English-language theatres, including the **English Theatre**, · *Kaiserstr. 52; tel: (069) 24 23 16 20*, the **Playhouse**, *Hansaallee 152, tel: (069) 83 24 34/28 02 27*, and the **Café Theater**, *Hamburger Allee 45, tel (069) 36 01 2 11/240*. Also ac-cessible to non-German speakers is the **Pupp-enzentrum puppet theatre**, *Diemelstr.9, tel: (069) 151 83 26*. The **Alte Oper**, *Opernplatz, tel: (069) 3601-2 11/240*, a meticulous reconstruction of the 19th-century opera house, is a venue for jazz and rock concerts as well as opera and classical ensembles. The city centre has more than 80 cinemas; however, many English-language movies are dubbed into German.

Shopping

Shopping is as extensive as you would expect in a prosperous modern city of this size, but Frankfurt offers little that is unique or uniquely affordable. The best buys are food and drink. **The Zeil**, the shopping precinct which runs east from the Hauptwache U-bahn station, is a new pedestrian mall with the highest sales turnover in Germany. It's a good deal less interesting than the nearby **Kleinmarkthalle**, off *Hasengasse*, a cornucopia of produce from all over the world (and a good place to stock up for a picnic or for food and drink for the next leg of your

trip). The **Grosse Bockenheimer Str.** is traditionally the location for Frankfurt's longest-established wine merchants, delicatessens and butchers; shop here for wine, cheese, smoked meats and dozens of kinds of sausage.

Sightseeing

Virtually every museum, gallery and other attraction offers discounts to young people and students of all ages. Frankfurt's major sightseeing attraction is undoubtedly the **Museumsufer** (Museum Row) along the banks of the Main. The city's museums cover every subject under the sun, some of them (like the **Bundespost-museum**, which exhibits paraphernalia from the history of Germany's post office and telephone company) calculated to appeal only to enthusiasts. Others are of more universal interest, like the **Stadelsches Kunstinstitut und Städtische Galerie**, *Schaumainkai 63*, with one of the world's most significant collections of art from the Middle Ages to the 20th century.

The **Goethemuseum/Goethehaus**, *Grosse Hirschgraben 23*, the poet's birthplace, has been carefully reconstructed and furnished from the his era and exhibits paintings, manuscripts and other relics of Frankfurt's most famous son. Nearby, the grand Gothic **Kaiserdom**, *Domstr.*, the cathedral, is worth a visit for treasures which include an altar dating from the 15th century.

The only part of the city which repays the stroller is the old **Sachsenhausen** district, reached by crossing the Alte Brücke (Old Bridge) and landmarked by the 15th-century **Kuhhirtenturm**, *Sachsenhäuser Ufer*, the last relic of its battlements. Here, some of its old-fashioned back alleys and squares have survived the building boom and there are plenty of pleasant old taverns to relax in.

Out of Town

Mountain and river scenery, historic towns and villages surround Frankfurt. **Kronberg**, a 25-minute ride from Konstablerwache or Hbf stations on S-bahn line 4, offers a fully restored castle dating from 1230 and a medieval town; nearby at **Königstein**, (DB bus no.917) are the ruins of a 10th-century castle.

Entertainment–Shopping–Sightseeing–Out of Town **169**

FRANKFURT
to
BERLIN

A historically significant route in Germany, this takes you through the former Iron Curtain and the heartland of the Weimar Republic (a brief hiatus between World War I and the Third Reich). Goethe and Bach are just two of the great artists whose influence on the culturally important region of Thuringia is still noticeable.

TRAINS

ETT tables: 750, 775, 670.

→ Fast Track

There are eight ICE trains daily between Frankfurt (Hbf) and Berlin (Zoo). All have dining-cars and carry a supplement. They leave every 2 hrs, the journey taking just under 5 hrs.

On Track

Frankfurt–Fulda

There is plenty of choice, with ICE trains hourly, IC/EC trains every two hours and an hourly local service. The journey usually takes a little under an hour.

Fulda–Eisenach

There are at least a dozen main line trains daily and the journey takes about 1 hr 20 mins.

Eisenach–Gotha

At least ten main line services operate every day, with a journey time of about 20 mins.

Gotha–Erfurt

There are at least ten trains a day, taking about 20 mins.

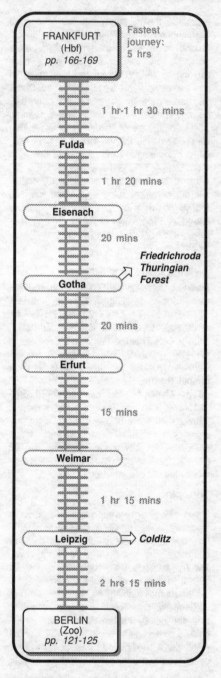

FRANKFURT (Hbf)
pp. 166-169

Fastest journey: 5 hrs

1 hr-1 hr 30 mins

Fulda

1 hr 20 mins

Eisenach

20 mins

Friedrichroda Thuringian Forest

Gotha

20 mins

Erfurt

15 mins

Weimar

1 hr 15 mins

Leipzig ⇨ *Colditz*

2 hrs 15 mins

BERLIN (Zoo)
pp. 121-125

Erfurt–Weimar
Trains are frequent and take about 15 mins.

Weimar–Leipzig
There are about six trains a day, taking about 1 hr 15 mins.

Leipzig–Berlin
There are at least 14 trains a day, the journey taking about 2 hrs 15 mins.

FULDA

Station: Hbf, *tel: (0661) 19419*. At the eastern end of the centre.
Tourist Office: *Schloss Str.1; tel: (0661) 10 23 45*. Mon–Fri 0830–1200 and 1400–1630, and Sat 0930–1200.

The **Dom** was built to house the *tomb of St Boniface* and is a perfect example of early Baroque. The high altar boasts a gilt *Assumption* between marble columns and the **Dommuseum** (accessible from the crypt) houses relics of the saint, including his head and the dagger with which he was murdered. The enormous **Stadtschloss** is the town hall, the ornate public rooms containing items ranging from portraits of Habsburg royalty to local faïence. A park leads to the **Orangerie**, an attractive Baroque building in front of which stands the *Floravase*, a lovely work topped by the goddess Flora.

EISENACH

Station: Hbf, *tel: (03691) 19419*.
Tourist Office: *Bahnhofstr.5; tel: (03691) 76162*. Open Mon 1000–1800, Tue–Fri 0900–1800, and Sat 0900–1500.

The splendid **Wartburg** was used by Wagner as the setting for *Tannhäuser*. A medieval castle with many later additions, it's an attractive complex where half-timbered buildings containing many splendid rooms surround two courtyards. Treasures in its museum include carvings by Riemenschneider and Dürer. The **Thüringer Museum**, in *Altstadt*, is devoted to local arts and crafts, wood-carving being a form at which Thuringians excelled during the Middle Ages.

The 15th-century **Lutherhaus**, *Lutherplatz*, is where Martin Luther lodged as a boy, the present half-timbered structure enclosing the original house. **Bachhaus**, *Frauenplan*, is furnished in period style, with documents about Bach's career and ancient musical instruments.

GOTHA

Station: Hbf, *tel: (03621) 19419*, at the southern end of town (tram nos.1/2/4 to centre), close to the **Thüringer Waldbahn**.
Tourist Office: *Markstr.2; tel: (03621) 54036*. Mon 1400–1700, Tue–Fri 0900–1900, and Sat 0900–1200.

The main gateway to the Thuringian Forest was the home of the Saxe-Coburg-Gotha dynasty, ancestors of the British royal family, and has an attractively restored *Altstadt*. The plain exterior of the massive **Schlossmuseum** gives no hint of the extraordinarily ornate decor inside, which mirrors the changing tastes of several centuries and contains such priceless objects as an elephant crafted by Dinglinger, the great Dresden goldsmith. The town has designed maps for over two centuries and the **Kartographisches Museum** is devoted to the craft.

- - - - - - - - - - - - - - - - - - - -

↷ Side Tracks from Gotha

In the **Thuringian Forest (Thüringer Wald)**, a good base (with lots of cheap accommodation) is **Friedrichroda**. **Tourist Office:** *Kurverwaltung, Gartenstr.9; tel: (03623) 446*. Travel there on the leisurely *Thüringer Waldbahn* rural tram, which allows you to absorb the scenery. This also stops at **Marienglashöhle** (lovely crystalline caves) and **Tabarz**, close to **Grosser Inselberg** (916m). Non-walkers can take a bus most of the way up. Hikers can enjoy all or part of the 168 km ridge-walk offered by *Rennsteig*, one of Germany's best trails.

- - - - - - - - - - - - - - - - - - - -

ERFURT

Station: Hbf, *tel: (0361) 19419*, is at the southeastern corner of the centre.
Tourist Office: *Bahnhofstr.37; tel: (0361) 26267*. Open Mon–Fri 0900–1800 and Sat

1000–1500. *Krämerbrücke 3; tel: (0361) 23436*. Open Mon–Fri 0900–1230 and 1330–1700, and Sat–Sun 0900–1100.

Accommodation

The few hotels are usually booked well in advance, but private rooms are often available. **Zimmervermittlung Brigitte Scheel**, *Paulinzeller Weg 23; tel: (0361) 41 38 38*, offer a 24-hour telephone booking service. **IYHF**: *Hochheimerstr.12; tel: (0361) 26705*, south of the centre (tram nos. 5/51).

Sightseeing

The stylish Thuringian capital dates from the 8th century and much of it survived the Allied bombs. Two hills to the west tower over the *Altstadt*. **Peterskirche**, once a magnificent Romanesque structure, dominates **Petersberg**, the larger hill, but the main attraction now is the view of the city. The smaller hill, **Domhügel**, is reached by monumental steps from **Domplatz**. The **Dom** was founded in the 8th century, but took several centuries to complete. Parts are Romanesque, but most Gothic. It is noted for *Gloriosa*, one of the world's largest bells, High Gothic choir stalls, 15th-century stained glass and an enormous hall. The distinctive triple-towered **Severikirche**, alongside, has a five-aisled nave that creates a false impression of size. The treasures include the fine pink sandstone sarcophagus of St Severus, an alabaster relief of St Michael and a 15th-century font.

Altstadt is a rewarding place to stroll, almost every street being lined with superb buildings. **Fischmarkt** contrasts the Renaissance **Zum breiten Herd** with the classically balanced **Zum roten Ochsen** and the 19th-century **Rathaus**, noted for the Romantic frescos inside with Thuringian themes.

Just south, **Prederigerkirche** has a plain façade that belies the gloriously intact Gothic interior. A magnificent *Annunciation* adorns the rood screen and the stained glass has floral motifs. On the other side of *Fischmarkt* is **Krämerbrücke**, a medieval bridge lined with 33 half-timbered shops that looks more like a medieval alley than a bridge: it's best appreciated from the waterside.

Just east of *Altstadt* is **Volkskunde**, a folklore museum about every aspect of Thuringian tradition.

In the 15th century, Erfurt was noted for its retables and a superb example can be seen in **Reglerkirche**, *Bahnhofstr*. To the north, in a Baroque palace, is **Angermuseum**, covering the decorative arts through the centuries.

Cyriaksburg, a castle south-west of the centre (bus no.2), houses a museum tracing the history of gardening and is set in large grounds that host a permanent garden show, *Internationale Gartenbauaustellung (Iga)*.

WEIMAR

Station: Hbf, *tel: (03643) 19419*, is 10-mins walk north of the centre (bus no.4).
Tourist Office: *Marktstr.4; tel: (03643) 2173*. Open Mon 1000–1800, Tue–Fri 0900–1800, and Sat 0900–1300.

Getting Around

The area of interest is concentrated in *Altstadt* and easily walkable.

Accommodation

There are few reasonable hotels, but the tourist office can arrange private rooms, as can **Werse & Reiseshop**, *Kleine Kirchgasse 3; tel: (03643) 3642*. **IYHF**: *Carl-August-Allee 13; tel: (03643) 2076*, 2 mins from Hbf; and *Zum Wilden Graben 12; tel: (03643) 3471*.

Sightseeing

Although it's of no great size, Weimar represents all that is best and worst in Germany. The entire *Altstadt* has been listed as a historical monument, steeped in the greatest of German culture, while, outside the town, Buchenwald represents the true horrors of the Nazi regime.

The largely neo-Classical **Schloss**, *Burgplatz 4*, houses a vast collection, including Dürer's *Hans and Elspeth Tucher* and outstanding 16th-century Cranach paintings.

The Gothic **Stadtkirche St Peter und Paul**, *Herderplatz*, contains a large triptych: either Lucas Cranach's last work or executed by Lucas

Cranach junior (one of three painter sons) as a memorial to his father.

Opposite the neo-Gothic **Rathaus** in **Marktplatz** is the eye-catching gabled **Cranachhaus**, where Cranach the Elder spent his last years, while **Bachstube** was where Bach lived during his stint as leader of the court orchestra.

Germany's two greatest writers both lived in Weimar. Schiller spent the last three years of his life at **Schillerhaus**, *Schillerstr.*, and his rooms are much as they were then, with drafts and early editions of his works. The nearby *Theaterplatz,* features a monument to Schiller and Goethe, both of whose works were first performed in the **Deutsches Nationaltheater**.

Goethehaus, *Frauenplan 1*, is in two parts, one a museum devoted to the author, the other an evocative Baroque mansion where he lived for some 50 years. **Goethepark**, to the east of the centre, contains the simple **Gartenhaus**, which was Goethe's first home in Weimar and later became his retreat. It contains a selection of his possessions and drawings. At the western edge of the park, the **Liszthaus** is the beautifully maintained residence of the Austro-Hungarian composer, who moved to Weimar in 1848 to direct the local orchestra for 11 years. He later returned, to spend the last 17 summers of his life at the house. His piano and some scores are among the exhibits.

LEIPZIG

Station: Leipzig's stations claim to be, respectively, the world's largest and the oldest still in use. The vast **Hbf,** *tel: (0341) 19419*, just northeast of *Altstadt*, dates from 1915 and amalgamates four earlier ones.

Bayerrischer Bahnhof, a few minutes south of Ring, was built in the 1840s, but destroyed by bombs. Only the neo-Classical façade has been restored, but the station is still the terminal for a few services.

Tourist Office: *Sachsenplatz 1; tel: (0341) 79590*. Just inside *Altstadt*, 4-mins walk from Hbf. Mon–Fri 0900–1900 and Sat 0900–1400.

Thomas Cook bureaux de change: *Dorotheenplatz 2–4* and at Leipzig–Halle airport.

Getting Around

There's a good tram network, but everything of interest is either within *Altstadt* or just outside it and easily walkable. Many place names are being altered, so ask the tourist office for a list of changes.

Accommodation

The hotels are very expensive and even private rooms are not cheap, but the situation may improve as Western tourism increases. Hotel chains: *Me.*

IYHF: *Käthe-Kollwitzstr.62; tel: (0341) 47 05 30*, west of the centre (tram nos.1/2); and *Gustav-Eschestr.4; tel: (0341) 57189*, a fair way north-west (tram nos.10/11/28), with a nearby **campsite:** *Am Auensee; tel: 0341) 52648.*

Sightseeing

Leipzig's attraction has never been aesthetic, but it's crammed with interest and has been a cultural centre for many centuries.

The 12th-century **Nikolaikirche**, *Nikolaistr.*, unremarkable from the outside, has a fascinating interior. Refurbished in the late 18th century, it combines simple Classical forms with Rococo decorations.

The heart of *Altstadt* is **Marktplatz**, dominated by the magnificent 16th-century **Altes Rathaus**. The **Neues Rathaus**, *Burgplatz,* is an incredible stylistic mishmash. It was built in 1899 and dominates the south of *Altstadt*.

The predominantly Gothic **Thomaskirche**, *Klostergasse,* is where Bach served as cantor for the last 27 years of his life (1723–1750). A monument to Bach (commissioned by Mendelssohn) stands outside and the **Bachmuseum** is across the street.

In the vast **Augustusplatz**, the subdued neo-Classical **Opernhaus** contrasts sharply with the very modern **Neue Gewandhaus**, which lays claim to being one of Europe's most beautiful concert halls. This is home to the great *Gewandhausorchester*, the oldest and largest orchestra in the world. The 34-storey **Universitätshochhaus** rises from the centre of the square, a relatively new home for the 15th-century university.

The **Grassi-Museum**, *Johannisplatz* (east of the centre), is a vast complex still far short of its potential, but two of the sections are already of general interest. The *Musikinstrumentenmuseum* (entered from *Täubschenweg*) contains over 3,500 historical musical instruments, some still used for recitals; *Museum für Völkerkunde* (entered from an interior courtyard) has ethnological displays from around the world, notably from the former USSR, the Far East and the Pacific.

⌔ Side Tracks from Leipzig

Colditz is a rather attractive little town dominated by the famous cliff-top **Castle**. It was largely ignored by the former Communist government, but is now mentioned in some tourist literature and there are plans to make it into a museum. The castle dates from the 11th century and underwent several changes of use before becoming a prison for Allied captives in World War II. A total of 130 prisoners succeeded in getting out, although only 30 made it all the way home. The tour includes a French tunnel that was discovered before it could be used. Start with a visit to the **Städtisches Museum**, which contains many items that provide a good background, including some ingenious devices fashioned by the POWs to aid their escapes. There are regular trains from Leipzig to the junction of Rochlitz, from where a scenic railway covers the 11 km upstream journey to Colditz.

FRANKFURT
to
MUNICH

There are several charming old Bavarian towns along this route, but one of the main attractions is Nuremberg, a place steeped in history and culture. Don't be put off by its grim 20th-century image, it is one of Germany's most interesting cities. It was here that the clarinet was invented and the first pocket-watch manufactured, and it's still a renowned producer of toys and gingerbread.

TRAINS

ETT tables: 760, 740, 750.

⟶ Fast Track

ICE trains (all with dining-cars) operate hourly from early morning to mid-evening between Frankfurt (Hbf) and Munich, running via Stuttgart, Ulm and Augsburg. The journey takes about 3 hrs 30 mins.

∿ On Track

Frankfurt–Würzburg

There are hourly trains throughout the day, the journey taking about 1 hr 20 mins.

Würzburg–Nuremberg (Nürnberg)

Trains run hourly during the day, taking just under an hour.

Nuremberg–Augsburg

The hourly ICE service takes just over an hour, while slower trains, every two hours, take 1hr 35 mins.

Augsburg–Munich (München)

Trains are frequent (roughly every half-hour),

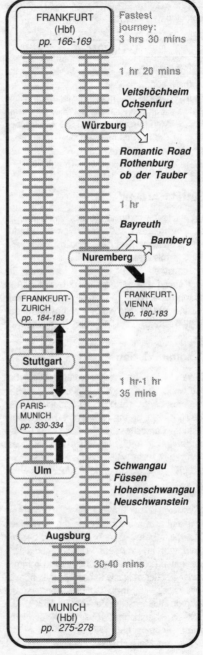

FRANKFURT
(Hbf)
pp. 166-169

Fastest journey:
3 hrs 30 mins

1 hr 20 mins

Veitshöchheim
Ochsenfurt

Würzburg

Romantic Road
Rothenburg
ob der Tauber

1 hr

Bayreuth
Bamberg

Nuremberg

FRANKFURT-
ZURICH
pp. 184-189

FRANKFURT-
VIENNA
pp. 180-183

Stuttgart

1 hr-1 hr
35 mins

PARIS-
MUNICH
pp. 330-334

Ulm

Schwangau
Füssen
Hohenschwangau
Neuschwanstein

Augsburg

30-40 mins

MUNICH
(Hbf)
pp. 275-278

but the type of service is very mixed and the journey time varies from 30 to 40 mins.

WÜRZBURG

Station: Hbf, *tel: (0931) 19419*. On the northern edge of *Altstadt*.
Tourist Offices: In front of Hbf, *tel: (0931) 37436*. Open Mon–Sat 0800–2000. *Haus Zum Falken, Marktplatz; tel: (0931) 37398*. Open Mon–Fri 0900–1800 and Sat 0900–1400. *Palais am Con-gress Centrum* (near *Friedensbrücke*); *tel: (0931) 37335*. Open Mon–Thur 0830–1600 and Fri 0830–1200.

Getting Around

The *Altstadt* is compact, lying between the river and the Residenz and centred on the **Markt**, where there is still a daily food market. Everything in this area is easily walkable.

The other area of interest is just across the river, linked to *Altstadt* by the 12th-century **Alte Mainbrücke**, but it's best to take the half-hourly bus (no. 9) from the western end of the bridge to the Festung, as that's a good 40-minute walk uphill.

Accommodation

There's a lack of cheap accommodation, but you could try around Hbf, especially on *Kaiserstr.* and *Bahnhofstr.* **IYHf**: *Burkarderstr.44; tel: (0931) 42590*, on the bank of the Main, below Festung. **Campsites:** *Winterhauserstr.160, Heldingsfeld; tel: (0931) 65598* (tram no. 3 to last stop, then 2 km walk); *Mergenheimerstr.136; tel: (0931) 72536* (tram no. 3: *Judenbühlweg*).

Sightseeing

Würzburg is the wine capital of Franconia (Franken) province, situated on the River Main. Declared a bishopric in 742, the town became an important religious centre, completely dominated by art-loving bishops, who commissioned a series of artists to beautify their homes. They chose well, including three masters: the sculptor Riemenschneider (1460–1531), the architect Neumann (1687–1753) and the painter Tiepolo (1696–1770).

Festung Marienberg is the city's symbol, a vast fortress that was the home of the bishops for four centuries. Little of the interior remains, but the tiny 8th-century **Marienkirche** is one of Germany's oldest churches and **Brunnenhaus** has a very old, deep 104m well. The **Mainfrankisches Museum**, also in the Festung, has a large collection of wood and stone statues by Riemenschneider and displays of other Franconian arts.

Kappelle, on the next hill to the south, is a graceful 18th-century pilgrimage church built by Neumann and later enlarged. It has twin onion-domed towers and a richly-decorated interior, with many frescos. The terrace provides tremendous views of the town. Also worth visiting on the west bank are **Burkhardkirche**, with its late-Gothic choir and *Madonna and Child* by Riemenschneider, and the early-Gothic **Deutschhauskirche**, which contains a number of fine carvings.

In the town itself, the **Residenz**, *Residenzplatz*, is a spectacular palace which replaced the Festung as the bishops' home. Designed by Neumann to symbolise their wealth and power it contains numerous brilliant frescos and sculptures, including a vast Tiepolo fresco on the staircase. Don't miss the sumptuous **Kaisersaal**, where the statues and paintings blend perfectly, or the incredibly intricate **Hofkirche**.

St Kilians Dom, *Hofstr.*, was rebuilt in the 1960s. The Irish St Kilian was responsible for converting the town to Christianity in the 7th century. Neighbouring **Neumünster**, *Kürschnerhof*, a pinkish Romanesque-Baroque building containing excellent sculptures and frescos, stands over the graves of St Kilian and other martyred Irish missionaries.

Marienkapelle, *Markt*, a lovely Gothic hall-church, has interesting sculptures above the portals, while **Stift Haug**, *Bahnhofstr.*, contains a *Crucifixion* by Tintoretto.

Side Tracks from Würzburg

In summer there are river cruises: downstream to **Veitshöchheim** (with a Rococo castle and gardens) or upstream, through wine-growing country, to such fortified towns as **Ochsenfurt**. For information, *tel: (0931) 91582*.

The **Romantic Road** (*Romantische Strasse*) runs for 350 km between Würzburg and Füssen. **Europabuses** operate daily in summer, making brief stops at the historic towns en route. Book three days in advance with **Deutsche Touring Büro,** *Am Römerhof 17, Frankfurt/Main 90; tel: (069) 790 3240.* Eurail and German Rail Passes cover Europabuses, but Inter-Rail does not.

To avoid the worst of the crowds, and have more time to explore, travel independently. The 'Jewel of the Romantic Road' is **Rothenburg ob der Tauber,** a completely intact 14th-century town that has been officially protected since the 19th century and is irresistibly photogenic. It can be reached by taking a train to **Steinach**, then a bus, the full journey taking just under an hour.

A pleasant 2 km-walk along the Tauber leads to **Detwang**, where Riemenschneider's *Crucifixion* can be seen in **Pfarrkirche**.

NUREMBERG (NÜRNBERG)

Station: **Hbf**, *tel: (0911) 19419*, just south of *Altstadt*'s medieval fortifications.

Tourist Office: In Hbf, *tel: (0911) 23 36 32.* Mon–Sat 0900–2000. **Branch:** *Hauptmarktplatz 18; tel: (0911) 23 36 35.* Mon–Sat 0900–1300 and 1400–1800, Sun 1000–1300 and 1400–1600. *Monatsmagazin* from the tourist office and *Plarrer* from news-vendors are good listings guides. For youth information, visit **Jugendinformation im Tratzenzwinger**, *Hintere Insel Schütt 20; tel: (0911) 224 815.*

Getting Around

The *Altstadt* is large (about 4 sq km) but best explored on foot. The River Pegnitz runs through the centre, with most of the old and reconstructed buildings to the north.

The city is amply provided with U-Bahn, streetcars and buses. A *Tageskarte* gives a day's travel on all the public transport and is worthwhile if you take more than a couple of rides.

Accommodation and Food

Cheap accommodation fills early in summer and it's worth paying the modest booking fee charged by the tourist office. **IYHF**: *Burg 2;* *tel: (0911) 24 13 52* or *22 10 24*, in the castle (U: *Plärrer*, then tram no.4). Booking is advisable. **Campsite:** *Volkspark; tel: (0911) 81 11 22* (tram no.12). Chain hotels include: *Nv, SC.*

The town is famous for *Bratwurst* and *Sauerwurst* (both sausages) and *Lebkuchen* (gingerbread). There are eating-places to suit all tastes and pockets. **Bratwurst Häusle**, *Rathausplatz*, is so famous it's almost a sight in its own right (expect it to be crowded).

Sightseeing

The city centre was reduced to little more than rubble in 1945, but post-war restoration was painstaking and you'd never guess that almost everything is of modern construction.

Nuremberg dates from the 11th century. By the 15th century it was a major cultural and trading centre, but it then declined until the 19th century. Today, past glories have been overshadowed by the Nazi regime. The Third Reich staged many rallies in the town, and the post-war trials resulted in 'Nuremberg' becoming almost synonymous with 'war-crimes'. The facts have not been swept under the carpet here and many of the grandiose Nazi buildings still stand in **Dutzendteich** (tram no. 9: *Luitpoldhain*), a south-eastern suburb which has become a recreational area dedicated to their victims.

The **Kaiserburg** is a good place to begin your exploration, as it provides good views to assist orientation. The earliest bit of it is the **Fünfeckturm**, a pentagonal 11th-century tower, while the 12th-century **Kaiserkapelle** is an unusual two-tier chapel with a tower over the chancel.

Below the fortress is **Tiergärtner Tor**, an attractive cobbled area flanked by half-timbered inns, where all manner of people converge in summer. The **Dürerhaus**, *Albrecht Dürer Str.*, was the actual home of Dürer, not a reconstruction. Furnished in period style, it's an evocative place which contains several of his original woodcuts. To the west, past **Neutor** (not too far a walk), is **Johannisfriedhof**, *Johannisstr.*, a medieval cemetery where Dürer and other local celebrities are buried. Many 16th–17th-century stones have carvings depicting some aspect of the deceased's life.

Back in *Altstadt*, inside **Altstadthof**, *Berg-*

str.19, is a brewery museum with a maze of underground passages where beer was stored. It produces dark beer to an unchanged 19th-century recipe and, despite the lack of free samples, few beer-drinkers are content with just one bottle.

The **Stadtmuseum**, in the pink, gabled **Fembohaus**, *Burgstr.15*, is worth visiting, to see the extraordinary decor. To the east is the city's oldest church, and one of its finest, the 13th-century twin-towered **Sebalduskirche**. Its exterior is covered with sculptures and the works of art inside include the bronze shrine of St Sebald.

Spielzeugmuseum, *Karlstr.15*, is about toy-making and heavy on the nostalgia. Nuremberg was, and remains, a centre of the craft and there is a toy fair every February. Further south are the half-timbered **Weinstadel**, a medieval wine depot overlooking a weeping willow-lined stretch of the River Pegnitz, and **Henkersteg**, a covered wooden bridge that spans it.

Immediately east of Sebalduskirche is the 17th-century **Altes Rathaus**, a building resembling a Venetian palace. Underneath it are dungeons and a torture chamber. Through **Rathausgasse** is a fun Renaissance fountain depicting a farmer carrying geese to market.

Hauptmarktplatz is the home of a food and flower market. In the centre is the **Schönerbrunnen**, an ornate pyramidal fountain with an iron ring hidden in the railing (not the obvious gold one). Should you find it, turn it three times and your wish will come true – maybe. **Frauenkirche** is a lovely little chapel containing some fine works of art and a superb 15th-century altar. Try to be in the square at noon, to watch the 16th-century clock on the façade.

A little south of the river, **Lorenzkirche**, *St Lorenzplatz* is a lovely edifice inspired by the great French churches. Among the art treasures it contains are a 20m-high stone tabernacle by Kraft and a suspended wooden *Annunciation* by Veit Stoss.

The **Germanisches Nationalmuseum**, *Kornmarkt*, is excellent and devoted to German science and culture. Exhibits include Dürer originals, old weapons, a goldsmith's creation of a tall ship and the first globe of the earth – made in 1490, so lacking America.

Königstor, one of the gates in the original ramparts, marks **Handwerkerhof**, an enclosed village where you can watch traditional craftsmen at work. Everything sold there can be found (cheaper) elsewhere in town however. To the west, just outside *Altstadt*, the **Verkehrsmuseum**, *Lessingstr.6*, is devoted to German railways and has many old locos, including the very first engine in Germany. Two manufacturers of model railways (Arnold and Fleischmann) are based in Nuremberg and you can visit their works – ask at the tourist office.

◤ Side Tracks from Nuremberg

For Wagner-lovers, a trip to **Bayreuth**, is mandatory: almost the whole town is connected with him. The annual festival (July–August) should be avoided unless you already have tickets and accommodation. There are frequent trains, taking about an hour.

Bamberg is a charming and little-visited 11th-century town astride a river, with a Rathaus on an island and a superb cathedral. Also of interest are the bishops' residence, St Michael's church and the humorist Ernst Hoffmann's house. There are several trains a day and the journey takes about 35 mins.

AUGSBURG

Station: **Hbf**, *tel: (0821) 19419*, 500m west of *Altstadt*.

Tourist Office: *Bahnhofstr.7; tel: (0821) 50 20 70*, halfway between Hbf and *Altstadt*. Open Mon–Fri 0900–1800 and Sat–Sun 1000–1400. A tiny booth by Hbf opens Mon–Fri 1000–2000 and Sat–Sun 0900–2000.

Getting Around

Altstadt is within the old city walls, many bits of which still exist, and everything of interest is within walking distance of the centre (measured from the Rathaus).

Accommodation

There's a dearth of cheap central accommodation, so ask the tourist office for something in the suburbs. **IYHF**: *Beim Pfaffenkeller 3; tel: (0821) 33909* (tram no. 2: *Stadtwerke*), close to the Dom.

Campingplatz Augusta: *tel: (0821) 70 75 75* (bus: *Autobahnsee*), open all year.

Sightseeing

Founded by Caesar Augustus in 15 BC, Augsburg had become immensely wealthy by the end of the 15th century, largely because of two families, the Welsers (who owned Venezuela!) and the Fuggers.

Jakob Fugger ('Fugger the Rich') was responsible for many of the town's finest buildings and also founded the **Fuggerei quarter** (a few blocks east of the Rathaus) in 1519 – the world's first welfare housing project. It's a walled enclosure of ivy-covered houses which are still a haven for poor Catholics of good character.

The onion-domed **Rathaus** is a Renaissance edifice that was painstakingly restored after the war. The *Goldener Saal* is particularly sumptuous, with a marble floor, a painted cedar ceiling and pillars adorned with gold leaf. There's a great view from the adjoining **Perlachturm** (70m watch-tower). A few blocks north is the architecturally confused **Hoher Dom**, which contains much of interest, including Romanesque bronze doors, Gothic sculptures, paintings by Holbein the Elder and 11th-century stained-glass windows. To the west, **Heilig-Kreuz-Kirche** is a paired Catholic/Protestant church containing Rubens' *Assumption*.

Heading back towards the centre, don't miss **Annaskirche**, *Annastr.*, whose Renaissance **Fuggerkapelle** was the inspiration for many others. Across the street, the **Maximiliansmuseum**, the 16th-century mansion of the Welsers, is home to the town museum.

A couple of blocks south, **Zeughaus** was the first of many municipal structures built by Elias Holl, an innovative creation featuring a striking bronze by the Mannerist Hans Reichle.

The **Schaezler Palace**, an 18th-century Rococo building, is part entertainment venue, part museum. The art gallery, reached via a magnificently ornate room, is home to some fine Holbeins and a Dürer portrait of Jakob Fugger. In front of the palace stands the **Herkulesbrunnen**, one of three bronze Renaissance fountains that adorn *Maximilianstr.*

Side Tracks from Augsburg

From Augsburg Hbf, buses run to the village of **Schwangau** and the town of **Füssen**, which mark the southern end of the Romantic Road (see p. 176). Although picturesque places in their own right, they are also convenient bases for visiting the three nearby **Bavarian Royal Castles**.

The oldest of these is **Hohenschwangau**, built in the early 19th century by Max II of Bavaria as a deliberate attempt to re-create a romantic past. The site had long been associated with the legendary Knights of the Swan.

Max's son, 'mad' King Ludwig II, surpassed his father in enthusiasm for castle-building. **Neuschwanstein**, towering on a rocky outcrop above Hohenschwangau, is the archetypal fairy-tale castle. Although the first to be built by Ludwig, it remained unfinished at the time of his death. The sumptuous apartments and halls, decorated with scenes of idealised medievalism inspired by the operas of Ludwig's protégé Wagner, mark the high point of 19th-century romanticism. The road up to the castle is steep, but buses and horse-drawn carriages are available, and the spectacle is worth the climb.

Some 20 km further east is **Linderhof**. Originally intended to rival Versailles, it became a small French-style château set in landscaped gardens, less breathtaking but with more charm than Ludwig's other creations. Among the oddities of Linderhof is the king's dining table, engineered to be lowered to the kitchens and raised again so that he could dine entirely alone, without even the presence of servants.

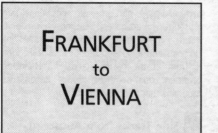

FRANKFURT
to
VIENNA

This route between Germany and Austria is known as the 'Route of Emperors and Kings'. It follows the River Danube (Donau) much of the way and incorporates two of Germany's most attractive old towns.

TRAINS

ETT tables: 66, 740, 800.

→ Fast Track

There are five EC trains daily (supplement payable) between Frankfurt (Hbf) and Vienna (Westbahnhof), plus one overnight express. The day trains have dining-cars and take about 7 hrs 45 mins. The overnight trains take about 8 hrs 20 mins and have a buffet service and sleepers.

∿ On Track

Frankfurt–Nuremberg–Regensburg

There are IC/EC trains between Frankfurt (Hbf) and Regensburg every two hours during the day. The journey takes nearly 3 hrs 30 mins, but there are dining cars. If you stop at Nuremberg, about 1 hr from Frankfurt (see p. 177), the onward journey to Regensburg takes 2 hrs 30 mins and trains operate roughly every hour during the day. You could also connect with the Frankfurt–Munich route from here (see p. 175).

Regensburg–Plattling–Passau

There are trains at least every two hours during the day. The full journey averages 1 hr 15 mins. Plattling is about half-way. You can reach the Bavarian Forest (*see Side Tracks, pp. 182*) by changing at Plattling, for Deggendorf – one of the many villages in the region.

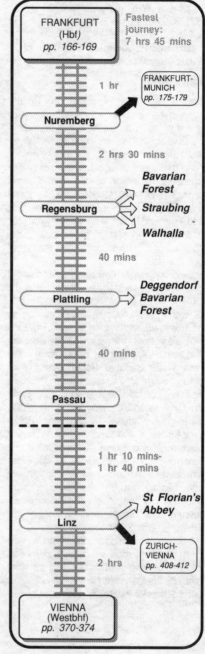

FRANKFURT (Hbf) *pp. 166-169*

Fastest journey: 7 hrs 45 mins

1 hr

FRANKFURT-MUNICH *pp. 175-179*

Nuremberg

2 hrs 30 mins

Bavarian Forest

Regensburg

Straubing

Walhalla

40 mins

Plattling

Deggendorf Bavarian Forest

40 mins

Passau

1 hr 10 mins- 1 hr 40 mins

St Florian's Abbey

Linz

2 hrs

ZURICH-VIENNA *pp. 408-412*

VIENNA (Westbhf) *pp. 370-374*

Passau–(Border)–Linz

Journey time varies from 1 hr 10 mins to 1 hr 40 mins, depending on whether you take an IC/EC train or an ordinary one: between them there is a service almost every hour. Border formalities are virtually non-existent. At Linz you can join the Zurich–Vienna route (*p. 408*).

Linz–Vienna

With both ordinary trains and (more frequent) IC/EC trains, the service is at least hourly and the journey usually takes under 2 hrs.

REGENSBURG

Station: Hbf, *tel: (0941) 19419*, is very central. **Tourist Office:** *Altes Rathaus; tel: (0941) 507 2141.* Mon–Fri 0830–1800, Sat 0900–1600 and Sun 0900–1200.

Getting Around

Everything of interest centres on *Altstadt*, a small area and easy to cover on foot. This is a place where legend and fact are almost inextricably interwoven and incorporated into much of the architecture. Some background knowledge greatly enhances your enjoyment and a little homework with a good guidebook will pay dividends. There is a very efficient **bus** service; timetables are available from *Ernst-Reuter-Platz 2*. **Danube Ferries** depart from between the Eiserne and Steinerne bridges.

Accommodation and Food

The only major chain hotel is *Ra*. There are some cheap central hotels, but you need to book in summer. Alternatively, you can pay for the tourist office to find you a room in a private home. **IYHF:** *Wohrdstr. 60; tel: (0941) 57402,* on an island in the Danube, 5-mins walk from the centre (bus no. 5: *Weissenburgstr.*). **Campsite:** (Mar–Oct) *Dunnerkeil, J Dirnberger, tel: (0941) 26839,* beside the Danube (bus no. 6: *Hans-Sachs-Str.,* then 3 km walk).

    Historische Wurstküche, *Weisselammgasse 3,* is Germany's oldest sausage house and sells nothing else. It's tiny and touristy, but part of the scene.

Sightseeing

The modern city is a booming industrial centre with a university that ensures it stays lively. **Altstadt** stands on the south bank of the Danube and was little damaged in the war. Many of the buildings date from a time when there were strong trading links with Venice and show a distinctly Italian influence. Many of the old streets are now pedestrianised and it's amazing that such a delightful place is not more on the tourist map.

    The 12th-century **Steinernebrücke** gives the best view of the medieval skyline. When it was built it represented the only safe crossing on the Danube and gave Regensburg tremendous strategic importance.

    Immediately to the south is **Domstadt**, an ecclesiastical complex centred on the magnificent **cathedral** (*Dom*). It's rewarding to explore, doubly so if you understand the 'in' jokes incorporated in the decor. A laughing angel near the transept seems absolutely appropriate. The Dom was started in the 13th century, but it was six centuries before the final touches (the 105m spires) were completed. Its attractions range from 14th-century stained-glass windows to a fine boys' choir (*Domspatzen*). In the **Treasury** (*Domschatz*) are some mouth-watering jewels and gold. During a September festival, the nearby goose fountain spouts beer instead of water (this is sold for charity).

    The exterior of **Alte Kapelle** belies the wealth of Rococo decorations inside, including a marble altar and rich frescos.

    The **Porta Praetoria** is part of the 2nd-century Roman defences and recent excavations have revealed Roman remains beneath the **Niedermunster**. The **Stadtmuseum**, *Dachauplatz*, has over 100 rooms about the town's cultural and artistic history.

    Scattered around the town are some twenty towers in the style of Italian fortified palaces. There were sixty originally, but they were never defensive, just status symbols – the higher the tower, the more important the owner. Most striking is the **Baumburger Turm**, *Watmarkt*, and the highest is the nine-storey **Goldener Turm**, *Wahlenstr.*, with a wine bar at the top.

Altes Rathaus, *Kohlenmarkt*, is a Gothic structure which is more interesting inside than out, so it's worth taking the **Reichstagsmuseum** tour. *Haidplatz* is dominated by the **Haus zum Goldenen Kreuz**, another place with a fascinating history. If you can spot the small stone mouse on the right-hand corner, you should rub it – to ensure your purse will never be empty.

The **Johannes-Kepler-Gedächtnishaus**, *Keplerstr. 5*, is dedicated to the scientist/astrologer (1571–1630) who made several significant contributions to our knowledge of both planetary movements and optics.

The south-western part of town was formerly a monastic quarter and many of the old buildings survive. **St Jakob**, just off *Bismarckplatz*, was marked by splendid sandstone figures. These have been eroded over the centuries, but you can still see that the main (Romanesque) portal is a mixture of pagan and Christian images. At the extreme southern end of the old city is the former Benedictine monastery of **St Emmeran**, once a great centre of learning. The Romanesque interior has been somewhat spoiled by over-ornamentation, but the 11th-century double portal survives and the crypt dates back to the 8th century. There are several superb sculptures on the monuments to historical figures.

The **Schloss Thurn und Taxis** consists of Benedictine buildings that were turned into luxurious residences in Napoleonic times. The Thurn und Taxis dynasty pioneered Europe's postal service in the 15th century and retained the monopoly until 1867. They now own much of Bavaria and the state rooms are open to the public when the family are not in residence. The **Marstallmuseum** has an enormous collection of carriages of all types.

Side Tracks from Regensburg

In summer there are a variety of cruises on the **Danube**. Destinations include **Walhalla**, where there's a 19th-century Greek temple modelled on the Parthenon and giving a splendid view to reward the steep climb, and **Straubing**, a market town dominated by a five-pointed Gothic tower and lined by the medieval façades characteristic of Bavaria's rural towns. The **Gäubodenmuseum** contains extensive Roman artefacts discovered in the region in 1950.

The **Bavarian Forest** (*Bayerischer Wald*) region encompasses 6,000 sq km of wooded peaks (60 over 1,000m), rivers, creeks and lots of tiny villages with churches, ruined castles and a traditional way of life. Within it the **Bavarian Forest National Park**, covering 8,000 hectares (20,000 acres), is strictly protected to safeguard the ecosystem and has countless marked trails (maps are sold in village tourist offices).

If you don't want to go alone, there's a good choice of walking tours. The lack of mass tourism means cheap accommodation is not difficult to find, but it also means that public transport is infrequent and there are seldom more than one or two buses a day.

For general information, contact **Fremdenverkehrsverband Ostbayern**, *Landshuterstr. 13, Regensburg; tel: (0941) 57186*. For information about hiking tours, contact **Nationalparkverwaltung Bayerischer Wald**, *Freyunstr. 2; 8352 Grafenau; tel: (08552) 42743*.

PASSAU

Station: Hbf, *tel: (0851) 19419*, west of the centre. Turn right and follow the Jugendherberge signs to Rathaus or (Mon–Fri 0630–1830) take the City-Bus.

Tourist Offices: **Main office:** *Rathausplatz 3; tel: (0851) 33421.* Mon–Fri 0830–1200 and 1300–1700, and Sat–Sun 0900–1300. They dispense a free monthly listing called *Aktuell*. **Branch:** At Hbf, Apr–Oct, Mon–Fri 0900–1700 and Sat–Sun 0900–1300.

Getting Around

With the exception of the palace-castle, everything of interest is easily walkable. **Ferries** leave from the docks along *Fritz-Schäffer-Promenade*, in front of the Rathaus. There is a 'Three Rivers Round Trip' tour of the city, which runs (Mar–Oct) when sufficient people have turned up.

Accommodation

Hotels include *HI*. There are some reasonably

cheap lodgings, but they fill early in summer and booking is recommended. The **IYHF** is housed in the palace-castle, *tel: (0851) 41351*, across the Danube. Cross the bridge by the docks and be prepared for a steep climb, or take the bus from *Rathausplatz* right to the door. Early booking is essential during school holidays. **Campsite:** *Halserstr. 34; tel: 41457*, by the River Ilz.

Sightseeing

Passau is a charming place on the German/ Austrian border, often by-passed but well worth a stop. The architecture is mainly Baroque, Rococo and neo-Classical because a major 17th-century fire destroyed most of the earlier buildings

The town is set on two peninsulas. The palace-castle is on the peninsula between the Danube and the Ilz and *Altstadt* on the one between the Danube and the Inn.

Veste Oberhaus was the former palace of the bishops and a prison for their enemies. It's a steep walk up, but there's a regular bus from *Rathausplatz*. The stronghold now contains the magnificent **Cultural History Museum** (54 rooms of art and artefacts spanning two millenia) and there's a marvellous view .

On the other peninsula, the lofty **Stephans-dom** with its green cupolas is a superb example of Italian Baroque architecture, with hundreds of cherubs on the ceiling and the world's largest church organ (over 17,000 pipes), which is used for noon concerts on weekdays. Behind the Dom is the cobbled *Residenzplatz*, lined with Renaissance dwellings including the **Treasury** (*Domschatz*), housed in the Residenz, which contains a marvellous collection of gold items and tapestries. Also on *Residenzplatz* is the small **Spielzeugmuseum**, a collection of 19th-century toys. Next to the ornate 14th-century **Rathaus** is the **Passauer Glasmuseum**, containing over 20,000 glass items spanning 150 years.

LINZ

Station: *Bahnhofstr.; tel: (0732) 17 17*, 2 km south of the centre (tram no. 3).
Tourist Information: *Hauptplatz 34; tel: (0732) 23 93 17 77*. Mon–Fri 0800–1800; June–Sept

also Sat–Sun 0800–1130 and 1230–1800. There's a smaller branch in the station; *tel: (0732) 23 93 17 73*. Mon–Sat 0800–1230 and 1330–1900, and Sun 1400–1900.

Getting Around

Ask the tourist office for *A Walk Through Linz's Old City*. Elsewhere there's an excellent tram and bus system. Tickets are available from machines at the stops and you can get (from Tabak stands) cards for 6 rides or for 24-hours unlimited travel. The tourist office provides route maps.

Accommodation

Hotels include *Nv*, *Pe* and *Ra*. Cheap lodgings are very hard to find in the centre. One of the few possibilities is *Wilder Mann, Goetherstr.14; tel: (0732) 24 05*, two blocks from the station.

There are three **IYHF hostels:** *Kapuzi-nerstr.14; tel: (0732) 78 27 20*, 10-mins walk west of *Hauptplatz* (tram no. 3: *Taubenmarkt*); *Blutenstr. 23; tel: (0732) 23 70 78*, in Lentia shopping centre (tram no. 3: *Reindlstr.*); *Stanglhofweg 3, Oberosterreich; tel: 66 44 34*, near the stadium (bus no. 27: *Froshberg*).

The nearest **campsite** is 10 km south-east, on *Pichlingersee* (hourly bus from the station).

Sightseeing

Perhaps best known as the place where Hitler spent his childhood, Linz straddles the River Danube. It has a well-preserved **Altstadt**, where a pedestrian zone of Baroque houses surrounds the large **Hauptplatz**. In the square, the Baroque **Altes Rathaus** is topped by an octagonal tower and astronomical clock. Just off it is the twin-towered 17th-century **Alter Dom**, *Domgasse*. The 15th-century **Schloss**, *Tummelplatz 10*, perched on a hill above Hauptplatz, offers great views and houses the **Landesmuseum**'s extensive collections of Bronze Age and Roman relics. The weaponry and folklore sections are also excellent.

Postlingbergbahn, *Landgutstr. 19* (at the end of bus line 3), is a funicular railway that climbs to the 18th-century twin-towered pil-grimage church of **Postlingberg** (537m), with its **Botanical Gardens** and panoramic views.

FRANKFURT
to
ZURICH

This route, between Germany and Switzerland, provides an opportunity to enjoy some mountain scenery, as well as visiting such diverse towns as Heidelberg (the setting for Sigmund Romberg's 'Student Prince') and Stuttgart – Europe's answer to Mo Town (Detroit).

TRAINS

ETT tables: 77, 760, 742, 74.

→ Fast Track

About three direct services run daily (supplement payable) from Frankfurt (Hbf) to Zurich (Hbf), one in the early morning and two in the afternoon, taking about 4 hrs. There is a dining-car on all services. The border is crossed at Basel, but it's not necessary to leave the train. Direct services take a different route to the On Track description given below (see route diagram opposite).

∿∿ On Track

Frankfurt–Mannheim

There's at least one train an hour, the journey averaging 45–50 mins. From Mannheim you can transfer to the Paris–Frankfurt route by taking a train to Saarbrücken.

Mannheim–Heidelberg

The service is at roughly half-hourly intervals, the journey taking 10–20 mins.

Heidelberg–Heilbronn

Trains are frequent by day and take 1 hr 30 mins.

Heilbronn–Stuttgart

Trains are irregularly spaced, but not normally

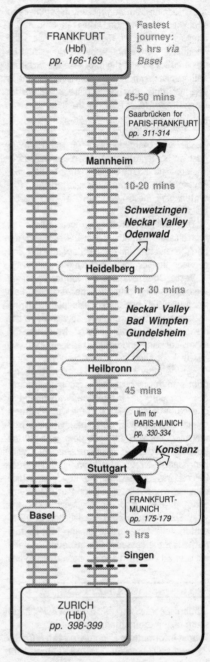

FRANKFURT
(Hbf)
pp. 166-169

Fastest journey: 5 hrs via Basel

45-50 mins

Saarbrücken for
PARIS-FRANKFURT
pp. 311-314

Mannheim

10-20 mins

Schwetzingen
Neckar Valley
Odenwald

Heidelberg

1 hr 30 mins

Neckar Valley
Bad Wimpfen
Gundelsheim

Heilbronn

45 mins

Ulm for
PARIS-MUNICH
pp. 330-334

Konstanz

Stuttgart

FRANKFURT-
MUNICH
pp. 175-179

3 hrs

Singen

Basel

ZURICH
(Hbf)
pp. 398-399

more than an hour apart. The journey averages 45 mins.

Stuttgart–(Border)–Zurich

Seven or eight trains run daily (half of which have refreshment service), operating at two-hour intervals. The journey takes about 3 hrs and the border (barely noticeable) is crossed at Singen.

MANNHEIM

Station: Hbf, *tel: (0621) 19419*, south-east of the centre.
Tourist Office: *Kaiserring 10; tel: (0621) 10 10 11*. Mon–Fri 0800–1800 and Sat 0830–1200.

Sightseeing

Mannheim's central street-grid was planned in the 18th century and this layout was widely copied in other towns, notably in North America. Little of the old town has survived, however, and even the reconstructed **Residenzschloss** is not particularly striking. The city's symbol is the **Wasserturm**, an impressive sandstone watertower. The **Kunsthalle** has one of Germany's finest collections of 19th–20th-century European art.

HEIDELBERG

Station: Hbf, *tel: (06221) 19419*, 1.5 km west of the centre. Buses run to the edge of *Altstadt*.
Tourist Office: directly in front of Hbf; *tel: (06221) 21341* or *27735*. Open Apr–Oct, Mon–Sat 0900–1900 and Sun 1000–1800; Nov–Mar 0900–1900. They issue a weekly listings guide, *Heidelberg diese Woche*.

Getting Around

Much of the *Altstadt*, the main area of interest, is pedestrianised and there's a funicular up to the Schloss. Elsewhere there's a good network of buses and trams.

Accommodation and Food

Finding a cheap bed is extremely difficult (virtually impossible in peak season), so book well in advance unless you are prepared to base yourself out of town in, say, Mannheim. Chain hotels include: *Hl.* **IYHF**: *Tiergartenstr.5; tel: (06221) 41 20 66*, near the zoo, about 4 km from the centre. Both **campsites** are east of the city: *Heidelberg-Schlierbach; tel: (06221) 80 25 06*, is by the Orthopaedic Clinic (bus no.35) and *Haide; tel: (06223) 2111*, is across the river from the Clinic.

Kneipen (student inns) are part of Heidelberg's scene. Many customers are tourists, but the bulk (in term-time) are still students and older taverns are decorated with all sorts of historical paraphernalia related to the fraternities.

Sightseeing

Heidelberg was virtually destroyed by Louis XIV, but rebuilt in the 17th century. It is extraordinarily photogenic and home to Germany's oldest university (founded 1386). It is a magnet for tourists and best avoided in peak season (July/August).

The largely ruined, but incredibly impressive, **Heidelberger Schloss** should not be missed. Things worth seeing include *Grosses Fass*, said to be the world's largest wine vat, and the reasonably intact *Apothekenmuseum*, with a 17th-century pharmacy and alchemist's laboratory.

Baroque mansions are scattered through **Altstadt** and one of the joys of the town is to just wander around looking at them. The Renaissance **Haus zum Ritter**, 14th-century **Heiliggeistkirche** and **Herkulesbrunnen** are on *Marktplatz*.

The other major square is *Universitätsplatz*, the location of **Alte Universität** (1712) and **Neue Universität** (1930) (the real 'new' campus is north-west of town). In the centre of the square is the **Löwenbrunnen**, a stone-lion fountain. Until 1914, students whose high spirits had got out of hand were confined in the special **students' prison** *Augustinerstr.*. Incarceration for a short period was regarded as an honour and self-portraits are common in the graffiti that covers the walls.

The **Kurpfalzisches/Palais Morass**, *Hauptstr. 97* is crammed with artefacts, including a fabulous 15th-century altarpiece by Riemenschneider and works by Dürer and Van der Weyden, while the **Völkerkunde/Palais Weimar**, *Hauptstr. 235*, has good exhibits from Africa.

Reach the north bank of the Neckar by

crossing **Karl-Theodor/Alte Brücke**, marked by a statue of the prince-elector on the south side. Once across, climb the very steep **Schlagenweg** staircase to **Philosophenweg**: the view was thought to inspire philosophic meditation. Further up **Heiligenberg** are a number of interesting ruins to reward the effort of the climb.

Side Tracks from Heidelberg

Schwetzingen (30 mins by frequent bus) is renowned for the 18th-century **Schwetzinger Palace**. The building itself is not vastly interesting, but the gardens are magnificent: extensive and full of statues, follies and fountains.

Cruises on the **River Neckar** are run by *Rhein-Neckar-Fahrgastschiffahrt* (tel: *(06221) 20181*) and *Personenschiffahrt Hornung* (tel: *(06221) 48 00 64*). They depart daily (May–Sept) from the quay by *Stadthalle*. The river is flanked bythe **Oden-wald**, an extensive forest amply scattered with villages below old castles on rocky crags. Cruises stop at some (**Neckarsteinach**, for instance, which has four ruined castles within 3 km).

HEILBRONN

Station: Hbf, tel: *(07131) 19419*, around 700m west of *Marktplatz*.
Tourist Office: *Rathaus, Marktplatz.*; tel: *(07131) 56 22 70*. Open Mon–Fri 0900–1730 and Sat 0900–1230.

Sightseeing

Much of the old town has been destroyed, but there are two surviving buildings of interest. The recreated Gothic Renaissance **Rathaus** is best-known for its 16th-century astronomical clock, which zips into activity every four hours (at 0400, 0800, 1200, 2000, and 2400). The Gothic **Kilianskirche** is the town's symbol, with its intricate 62m belfry topped by a figure bearing Heilbronn's coat of arms. It has a superbly carved altarpiece and marks the spot of the supposedly miraculous well for which the town was named. If you like wine, the September **Heilbronner Herbst** is the best time for a visit,

when around 200 vintages are available in *Marktplatz* and bands accompany the drinking.

Side Tracks from Heilbronn

From May to October **River Neckar cruises** are available from just below the bridge near *Marktplatz*. These go downstream to Bad Wimpfen and Gundelsheim twice a day. For information, tel: *(07131) 85430*.

Bad Wimpfen is a picturesque old town above the river. Its cobblestoned streets are lined with asymmetrical half-timbered houses and there are remains of a 13th-century castle with a high blue tower. The little *Steinhaus Museum* contains Roman artefacts and the *Puppenmuseum* (Doll museum) is interesting.

Gundelsheim, in the shadow of *Schloss Horneck*, is the best point from which to reach *Burg Guttenberg*, which is impressive in itself and contains a very interesting museum. The prime attraction, however, is an enormous collection of birds of prey. There are twice-daily demonstrations showing some of them in free flight. Several dozen are released each year to build up the natural populations of endangered species.

STUTTGART

Station: Hbf, tel: *(0711) 19419*, is very central, to the west of *Schlossgarten*.
Tourist Office: *Königstr.1A;* tel: *(0711) 222 8240*, by Hbf. Mon–Fri 0930–2030, Sat 0930–1800 and Sun 1100/1300–1800. They sell excellent maps and distribute transport timetables, as well as museum, gallery and theatre guides. **Youth information**: contact Jugendinformation, *Hohe Str.9*; tel: *(0711) 2268001*.

Stuttgart Live and *Ketchup* (both from newsagents) give listings of what's on, while the tourist office publish a full monthly guide, *Stuttgarter Monatsspiegel*.

Getting Around

The city centre is compact and largely pedestrianised, but many sights are outside this area and it's worth getting a 24-hour pass which covers all the buses, trams and trains in the area.

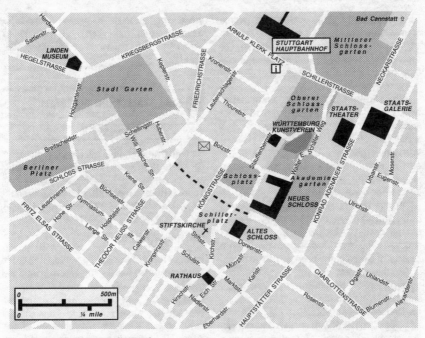

Accommodation and Food

Most hotels in Stuttgart break the bank, but there are a few reasonable places and you can usually get private rooms – ask the tourist office. Chain hotels include: *Ic.* **IYHF:** *Hausmannstr.27; tel: (0711) 24 15 83*, 15-mins uphill walk east from Hbf (or U15/16: *Eugensplatz*). If you have no luck in Stuttgart, try **Ludwigsburg**: *Gemsenbergstr.21; tel: (0714) 51564* (S: 15 mins, then 10-mins walk). **Campsite:** *Mercedesstr.40, Cannstatter Wasen; tel: (0711) 55 66 96* (Bad Cannstatt; tram nos.1/2). Open all year.

The local wines are excellent and can be sampled at *Weinstuben*, comfortable places with reasonable prices and good German food.

Sightseeing

The city began life around 950, as a stud farm (*Stutengarten*: hence the horse on the coat-of-arms), but became important only in the 19th century. There is little in the way of historic sights, but it's a lively place with many excellent museums (most of them free). Although one of Europe's most prosperous manufacturing cities,

Stuttgart has a somewhat suburban atmosphere, probably because about three-quarters of its area consists of parks, farms, orchards and vineyards.

Schlossgarten is an enormous park (nude sunbathing OK), extending north from **Schlossplatz** to the river. The northern part is **Rosensteinpark** and the extreme north-eastern corner is **Wilhelma**, a complex that includes a natural history museum, a Moorish garden with a large lily pond and a zoo holding over 9,000 animals.

The new wing of **Staatsgalerie Stuttgart**, *Konrad-Adenauer Str.30*, was finished in 1984

Besenvirtschaften

Besenvirtschaften is a tradition in the Stuttgart area, whereby many wine-growers hang a broom outside their houses when the new wine is ready. As long as the broom is displayed (Nov–Mar), you can treat the house as an informal pub and pop in to sample the brew (at well-below-normal prices).

---

and was very controversial, but has since become acknowledged as a fine example of modern architecture. One room is given over to *The Legend of Perseus* by Edward Burne-Jones and other exhibits include the finest Picasso collection in the country.

Altes Schloss, *Schillerplatz*, encompasses what remains of the 14th-century castle that replaced the stud farm. The rest of the building is a Renaissance palace, housing the excellent **Württembergisches Landesmuseum**. The eclectic exhibits include 19th-century crown jewels, Swabian sculptures, stained glass, an intact Celtic grave and Renaissance clocks.

An attractive, if odd, appearance is presented by the **Stiftskirche**, just off the square, the result of 15th-century additions to a much earlier structure. The choir has superb Renaissance carvings of eleven of the rulers of Württemberg.

On the western side of town, near the university, are the **Hospitalkirche**, where there's a monumental sculpture of the *Crucifixion*, and the **Lindenmuseum**, *Hegelplatz 1*, a fascinating ethnological museum with sections on American Indians, the South Seas, Africa, the Orient and Asia. On a hill to the north-west, **Hohenpark Killesberg** contains such diverse attractions as a beer garden, a flamingo pond, a miniature railway and domestic animals (which make it very appealing to children).

Bad Cannstatt, across the river from Rosensteinpark, is now part of Stuttgart (S: nos. 1/2/3) and provides one of its recreational areas, **Kurpark**, a restful spot with mineral springs and willow-shaded paths. Cannstatt is the home (every Sept–Oct since 1818) of **Volksfest**, a huge beer festival that is second only to Munich's Oktoberfest.

In 1886 Gottlieb Daimler and Carl Benz (quite independently) invented motor cars and opened factories to produce them. These were later combined and are now at **Unterturkheim**, south of Bad Cannstatt. The **Daimler-Benz Museum** (S1: *Neckarstadion*) displays over 70 historical models (in mint condition), ranging from the first-ever motorbike (invented by Daimler a year before his car) to futuristic experimental vehicles. In the northern suburb of **Zuffenhausen** (S6: *Neuwirtshaus*), are their arch-rivals, **Porsche-werk**. This museum is smaller (around 50 vehicles, mostly racing-cars), but Porsche do permit tours of their works. Book ahead; *tel: (0711) 827 5685.*

Side Track from Stuttgart

KONSTANZ

Station: Hbf, *tel: (07531) 19419*, is between *Bahnhofplatz*, the eastern boundary of *Altstadt*, and the harbour.

Tourist Office: *Bahnhofplatz 13; tel: (07531) 28 43 76*. Mon–Fri 0800–2000, Sat 0930–1330 and 1600–1900, and Sun 1000–1300.

Getting Around

There's a maze of different passes covering buses and/or ferries, so spend a little time exploring the possibilities.

Most of the ferries leave from the quay behind Hbf and fares are reasonable. Frequency is seasonal, but there are timetables at all the quays. The largest operator is the DB-run **Bodensee-Verkehrsdienst**, *Hafenstr.6; tel: (07531) 28 13 98*. DB rail passes are valid.

Accommodation

Book well ahead as, besides the hostels and campsite, there's nothing cheap in town other than reasonably priced private homes. **IYHF:** *Zur Allmannshohe 18; tel: (07531) 32260*, (bus no.4). **Jugendherberge Kreuzlingen**, *tel: (072) 75 26 63*. Although in Switzerland, it's actually closer to the centre than the IYHF. Formalities are minimal, so just walk to the border and get directions from the guard. **Camping,** *Litzelstetten-Mainau, Dietmar Heinert; tel: (07531) 44321*. There are other sites around the lake.

Sightseeing

Most of Konstanz is in Germany, but the southern section spills into Switzerland. It's the largest settlement on **Lake Constance (Bodensee)**, an enormous body of water forming part of the German/Swiss/Austrian border.

Trains from Stuttgart and Konstanz are via Singen, with several good connections every day, the full journey taking around 2 hrs 30 mins. In summer you need not return to Stuttgart, but can take a lake ferry between Konstanz and Schaffhausen (taking 4 hrs 20 mins), plus a train between Schaffhausen and Zurich (about 40 mins). There are reasonable connections.

Owing to its Swiss area, Konstanz was not targeted by Allied bombers and retains an attractive old quarter, **Niederburg**, where little alleys wind between half-timbered buildings with beautifully decorated façades. Elaborate frescos on the Renaissance **Rathaus** depict the town's history. The Romanesque **Münster** dates from the 11th century, but many bits were added later.

Around Lake Constance

Mainau (bus no. 4: *Staad* or ferry) is a delightful 45-hectare island linked by a footbridge to the north-east corner of town. A lush, colourful garden surrounds a Baroque palace that was used by the Teutonic Knights for over five centuries and is still inhabited, although the richly ornamented chapel is open to the public.

Ferry destinations include: **Meersburg**, an atmospheric hillside town with a picturesque Markt and very old inhabited castle; **Unteruhldingen**, which is home to an open-air museum (with recreations of Stone Age dwellings) and a marvellous basilica that is worth the 20-mins uphill walk; and **Uberlingen**, a strikingly attractive town with a Gothic Münster and interesting old buildings.

The Konstanz–Schaffhausen ferries call at **Reichenau**, which has three 9th-century monasteries, each surrounded by a village and all worth a visit. There are also regular buses from Konstanz. Not far away is **Wollmatinger Ried**, a protected marshland with rich bird life that can be visited Apr–Oct: details from the information desk in Reichenau station.

ISTANBUL

Istanbul, the city of three names, bestrides the Bosphorus, linking Europe and Asia. It is a fabulous metropolis crammed with the splendour of the Byzantine and Ottoman empires, of which it was successively the capital.

Originally a Greek settlement called Byzantium, the city was renamed Constantinople in AD 330, when the Emperor Constantine established it as capital of the Byzantine or Eastern Roman Empire. Known as New Rome, Constantinople became the most influential city in Europe. Over the centuries, it withstood attacks by Goths, Persians and Arabs, before finally falling to the Turks under Sultan Mehmet II in 1453, when it became Istanbul. During the glory years of the Ottoman sultans (in the 16th century and beyond) Istanbul, capital of a burgeoning empire, became a dazzling and vibrant city packed with fine mosques and palaces.

In 1923, following the fall of the Ottomans, the great reformer, Atatürk, leader of the Turkish Republic, moved the seat of government to Ankara. After almost 1,600 years, Istanbul had lost its capital status, but not its importance, its strategic value and its sheer excitement.

Tourist Information

Main Office: 57 Meşrutiyet Cad., Beyoğlu; tel: 245 6875 or 243 3472. **Branches:** Atatürk Airport; tel: 573 7399 or 573 4136; Karaköy Maritime Station; tel: 249 5776; Hilton Hotel, Cumhuriyet Cad., Harbiye; tel: 233 0592; and Sultanahmet Meydani; tel: 518 1802 (between Aya Sofya and the Blue Mosque). Tourist office hours are Mon–Fri 0830–1230 and 1330–1730. All distribute free maps and guides to Istanbul (in English) and have details on local transport.

If you have any problems, look for the special tourist police, who can be recognised by their beige uniforms and maroon berets. They can also be telephoned on: 527 4503 or 528 5369.

Arriving and Departing

Airport

Atatürk Airport (tel: 573 7617 or 573 3530) is in Yeşilköy, 15 km west of Istanbul. Buses run every half-hour between Atatürk and the THY (Turkish Airlines) terminal at Şişhane.

Stations

There are two rail terminals. **Sirkeçi Station** (tel: 527 0050 or 520 6575), near the waterfront at Eminönü express tram or 10-mins walk beside tram line to Sultanahmet): trains to Europe via Greece or Bulgaria. The bureau de change in the station will exchange only cash, but there are others immediately outside and automatic cash dispensers in the forecourt.

Rail services to Asian Turkey and beyond use **Haydarpaşa Station** (tel: 336 0475), across the Bosphorus (by ferry).

NB In Greek railway timetables Istanbul is still referred to as (in Cyrillic) as Constantinopolis.

Getting Around

Istanbul is separated into European and Asian halves by the Bosphorus. The western (European) half is itself split by the Golden Horn (Haliç), an inlet of the Bosphorus. Most of the interesting sights are in Sultanahmet, south of the Golden Horn in the Old Stamboul area.

Express Tram

There is one express tram line, running from Sirkeçi station west along Divan Yolu and Millet Cad., out to the old city walls. Buy tickets from kiosks by the stops: place them in metal containers at the entrance to the platforms.

Buses

Large fleets of buses cover most of Istanbul, but routes can be confusing and there is no bus map to consult, so ask for details at major stops or tourist offices. The major departure points are Taksim Square, Eminönü (near the Galata Bridge) and Beyazit. Tickets can be bought at kiosks or from street vendors and are surrendered into mysterious sucking machines on board. Depending on the route taken, one or two tickets may be required.

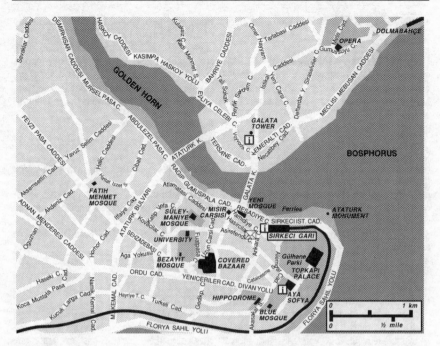

Taxis

The yellow taxis in Istanbul offer a simpler alternative to the buses. Fares are reasonable, but ensure that the driver starts the meter when you get in. Fares double between midnight and 0600. The unique *Dolmus*, communal taxis, run on set routes and cram remarkable numbers of passengers into huge decrepit American cars.

Ferries

Ferries run regularly across the Bosphorus, between *Karaköy* on the European side and *Haydarpaşa* and *Kadiköy*; and between *Eminönü* on the European side and *Üsküdar*. Schedules can be confusing and piers chaotic, so ask for details at the tourist office, or consult the *Thomas Cook Guide to Greek Island Hopping* (see p. 21).

Living in Istanbul

Accommodation

Chains include *Hl, Hn, Pe, Ra, Sh, Pu*. Most budget accommodation lies in the *Sultanahmet* district, particularly in the back streets between *Sultanahmet Square* and the water. **IYHF:** *6 Caferiye Sok; tel: 513 6150*. There is also a collection of similarly priced private hostels. Although basic and usually crowded, these are cheap and marvellously placed for Istanbul's main sights, only 2 mins walk to the Blue Mosque. There are often a few people hawking rooms to arriving rail passengers, but they are usually touting for establishments far from the centre. Make sure you know where they are and how to get there before agreeing to anything.

Some of Istanbul's top range hotels congregate north of the Golden Horn in *Taksim* and *Harbiye*, along or near *Cumhuriyet Cad.*. As well as being a considerable distance from the main sights, this is one of Istanbul's most characterless areas. There are, however, plenty of hotels south of the Golden Horn, so it is possible to stay in *Old Stamboul* without having to slum it, with a particular concentration of hotels of all categories in *Beyazit*, *Laleli* and *Aksaray*. The tourist offices have a comprehensive list.

There are four **campsites** in and around

Istanbul, all some distance from the centre.

Communications

The **main PTT office** is at 25 Yeni Postane Cad., near Sirkeçi Station. However there are many branches throughout Istanbul which generally have shorter queues, both for postal services and for making telephone calls. You can make international calls at all the major PTT offices.

Pay phones require *jetons* (tokens), which come in small, medium and large sizes and can be bought from kiosks. Few pay phones seem to function. A small *jeton* should suffice for a local call; long-distance attempts require many large ones. Some new card phones are being introduced (cards available from PTT offices). The dialling code for Istanbul is 212 (north of the Bosphorus), or 216 (south of the Bosphorus).

Eating and Drinking

Istanbul's eating options are as varied and colourful as the city itself, but be prepared to head away from the tourist centres for the best deals. Restaurants around *Sultanahmet* are certainly adequate, but you can find more character (and lower prices) elsewhere. Istanbul, located near two seas, is naturally a great place for seafood. Fish restaurants cluster in *Kumkapi* on the south coast of *Stamboul*, west of *Sultanahmet*. This area is lively and entertaining at night and you may find gypsy musicians accompanying your meal.

North of the Golden Horn, in *Beyoğlu*, *Çiçek Paşaji* (Flower Passage), is an alleyway packed with restaurants accompanied by more gypsy musicians. The passage has become quite touristy in recent years but still represents the best option for eating in the newer parts of the city.

Throughout *Stamboul* are street sellers and kiosks selling fish, lamb or chicken kebabs (usually served in bread not pitta), Turkish sweets and Western foodstuffs like corn-on-the-cob.

Bakirköy, further along the railway line towards the airport, is another good area. Further afield, the settlements on either side of the Bosphorus are renowned for their seafood restaurants, which often afford dramatic views across the straits. These include *Ortaköy*, by the European end of the Bosphorus bridge, where,

along with much eating, there is live music and dancing. Further north, *Humeli Kavaği* (European side), and *Anadolu Kavaği* (Asian side), are popular destinations amongst day-trippers on Bosphorus excursions. It's possible to sail up, eat, then sail back to Istanbul. Both towns seem to revolve around their copious fish restaurants.

Embassies and Consulates

Australia: *58 Tepecik Yolu, Etiler; tel: 257 7050.*
Canada: *107 Buyukdere Cad., Gayrettepe; tel: 272 5174.*
New Zealand: has no diplomatic representation, but the British Embassy should be able to help if you have problems.
UK: *34 Meşrutiyet Cad., Beyoğlu; tel: 244 7540.*
USA: *104–108 Meşrutiyet, Tepebaşi; tel: 251 3602.*

Money

There are plenty of bureaux de change around Istanbul, especially in *Sultanahmet* and in the covered market. Commissions and rates vary considerably, so it is worth checking several offices. Due to extremely high inflation, exchange rates date rapidly, although prices stay reasonably constant in terms of Western currencies. Automatic cash dispensers are becoming more common and are convenient; it is often cheaper to get a cash advance on a credit card and pay the handling charge than to pay commission at a bank or bureau.

Ekin Tourism, *Cumhuriyet Caddesi 295, Harbaye*, the **Thomas Cook** network member in Istanbul offers emergency assistance in the case of lost or stolen Thomas Cook travellers' cheques.

Entertainment

The best areas for nightlife are those with good eating possibilities: *Kumkapi*, with its many bars and restaurants, and *Çiçek Paşaji*, in *Beyoğlu*. The disco scene is concentrated around *Harbiye* and *Taksim* but is expensive and unappealing. The international arts festival is in June and July. Its main venues are the **Cemal Resit Rey Hall**, *Harbiye*, and the **Atatürk Cultural Center**, *Taksim*.

Shopping

Shopping and street life provide the best of the city's entertainment. The most famous of the markets is the **Kapali Çarşi (Covered Bazaar)**, *Beyazit*: go along *Divan Yolu* from *Sultanahmet Square*. There are thousands of shops and stalls here, roughly grouped according to merchandise, with whole alleys selling gold, silver, brass or leather. If you are going to buy anything, haggle hard. Even if you reduce the original price to a third, you are probably still paying too much in local terms. However, the atmosphere is free and worth sampling. The **Misir Çarşisi**, the spice bazaar near the Yeni Mosque, is less touristy and equally interesting.

Sightseeing

Istanbul is full of monumental buildings of such presence that each would, on its own, dominate many lesser cities. Here they fight for prominence, creating a memorable skyline of domes and minarets, best seen from the Bosphorus at dawn, or the top of the **Galata Tower**, north of the Golden Horn. Built in 1348 by the Genoese, this now serves as a club and bar.

Aya Sofya

Nowhere is the glut of memorable landmarks more evident than in *Sultanahmet*, where the Aya Sofya museum and the Blue Mosque sit squarely opposite one another.

Work on **Aya Sofya**, formerly the Basilica of St Sophia, was started by Constantine in AD 347, but its present form is mainly due to substantial reconstruction by Emperor Justinian in the 6th century. St Sophia served as the cathedral of Constantinople until the Turkish occupation of 1453, when it was converted into a mosque. In 1935 Atatürk turned it into a museum; a convenient non-secular label, as Aya Sofya has few conventional exhibits. The building is massive, although its bulk can seem drab compared to the more flamboyant mosques it was to inspire. With a dome 31m in diameter and 55m high, Aya Sofya was the the largest domed structure in the world until St Peter's in Rome was built. Its interior impresses more with its size than its decoration, although

there are some mosaics around the gallery (head up the sloped flagstone walkway). The stark interior spaces are occasionally used as film sets, so you may double take when you come across knights in chain mail wandering around.

The Blue Mosque

Following the Turkish occupation, many mosques were built which imitated Aya Sofya to varying degrees. None was more blatant than the **Sultan Ahmet Mosque**, commonly known as the **Blue Mosque**. Built in 1609–1616 for Sultan Ahmet I, the Blue Mosque clearly borrows architectural forms from Aya Sofya; it has been conjectured that Ahmet was deliberately trying to outdo Justinian's efforts. Sitting either side of *Sultanahmet Square*, the two buildings form one of Istanbul's most dramatic cityscapes. The flamboyant Ahmet equipped his mosque with six minarets, a move which caused ructions with the religious authorities as it equalled the number at Mecca. Ahmet defused the situation by paying for a seventh to be built at Mecca.

The exterior of the Blue Mosque is more appealing than Aya Sofya's, almost mesmeric with its sequence of nested half-domes. The 'blue' appellation comes from its interior: blue and white Iznik tiles pick up the gentle washed light that filters in through the windows. It is certainly worth braving the touts and hustlers outside in order to view the interior. Entry is permitted outside prayer times. Be polite but firm with the many people who will try to convince you that it is necessary to pay ridiculously large sums for a tour, or to be let in, or to have your shoes looked after. Locals simply walk in carrying their footwear. On summer evenings a rather brash sound and light show redeems itself with some captivating floodlighting.

The **Hippodrome**, focus of Byzantine life in Istanbul, was sited in what is now part of *Sultanahmet Square*. You can see some remains including an Obelisk and the Serpentine Column. Across from the Hippodrome, the **Ibrahim Paşa Palace** houses the **Museum of Turkish and Islamic Art**, including some priceless ancient Persian carpets.

On the other side of the Blue Mosque are the **Mosaic Museum**, with some Byzantine mosaics, and the quaintly named **Turkish Carpets Museum**. This latter represents the more staid end of the carpet industry in Istanbul.

The Topkapi

Behind Aya Sofya, at the end of the peninsula, sprawls the magnificent **Topkapi Palace**, seat of the Ottoman Sultans from the 15th to the 19th centuries. The complex has now been converted into an encyclopaedic collection of the Imperial treasures, stretching through three courtyards. Allow yourself at least a full day to take in the cream of the exhibits, which include Islamic armour, imperial robes, jewellery and precious *objets*, porcelain and miniatures.

There is a quite staggering and hypnotic level of ostentation in the over-bejewelled daggers and great balls of emeralds in **The Treasury**. Look out for the **Pavilion of the Holy Mantle**, which houses religious artifacts, including sacred relics of Mohammed. One star attraction is the extensive **Harem**, one of the best preserved in the world, which in its prime housed about 500 concubines and their eunuch attendants. The Harem can only be seen on tours; book a few hours ahead. There are great views over the Bosphorus from the Palace terrace.

Clustered around the Topkapi is a supporting cast of first-rate museums. Signposted off the first court of the Topkapi are the **Archaeological Museums**: consisting of the **Archaeological Museum** itself, guardian of the Alexander Sarcophagus, the **Museum of the Ancient Orient** and **Çinili Kosk**, the tiled pavilion, built by Mehmet the Conqueror. The 18th-century **Ahmet III Fountain** stands at the entrance to the Topkapi. The **Church of St Irene**, the first built in Constantinople, pre-dating even Aya Sofya, is now also a museum.

Out to the west of Stamboul are the old **City Walls**, now partially restored. Built in the 5th century by Theodosius, they stretch from the Sea of Marmara to the Golden Horn, protecting all the land approaches to the city.

Mosques

Elsewhere are many other superb mosques, such as the magnificent **Süleymaniye Mosque**, designed by Sinan, one of the great Ottoman architects, for Süleymaniye the Magnificent, who is buried in the adjacent graveyard. Although it has only four minarets, the Süleymaniye is larger than the Blue. The **Yeni Mosque** (meaning 'new', although built between 1597 and 1633) is unmissable to those arriving at Eminönü or crossing the Galata Bridge. There are a miserly two minarets here. Work started on the **Fatih Mosque** only ten years after the Turkish conquest. The mosque is named after Istanbul's conqueror, Fatih Sultan Mehmet, who is buried there. Istanbul's oldest mosque, however, is the **Beyazit**, next to the covered market.

The Bosphorus

The Bosphorus strait, leading north from the Sea of Marmara to the Black Sea, is sprinkled with impressive imperial palaces and pavilions built by a succession of sultans. The best way to see them is by **boat**; popular excursion trips run up to *Rumeli Kavaği* and *Anadolu Kavaği* from *Eminönü, pier 3*. On Monday to Saturday, three boats run each way; on Sundays and bank holidays there are five each way and prices are halved.

The most prominent palace en route is the **Dolmabahçe**, which has a 600m water frontage. Built by Sultan Abdulmecit in the 19th century, this served as the final seat of the Ottoman sultans. Atatürk died here in 1938. Further north is the **Ciragan Palace**, now a hotel. On a hill set back from the Bosphorus is the **Yildiz Palace** complex, built by Sultan Abdulhamit, replete with exotic gardens.

The Asian bank also has its fair share of imperial residences. Just north of the **Bosphorus Bridge**, the first to join continents, is the **Beylerbeyi Palace**, another 19th-century construction, this time the work of Sultan Abdulaziz. The 19th-century sultans took turns to adorn the Bosphorus with extra palaces. Further north the **Göksu** or **Küçüsku Palace** served as the summer residence of Abdulmecit. The second bridge across the Bosphorus, the **Fatih Sultan Mehmet Bridge,** is to the north.

The boat-trip goes no further than **Kavaği** but, from the fortifications overlooking **Anadolu Kavaği**, you can look out to the massive expanses of the Black Sea.

ISTANBUL
to
BUDAPEST

This route links Istanbul, on the Europe/Asia frontier, to Budapest, at the heart of central Europe. It winds across Bulgaria and Romania, two countries which until recently were inaccessible to the independent traveller. Passing through both Sofia (Sofija) and Bucharest (Bucureşti), the route provides an insight into areas of Eastern Europe still seldom travelled by Westerners: trains are virtually devoid of backpackers.

TRAINS

ETT tables: 97b, 965, 960, 950.

→ **Fast Track**

There is one direct train a day between **Istanbul** and **Budapest**, which takes 17 hrs. However, this is via Belgrade and, due to the situation in former Yugoslavia, this route is not recommended. Details are not included. There are no other direct services and you usually have to change trains in both Sofia and Bucharest. Three times a week, however, there are through carriages between Istanbul and Bucharest, which make it possible to avoid the change in Sofia.

The Balkan Express runs overnight between **Istanbul** and **Sofia** (taking about 12 hrs). Couch-ettes are available but no refreshment service. There is only one overnight train between **Sofia** and **Bucharest**. It has sleeping-cars and couchettes, but no refreshment facilities. Between **Bucharest** and **Budapest**, there are three over-night trains, the Ovidius, the Dacia Express and the Balt Orient Express. All carry first- and second-class sleeping-cars and couchettes, but no refreshments. In

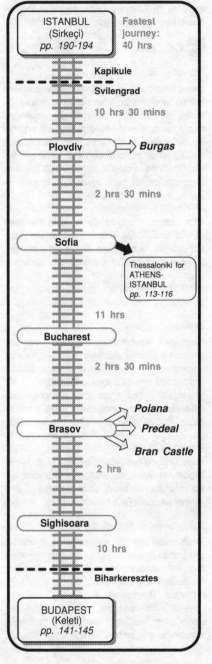

ISTANBUL (Sirkeçi) pp. 190-194

Fastest journey: 40 hrs

Kapikule
Svilengrad

10 hrs 30 mins

Plovdiv ⟹ *Burgas*

2 hrs 30 mins

Sofia

Thessaloniki for ATHENS-ISTANBUL pp. 113-116

11 hrs

Bucharest

2 hrs 30 mins

Poiana
Brasov ⟹ *Predeal*
Bran Castle

2 hrs

Sighisoara

10 hrs

Biharkeresztes

BUDAPEST (Keleti) pp. 141-145

---

addition, the Pannonia Ex-press runs during the day, taking about 17 hrs.

On Track

Istanbul–(Border)–Plovdiv

The Balkan Express runs overnight between Istanbul and Plovdiv. The journey averages 10 hrs 30 mins. The train carries sleeping compartments, but crosses the border early in the morning and suffers interruptions from both Turkish and Bulgarian Customs and Immigration officials, so don't expect a good night's sleep. There's no refreshment service.

Plovdiv–Sofia

There are ten express trains daily between Plovdiv and Sofia. The journey should take about 2 hrs 30 mins, but delays are common. Some of the faster trains require reservations.

Sofia–(Border)–Bucharest

See Fast Track for details of this leg.

Bucharest–Braşov

There are a number of express trains every day between Bucharest and Braşov. All require seat reservations. Half are long-distance overnight services which reach Braşov in the small hours of the morning and there can be long gaps between the other. The journey takes 2 hrs 30 mins–3 hrs 30 mins.

Braşov–Sighişoara

There are express trains each day between Braşov and Sighişoara, although four of these are in the early hours of the morning. The journey takes about 2 hrs.

Sighişoara–(Border)–Budapest

There are three trains daily between Sighişoara and Budapest (Keleti), for all of which reservations are necessary. Timings at Sighişoara are not always very convenient, choose your train with care. The journey averages 10 hrs. The Romania/Hungary border crossing is time-consuming and thorough: you can expect your compartment to be searched.

PLOVDIV

Station: tel: (032) 22 27 29, about 1 km south-west of the centre. There are no exchange facilities at the station so travellers arriving from Turkey must walk into town in order to obtain Bulgarian currency.

Tourist Information: Balkantourist's privatised successor, **Puldin Tours**, has not yet established a permanent office in central Plovdiv; call their head office, tel: (032) 55 28 07, for the latest details. Currently the best sources of tourist information are the hotel information desks. **Hotel Trimontium**, tel: (032) 23 491, in the central square, is helpful and sells reasonable city maps: open 0700–2200. The **Old Plovdiv Agency**, Hotel Bulgaria, Evtimi St; tel: (032) 22 55 64, also has maps.

Getting Around

It is 10–15-mins walk north-east along tree-lined Ivan Yazov St, diagonally across from the station, to Plovdiv's central square. Here you will find Hotel Trimontium and the main post office and telephone building. Kolarov St (which may soon be renamed Battenberg St), the pedestrianised main street, leads north towards the old town. Buses and trolley-buses run throughout Plovdiv, but much of the hilly old town is only accessible on foot. Remember that many streets are being renamed and maps can rapidly become out-of-date.

Accommodation

Hotel chains with properties in the city include Nv. Several commercial agencies arranging accommodation in private rooms have opened rec-ently. They can also change money. Look for the signs, particularly along Kolarov St. Plovdiv has six hotels, but even the cheaper ones cost more than a private room. You may also find locals offering private accommodation.

Sightseeing

Plovdiv, Philippopolis to the Macedonians and Trimontium to the Romans, was described by Lucian in the 2nd century AD as 'the largest and most beautiful of all cities in Thrace'. Until the late 19th century Plovdiv was more populous than Sofia and was the centre of Bulgarian cultural life. The unification of Bulgaria was announced here in 1885; Sofia became capital of the unified state and Plovdiv's influence slowly declined. Now Bulgaria's second city, Plovdiv is decidedly not a thing of beauty, ringed by depressing industrial buildings and tower blocks. However, there is still much of interest in the central old town, where the coarsely cobbled streets, cluttered with Plovdiv Revival period houses and dotted with Roman remains, possess a charm and character not found in Sofia.

Archaeological finds date Plovdiv to around 4000 BC, and the city was occupied by Thracians and Macedonians before the Romans took over in 72 BC. Remains of Trimontium, the city of the three hills, include the partially restored 2nd-century marble **Amphitheatre**, one of Bulgaria's most notable archaeological sites. Nestling in the old town, the amphitheatre affords stark views over the modern Plovdiv suburbs to the mountains beyond. Gladiator tournaments took place in the **Philippopolis Stadium**, the few surviving seats of which are opposite a concrete cocktail bar terrace on *Piaţa Noemvri 19*, in the heart of the city. The remains of the **Roman Forum**, including marble floors, can be seen in the central square near Hotel Trimontium.

The city's most important contribution to recent Bulgarian culture is the **Plovdiv National Revival period house**. A cluster of fine examples of the style, mainly from the early 19th century, can be found towards the north end of the old town. The **Balabanov House** now hosts recitals and exhibits works by contemporary Bulgarian painters; the **Lamartine House** includes a museum room dedicated to the French writer and statesman. The **Ethnographic Museum**, *Argit Koyumdjioglu House*, has exhibits on the local culture, while the **Archaeological Museum**, *1 Piaţa Saedineni*, contains relics from Plovdiv's earliest days right up to the National Revival.

– – – – – – – – – – – – – – – – – – –
Side Track from Plovdiv

Four trains a day run east to **Burgas** on the Black Sea, from where you can explore Bulgaria's tourist resorts. The journey takes about 4 hrs 30 mins. Having long been a favourite destination for Eastern Europeans, the Black Sea coast is rapidly establishing popularity with Western travellers.

– – – – – – – – – – – – – – – – – – –

SOFIA (SOFIJA)

Airport: **Sofia International,** *tel: (02) 88 44 33*, is 11 km from the centre. Telephone *(02) 72 06 72* for information on international flights or *72 24 14* for domestic flights.
Station: *tel: (02) 31 111*, about 1.5 km north of the centre.
Tourist Information: Balkantourist, *27 Stambolijski Blvd; tel: (02) 88 44 30*, is a useful first stop for information. There are a number of private agencies which can help find a room or change money. These include: **InterBalkan**, which has offices at the airport (*tel: (02) 32 21 90*) and the station (*tel: (02) 72 01 57*); **Balkantourist Travel Service**, an offshoot of Balkantourist, *3 Stara Planina St*; and **Rila**, *5 Gurko St; tel: (02) 87 07 77*. Rila can make international train reservations and sell tickets. Tickets are also sold by the **Travel Centre**, underneath the National Palace of Culture, *1 Bulgaria Square*. Expect to pay for printed information.

Getting Around

Central Sofia is fairly compact and most areas of interest can be reached on foot. Maps tend to be clear and easy to follow, but remember that street names may have changed. There is a large network of trams, trolley-buses and buses; stops display the routes of each service using them. Buy tickets from kiosks or street vendors near stops. A one-day pass is good value if you are planning more than three rides, but tickets are extremely cheap. Trams (nos. 1/7) run from the station along *Dimitrov St* and *Vitosha Blvd* through the town centre.

Living in Sofia

Accommodation

The mechanisms for finding accommodation in

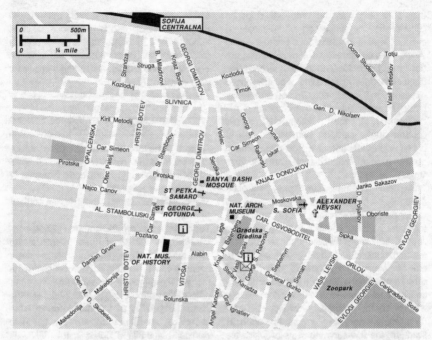

Sofia are also in a state of flux. **Balkantourist** book rooms in hotels and private apartments. More convenient are the agencies in the station, which offer reasonably priced and fairly central private rooms. Holders of ISIC cards can often get discounts. Ensure that whenever you book a room, the agency stamps your statistical card; most tend to be efficient and well-organised in this regard. Private rooms are good value, but expect prices to rise rapidly to Western – or at least Hungarian – levels soon. Sofia also has a collection of extremely expensive high-class hotels catering to business and diplomatic visitors to the capital. Hotel chains with property in the city: *Sh*.

Absurdly, some hotel guides cost money – and often they cover only hotels with two or more stars. Ask at the tourist agencies if you want details of cheaper establishments.

Communications

The **main post office** is at *2 Gurko St*, opposite the Rila agency. International phone calls can be dialled directly, with the minimum of fuss, from the **central telephone office** on *Stefan Karadza St*, diagonally behind the post office.

Eating and Drinking

Many of Sofia's restaurants are still rather dour and cheap, but they are gradually becoming less grim and more expensive as free enterprise takes hold.

Head for *Vitoša Blvd* and the surrounding side streets for a large collection of eateries. Bulgarian-style fast-food joints and self-service greasy-spoons abound, with food that is unimaginative, but reasonably filling.

By paying a little more, it is possible to get an excellent meal from one of the smart pizza or burger places that have opened in recent years. Aimed at the locals (despite receipts printed in English), these are still far cheaper than the upmarket restaurants designed for Western business visitors.

One of the best aspects of Sofia's culinary scene is the abundance of street cafés serving good cheap coffee (just a few pennies) and excellent cakes.

Embassies

UK: *65 Levski Blvd; tel: (02) 88 53 61.*
USA: *1 Saborna St; tel: (02) 88 48 01.*
Citizens of **Canada**, **Australia**, and **New Zealand** should use the UK embassy.

Money

Bureaux de change have sprouted all over central Sofia, including some open 24 hrs ('non-stop') on *Vitoša Blvd*. There are plenty of exchange facilities in the central station. Check rates and commissions as it is often possible to get a better deal at bureaux than at banks. Little of the black market remains.

Entertainment

New street cafés and bars are gradually bringing the crowds to Sofia's streets, although much of the centre remains strangely soulless, with anonymous blocks lining empty streets. There are nightclubs, but most cater to the guests of the top hotels. Local clubs often consist of a few primitive poker machines, a pool table and a bar. The best street life is on *Vitoša Blvd*, especially down at the south end towards *Patriarch Evtimi St*, where crowds of teenagers hang out doing nothing, in true Western style. Sofia's cinemas are very cheap and tend to show films with the original sound-track, merely adding subtitles.

Sightseeing

Sofia was a Thracian and Roman settlement before becoming the headquarters for the Turkish governor during the occupation of the Balkans. However, until it was declared capital of the unified Bulgaria, the city tended to be eclipsed by Plovdiv in terms of cultural importance. Today Sofia is a modern institutional city with a capital's quota of museums and churches, although none of them is compelling. Currently the most captivating aspects of the city are the manifestations of its change from Communist rule to Free Enterprise. The statue of Lenin has disappeared from *Lenin Square*, street cafés are gradually bringing life to the broad drab boulevards, washing-machines share shop space with jeans and fruit juices,

while BMWs and sharp suits mingle with Trabants and unstylish synthetics.

Sofia was named after the 6th-century **St Sofia Basilica**, *Alexander Nevski Pl*. The dim interior is occasionally open to visitors. On one flank of the church the *Eternal Flame* flickers in memory of the Bulgarian war dead.

The best photo opportunity in Sofia is undoubtedly the **St Alexander Nevski Cathedral**, a neo-Byzantine, gold-domed tribute to the Russians who died in the Russian-Turkish war of 1878. In the crypt, a collection of Bulgarian icons traces the development of Bulgarian icon-painting, from medieval times to the National Revival period of the 18th and 19th centuries.

The 4th-century **St George Rotunda** provides an impressive block to the flow of *Dimitrov* and *Vitoša Blvds*. Its interior is being restored – and has been for some years. Within a few hundred yards are the 16th-century **Banya Bashi Mosque**, *Dimitrov Blvd*, and the 14th-century **St Petka Samardjiiska Church**, built below street level and now suffering the indignity of standing in a pedestrian underpass by the TSUM department store.

You can see relics from Bulgaria's eventful history in the **National Archaeological Museum**, *2 Saborna Blvd*, and the **National Museum of History**, *2 Vitoša Blvd*. The 11th-century **Boyana Church**, at the foot of the Vitoša mountains, is Sofia's contribution to the World Cultural Heritage List.

BUCHAREST (BUCUREŞTI)

Airport: Otopeni *(tel: (01) 633 66 02)* is 16 km from the centre.
Stations: Virtually all trains stop at **Gara de Nord**, *tel: 952*, but there are occasional services to **Băneasa**, **Obor** or **Basarab** stations. Advance tickets and reservations (obligatory for all except the slowest trains) can be obtained at the **CFR agencies** in the centre. For domestic reservations and tickets: *10–14 Str. Domnita Anastasi; tel: (01) 613 26 44* and *132 Calea Grivitei; tel: (01) 650 72 47*. For international journeys: *2 Piaţa Unirii; tel: (01) 613 40 08*. Allow plenty of time. Queues are not as bad as a few years ago,

but delays do still occur.

Tourist Information: the helpful **ONT-Carpati Information Office**, *7 Magheru Blvd; tel: (01) 312 09 15* or *614 07 59* (metro: *Piaţa Romana*), can arrange accommodation and sell an up-to-date map of Bucharest, but there is virtually no other printed information. Mon–Fri 0800–2000, Sat 0800–1530, and Sun 0800–1400. There are **branches** at Otopeni airport and in Gara de Nord. The latter has multi-lingual staff. The private agencies now opening up cater mainly for Romanians.

Getting Around

Distances in central Bucharest are deceptively long and it takes stamina to explore the city entirely on foot. The ONT map is valuable, and currently accurate. Remember that almost half the streets have been renamed in the past few years.

Metro, Buses and Trolley-buses

The **metro** is fairly comprehensive, frequent and fast, serving Gara de Nord and much of central Bucharest. Get change for the turnstiles from the kiosks in each station. There are three main lines, though some of the route maps in trains and stations are unnecessarily obtuse.

Buses and **trolley-buses** also run throughout central Bucharest and cover outlying areas not served by the metro. Buy tickets from orange kiosks marked RATB before boarding. For route details check the map on display at major stops or get a copy from a kiosk.

Taxis

Some taxis belong to state companies, others to private companies, and many to independent operators, official and otherwise. It is possible to bargain over fares with some drivers and not with others. Whichever type you take, it is likely you will pay over the odds, although the fare will still be very cheap by Western standards.

Living in Bucharest

Accommodation

ONT can arrange rooms in centrally located private houses. You pay for the convenience,

however, as around 30% of the charge goes to the tourist office. Ask if the price includes breakfast – you may be grateful for whatever food is on offer.

Rail travellers are approached fairly frequently by individuals with unofficial private rooms on offer. These are invariably cheaper than agency rooms. As always, ask to have the location pointed out on a map, so you don't end up in a distant suburb, and don't part with large sums of money before seeing the room. Hosts in private lodgings can often be eager to chat with their guests and may turn out to be the best source of information on the intricacies of modern Bucharest.

The cheapest one-star hotels are no more expensive than private agency rooms, but are generally characterless. Western-style hotels, such as the *Ic*, are available at prices designed more for expense accounts than budget travellers. **Camp-sites** have a very poor reputation in Bucharest, although the ONT can supply details of these and the student hostels of variable quality that are open during the summer.

Communications

The **main post office**, *Str. Matei Millo* , is around the corner from the **main telephone office**, *37 Calea Victoriei*. It is possible to make international calls here, but you must hand the operator the number you want to call and prepay for at least three minutes. You may have to pay a small charge even if there is no answer.

It is easier to call abroad from one of the new hi-tech call boxes: dial *2 for instructions in English. You will need plenty, but not excessive amounts, of coins. For telephone information *tel: 951*. Telephone numbers in Bucharest have recently changed from six to seven digits. Most numbers have been prefixed with '6', but there are a few exceptions. The dialling code for Bucharest is 01.

Eating and Drinking

Bucharest can be hard on the stomach. The proliferation of shiny Coca-Cola and Pepsi signs adorning shops and cafés hides the fact that there is little inside except for the soft drinks.

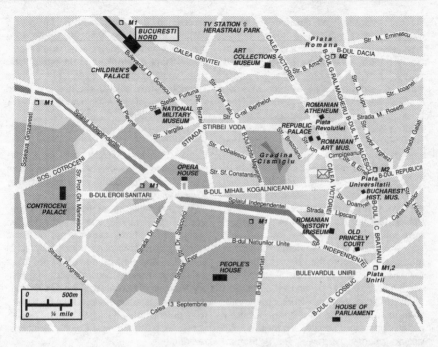

Many of Bucharest's eating joints offer little more than sad hamburgers.

There are occasional food stalls offering reasonable snacks, especially around Piaţa Universităţii and the Lipscani St area; but queues form rapidly whenever anything slightly out of the ordinary appears at a street stall, seemingly regardless of its actual quality.

Some rather more appetising restaurants, such as fried chicken outlets, have opened in the past few years and, although more expensive than the grimmer eateries, they are still extremely cheap for Westerners. There are some restaurants designed for foreigners, but expect to pay seven or eight times as much as in a local restaurant.

Bottled water is fairly scarce and far more expensive than bottled soft drinks.

Embassies

Canada: *36 Nicolae Iorga St; tel: (01) 650 63 30.*
UK: *24 Jules Michelet St; tel: (01) 611 16 34.*
USA: *7–9 Tudor Arghezi St; tel: (01) 210 4042.*

Citizens of **Australia** and **New Zealand** should use the UK embassy.

Money

You can change money safely at the ONT, but their commission is high. Many other bureaux de change exist throughout Bucharest – check rates, as they can vary from office to office. It is extremely risky changing money on the black market. Be especially careful at Gara de Nord; there are countless stories of travellers being ripped off there.

Sightseeing

Bucharest, once a city of grandeur and style, suffered badly from the excesses of the Socialist dictator Nicolae Ceauşescu. For centuries the seat of the Princes of Wallachia, the city became capital of Romania in 1859 and flourished thereafter. Between the two world wars, it became known as Little Paris, with elegant residential quarters and boulevards, a French-speaking aristocracy and even a down-scale Triumphal Arch. Ceauşescu destroyed much of the city's elegance and replaced the stylish neighbourhoods with brutal tower blocks, massive ceremonial avenues and a palace to rival the most extraordinary of follies. A sad piece of local self-mockery is that he turned Bucharest into Little Sofia or Little Moscow. Now, under the National Salvation Front government that replaced Ceauşescu after the 1989 revolution, Bucharest is still poor and dour, but there is a fragile sense of optimism amongst its inhabitants.

Little remains of the Gallic style that once distinguished the city; the centre is grim and harsh, dotted with memorials to casualties of the revolution that overthrew Ceauşescu. **Piaţa Universităţii** (metro: *Universităţii*), the *Tiananmen Square* of Bucharest, is scattered with ancient crosses and modern plaques brought in to commemorate both the 1989 revolution and the later civic disruption (April–June 1990) which was suppressed by Ion Iliescu, president of the National Salvation Front government. Students gather here, next to revolutionary posters and daubed slogans, and there is still a vibrancy amongst the crowds. The **TV Station**, *Calea Dorobantilor* (metro: *Aviatorilor*), was a prime target during the revolution, and crosses commemorate casualties of the fighting. Throughout the city it is possible to detect bullet marks on strategically located buildings.

Testimony to Ceauşescu's reign, as opposed to his overthrow, lies in the massive **House of the Republic** (or **People's House**) (metro: *Izvor*). Ceauşescu destroyed 40,000 homes – almost a fifth of Bucharest – and eliminated some of the most stylish quarters in order to clear the area for the project, which nearly wiped out Romania's foreign currency reserves. The sheer scale of the building is stunning. Ask at the ONT office about the possibilities of tours. Ceauşescu also built the **Victory of Socialism Boulevard** (now **B-dul Unirii**), a soulless ceremonial avenue lead-ing to the People's House. *B-dul Unirii* is lined with ten-storey luxury apartment blocks, some unfinished or unfurbished, yet behind them in the back streets forgotten slums remain.

You can take a breather in the centre of town in **Grădina Cişmigiu Park** and flower garden, on *B-dul Kogălniceanu* . It is also possible to get away from Bucharest's hard grey centre and intimidating suburbs in the area around **Piaţa Aviatorilor** and **Herăstrău Park**. Here wide cobbled avenues lead to the **Triumphal Arch**, erected after the First World War and one of the reminders of Bucharest's Parisian aspirations.

Museums

Bucharest's more traditional sights are skeletal, many undergoing renovation or reorganisation. Expect many of the institutions to be guarded by soldiers with assault rifles.

The **Art Museum of Romania**, *1 Ştirbei Voda, Piaţa Revolutiei*, approached across an overgrown courtyard, currently has only two rooms open. *Piaţa Revolutiei* is itself fairly typical of central Bucharest, a mix of shabby older buildings and severe modern blocks. The **History Museum of Bucharest**, *2 B-dul I.C.Bratianu* , has some interesting artefacts from Bucharest's more distant past, including links with Dracula's father, yet seems incomplete without details of recent events.

If you need to pass a few hours in central Bucharest, you could also try the **History Museum of Romania**, *12 Calea Victoriei*, the **Art Museum**, *111 Calea Victoriei*, or the **George Enescu Museum**, *141 Calea Victoriei*, but don't expect a riveting experience or to find many others sharing it with you.

The **Village Museum**, *28-30 Şos. Kiseleff*, 5 mins north of the Triumphal Arch, used to be a favourite destination for official tour parties. The open-air collection of village houses, barns, sheds and windmills from 71 sites across the state offers a packaged but fascinating view of the Romanian countryside. Communist-style manning procedures mean that the only buildings whose interiors are open to the public are those with attendants sitting inside. The museum is beside **Herăstrău Park**, a fine retreat whose more wooded areas provide cover for trysting couples.

BRAŞOV

Station: *tel: 952*, about 2 km north of the old

town. Make train reservations at the **CFR Agency**, *53 Republicii St; tel: (068) 14 29 12*. Bus no.4 runs from the station to Piaţa Sfatului and Piaţa Unirii in the old town. The route to the centre is well signposted, but is at least 30-mins walk.

Tourist Office: *B-dul Eroilor; tel: (068) 14 16 48*, in the lobby of the Aro Palace Hotel, near the old town. Mon–Fri 0800–1600. When the office is closed, ask for a map at the hotel reception desk.

Getting Around

Once in the old town, everything of interest is accessible on foot and much of central Braşov is pedestrianised.

Accommodation

There are several well-appointed hotels, but expect to pay Western prices. Local residents gather outside the major hotels in order to offer private rooms to visitors: head for the hotel area around *B-dul Eroilor* and *Republicii St* and look expectant. A backpack .is usually indication enough.

Sightseeing

This Transylvanian town, situated close to Wallachia and Moldavia, has been an important commercial and cultural centre since the 14th century. The well-preserved old centre, spectacularly nestled beneath Mt Timpa, provides a fascinating picture of Romania's past.

The dismal housing estates of Braşov's suburbs between station and old town are in stark contrast to the marvellously preserved centre. The 14th-century **Black Church**, *Curtea Bisericii Negre St*, is considered the definitive example of Gothic architecture in Romania. Exhibits include old prints of the town and detail the life of Johannes Honterus, the 16th-century publisher and humanist. The 15th-century **Town Hall**, *Piaţa Sfatului*, was known as Trumpet's Tower, since warnings of danger to the town were sounded from the tower. Inside, the **Regional History Museum** displays the oldest existing document written in Romanian. **Piaţa Sfatului** is also an unlikely venue for

occasional heavy metal rock concerts. Towards the far end of the old town, in *Piaţa Unirii*, the **Museum of Romanian Culture** is housed in what was the first Romanian language school.

The unusually lively main shopping street, *Republicii St*, leads down to *B-dul Eroilor*, where heavy fighting took place during the 1989 revolution. Bullet holes deeply scar the concrete around the bottom of the Modarom building. Across the street a **Memorial Park** contains the fresh stark graves of 20 of the 62 people who died in Braşov in December 1989. Most of the casualties were in their early twenties, but there is one grave of a six-year-old child.

A cable-car runs up the 900m **Mt Timpa**, with views north and east over Braşov. Foreigners pay more than Romanians, but to save money (or for exercise) you can walk down (or up) the mountain on a zigzag path beneath the cable-car. The trees at the top mean that some of the best views of the old town are provided by the ride itself.

Side Track from Braşov

Braşov is situated near the winter resorts of **Predeal** and **Poiana Braşov**. However, the most popular excursion from the town is to **Bran Castle**, infamous lair of Vlad the Impaler, better known as Count Dracula. The castle is 26 km from Braşov and accessible by bus. There are regular tours.

SIGHIŞOARA

Station: *tel: (65) 771 886*, about 1 km from the centre. Make reservations at the **CFR Agency**, *2 Decembrie 1 St; tel: 771 820*.

Tourist Office: The former OJT bureau is in *Hotel Steaua*.

Sighişoara is another well-preserved Transylvanian town. The **Clock Tower**, set within the ruins of the medieval fortifications, is Sighişoara's most distinctive sight. Dracula enthusiasts can view the house of his father, Vlad Tepeş.

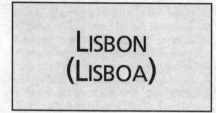

LISBON (LISBOA)

Lisbon lies on seven low hills at the estuary of the River Tagus (Tejo). The city's name is said by some to derive from Alis Ubbo, the Phoenician for 'delightful little port'. Almost wiped out by a massive earthquake in 1755 (the ancient 11-mile-long aqueduct was, remarkably, left standing and still supplies water to the city), Lisbon was redesigned on a grid system and rebuilt on a grand scale by the Marques do Pombal. It's a relatively small city by European standards and charms all visitors. You need at least 2–3 days to explore the flower-bedecked old districts of narrow streets. The modern section is full of open squares and wide esplanades paved with artistically arranged mosaics.

Tourist Information

The main tourist office is in the *Praça dos Restauradores* (Palacio Foz); *tel: 346 36 43* or *58*, open Mon–Sat 0900–2000 and Sun 1000–1800. They arrange accommodation (without taking commission), which can be hard to find at Easter and in midsummer. There is a second branch at *Pavilhao Carlos Lopes, Parque Eduardo VII, 1000 Lisbon; tel: 54 97 20/52 89 49/54 99 98*, open Mon–Sat 0900–1900.

Thomas Cook network member Marcus & Harting (*Rossio 50; tel: (01) 346 9279*) offers bureau de change and other travel serrvices.

Arriving and Departing

Airport

Portela de Sacavem Airport (*tel: 80 20 60*) is 7 km north of the city, with no train link. There are buses to all rail stations, but taxis are not expensive.

Stations

There are several railway stations in Lisbon.

Santa Apolónia Station on the banks of the *Tagus* near *Alfama; tel: 86 41 42* is the main station, handling all international trains, and those to east and north Portugal. There is an information office in the station will help book accommodation. Bus no 9 links Santa Apolónia to Rossio (which is central), but taxis are cheap.

Rossio Station (*tel: 346 50 22*) serves the west. **Cais do Sodre Station** on *Avenida Vinte e Quatro de Julho; tel: 347 01 81* doubles as the quay for the Tagus ferries and as the station handling the local coastal rail service.

Terreiro do Paco Station (*tel: 87 50 58*) is the terminal for the ferries across the Tagus to **Barreiro**, which is the station for trains to southern Portugal. Some rail passes can be used for this 25-min ferry crossing and many people do it for fun, as it provides a panoramic view of Lisbon. There are departures every 30 mins.

Campolide, the first stop on the Rossio line, is for commuters, so don't get off there.

Getting Around

Make a point of getting a walking map of the Alfama district. Public transport in Lisbon is cheap, efficient and varied, consisting of buses, trams, the metro and funiculars (*elevadores*) (between different levels of the city).

Tickets

Train tickets are available from any travel agency or the Rossio and Santa Apolónia stations.

Carris, the Lisbon public transportation company sells books of tickets which cover all Lisbon's public transport from all their kiosks.

Metro (Subway) and Trams

The metro is fast and frequent, but operates only in the city centre: if you haven't got a book of tickets or tourist pass, buy one at the entrance barrier. The 19th-century trams are still an integral part of the transport system and are easy to use. Carris offer tram tours: a slow and picturesque way to see the city.

River Journeys

In summer there are daily (and nightly) trips on the **River Tagus**, leaving from *Terreiro do Paco; tel: 87 50 58.*

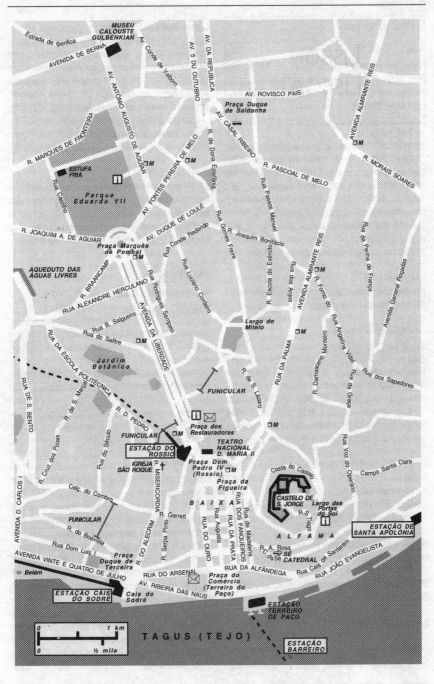

TAGUS (TEJO)

Living in Lisbon

Accommodation

Hotel groups here include *Ch, Hl, Ic, Mr, Nv, Pe, Pu* and *Sh*. The vast majority of cheap places are in the centre of town, on and around Avenida Liberdade. If these are full, try Avenida Almirante Reis (to the east). Out of season you may be able to find something for around Esc. 3000, but allow much more at Easter and in midsummer.

IYHF: *Rua Andrade Corvo 46; tel: 53 26 96.*
Campsite: Parque da Camara Municipal de Lisboa-Monsanto (on the road to Benfica); *tel: 70 20 61*, which has a pool (take bus no 43 from Rossio to *Parque Florestal Monsanto*); Clube de Campismo de Lisboa (*Costa da Caparica; tel: 290 01 00*) is 5 km out of town, with a beach (metro to *Palhava* or the bus from *Praça Espanha*).

Communications

The *Praça dos Restauradores* post office is open 0900–2200 and has a poste restante facility.

Eating and Drinking

Lisbon's restaurants are cheap and offer a wide choice. The *Bairro Alto* is patronised by locals, and particularly cheap, as are the restaurants in *Alfama*. *Baixa* is aimed at tourists and more expensive, but still good value. If you're really hard-up, there are food stalls in the market behind Cais do Sodre station. Students can also use the *cantinas* on the university campus.

Embassies and Consulates

Australia *Avenida da Liberdade 244; tel: 52 33 50* or *52 34 21*.
Canada *4th Floor, Avenida da Liberdade 144-156-4; tel: 347 48 92*.
New Zealand New Zealand affairs are handled by the British Embassy.
UK *Rua Sao Domingos a Lapa 37; tel: 396 11 91* or *47*.
USA *Avenida das Forcas Armadas; tel: 726 66 00*.

Entertainment

Nightlife

There are also many bars, discos and nightclubs.

Lisbon has several *casas de fado* and *adegas tipicas* (wine cellars), which feature *fado* singing and guitar playing; there may be an entrance fee or cover charge. If not, you are expected to buy a reasonable amount to eat or drink. Performances usually begin around 2200, but the best singers seldom appear until much later and it's quite usual for the *fado* places to stay open until 0330.

Bullfights are held at the *Campo Pequeno* on most Thursday evenings from July to September.

Theatres, Cinemas and Concerts

There are frequent performances of operas and ballets, and many theatres and cinemas. The latter show films in their original language (with Portuguese subtitles) and charge half-price on Mondays, but you must book in advance.

Shopping

The **Baixa** and **Chiado** districts are good for shopping of all kinds, while the **Rua do Ouro** is a centre for jewellery. The neo-modern **Amoreiras** shopping centre on *Avenida Engeneiro Duarte Pacheco* is a complex which has a range of shops and is open daily 1000–2400.

There's a daily dawn **fish and flower** market opposite *Cais Sodre*. Lisbon's **flea market** *Feira da Ladro* is held in the *Campo de Santa Clara* on Tuesday (morning) and Saturday (all day).

Sightseeing

Museums

The picture gallery of the **Museu Nacional de Arte Antiga** on *Rue das Janelas Verdes* (take the tram) is home to a 15th-century polyptych which is a masterpiece of Portuguese art. Other exhibits include tapestries, silver and gold plate, ceramics, ancient sculptures, porcelain and oriental rugs.

The **Calouste Gulbenkian Museum** on *Avenida de Berna* (metro: *Praça de Espana*) houses the millionaire's private collection of everything from paintings and engravings to furniture and sculpture. The museum stands in a delightful 17-acre park. Next door is the **Centro de Arte Moderna Calouste Gulbenkian**, *Rua Dr Nicolau Bettencourt*, with exhibits by important 20th-century Portuguese painters and sculptors.

The **National Tile Museum,** on *Rua da Madre de Deus 4B* (take the tram) is in the cloisters of a 16th-century convent which was badly damaged in the earthquake, but restored in the original Manueline style. The cloister survived and *azulejos* there include a depiction of Lisbon before the earthquake.

Among the exhibits in the **Museu de Arte Sacra** adjoining *Sao Roque* (metro: *Restauradores*, then take the funicular up) are some outstanding examples of the work of Italian goldsmiths. The 18th-century **Paco de Belem** on *Praça Afonso de Albuquerque* was a royal palace and is now the official residence of Portugal's President. The former riding school houses the **Museu Nacional das Coches**: on display are some 60 richly decorated ceremonial carriages.

Sights

Alfama (metro: *Rossio*) is the old Moorish quarter and little changed since the 12th century, with winding cobbled streets, white-washed houses and lots of dead ends. One of the few areas to survive the earthquake of 1755, it's a marvellous place to explore on foot.

The medieval **Castle of Sao Jorge** (metro: *Rossio*) has ten towers linked by massive battlements and stands on one of the seven hills. Some parts date back to the 5th and 6th centuries. A royal residence for four centuries, later it served as a prison. Nowadays peacocks stroll beneath the ivy-shrouded yellow sandstone battlements and you have a superb view over the city. (It's a stiff climb and not easy to find your way to it, so get a good map – or a taxi.)

The **Bairro Alto** (Upper Town; Metro: Restauradores) is linked to the Lower Town (*Avenida da Liberdade*) by the *Elevador da Gloria* (a funicular railway). Another maze of narrow streets that survived the earthquake, it consists mainly of early 18th-century houses, some still residential and others home to much of the city's nightlife.

The marble-arcaded **Praça do Comercio** (metro: *Rossio*) has a really impressive triumphal arch that bears close examination. The **Praça dos Restauradores** is an exuberant 19th-century structure in Manueline style, part of which is now a shopping mall and part the Rossio Station. The

Praça da Figueira (metro: *Rossio*) was settled by crusaders brought in to retake the city from the Moors in 1147 and there are enough remains of the walls and gates to convey an impression of the city as it was then.

The exterior of the **Church of Sao Roque** by Rossio Station gives no clue to the elegantly decorated 16th-century interior. It's marvellous 18th-century chapel, dedicated to St John the Baptist, was constructed in Rome (of marble and alabaster, gold, silver and precious stones), then shipped in its entirety to Lisbon.

The **Parque Eduardo VII** (metro: *Parque/Marques*) was named for the English monarch, after he visited Lisbon. It is a landscaped park with a lake, a children's play area, a good view of lower Lisbon and very attractive tropical gardens.

Belem (take the tram) is a riverside suburb. The modern **Monument of the Discoveries** on the river bank is dedicated to the naval explorers who sailed from here and there are various other monuments, museums and fine buildings which make it worth spending some time in the area.

The **Belem Tower**, with its lace-like loggia, is an exquisite example of Manueline architecture. It was built (1512–1521) to protect the harbour entrance and the fifth-floor has a great view across the estuary. The tower was restored in 1845 and is furnished in period style.

The **Jeronimos Monastery**, inland from the Monument, began life as a chapel for Henry the Navigator's seamen. Vasco da Gama was royally received in the chapel when he returned from his triumphant voyages and the present splendid building was commissioned by the king in thanks for the successes of all the Portuguese explorers. It was designed by Boytac, the best of the Manueline architects, and construction began in 1502. The magnificent south door is widely acknowledged as the finest example of the style. The High Renaissance choir was a 16th century addition. Other features of the monastery include some amazing carvings, a series of grand tombs (including da Gama's) and the two-storey cloister. The wings of the complex are home to museums and a planetarium.

The **Se Patriarchal** (Cathedral) on *Largo da Se* (metro: *Rossio*) was once a fortress. There are some notable 14th-century tombs, a Baroque crib, a magnificent Romanesque screen and a fine collection of religious art.

Views of Lisbon

From the **Tagus Bridge**, the second longest suspension bridge in Europe, there is a panoramic view of Lisbon.

Side Tracks from Lisbon

FATIMA

Tourist Office: *Avenida D Jose Alves Correira da Silva: tel: 53 11 39.*

Fatima has been a pilgrimage centre since the Virgin Mary appeared there on 13 May 1917 – and again on the 13th day of the following 4 months. Word spread and on 13 October a crowd had gathered. Mary did not appear, but the assembled throng (some 70,000 people) witnessed the sun spinning in the sky. Ceremonies are held every year on the 13th day of all 4 months, but May and October are the biggest. There are several buses from Lisbon every day and the journey takes about two hours. The **Chapel of the Apparition** contains a fountain fed by a spring said to have miraculous curative powers.

OBIDOS

Tourist Office: *Rua Direita; tel: 95 52 31.*
An enchanting medieval walled town, Obidos has winding streets and small white-washed houses, their balconies brimming with flowers. It's so attractive that it has been declared a national monument. There are trains from Lisbon (Rossio) and the journey takes about two hours.

At one time a lagoon reached almost to the town, but the waters receded and Obidos lost its strategic importance (and avoided the over-building common elsewhere). The many places of interest include the 12th–13th-century **Castle**, the 15th–18th-century **Church of the Misericordia**, the **Church of Santa Maria** and the 18th-century **Town Gate**.

QUELUZ

Queluz is the home of a small, pink Rococo building that was inspired by Versailles and is arguably the prettiest palace in the world. It was the summer residence of the Bragança kings and is still used to house very important visitors, so check that it will be open. The interior of the palace is exquisitely furnished and the formal gardens have changed little since the 18th century. The palace is the setting for many cultural events each year, including a month-long garden festival for which all the participants wear medieval costumes. There are trains from Lisbon (Rossio) every 15 minutes and the journey takes 20 minutes.

SINTRA

Tourist Office: *Praça da Republica; tel: 23 39 19.*
The station is a 15-min walk from the town.

Sintra is a beautiful town, which has a timeless quality enhanced by the horse-drawn carriages that are still for hire in the main square. The trains to Queluz continue to Sintra (the full journey taking 40 minutes), so both can be visited in one day-trip.

The central **National Palace** is a complex of mixed architectural styles, including two remarkable conical chimneys. The original **Moorish Castle** (now in ruins) stands on a hill above the town and even higher is the Bavarian-castle-inspired **Pena Palace**, which is furnished in early 20th-century style and surrounded by nearly 500 acres of gardens.

ESTORIL AND CASCAIS

These are both stylish resorts with good hotels, nightlife and diverse facilities. They are a short and scenic train ride west of Lisbon. Trains run every 15/20 minutes from Cais da Sodre, stopping at several resorts and taking 30–35 minutes for the full journey to Cascais (26 km). Estoril is a couple of stops earlier.

LISBON
to
SANTIAGO DE COMPOSTELA

This route leads from Lisbon, capital of Portugal into north-west Spain, through the wild Rías Bajas of Galicia. Places of interest include the university town of Coimbra, Oporto (Porto) – home of the port trade – and the pilgrimage centre of Bom Jesus do Monte.

TRAINS

ETT tables: 445, 446, 439.

 Fast Track

An express service runs Lisbon (Santa Apolónia)–Oporto (Campanha), taking just over 3 hrs (6 hrs on slower trains). You must change to a local service at Oporto and then at Vigo, adding 8 hrs more to the journey. There are often long waits between trains (not all offer refreshments).

～～ On Track

Lisbon–Coimbra

Daily trains run frequently from Lisbon (Santa Apolónia) to Coimbra (B). The journey takes about 2 hrs on direct Alfa trains (supplement payable), almost 3 hrs on others. Most have a buffet service.

Coimbra–Oporto

Over a dozen trains run regularly from Coimbra (B) to Oporto (Campanha). The journey takes less than 1 hr 30 mins on Alfa services (supplement payable) and over 2 hrs on others.

Oporto–Viana do Castelo

About ten trains a day run between Oporto

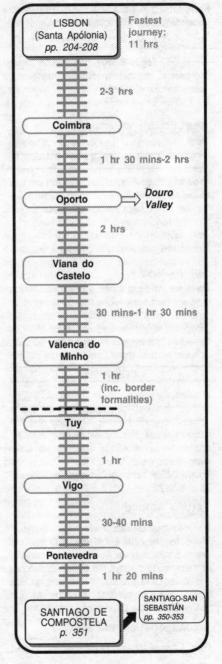

LISBON
(Santa Apólonia)
pp. 204-208

Fastest journey: 11 hrs

2-3 hrs

Coimbra

1 hr 30 mins-2 hrs

Oporto ⟹ *Douro Valley*

2 hrs

Viana do Castelo

30 mins-1 hr 30 mins

Valenca do Minho

1 hr (inc. border formalities)

Tuy

1 hr

Vigo

30-40 mins

Pontevedra

1 hr 20 mins

SANTIAGO DE COMPOSTELA
p. 351

SANTIAGO-SAN SEBASTIÁN
pp. 350-353

(Campanha) and Viana do Castelo, but they are unevenly spaced. Average journey time: 2 hrs, faster on IR trains; slower on stopping services.

Viana do Castelo–Valenca do Minho

There are at least five trains daily from Viana do Castelo to Valenca do Minho. Journey times vary from 30 mins to 1 hr 30 mins.

Valenca do Minho–(Border)–Tuy

Three trains run daily. The journey takes about 10 mins, but border procedures can last over an hour if you stay on the train. Many people prefer to walk: this takes about 20 mins on the Portuguese side and another 20 mins on the Spanish side, but reduces border formalities.

Tuy–Vigo

Three trains run daily, taking about 1 hr.

Vigo–Pontevedra

There are six–eight trains a day, but intervals between them vary. Trains take 30–40 mins.

Pontevedra–Santiago de Compostela

Six–eight trains leave daily, taking 1 hr 20 mins.

COIMBRA

Stations: the central station, Coimbra A (*tel: (39) 272 63*), is about four blocks from the tourist office. Coimbra B handles long-distance trains (including those from Lisbon). 3 km north-west of town (*tel: (39) 349 98*). There are trains between them, which take 5 mins.
Tourist Office: *Largo da Portagem; tel: (39) 238 86* or *330 28*.

Getting Around

The main **bus station**, *Avda Fernao de Magalhaes; tel: (39) 270 83*, is 15-mins walk from the centre. Across the river from the main town are Portugal dos Pequenitos (on top of a steep hill) and Santa Clara (partially submerged, so you have to visit it by boat). Other places of major interest are walkable.

Accommodation and Food

There are several hotels of different grades, but you won't get decent accommodation for less than 2000$00. Near the station, the slightly seedy *Rua da Sota* area is the area to look for cheap, but very basic, lodgings. **IYHF**, *Rua Henriques Seco 12–14; tel: (39) 229 55*; **Campsite**: the *Municipal Sports Complex* (entrance from *Praça 25 de Abril); tel: (39) 71 29 97*.

There are cheap eating-places all over the centre: really basic food is available on *Beco do Forno* and *Rua dos Gatos* (alleys between *Largo da Portagem* and *Rua do Soto*).

Sightseeing

Coimbra was a centre of the Portuguese Renaissance and is the seat of one of the oldest universities in the world. The town overlooks the River Mondego and is a charming place with many fine old buildings, twisting streets, white-washed terraced houses, parks and gardens. It is also noted for its own student-influenced *fado* (melancholy Portuguese folk song).

The **University** is a Baroque fantasy, with a particularly interesting library. The **Se Velha** (cathedral) is arguably the finest Romanesque building in Portugal, while the south wing of the 16th-century **Santa Cruz** is a decorative church complex. The **Machado de Castro Museum** is housed in a former bishop's palace. The **Convent of Santa Clara** is gradually sinking and much of it is now underground. **Portugal dos Pequenitos**, an educational playground for children, is also fascinating for adults.

OPORTO (PORTO)

Stations: Campanha, *Pina da Estacao; tel: (2) 56 41 41*, near the south-east edge of town is the international station. **Sao Bento**, near *Prace Liberdade; tel: (2) 200 27 22*, is far more central. It handles local and regional services and is lined with beautiful *azulejos* (decorative Portuguese tiles). All Sao Bento trains stop at Campanha (about 5 mins away).
Tourist Offices: *Praça Dom Joao I, 43; tel: (02) 31 75 14* and *Rua Clube dos Fenianos 25; tel: (02) 32 33 03*.

Getting Around

Oporto's public transport company is STCP;

tourist tickets can be obtained from their kiosks. Trams, buses and trolley-buses all serve the city. Several private coach companies operate multi-lingual tours in the Costa Verde area. Ribeira, the riverside area, is the oldest part of town and the place for ferry excursions (from Cais da Ribeira). These operate Mar–Dec (pre-book for night trips) *tel: (02) 32 42 36/38 41 61.*

Accommodation

Hotels range from one- to five-star. Major hotels include: *Md, Nv, Sh.* For cheap lodgings, try the central area around *Ada dos Aliados.* Avoid the dock-side Ribeira. There's a **Youth Hostel** at *Rua Rodrigues Lobo 98; tel: (02) 606 55 35* and a convenient **Campsite** at *Parque de Prelada, Rua Monte de Burgos; tel: (02) 81 26 15.* There are also two in Gaia.

Sightseeing

The Romans built Portus and Cale at the mouth of the River Douro. The twin settlements prospered and gave their name to the whole country. Oporto also gave its name to the fortified wine and is still home of the port trade as well as Portugal's second city. The main attraction of the city is the port lodges, to be found in the suburb of **Vila Nova de Gaia**, linked to the city centre by the double-decker **Dom Luis I Bridge**. Tours of the lodges in-clude a tasting. From **Serra do Pilar** (by the bridge) there are spectacular views.

In the old town, near the river, are numerous fascinating churches and museums. The best of the churches include the **Cathedral (Se)**, *Terreiro de Se*, with architectural styles ranging from the 12th–18th century. The **Church of Sao Francisco**, *Rua Nova da Alfandega*, has a Gothic façade and an exquisite Baroque interior. For superb *talha dourado* (intricate guilding), see the altar of **Sao Bento**, *Rua Sao Bento da Vitoria*. The Baroque façade of the **Misericordia Church**, *Rua das Flores*, is famous.

The **Ethnographical Museum**, *Rua Belomonte*, has excellent displays about the region, including a reconstruction of a winery. The **Soares dos Reis Museum**, housed in the Carrancas Palace, *Rua D. Manuel II*, is famed for its collection of the decorative arts, including Portuguese faïence.

The **Torre dos Clerigos**, *Rua Clerigos*, is Oporto's symbol, a bell-tower (225 steps) that affords a magnificent view. The **Palacio da Bolsa**, *Rua Infante de Henrique*, is now the Stock Exchange, but contains an elaborate Arab Hall. The central **Praça da Liberdade** is surrounded by buildings of interest and dominated by an equestrian statue. The **Jardim do Palacio de Cristal**, *Rua D. Manuel II*, is the setting for a pavilion which hosts many sporting and artistic events.

Side Tracks from Oporto

Buses run from Oporto to **Braga** every half-hour and take about 1 hr 30 mins. Braga is a place where religion matters and the **Cathedral** is Portugal's oldest, richly ornamented and full of priceless artefacts. From *Avda Central*, take a bus to the pilgrimage site of **Bom Jesus do Monte** (5 km east). The gardens are delightful and there's a funicular if you can't face the 116m climb up the ornate Staircase of the Five Senses to the attractive Chapel of the Miracles. **Tourist Office**: *Avda da Liberdade 1; tel: (053) 225 50.*

VIANA DO CASTELO

Station: *tel: (058) 82 22 96* or *82 31 94.* This is near the town centre.
Tourist Office: *Rua do Hospital Velho; tel: (058) 82 26 20* or *82 78 73.*

Accommodation

Pensions are easy to find, but not necessarily cheap. Rooms in private houses are often a better bet – advertised by cards in the windows.

Campsites: *Orbiturna Praia do Cabedelo; tel: (058) 221 67* and *Campismo Inatel Praia do Cabedelo; tel: (058) 232 42.* Both are by Cabedelo beach and, in season, there's a rather dilapidated ferry from Largo 5 de Outubro.

Sightseeing

This old fortress town is a pleasant resort on the River Lima. On one side of the river is the beach, on the other the charming little town which is noted for Renaissance and Manueline architecture. It's also a centre of Portuguese folklore and famous for handicrafts. With the exception of Santa Lucia (accessible by funicular from *Avda 25 de Abril)*, interesting sites are walkable.

The central square, **Praça de Republica** has a fountain that has been copied all over the region. The **Misericordia Church** contains 17th-century *azulejos* and some impressive *talha dourado*, while the neo-Byzantine church of **Santa Lucia** is impressive in itself and affords a panoramic view of the town. The **Municipal Museum** is one of the best in Portugal, with particularly fine glazed earthenware and furniture. Viana do Castelo's *Romaria* (in August) is the biggest festival in the country, held to honour Our Lady of Agony.

VALENCA DO MINHO

Station: *tel: (051) 82 41 55* or *55 35 36*. This is on the east side of the new town.
Tourist Office: *Ada de Espanha; tel: (051) 233 74.*

The ancient town overlooks the Minho river and guards the border with Spain. The former stronghold consisted of two fortresses and many of the 17th–18th-century walls have survived. These, together with the narrow streets lined with white houses, impart a medieval flavour.

TUY (TUI)

Station: *tel: (986) 60 08 13*. This is central.
Tourist Office: *tel: (986) 60 17 89.*

A bridge connects this tiered Spanish town to Portugal. Tuy has grown around the **Cathedral of San Telmo**, the remains of which are now covered by lichen. The 13th-century cloister has twin columns and carved choir-stalls. There are also an ornate 14th-century porch and some fine Gothic sepulchres. Visit the churches of **Santo Domingo** and **San Bartolome**, if time permits.

VIGO

Station: *tel: (986) 43 33 69*. This is central.
Tourist Office: *Jardines de las Avdas s/n; tel: (986) 43 05 77.*

Vigo is a major port on a bay guarded by the Isla Cies archipelago. The seafront is a hive of activity early in the morning and there's a lively

fish market (*Pescadería*). There are some attractive arcaded houses near the harbour and **Castro Castle**, on a hill behind the town, provides a magnificent view. The **Isla Cies** are reached by ferry from Vigo. One of them is a bird sanctuary, but the other two can be visited. They are joined by a causeway, with the Atlantic on one side and a quiet lagoon on the other. If you book ahead (*tel: (986) 42 16 22)*, it is possible to camp there.

PONTEVEDRA

Station: *tel: (986) 86 31 63*. This is central.
Tourist Office: *General Mola 2; tel: (986) 85 08 14.*

Accommodation

Budget accommodation is limited. There are some *fondas* (inexpensive guest houses) on *Plaza Teucro* and *Calle Charino* and *hostales* at *Andrés Mellado 11* and *Virgen del Camino 70*.

Sightseeing

Pontevedra, a typical old Galician town, is an attractive place. Situated on the River Ponteve-dra, it began life as a port, but its importance dwindled as the old harbour silted up and it was by-passed by the progress that has ruined other such settlements. There's a new city, but it has grown without disturbing the old one. Parts of the original walls are visible and the old town consists of a maze of narrow, twisting cobbled streets, arcaded squares with carved stone cross-es and low houses with flower-filled balconies. Sights are in the small old city and walkable.

La Peregrina, an unusual chapel in the shape of a seashell, is situated by the partly arcaded main square, the **Herrería**, on the boundary be-tween the old and new areas. The Gothic façade of the **Convent of San Francisco** looks onto the Herrería.

The **Iglesia de Santa María la Mayor**, *Isabel II*, has an impressive Plateresque façade and is surrounded by gardens. **Santo Domingo Church** by the *Jardines Vincenti* is largely in ruins but the surviving wing holds the **Archaeological Museum**. The **Provincial Museum**, *Plaza de Lena*, is housed in two old mansions linked by an arch.

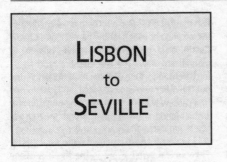

LISBON
to
SEVILLE

This somewhat tortuous route takes you from from the Portuguese capital into southern Spain, offering the opportunity to sample the pleasures of the Algarve.

TRAINS

ETT tables: 449, 429, 425.

→ Fast Track

With no through trains and no direct line, there is no way to cover this route quickly.

⇝ On Track

Lisbon (Lisboa)–Sétubal

There are services throughout the day (with a maximum wait of 2 hours) between Lisbon (Terreiro do Pago Pier) and Sétubal. The total journey time is about 1 hr 15 mins, including a 30-min Tagus ferry crossing (rail passes valid).

Sétubal–Albufeira

There are four trains every day. They take 3–4 hrs and there may not be a refreshment service.

Albufeira–Faro

There are over a dozen trains between Albufeira and Faro every day, taking 30 mins–1 hr.

Faro–Vila Real de Santo António

There are at least 10 trains a day. The journey takes 1 hr to 1 hr 30 mins.

Vila Real de Santo António–(Border)–Ayamonte–Huelva

There is no railway between these points. Vila railway station is adjacent to the ferry to

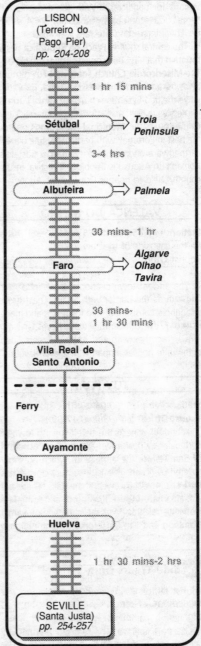

LISBON
(Terreiro do
Pago Pier)
pp. 204-208

1 hr 15 mins

Sétubal ⇒ *Troia Peninsula*

3-4 hrs

Albufeira ⇒ *Palmela*

30 mins- 1 hr

Faro ⇒ *Algarve Olhao Tavira*

30 mins-
1 hr 30 mins

Vila Real de
Santo Antonio

Ferry

Ayamonte

Bus

Huelva

1 hr 30 mins-2 hrs

SEVILLE
(Santa Justa)
pp. 254-257

Ayamonte, but the Ayamonte bus station is a 10-min walk from the ferry at that end. There are six to ten buses daily between Ayamonte and Huelva but at Huelva the bus station is some distance from the train station and the best way to cover that leg is by taxi. There is no set schedule for either the buses or the ferries, so it is very difficult to plan ahead and you should make enquiries locally to see what connections are available. The actual river crossing is very short. There is a fairly new road bridge linking Portugal and Spain and it is possible that a bus link between Vila Real and Ayamonte/Huelva will be introduced.

Huelva–Seville (Sevilla)

There are three trains a day between Huelva (Termino) and Seville (Santa Justa). The journey takes 1 hr 30 mins to 2 hrs.

SÉTUBAL

Station: *Estrada de Sétubal; tel: (65) 268 45.* About 1 km east of the centre.
Tourist Office: *Praça de Quebedo; tel: (65) 295 07.*

Sétubal is a large port and resort offering a range of sporting facilities, but it's somewhat short on charm. The town is a mixture of broad modern roads and old cobbled lanes lined with white houses. The ramparts of the 16th-century **Castelo de São Filipe** offer a panoramic view and the harbour area is an interesting place for a stroll. The 15th-century **Church of Jesus** is built of marble and was possibly the first major structure in the Manueline style, which is perfectly illustrated by the twisted pillars and the ribs supporting the vault. There's a **Municipal Museum** in the Gothic cloister which has a large collection of Portuguese Primitive paintings and 15th–16th-century *azulejos*.

Side Tracks from Sétubal

At the tip of the **Troia Peninsula** is a large modern tourist complex with a great range of facilities. It is accessible by ferry from Sétubal.

The peninsula is a promontory with an estuary on one side and the Atlantic on the other. The waters of the estuary are calm and the beaches are usually crowded. The Atlantic side is much quieter and has good waves, and is preferred by people who enjoy sea-swimming.

The base of the promontory and part of the mainland form an area of marshland, dunes and mud flats which has been made a nature reserve for a variety of waterfowl. Dolphins and sea otters are occasionally seen in the estuary.

Situated 9 km from Sétubal (access by bus), **Palmela** is a tiered village in the foothills of the Serra da Arrabida, dominated by a 12th-century **castle**. It is in a rich farming district and famous for wine, with colourful grape harvest festivals every Sept–Oct. The 18th-century **St Peter's Church** has an interior almost entirely covered with *azulejos* depicting scenes from the saint's life. There is a **tourist office** at *Largo do Chafariz; tel: (065) 235 00 89.*

ALBUFEIRA

Station: *Estrada de Albufeira; tel: (089) 57 16 16.* This is about 7 km north of town, but there are good bus connections.
Tourist Office: *Rua 5 de Outubro; tel: (089) 51 21 44.*

Once an Arab stronghold, Albufeira is now one of the biggest package-holiday resorts on the Algarve coast, with high-rise hotels and apartment blocks swamping the charm of what was a quiet fishing village. (The nightlife here is good). By day you can see the colourful fishing boats drawn up on the beach, and the fishermen mending their nets, by night you can watch their lights bobbing out at sea as they trawl for sardines. The main beach is reached by cliffside steps or through a tunnel. It's attractive and safe, but definitely overcrowded in season.

FARO

Airport: RN buses (nos 17/18) operate between airport and town centre, a 30-min journey, but taxis are cheap and take about 20 mins. For 24-hour information *tel: (089) 81 82 81.*
Station: *Avenida de Republica; tel: (089) 431 75.*

Tourist Office: *Rua da Misericordia 8–12; tel: (089) 80 36 04.* There is a **regional tourist office** at *Rua Ataide de Oliveira 100, 8000 Faro; tel: (089) 80 36 67.*

This is the capital of, and main point of access to, the Algarve. The original city was largely destroyed by the earthquake of 1755, although a little of the old town did survive. Nowadays it is a busy industrial town and port, where the main attraction is the shopping. The bizarre **Capela dos Ossos** behind the *Igreja do Carmo* (Church) on *Largo do Carmo* is lined with skulls and bones. The **Cathedral** (*Largo de Se*) is mostly 17th/18th century. The interior of the **Church of São Francisco** (*Largo de São Francisco*) has panels of 18th-century *azulejos* and a chancel with *talha dourado* decorations.

- -

⤺ Side Track from Faro

THE ALGARVE

There are lots of cheap and convenient buses throughout the area. Occupying the south of Portugal, the Algarve is noted for picturesque villages and varied tourist facilities; from casinos and golf courses to horse-riding, handicraft shops and Roman remains. Some of its many resorts are well planned to merge with nature, others are horrendous eyesores. Inland, there are great orchards of almonds, figs and oranges, particularly attractive in Jan–early Feb.

The main area of development is the stretch from Faro to the west, which is rocky and very picturesque, with lots of small sheltered beaches. The dramatic windswept promontory of **Cape St Vincent** (near **Sagres**, at the far south-west of the country) was once thought to be on the edge of the world and the meeting place of the gods. The east (between Faro and the Spanish border) is less dramatic, featuring long stretches of sand and pine groves. It is little developed and the **Ria Formosa** is a peaceful seabird reserve.

About 9 km from Faro, **Olhao** is a 17th-century town known for its lively fish market and relatively untouched by tourism. The local style of building resulted from the 18th-century fishermen's contact with their North African counterparts (rather than the more usual Moorish occupation), with, typically, 2/3-storey square terraced houses whose flat roofs are used as terraces. It's just a good place to get the feel of the 'real' Portugal and you can get boats to the quiet offshore islands of **Culatra** and **Armona** for a swim from a quiet beach. There is a **tourist office** at *Largo da Lagoa; tel: (089) 71 39 36.*

A town of Roman origin, 22 km from Olhao, **Tavira** virtually began all over again after the devastating earthquake in 1755. It is a charming place with pastel-coloured houses, miniature domes, ornate bell-towers, low bridges and twisting streets. Despite the long beaches nearby, tourism has not yet taken over and churches are a greater feature than hotels. However, the churches are usually closed outside the hours of worship, so you have to find the keyholders if you want to look inside. The market sells local produce at one end and fresh seafood at the other. The **tourist office** is at *Praça da Republica; tel: (81) 225 11.*

- -

VILA REAL DE SANTO ANTÓNIO

Station: *Estrada de Vila Real de Santo António; tel: (059) 431 75.* This is near the centre of town. **Tourist Office:** *Avenida da Republica; tel: (059) 432 72.*

The original frontier town was destroyed by a tidal wave in the early 17th century and the Marques do Pombal laid out the new one centred on a square with a black and white mosaic pavement radiating from a central obelisk and surrounded by orange trees. The town is now a fishing and commercial port.

HUELVA

Station: Termino *Avenida de Italia; tel: (955) 24 89 02.* Only 5 mins walk from the centre. **Tourist Office:** *Vazquez Lopez 5; tel: (955) 25 74 03.*

There's a good **Archaeological Museum**, which includes local finds and Romanesque sculptures, but Huelva is basically an industrial town which swamps the few buildings of interest, such as the Baroque **Cathedral.**

LONDON

London is one of the world's greatest cities, with something for everyone, from fine art and history to superb shopping and theatre. Allow an absolute minimum of 4–5 days if you are to get any sort of feeling for what's on.

Tourist Information

The tourist information centre in **Victoria Station** can provide information and a hotel booking service (for anywhere in the UK) to personal callers; open Mon–Sat 0800–1900 and Sun 0800–1700. You can get information by phone via a recorded message; tel: (0839) 123, followed by a series of different codes according to the subject in which you are interested (calls cost £0.36 per minute cheap rate and £0.48 per minute at all other times, however). For a list of the subjects and codes tel: (071) 971 0026.

Arriving and Departing

Airports

Heathrow Airport is 24 km west of London. The Piccadilly tube (subway) and Airbuses A1 and A2 serve all four terminals, from various pick-up points in central London. Allow an hour for the journey. There are also regular Green Line buses and National Express coaches from the airport to Victoria Coach Station. There is a tourist information desk located by the underground station for Terminals 1, 2 and 3.

Gatwick Airport is 43 km south of London. Express trains depart, every 15 mins during the day, for Victoria Station (journey time: 30 mins). The cheaper Flightline 777 bus service takes 60–70 mins. There is a tourist information desk on the arrival concourse of the South Terminal.

Buses

Victoria Coach Station Buckingham Palace Rd, SW1; tel: (071) 730 0202, is the main London

terminal for long-distance coaches. Green Line buses (tel: (081) 668 7261) operate within a 40-mile radius of London; other areas are covered mainly by National Express.

Stations

There are 16 British Rail stations in central London, all well-equipped with WCs, cafés, bars and restaurants, newsagents and other shops (all are linked by London Underground). The most important are:

Victoria (tel: (071) 928 5100). An almost obligatory stop for international travellers, Victoria is the terminal of the Gatwick Express and also handles most of the boat-train services to France and Belgium. Other services cover the south-east counties: Kent, East Surrey and Sussex. Victoria is also home to a number of useful information desks, such as the British Rail European office, the main London Tourist Board office and a hotel-booking desk. There is a Travellers' Aid office on platform 10, which can help with all sorts of problems, including lost passports.

Waterloo (tel: (071) 928 5100). Traditionally covering the south-west counties, Waterloo handles boat-trains via Portsmouth to France and Spain. It will soon assume a more glamorous role as the London terminal for EuroTunnel passenger trains (see p. 29).

King's Cross (tel: (071) 278 2477) currently handles services to the north-east and Scotland.

Other main stations include: **Euston** (tel: (071) 387 7070) for trains to the West Midlands, north-west and Scotland; **Liverpool St** (tel: (071) 928 5100) for trains to East Anglia, including boat-trains to Harwich for ferries to the Netherlands; **Paddington** (tel: (071) 262 6767) for trains to Wales and the West Country; **St Pancras** (tel: (071) 387 7070) for trains to Sheffield and the East Midlands. St Pancras is destined (in 2005) to become the second London international station for trains travelling via the EuroTunnel to cities north of London.

Getting Around

The first thing you should do on arrival is arm yourself with a good street guide: try the A–Z Map of London (available for £1.95 from most

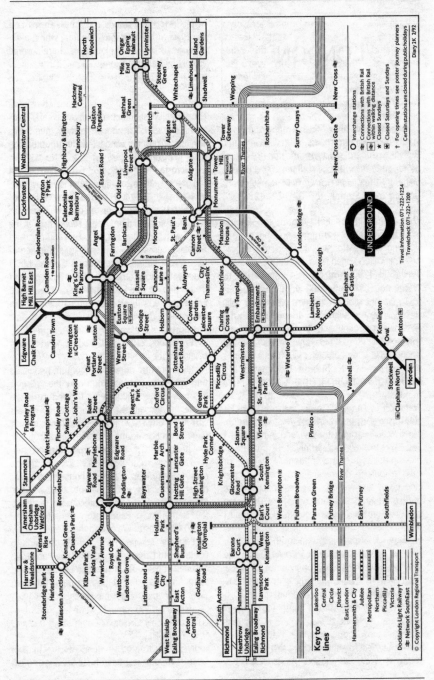

newsagents). This covers the central area on a scale of 6 in. to the mile, highlights places of interest and has a full-colour map of the underground, plus maps showing the West End cinemas and theatres. For more detail and a much wider area, buy the full *A–Z* and *Nicholson Street Guides*, also available from most newsagents.

Free bus and underground maps and other information about London Transport (LT), including the various types of tickets, should be available in most tube stations. If you draw a blank, try the main LT office in **St James's Park Underground Station** (*tel: (071) 222 1234* – 24 hours a day). Travel during rush hour (primarily Mon–Fri 0815–0945 and 1700–1830) is no fun at all, so avoid it if you can.

Tickets

Single tickets are expensive in comparison to Travelcards (£3.70; available from most stations and many newsagents). These cover all public transport services within London, giving you the freedom to hop on and off buses, tubes and some local trains. One-day passes can be bought and used only after 0930 and are not valid for travel on Night buses (designated 'N'). Others (valid for one week, one month, three months or one year) can be used at any time. Transport in London is arranged in a series of concentric circles (zones) spreading out through the suburbs. A ticket for Zones 1 and 2 should cover most tourist destinations.

The Underground

Commonly known as 'The Tube', London's underground railway (subway) system is extensive, efficient and usually the quickest way to get around. On the down-side, it can be dirty, impossibly crowded and claustrophobic during rush hours. The hours of operating vary slightly from line to line, but most services run Mon–Sat from 0530 to around midnight and Sun 0700–2330. Smoking is strictly forbidden.

Each line is designated a name and a colour and maps displaying this are found at frequent intervals throughout stations. Platforms are clearly labelled to show if the trains are north, south, east or west bound. As an additional help, destination boards on the platforms and the front of the train give the final stop.

Keep your ticket handy: there are occasional inspections and you need to put it through a turnstile machine to get out of the station.

Buses

London's bright red double-decker buses have become a tourist attraction in their own right. The roads are often congested and travel can be slow, but some of the routes (e.g. No. 12) are excellent for sightseeing and the view from the top deck is always great. Most services run: Mon–Sat 0600–2400 and Sun 0730–2300. Restricted services operate out of Trafalgar Square through the night. Night bus stops have blue and yellow signs.

Older buses have an open platform at the back and a conductor to issue tickets. More modern buses have doors and you must pay the driver before you take your seat. Keep your ticket until you reach your destination as there are random checks.

Buses do not always go the full length of the route, so check the destination board on the front or back.

There are bus stops every few hundred yards throughout central London, with the relevant bus numbers clearly shown. The red signs are request stops and the bus will not halt unless you flag it down – or ring the bell (once only) if you are on board.

Special tourist buses, some open-topped, take in the major sights and may provide a running commentary during the journey. Major departure points for these are *Marble Arch*, *Victoria, Haymarket* and *Green Park*.

River Journeys

East to the Tower of London, St Catherine's Dock and Greenwich: **Catamaran Cruises**, *Charing Cross Pier, Victoria Embankment, WC2; tel: (071) 839 3572* (tube: *Embankment*), run daily cruises throughout the year. Open 0800–1800 (until 2130 or later in summer). Closed only Christmas Day, Boxing Day and New Year's Day.

West to Kew, Richmond and Hampton Court: **Westminster Passenger Services**, *West-*

minster Pier, Victoria Embankment, SW1; tel: (071) 930 2062 (tube: Westminster), run daily cruises from the week before Easter to late-September and a limited service in October. Open summer Mon–Fri 0900–1600, but an answerphone is monitored throughout the year.

Taxis

London's famous 'black' cabs are often covered by advertisements and may not always be black, but their shape is nevertheless distinctive. Fares are not cheap, but taxis are metered and the drivers have to pass a rigorous test on their knowledge of London. There are extra (metered) charges for: a lot of baggage; more than one passenger; travelling in the evening (after 2000) or at weekends.

There are taxi ranks at key positions, but you can also hail them in the street. When a taxi is free, the light at the front is on. Avoid the (unlicensed) minicabs which tout for business on the street.

Living in London

Accommodation

London has an enormous range of accommodation, from world-renowned hotels with mega-high prices, such as the Ritz and Savoy, to youth hostels (see below).

All the major international hotel chains are represented. Further down the scale, there are plenty of small hotels, ranging from dire flea-pits to clean establishments with modest facilities. Prices start at around £25 per person for something half-way decent. The Paddington, Victoria and Earls Court areas, in particular, have a good range.

The best bet for cheap accommodation is the **IYHF**, which has seven hostels in London. If you are not already a member, full details can be obtained from their central information office (tel: (071) 248 6547).

The London Tourist Board (tel: (071) 824 8844) will take hotel bookings by phone up to six weeks in advance if you have an Access or Visa card. Alternatively, for a small fee, you can book at the **Thomas Cook Hotel Booking Desks** at Heathrow (daily 0800–1830) or at Victoria Station (Mon–Sat 0800–1900 and Sun 0800–1700).

Camping in central London is not possible. The parks are locked at around midnight and patrolled until they re-open. The city spreads for miles in every direction and the nearest campsites are some way out of town. If you are interested, contact the **Camping and Caravanning Club** 11 Lower Grosvenor Place, SW1; tel: (071) 828 1012.

Communications

Post offices are usually open Mon–Fri 0900–1730 and Sat 0900–1230, although some small branches close for lunch. A limited range of stamps is available from many shops and hotels. The post office near Trafalgar Square (24/28 William IV St, WC2 4DL) is a major branch that has a poste restante facility. It is open Mon–Fri 0830–1830.

When making telephone calls, both the length of the call and the time of day affect the cost. There are two time bands: the cheapest is Mon–Fri 1800–0800 and all weekend; the more expensive is Mon–Fri 0800–1800. Blue Mercury phones are usually cheaper than green BT ones. Coin, card, and credit card phones are all easily available.

London numbers have two area codes. The current ones are 071 for the centre, 081 for outlying areas, both followed by seven digits. From 16 April 1995, these will become 0171 and 0181 respectively.

To phone the national operator, tel: 100; for the international operator, tel: 155.

To phone the UK from abroad: tel. the appropriate international code, followed by the country code (44), followed by the area code without the first 0. Area codes will all be changed from 16 April 1995 to include a 1 after the 0. To call abroad from the UK: tel: 010, followed by the country code, then the number. From 16 April 1995, 010 will become 00.

Eating and Drinking

London is a superb hunting ground for food, with restaurants of every conceivable type, from traditional British to those of countries you probably couldn't pin-point on a map. The cost

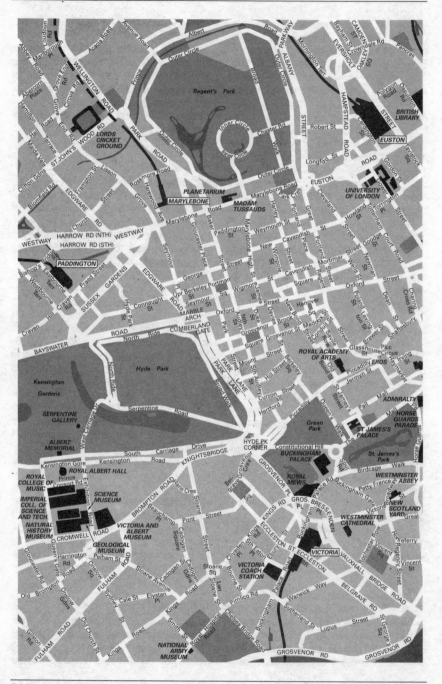

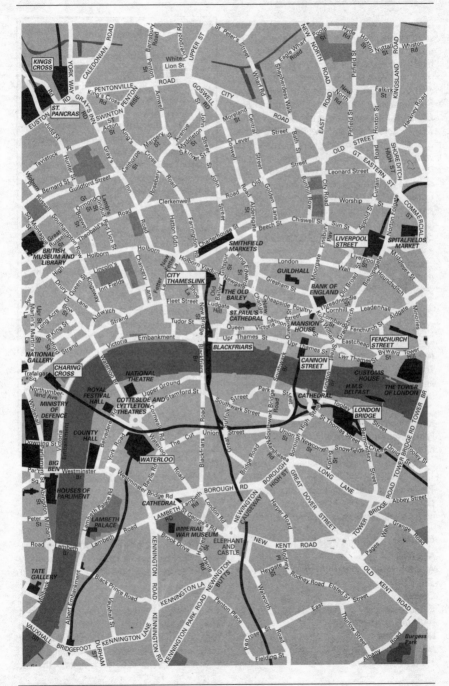

is equally varied: from fast-food chains, where you can get something filling for about £2, to places with no prices on the menu that cost more than you would spend on food in a year.

In the **West End**, Soho and Covent Garden offer the best array of restaurants. Slightly away from the centre, Queensway, Victoria and Earls Court areas are very lively in the evenings, with a wide range of cheap and cheerful eating places.

Food in pubs and wine bars is usually good value. Italian, Chinese and Indian restaurants are common and many are excellent, with a wide range of cheap dishes on offer. Many serve food to take out, as do most kebab places and fish and chip shops. Places with a menu in several languages or that display a Union Jack are designed for tourists and tend to be over-priced and often poor quality.

Most restaurants and cafés display menus outside. If a service charge is not noted separately on the bill, leave a tip of at least 10%.

Pubs

There are pubs on every street, including historic inns reputed to have been frequented by everyone from Ben Jonson to Charles Dickens. There are several books devoted to the subject and even organised 'pub crawls', which combine a historic walk with an evening's drinking. If this appeals to you, just turn up at Temple tube station at 1930 any Friday evening and join Peter Westbrook (tel: (081) 883 2656) for one of his organised tours.

Standard pub opening times are Mon–Sat 1100–2300, Sun 1200–1500 and 1930–2230. The minimum age limit for drinking alcohol in public places is 18. Children are not allowed in unless a separate area is provided for them.

Embassies and Consulates

Australia
Australia House, Strand, WC2B 4LA; tel: (071) 379 4334
Canada
Consular Section, 1 Grosvenor Square, W1X 0AB; tel: (071) 258 6316
New Zealand
New Zealand House, 80 Haymarket, SW1Y 4TQ; tel: (071) 930 8422

Thomas Cook

Thomas Cook travellers' cheque emergency refund number:
tel: 0800 622101 (freephone)

The following Thomas Cook locations can offer: commission-free encashment of Thomas Cook travellers' cheques; emergency assistance in the case of lost or stolen Thomas Cook travellers' cheques and MasterCard cards (locations marked *); extended opening outside banking hours (locations marked **).

45, Berkeley St * **, 45 Berkeley St, Mayfair, W1A 1EB; tel: (071) 499 4000 (tube: Green Park). The main London office of the company, this branch also has a visa application and emergency assistance service, and a health clinic and vaccination centre; open: Mon–Fri 0830 (1000 Wed) –1730 and Sat 0900–1600.

126 Queensway * **
92 Kensington High St * **
21 Old Brompton Rd * **
Piccadilly Circus Underground Station* **
No 1 Marble Arch **
Selfridges Ltd, 400 Oxford St * **
South Kensington Underground Station* **
378 Strand *
100 Victoria St * **

USA
24 Grosvenor Square, W1A 1AE; tel: (071) 499 9000

Money

There are banks and bureaux de change on virtually every main street. **Thomas Cook** travellers' cheques can be cashed free of commission in the bureaux listed above.

Security

Unfortunately, London is just as prone to street crime as most major cities and you should exercise caution. There are the usual number of pickpockets, bag-snatchers, con-men and so on. It is reasonably safe to walk around the city centre in the late evening as streets are well-lit and generally busy, but women on their own should avoid the *King's Cross* area.

Entertainment

There are several publications listing London's entertainments, of which the best are the weekly magazines *Time Out* (£1.40) and *What's On* (£1.00), available from all newsagents. The daily *Evening Standard* also has excellent theatre and cinema listings.

Nightlife

Almost everything is on offer, including casinos, jazz clubs, discos, gay clubs and pub entertainment. Most clubs offer one-night membership at the door. There is often a dress code, which might be a jacket and tie or could just depend on whether you look trendy enough. Jeans and trainers are out, no matter what. The larger rock venues are all a little way out of the city centre, as are many of the pubs with the best entertainment.

The chief problem is that almost the entire city shuts by midnight. Those places that do stay open late usually increase their entrance charges at around 2200 and many places charge more at weekends.

Theatres, Cinemas and Concerts

London is one of the world's greatest centres of theatre and music. In addition to the Royal National Theatre (*South Bank Centre* – see below) and the Royal Shakespeare Company (*Barbican Centre*), there are about 50 theatres in central London. Most of them are in the *West End*.

West End theatre tickets are expensive, but there is a kiosk in *Leicester Square* (the south side) which sells half-price tickets for performances the same day. If you want to book ahead, go to the theatre itself as most agents charge a hefty handling fee. Seats for the big musicals are often hard to get, but it's always worth queuing for returns.

Away from the centre, a number of fringe theatres offer small-scale or alternative productions, at reasonable prices.

There are classical music concerts in a wide variety of venues, from ultra-cheap lunch time performances in churches to major symphonies in famous venues. If you are in London in July/August, make a real effort to get to the Proms, a superb series of concerts at the **Royal Albert Hall**, *Kensington Gore*, (tube: *Knightsbridge/South Kensington*; bus nos. 9/9A/10/52/C1 stop right outside). There are many standing-room tickets at low prices for those prepared to queue.

There are dozens of cinemas in the *West End* and there's often a discount for the first showing on weekdays. Most are expensive and you'll find the same films at a lower price a little way out of the centre.

The South Bank Centre (tube: *Embankment*, plus a walk over Hungerford Bridge; or Waterloo – slightly closer, but with a less pleasant walk) is an outstanding entertainment complex. Attractions include: **National Theatre (NT)** (three different auditoriums); **National Film Theatre (NFT)**; **Museum of the Moving Image (MOMI)** – a must for cinema buffs; **Hayward Gallery** (frequent exhibitions of contemporary art); **Royal Festival Hall** (musical performances from symphonies to jazz); and **Queen Elizabeth Hall** (solo and small group performances). Prices are slightly lower than in the *West End* and there are free performances on the embankment and in the lobby of the NT.

Shopping

The *West End* is full of famous shopping areas. For serious shopping, including many department stores, try *Oxford St* and *Regent St* (home to Hamleys toy shop). For designer clothes and up-market window shopping, try *Bond St*, *South Moulton St* and *Brompton Rd* (home of Harrods). For books: *Charing Cross Rd*. For trendy boutiques: *Covent Garden*. Fortnum and Masons, on *Piccadilly*, is an unbelievable food paradise.

Some of London's street markets are tourist attractions in themselves. Amongst the best are **Portobello Rd** (tube: *Ladbroke Grove/Notting Hill Gate*, Mon–Sat, best Sat morning); **Petticoat Lane**, *Middlesex/Goulston Sts*, Sun morning (tube: *Liverpool St*); and *Camden Lock*, Sat–Sun (tube: *Chalk Farm*).

Sightseeing

You don't need to spend huge amounts of money, because many of London's attractions can be admired from the outside and some museums and galleries are free. This is only the briefest listing of the very best. Most places open daily, all year round, but check current times before you go.

Art Galleries

Of the countless art galleries, there are three which are outstanding – and admission is free, except for special exhibitions. The **National Gallery** (12th–19th century art) and **National Portrait Gallery** are neighbours in *Trafalgar Square* (tube: *Charing Cross* or *Leicester Square*). The **Tate Gallery** *Millbank SW1* (tube: *Westminster/Pimlico*) is home to impressionist and more modern works.

Museums

The (free entrance) **British Museum** *Great Russell St, WC1* (tube: *Russell Square*) is a treasure trove of original artefacts from ancient Egyptian sculptures onwards. The fascinating **Imperial War Museum** *Lambeth Rd, SE1* (tube: *Lambeth North*) offers a history of warfare

---

Thomas Cook Leisure Line

Calls cost 36p per minute cheap rate and 48p per minute at all other times, plus any hotel surcharge (as at date of this book).

Accommodation Late Availability
tel: (0839) 168 134

Sightseeing Tours
tel: (0839) 168 135

UK Short Break Specials
tel: (0839) 168 136

Overseas Rail Information
tel: (0839) 168 137

Thomas Cook Exchange Rates Line
tel: (0839) 401 119

UK Weathercall
tel: (0839) 500 928 (London Area)
tel: (0839) 500 400 (National)

---

through the ages; open daily but free on Friday only. The **Museum of London** *London Wall, EC2* (tube: *Barbican/St Paul's/Moorgate*) offers a beautifully displayed history of the city from 400,000 BC to the 20th century.

Clustered together near *South Kensington* tube are three other great museums. The **Natural History Museum**, with many hands-on exhibits and a brilliant dinosaur display, and the **Science Museum** (free after 1630) are both on *Exhibition Rd*. The **Victoria and Albert Museum** on *Cromwell Rd* (voluntary donations) houses the national furniture, china and glass collections, among other things.

Sights

Buckingham Palace, *The Mall/Buckingham Palace Rd, SW1* (tube: *Victoria/St James's Park*). Some State apartments are open to the public mid-summer. The Royal Mews (horses and State coaches) can be visited year round. The Changing of the Guard takes place in the forecourt (visible from the street) every morning or every second morning (depending on the season).

The **Houses of Parliament** and **Westminster Abbey** are at *Parliament Square, SW1* (tube: *Westminster*). If you want to hear a debate in the House of Commons, expect to queue. Westminster Abbey opens daily (except Sundays), but there is a charge for the most interesting parts.

In the City of London are Sir Christopher Wren's **St Paul's Cathedral** *Ludgate Hill, EC4* (tube: *St Paul's*) and the **Tower of London** *Tower Hill, EC3* (tube: *Tower Hill*), built by William the Conqueror, once jail to traitors and now home of the Crown Jewels and Beefeaters.

Side Tracks from London

Just outside central London and easily accessible by train, bus or boat (see River Journeys) are the magnificent **Kew Botanical Gardens**, and superb Tudor palace **Hampton Court**. Heading the other way, spend a day at **Greenwich** home to the **Maritime Museum**, **Naval College**, **Royal Observatory**, and the **Cutty Sark**.

LONDON
to
AMSTERDAM

Many of the Netherlands' major towns lie between Hook of Holland and Amsterdam and are included in this route, but the excellent rail network makes it easy to reach other places too.

TRAINS

ETT tables: 12, 15, 220.

⟶ Fast Track

London–Amsterdam

Between London (Liverpool Street) and Amsterdam (Centraal) there are two daily services, morning and evening, using the Harwich–Hook of Holland sea crossing. The day journey takes about 12 hrs – an hour or so quicker than the night service. All trains offer both first- and second-class travel. On Sundays at some times of year the journey between Liverpool Street and Harwich is by bus. Sailing time is about 7 hrs during the day and about 9 hrs at night. Advance booking is necessary for berths on the overnight ferry. There are border formalities at Harwich and the Hook of Holland.

The introduction of **Channel Tunnel** services (see p. 29) will make it possible to travel from London (Waterloo) to Amsterdam via Brussels.

⟿ On Track

It's unlikely you'll have to wait more than half an hour on any leg of the journey. Approx. journey times on the suggested route are: *Hook of Holland (Hoek Van Holland)–Rotterdam* 30 mins; *Rotterdam–Delft* 15 mins; *Delft–The Hague* 10 mins; *The Hague–Leiden* 15 mins; *Leiden–Haarlem* 25 mins; and *Haarlem–Amsterdam* 15 mins.

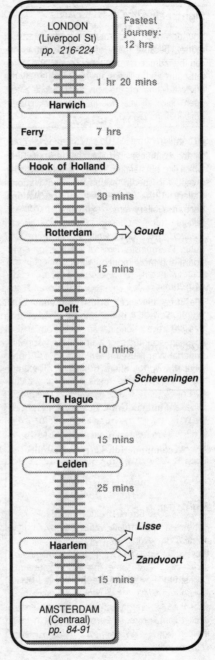

Route

HOOK OF HOLLAND
(HOEK VAN HOLLAND)

Ferries and **trains** share a terminal, separated only by customs and immigration formalities, so you just walk between them. For information, *tel: (01747) 89333.*

ROTTERDAM

Station: Centraal Station (CS) and the bus station are together on the edge of the centre. (This is an area to be avoided at night.) There's a tourist information booth at CS.
Tourist Office: *Coolsingel 67; tel: (010) 413 6000.* They can provide *This Month,* a free listing of events.

Getting Around

There are two metro lines, which connect in the centre: blue runs north–south and red runs east–west. There's also an efficient tram and bus service. The main area of interest is around the waterfront, where walking is the best form of transport.

Accommodation

Major hotels include *GT, Hn* and *Nv.* There are two areas with cheap hotels about 1 km southwest of CS (try *'s Gravendijkwal* and *Heemraadsingel*) and just north of CS (try *Provenierssingel*). The **IYHF**, at *Rochussenstraat 107; tel: (010) 436 5763,* is 3 km from CS (tram nos. 4/6). Mid-Jun–mid-Aug there's dormitory accommodation at **Sleep In**, *Mauritsweg 291: tel: (010) 121 420* or *143 256,* 5 mins walk south of CS.

Sightseeing

Rotterdam was virtually wiped out by German air-raids in World War II and it's now a thoroughly modern place, noted for imaginative architecture and some interesting museums. Situated at the delta of the rivers Rhine, Maas/Meuse and Waal, it has been a major harbour since the 14th century and is now has the world's largest container port, **Europoort** – boat tours leave from *Willemsplein* (blue metro: *Leuvehaven*).

There's little of interest in the centre, but don't miss the enormous **Museum Boymans-Van Beuningen**, *Mathenesserlaan 18* (red metro: *Eendrachtsplein* or tram no. 5 from CS). Among the major sections are: the Surrealists, Rembrandt (and his pupils), early Dutch painters (including Breughel and Bosch) and the Van der Vorm collection (ranging from Dürer to Cézanne, Gauguin to Munch). The **Maritiem Museum Prins Hendrik**, *Leuvehaven 1* (red metro: *Churchillplein*), is an open-air museum devoted to the city's long maritime history and there's constant renovation in progress. You can board the *Museumschip De Buffel*, a 19th-century vessel of war which is moored alongside. **Museum voor Land en Volkenkunde**, *Willkemskade 25,* is devoted to geography and ethnography. Towering above the adjacent park is the 185m **Euromast**, *Parkhaven 20* (red metro: *Dijks*), with external lifts going to the revolving summit, for panoramic views of the long (37 km) waterfront.

The most striking buildings are located around **Oude Haven**, the old harbour. The **Gemeentebiblioteek (**Central Library**)** is a pyramidal structure with escalators that provide great views of the old port. Nearby are futuristic cube houses, one of which, **Kijk Kubus**, *Overblaak 70,* is open to the public – nice to visit, but you might not want to live there.

The neighbouring **Delfshaven** district (tram nos. 4/6) escaped the bombs and is an attractive area where old warehouses have been converted into upmarket flats. The Pilgrim Fathers set sail from here in 1620, but their ship proved to be unseaworthy, so they docked at Plymouth and transferred to the *Mayflower* before attempting the Atlantic crossing. **Dubbelde Palmboom Museum**, *Voorhaven 12,* is housed in one of the 19th-century warehouses and is devoted to the history of the delta.

- - - - - - - - - - - - - - - - - -

🔁 Side Track from Rotterdam

GOUDA

Gouda is 25 mins from Rotterdam by hourly train. **Train** and **bus stations** are together, 10–

15 mins walk from Markt, around which are all the main sights of the pretty little town.
Tourist Office: *Markt 27; tel: (01820) 13666/13298.*

Accommodation

There's no IYHF, but there is a hostel at *Westhaven 46; tel: (01820) 12879.*

Sightseeing

Gouda exemplifies small-town Holland, with a ring of quiet canals around ancient buildings. 225
The ornate 15th-century **Stadhuis**, *Markt*, contains carved fireplaces and 17th-century tapestries. It's a cheerful place that is very popular for weddings, but you can explore between the ceremonies. Behind the Stadhuis is **Waag**, the 17th-century weigh-house. Every Thursday morning in July and August it's opened for trading and suitably costumed farmers weigh their cheeses by traditional methods (strictly for the benefit of tourists).

St Janskerk, just south of the square, is a 16th-century cruciform structure that is famous for its length (123m) and its 70 superb stained-glass windows, the best of which are 16th century and have biblical themes. Behind the church is *Achter de Kerk*, on which is the ornate 17th-century **Lazaruspoortje**. Once the entrance to a hospital for lepers, it is now the back gate to **Het Catharina Gasthuis**, a complex of 14th–17th-century buildings which houses a fascinating municipal museum with some excellent early religious art, a torture chamber and a gruesome operating room. The **De Monriaan Museum**, *Westhaven 29* (covered by the same ticket), is an old tobacco shop displaying clay pipes.

At **Het Tin en Karamiek Huis**, *Lange Groenendaal 73*, you can watch craftsmen decorating china with the Delft designs (85% of Delft ware is made in Gouda) and also producing the rarer (and richer) Gouda designs.

De Roode Leeuw, *Vest 65*, is the last working flour mill in the country which is still the home of the miller. You can climb inside while it's turning.

VVV can provide you with details of dairy farms around the town which will allow you to watch the famous cheese being made. There are five different types of Gouda – as a contrast, the town also produces excellent syrup waffles.

DELFT

Station: a short walk from the centre of town.
Tourist Office: *Markt 85; tel: (015) 126 100.*

Delft is a place of great charm – arguably the most attractive town in a country full of them – and it's easy to explore on foot. Boat-trips along the unspoiled canal system are possible from April to October and horse-drawn carriages can be hired in **Markt**, the main square. When Chinese porcelain reached Delft, it inspired the local potters and their lovely blue and white designs made the town famous. **De Porceleyne Fles** has hourly demonstrations and visits can be made to **De Delftse Pauw** to watch the artists at work. **Het Prinsenhof** exhibits tapestries, paintings and pottery of the Delft school, as well as contemporary art. Across the road is **Oude Kerk**, which has an alarmingly leaning tower. **Oude Delft** is the town's oldest canal and there's a superb collection of antique Delftware and decorative tiles at the **Huis Lambert van Meerten**.

THE HAGUE (DEN HAAG)

Stations: Hollandse Spoor (HS), 1 km south of CS, serves Amsterdam and Rotterdam, but **Centraal (CS)** is more convenient (5 mins walk from centre) and serves most other places. Regular trains and trams (nos. 9/12) link them.
Tourist Office: *Koningin Julianaplein 30; tel: (070) 354 6200*, close to CS.

Accommodation and Food

Ther are many chain hotels, including *GT, Ic, Nv, Pu* and *Sf*. There are cheap hotels near HS, but the area is not recommended and, if money is a consideration, it's better to base yourself at Scheveningen (*see below*). If you prefer to stay in town, ask VVV about private rooms.

The **IYHF** is at *Monsterseweg 4; tel: (070) 397 0011*, 8 km west of town near Kijkduin beach (bus nos. 122/123/124 from CS plus a 10-mins (signposted) walk: tell the driver you want the hostel). Close to it are a small cheap hotel and a campsite.

For cheap eating, try *Herenstraat* (near the Binnenhof). There are many bars in the streets east of *Lange Voorhout*.

Sightseeing

Many of the major sights can be visited on foot and there's a good network of buses and trams if you want to go further afield. Boat trips can be booked through **Rondvaartbedrijf RVH**, *Spui 256; tel: (070) 346 2473*, near CS.

The administrative capital of the Netherlands is a pleasant town with wide boulevards and graceful architecture, a tranquil place except when it hosts a variety of lively summer festivals: notably the 10-day **Pasar Malam Besar** (Indonesian market). Other regular events involve horses, kites and jazz.

The city centre is the **Binnenhof**, the courtyard of William II's residence when he founded the town (in 1247) by building a hunting lodge. The city's official name is still *'s Gravenhage* (Count's Hedge). The 13th-century **Ridderzaal (Knights' Hall)** is the home of the Dutch parliament and many official ceremonies take place here. At other times it can be visited, as can the government chambers when parliament is not sitting.

Mauritshuis Museum, *Plein 29*, is a Renaissance mansion that houses the best of the Royal Collection: Rembrandt, Vermeer, Memling, Brouwer, van Dyck, Rubens and Steen are all well represented. If you want more, the rest (included in the same ticket) is in the **Schildergallerij Prins Willem V**, *Buitenhof 35*, which is virtually wallpapered with paintings. Next door is **Rijksmuseum Gevangenpoort**, a prison for over four centuries that contains a gruesome range of instruments of torture.

Panorama Mesdag, *Zeestraat 65b*, is a realistic circular view of Scheveningen painted by Hendrik Mesdag in 1881. His house, now a museum, is just round the corner, at *Laan van Meerdevoort 7*. Ten minutes away (by tram no. 4) is the 1990s version of a panorama, at **Omniversum (Space Theatre)**, *President Kennedylaan 5*, utilising lasers, films and sound effects for hourly performances.

The town has a host of palaces, but most can be viewed only from the outside. An exception is the huge **Vredespaleis (Peace Palace)**, *Carnegieplein 2*, which was financed by Andrew Carnegie. It houses the International Court of Justice, and is a strange architectural mishmash containing a display of items donated by various world leaders. It's closed when the Court is in session.

The municipal museum, **Gemeentemuseum**, *Stadhouderslaan 41* (bus no. 4 from CS), is a 'must'. It offers superb glass and silverware, beautifully reconstructed period rooms, a wide range of musical instruments, Islamic ceramics, period costumes and a superb range of modern art, including the world's largest collection of paintings by Mondriaan.

Madurodam, *Haringkade 175* (half-way to Scheveningen, tram nos. 1/9), is a miniature town (scale 1:25) that includes models of the nation's landmarks. It's usually very crowded, but children (and many adults) love it.

Side Track from The Hague

Scheveningen is a North Sea resort about 4 km from the city centre (from which there are frequent buses and trams). It centres on the 19th-century **Kurhaus Hotel**, in which there's a casino. Among the other attractions are a long sandy beach and a model of Jules Verne's *Nautilus*. There's a fireworks display every Friday evening in July and August. Hotels here are a bit cheaper than in town: details from **VVV**, *Gevers Deyjnootweg 126; tel: (070) 354 6200*.

LEIDEN

Station: the rail and bus stations are together on the north-west edge of town, about 10-mins walk from the centre.

Tourist Office: *Stationsplein 210; tel: (071) 146 846*. Across the street from the station.

Leiden is a delightful little town, with some user-friendly museums, that is well worth a visit. Everything of interest is within easy walking distance of the centre. The medieval quarter centres on **St Pieterskerk**. On *Rapenburg* are the earliest part of the **University** (founded 1574) and its **Hortus Botanicus**, which is among the world's oldest botanical gardens. **Van Oudenheden** is an excellent archaeological museum that includes a complete 1st-century AD Egyptian temple. **De Lakenhal** covers the history of the town: the period-furnished rooms include a kitchen and a brewery and Van Leyden's *Last Judgment* is among the fine paintings. Nearby is **Molenmuseum de Valk**, a museum about windmills, while **Voor Volkenkunde** contains spectacularly good Japanese and Indonesian exhibits.

HAARLEM

Station: this was built in 1908 and the style is art deco. It's about 10-mins walk north of the centre, but buses stop right outside.
Tourist Office: *Stationsplein 1; tel: (023) 319 059.*

Accommodation

The choice of hotels is better if you base yourself in Zandvoort (*see Side Tracks below*), where there is more choice. If you do want to be central, ask VVV about private rooms. The **IYHF** is at *Jan Gijzenpad 3; tel: (023) 373 793*, 3 km north of the station and 10 mins on frequent buses (nos. 2/6). In spring and summer there's the option of camping in the dunes along *Zeeweg* (bus no. 81 to Bloemendaal-aan-Zee).

Sightseeing

Haarlem is a peaceful provincial town on the River Spaarne, a picturesque place, much of which looks as if it's straight out of a 17th-century painting. The central **Grote Markt** is a perfect example of this and the town's religious past shows in the homilies carved on many facades. It's small enough to explore on foot, but there are plenty of buses.

The **Stadhuis**, *Grote Markt*, has expanded over the centuries and has a lavishly decorated interior that can be viewed when it's not in use. Also in the square is **St Bavokerk/Grote Kerk**, which was completed in the mid-16th century and became a popular subject for 17th-century

painters. Inside is an enormous Baroque pipe organ, which was played by Mozart and is still used for recitals.

The town's main attraction is the **Frans Hals Museum**, *Groot Heiligland 62* (15-mins stroll south from the square), a 17th-century almshouse where Hals ended his days. It contains several of his paintings. Two other things of particular interest are a delicate 18th-century doll's house and a workshop where you can watch the art restorers.

A once-private collection that dates from the 18th century can be seen at **Teylers Museum**, *Spaarne 16*. The diverse exhibits include old scientific instruments, fossils and drawings – some by Raphael, Michelangelo and Rembrandt.

Provinciehuis Noord-Holland was built by an eccentric 18th-century collector and is incredibly ornate. Guided tours have to be arranged by VVV, but it's worth making the effort.

Hofjes (take *Lange Annastraat* north from the 17th-century **Nieuwe Kerk**) are the attractive courtyards of ancient almshouses. Many are still inhabited, but the residents don't take exception if you (discreetly) have a quick look.

◣ Side Tracks from Haarlem

Zandvoort (10 mins by train and frequent buses in summer) is the beach for Haarlem and has plenty of cheap pensions (**VVV**, *Schoolplein 1; tel: (02507) 17947*, can supply information). It's a large resort with a dolphinarium, a casino, lots of good beaches (including a long one for nudists) and a dune reserve to the south.

Lisse (**VVV**, *Grachtweg 53a; tel: (02521) 14262/15263*) is easily reached by bus (nos. 50/51) from Haarlem station: get a combined bus/entrance ticket. Trains and buses run also from Amsterdam and Leiden. Lisse is the centre of the Dutch bulb-growing region and its **Museum voor Bloemenbollenstreek** is devoted to bulb culture. The **Keukenhof Gardens** (a 70-acre park, with 16 km of paths) are the showcase of the Dutch bulb industry – take a picnic to avoid overcrowded cafés. The season stretches from late-March to late-May, but the tulips and other flowers are at their best in April.

LONDON to BRUSSELS

This route to the Belgian capital through Flanders includes the medieval towns of Bruges and Ghent. Distances are short and the comprehensive train network is an invitation to wander.

TRAINS

ETT tables: 12, 500, 200.

→ Fast Track

Trains leave London (Victoria) for Ramsgate, from where there are ferry and jetfoil connections to Ostend. From Ostend the journey is by train to Brussels (Nord and Midi). Total journey time is about 8 hrs 30 mins. For details of the ferry services see p. 234. From late summer 1994, direct trains through the Channel Tunnel (see p. 29) will eventually operate hourly, cutting the time to about 3 hrs 10 mins.

⤳ On Line

London (Victoria)–Ramsgate

There are about 2 trains per hour, approximate journey time: 1 hr 45 mins.

Ramsgate–Ostend (Oostende)

Ferry details on p. 234.

Ostend–Bruges (Brugge)

Trains operate at intervals of roughly 30 mins and the journey time is about 15 mins.

Bruges–Ghent (Gent)

Trains run nearly every 30 mins between Bruges and Ghent (Sint-Pieters). The journey time is about 30 mins.

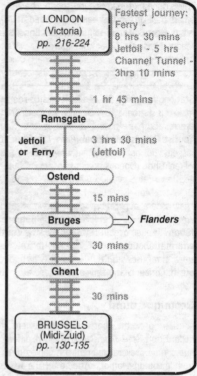

Ghent–Brussels (Bruxelles)

Trains run between Ghent (Sint-Pieters) and Brussels (Midi/Zuid) at intervals of approximately half an hour and the journey takes about 30 mins.

OSTEND (OOSTENDE)

Station: tel: (059) 70 08 81. The ferry terminal and rail station are close together, separated by Customs and Immigration, and only a few minutes walk from the centre of town.

Tourist Office: Monacoplein 2; tel: (059) 70 11 99.

This once-fashionable resort is now primarily a terminal for the cross-Channel ferries, but it is still the busiest beach resort in Belgium. The tall ship **Mercator** (moored opposite Maritime Station), which was a training vessel for the merchant navy, is now a maritime museum. The house where the Expressionist painter James Ensor lived is a museum devoted to him: **James Ensorhuis**, *Vlaanderenstraat 27*.

BRUGES (BRUGGE)

Station: *tel: (050) 38 23 82*. This is beside the main bus station, a 15–20-min walk south of the centre, and has a hotel booking service.

Tourist Offices: Municipal, *Burg 11; tel: (050) 44 86 86*, is housed in the 18th-century Gerechtshof. Open Apr–Sept, Mon–Fri 0930–1830 and Sat–Sun 1000–1200 and 1400–1830; Oct–Mar, Mon–Sat 0930–1245 and 1400–1745. They issue a publication called *Agenda Brugge* which details all the local events. **Regional**, *Kasteel Tillegem; tel: (050) 38 02 96*. The **Youth Information Centre**, *JAC, Kleine Hertsbergestraat 1; tel: (050) 33 83 06*, has lists of budget accommodation and serves as a general youth help centre.

Getting Around

A boat-trip on the canals is a must. There are departures every 15 mins or so from five different quays, run by several different companies (details from the tourist office). After that, the easiest way to explore is on foot, as most places of interest centre on two almost adjoining squares, Markt and Burg, linked by Breidelstraat. The tourist office can suggest good walking routes. You can also take a horse-drawn carriage from the Town Hall: pleasant, but not cheap.

Accommodation

As a major tourist city Bruges offers a good range of hotels, including *Hl, Nv* and *Pu*. There are several small lodging-places along *'t Zand* (west of *Markt*). The **IYHF**, *4/Assebroek, Baron Ruzettelaan 143; tel: (50) 35 26 79*, is about 2 km south of Markt (bus no 2), but there are some private hostels which are more central. Of special interest is the **Bauhaus**, *Langestraat 135–137; tel: (50) 34 10 93*, (bus no 7 from the station). This is very good value and the bar is a popular nightspot with the locals. The nearest **campsite** is St. Michiel, *Tillegemstraat 55; tel: 38 08 19*, 3 km south-west of the station (bus no 7).

Sightseeing

Bruges, the capital of Flanders, is an enchanting and almost perfectly preserved medieval town with a wide range of architectural styles. There is a large student population so, despite its historic attractions, the town is by no means out of touch with the twentieth century.

Three sides of **Markt** consist of gabled guild houses flying medieval banners. **Belfort**, an octagonal 79 m belfry, dominates Bruges. It is a mainly 13th-century structure, but the top storey was added in the 15th century. There are 366 steps to reach the remarkable 47-bell carillon, which rings on the slightest pretext. The great **Hallen** (market), at the foot of the belfry, took over 350 years to complete.

Burg is a cobbled square surrounded by monumental buildings spanning five centuries. These include the Renaissance **Oude Griffie** (Recorder's house); the Baroque **Proosdij** (deanery – not open to the public), the neo-Classical **Gerechtshof** (Court of Justice) and the **Bruges Vrije Museum**: an old magistrate's hall with a superb Renaissance chimneypiece. The 14th-century **Stadhuis** (Town Hall) has sandstone turrets and features a particularly magnificent hall with a vaulted ceiling. The **Baziliek van Het Heilig Bloed** is a Romanesque basilica named for the drop of Holy Blood that is contained in a crystal phial – every Ascension Day this is paraded through the streets in a magnificent gold and silver reliquary.

The **Dijver** is one of the canals, and **Dijverstraat** the canal bank. Every weekend it hosts an antiques and flea market and it is home to two of the city's museums. **Groeningemuseum** (no 12) houses a particularly fine collection of Flemish art from the 14th century to date. Jan van Eyck (who spent the last eleven years of his life in Bruges) is especially well represented. **Gruuthusemuseum** (no 17) is a 15th-century mansion which has fantastic rose-coloured stone tracery and an amazing diversity of exhibits, ranging from lace to weaponry.

Onze-Lieve Vrouwekerk (Church of Our Lady), *Katelijnestraat*, is an architectural mishmash, including Belgium's highest spire (about 120 m). Among the many treasures it contains is a truly beautiful marble *Madonna and Child* by Michelangelo. A little to the south is **Minnewater**, a park with a 16th-century lock-keeper's house and a canal bridge leading to the peaceful 13th-century **Beguinage**.

Sint-Janshospital, *Mariastraat 38*, was once a hospital. Among its patients was the 15th-century Flemish Primitive painter Hans Memling and it is now a museum devoted to his work. Some of the original hospital survives, notably the well-preserved dispensary. A couple of blocks west is the **Kathedral Sint Salvator**, an 18th-century structure with a 13th-century choir that is worthy of close examination.

Huidevettersplein, between Groene Rei and Rozenhoedkaai, is an area of picturesque buildings and terraced cafés that is popular with street artists, so this is the place to come if you want a (literally) personal souvenir. In the summer months, puppet operas are staged at the **Marionette Theatre**, *Sint-Jakobstraat 36*.

GHENT (GENT)

Station: there are three stations, but the main one is **Sint-Pieters** (*tel: (091) 22 44 44*), 2 km south of the centre (take tram nos 1/2/10/11/12 to Korenmarkt).

Tourist Offices: Municipal, *Crypt Stadhuis, Botermarkt 64; tel: (091) 24 15 55*. Open daily 0930–1830 (closing at 1630 in winter). **Provincial**, *Koningin Maria-Hendrikaplein 64; tel: (091) 22 16 37*. Open Mon–Fri 0830–1200 and 1315–1645.

Getting Around

Most of the interesting places are in the small city centre and within easy walking distance of each other. Many different boat excursions and taxi tours are available. Timetables for the public transport (buses and trams) can be obtained from **Maatschappij voor het Intercommunal Vervoer te Gent**, *Brusselsesteenweg 323*.

Accommodation

Major hotels represented include *HI*, *Ib* and *Nv*. For travellers on a budget there are some reasonable lodging-places near the station and rooms are available at the university during the summer vacation (details from the tourist office). The best **campsite** is Blaarmeersen, *Zuiderlaan 12; tel: (091) 21 53 99*, north-west of the station (bus nos 51/52/53).

Sightseeing

Although its claim is disputed by other towns in the area, Ghent is generally considered to be the heart of the Flemish culture. It's a lively place during the university year and peaceful at other times.

Sint-Baafskathedraal, *Limburgstraat*, is a Gothic cathedral with marble ornamentation that is home to Van Eyck's 15th-century masterpiece *The Adoration of the Mystic Lamb*, as well as a 12th-century crypt and ornate guild chapels. **Sint-Michielskerk**, *Sint-Michielstraat*, contains many important religious works of art, including Van Dyck's *Christ Dying on the Cross*. **Sint-Niklaaskerk**, *Korenmarkt*, is the third of Ghent's great churches, but is currently undergoing renovation.

Korenlei, by *Sint-Michielsbrug*, was the heart of the medieval port and is the point from which boat tours leave. It is a picturesque area, with many 18th-century houses, and epitomises the charm of the old town. The 15th-century **Lakenhalle** (Cloth Hall) adjoins the 14th-century **Belfort** (Belfry), *Sint-Baafsplein*. You can take a lift to the top (90 m) for a superb view of the city.

Gravensteen, *Sint-Veerleplein*, is a forbidding 12th-century castle which still dominates its surroundings. It has been put to various uses over the centuries, but the ramparts and torture chamber remain, complete with explanations of how the gruesome instruments were used.

The **Stadhuis** (Town Hall), *Botermarkt*, has a spectacular exterior, the architectural styles ranging from 15th-century Flamboyant Gothic to 18th-century Baroque, with numerous detailed statues of famous figures. On a guided tour, you can see the magnificently decorated *Pacificatiezaal*. The attractive **Museum Voor Sierkunst**, *Jan Breydelstraat 5*, has rooms in period style. The **Museum Voor Volkskunde**, *Kraanlei 65*, is a series of converted almshouses depicting how people lived at the turn of the century.

LONDON
to
PARIS

There is little of major interest on this route, but it's worth at least allowing a few hours for Boulogne.

TRAINS

ETT tables: 10, 102

→ Fast Track

There are several different possibilities on this route. For all sea crossings, the London terminal is Victoria, but for Channel Tunnel trains it is Waterloo International. In Paris, use the Gare du Nord (St-Lazare for Newhaven–Dieppe route). Refreshments are available on the ferries, but seldom on the trains. For details of all the ferries see the next page, and for the Tunnel p. 29.

∿ On Track

Calais–Boulogne

On weekdays there are at least half a dozen trains every day between Calais (Ville) and Boulogne (Ville), but they run at irregular intervals. The weekend service varies considerably. Journey time is 30–45 mins.

Boulogne–Paris

There are at least six trains each day between Boulogne (Ville) and Paris (Nord), taking 2 hrs 15 mins–2 hrs 50 mins. Some of the trains have a refreshment service.

CALAIS

Stations: *Maritime; tel: 21 46 81 65* is by the docks and *Ville; tel: 21 46 81 66* is 5 min-walk from *pl. d'Armes*. Only trains connnecting with

ferries stop at Maritime. Shuttle buses meet all cross-Channel vessels and provide free transport to the centre, from where everything of interest is walkable.

Tourist Office: *12 blvd Georges Clemenceau; tel: 21 96 26 40*. Mon–Sat 0900–1230 and 1400–1830 (July–mid-Sept until 2200).

In front of the picturesque **Town Hall** stands the town's most famous sight, Rodin's superb sculpture of the Burghers of Calais, who saved the town from destruction by the English in 1347. There are also remains of a 13th-century **Watch-tower**, 17th-century **fortifications**, and a couple of **museums**, one about World War II and another (the Fine Arts) partly devoted to machine-made lace.

BOULOGNE

Stations: *Maritime; tel: 21 80 44 40*, is at the docks and *Ville; tel: 21 80 50 50*, is in the centre. Only trains connnecting with ferries stop at Maritime.

Tourist Office: *quai de la Poste; tel: 21 31 68 38*. June–Sept, Sun–Thur 1000–1900 and Fri–Sat 1000–2100; Oct–May, Tue–Sat 0900–1200 and 1400–1800.

Sightseeing

The main reason for a stop in Boulogne is undoubtedly **Nausicaa**, a must for anyone who is at all interested in marine life. It is Europe's largest complex of the kind, devoted to understanding and explaining the marine environment. Opened only in 1991, its facilities include a reference library, a cinema showing documentaries, the piped songs of whales and an experimental centre. Over 300 species of all types (from shrimps to sharks) can be seen in enormous tanks arranged in such a way that you get very close to the creatures (some fish can even be touched) and you almost feel that you, too, are under the sea.

The minor attractions of the fishing port are the 19th-century **Basilique de Notre-Dame**, with crypts containing the remains of a Roman temple, a 12th-century **Belfry** that affords a great view of the port and a 13th-century fortified **Château** that is now a museum.

Cross-Channel Ferries with Rail Connections

Crossing the English Channel by sea (as opposed to by Tunnel – see p. 29) can be a confusing business, with regular ferries, hydrofoils, hovercrafts, etc from England to France, Belgium and the Netherlands, with a widely differing collection of fares and discounts. The price can vary dramatically, and you cannot assume that the shortest crossing is the cheapest. All Channel trains out of London are meant to connect with particular sailings. With the advent of the Channel Tunnel, however, British Rail will no longer actively schedule services for the convenience of ferry passengers. This panel concentrates on the shorter and most popular crossings. For the full range, see the *Thomas Cook European Timetable.*

Cross-Channel Companies

Hoverspeed: Maybrook House, Queen's Garden, Dover, Kent CT17 9UQ; tel: (0304) 240 241. 50% discount for Inter-rail.

Sally Line/Oostende Line: Argyle Centre, York St, Ramsgate CT11 9DS; tel: (0843) 595 522. 50% for Inter-railers ; 35% off for Eurail.

Sealink Stena Line: Charter House, Park St, Ashford, Kent TN24 8EX; tel: (0233) 647 047. 50% discount for Inter-rail.

Best Options

The following routes are linked to connecting train services and offer the best options for the main cross-Channel journeys.

London–Amsterdam

Ramsgate–Oostend Channel crossing 3 hrs 45 mins – 4 hrs 30 mins on the ferry (3 sailings daily); 1 hr 45 mins on the jetfoil (4 crossings daily). Total journey time 11 hrs 15 mins – 12 hrs 20 mins by ferry; 8 hrs 15 mins – 9 hrs 30 mins by jetfoil. Reservations are necessary on all crossings. It is necessary to change trains at Rosendaal (the Belgian–Dutch border) with 5–15 min wait.

Harwich–Hook of Holland Channel crossing 7 hrs (2 sailings daily, including one over-

night). Total journey time 11 hrs – 13 hrs 45 mins. Reservations required for night sailing.

London–Brussels

Ramsgate–Oostend Channel crossing 3 hrs 45 mins – 4 hrs 30 mins on the ferry (3 sailings daily); 1 hr 45 mins on the jetfoil (4 crossings daily). Total journey time is 8 hrs 5 mins – 9 hrs 20 mins (by ferry) or 5 hrs 50 mins – 6 hrs 50 mins (by jetfoil). Reservations needed for all crossings.

London–Paris

Dover–Calais Channel crossing 1hr 15 mins–1 hr 30 mins; total journey time 7–8 hrs (by ferry; 50 sailings a day). (The crossing by Hovercraft takes 35 mins, with 14 sailings a day, and the SeaCat has 8 daily sailings, taking 50 mins, but no trains connect with either of these services).

Folkestone–Boulogne Channel crossing 55 mins (by SeaCat; 1–2 sailings daily); total journey time 6 hrs.

Newhaven–Dieppe Channel crossing 4 hrs; total journey time 9 hrs. There are 2 services daily including one overnight at reduced fares – this is an inconvenient service but is preferred by some because of the low fare.

Catching the Ferry

At Calais (Maritime), Ostend, Harwich (Parkeston Quay), Hook of Holland (Haven), Newhaven (Marine), Folkestone (Harbour) and Boulogne (Maritime), the train will take you to the ferry berth, leaving you only a short walk with your luggage. At Dover the Channel trains stop at the Western Docks station with a free bus connection to the ferries at Eastern Docks. At Dieppe and Ramsgate there are connecting buses between the town station and the port. With the advent of the Channel Tunnel, the stations at Calais (Maritime), Newhaven (Marine), Folkstone (Harbour), Boulogne (Maritime) and Dover (Western Docks) may all eventually close, with connections to the ferries being made from the respective 'town' stations.

MADRID

Madrid is a large, modern city with both the benefits and disadvantages common to such places. The area of interest to visitors is small and easy to get around. Puerta del Sol, although not attractive in itself, is in the centre of the city (and of Spain, since it is the place from which all distances in the country are measured). It is an excellent spot to get your bearings.

Tourist Information

Regional/provincial office: *Edificio Torre de Madrid, Princesa 1, Plaza de España; tel: 541 23 25* open Mon–Fri 0900–1900 and Sat 0930–1330. This is due for renovation, however, and may be temporarily closed. **Branch office:** *Duque de Medinaceli 2; tel: 429 49 51* and *429 44 87*, open Mon–Fri 0900–1900 and Sat 0900–1300/1330. **Municipal office:** *Plaza Mayor 3; tel: 266 54 77*, open Mon–Fri 1000–1400, 1600–2000 and Sat 1000–1400. **Chamartín station** (opposite Platforms 10/11): (*tel: 315 99 76*) open Mon–Fri 0800–2000 and Sat 0800–1300) This office provides leaflets on rail excursions and usually has some in English. If it's closed, try the hotel office opposite Platforms 6/7. **Viajes TIVE** *Calle Fernando el Catolico 88; tel: 543 02 08.* In summer there are temporary tourist (*turismo*) stands in tourist areas. The **Thomas Cook** network member in Madrid, **Viajes International Expreso**, *Fernando el Catolico 61; tel: 549 501 3*, can find accommodation and make travel arrangements.

Arriving and Departing

Airport

Madrid Barajas Airport (*tel: 305 83 43*) is about 16 km north-east of town. There is a tourist office in the International Arrivals Hall (*tel: 205 86 56*), open Mon–Fri 0800–2000 and Sat 0800–1300. A bus operates every 10–15 minutes between the airport and Plaza de Colón in the centre of town. The journey takes about 30 mins (*tel: 431 61 92*).

Stations

Chamartín Station (*Avenida Pio XII; tel: 314 12 22*) is in the northern suburbs. It is Madrid's main station (a very modern place with every conceivable facility) and handles trains to the north, north-east and north-west, including those for France. It is also the terminal for some of the south-bound trains, but most of those stop at Atocha en route.

Part of **Atocha Station** (*Avenida Ciudad de Barcelona; tel: 530 50 36*) is the main terminal for the southern, eastern and western services, and also for trains to Portugal. The older part of the station, **Puerta de Atocha** (*Glorieta Emperador Carlos V; tel: 396 91 80*), is now the terminal for the AVE via Córdoba to Seville.

El Norte Station, also known as **Principe Pío** (*tel: 541 22 25*), is to the west of town, below the Plaza de España. This is now only a suburban station.

All the mainline railway stations are connected to the metro and there is also a special *Apeadero* underground link between Chamartín and Atocha, on which Inter-Rail passes are valid. The *Apeadero* uses Platform 1 in Chamartín, but has its own terminal in Atocha. The main **RENFE** office is at *Calle Alcala 44; tel: 530 02 02* (metro: *Banco de España*).

Getting Around

Excellent street maps can be picked up at the tourist offices or bought at news-stands.

The Metro

The metro (subway) (*tel: 435 22 66* and *552 49 00*) is cheap, efficient and easy to use. The lines are colour-coded and marked according to the last destination. It operates 0600–0130 and free colour maps are available from ticket offices, tourist offices and most hotels. There's a flat fare (Ptas 125), but you save by buying *tacos* (books of ten tickets for Ptas 490).

Buses

The bus system is comprehensive, efficient and the same price as the metro, but not as easy to master. You can get a map of the whole bus system (*Plano de los Transportes*) from the EMT booths on *Plaza de la Cibeles, Callao* or *Puerta del Sol* (*tel: 401 99 00*). There are also route plans on the bus stops (*paradas*). The regular city buses are red and most operate 0600–midnight (there are a few night services from *Plaza de la Cibeles*, with stops marked 'N', but it's safer to stick to taxis if you are out late). There are also smaller, quicker, yellow buses. You save by getting a *Bonobus* ticket (ten rides: Ptas 490). Most long-distance buses pass through the central **Estación del Sur** (*tel: 468 42 00*; metro: *Palos de la Frontera*).

Taxis

Taxis provide an inexpensive way of getting around the centre late at night *tel: 247 82 00* or *445 90 08* or *447 51 80*.

Living in Madrid

Accommodation

Madrid offers the wide range of accommodation that you would expect to find in a major city. Among the main hotel groups you will find *Ch, Hl, Ic, Ml, Nv* and *Pu*.

Brujula is an accommodation service with offices at the airport, bus station, Atocha and Chamartín train stations and on the 6th floor (above the tourist office) of the *Torre de Madrid; tel: 248 97 05*. It covers the whole of Spain and you pay only for long-distance calls.

There is cheap accommodation around Atocha station, but it's not a very pleasant area at night. Try around *Plaza Santa Ana* and on the side streets off *Gran Vía: Calle Fuen-carral*, for instance, is virtually lined with places offering cheap lodgings.

IYHF hostels are located at *Calle Santa Cruz de Marcenado 28; tel: 247 45 3* (metro: *Arguelles*) and at *Richard Schirrmann, Casa de Campo; tel: 463 56 99* (metro: *Lago*).

Madrid's **campsites** are both out of town, but compensate by having enough facilities to be self-contained. *Camping Madrid; tel: 302 28 35* even has a swimming pool; it is 11 km from town on the N-1 road to Burgos (take the metro to Plaza Castilla, then bus nos 151/154/155 to Iglesia de los Dominicos). *Camping Osuna: tel:*

741 05 10 is somewhat noisy, as it is under a flight path. It is 15.5 km from town on the Ajalvir–Vicalvaro road. Take the metro to Canillejas, then bus no 105 to Avenida Logrono.

Communications

The main **post office** is in the Palacio de Comunicaciones, *Plaza de la Cibeles* (metro: *Banco*); open Mon–Fri 0900–1400 (until 2200 for some services) and Sat 0900–1300. Even if you don't want to use it, it's worth a visit just to see the building.

Many Madrid telephone numbers beginning with a 2 are being changed to begin with a 5, but this is not happening overnight and there is no real way of being sure which numbers have already been changed. If you try a 2 and can't get through, substitute a 5 – and vice versa.

If you want to make an international call, the main **Telefónica office** is at *Gran Vía 30*; open daily 0900–midnight. There are branches at *Calle Virgen de los Peligros* and the *Palacio de Comunicaciones*.

Eating and Drinking

Restaurantes típicos are places with some atmosphere that specialise in Spanish cuisine. You should book if you want to go to a Catalan or top seafood restaurant.

The old town area south-west of *Plaza Mayor* is good for restaurants. Arguelles has a range of cheap eating-places, so do *Calles Echegaray* and *Manuel Fernandez Gonzalez* (near *Plaza Santa Ana*). There are also many *tapas* bars around *Plaza Mayor* and *Plaza Santa Ana*. Two good areas for eating cheaply are Huertas and the old town to the south-west of Plaza Mayor.

Chiringuitos are beer gardens with discos: there are quite a few on Paseo de la Castellana and Paseo del Prado.

Embassies and Consulates

Australia *Paseo Castellana 143; tel: 579 04 28.*
Canada *Calle Nunez de Balboa 35; tel: 431 43 00.*
New Zealand *Plaza Lealtad 2 (3rd Floor); tel: 523 02 26.*
UK *Calle Fernando el Santo 16; tel: 319 02 80.*
USA *Calle Serrano 75; tel: 262 80 20.*

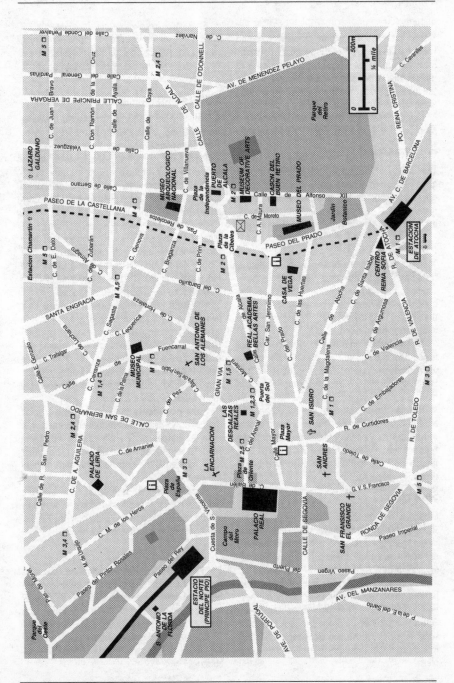

Security

Madrid has most of the crime problems common to large cities throughout the world, but in many areas you are just as safe by night as by day since the Madrileños are sociable people and most of the streets are crowded in the evenings. Women alone should not linger around the seedier parts of Huertas, Malasana or Chueca, but can avoid problems if they head straight for their target.

Entertainment

The *Guía del Ocio* is a weekly publication that gives listings of what's on, including theatre, opera and cabaret and is available from most news-stands. There's also a handout from hotels, etc, called *En Madrid* with similar information.

Nightlife

There's excellent nightlife, with numerous restaurants, bars and dance venues. Live music can be found easily. At weekends most bars stay open until 0300 and many close much later than that. Discos tend to have a cover charge, but bars with dance floors don't.

The **Malasana** area (metro: *Bilbao/Tribunal*) is good for music and bars and popular with a wide range of age groups. It centres on the Plaza Dos de Mayo, Calle de Velarde and Calle de Ruiz.

Huertas (metro: *Anton Martín*) is the area around Plaza Santa Ana and has a huge variety of bars that stay open until all hours. **Paseo del Prado** (metro: *Atocha/Banco de España*) is a rather more up-market area with smart and expensive cafe-bars.

Shopping

Madrid is not the best place in the world for shopping but, if you like to window-shop, several of the main upmarket shopping streets run off, or parallel to, *Calle Serrano*, which is the Spanish equivalent of Knightsbridge or Fifth Avenue.

If you don't like to come away empty-handed, food, such as wine or oil, is the best buy because it's fairly cheap throughout Spain. Get it from corner shops in the back streets or supermarkets. The **Museo de Jamón** (near Sol) is a shop, not a museum, but it's rather a fun place.

El Rastro (metro: *Latina*) is a flea-market which is something of a Sunday-morning institution. It's best to go early because it can be impossibly crowded by midday and begins to pack up around 1400.

Sightseeing

A leaflet called *Conozcamos Madrid* (available from the municipal tourist office) lists walking tours for Spanish-speakers.

Plaza Mayor (metro: *Sol*) is a stately square surrounded by grandiose 17th-century buildings, at which time it was a centre for Spanish society and the place where such pleasant entertainments as bullfighting and the Inquisition's *autos-da-fe* were staged. Today, the pleasures are more civilised: you can sit at a pavement café, admire the equestrian statue of King Philip III and watch the world go by. The old Hapsburg area to the south-west of Plaza Mayor is the most attractive in Madrid.

The **Retiro** (metro: *Retiro/Atocha*) is a park laid out in the 17th century, a cool place with wooded corners, formal avenues, brilliant flowers and a large boating lake. Adjoining it is the **Jardín Botanico** (metro: *Atocha*), a delightful place with three separate terraces, some of which feature vegetables as well as the more usual shrubs and flowers.

Plaza de Oriente (metro: *Opera*) is a small garden opposite the palace that is adorned with over 40 statues of Spanish royalty, notably a splendid equestrian statue of Philip IV. Another lovely garden is the **Campo del Marco**, behind the palace.

Plaza de la Villa is a small square in the oldest part of Madrid. It is surrounded by mainly 16th- and 17th-century buildings in Renaissance, Mudejar and Baroque style.

Galleries and Museums

The **Prado** (metro: *Atocha/Banco de España*) is one of the world's greatest art galleries, with individual sections devoted to Goya, Velazquez, Murillo, Zurbaran and El Greco. The Italian and Flemish schools are also very well represented.

Picasso's masterpiece *Guernica* is in the new art museum **Centro Reina Sofia** (metro: *Atocha*).

The **National Archaeological Museum** (metro: *Serrano* and *Colón*) contains a major collection of articles from all over Spain, including some stone-carved Iberian mother-goddesses from the 4th century BC. In the grounds is a full-scale reproduction of the Altamira Caves: they contain one of the world's greatest sets of early cave paintings.

The late Renaissance **Palacio Real** (metro: *Opera*) is an 18th-century building of Italian design, with colonnaded arches. The state rooms (they are still used as such from time to time) were decorated in the 18th and 19th centuries and are full of priceless treasures: Tiepolo frescoes, magnificent tapestries, glittering chandeliers, decorative clocks, silverware, gilt ornamentation and works by a variety of famous artists – which are rather swamped by their surroundings. There are also an 18th-century pharmacy, a huge hall lined by prancing horses and an interesting armoury.

The **Museum of Decorative Arts** (metro: *Retiro*) displays a stunning collection of furniture, ceramics, porcelain, glass, leather, dolls' houses, together with a wide range of other handicrafts.

At the **Tapestry Factory** (metro: *Menendez Pelayo*) you can watch tapestries being made by traditional methods. There's also a display of Goya cartoons.

The 16th-century **Convento de las Descalzas Reales** (metro: *Sol*) was a convent for noblewomen and handsomely endowed by their families. It still houses a closed order, but parts of it are open: it has a superb collection of 16th- and 17th-century religious art (fittingly displayed in a series of shrines) and many other treasures, including a magnificent series of tapestries with Rubens designs.

Lázaro Galdiano (metro: *Ruben Darío/ Avenida de America*) is a major museum with a superb collection of ivory and enamel work, jewellery and paintings.

The **Thyssen-Bornemisza** museum (metro: *Banco de España*) is one of Madrid's newest attractions. After lending the city his priceless 800-piece art collection for a limited period, Baron Thyssen decided (in 1993) that it should be permanently on display to the public.

The small **Convent of the Incarnation** (metro: *Santo Domingo*) has a unique room that is totally lined with reliquaries (over 1,500 of them). Some are exquisite, others grotesque, but the whole place is amazing.

Side Tracks from Madrid

Remember that seat reservations are essential for most trains. Where they are not possible, you should arrive early.

EL ESCORIAL

Tourist Office: *Calle Floridablanca 10; tel: 890 15 54.*

This is 52 km from Madrid and there are several trains every day (from Chamartín station, stopping at Atocha, and taking about an hour), but the Escorial railway station is a little out of town and it's a long uphill walk, so it's better to take a local shuttle bus to the centre. The **Empresa Herranz** buses (*tel: 543 81 67*) are faster than the trains and take you right to the palace. There are around 15 a day and the journey takes an hour, departing from *Calle Fernandez de los Ríos* (metro: *Moncloa*).

El Escorial is a magnificent 16th-century complex that includes a monastery, a church, a library with nearly 3,000 5th–18th-century documents and a mausoleum. Many notable works of art are on display in the complex, some forming an intrinsic part of the decor.

The actual palace is of particular interest, the austere quarters of Philip II being in marked contrast to the luxurious apartments used by the Bourbons.

AVILA AND SEGOVIA

Both towns are easily accessible by train from Chamartín or Principe Pío. Alternatively, you could take the bus (*tel: 230 48 00*) from *Paseo de la Florida 11* (next to Norte station). The journey takes 1 hr 30 mins–2 hrs.

Avila Tourist Office *Plaza de la Catedral 4; tel: 35 71 26.* The bus and train stations are about a mile from the centre, but you can get a tram. The town's main attractions are the

Cathedral, the **Basilica of San Vincente** and the **Monastery of Santo Tomas** plus many buildings associated with **Saint Teresa of Avila**.

Segovia Tourist Office *Plaza Mayor 10; tel: 43 03 28*. Bus no 3 will get you from the bus or train station to the centre. There are a remarkable number of attractions for a small place, the most notable being the **Cathedral**, the **Alcazar** and the **Roman aqueduct**.

TOLEDO

Station: *Paseo de la Rosa; tel: 22 12 72*.
Tourist Offices: The main office is at *Puerta Nueva de Bisagra s/n; tel: 22 08 43*. There is also a branch at *Plaza Zocodover; tel: 22 14 00*.

Between Madrid (Atocha) and Toledo there are eight trains a day and the journey time is 1 to 1 hr 30 mins. There are also plenty of buses every day, the journey taking about 1 hr 30 mins.

Accommodation

It can be difficult to find space on summer weekends. The best cheap accommodation is in the old town: try around Juan Labrador, Descalzos and Perala. There is a **IYHF** on the outskirts of town in a wing of *Castillo San Servando; tel: 22 45 54*. The **university** sometimes has rooms available.

Campsites are located at *Circo Romano 21* (10 mins walk from Puerta de Bisagra but not very comfortable) and *El Greco*: much better facilities, but 1.5 km out of town, on the road to Madrid.

Getting Around

To get into the city centre (either the main tourist office or Plaza Zocodover) from either the railway station or the bus terminal, take bus nos 5/6 (every 15 mins). If you prefer to walk (it's a pleasant route), allow around 20 minutes.

The authorities are planning to ban normal traffic from the old town. When this happens they will provide some type of special ride to take visitors to the places of major interest, which are close enough together for walking between them to be sensible. However, the old town is a labyrinthine place (and many of the street names are not marked), so get a map and refer to it often to keep track of where you are.

Sightseeing

The main buildings in Toledo are perched on a hill, surrounded by ancient walls and with the River Tagus forming a natural moat on three sides. It's a place with history in every street and you can easily understand how it inspired El Greco, who lived and worked here for nearly 40 years.

Inevitably, there are hordes of tourists and the tacky shops and stalls that spring up to cash in on them, but they do sell souvenirs which relate specifically to the town. The triangular **Plaza Zocodover**, with its arcades and cafés, is the animated centre. Heading off it are Calle del Comercio (which leads towards the cathedral and many other monuments) and Cuesta del Alcazar, which goes where its name suggests.

The **Alcazar** (old fortress) has been rebuilt many times and the current structure dates largely from the 1930s. It houses a museum which is a must for anyone interested in military matters.

Museo de Santa Cruz just east of Plaza de Zocodover contains some notable religious paintings and a 15th-century zodiacal tapestry.

Toledo **Cathedral** is a fascinating mixture of styles, having taken over 250 years to complete. It's a marvellous place, with stained-glass windows to light your exploration, elaborate decorations and countless works of art, notably the *Transparente*: a marble sculpture positioned to catch the light in a most dramatic way.

In the **Aljama**, the old Jewish quarter on the west side of the old quarter, are the only two surviving synagogues. **El Transito** is a 14th-century Mudejar edifice with a ceiling of carved cedar, silk-covered walls and Hebrew texts. The 12th-century synagogue of **Santa María la Blanca** is very different: its conversion into a Christian church did not affect the basic layout of the lovely interior, where 5 aisles are formed by 24 pillars supporting arches with unusual capitals and stone carvings.

MADRID
to
BARCELONA

This route leads from the centre of Spain to Valencia, crossing La Mancha (home of Don Quixote), and then follows the eastern coast to Barcelona. It will appeal to anyone who has a feel for history.

TRAINS

ETT tables: 410, 420, 419, 415.

→ Fast Track

The quick journey is via Zaragoza, unlike the full route below. Most trains serve Chamartín in Madrid and Sants in Barcelona, but a few stop at the other stations as well (or instead), so check carefully before travelling. The ordinary trains operate at least once a day (taking 8 hrs–8 hrs 30 mins) and at least three times a night (with sleepers, taking 8 hrs 30 mins–9 hrs 30 mins). There are also three Talgos a day, which take only 6–7 hours, but carry a supplement. All the trains have a refreshment service.

∿ On Track

Madrid–Aranjuez

There are at least a dozen trains a day (Talgo and otherwise) between Madrid (normally Chamartín, but some use Atocha) and Aranjuez. The journey time varies considerably from 25 mins to 1 hr 30 mins.

Aranjuez–Cuenca

There are four to six trains a day, the journey taking about 2 hrs.

Cuenca–Valencia

There are three trains a day between Cuenca

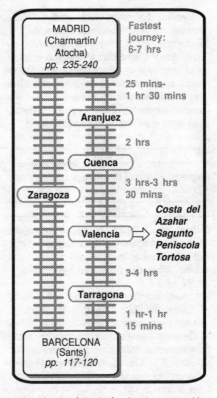

and Valencia (Término), the journey taking about 3 hrs–3 hrs 45 mins.

Valencia–Tarragona

There are at least eight trains a day between Valencia (Término) and Tarragona. Journey time is around 3–4 hrs. Some call at Valencia-Cabanyal as well. Most trains have a buffet .

Tarragona–Barcelona

There is a good service between Tarragona and Barcelona (mostly Sants): 1 hr–1 hr 15 mins.

ARANJUEZ

Station: *tel: 891 02 02.* 1 km outside town, the station is a 10-minute (signposted) walk from the palace.
Tourist Office: *Puente de Barcas s/n; tel: 891 04 27.*

Situated on the south bank of the Tagus, Aranjuez has just one major attraction: a palace-museum.

The **Royal Palace** started life as a country house that was presented to Ferdinand and Isabella, but the present structure dates from the 18th century and is a succession of opulently-furnished rooms full of marble mosaics, crystal chandeliers, Flemish tapestries and the like. In the gardens are ancient elms, the **Casita del Labrador** (strongly resembling the Petit Trianon at Versailles) and the **Casa de Marinos** (where the pleasure boats of six sovereigns can be seen).

CUENCA

Station: *tel: 22 07 20.* The road leads straight up to the old town, but it's a hard climb and most people prefer to take a bus (nos 1/2).

Tourist Office: *Calle Dalmacio Garcia Izcara 8; tel: 22 22 31.*

The main attraction is the old town itself, particularly the **Casas Colgadas**: tiered houses that hang over a sheer chasm.

The old quarter is a delightful place, just made for hill-walking; there are arches where houses span the alleys, finely carved wooden balconies, armorial bearings, impressive doorways and some breath-taking views.

The authorities are planning to close the old town to normal traffic but, when they do, there will be a special shuttle service.

The central **Plaza Mayor** is about the only level part of the old town. Don't be put off by the exterior of the **Cathedral**: the interior is very fine and houses a good treasury. The best museums are the **Diocesan Museum** and the **Museo de Arte Abstracto**. The latter is in one of the hanging houses and gives you the chance to inspect the carved balconies at close quarters. For a fine view, try the **Puente San Pablo**.

VALENCIA

Stations: There are two major RENFE stations: **Término del Norte** (*tel: (6) 352 93 62*), which is centrally located and **Cabanyal** (*tel: (6) 356 21 67*), which is the station serving the ferries and is 5 mins (by rail) from Término del Norte.

There is also a **FEVE** station (for local towns) near *Museo de Bellas Artes* opposite Torres Serranos.

Tourist Offices: *Calle de la Paz 48; tel: (6) 352 40 00* and *Plaza Ayuntamiento 1; tel: (6) 351 04 17.* At Norte *tel: (6) 352 28 82,* at Manises *tel: (6) 153 03 25.*

The lively modern city is a place with many lush parks and gardens, elaborate Baroque facades and orange groves. Paella (traditionally eaten for lunch, not in the evening) originated here.

Valencia is also famous for *Fallas,* a week-long festival in mid-March which centres on a competition to produce the best *ninot* (papier mâché doll). The whole town celebrates as the entries are paraded through the streets and (on the last night) ritually burned, to the accompaniment of an enormous fireworks display.

Getting Around

The area covered by the old town (where most sights of interest are located) is small and you can easily walk between them. There is a good bus service during the day but you may have to get a taxi at night if you're out late.

EMT buses operate throughout the city (*tel: (6) 352 83 99*). You can buy tickets either when you board or from news-stands: they are available in books of ten, which represent a saving. Most buses can be boarded in Plaza Ayuntamiento.

Accommodation

There are some really cheap places in the area of Norte (notably on *Calle Bailen* and *Calle Pelayo*), but they are not very salubrious and you may prefer to spend a bit more and stay either out by the beach or in the centre. Good areas to try are around *Plaza Ayuntamiento* and *Plaza Mercat* – but avoid Barrio Chino (the red-light district).

IYHF: La Paz on *Colegio Mayor, Avenida del Puerto 69. tel: (6) 361 74 59* (halfway between *Plaza Ayuntamiento* and the ferry terminal – bus no19).

The most convenient **Campsite** is El Saler, which has a good beach and is located 10 km south of the city (bus from Puerta del Mar, at the end of Glorieta Park).

Sightseeing

Many historical structures were destroyed by inept town planners and the Spanish Civil War put paid to most of the rest, so the town is largely modern, but two medieval gates survive (**Torres de Serranos** and **Torres de Cuarte**) and there is an old quarter with some pleasant squares and (rather run-down) Baroque mansions.

Plaza del Ayuntamiento (also called **Plaza del Pais Valenciano**) is the hub of the city. A few hundred metres to the north, extending to the River Turia, is the old quarter, **Barrio del Carmen**. **Plaza de la Virgen** is dominated by two octagonal towers: the Baroque spire of **Santa Catalina** and the **Miguelete**, which is the unfinished tower of the cathedral.

The **Cathedral** is the town's most interesting building: a mixture of styles. A 1st-century agate chalice adorned with gold and pearls is said to be the Holy Grail and is displayed behind the altar, against alabaster reliefs.

Next door is **Nuestra Señora de los Desamparados** and just across the way is the **Palacio de la Generalidad**, which has two tower rooms with gilded ceilings.

The Gothic **Lonja de la Seda** (*Calle Caballeros*), with its exquisitely designed interior, is a reminder that Valencia was prominent in the 15th-century silk trade. Across the street is the **Mercado Central** (market), an ornate building with a stained glass ceiling and many *azulejos*.

The **Colegio del Patriarca**, *Plaza Patriarca*, contains a small art museum with sculptures, tapestries, *azulejos* and a variety of paintings. The **Palacio de Dos Aguas**, *Riconda García Sanchíz*, has an extraordinary alabaster doorway and contains the **Ceramics Museum**: a vast range of exhibits, from the Iberian period to the present day. The neighbouring **San Juan de la Cruz** is almost as decorative.

◠ Side Tracks from Valencia

Transmediterránea on *Avenida Manuel Soto* (tel: *(6) 367 07 04*) operate regular ferries to the **Balearic Islands** – Majorca, Minorca and Ibiza – from Estación Maritima (*tel: (6) 323 75 80*).

The coastal strip from Valencia to Castellon, the **Costa del Azahar**, is named after the orange blossom that grows there, sheltered from the harsh *meseta* wind by the mountains which rise steeply a few kilometres inland from the sea. This area, along the western Mediterranean coast, has generally suffered the consequences of mass tourism, but it is still worth a visit.

Sagunto has the remains of a 2nd-century amphitheatre (*Teatro Romano*) and is crowned by the ruins of a citadel giving good views. Further north, **Peniscola** stands on a small peninsula, a charming village of whitewashed houses and winding streets surrounding a spectacular 14th-century castle.

Towards **Tortosa**, the **Delta de l'Ebre** Natural Park, with its long, deserted beaches and sand dunes, is home to some 60% of all European bird species (not accessible by public transport).

TARRAGONA

Station: *Plaza de la Estacion s/n; tel: (77) 23 13 59*. This is centrally located.
Tourist Office: *Rambla Nova 46; tel: (77) 23 21 43*.

Founded in 218 BC, Tarragona prospered under the Romans and many traces of their city have survived, including bits of temples, forums and a theatre. There are also a necropolis and an aqueduct, a little way out of town.

The city is in two parts: the medieval walled town is on a limestone bluff overlooking the sea and the modern town is lower down, **Rambla Vella** being the dividing line. The **Paseo Arqueologico** is lined on one side by 3rd-century BC Roman walls. The **Museo Arqueologico** is crammed with impressive Roman sculptures, bronzes and mosaics. The neighbouring **Museum of History** is unusually well-laid-out, built over Roman walls.

La Seu (the cathedral) should not be missed. It is a beautiful church that is a superb example of the transition from Romanesque to Gothic. The interior includes rose windows and a gilded alabaster retable and is full of fascinating detail.

MADRID to LISBON

This route, linkis Spain and Portugal through Estremadura, the historic homeland of the Conquistadores. Its delightful old towns owed their prosperity to the vast wealth brought back from the Americas by these adventurers .

TRAINS

ETT tables: 80, 433, 445.

→ Fast Track

There are two services daily between Madrid and Lisbon (Santa Apolónia). The daytime train Luis Camoens (to/from Atocha) takes about 8 hrs and carries a supplement. The overnight train Estrella Lusitania (which departs from Chamartín) takes nearer 10 hrs, but has first- and second-class seating, couchettes and sleepers. There are dining cars and through carriages on both trains, so no change is necessary at the border, but seat reservations are required.

∿ On Track

Madrid–Talavera de la Reina

There are six trains daily between Madrid and Talavera; two are Talgos (supplement payable) however, and those departing from Chamartín are very slow, so the three which use Atocha are the best bet: they take about 1 hr 30 mins.

Talavera de la Reina–Cáceres

There are four fast trains and two Talgos every day; journey time is about 2 hrs 30 mins.

Cáceres–Valencia de Alcantara

There are two trains a day, the journey taking around 1 hr 30 mins.

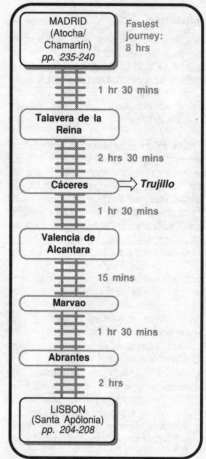

MADRID (Atocha/Chamartín) *pp. 235-240* — Fastest journey: 8 hrs

1 hr 30 mins

Talavera de la Reina

2 hrs 30 mins

Cáceres ⟹ *Trujillo*

1 hr 30 mins

Valencia de Alcantara

15 mins

Marvao

1 hr 30 mins

Abrantes

2 hrs

LISBON (Santa Apólonia) *pp. 204-208*

Valencia de Alcantara–(Border)–Marvão

There are two trains daily. A supplement is payable for the Luis de Camoens, but it operates in the early evening (taking 15 mins). The Estrella Lusitania departs in the early hours of the morning.

Marvão–Abrantes

There are two trains daily, but only one (the Talgo) operates during the day. You have a choice between paying the supplement for this or travelling by the other in the early hours of the morning. The journey takes about 1 hr 30 mins.

Abrantes–Lisbon (Lisboa)

Seven trains a day run between Abrantes and Lisbon (Santa Apolónia). The journey takes about 2 hrs.

TALAVERA DE LA REINA

Station: *tel: (925) 80 13 88.* This is about 1 km from the city centre.

Talavera is the centre of a ceramics industry and famous for the attractive blue and yellow tiles (*azulejos*) which have been produced here since the 15th century: these can be seen adorning many buildings. The **Museo Ruiz de Luna** displays 15th–19th-century pottery. The **Capilla de Nuestra Señora del Prado** is adorned with 16th–18th-century tiles.

CÁCERES

Station: the bus and train stations are together, about 1.5 km out of town on *Avenida Alemania; tel: (927) 22 08 31.* There is a free bus transfer every half-hour between the station and the centre, from where there are signs to the Plaza Mayor.
Tourist Office: *Plaza Mayor 37; tel: (927) 24 63 47.*

Accommodation

There is a good choice of hotels, including *Ml* and *Pr*; the best area for both staying and eating cheaply is in the vicinity of *Plaza Mayor.*

IYHF: *Colegio 'Donoso Cortés', Rda de San Francisco s/n; tel: (927) 22 89 01.*

Getting Around

There are buses and taxis, but the way to explore the old town is on foot. The places of interest are almost all around (or just off) either the *Plaza de Santa María* or the *Plaza San Mateo*, and the two plazas are not far apart. It's easy to get lost in the maze of streets, however, so arm yourself with a good map of the old town.

Sightseeing

Cáceres is a truly charming place crammed with so much of interest that it has been declared a World Heritage site. Yet it is relatively unknown and visitors are still almost outnumbered by the storks that have built nests on every conceivable perch. The ancient city walls surround a largely intact old town which is a marvellous place to explore. Do go back after dark, just to absorb the atmosphere; you really feel that you have stepped into another century.

The cobbled, partially-arcaded **Plaza Mayor** borders the old town and is the obvious place from which to start exploring. On one side is the **Torre del Horno**, a well-preserved Moorish structure of mud-brick. On the other side is the **Torre de Bujaco**, a Moorish tower on Roman foundations. The **Arco de la Estrella** leads to the areas of interest.

The **Plaza de Santa María** is lined with fine buildings, including the Gothic **Cathedral**, which contains sarcophagi and a 16th-century retable; the **Palacio de Mayoralgo**; and the 16th-century **Episcopal Palace**, decorated with engravings of the Old and New Worlds.

The **Casa Toledo-Moctezuma** was built by the grandson of Tecuixpo Istlaxoohitl (a.k.a. Isobel Moctezuma), an Aztec princess who married Juan Cano de Saavedra, a follower of Cortés.

The **Carvajal Palace** houses the tourism and craft council but you can visit the chapel and the first floor gallery (decorated in 19th-century style). Almost next door is the **Palacio de los Golfines de Abajo**, which has an impressive Plateresque facade and twin-arched Romanesque windows. There are many other old mansions with imposing coats of arms and gargoyles. A little to the south, at the top of the hill on which the old city stands, is the 15th-century Gothic **Church of San Mateo** (*Plaza San Mateo*), a place which is a fascinating mixture of external styles and contains a Baroque altarpiece as well as the tombs of many nobles. The 15th-century **San Francisco Javier** has a fine late-Gothic church and cloister.

The **Casa de las Veletas** was built on the foundations of a Moorish citadel and contains an Almohade water cistern (*aljibe*) with a vaulted ceiling supported by horseshoe arches. It houses a small provincial museum. The **Casa de los Pereros** holds constantly changing exhibitions of contemporary art.

◈ Side Track from Cáceres

From Cáceres you can get to **Trujillo**; there is no rail link, but there are about a dozen buses a day from the main bus station in Cáceres. The 5 km journey takes about half an hour.

Although a 10th-century **Moorish Castle** overlooks the town (which is 5 km east of Cáceres), Trujillo is a place built largely from the proceeds of the Peruvian conquests and known as the 'Cradle of the Conquistadores'.

The **Tourist Office** at *Plaza de España s/n (tel: (927) 32 06 53)* provides good maps which include some background about the families who commissioned the town's main buildings.

From the bus station, it's an uphill walk to **Plaza Mayor**, at the heart of the town. The square is built on different levels, connected by steps, and lined with once-magnificent palace-mansions, arcades and whitewashed houses. It is dominated by a bronze statue of Francisco Pizarro, mounted and in full regalia. The beautiful Plateresque **Palacio de la Conquista** was built by Hernando Pizarro (the elaborate window grilles and corner balcony are particularly attractive) and there are many other 16th/17th-century seigneurial mansions with lavish armorial bearings.

The **Calle de Ballesteros** leads from the square up to the old walls (passing the domed **Torre del Alfiler**), in which there is a gateway that gives access to the 13th-century Romanesque-Gothic church of **Santa María la Mayor**. This is on the site of an Arab mosque and contains Roman sarcophagi as well as the tombs of the Pizarros and other Spanish heroes. The winged retable by Fernando Gallego has 25 panels depicting a range of religious subjects.

VALENCIA DE ALCANTARA

Station: *Estación RENFE; tel: (927) 58 00 72.* This is about 2.5 km from the city centre.

The Spanish frontier town is a small, pleasant place with old walls and a ruined 13th-century Moorish castle. Within the walls are the 13th-century **Iglesia de la Encarnación**, which has a fine Gothic facade, and the 16th-century **Iglesia de Nuestra Señora del Rocamador**, with a figure of Christ, attributed to Berruguete.

Some nearby dolmens testify to the presence of man in prehistoric times.

MARVÃO

Station: Marvão's own station, Beira, is not very near the town. Better to get off at **Castelo de Vide** station, which is itself some 13 km away and take a taxi to Marvão (there are no buses). **Tourist Office:** *Rua do Dr Matos Magalhaes; tel: 932 26.*

Marvão is a small, remote medieval town, perched high on a peak of the ridge which forms a natural border with Spain. It is dominated by a 13th-century **Castle** on a wooded hill above the town, from which there are fine views in every direction. There are several pretty chapels with Renaissance touches.

ABRANTES

Station: Rossio S, *tel: (041) 314 06* or *314 66*. This is about 4 km south of the town centre, on the other side of the River Tagus.
Tourist Office: *Largo da Feira; tel: (041) 225 55.*

Perched high above the Tagus, Abrantes was built to defend the old Beira province. It is a small place and retains much of its original character. Above the town, approached through a maze of flower-bedecked alleys, are the remains of the 14th-century **Castle** built by King Dinis. The keep has been partially restored and is now a belvedere offering panoramic views of the town, the Tagus Valley and the mountains. The 13th-century **Church of Santa Maria do Castelo** (in the castle grounds) was restored in the 15th century and houses a museum containing an interesting collection of Gothic works of art and *azulejos*.

The **Church of São João Baptista**, rebuilt in the 16th century, has some excellent wood carvings and a Renaissance ceiling. The 16th-century **Church of the Misericordia** and 15th-century **Convent of São Domingas** are also worth a visit.

MADRID
to
MÁLAGA

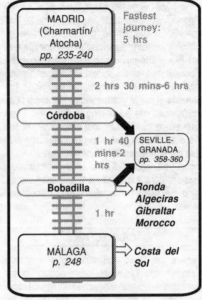

This route connects the Spanish capital with the Mediterranean coast. Its principal interest is in its side-tracks into the historic region of Andalusia and the popular seaside resorts of the Costa del Sol, and the opportunity it gives to visit the British enclave of Gibraltar and even Morocco.

TRAINS

ETT tables: 425, 426.

→ Fast Track

There are 2 direct Talgo services on the AVE fast line, 2 conventional expresses and an overnight sleeping car/couchette train (with second-class seats). The fastest journey, by the Talgo services, is 4 hrs 40 mins.

∿∿ On track

Madrid–Córdoba–Bobadilla

This route coincides with the Seville–Granada route, p. 358, as far as Bobadilla, and the same train information applies. From Córdoba or Bobadilla you can switch to that route before resuming your journey to the coast. For the description of Córdoba, see p. 359.

Bobadilla–Málaga

There are 11 trains a day, but 5 of these leave before 1000 from Bobadilla or after 1900 from Málaga and there are long gaps between other services. The journey takes about 1 hr.

BOBADILLA

From this stop you can detour to Seville ·or Granada (see above) or to take the following Side-track, which leads via the picturesque town of Ronda before terminating at Algeciras, virtually the southernmost point in Spain.

⌒ Side tracks from Bobadilla

Five daily trains from Bobadilla (but only 3 of these depart at a rerasonable hour) take just over 1 hr to reach Ronda, and another 1 hr 45 mins more to Algeciras. From Algeciras, itself an industrialised port of little tourist interest, it is possible to visit the British colony of Gibraltar, or even take a ferry to **Morocco**.

RONDA

Tourist Office: *Plaza de España; tel: (952) 87 12 72.*

Ronda is a small town of pre-Roman origin set in the midst of the rugged Serrania de Ronda mountains. Its main claim to fame is the impressive 18th-century bridge, the **Puente Nuevo**, spanning a deep gorge which divides the town in half. The view from the bridge is astonishing – even more so is the sight of the bridge from below, although this entails a fairly long walk from the town. It was in Ronda that Pedro Romero invented the modern style of bullfighting – on foot rather than from horseback – and the bullring, a short walk from the bridge, is one of the oldest, and certainly the smallest, in Spain. Close by the bullring is the **Alameda**, a public garden laid out by the side of the ravine with stunning views over the surrounding plains. On the other side of the bridge is the Moorish quarter; the attractive **Casa del Rey Moro** (house of the Moorish King) despite its name is an early 18th-century mansion. Ronda is at its most charming during one of the many fiestas which occur throughout the year.

GIBRALTAR

There is no direct rail connection. Frequent buses run from **Algeciras**, taking about 50 mins to reach the Spanish frontier town of **La Linéa**. From here you literally walk across the border into Gibraltar (passports needed). It is also possible to take a bus from Málaga or any of the other coastal resorts (up to 2 hrs).
Tourist Office: *Cathedral Square; tel: 76400*
Thomas Cook network member: Lucas Imossi Travel, *1–5 Irish Town; tel: 73525.*

The Rock of Gibraltar reaches a height of 430 m, occupying a strategic position at the southern tip of Spain that has made it a military prize since ancient times. In 1704 Gibraltar was seized by the Royal Navy, and despite several attempts at reconquest it has remained in British hands, becoming a Crown Colony in 1830. The population is of mainly Genoese and Spanish descent, but the ambience tries to be as British as possible, from English-style pubs to the **Changing of the Guard** every Monday morning outside the Governor's residence (*Main St*). To remind yourself you are nearly in North Africa, and to enjoy stunning views across the Straits towards the Atlas Mountains, take one of the **cable cars** that run all day from *Alameda Gardens* to the summit. They stop halfway up at the den of the famous **Barbary apes**, which live in packs on the upper reaches of the Rock.

The British military presence is low-key these days, but the **Upper Galleries**, 100 m of tunnels excavated at the end of the 18th century to provide artillery positions, are evidence of Gibraltars embattled past.

MÁLAGA

Station: RENFE, in the city centre; *tel. (95) 236 02 02*. Local trains for the coastal resorts leave from here as well (at a different level), and this railway is also served by another centrally located station, Centro Alameda.
Tourist Office: *C. Marqués de Larios 5; tel: 21 34 45.*

The fourth-largest city in Spain and a busy working port, Málaga is the communications centre for the holiday coasts on either side of it. It makes few concessions to tourism, but the resolutely Spanish character of its streets, restaurants and hotels can be refreshing in the midst of the international and commercialised atmosphere of the rest of the Costa del Sol.

Málaga's historic past is most evident in the area near the port. The long, shady walks of the **Paseo del Parque** are overlooked by the 8th-century **Alcazaba**, a fort built by the Moors on Roman foundations, and the **Gibralfaro** castle, of even older origin. Just off the Paseo is the **Cathedral**, set in a secluded square and noteworthy for its stump of a tower, unfinished because the money for its construction was diverted to support the American forces in the War of Independence.

Side tracks from Málaga

A frequent train service runs west from Málaga (Centro-Alameda and RENFE stations) along the **Costa del Sol**, connecting it to the airport and the busy resorts of **Torremolinos**, **Benalmádena** and **Fuengirola**. Málaga is also at the centre of a bus network reaching out further west to many smaller resorts, and **Marbella**, **Estepona** and as far as **Gibraltar**. Eastwards it is possible to reach **Nerja**, famous for its caves, and assorted seaside towns all the way to **Almeria**.

MARSEILLE

Cosmopolitan gateway to the Mediterranean, Marseille will surprise and invigorate, a far cry from the gritty image known through films.

Tourist Information

Main tourist office: *4 Canebière; tel: 91 54 91 11.* Open summer 0830–2000 daily; winter Mon–Sat 0900–1930, Sun 1000–1700. Service is very helpful. The information desk at Gare St Charles (*tel: 91 50 59 18*) is open summer 0800–2000 daily; winter closed lunchtime and open until 1800, closed at weekends. An information office for younger travellers, **Centre Information Jeunesse**, is at *4 rue de la Visitation; tel: 91 49 91 55.* The **Thomas Cook** network member, Via Voyages, *1 Bis, La Canebière; tel: 91 90 07 37,* provides travel services to visitors.

Arriving and Departing

The main **station** is **Gare St Charles**, just under 1 km west of the Vieux Port at *av. P. Semard; tel: 91 08 50 50.* For reservations *tel: 91 08 84 12.* Information is available Mon–Sat 0900–1300 and 1600–1900. For the centre of town, either take the metro or head down the ornamental *Marseillaise* steps, take *blvd D'Athenes/blvd Dugommier* to *La Canebière,* and turn right. The **SNCF** office at the tourist office handles information and reservations and is often less stressful than St Charles.

The **Inter-City bus station** is next door to St Charles (turn right out of the station) with connections to most towns in the south of France. **Ferry services** are operated by **SNCM**, *61 blvd des Dames; tel: 91 56 32 00* (metro: Joliette). Services depart from here to Corsica, North Africa, and Italy.

Getting Around

Metro and Buses

Both the metro (subway) – easy, efficient, and safe – and the bus network are operated by RTM. There are two metro lines, intersecting at Gare St-Charles (down the escalators), which serve most of the city. **Line 1** (blue) runs east–west and serves the Vieux Port area. **Line 2** (orange) runs north–south. The metro stops at 2100. Most local buses pass through the Vieux Port/Canebière area. Night buses run from La Bourse, just north of La Canebière. A good map of bus and Metro routes, the Plan du Réseau, is available from the tourist office or **RTM** office at La Bourse, *6–8 rue de Fabres, tel: 91 91 92 10.*

Tickets are available at all metro stations and on all buses and are transferable between the metro and buses. Books (*carnets*) of ten tickets are good value.

Taxis

These are available from the station exit or *tel: 91 03 60 03.*

Living in Marseille

Accommodation

Vieux Port is the area which contains the most upmarket accomodation. Major hotel chains in Marseille include *Me, Nv, Pu* and *Sf.* For cheap, functional and tranquil hotels try the areas between *blvd Garibaldi* and Réformés Canebière Metro station (*allée Gambetta*), and around the Préfecture (*rue Montgrand*). **IYHF hostels**: **Bois-Luzy** (closed 1030–1700), *76 av. Bois-Luzy; tel: 91 49 06 18* (take bus no 8 from the Bourse) and **Bonneveine**, *47 av. J.Vidal; tel: 91 73 21 81,* to the south, near the beach in a quiet residential district (metro to Castellane, then bus no 19 or 44 to Vidal-Collet).

Communications

The **post office** is at *1 pl. de l'Hôtel des Postes,* near the Bourse. Poste restante facilities are available Mon–Fri 0800–1900 and Sat 0800–1200.

Eating and Drinking

Marseille provides for all tastes and all pockets. For *bouillabaisse* (its famous fish stew), at a cost, head to the **Vieux Port**, where a vibrant fish market offers a glimpse of the *Marseillais* temperament at its most entertaining, and the

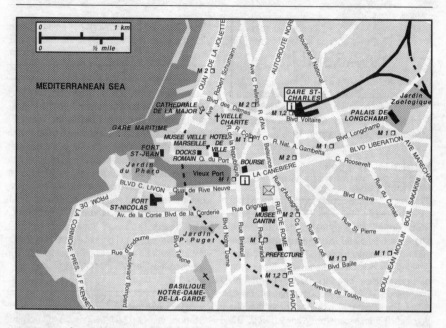

restaurants of **quai de Rive Neuve**. Oyster bars and several ethnic and fast-food restaurants are found around **pl. Thiers**. The other centre of culinary Marseille is at **cours Julien** and **cours D'Estienne d'Orves**, where couscous, Vietnamese, Iranian, Russian and old fashioned French food is available. A daily market enlivens the quarter around **Noailles** metro station.

Entertainment

The city's football team, L'Olympique de Marseille, is world-class. Tickets start at around FFr. 100 and are available from *Stade Velodrome, bd Michelet; tel: 91 07 77.28* (metro: *Rond Point du Prado*).

Nightlife

Marseille's nightlife is generally safe and notoriously dull. To be extra cautious, avoid streets to the south-west of the train station (north of La Canebière). The Opéra, Marseille's historical red-light district, is often lively but not dangerous. *Pl. Thiers* is the centre of nocturnal festivities, with trendy bars, restaurants and mediocre nightclubs. Otherwise, try the live music haunts around *cours Julien*.

Sightseeing

There has been a port in the **Vieux Port** area for 2,600 years; remains of the Roman version are found in **Le Jardin des Vestiges** behind the Bourse shopping complex (metro: *Vieux Port*), which houses the self-explanatory **Musée d'Histoire de Marseille**. La Canebière ('Can o' beer' to English sailors last century) is the second most famous street in France (after the Champs-Élysées). At number 7, **Le Musée de la Marine**, charts Marseille's relationship with the sea.

In the **Panier District**, north of the port, the **Musée du Vieux Marseille**, *rue de la Prison*, contains two centuries' worth of fascinating junk, while German explosives in 1943 revealed the ancient Roman docks, now on display in the **Musée des Docks Romains**, *pl. de Vivaux*. **Vieille Charité**, once a lunatic asylum, is a fine baroque church now housing innovative art exhibitions.

South of the Canebière, **Musée Cantini**, *19 rue Grignan*, boasts modern art, whilst the **Musée des Beaux Arts** to the east (metro: *Longchamp/Cinq Avenues*) contains lively impressionists. Given time, visit **Château d'If**, the skeletal island in the bay (boat from *quai des*

Belges; tel: 91 59 02 30) home of Dumas' Count of Monte Cristo, offering a magnificent vista of Marseille.

End any visit to Marseille at **Notre-Dame-de-la-Garde**, the white church with a spectacular view down over the city (take bus no 60 from the Vieux Port). In the distance is Le Corbusier's **Unité d'habitation** on *blvd Michelet*, a giant minimalist apartment complex built in 1945.

- - - - - - - - - - - - - - - - - - -

◠ Side Tracks from Marseille

AIX-EN-PROVENCE

Station: *tel: 42 89 09 79* or *91 08 50 50*. Hourly connections to Marseille (journey time: 30 mins). For the town centre, walk 250 m northwards up *av. Victor Hugo* to La Rotonde.

Tourist Office: *pl. du Général de Gaulle, tel 42 16 11 61*; guided tours of Aix are available daily in summer at 1000, 1530, and 2100 and are conducted in English on Wednesdays at 1000 (cost: FFr. 50).

So close, but a different world to Marseille, Aix is a town of culture, grace and charm and the birthplace of the great Impressionist painter, Cézanne. Head towards the *cours Mirabeau*, to sit, sip coffee and people-watch (Les Deux Garçons is the most famous café), and admire the street's many gracious 17th-century mansions. Aix's museums are dull, the best being **Musée des Tapisseries**, with beautiful textiles, housed in the Archbishop's Palace, just behind the **Cathédrale de Saint-Sauveur**, a building with a mix of almost every architectural period and a small, beautiful Romanesque **cloister**.

Cézanne despised his home town, but his studio, **L'Atelier Cézanne**, *9, av. Paul Cézanne*, off *av. Pasteur*, is lovingly preserved. Alternatively, follow the **Cézanne Trail** brochure from the tourist office, or hire a bike and take off into the countryside that stars in his paintings, along the D17 to **Le Tholonet**, or D10 to **Vauvenargues** (and Picasso's grave). Aix's **markets** are also a delight; head to *pl. des Prêcheurs* for flowers, *pl. Richelme* for vegetables. *Cours Sextius* and its back streets have numerous bars and small clubs. There is a huge music festival every July (*tel: 42 17 34 00* for information).

BANDOL

Station: *tel: 94 32 21 29*, 10 mins from the port.
Tourist Office: by the port; *tel: 94 29 41 35*.

Bandol is a stop on the Toulon–Marseille TGV. A resort town, and therefore expensive, Bandol has pretty beaches and a Mediterranean ambience. The wine here is exquisite: try the **Maison des Vins** next to the tourist office for an introduction. Apart from the beaches, Bandol is a good base for excursions. **Île de Bendor** (boats from the port) is an island owned by pastis baron Paul Ricard. Nearby at **Sanary-sur-Mer** is an impressive zoo, with flocks of exotic birds. Or you could take a bike ride along the coast to **St Cyr-les-Lecques**.

CASSIS

Station: *tel: 42 01 01 18*. This is 3 km from the sea. Alternatively, take a bus (*tel: 42 73 18 00*) from Marseille; these stop at the central square.
Tourist Office: *pl. P. Baragnon; tel: 42 01 71 17*.

A picturesque port in winter, a tourist spot in summer. The *calanques* from here to Marseille are stunning – tiny fjords of crystal water and white rock. Footpaths lead west, or take a boat trip from Cassis port. Some of the best wine in the area is available here.

LA CIOTAT

Station: *tel:* La Ciotat *42 83 08 63*, Marseille: *91 08 50 50*. This is located 3 km from town and the beaches, but a regular bus service runs every 20 mins until 2100.
Tourist Office: *blvd Anatole France* (by the Vieux Port) *tel: 42 08 61 32*.

La Ciotat is on the main Marseille–Nice line (see p. 257); it has long, sandy beaches and a quirky Vieux Port. Louis Lumière shot the first motion picture here, of a train pulling into La Ciotat station. A good place to hire bikes and head up to **Cap Canaille** (the tallest sea cliff in Europe) or down to Cassis.

- - - - - - - - - - - - - - - - - - -

MARSEILLE
to
BARCELONA

This route takes you along two very different and extremely popular stretches of Mediterranean coast, from the French Riviera through the wild marshes of the Camargue and the heavily built-up Costa Brava, to Spain's trendiest city, Barcelona.

TRAINS

ETT tables: 81, 151, 163, 162, 416.

→ Fast Track

There is one through day service with a change of train at Avignon, taking 6 hrs 30 mins, with a restaurant car between Avignon and Barcelona.

∿ On Track

Marseille–Arles

At least ten trains run daily from Marseille (St Charles) to Arles, taking 45–55 mins.

Arles–Tarascon

Six trains run daily, taking just under 10 mins.

Tarascon–Nîmes

There are several trains daily, taking 20 mins.

Nîmes–Montpellier

Many trains run daily but depart infrequently, so plan carefully. Journey time is 30–45 mins.

Montpellier–Béziers

There are many trains departing frequently and taking about 45 mins, except in the evening.

Béziers–Narbonne

There are frequent trains, and you should not

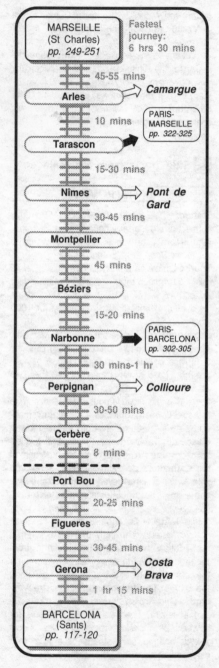

MARSEILLE (St Charles) pp. 249-251

Fastest journey: 6 hrs 30 mins

45-55 mins

Arles ⟹ *Camargue*

10 mins

PARIS-MARSEILLE pp. 322-325

Tarascon

15-30 mins

Nîmes ⟹ *Pont de Gard*

30-45 mins

Montpellier

45 mins

Béziers

15-20 mins

Narbonne ➤ PARIS-BARCELONA pp. 302-305

30 mins-1 hr

Perpignan ⟹ *Collioure*

30-50 mins

Cerbère

8 mins

Port Bou

20-25 mins

Figueres

30-45 mins

Gerona ⟹ *Costa Brava*

1 hr 15 mins

BARCELONA (Sants) pp. 117-120

have to wait more than 1 hr other than in the evening. The journey takes 15–20 mins.

Narbonne–Perpignan

Trains are frequent but irregular. Some take up to twice as long to do the journey as others. Average journey times: 30 mins–1 hr.

Perpignan–Cerbère

Trains are frequent but irregular. Journey time varies from 30–50 mins.

Cerbère–(Border)–Port Bou

Some ten trains run daily, taking about 8 mins.

Port Bou–Figueres

There are over a dozen trains a day. The journey takes 20–25 mins.

Figueres–Gerona (Girona)

Trains are frequent and take 30–45 mins. There are some Talgos, but they are not much faster and it's not worth paying a supplement.

Gerona–Barcelona

Trains are frequent, the journey taking roughly 1 hr 15 mins to Barcelona (Sants). Many also stop at Barcelona (Passeig de Gracia), about 5 mins before Sants. There are also Talgos and EC trains (supplement payable), but the journey time is much the same as on the ordinary trains. These use Barcelona França.

ARLES

Station: tel: 90 96 43 94. Information desk open 0900–1800 (closed at lunch time during winter). For the arena, walk down av. Talabot and along rue Laclavière.

Tourist office: take bus no.4. The main office for tourist information is at Esplanade des Lices; tel 90 49 36 90. Open daily 0900–1900 during summer; closed for lunch during winter. Hotel reservations can be made here. There is an office in the station, which closes from 1300–1630.

Getting Around

Most major sights and museums are tucked into a tiny old town and are easily accessible on foot.

Accommodation and Food

Chains include BW, Me. There are several inexpensive hotels around pl. du Forum and pl. Voltaire, where you will also find the liveliest cafés. For small but good quality restaurants, try around pl. du Forum, and rue du 4 Septembre. **IYHF**, 20 av. Foch; tel 90 96 18 25, is south of town (bus no.4 from the station, then bus no. 3 from blvd des Lices to Fournier).

Sightseeing

Ancient Rome meets Van Gogh and black bulls in Arles, spiritual heart of Provence, and perfect for relaxing and drinking up history. In July, the music, dance and theatre festival fills the streets.

This is one of the best preserved Roman towns in the world. To visit all monuments and museums, buy a 'global' ticket from the tourist office. The **Arènes**, rue des Arènes, is a mini Coliseum, still used for bull fights from Easter to September. The **Théâtre Antique**, rue du Cloître, is also still used for productions. Nearby, on the central pl. de la République, are the beautiful Romanesque **Église de St-Trophim** and the **Musée Lapidaire Paien**. In the town centre, **Musée Arlaten**, rue de la République, is dedicated to local history and traditions, whilst **Musée Réattu**, rue du Grand Prieuré, has a collection of Picasso drawings. The tourist office runs Van Gogh tours, but none of the artist's works are here in the town where he cut off his ear.

Side Tracks from Arles

The **Camargue** is a wilderness of marshland and rice fields roamed by white horses and black bulls. Its lagoons pink with flamingoes, the Camargue is best seen by bike or horse (bike hire in Arles, horse hire throughout the area). Get there either by bus (bus station is opposite the railway station; tel: 90 49 38 01), **Cars des Camargue** (tel: 90 96 36 25) or hire a **bike** from the train station (tel: 90 96 43 94) or Dall'Oppio, at 10 rue Portagnel; tel: 90 96 46 83.

On the coast, **Saintes-Maries-de-la-Mer** is a gypsy shrine and site of an international gypsy festival in May.

TARASCON

Station: *tel: 90 91 04 82*. For centre-ville, head right; for the river and château, head left.
Tourist Office: *59 rue des Halles; tel: 90 91 03 52*.

Due to heavy bombing during World War II, this is a drab town on the Rhône, but the **Château du Roi René**, a fairy-tale 15th-century castle on the river (guided tours, closed Tues), is worth a visit. In the **House of Tartarin**, based on Daudet's famous fictional character, you will find a model of the legendary **Tarasque** dragon, which lives in the Rhône and was banished to its depths by Saint Martha's crucifix, an event celebrated in a festival every June. There are several good, cheap places to stay and eat in the square by the station. **IYHF**: *31 blvd Gambetta; tel: 90 91 04 08*.

NÎMES

Station: *tel: 66 23 50 50* Mon–Fri 0800–1800' Sat 0900–1215 and 1400–1800 for informatio-nor; *tel: 66 78 79 79* for reservations. For the centre of town and the tourist office, head down *av. Feucheres* to *esplanade Charles de Gaulle*, then along *blvd Victor Hugo*.
Bus Station: *rue Ste. Felicité* (behind train station); *tel: 66 29 52 00*. Buses depart from here for Uzes, Pont du Gard and Camargue.
Tourist Office: *6 rue Auguste; tel: 66 67 29 11*. Open daily 0800–1900 summer; closed for lunch winter. Currency exchange and hotel reservation facilities are available. There is also a tourist office (hotel reservations) in the station (*tel: 66 84 18 13*), open daily 0930–1230 and 1430–1830.

Accommodation and Food

IYHF, *chemin de la Cigale; tel: 66 23 25 04*, is 2 km from the centre (bus no.20 from the station; departs hourly). Otherwise, try *blvd des Arènes*, or around *blvd Amiral Courbet*. Side-streets off *blvd Victor Hugo* are laden with good-quality, inexpensive restaurants. Try *rue Fresque* and *rue de l'Etoile*. For animated bars, head for the places around the arena, *blvd Victor Hugo* and *blvd des Arènes*. During the feria in February, May and September this area is crazed.

Sightseeing

As well as some fine medieval streets in the area around the **Cathédrale de St Castor**, *pl. aux Herbes*, and several museums, the town is full of impressive Roman sites. The **Arènes**, *rue de la République*, is a huge amphitheare still used to host feria bullfights, when would-be Heming-ways flock to Nîmes. The **Maison Carreé**, *blvd Général Perrier*, an immaculate 1st-century temple, now houses the **Musée d'Antiquités**. Next door is the hyper-modern **Centre d'Art Contemporain**, designed by Norman Foster. To the west, the 18th-century **Jardin de la Fontaine**, off *av. Jean-Jaurès* and below the romantic **Temple of Diana**, was France's first public garden. Further north rises the **Tour Magne**, a 30-metre octagonal Roman tower.

Side Tracks from Nîmes

The **Pont de Gard** is a spectacular Roman aque-duct 48 m above the Gard river. Buses run eight times a day from Nîmes. The site attracts 2 million visitors a year. Water was brought to the aqueduct from **Uzès**, a delightful medieval village centred on a formidable castle, which today has waxworks and holographic ghosts.

MONTPELLIER

Station: *pl. Auguste-Gilbert; tel: 67 58 50 50* or *67 58 43 06* (reservations). The information desk opens Mon–Sat 0800–1900; Sunday 0800–1700 (closed at lunch time). For the centre of town head north, along *rue Maguelone*.
Tourist Office: main office is at *allée du Tourisme, Le Triangle*, (off *pl. de la Comédie*) *tel: 67 58 67 58*. Open summer Mon–Sat 0900–2000; Sunday 0900–1300. Open winter 0900–1800, closed Sunday. Hotel reservations, currency ex-change facilities, and tours of the city are avail-able. There is also a tourist office at the station, open Mon-Fri 0900–1200 and 1400–1800.

Sightseeing

High-tech, young and trendy, Montpellier has the required selection of old houses but most of all is fun to visit. The **Vieille Ville** (old town) houses many 17th- and 18th-century mansions (free guides from the tourist office) and cobbled streets. To the west the **Arc de Triomphe** leads to a small park and a fine **Aqueduct**. In contrast, to the east, the **Antigone** housing complex is stunningly neo-classical. **Musée Fabre**, *13 rue Montpellieret*, has fine 19th-century art.

Most of all, Montpellier is a place to stroll and sip strong coffee, in the hip bars and clubs in and around the **pl. de la Comédie**. As this is a university town, with 40,000 poverty-stricken students to feed, there are hundreds of inexpensive, good quality eating places, bars and hotels. Look in the north-west district around the university, which is full of ethnic 'restos', and between the *pl. de la Comédie* and the station.

BÉZIERS

Station: *tel: 67 62 50 50* or *67 49 61 89* (reservations). Information desk opens 0900–1800. For the centre of town, head north along *av. Gambetta*, and *av. Alphonse Mas*.
Tourist Office: *27 rue 4 Septembre*, off *pl. G. Péri; tel: 67 49 24 19*. Details of local wine festivals are also available here.

Sightseeing

This is a lively town with an attractive old centre and vineyards clinging to its outskirts. The gothic **Cathédrale de St-Nazaire**, founded in the early 13th century, replaced an earlier one burned down during the Albigensian Crusade in 1209, with 20,000 people locked inside. Visit the **Musée du Vieux Biterrois et du Vin** (*7 rue Massol*), housed in a 14th-century Dominican convent. Romantics should head to **Plateau des Poétes** (north of station). West of the town, the **Canal du Midi** leads from the Mediterranean to the Atlantic. Day cruises travel through locks and vineyards from Béziers. Regular buses leave *pl. Jean-Jaurès* for nearby long, sandy beaches.

NARBONNE

Station: *tel: 68 47 50 50* or *68 32 38 83* (reservations); 10-min walk north-east of town centre, turn right along *blvd Frédéric Mistral* to

the river, and left along *rue Jean-Jaurès*. Information available 0730–1900 (closed lunch time).
Tourist Office: *pl. Salengro; tel: 68 65 16 50*.

Sightseeing

A fine Midi town, lapped by vineyards and with good beaches nearby, Narbonne is dominated by the magnificent Gothic **Cathédrale St. Juste**, designed to be one of the biggest churches in Christendom, but never finished because the authorities would not allow the town walls to be pulled down to build the nave. It has some lovely stained glass and is worth a climb to the towers. The opulent **Palais des Archevêques** next door houses an art and archaeology museum. **L'Horreum** (*16 rue Rouget-de-l'Isle*), is a preserved Roman granary, still under excavation.

PERPIGNAN

Station: *tel: 68 35 50 50* or *68 34 73 11* (reservations). Information desk open 0800–1930. For the town centre (600m) go along *av. de Gaulle*, then left along *quai de Lattre de Tassigny*.
Bus Station: *av. du Général Leclerc; tel: 68 35 29 02* (north of train station, off *pl. de la Résistance*). Regular services to the beaches are available from here (take bus no.1, or *Car Inter 66*).
Tourist Office: Regional office is at *quai de Lattre de Tassigny; tel: 68 34 29 94*, open summer 0900–2000; winter 0900–1900. The town office is at *pl. Armand-Lanoux; tel: 68 66 30 30* (30-mins walk from the station), open at similar hours.

Accommodation and Food

IYHF, *allée Marc-Pierre; tel: 68 34 63 32* is between the train and bus stations behind Parc Pépinière. Cheaper hotels are located off *pl. de Verdun*, or near the station along *av. de Gaulle*. **Camping** is available to the west at La Garrigole (bus no. 2 from the station). Spanish influence and local wine combine to make lively restaurants; try around *pl. de Verdun*.

Sightseeing

Almost Spanish, the town is wealthy, ancient and overrun in summer. The 15th-century fortified gatehouse, **Le Castillet** (*quai Sadi-Carnot*) in the old town, houses a Catalan museum. **Pl. de Loge** is 14th-century and still lively, while the **Cathédrale St. Jean** (*pl. Gambetta*), is gothically grand. The impressive **Citadelle**, to the south, off the *pl. des Esplanade*, protects the imposing 13th-century **Palais des Rois de Majorque**.

Side Track from Perpignan

Collioure is a picture-postcard ex-fishing village, 'discovered' by Matisse and Picasso. The **Château** looks over the village and old port, where artists still paint. Regular trains from Perpignan.

FIGUERES

Station: *tel: (972) 50 46 61*. Central.
Tourist Office: *Plaza del Sol; tel: (972)50 31 55.* Open Mon–Fri 0830/0900–1900/2000 (until 1500 in winter) and Sat 0900–1300/1400.

Sightseeing

The **Salvador Dalí Museum**, signposted from the station, is the only real attraction. Whether you consider Dalí a genius or a madman (or both), the surreal museum is likely to confirm your views of the man. It's a bizarre place that Dalí designed himself (even to his own grave). There's no guide book, as he wanted visitors to use their imagination, but the attendants are more than happy to answer questions. The **Museu Juguete** (*Rambla 10*), is also interesting – a collection of around 4,500 19th-century dolls and models assembled by one man.

GERONA (GIRONA)

Station: *tel: (972) 20 46 78*. In the new town, a 10-min walk from the river and Pont de Pedra.
Bus Station: *tel: (972) 21 23 19* (just round the corner from the train station).
Tourist Office: *Rambla Llibertat 1; tel: (972) 20 26 79* (near the Pont de Pedra). There's also a tourist office at the train station.

Accommodation

There is plenty of cheap accommodation, with all the best places to be found in the old town – try around the cathedral and *Calle Santa Clara*. From October to June, however, rooms can be hard to find because so many lodgings are full of students. **IYHF**, *AJ Ceruari de Girona, Calle Ciutadans 9; tel: (972) 20 15 54.*

Sightseeing

This medieval walled town, on one side of the River Onyar, is connected by the Pont de Pedra to a prosperous new city. Take time to wander through the narrow medieval streets, seeing the **Casas del Onyar** (picturesque houses which overhang the river) and exploring the churches.

El Call (old Jewish quarter), on *Calle Forca*, is an evocative area leading to the **Cathedral** and **Museu d'Art**. The Gothic Cathedral, heart of the old town, is approached by a 90-step 17th-century stairway. The interior has a single-naved vault with a 22m span (largest in the world). The altarpiece is of 14th-century silver and enamel.

The 11th-century **Baños Arabes** (Roman Baths) were rebuilt; the present ones are 13th-century Romanesque with Moorish touches. The **Diocesan Museum**, housed in a splendid Renaissance bishop's palace, has a wealth of beautifully displayed paintings and carvings from the Romanesque period to the 20th century.

The 11th–12th-century Romanesque Benedictine **Monastery Sant Pere de Galligants**, *Carrer de Santa Llucia*, now houses the archaeological museum. The **Palacio de los Agullana** is a fine town palace from the 14th–17th cen-turies which, together with the **Sant Marti Sacosta Church**, forms an attractive Baroque area.

Side Tracks from Gerona

Gerona is the transportation hub for the **Costa Brava**, with scores of buses daily to the coastal resorts. You can also get there easily by bus from Figueres.

This once-beautiful, rugged coast is now little more than a succession of tourist developments, especially in the south, but man can seldom destroy nature completely, and in many places the roads are forced to zigzag inland to get from one resort to the next, leaving some inaccessible stretches of coastline unspoiled.

MARSEILLE to NICE

This route passes some of the world's best-known jet-set towns as it follows the legendary Côte d'Azur, playground of the rich and famous – and of envious backpackers forced by cost to sleep on the beach. Combine it with the Nice–Genoa route (p. 286) for a complete tour of the French and Italian Rivieras.

TRAINS

ETT tables: 164.

 Fast Track

There is no really fast track on this route. However, most travellers to this area will want to enjoy a leisurely journey, so it shouldn't matter. There are express trains which call only at Toulon, St-Raphaël, Cannes and Antibes. Nice is usually the changing point for journeys further along the Riviera towards Italy (*see Nice–Genoa route, p. 286*).

On Track

Marseille–Toulon

There are regular non-stop trains (including some TGVs) running daily between Marseille and Toulon. Journey time: 45 mins. In addition, there are another dozen stopping trains. From Marseille to La Ciotat, the journey time is 30 mins; from La Ciotat to Bandol takes 10–15 mins; and from Bandol to Toulon, 10–15 mins.

Toulon–Fréjus/St-Raphaël–Cannes

There are at least 20 trains a day between Toulon and Cannes, plus some TGVs. All of them stop at Fréjus/St-Raphaël. The total journey time is 1 hr 20 mins, while the leg from Toulon to St-Raphaël

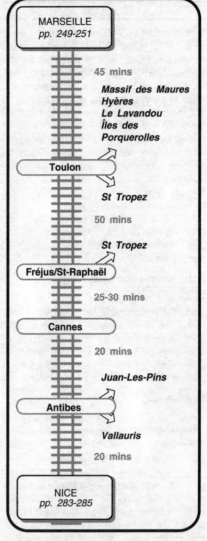

takes about 50 mins and the leg from St-Raphaël takes about 25–30 mins.

Cannes–Antibes–Nice

Regular services stop at Juan-Les-Pins, Antibes, Cagnes-sur-Mer and Nice. Total journey from Cannes to Nice is only 40 minutes.

TOULON

Station: *tel: 94 91 50 50* (for information, open 0900–1900); *tel: 94 22 39 19* (for reservations). The station is located north of the centre. For the centre of town, cross *pl. Albert 1er*, and head south down *av. Vauban*. The old town and sea front are south of *av. Général Leclerc*.

Bus station: Gare Routière, next to the train station; *tel: 94 93 11 39*.

Ferries: SNCM; *tel: 94 16 66 66*. Daily sailings to Corsica, weekly sailings to Sardinia. Tours of Toulon's harbour are available from *quai Stalingrad*.

Tourist Office: *8 av. Colbert, tel: 94 22 08 22*. Open summer 0800–1900; winter 0830–1830. There is also a tourist Information desk at the station, *tel: 94 62 73 87*. Open summer 0730–2000; winter 0830–1200 and 1400–1830, closed Sunday.

Accommodation and Food

Toulon is a cheap place to stay, but quality is short. *Rue Jean-Jaurès* (down *Jean Moulin* from *Leclerc*) has several acceptable hotels and a few good value restaurants. The old town offers dingy pizza places, and a less than welcoming atmosphere. Otherwise, try the corniche road to the east (take bus no 23 from the station).

Sightseeing

Toulon, France's number two naval base, is suffering economic hardship and can be a depressing place. The old town has a quirky potential but manages to stay seedy.

Lovers of sleaze will enjoy the quarter around **pl. des Armes**. Otherwise, the **Musée Naval**, *pl. Monsenergue*, traces the city's marine development. Toulon is best viewed from **Mont Faron**, 500m above the Mediterranean, where there is a **zoo** and **museum** recalling the Allied invasion of Provence in 1944 (take bus no 40 from the station to where a *téléphérique* winches up to the summit).

◠ Side Tracks from Toulon

The **Massif des Maures** to the east of Toulon has the least spoilt coastline in Provence. The **coast road** is served by hourly **Sodetrav** buses between Toulon and St-Raphaël. Sandy bays mark the coast: **Hyères** and **Le Lavandou** are smart resorts, with lively nightlife in season, deserted bars in winter. Off Hyères are the **Îles de Porquerolles**, three remarkably untouched islands, one of which is a protected national park, offering some of the most beautiful beaches in France. Boats depart regularly from Hyères, Le Lavandou and Toulon (around FFr.100 return).

ST-TROPEZ

Accessible only by Sodetrav bus from Toulon or St-Raphaël, or by boat from Ste Maxime across the bay, St-Tropez – often abbreviated to *St-Trop* ('Saint Too Much') – can be a disappointment. The legendary beaches are in fact 5 km from the town. Bike hire is advisable to explore the pretty villages of **Ramatuelle** and **Gassin**, as well as 20 km of beaches.

The **Bus Station**, *av. de Gaulle, tel: 94 95 24 82*, is close to the port (nowhere is far in St-Trop).

Thomas Cook bureau de change: *quai Gabriel Peri*.

Accommodation and Food

These are both expensive. Try campsites to the south along the coast for reasonable accommodation and look away from the port (take the rue de la Citadelle) for some good, small restaurants. Amongst the bars, **Sénéquier** on the port is still the place to be seen. Inland from the port, **pl. des Lices** is a must, with its plane trees and gnarled blvdes players. The still bohemian **Café des Arts** was painted by Signac.

Sightseeing

Strolling is what Tropeziennes do best. But find time for **Musée de l'Annociade**, the region's finest art museum in a converted chapel on the west side of the port, boasting a dazzling array of impressionists from Cézanne, Matisse, Bonnard, to Signac and Dufy. A walk up to the **Citadelle** offers good views, and a confrontation with the town's haughty peacocks. There are two small **beaches** in town. From the base of the Citadelle, and the seaside cemetery, continue along the path to **plage des Graniers**, the closest 'real' beach. Otherwise, hitch or cycle the D93 south. **Tahiti** beach has the jet-set crowd, **Pampelonne** the older stalwarts.

_____

FRÉJUS/ST-RAPHAËL

Barely a kilometre apart, each commune has its own station and tourist office. Fréjus-Plage is a strip of tacky bars and restaurants, St-Raphaël its more upmarket continuation, and Fréjus town an interesting, if schizophrenic, historic resort.

Stations: Gare de Fréjus, *tel: 94 95 16 90*. Gare de St-Raphaël, *tel: 94 91 50 50* (for information, open 0900–1900); *tel: 94 22 39 19* (for reservations). For the sea, exit the station and head right 200 m.

Bus station: St-Raphaël, behind the train station, *tel: 94 95 24 82*. For Nice/Marseille: Cars Phocéens, *tel: 93 85 66 61*. For St-Tropez and Toulon: Sodetrav, *tel: 94 95 24 82*. Buses inland for Bagnols, Fayence, and Les Adrets: Gagnard, *tel: 93 36 27 97*.

Tourist Offices: Fréjus, *325 rue Jean-Jaurès; tel: 94 51 54 14*. Fréjus-Plage, *blvd de la Libération; tel: 94 51 48 42*. St-Raphaël (opposite the station) *tel: 94 95 16 87*. Open summer 0900–1900; winter 0900–1800.

Accommodation and Food

The **IYHF** (*Chemin du Counillier; tel: 94 52 18 75*) on the RN7 towards Cannes is 2 km from Fréjus town and 4.5 km from the sea. (there is a bus from St-Raphaël bus station at 1800 each night, returning each morning).

Even better is **Centre International du Manoir** (*Chemin l'Escale; tel: 94 95 20 58*) next to the station at Bouloris, 5 km from St-Raphaël, 100 m from the sea. (Buses depart every 30 minutes from St-Raphaël bus station). Camp at **Parc de Camping de Saint-Aygulf**, off the RN 98 to the west of Fréjus (*tel: 94 81 20 14*). By the beach, 4 km from Fréjus station (take bus no 29 in the direction of St-Aygulf from St-Raphaël bus station). **Holiday Green** (*route de Bagnols, tel: 94 40 88 20*), is an anglophile campsite 6 km north of the sea (take bus no 11 in the direction of Bagnols, from St-Raphaël). Otherwise, accom-

modation is not cheap. The best bets are back from the sea in Fréjus-Plage.

If self-catering, try St-Raphaël's daily fish market at *pl. Ortolan* and the food market in *pl. Victor-Hugo* (get to both early). Otherwise, the best value food is found in Fréjus town, around *pl. Agricola* (pizzerias and crêperies). In St-Raphaël, try to the east of the casino and just back from the sea, on *promenade R. Coty*. Otherwise, Fréjus-Plage is littered with fast-food stands. The best nightlife is to be found around the new port and casino area in St-Raphaël.

Sightseeing

Fréjus was a Roman port, created by Julius Caesar in 49 BC. The **Roman remains** are scattered throughout the town; only one is organised (the **Arènes**, off *av. du XV Corps*, open morning and afternoon) but a glimpse through the fence at this is probably enough. The 11th–13th-century **Cathedral** was the first gothic church in Provence. St-Raphaël has little to offer. If you have the time, and money, take a **boat** along the coast. **Les Bâteaux Bleus** (*tel: 94 95 17 46*) leave from the Vieux Port of St-Raphaël for St-Tropez and St Aygulf, and offer day excursions to the **Iles de Porquerolles**.

CANNES

Station: *tel: 93 99 50 50* (for information, open 0800–2100); *tel: 93 88 89 93* (for reservations). For the sea, head down *rue des Serbes* (250 m).

Bus Stations: *tel: 93 39 31 37*. Buses to Vallauris, Golfe-Juan, Place de l'Hôtel de Ville: *tel: 93 39 11 39*. Buses to Juan-les-Pins, Antibes, Nice, Grasse, Vallauris, local buses.

Tourist Information: Main office, *Palais de Festivals, esplanade Georges-Pompidou; tel: 93 39 01 01*. There is a tourist information desk at the station (*tel: 93 99 19 77*). Both the above open summer 0900–2000; winter, Mon–Sat 0900–1230 and 1400–1830. Services include hotel reservations and car rentals.

Post Office: *22 Bivouac de Napoléon; tel: 93 39 14 11*.

The **Film Festival** is held in the second week in May, in the Palais des Festivals. Public tickets for films outside the main competition are sold daily from the office next to Tourist Information.

Accommodation and Food

Cannes has the range of hotels you would expect of a major convention centre, including some very luxurious ones. Chains represented include BW, Ch, Hn, Ic, Nv, Pu and Sf. Cheaper hotels are to be found away from the seafront. Try *rue Maréchal-Joffre*, from *pl. du 18 Juin* (turn right from the station), *rue Fortville*, and surrounding side-streets. Good food abounds in Cannes. Avoid the tourist traps on the front and try *rue Felix Faure*, which runs parallel to the sea, or *quai St Pierre*, by the port, instead. *Rue Mace* and *rue Felix-Faure* have some interesting bars and clubs. The *Croisette* is expensive, although casino discos usually do not charge (but drinks are exorbitant).

Sightseeing

Glitzy Cannes, twinned with Beverly Hills, is surprisingly welcoming to those without MGM contracts or family jewels. Wander away from the glamorous *blvd de la Croisette* for small winding streets and hidden squares.

Cannes specialises in second-hand glamour – promenades along the *Croisette*, gawking at the stars' hand prints outside the **Palais des Festivals**. There are few specific sights. Climb *rue Saint-Antoine* to the hill of **Le Suquet**, the oldest quarter. Here, the **Musée de la Castre** in the château has antiquities and a history of the town. Off Cannes, the **Îles de Lérins** are an antidote to chic, offering a monastery, fortress (home of the Man in the Iron Mask) and pine woods. There are daily departures from the quay by the Casino (*tel: 93 39 11 82*).

ANTIBES

Station: *av. Robert-Soleau; tel: 93 99 50 50* (for information, open 0830–1900); *tel: 93 88 89 93* (for reservations). For the centre of town, head down *av. Robert Soleau* to *pl. Général de Gaulle*. From here *blvd Albert 1er* leads to the sea.
Bus Station: *Gare Routière, rue de la République*. Local coastal buses from *pl. Général de Gaulle*.
Tourist Office: *11 pl. Général de Gaulle; tel: 93 33 95 64*. Open summer, Mon–Sat 0900–2000 and Sunday morning; winter, Mon–Fri 0900–1200, 1400–1800 and Saturday morning.

Accommodation and Food

The **IYHF** (*blvd de la Garoupe, tel: 93 61 34 40*) is 3 km from Antibes, under pines by the sea on Cap d'Antibes (bus from *pl. Général de Gaulle*); full in summer. In Antibes itself, try around the bus station. *Pl. Nationale* and the surrounding side streets offer several inexpensive restaurants, while *rue Aubernon*, just up from the port, has many bistros often frequented by yachting types.

Sightseeing

Mixed chic and tackiness, Antibes is a pleasure port (not for Anglophobes) with a long history and a relaxed atmosphere. Take a walk through the port to ogle some of the biggest boats in the Northern Med. Do not miss the **Musée Picasso**, in the Château Grimaldi, above the sea, displaying some of Picasso's most entertaining pottery, and his delightful *Joie de Vivre*. The **Musée Archéologique**, in the bastion St André at the southern end of the sea wall, contains traces of Antibes' Greek and Roman past.

- - - - - - - - - - - - - - - - - - -

〰 Side Tracks from Antibes

Juan-Les-Pins is the playground of the coast, where the **Côte d'Azur** originated one summer in 1921. There are lively beaches, bars, discos and a Jazz festival in July. Buses depart from Antibes' *pl. Charles de Gaulle*. Many of the beaches are private, but there is still public space.

Just inland to the west of Antibes, **Vallauris** is pottery capital of the Riviera, famous for ceramics since 1500; Picasso came here in 1946 to make pots. Today his huge fresco *War and Peace* is in the small **Picasso Museum**.

- - - - - - - - - - - - - - - - - - -

MILAN (MILANO)

Milan is the commercial hub of Italy, a city packed with banks and financial institutions, which boasts a standard of living high even for the wealthy north of Italy. It is also deeply style-conscious, as befits one of Europe's top fashion centre. Be prepared for inflated prices.

A Celtic and Roman settlement, Milan gained importance during the Middle Ages, under the authority of a series of influential bishops, and, even then, was known for its money changers. The Visconti and Sforza families ruled Milan during most of the 13th to 16th centuries. The Viscontis started construction on the Duomo, while the Sforzas built the castle and brought to Milan many of the top artists and thinkers of the time, including Leonardo da Vinci.

Tourist Information

Main APT office: *Palazzo del Turismo, 1 Via Marconi; tel: (02) 809 662*, to the right of the Duomo. Free maps and guides to Milan in English. Open Mon–Sat 0800–2000, Sun 0900–1200 and 1330–1700. Branch: *Stazione Centrale; tel: (02) 669 0532.*

Arriving and Departing

Airports

Malpensa, about 50 km north-west of Milan, servestpdel
 intercontinental and charter flights. **Linate**, 7 km from Milan, handles domestic and European flights. Buses to and from both airports depart from the **bus terminal**: *Piazza Luigi di Savoia; tel: (02) 6698 4509*, right beside Stazione Centrale. For information on flights from either airport, *tel: (02) 7485 2200.*

Stations

The vast majority of trains serve the monu-mental and fully-equipped **Stazione Centrale**, *Piazza Duca d'Aosta; tel: (02) 675 001* (metro lines 2/3). Some trains stop instead at **Stazione Porta Garibaldi** *(tel: (02) 655 2078)* or **Stazione Lambrate** (*tel: (02) 675 001*), both served by metro line 2. Milan's prime position in the heart of northern Italy always helped its trade; now the city acts as the key node in Italy's railway system.

Getting Around

Metro, Buses and Trams

The same tickets are used for all public transport. Single tickets (L.1200) are good for one journey on the metro or 1 hr 15 mins travel on the buses. Tickets are available from machines in metro stations or from tobacco-nists (*tabacchi*) and newspaper kiosks. A day pass (L.3800) and two-day pass (L.6600) are available from underground stations.

The metro, **Metropolitana Milano (MM)**, is clean, efficient and easy to use. There are three colour-coded lines. Cancel tickets in the gates at station entrances.

The **bus** and **tram** systems are more comprehensive and consequently more compli-cated, but stops have details of each route serving them. Buy tickets in advance and validate them in the machines on board.

Taxis

Milan's taxis are yellow and can be expensive. There's a substantial flat fare to start with and extra charges are applied for baggage and travel on holidays or late at night. There are large ranks at *Stazione Centrale* and *Piazza Duomo* and cabs can also be booked by phone or hailed on the street. Avoid touts offering unofficial taxis.

Living in Milan

Accommodation

Accommodation in Milan does not escape the inflated prices of the rest of the city, but there are plenty of pensions around the station and the town centre. Major hotel groups are well represented and include *Ch, Ex, Hl, Hn, Ib, Nv*

---

and *Ra*. The tourist office will provide a full list of accommodation. Alternatively, the **Hotel Reservation Milan** service, *24 Via Palestro; tel: (02) 7600 7978*, can help find a room.

IYHF: *2 Via Martino Bassi; tel: (02) 3926 7095*, (metro line 1 to QT8 station). **Camping**: *Via G Airaghi; tel: (02) 4820 0134*. Open all year.

Communications

The **central post office**, *1 Piazza Cordusio; tel: (02) 869 2069*, is open 24 hrs for telexes, faxes and telegrams.

Public **telephone offices** can be found at *Galleria V Emanuele II, 4 Via Cordusio*, and *Stazione Centrale*. Public phones take either coins or phonecards, the latter available from automatic cash dispensers and kiosks.

The dialling code for Milan is 02. To phone Milan from abroad: *tel: 39 (Italy) + 2 (Milan) + number*; to phone Milan from elsewhere in Italy: *tel: 02 + number. (See also p. 52.)*

Eating and Drinking

The Milanese take their food seriously and are prepared to pay substantial sums for their meals, so restaurants are generally expensive. Better value eateries include the lunch spots catering to office workers, with many reasonable self-service restaurants around the town centre. At lunch-time, customers often eat standing up. *Pizzerie* and Chinese restaurants offer reasonably priced evening meals. Bars tend to serve more coffee than alcohol, along with *panini* – filled rolls in a multitude of varieties.

Regional specialities include *cotoletta alla milanese*, an Italian version of *Wiener schnitzel*, *risotto alla milanese* (rice dish) and the vegetable and pork *minestrone*. Despite being inland, Milan has excellent fish, fresh from the coast.

Money

There is no shortage of bureaux de change in Milan; sometimes it seems as if every third building is a bank. At weekends, exchange facilities are available in *Piazza Duomo* and *Stazione Centrale* and in both airports. Automatic machines that convert cash are located in the town centre and in Stazione Centrale.

Consulates

Australia *2 Via Borgogna; tel: (02) 7601 3330*.
Canada *19 Via Vittor Pisani; tel: (02) 669 7451*.
UK *7 Via S. Paolo; tel: (02) 869 3442*.
USA *2 Via Principe Amadeo; tel: (02) 290 351*.

Entertainment

Milan's daily newspapers, *La Repubblica* and *Corriere della Sera*, produce weekly supplements detailing Milan's entertainment and nightlife.

The city's most famous institution is the grand **La Scala** opera house. Donizetti, Puccini and Verdi all staged operas here. Tickets are extremely elusive, but you may be able to get them on Mondays, for a performance of classical music rather than opera. The **Conservatorio** also hosts concerts. Cinemas cluster around *Corso Vittorio Emanuele*, near *Piazza Duomo*.

Nightclubs tend to close around 0200–0300. **Le Scimmie** (Monkeys) is one of the most famous.

Two of the more trendy areas of town are **Porta Ticinese** and **Brera**. The *Porta Ticinese* and the *Navigli* (canals) district is home to a high concentration of bars and venues (the actual *Porta Ticinese* is a remnant of the 14th-century city ramparts). Cafés and bars also dot the small streets around *Brera*.

Via Brera is the showcase of Milan's fashion industry. The Milanese care about their clothes and smart dress is the norm for almost all nightlife throughout the city, even informal promenading.

Sightseeing

Milan's signature building is undoubtedly the **Duomo** (Cathedral), *Piazza Duomo* (metro: *Duomo*). Work started in 1386, but it was not until 1958 that the last pinnacles were finished. The Duomo is a magical and extravagant Gothic structure, both longer and wider than St Paul's in London, overflowing with belfries, statues and pinnacles in white marble. The comparatively stark interior contains fine stained glass and works of art dating back to before the cathedral's construction. Stairs lead up to, over

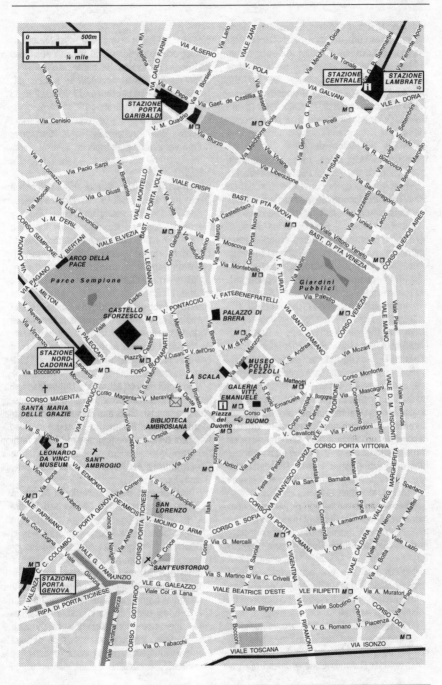

and around the extensive roof system, from where you can obtain a fine view of Milan and can examine close-up some of the adornments to the cathedral's exterior. The **Cathedral Museum** (in the Royal Palace just by the Duomo) houses sculptures, carvings and glass.

On the north side of *Piazza Duomo* is the **Galleria Vittorio Emanuele II**, a monumental 19th-century iron and glass shopping mall known as the **Salon de Milan**. This leads through to *Piazza Scala*, home of **La Scala** (more properly the Teatro alla Scala), probably the most famous opera house in the world. **La Scala Theatre Museum**, in the building, exhibits mementoes from the history of opera.

The **Pinacoteca di Brera**, *28 Via Brera*, is Milan's finest art gallery. The collection concentrates on Italian artists of the 14th–19th centuries, although foreign schools of the 17th–18th centuries are also represented. Notable works include Raphael's *Marriage of the Virgin* and Mantegna's *Dead Christ*. The gallery is housed in part of the **Palazzo di Brera**; in the courtyard stands a statue of Napoleon I from 1809, four years after he was crowned King of Italy in the Duomo.

Further priceless art works are displayed in the **Ambrosiana Gallery**, *2 Piazza Pio XI* (metro: *Duomo* or *Cordusio*). Works by Leonardo da Vinci include the portrait of the musician Caffurio. Caravaggio's *Basket of Fruit* and Raphael's cartoons for the Vatican are other star attractions. The gallery takes up part of the **Biblioteca Ambrosiana**, a library founded in the early 17th century, which houses a Virgil manuscript and other rarities.

Milan's single most famous painting, Leonardo Da Vinci's *Last Supper* (1495–1497), now hangs in the old Dominican monastery refectory next to **Santa Maria Delle Grazie** (metro: *Cadorna*). The *Last Supper*, depicting Jesus saying 'One of you will betray me', attracts large crowds and a hefty entrance fee. The church itself, a Renaissance building designed by Solari, is also worth a look.

The **Basilica of Sant'Ambrogio** (metro: *Sant'Ambrogio*) was built in the late 4th century by St Ambrose, the Bishop of Milan. Most of what is standing today dates from the 12th century, although the smaller campanile, 300 years older, is one of the most ancient in the region. So eloquent and smooth in speech was St Ambrose that his name was given to honey liqueur. His remains now lie in the crypt. The **Basilica of San Lorenzo**, *39 Corso di Porta Ticinese*, has a similar history to Sant'Ambrogio, built around AD 500 and reconstructed some 700 years later. A notable portico of 16 columns from a Roman temple stands in front.

Castello Sforzesco

Sforza Castle, *Piazza Castello*, at the end of Via Dante (metro: *Cairoli*), is a distinctive, heavy fortress, with walls nearly 12 ft thick. Built by Francesco Sforza on top of an earlier Visconti fortress, the castle now houses an encyclopaedic collection of galleries and museums, displaying everything from arms to furniture, from Egyptian art to musical instruments. The pick of the bunch is probably the **Museum of Antique Art**, with some valuable works by Michelangelo. Behind the castle is **Sempione Park**, the largest green space in central Milan. At the far end is the **Arco Della Pace** (Arch of Peace), which has seen many wars in its 150-year lifetime.

The **Poldi Pezzoli Museum**, *12 Via Manzoni* (metro: *Montenapoleone*), was originally assembled by Gian Giacomo Poldi Pezzoli, a well-to-do Milanese collector. The museum includes fine Botticelli and Mantegna paintings. Twentieth-century Italian art is displayed at the **Contemporary Art Museum**, *9 Palazzo Reale*, *Piazza Duomo*.

The **Leonardo da Vinci National Museum of Science and Industry**, *21 Via San Vittore* (metro: *Sant'Ambrogio*), is not just an attempt to capitalise on the great man's name. In addition to exhibits on the evolution of science, the museum has displays of Leonardo's own ideas, including a model of his famous airscrew, precursor of the helicopter.

In the Western suburbs stands a modern structure as distinctive and monumental as either the Duomo or Sforza Castle. The **San Siro Stadium**, a futuristic construction of steel lattices and huge concrete cylinders, is visible for miles in all directions.

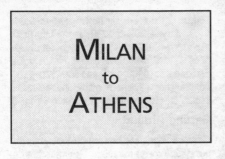

MILAN
to
ATHENS

A link between the two great civilisations of ancient Europe, this journey runs down the east coast of Italy, across the Ionian Sea and through the Greek Peloponnese.

TRAINS

ETT tables: 99, 370, 388, 390, 1525, 980.

 Fast Track

This involves changes and a ferry journey (see On Track) and so is not a truly fast route. In July–Aug the whole journey takes about 37 hrs. At other times, poor connections add to its length.

Between **Milan** (Centrale) and **Brindisi** (Centrale) there are two IC services, with dining cars, during the day, and more trains overnight, most with couchettes. The journey takes 10 hrs by day, 12 by night. July–August the Parthenon Express between Milan (Lambrate) and Brindisi (Marittima) connects with ferry services (Milan departure is early in the morning.) In other months you may have a long wait for the boat.

Nine trains run daily between **Patras** and **Athens**. Some are IC and require reservations, but the last evening service from Patras does not. The journey takes 3 hrs 30 mins – 4 hrs 30 mins. Not all trains have refreshment services.

On Track

Milan–Bologna

Two to three trains run every hour, throughout the day. Non-stop IC services take about 1 hr 30 mins, slower stopping trains about 2 hrs 30 mins.

Bologna–Ravenna

Nine trains run daily, taking about one hour.

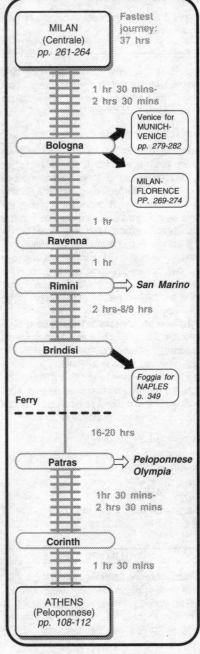

MILAN
(Centrale)
pp. 261-264

Fastest journey: 37 hrs

1 hr 30 mins–
2 hrs 30 mins

Bologna

Venice for
MUNICH-
VENICE
pp. 279-282

MILAN-
FLORENCE
PP. 269-274

1 hr

Ravenna

1 hr

Rimini ⇨ *San Marino*

2 hrs-8/9 hrs

Brindisi

Foggia for
NAPLES
p. 349

Ferry

16-20 hrs

Patras ⇨ *Peloponnese
Olympia*

1hr 30 mins-
2 hrs 30 mins

Corinth

1 hr 30 mins

ATHENS
(Peloponnese)
pp. 108-112

Ravenna–Rimini

There are twelve trains daily (eight on Sun), taking about one hour.

Rimini–Brindisi

Two IC trains, with dining-cars, run daily (supplement payable); the journey takes about 7 hrs. There are several overnight services (taking 9 hrs), mostly with couchettes.

Brindisi–(Border)–Patras

Ferries run at least twice a day in high season (reservations recommended), once daily at other times. Journey time is about 16 hrs direct or about 20 via Corfu and Igoumenitsa. Dining facilities and duty-free shops are available, but there are no berths (seats recline). Check in two hours before departure usually enforced only in high season. Border formalities are minimal. In Brindisi you must show your passport and have your ferry boarding-pass stamped by police in the building above Stazione Marittima. In Patras, police and customs are in the Customs House, on *Iroon Polytechniou St.*

Hellenic Mediterranean Lines, *8 Corso Garibaldi; tel: (0831) 528 531*, and **Adriatica Navigazione**, *85–87 Corso Garibaldi; tel: (0831) 523 825*, offer free passage to Inter-Rail and Eurail pass holders between Brindisi and Patras, although a L.10,000 port tax must be paid. Additionally, June–Oct, Eurail pass holders must pay L.15,000 high-season supplement.

Patras–Corinth (Korinthos)

Nine trains run daily, taking 1 hr 30 mins–2 hrs 30 mins.

Corinth–Athens

There are 14 trains a day, taking about 1 hr 30 mins.

BOLOGNA

Station: **Stazione Centrale**, *tel: (051) 246 490*, 1 km north of *piazza Maggiore*; walk along *Via del'Indipendenza* (or take bus nos.25/30). A memorial to casualties of the 1980 station bombing stands by the renovated station entrance.

Tourist Offices: railway station, *tel: (051) 246 541*, Mon–Sat 0900–1230 and 1430–1830; airport, *tel: (051) 381 732*, Mon–Sat 0900–1300; and *6 piazza Maggiore; tel: (051) 239 660*, Mon–Sat 0900–1900 and Sun 0900–1300. All branches have free maps and guides in English (ask for the listing *A Guest in Bologna*).

Getting Around

Central Bologna can be seen on foot. The local bus system covers the suburbs (tourist office can issue a route map). Tickets, available from tobacconists' kiosks, are good for one hour once validated on board. An 8-trip pass is available.

Accommodation

The tourist office has a wide-ranging list of hotels and pensions in all categories. **IYHF**: *5* and *14 Via Viadagola; tel: (051) 501 810*, 6 km from the centre. **Camping**: *Città di Bologna; tel: (051) 325 016* (bus no.25A/30), open all year.

Sightseeing

Bologna's university, founded in the 11th century, is the oldest in Europe and its buildings are scattered through the city. The medieval town itself, crammed with churches, towers, palaces and porticoes, is one of the best preserved in Italy and provides the visitor with a rich catalogue of architectural gems. Despite its antiquity, however, Bologna is not stuck in the past; interwoven with the array of monuments is a vibrant, commercial city.

The 16th-century **Palazzo dell'Archiginnasio**, *Via dell'Archiginnasio*, was the university's first permanent home; today that honour goes to **Palazzo Poggi**, *Via Zamboni*. The university maintains 21 museums created from work and research by its scholars, although many, such as the **Museum of Domestic Animals' Anatomy**, are of academic interest only. A booklet available from the tourist office locates and describes important university buildings and museums.

The central square, **piazza Maggiore**, is a good place from which to start absorbing Bologna's architectural treasures. On the four sides of the 13th-century square lie the **Palazzo Comunale** (the town hall, which now houses Bologna's modern art collection), the 15th-century **Palazzo del Podesta**, the **Palazzo dei Banchi** and the **Basilica of San Petronio**. The **Fountain of Neptune**, built in 1564, spouts in the north-west corner. At **piazza San Stefano**, the **Churches of San Stefano** (**Crucifisso, Santo Sepolcro, Trinita, San Vitale** and **Sant'Agricola**) make up a complex, replete with cloisters and courtyards, that has retained its ancient atmosphere through the centuries.

The Bolognese architectural portfolio is also notable for its towers and porticoes. Towers, highly fashionable in the 13th century, were built as a sign of wealth, but sometimes served as fire-escapes from the lower wooden buildings. The two most distinctive examples still standing are the 98m **Asinelli** and its inferior partner the **Garisenda**, by *piazza di Porta Ravegnana*. Bologna's porticoes stretch throughout the city in a variety of styles, ranging from medieval through Renaissance to modern.

Connections

From Bologna it is possible to travel north-east to Venice *(see p. 366)* or south-west to Florence *(see p. 157)* and Rome *(see p. 341)*.

RAVENNA

Station: *tel: (0544) 36 450*, about 500m east of town; walk down *Viale Farini* and *Via Diaz*.
Tourist Office: *8 Via Salara; tel: (0544) 35 404*; in the centre of town.

Sightseeing

Ravenna is compact and its centre pedestrianised. Its quiet air today belies its former pre-eminence, both as a capital of the Roman empire in the 5th century AD, and as the centre of Byzantine rulers in Italy during the 6th and 7th centuries AD. Remnants of these periods include a fine collection of vivid mosaics.

The major sights cluster in the north-west corner of the old town. The 6th-century **Basilica of San Vitale** features depictions of the Byzantine Emperor Justinian and Empress Theodora. The **Mausoleum of Galla Placidia**, lined with old mosaics in deep rich colours, and the **National Museum** are in the grounds. In the south-west of town, the **Archiepiscopal Museum** has more

relics from Ravenna's rich history. The 6th-century **Arian Baptistery**, *Via Ariani*, is one of the few original Arian buildings still standing, a relic from the reign of Theodoric the Goth.

RIMINI

Station: *tel: (0541) 53 512*; between Rimini old town and the sea.
Tourist Offices: *1 Piazzale C Battisti; tel: (0541) 51 331*, outside the station, and *3 Piazzale Indipendenza; tel: (0541) 51 101*, on the waterfront. Many nearby beach resorts also have seasonal offices. *Instantaneo* (ask at tourist offices), has comprehensive practical information.

Getting Around

Frequent buses run along the coast and around Rimini. The tourist office and bus information booth outside the train station has details.

Accommodation

Almost every building close to the beach offers accommodation. The huge list at the tourist office, coupled with the clusters of signs advertising rooms, can be bewildering; try the booking service in the station. **IYHF:** *Via Flaminia 300; tel: (0541) 373 216*, near the airport, is 10-mins walk from the seafront at Miramare.

Sightseeing

Rimini, heart of the Adriatic Riviera and little more than one long beach, stretches from **Viserbella** in the north through **Viserba, Rivabella, Marina Centro** and **Bellariva** to **Miramare**. It is totally dependent on tourism and unashamedly supplies what its visitors want. Regimented sun-loungers, parasols and beach paraphernalia are lined up for miles on end, backed by an unbroken chain of amusement arcades, gift shops and restaurants. The seafront is a place dedicated to fun. The centre of town has some more sober attractions, including the **Civic Museum**.

Side Track from Rimini

Most people visit **San Marino**, a 1,700-year-old independent republic covering just 23 square miles, purely for its novelty value. However, there are fine views of the coast and the Apennines from the main ridge. Several buses run daily from Rimini, the journey taking 45 mins.

BRINDISI

Stations: major trains stop at **Centrale**, *tel:* *(0831) 521 975*; two per day call at **Marittima**, by the port (from Centrale, walk straight down *Corso Umberto* and *Corso Garibaldi*).
Ferries: *Via R Margherita* (for ferries to Greece).
Tourist Office: head office, *88 Via Cristoforo Colombo; tel: (0831) 562 126* (normal office hours). In high season there is also a branch at the port: *Via R Margherita; tel: (0831) 521 944.*

Sightseeing

Brindisi's existence has always been reliant on its natural port, which was prized by the Romans as a haven for their fleet. The poet Virgil, who described it in *The Aeneid*, later died here. In the 19th century the town was an important stop on the London–India mail route, today it sees thousands of backpackers en route to the Greek ferries.

Brindisi's few interesting remains include **Roman columns**, parts of the city gates at **Porta Lecce** and **Porta Mesagne**, and the **Cathedral** (built 1098–1132) containing ancient mosaics.

Side Tracks from Brindisi

About half of the ferries between Brindisi and Patras stop at Corfu and Igoumenitsa. The Ionian island of **Corfu** is popular primarily for its beaches and resorts, but the town does have some distinguished Venetian architecture. **Igoumenitsa** is a good base for exploring the rugged mountainous interior of northern Greece.

PATRAS

Station: *tel: (061) 277 441.*
Ferries: *Iroon Polytechniou St* (for **Italy** and the **Ionian Islands**). Port tax: Dr.1,500, high-season

supplement to Brindisi: Dr.2,500. **Port Authority**: *Othonos Amalias St; tel: (061) 341 002* (many ferry agencies are on the coast road).
Tourist Office: *110 Iroon Polytechniou; tel: (061) 653 358*, in the Customs House. **Tourist Police:** *53 Patreos St; tel: (061) 220 902.*

Sightseeing

Agios Andreas is one of the largest churches in Greece, with a 43m-high dome surrounded by a dozen lower-domed bell-towers (representing Jesus and the 12 apostles). The ruined **Venetian Castle** offers a view making the climb worthwhile. There are also a reconstructed **Roman Theatre** and an **Archaeological Museum**.

Side Tracks from Patras

From Patras trains run south through the **western Peloponnese**, taking 2–3 hrs to reach **Pirghos**, from where it's 30 mins (by train) to **Olympia**, site of the Olympic Games of ancient Greece..

CORINTH (KORINTHOS)

Station: *tel: 22 520*, 500m from the centre.
Tourist Police: *51 Ermou St; tel: 23 282.*

Sightseeing

New Corinth, near the dramatically sheer gorge of the Corinth Canal, is linked by bus to its ancient namesake. It is unremittingly modern, but lively; in the evening artists display their wares down by the waterfront.

Old Corinth (7 km away) is spectacularly set between mountains and sea and dominated by the surviving columns of the 6th-century BC **Temple of Apollo**. Remnants of the central **forum** are flanked by the occasional row of crumbling ancient shop buildings. You can also discover (unmarked) toilet pits that have survived through the centuries. The **Fountain of Peirene** was built during the Roman occupation of Corinth and still functions, just: it is possible to hear faint dripping from the spring deep in the arches. On the mountain top above Old Corinth are **Acrocorinth** and a **Venetian Fortress**.

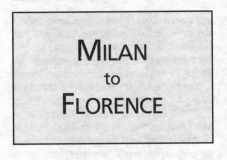

MILAN
to
FLORENCE

This Italian route moves between Lombardy and Tuscany via Liguria, providing a chance to enjoy some of Italy's best coastline, lovely countryside and several charming medieval towns. In particular, do not miss the opportunity to see the Tuscan cities of Siena and Lucca.

TRAINS

ETT tables: 370, 355, 360, 369.

➔ Fast Track

Twelve IC trains run daily (supplement charged) from Milan (Centrale/Piazza Garibaldi) to Florence (SMN), taking 3 hrs (most offer refreshments); two Pendolino trains (supplement charged) also run to Florence (Rifredi), taking 2 hrs 30 mins.

⌇ On Track

Milan (Milano)–Pavia

Trains from Milan (Centrale) are frequent; the journey takes about 25 mins.

Pavia–Genoa (Genova)

Trains to Genoa (Porta Principe) are frequent, but there are long gaps between some; the journey averages 2 hrs.

Genoa–Santa Margherita Ligure

Trains from Genoa (Porta Principe) are frequent but irregular (long intervals between some); the journey takes about 30 mins.

Santa Margherita Ligure–Rapallo

Trains are frequent but irregular (long intervals between some). The journey takes 10 mins.

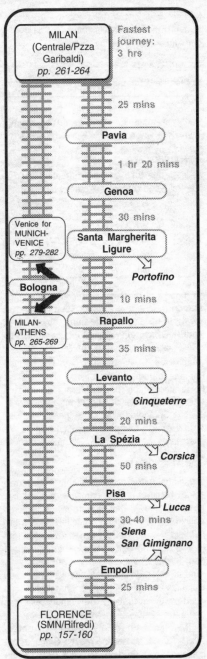

Rapallo–Levanto

At least twelve trains run daily; the journey averages 35 mins.

Levanto–La Spézia

Several trains run daily, taking about 20 mins.

La Spézia–Pisa

Plenty of trains run, but depart at irregular intervals. The journey time is around 50 mins.

Pisa–Empoli

At least one train an hour runs between Pisa (Centrale) and Empoli, the journey taking 30–40 mins.

Empoli–Florence (Firenze)

Trains depart hourly for Florence (SMN), taking about 25 mins. Some trains also use Rifredi.

PAVIA

Station: *tel: (0382) 23 000.* West, in modern town: 10-mins walk from centre (bus nos.3/6). **Tourist Office:** *Via Fabio Filzi 2; tel: (0382) 22 156* (near station). Mon–Sat 0930–1230 and 1430–1800.

Accommodation

There's a shortage of budget accommodation. Try the **Splendide**, *Via XX Settembre 11; tel: (0382) 24 703.* **Camping** (May–Sept), Ticino, *Via Mascherpa 10; tel: (0382) 525 362* (bus no.4).

Sightseeing

The old town itself is the main attraction, known for its medieval towers, attractive churches and peaceful squares. The **Duomo** was completed only in the 1930s and is an architectural mess, not helped by the collapse of a tower in 1989. Far nicer is the 12th-century Romanesque church of **San Michele**, *Via Cavallotti*, with its yellow sandstone façade and friezes depicting mythical creatures and symbolising the struggle between good and evil. It contains 14th-century bas-reliefs and a 7th-century silver cross.

The huge 14th-century **Castello Visconteo**, *Strada Nuova*, houses the **Museo Civico**, which contains an interesting archaeological section

and some reasonable Venetian paintings. Behind the castle, the Lombard-Romanesque church of **San Pietro in Ciel d'Oro**, *Via Griziotti*, contains the **reliquary of St Augustine**, a Gothic marble ark on the high altar.

The highlight of the area is the **Certosa di Pavia**, a Carthusian monastery, 8 km north of town with an incredible façade, including Carrara marble transported from 250 km away. The mass of exterior ornamentation creates an amazingly harmonious whole reflecting the major styles of three centuries. The interior of the church is Gothic, filled with paintings, statues and tombs and as elaborately decorated as the flamboyant exterior. The rest of the monastery can be seen by joining a guided tour. Buses are frequent (from *Piazza Piave*), then there's a 1.5 km walk to the entrance.

GENOA (GENOVA)

For information about Genoa, see p. 288.

SANTA MARGHERITA LIGURE

Station: *tel: (0185) 286 630,* at the top of *Via Roma*, which leads to *Via XXV Aprile*. **Tourist Office:** *Via XXV Aprile 26; tel: (0185) 287 485.* Summer, daily 0900–1230 and 1530–1900. Winter, Mon–Sat 0800–1145 and 1515–1745.

This attractive little resort with some cheap, pleasant hotels is a good base for visiting other coastal towns. The richly decorated interior of the **Basilica di Santa Margherita** is worth seeing.

Side Track from Santa Margherita Ligure

Portofino, a beautifully sited upmarket resort, makes an interesting day-trip by bus. Besides the obvious attractions, the town is famous for antique lace and the museum has a section devoted to the subject. **Monte Portofino**, just outside the town, is a 610m-long headland that is a nature reserve, with over 700 species of wildflowers and shrubs. **Tigullio**, *Via Palestro 8; tel: (0185) 284 670,* operate both buses and ferries from Santa Margherita to Portofino (and other resorts), leaving from *Piazza Martiri della Libertà* and the adjoining quay.

RAPALLO

Station: *tel: (0185) 50 347.*
Tourist Office: *Via Diaz 9; tel: (0185) 51 282.* Open daily 0930–1230 and 1600–1900.

A once-beautiful resort haunted by writers, Rapallo is now hectic and expensive, with a large marina, but there is an attractive old area with cobbled streets. Keen walkers can enjoy the scenery while following footpaths up to the hill village of **Montallegro**, with its 16th-century **Santuario**. The less energetic can get a cable-car up from *Via Castegneto.*

LEVANTO

Station: La Spézia *(see below)* handles enquiries concerning Levanto.
Tourist Office: *Piazza Colombo 12; tel: (0187) 808 125.* They have details about **Cinque Terre** (see below).

A quiet little town with a long beach, good Wednesday market and plenty of cheap hotels. The real point of stopping here is to use it as a good base for exploring the Cinque Terre.

◠ Side Tracks from Levanto

The **Cinque Terre** consists of five isolated fishing villages (**Monterosso, Vernazza, Corniglia, Manarola** and **Riomaggiore**), sheltered by cliffs and virtually unknown until the railway reached them. Each has a distinctive character and it's worth going to all five. The hourly trains take only a few minutes between each village. You can also walk between them, enjoying dramatic coastal scenery, but check what is involved first because the maps can be deceptive.

LA SPÉZIA

Station: *tel: (0187) 35 373.* Turn left on *Via Siffredi* for the centre.

Tourist Office: *Via Mazzini 47; tel: (0187) 36 000,* by the seafront. Mon–Thur 0800–1400 and 1430–1730; Fri–Sat 0800–1300.

Most of the old town was destroyed by Allied bombers, but La Spézia lies on a wonderful natural harbour and the surrounding hills are studded with old Genoese castles. The church of **Santa Maria** has survived, a 14th-century structure rebuilt in the 17th–18th centuries. The **Museo Navale** contains maritime objects from the 16th century onwards and the **Museo Civico** houses ancient Ligurian artefacts.

◠ Side Track from La Spézia

From La Spézia you can reach **Corsica** (journey time: 5 hrs). In summer there are daily ferries (to Bastia), operated by **Corsica Ferries**, *Molo Italia; tel: (0187) 21 282,* and **Navarma Lines**, *Via Tolone 14; tel: (0187) 21 844.*

PISA

Station: Centrale, *tel: (050) 42 291* or *41 385,* south of the River Arno and 20-mins walk from the Leaning Tower (bus no.1).
Buses: APT, *Piazza Sant'Antonio; tel: (050) 23 384,* and **Lazzi,** *Piazza Vittorio Emanuele; tel: (050) 46 288,* between them cover all Tuscany.
Tourist Offices: *Piazza della Stazione 11; tel: (050) 42 291,* Mon–Sat 0900–1300 and 1500–1900. *Campo dei Miracoli; tel: (050) 560 464.* Mon–Fri 0900–1500 and (Tue–Thur) 1530–1830; Sat 0900–1200 and 1500–1800.

Accommodation

There are several good budget hotels around *Campo dei Miracoli,* but they are popular and in term-time students fill the best. **Campsite:** Campeggio Torre Pendente, *Viale Cascine 86; tel: (050) 560 665,* 1 km west of the Leaning Tower, signposted from *Piazza Manin.*

Sightseeing

Pisa was a major Mediterranean maritime power around the 12th century. The innovative architecture of this period, characterised by distinctive stripes of marble and blind arcades, became

---

known as Pisan-Romanesque. Some of Italy's finest medieval sculptures are here, many by Nicola and Giovanni Pisano (father and son) and other Pisanos (unrelated). The main centre of interest is the **Campo dei Miracoli** (Field of Miracles).

The 11th-century four-tiered **Duomo**, one of Italy's finest cathedrals was the first Tuscan building to use marble in horizontal stripes (a Moorish idea). The original bronze entrance, **Portale di San Ranieri**, was cast around 1180. A 16th-century fire destroyed much of the interior but some of Cosmati's lovely floor survived, as did the 14th-century mosaic of Christ by Cimabue and a superbly sculpted pulpit by Giovanni Pisano. Some lovely ivory carvings, also by him, are in the new **Museo dell' Opera del Duomo**, which contains an enormous selection of Roman sarcophagi and medieval works of art. Construction of the circular **Baptistery** was interrupted by a lack of funds. The three lower storeys consist of Romanesque arcades. The top half, in Gothic style, with pinnacles and a dome, was added later (by the Pisanos). It has a pulpit superbly carved by Nicola Pisano.

The **Leaning Tower (Torre Pendente)** began life in 1173, as a campanile for the Duomo. When it was 10m high it began to tilt and the architect fled. Construction continued, however, with successive architects trying unsuccessfully to restore the balance. It is now 5m off true, visitors can no longer go inside and the architects continue to spend their days arguing about how to prop it up.

The north of the square is bounded by the white marble wall of what has been called the world's most beautiful cemetery, **Camposanto**. Allied bombing destroyed most of the famed frescos, but some fragments survived. Don't miss the macabre (anonymous) 14th-century cycle *Triumph of Death*.

Piazza dei Cavalieri was laid out by Vasari around 1560 and **Palazzo dei Cavalieri** became the headquarters of the Knights of St Stephen. Their adjoining church, **Santo Stefano**, has a lovely wooden ceiling and houses banners captured from the Turks during the battle of Lepanto (1571). Across the square is the architecturally interesting **Palazzo dell'Orologio**.

Not far from **Ponte di Mezzo**, on the north bank of the Arno, is the **Museo Nazionale di San Matteo**, *Lungarno Mediceo*, where many important artistic works from Pisa's old churches are now kept. On the south bank, west of the bridge, is the tiny **Santa Maria della Spina**, *Lungarno Gambacorti*, a lovely example of Gothic art, enlarged in 1323. The exterior has many delicate ornamental touches.

Certosa di Pisa (12 km to the east and served by regular APT buses) is an enormous 14th-century Carthusian monastery with a frescoed church where all eleven chapels are painted in pastel colours. Each three-room cell has its own little patch of garden.

◠ Side Track from Pisa

LUCCA

Station: *tel: (0583) 47 013*. Just outside the city walls, an easy walk to the centre. There are frequent trains from Pisa, taking about 30 mins. **Tourist Offices:** *Piazza Verdi* (just inside western city walls); *tel: (0583) 53 592*. Open 0900–1900. *Via Vittorio Veneto 40; tel: (0583) 493 639* (central). Mon–Sat 0900–1230 and 1500–1900.

Accommodation

Finding space is always a problem, so book ahead. An accommodation service is provided by **CIV-EX**, *Via Veneto 28; tel: (0583) 56 741*. Non-bookers may have to stay overnight in Pisa or Viareggio. **IYHF:** *Via del Brennero 673; tel: (0583) 341 811*. Open Mar–Oct. **Camping** is possible behind the hostel.

Sightseeing

The old town is one of the most picturesque in Tuscany. The streets are dotted with palaces, towers and decorative old churches, most dating from Lucca's heyday (11th–14th centuries).

Start with a stroll around part of the 4 km of ancient walls that enclose the old city and are themselves encircled by a green belt, a buffer between the medieval and modern towns. Some bastions have been restored and you can get a good idea of the town's layout.

The Romanesque **Duomo di San Martino**, in

the south of the centre, has an oddly harmonious asymmetrical façade, with individually designed columns and loggias. Many of the exterior bas-reliefs are by Nicola Pisano. The Gothic interior houses several works by Civitali, notably the *Tempietto*, a gilt and marble octagon constructed to honour the *Volto Santo* (Holy Face), and a crucifix believed to be a true likeness of Christ because it was carved by Nicodemus, who witnessed the Crucifixion. There are many other excellent carvings and paintings, such as the early 15th-century *Tomb of Ilaria del Carretto* (a delicate masterpiece by Jacopo della Quercia) and Tintoretto's *Last Supper*.

The central church of **San Michele in Foro** has a remarkable façade, a multi-tiered affair of striped marble loggias with a diversity of supporting pillars, all topped by a huge bronze of Archangel Michael. Funds ran out before the interior could be completed. Almost opposite, the **Casa di Puccini**, *Via di Poggio 30*, is now a small museum devoted to the composer, with his music as a background to most tours.

Near the western city wall is the **Pinacoteca Nazionale**, housed in *Palazzo Mansi, Via Galli Tassi 43*. The 17th-century palace is of rather more interest than the pictures it displays, the over-decorated interior including a particularly spectacular gilded bridal suite.

Torre delle Ore, a 15th-century clock tower, adjoins the church of **San Frediano** (just inside middle of northern town wall). A fairly plain structure, it's topped by a magnificent 13th-century polychromatic mosaic of *The Ascension*. The interior is subtly attractive, featuring many fairly plain (but varied) columns and subdued lighting. Artistic treasures include *Fonta Lustrale*, a 12th-century font on which three different craftsmen worked, pavement tombs, 16th-century frescos and a lace-clad mummy.

Just south-east is the **Piazza del Anfiteatro**, an area of medieval buildings incorporating several arches and columns of the original Roman amphitheatre, from which the oval shape derives. Further south-east is **Palazzo Guinigi**, *Via Sant'Andrea*, a rambling complex of interconnected medieval buildings. A climb of 230 steps leads up a turreted tower with an oak sprouting from the top.

The city's main museum, **Museo Nazionale Guinigi**, east of the centre on *Via della Quarquonia*, contains a huge and varied collection of local Romanesque and Renaissance art.

EMPOLI

Station: *tel: (0571) 74 297*.

If you have to wait here for a connection, it's worth having a look at the 5th-century green and white **Collegiata**, *Piazza Farinata degli Uberti*, and the adjacent **Pinacoteca San Andrea**, containing worthwhile sculptures and paintings.

Side Tracks from Empoli

SIENA

Station: *tel: (0577) 280 115*, 2 km north-east (in valley below town). It is a 45-mins walk to the centre, but there are regular shuttle buses (tickets from machine by entrance). Siena is about 1 hr from Empoli by train.
Buses: Long-distance buses (covering all Tuscany), run by **Lazzi** and **Train**, leave from *Piazza San Domenico* bus station (*tel: (0577) 221 221*).
Tourist Office: *Via di Città 43; tel: (0577) 42 209*. Mon–Fri 0900–1300 and 1600–1900, and Sat 0830–1300. **Branch:** *Il Campo 56; tel: (0577) 280 551*. Mon–Sat 0830–1930. There are also booths in the train and bus stations.

Getting Around

Il Campo is the central square and focal point of Siena. The surrounding area is mostly pedestrianised.

Accommodation

Private rooms are best value, but you often have to stay at least a week and they can be full of students in term-time. There are relatively few hotels, which are often full. For the Palio (early July and mid-Aug), either book well ahead or stay up all night (many do). At other times, if the tourist office can't help, try the **Cooperativa Hotels Promotion** booth opposite San Domenico, *Via Curtatone; tel: (0577) 228 084*. Mon–

Sat 0830-1900. **IYHF:** *Via Florentina 89; tel: (0577) 52 212*, 2 km north-west of centre (bus nos.4/15). A more central **hostel** is: *Casa del Pellegrino, Via Camporegio; tel: (0577) 44 177*, behind San Domenico. **Campsite:** *Campeggio Colleverde, Strada di Scacciapensieri 47; tel: (0577) 280 044*, 2 km north (bus no.8).

Sightseeing

Siena, a major European power in the 12th/13th century, never recovered from an outbreak of the plague in 1348. This meant that it was bypassed for several centuries and has thus changed little since the Middle Ages.

There were originally 60 ancient *contrade* (wards named after animals), of which 17 remain, each with its own church, museum and central square with a fountain featuring the relevant animal. Rivalry between wards is strong, reaching a head in the twice-yearly **Palio**, the frantic, no-holds-barred horse race around the Campo for which the city is best known. Only 10 horses can participate, so lots are drawn to decide which wards will be represented and the whole thing is regarded as a matter of honour by the locals, with rehearsals for days beforehand and excitement mounting to fever-pitch. Races last only 70 seconds or so, but are preceded by a 2-hour procession. Get there early if you want to watch – standing in the centre is free, if crowded.

The asymmetrical **Campo** dates from 1347. Marking the spot where several *contrade* converge, it is regarded as neutral territory and is the focus of the city's life. The arcaded and turreted **Palazzo Pubblico**, on the south side, still performs its traditional role as the town hall and its bell-tower, the 102m **Torre del Mangia**, soars above the town, providing superb views. Some rooms house the excellent **Museo Civico**. Give priority to the *Sala dei Nove* and *Sala del Mappamondo*, containing the greatest treasures: Lorenzetti's *Allegories of Good and Bad Government* and Martini's *Maestà* and *Portrait of Guidoriccio da Fogliano*.

The **Duomo**, a few blocks west of Campo, is one of the finest anywhere. The exterior includes marble of several colours and the interior is dazzling, with no inch left unadorned and particularly striking use made of marble stripes. The

façade was redesigned in 1284, a rose window added in the 14th century and some mosaics date from the 19th century. The floor comprises 56 separate sections, on which over 40 artists worked for nearly two centuries. The elaborate 1265 pulpit is one of Nicola Pisano's best and there's a notable Donatello bronze. The **Biblioteca Piccolomini** has some superb frescos by Pinturicchio. The **Baptistery** (below the Duomo) and the **Museo dell' Opera del Duomo**, contain many other Sienese masterpieces.

Terzo di Città, (south-west of Campo), has some of the city's finest private palaces, such as the **Palazzo Chigi-Saracini**, *Via di Citta 82*. The **Pinacoteca Nazionale**, *Via San Pietro 29*, in a 14th-century palace, has a wide-ranging, chronologically arranged selection of Sienese art.

In **Terzo di San Martino**, south-east of Campo, is **Santa Maria dei Servi**, a massive monastic church with two frescos of the *Massacre of the Innocents*: a Gothic one by Lorenzetti and a Renaissance one by Giovani (both in the chapels) and some fine altarpieces.

Terzo di Camollia, north of Campo, houses two monastic churches. **San Domenico**, to the west, was founded in 1125 and houses the reliquary containing St Catherine of Siena's head and some dramatic Il Sodoma frescos. The enormous **San Francesco**, to the east, contains Lorenzetti frescos and the adjacent **Oratorio di San Bernadino** (keyholder at no.22) has an interior positively glowing with frescos.

SAN GIMIGNANO

San Gimignano (32 km north-west, half-hourly buses from Siena, via Poggibonsi) is a typical medieval hill town (even the hordes of tourists can't spoil the atmosphere), which was noted for its 70 towers, partly defensive and partly status symbols, of which 14 survive. Around *Piazza del Duomo* (central) are some superb medieval buildings. The tourist office is on the main square.

Volterra (regular Lazzi buses from Siena) is an Etruscan hill town noted for the alabaster that has been mined since time immemorial. It is home to the country's best Etruscan museum.

MUNICH (MÜNCHEN)

Other German cities are famed for high culture, high jinks, or big business. Munich, capital of Bavaria, is best known for its beer, sausages, and a laid-back approach to life. However, the city also offers plenty to see and do. Allow at least two days, especially if you plan to do any serious drinking.

Tourist Information

Fremdenverkehrsamt der Landeshauptstadt München (Munich Tourist Board), *Postfach, 80313 München; tel: (089) 2 39 11* (0900–.1500, Fri 0900–1230), has information centres at Hauptbahnhof (Hbf) (main railway station), Bayerstr. entrance; *tel: (089) 2391 256/257*, open Mon–Sat 0800–2200, Sun 1100–1900; at Munich Franz-Josef Strauss Airport, Central Building; *tel: (089) 97 59 28 15*, open Mon–Sat 0830–2200, Sun and hols 1300–2100; and in the city centre at *Rindermarkt/Pettenbeckstr.*, open Mon–Fri 0930–1800. A good city map is available free from all information centres. **Youth information**: try Jugendinformation, *Paul-Heyse-Str.22; tel: (089) 51410660.*

Arriving and Departing

Airport

Munich's **Franz Josef Strauss Airport**, is Germany's second international hub (after Frankfurt). Flight information, *tel: (089) 97 52 13 13.*

  S-Bahn line S8 runs every 20 minutes from Hbf via the city centre to the airport between 0333 and 1153. First service from the airport is at 0355, last service at 0055. For the city centre, get off at *Marienplatz*. Journey time is 36 minutes. **Buses** run every 20 minutes between 0310 and 2130 connecting the airport with the Hbf, journey time about 45 minutes.

Stations

Hauptbahnhof München, *Bahnhofplatz* (about 1.5 km from *Marienplatz*) is Munich's main railway station, and southern Germany's most important rail junction, with connections into southern, central and south-east Europe. Time-table information: *tel: (089) 19419*; fare information: *tel: (089) 55414*; ticket reservations: *tel: (089) 128 5857*; seat, sleeper and couchette reservations: *tel: (089) 1223 2333*; recorded information: *tel: (089) 11531 35.*

Getting Around

You can get around the 3–4 sq km of the compact city centre easily on foot, and Munich rewards walkers more than most German cities, with its wide boulevards, gracious neo-classical buildings and neatly laid-out parks. For trips further afield, use the public transport system which combines buses, trams, S-Bahn (overground) and U-Bahn (underground) trains.

Tickets

Buy them at stations, newsagents, hotel desks and campsites. **Tageskarten** (day tickets), which give unlimited access to the system for two adults and three children, are good value even for two adults alone, if they plan to see a lot of the city. They cost DM8 (inner zone only) or DM16 and are valid 0900–0200. Otherwise, buy **streifenkarten** (strip tickets: DM10) good for 10 trips, or single tickets. All tickets must be validated in the machine provided on boarding. Tickets are valid for all forms of transport. A ticket good for all trains and buses and valid for the length of your stay is sold as part of the **Münchner Schlüssel** (Key to Munich) discount package offered by the tourist board (see Sightseeing).

Buses, trams and U-Bahn

The public transport system is superb, with no-where more than half a block's walk away from a stop or station. Everything runs 0430–0200. Get network map, timetables, and further information about tickets and discounts from the municipal transport authority, **München Verkehrs und Tarifverband** (MVT), *Thiersch-str. 2, 80538 München, tel: (089) 23 80 30.*

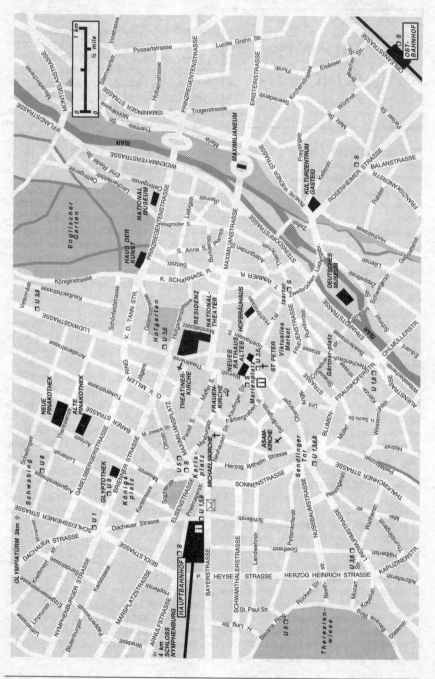

S-Bahn

You can get information on S-Bahn routes, tickets and timetables from **Deutsche Bahn** (German Federal Railways) on *(089) 557 575*.

Taxis

Official taxis are cream-coloured, plentiful and reliable. Per-kilometre charge is roughly equivalent to two single MVT tickets.

Living in Munich

Accommodation

Finding accommodation is rarely a problem except during the city's biggest tourist attractions, the annual Oktoberfest beer festival and *Fasching*, the Bacchanalian carnival which precedes Ash Wednesday. You can book rooms at all prices through the tourist board offices at the airport, in the station, and in the city centre, but they do not take bookings by telephone. International chains with property in the city include *Ch, BW, Hl, Me, Hn, Ma, Pe, Nv, Ra, Ic, Ex.*

The seasonal boom in visitors to the beer festival means Munich has a better-than-average supply of budget accommodation for younger travellers. There are two large IYHF hostels: **Jugendherberge**, *W-8000 Munich 19, tel: (089) 13 11 56* with 509 beds and **Jugendherberge**, *W-8000, Munich 70 JGH, tel: (089) 723 65 50* with 344 beds. Further information on youth hostels in the region from **Deutsches Jugendherbergswerk**, *Postfach 14 55, 4930 Detmold, tel: 05231 7 40 10.* Tourist board offices also provide a hotel list which includes almost 2000 beds in hostels and dormitories run by other organisations in the city, but these cannot be booked through the tourist office.

Munich's warm summers encourage camping, and there are three campsites in the suburbs: **München Langwieder See**, *Eschenriederstr. 119, München 60, tel: (089) 814 15 66*; **München Thalkirchen**, *Zentrallandstr. 49, Munich 70, tel: (089) 723 17 07*; and **München Obermenzing**, *Lochhausener Str.59, München 60, tel: (089) 811 22 35.*

Communications

Postamt 32, Bahnhofplatz 1, tel: (089) 53 88 27

30/27 33, is the post office closest to the railway station, open 24 hours for telephone calls, poste restante, and cheque and currency exchange. All mail addressed via poste restante is held here.

To phone Munich from abroad: *tel: 49 (Germany) + 89 (Munich) + number.* To phone Munich from elsewhere in Germany: *tel: (089) + number.*

Eating and Drinking

Munich is preoccupied with food and drink, perhaps more than anywhere else in a country not noted for asceticism. These come to a head at the annual beer festival in October, when Bavarians and their foreign guests attempt to outdo each other in excess, and at Fasching, the pre-Lent carnival. The city's favourite snack is the *weisswurst*, a white sausage flavoured with herbs and spices. Munich is famous, too, for its many kinds of bread, but still more famous for its beers, from refreshing pilsner-type *steins* to the extra-strong *starkbiers*. Each brewery maintains its own beer-hall, including the legendary *Hofbraühaus*. Fewer foreign snacks have made their way onto Munich's streets than in any other German cities, but if you are on a budget a bowl of *gulaschsuppe* – originally a Hungarian import, now popular all over Germany – will fill you up nourishingly and make your marks go further.

The best place for cheap eats is the Viktualienmarkt, the produce market where a score of traditional taverns sell beer, schnapps, sausage and soup. It also has a popular beer garden.

Consulates

Australia: none, nearest is in Berlin.
Canada: *Am Thal 29; tel: (089) 222 661*
New Zealand: none, nearest is in Berlin.
UK: *Amalienstr.62; tel: (089) 394 015*
USA: *Koniginstr. 5; tel: (089) 230 11.*

Money

You can change money at most city centre banks and at main post offices (*see Communications)* as well as at exchange offices in Hbf and the airport. All major credit cards are widely accepted.

Entertainment

Munich offers a full gamut of high and low culture, from a summer opera festival to the brass band rhythms of the **Oktoberfest** (held for two weeks in late September in the Theresienwiese park) and other popular occasions. There are also plenty of rock, jazz and blues bars providing a venue for home-grown and visiting bands.

The Munich tourist office publishes a monthly programme, *Monatsprogramm*, available free or very cheaply from the information offices, news-stands, bookshops and in many hotels and pensions. It lists all kinds of events, from live music to museum and art gallery exhibitions.

Theatres, Cinemas and Concerts

The **Nationaltheater** (Bavarian State Opera House) is the venue for opera, ballet and classical concerts (also performed in the **Gasteig Kulturzentrum** and in the **Staastheater** and **Gärtnerplatz**). Free lunchtime concerts are given daily at the Gasteig Kulturzentrum by students of the Richard Strauss Conservatorium. It's worth checking with the tourist office for details of other free concerts, which are frequent. Munich has several **cinemas**, some showing English-language movies which are subtitled into German rather than dubbed.

Shopping

The **Karlsplatz** shopping mall mingles department stores, supermarkets and fashion stores, while the city's most elegant designer showrooms are along **Theatinerstr.** and **Maximilianstr.** There are expensive antique stores in the **Briennerstr.** and **Ottostr.** area, cheaper ones along *Turkenstr.* in **Schwabing**, traditionally the city's bohemian quarter and still a good place to look for the off-beat. Head for the **Viktualienmarkt** to stock up on wonderful bread, cheese and sausage for your next train journey or for a picnic. If you visit Munich in December, visit the **Christkindlmarkt** (Christ Child Market) on the *Marienplatz*, which runs from late November to Christmas Eve. Candle-lit stalls sell mulled wine, snacks, and gifts and best buys include traditional Bavarian Christmas decorations.

Sightseeing

The tourist board operates a scheme called **Münchner Schlüssel** (Key to Munich) based on a book of coupons which allows reduced entrance charges to museums, theatres and special attractions, suggestions to help you plan your visit and a public transport ticket valid for the duration of your stay. Munich's sights include the 15th-century **Frauenkirche cathedral**, *Frauenplatz*, with its twin onion domes, the **Altes Rathaus** (Old Town Hall) dating from the middle ages and now housing a delightful toy museum, and the 19th-century **Neues Rathaus**, both on the **Marienplatz**, the city's central square. Be there at 1100 or 2100, when the **Glockenspiel**, an ornate musical clock, strikes the hour. Also worth seeing are the ornate Baroque Rococo **Asamkirche**, *Sendlinger Str.61/2*, and the open-air produce market, the **Viktualienmarkt**. Along the *Ludwigstr.* are some of the city's finest 18th- and 19th-century buildings. The **Residenz**, *Max-Joseph-Platz 3*, the Baroque palace of the city's Wittelsbach princes, houses several museums and overlooks the manicured lawns and flowerbeds of the **Hofgarten**, the city's most imposing park. Chief among Munich's museums are the **Alte Pinakothek**, *Barerstr.27*, with canvases by some of the greatest old masters, and the **Neue Pinakothek**, *Barerstr.29*, with a fine collection of 19th-century European art. **Schloss Nymphenburg**, summer palace of the Wittelsbachs, is worth visiting for its gardens, interiors and portrait gallery (U-Bahn: *Rotkreuzplatz*, then tram no.12).

It's also possible to tour the film studios, **Bavaria Filmstadt**, *Bavariafilmplatz 7*, visit **BMW Museum**, *Petuelring 130*, and the museum of technology, the **Deutsches Museum**, *Museuminsel 1*.

View of Munich

An unparalleled view is offered from the 290m-high **Olympiaturm** (Olympic Tower), in the Olympic park north of the city centre, which has three viewing platforms – two open, one enclosed – at the 190m level, with a revolving restaurant. (Open 0900 – midnight, last ascent 2330; U-Bahn 3 to *Olympiazentrum*).

MUNICH
to
VENICE

The main attraction of this route is the scenery. It follows the Alps between Germany and Italy, with a stop in Austria en route. To see more of Austria, join the Zurich–Vienna route in Innsbruck (see p. 408). Sit on the right from Munich (or left from Innsbruck) for the best views between them: a breathtakingly scenic stretch.

TRAINS

ETT tables: 76, 785, 380, 350.

→ Fast Track

Two trains daily run Munich (Hbf)–Venice (Santa Lucia). The day train (dining-car; supplement charged) takes 7 hrs 15 mins. The overnight train (no supplement) takes 9 hrs 15 mins (couchettes; no refreshment service). Borders are crossed at Kufstein and Brennero (minimal formalities). All trains call at Venice (Mestre) en route.

On Track

Munich (München)–Garmisch-Partenkirchen

The service is hourly for most of the day and the journey time averages 1 hr 20 mins.

Garmisch-Partenkirchen–(Border)– Innsbruck

Seven trains daily (more if you change at Mittenwald), taking about 1 hr 30 mins direct. The border is at Schamitz (minimal formalities). You must always change trains at Innsbruck; three–four services a day provide reasonable onward connections.

Innsbruck–(Border)–Verona

Four EC trains daily (dining-cars; supplement)

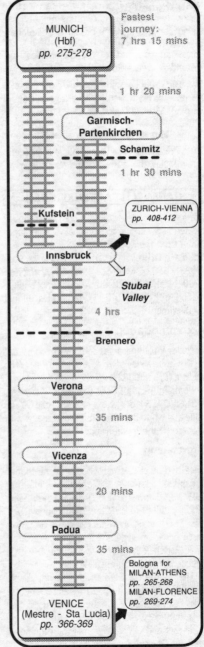

Fastest journey: 7 hrs 15 mins

MUNICH (Hbf) pp. 275-278

1 hr 20 mins

Garmisch-Partenkirchen

Schamitz

1 hr 30 mins

ZURICH-VIENNA pp. 408-412

Kufstein

Innsbruck

Stubai Valley

4 hrs

Brennero

Verona

35 mins

Vicenza

20 mins

Padua

35 mins

Bologna for MILAN-ATHENS pp. 265-268 MILAN-FLORENCE pp. 269-274

VENICE (Mestre - Sta Lucia) pp. 366-369

taking about 5 hrs 30 mins. There is also one train daily with no supplement or refreshment service, taking about 6 hrs. The border is at Brennero (minimal formalities).

Verona–Vicenza–Padua (Padova)

Trains are frequent (although there is a gap of 3 hrs mid-morning). Verona–Vicenza takes about 35 mins, Vicenza–Padua about 20 mins.

Padua–Venice (Venezia)

The service to Venice (Santa Lucia) is frequent, but irregular, the journey taking about 35 mins.

GARMISCH-PARTENKIRCHEN

Station: Hbf, *tel: (08221) 19419*, centrally located between the two original villages, about 100m from the **Zugspitzbahn**.
Tourist Office: *Richard-Strauss-Platz; tel: (08221) 18022*. Mon–Sat 0800–1800, and Sun 1000–1200. When closed, recorded hotel information *(tel: (08821) 19412)*, includes budget establishments.

Accommodation

There are lots of pensions and private rooms, but most require a stay of at least three nights. **IYHF:** *Jochstr.10; tel (08821) 29 80*, 4 km from town, in *Burgrain* (bus nos.6/7). **Camping**, *Zugspitze; tel: (08821) 31 80*, west, near Grainau village (blue and white bus from Hbf). Hotel chains with property in the town include: *Ra*

Sightseeing

Once two quiet Bavarian villages at the foot of **Zugspitze** (Germany's highest mountain at 2,966m), Garmisch and Partenkirchen were officially united to host the 1936 Winter Olympics. They retain individual personalities, Garmisch being an expensive and upmarket area, while Partenkirchen is fairly traditional, with a selection of cheapish hostelries.

The town, now Germany's most popular ski resort, has 68 miles of alpine runs and 93 miles of cross-country trails and in summer is a good base for mountain walking and climbing, with nine cable-cars and a cogwheel railway running all year. The **Olympic Ice Stadium** is also open year-round. The **Heimatmuseum** is a fun place that displays things like Bavarian carnival masks and historic mountaineering photographs.

Most visitors want to ascend **Zugspitze**, for which the base is **Eibsee**, a mountain lake reached by the Zugspitzbahn cog railway. Once at Eibsee, you can take the Eibseebahn cable-car to the summit or continue by rack railway through a winding tunnel to the **Hotel Schnee-fernhaus** (2,650m), from where the Gipfelbahn cable-car goes to the summit. You can walk to the Customs border post at **Zugspitzkamm** (2,805m) and take the Tiroler Zugspitzbahn cable-car to **Ehrwald** (in Austria). Whichever route you take, the views are fantastic and many people go up one way and down another. Eurail passes give discounts. Other local peaks accessible by cable-car are: **Osterfelderkopf** (2,050m), **Wank** (1,780m), **Kreuzeck** (1,650m), **Eckbauer** (1,238m) and **Hausberg** (1,330m). The last is the base for exploring the spectacular **Partnachklamm Gorge**. There is no cable-car up **Alpspitze** (2,628m), but this is popular with walkers.

INNSBRUCK

For information about Innsbruck, see p. 409.

VERONA

Station: *tel: (045) 590 688*, 15–20 mins walk south of the centre (bus nos.1/8/51/58).
Tourist Office: *Via Dietro Anfiteatro 6; tel: (045) 592 828*. **Branch:** *piazza delle Erbe 38; tel: (045) 803 0086*. Both open Sat 0800–1900/2000 and Sun 0900–1400. *Verona For You* lists entertainments.

Getting Around

Walking is undoubtedly the best way to explore the centre. Get buses to travel further afield.

Accommodation

Plenty of cheap hotels and student accommodation (booking is essential for the opera season: July–Aug). Hotel chains with property in the town include: *Hl*. **IYHF:** *Salita Fontana del Ferro 15; tel: (045) 590 360*, 3 km from the station, across Ponte Nuovo (bus nos.2/20/32/59); permits camping in the grounds. **Campsite:** *Via Castel San Pietro 2; tel: (045) 592 027*, mid-June–mid-Sept, walkable from centre (bus no.3).

Sightseeing

Verona was at its peak in the 13th century, when ruled by the della Scala (Scaligeri) family, great art lovers. They commissioned works which impart considerable charm to the modern town. With lots of romantic rose-coloured marble, Verona is a good setting for **Romeo and Juliet**, but Juliet's house, *Via Cappello*, isn't worth the entrance fee. Her 'tomb', *Via del Pontiere*, is a restful spot.

The most significant of the many Roman remains is the **Arena**, *piazza Bra*, which seats 20,000: one of the world's largest amphitheatres. The inner complex is virtually intact, complete with its 44 tiers of pink marble. It holds an annual opera and ballet festival which always includes a spectacular production of *Aida* (well worth attending, but hire a cushion).

Across the river, the **Museo Archeologico** displays Greek, Roman and Etruscan artefacts. There are good views from the terraces and the grounds contain the **Teatro Romano**, another ancient entertainment centre still used for performances, some of which are free. These include Shakespeare (in Italian), jazz and ballet.

Other Roman remains include several monumental arches and parts of excavated streets. **Piazza delle Erbe**, originally the Roman forum and now the site of a colourful flea market, is the heart of the city and surrounded by Renaissance palaces. The **Arco della Costa** leads to *Piazza dei Signori*, also surrounded by impressive old buildings, including the **Palazzo degli Scaligeri** and graceful 15th-century **Loggia del Consiglio**.

Near the square, by the Romanesque church of **Santa Maria Antica**, are the extraordinarily ornate Gothic tombs of the dynasty, **Arche Scaligeri**. An equestrian statue that once topped one of them now stands outside **Castelvecchio Museum**, *Corso Cavour*, which houses weapons, jewellery and some notable religious paintings. The excellent works by little-known medieval artists rival those of the acknowledged masters, also displayed.

Just north-west of the centre is **Chiesa di San Zeno Maggiore**, a superb example of the Romanesque style which contains a notable *Madonna* altarpiece by Mantegna and magnificent 11th–12th-century bronze doors which created a nationwide demand for similar portals.

Sant'Anastasia is a mainly Gothic church with 14th-century exterior carvings. Inside, Pisanello's *St George and the Princess* is of particular interest. *Via Duomo* leads to the striped red and white marble **Duomo**, a blend of Romanesque and Gothic that contains an *Assumption* by Titian and a choir by Sansovino.

VICENZA

Station: *tel: (0444) 325 045*, 10 mins walk south of the centre (bus nos.1/7).
Tourist Office: *piazza Matteotti 12; tel: (0444) 320 854*. Mon–Sat 0900–1230 and 1500–1800; Sun 0900-1230.

Getting Around

Most places of interest are in the old centre, and easily walkable; there is a good bus network.

Accommodation

The cheapest hotels are away from the centre or in noisy locations, so it's worth considering two-star places. Book ahead for summer and autumn. **Camping:** *Campeggio Vicenza, Strada Pelosa 241; tel: (0444) 582 311*, 20 mins by bus (no.1) from the station.

Sightseeing

A prosperous provincial city with a well-preserved medieval centre, Vicenza was largely rebuilt in the 16th century, to designs by Andrea di Pietro della Gondola, better known as Palladio. He gave his name to the Palladian style: an elegant form of architecture that applied Renaissance concepts to Classical forms.

Porta Castello (all that remains of the medieval castle), marks the start of *Corso Palladio*, which is the old town's main road and lined with imposing palaces, and *Contrà Porti* is another street with several fine buildings. The Gothic **Duomo**, about a block from Porta Castello, is a post-war reconstruction.

The **Piazza dei Signori** was the Roman forum and is still the hub of the city. It is noted for the magnificent **Basilica**, a medieval palace which was once in severe danger of collapsing. Palladio's first public project, he was to shore it up using Ionic and Doric columns, saving it and establishing his reputation.

Palazzo Chiericati, *piazza Matteotti*, also by Palladio, houses the well-stocked **Museo Civico**, containing paintings by such masters as Tintoretto and Memling. The ticket also covers **Teatro Olimpico**, the oldest indoor theatre in Europe, opened in 1585 and still in use during the summer months. It was Palladio's last work, and possibly his finest, based on ancient Roman theatres and with superb acoustics. Also in the square, the 13th-century Dominican church of **Santa Corona** has two great paintings: Bellini's *Baptism of Christ* and Veronese's *Adoration of the Magi*. A third masterpiece, Vecchio's *Madonna and Child*, is in nearby **Santo Stefano**.

About 1.5 km south-east of the centre (bus nos.8/13) are two notable villas: **Villa Valmarana dei Nani**, an 18th-century country house with marvellous Tiepolo frescos; and **La Rotonda**, Palladio's most famous creation, which inspired great architects from all over the world. Go on Wednesday, so you can see inside.

PADUA (PADOVA)

Station: Stazione Ferroviaria, *tel: (049) 875 1800*, at the northern edge of town.
Tourist Office: APT, in the station; tel: (049) 875 2077. Mon–Sat 0900–1800 and Sun 0900–1200. *Padova Welcome* is a very informative booklet about the town and area.

Accommodation

Plenty of choice (try around *piazza del Santo* but booking is advisable. University rooms may be available in summer, *tel: (049) 828 3111.* **IYHF:** *Via Aleardi 30; tel: (049) 875 2219* (bus nos.3/8/12). **Camping:** Montegrotto Terme, *Strada Romana Apponese; tel: (049) 793 400* (15 mins by train). It has a pool and thermal baths.

Getting Around

The major attractions: the Scrovegni chapel and Il Santo are about 1km apart (there are buses).

Sightseeing

Padua, extensively damaged in World War II, has a history dating from 45 BC and there are remnants of its glorious past. The university (1222) is associated with Galileo, Dante and Petrarch, while Mantegna, Giotto and Donatello contributed to the city's artistic inheritance.

One work of art is, in itself, strong reason to visit Padua: a glorious three-tier depiction of scenes from the lives of Mary and Jesus (in the **Cappella degli Scrovegni**, *Corso Garibaldi*). This Giotto masterpiece consists of 36 panels, took 3 years to complete and is in virtually perfect condition. The adjacent **Museo Civico** holds mainly 14th–18th-century works. The neighbouring **Eremitani** church, rebuilt in the original 14th-century style, has a beautifully carved wooden ceiling, but only a few scraps survive of its famous Mantegna frescos.

Padua's other major attraction is **'Il Santo'** – the **Basilica di Sant'Antonio**, *piazza del Santo*. This is a mixture of architectural styles (with a distinctly oriental flavour) and a major pilgrimage centre, miraculous powers being attributed to the tongue and jaw of St Anthony, kept in a head-shaped reliquary. The chapel contains 16th-century panels about his life, but more notable are Donatello's bronze sculptures on the high altar and marble reliefs by Lombardo. Donatello's superb *Monument to Gattamelata*, the central point of the square, was the first major bronze of the Renaissance and influenced the whole Italian Renaissance movement. The **Oratorio di San Giorgio** is home to some fine frescos, while the works in the nearby 15th-century **Scuola del Santo** include early Titians. Just to the south is the **Orto Botanico**. Established in 1545, it was originally the university's herb garden and has changed little since.

There are some attractive 15th–16th-century buildings on *piazza dei Signori*. Just to the south of this is the **Duomo**, a not very exciting cathedral adjacent to the Romanesque **Baptistery**, lined with lovely 14th-century frescos.

The 16th-century **University Building**, *Via VIII Febbraio*, where Galileo lectured, is worth a visit to see the old anatomy theatre.

NICE

Queen of the Riviera, Nice attracts 4 million visitors a year. With 240 hotels, countless restaurants and clubs it is a vibrant place. Yet the city has a harsher under-side with petty crime rife. Although an ancient city (founded in 350 BC), Nice only became part of France in the 19th century.

Tourist Information

The **Tourist Office** (tel: 93 87 07 007) is next to the station, to the left of the station steps. Open summer 0845–1830; winter 0845–1215 and 1400–1745. Closed Sundays. An efficient hotel reservation service is also available. **Youth Information**: Centre d'Information Jeunesse, rue Gioffredo 19; tel: 93 80 93 93.

Arriving and Departing

Airport

Nice Côte d'Azur Airport is 6 km west of Nice. For information tel: 93 21 30 12. There are tourist information desks in both terminals which can be contacted through the general airport information line. Hotel reservation desks are also located nearby. A bank and bureau de change facilities are available in Terminal 1. Auto Nice Transport (tel: 93 56 35 40) operate a **bus** service from the airport to Gare Routière bus station, which departs every 20 mins from 0605 until 2325. The approximate journey time is 20 mins.

A taxi from the airport to the city centre takes around 10 mins and costs approximately FFr. 20.

There are also services, operated by Rapides Côtes d'Azur (tel: 93 55 24 00), which depart from the airport to Cannes, Antibes, Juan les Pins, Monte Carlo and Menton.

Stations

Nice-Ville, av. Thiers, is the principal railway station (tel: 93 87 50 50 for information, 0700–2200; tel: 93 88 89 93 for reservations). There is also a smaller station, Gare de Sud, which serves private lines. To get to the centre of town, from the station, turn left to av. Jean Médecin, right down to pl. Masséna (300m), and right again towards the sea.

Getting Around

Buses

Gare Routière **bus station** is at promenade de Peillon; tel: 93 85 61 81. Local bus services depart from pl. Masséna. You can purchase tickets on the bus or get a seven-day, five-day or one-day pass in advance. Information is available from 10 rue Félix-Fauré; tel: 93 62 08 08.

Ferries

Services depart from **SNCM**, 3 av. Gustave-V, tel: 93 13 66 66. There are regular crossings from here to Corsica.

Living in Nice

Accommodation

Nice has three **IYHF** hostels, all far from the centre. The first, **Nice** hostel, is on Mt Alban (tel: 93 89 23 64), which is 4 km out of town and uphill! (take bus no.5 from the station to Jean-Jaurès, then no.14 to the hostel). The hostel is open from 1000 and it is not possible to make reservations in advance. **Clairvallon** hostel, av. Scuderi; tel: 93 81 27 63, is in Cimiez to the north of the centre (take bus no.15 or no.22 and stop at 'Scuderi'), in a park with pool. Near the airport, **Magnan** hostel, 31 rue Louis-de-Coppet, is welcoming (take bus no.23 from the station). International hotel groups with properties in the area include: Ch, BW, GT, Hl, Me, Md, Nv, Sf, Pu.

A very wide choice of good value accommodation can be found near the station at rue d'Angleterre, rue de Suisse, av. Durante, rue Paganini and in Vieille Ville (Old Nice), around pl. St François, to the north. Camping facilities are distant from the centre, at Villeneuve-Loubet to

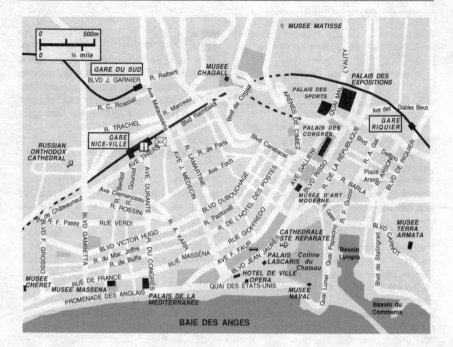

the west, (10 mins by train). Sleeping on the beach is not advised.

Communications

The **post office** is located at *23 av. Thiers* (turn right at the station). The **Post Restante** is at *pl. Wilson*, two blocks north-east of the bus station (*tel: 93 85 98 63*).

Eating and Drinking

A culinary paradise, Nice is influenced by its neighbours, Italy and the Mediterranean. Old Nice contains countless restaurants. The best value are *socca* joints, a thin bread-like substance made from fried chick-pea dough, delicious and cheap (try *rue St Réparate* and its side-streets in search of this). North of the old town, *pl. Garibaldi* boasts the best shellfish, and good *socca*. *Cours Saleya* has sea-food places but is mostly over-priced. The Zone Piétonne, off *Jean Médecin*, has pizza places and bistros. Nice (*Niçois)* fast-food includes the huge *pan bagnat*, thick sandwiches with tuna, anchovies and

salad, aforementioned *socca*, and great pizzas.

Money

Thomas Cook foreign exchange offices are located at Nice-Ville, *2 pl. Magenta*, and *13 av. Thiers.*

Entertainment

In summer, Nice grinds till well past dawn. Bars shut around 0300, when everyone heads to the beach. Saunter along *rue de la Préfecture* in old Nice or side-streets off *pl. Rossetti* by the cathedral.

Nightlife

Stroll the cours Saleya at night, and watch the world and its poodle go by. Clubs are expensive; many bars have music and in summer everyone just dances on the tables.

Theatres, Cinemas and Concerts

In July the **Jazz Festival** is not to be missed; great names of world jazz appear in Nice's

Roman amphitheatre and gardens in Cimiez (tickets are available usually up until the event from **FNAC**, *Nice Etoile shopping mall, av. Jean Médecin*).

In February, the **Nice Carnival** is an overblown parade, ostensibly for the tourists but also the largest Mardi Gras celebration in France. A series of spectacular flower parades leads up to the final fireworks nights. Information is available from the Comité des Fêtes, *5 Promenade des Anglais, tel: 93 87 16 28.*

Sightseeing

Nice's museums are free and easily accessible by local bus. The newly refurbished **Musée Matisse** (take bus no.15, 17, 20 or 22) is in a 17th-century villa amongst the Roman ruins of Cimiez (beautiful paintings and sketches in a beautiful setting). Also in Cimiez, the **Musée Marc Chagall** on *av. du Dr Ménard*, (take bus no.15) is a graceful temple to Chagall's genius and beautifully lit to display his huge biblical canvases. In the centre of town, the **Musée d'Art Moderne et d'art Contemporain**, on *blvd Jean Jaurès*, (take bus no.5 or 17) is an unmistakable white marble cliff, filled by strangely fascinating squashed cars, pop art and nightmarish blue men. To the west of the centre, just up from the sea, the **Musée des Beaux-Arts Jules-Cheret** on 33 *av. des Baumettes*, (take bus no.38) contains a small collection of Dufys, Sisleys and others. To the east, **Musée Terra Amata** on *25 blvd Carnot* (take bus no.1, 2, 7, 9, 10 or 14) has displays of prehistoric inhabitants of Nice, from 400,000 years ago. **Vielle Ville** (Old Nice) seems more Italian than French (which it was until 1860). Wander the narrow streets, to **Palais Lascaris** on *15 rue Droite*, a 17th-century palace/museum. Beyond, steps lead up to the **Château**, site of ancient Greek Nikaia, with a park, small naval museum and breathtaking view. At sunset, stroll the **promenade des Anglais** as the lights begin to shimmer and the **Hotel Negresco** lights up like an elaborate wedding cake.

Side Tracks from Nice

Renoir spent the last years of his life in **Cagnes-Sur-Mer**, buying an isolated house in an olive grove overlooking the sea. Today, this is the delightful **Musée Renoir**, with rooms as he kept them 80 years ago (from the train station, take the bus to Beal-Les Colettes). Above the coast, **Haut de Cagnes** is a medieval Citadelle, whose Château is now an art museum.

There is an hourly service from Nice bus station that will take you to **St Paul-de-Vence**, a picturesque *village perche*, home to artists and tourists. Wander through the narrow medieval streets and sip coffee watching the *boule* players (*boulistes*) argue another round. The most interesting modern art museum in France, **The Fondation Maeght**, is here, purpose-built by the Maeghts, who were friends of Matisse. The garden is a quirky sculpture park, designed by Miró.

Villefranche-sur-Mer, one of the deepest ports on the coast, is today home to cruise ships, with a lively beach right below the train station and an Italianesque waterfront. The little **Chapelle St-Pierre** was painted outside and inside by Jean Cocteau in 1957.

Inaccessible by train, **St-Jean-Cap-Ferrat** is a walk up from Villefranche beach, or a bus ride from Nice bus station. This peninsula contains the prettiest beaches in the region, and some of the world's most expensive homes. The port is lined with restaurants, tranquil even in high season, and surprisingly inexpensive.

The only vila open is the Fondation Ephrusoi-de-Rothschild, which is home to superb furnishings and a splendid fine art collection.

Perched 427m above the Mediterranean, **Eze** has a spectacular view. The train station is by the sea, but steps climb up the cliff to the village, consisting of narrow streets, arty boutiques, and a Jardin Exotique full of incongruous cacti.

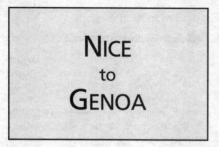

NICE
to
GENOA

This route takes you from Nice to the principality of Monaco, across the Italian Riviera di Ponente and connects with the Milan–Florence route (p. 269) at Genoa.

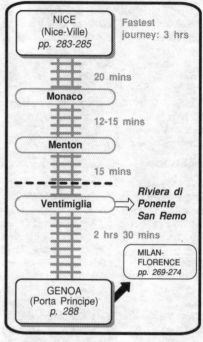

NICE (Nice-Ville) pp. 283-285 — Fastest journey: 3 hrs

20 mins

Monaco

12-15 mins

Menton

15 mins

Ventimiglia ⟹ **Riviera di Ponente San Remo**

2 hrs 30 mins

MILAN-FLORENCE pp. 269-274

GENOA (Porta Principe) p. 288

TRAINS

ETT tables: 90, 164, 355.

➡ Fast Track

Four daily trains (more in summer) run between Nice (Ville) and Genoa (Porta Principe). Other services are available, but require a change of train at Ventimiglia and add an extra 20–30 minutes to the journey, as you will have to allow time for customs checks. The approximate journey time on the through services is between 3–4 hrs.

〰 On Track

Nice–Monaco

There are dozens of trains per day between these two stops. The average journey time is 20 mins.

Monaco–Menton

Dozens of trains run daily, taking 12–15 mins.

Menton–(Border)–Ventimiglia

Services run regularly along this route, taking 15 mins.

Ventimiglia–Genoa (Genova)

There are about 20 trains per day along this coast. Most stop frequently but as the line is very scenic this is an advantage. Some faster IC trains operate, but a supplement is payable.

MONACO

Station: *tel: 93 87 50 50.* Information is available 0900–1845. For the Royal Palace head straight down to *pl. d'Armes*, continue towards the port and a footpath leads up onto the palace rock. For the Casino, turn left at the port along *blvd Albert 1er*, and up the hill along *av. d'Ostende* (500m). Otherwise, take bus no.4 from the station.

Tourist Office: *2A blvd des Moulins; tel: 93 30 87 01* (near the Casino). Open Mon–Sat 0900–1900 and Sunday mornings only.

Post Office: *pl. Beaumarchais* (you can't buy stamps anywhere else).

Accommodation and Food

Unsurprisingly expensive for hotels. The Centre de la Jeunesse Princesse-Stéphanie is a **youth hostel** on *24 av. Prince-Pierre*, 100m from the station and a godsend, for 16–26 year olds. Otherwise, try hotels on *rue de la Turbie* near the station. This is also one of the best places for reasonably priced pizzas (otherwise, try the snack bars on the *quai Albert 1er*).

Nightlife

There are three casinos. The **official Casino** charges FFr. 50 entrance fee, smart dress required. **Café de Paris**, next to the 'official' one, and **Loess**, down steps at the north end of the 'official' one, have free entry and less strict dress codes – over 21 applies, but not rigidly. Bars in Monaco are fun, but usually expensive. Try side streets off *rue Grimaldi* behind the port. Monaco is an enjoyable wandering ground at night, and watching is free.

Sightseeing

Flash, fast and finely manicured, Monaco will live up to expectations. Do not expect any bargains, but it costs little to wander, look and brush with opulence.

The **Casino** is the heart of Monte-Carlo (the city within the Principality of Monaco), designed by Garnier, and worth a look for the interior gilt alone. The **Musée National** (*17 av. Princesse Grace)* is stuffed full of dolls and figurines while the **Royal Palace**, up on the rock, is small and not so regal (changing of the guard takes place at 1155 precisely). Here, too, is the **Waxwork Museum**, with waxen Stephanies and Carolines next door to the real thing.

Monaco's greatest attraction is the **Musée Océanographique** (*av. St Martin)*, at the southern edge of the rock, one of the world's great aquariums, developed by Jacques Cousteau.

Above the skyscrapers, the **Jardin Exotique** (bus no. 2) sprouts 7,000 tropical plants.

MENTON

Station: *tel: 93 87 50 50.* Information is available daily 0900–1830. For the sea, head down *rue Edouard VII* from *pl. Victoria*.
Bus Station: *Esplanade Carei, route de Sospel; tel: 93 55 24 00.* North of the station, buses to hinterland.
Tourist Information: *Palais de l'Europe, av. Boyer* (left from station then right) open 0900–1800.

Accommodation

There is a **Youth Hostel** (*plateau St. Michel, route des Ciappas; tel: 93 35 93 14)* which you can reach by catching a minibus from the bus station. Next door is a campsite with a superb view over the Mediterranean. For hotels, try *rue Albert 1er*, near the station.

This is not a great place to eat. Italian-influenced restaurants are best, in the old town, around *rue St. Michel*. There is a lively market in *pl. aux Herbes*, which sells good lemons.

Sightseeing

Almost Italy, Menton is a retirement town with charm, long stony beaches and a lemon festival. It is worth at least an afternoon's visit. The lemon festival takes place in February, whilst August hosts a chamber music festival. Wander around the old town, constructed by the Grimaldis in the 15th-century. **Église St. Michel**, built in 1640, is particularly impressive. To the west, the **Palais Carnoles** belonged to a Monaco Prince and now houses an interesting art collection (impressionists/modern). In the **Hotel de Ville**, the **Salle des Mariages** was lavishly decorated by Jean Cocteau. There is a colourful **Musée Jean-Cocteau** (*bastion du Vieux-Port)* at the east end of the beaches.

VENTIMIGLIA

Ventimiglia, which is right on the French/Italian border, has a Roman theatre and a noteworthy old town, parts of which date back to the 12th century. There is also an excellent beach here.

– – – – – – – – – – – – – – – – – – –

🔊 Side Tracks from Ventimiglia

The beaches along the **Riviera di Ponente** (the coastal strip from Ventimiglia to Genoa) attract many visitors, but the locals remain more interested in their thriving olive oil industry.

A little further on from Ventimiglia, you come to **San Remo**, the largest resort on the Italian Riviera, stretched out around an 8 km bay. The old town, with its narrow streets, steep steps and arches, and bits of the new town (such as the palm-lined *Corso dell' Imperatice)*

---

will be of interest. A short bus ride away is the small coastal resort of **Arma di Taggia**.

Further along the coast, there are several other popular resorts, including **Alanio**, famed for its splendid gardens and a main street dating back to the 16th century and **Albenga** and **Pietra Ligure**, both smaller towns with fine, old centres. **Savona**, best known for a fine cathedral and its ship-breaking industry, marks the end of the best beaches as you head towards the industrial outer reaches of Genoa.

GENOA (GENOVA)

Stations: Stazione Principe, *tel: (10) 241 21*, handles trains to the west. Take bus no.40 from here to get to the city centre. Stazione Brignole, (*tel: (10) 58 63 50*), is further east and handles trains to the south and east, take bus no.41 from here to get to the city centre. Trains to the north use both stations; use bus no.37 to transfer between them.

Tourist Offices: City centre: *Via Roma 11; tel: (10) 58 14 07*. Open Mon–Thur 0800–1400 and 1600–12800; Fri–Sat 0800–1300 and at *Via Porta degli Archi 10–5; tel: (10) 54 15 41*. There are also tourist offices at both Principe (*tel: (10) 26 26 33*) and Brignole (*tel: (10) 56 20 56*) stations, which open daily 0800–2000.

Getting Around

The old part of town centres on the docks and is easily explored on foot (during the day; it's not safe at night). Elsewhere, there's a good bus service and ATM kiosks sell tourist tickets which provide unlimited travel for one day (price L. 1.200). There is also a funicular from *Plaza del Portello* to *Sant'Anna*, high on the hill on which the town is built. There's a great view from the top and the journey is worthwhile in itself.

Accommodation and Food

Cheap accommodation is easy to find, but some of it is very tacky. Try the roads on the outskirts of the old town and (near Brignole) *Via XX Septembre* and *Piazza Colombo*. There is one **Youth Hostel** (*Via Constanzi; tel: (10) 58 64*

07). The cheapest eating places for lunch are in the dock area, but most close in the evening. Street stalls all over the city sell fried seafood and chickpea pancakes.

Sightseeing

Genoa, 'La Superba', was once a proud maritime republic ruled by a doge. Today's city has little charm, but there is an interesting old town, with a maze of tiny alleys and many old palaces and mansions. It is centred on the port, to the south and south-west of the modern city.

The **Palazzo Ducale** (*Piazza Matteotti)* was once the seat of the doge. Across the street is **Gesu Church**, which contains two Rubens and a Guid-eo Reni. The nearby **Cattedrale di San Lorenzo** has some unusual artefacts: the reliquary of John the Baptist on which his severed head is reputed to have rested and a dish said to have been used at the Last Supper. The **Museo d'Arte Orientale** is housed in the Villetta di Negro, off *piazza Corvetto*. The mosaic spire of **Sant'Agostino** points the way to the **Museo dell'Architettura e Scultura Ligure**, built around the cloister of a 13th-century monastery and containing ancient maps of Genoa, as well as wood-carvings and many artefacts from different periods, as far back as Roman times. **Piazza Caricamento** is on the waterfront, and always a hive of activity with market stalls and many cafés. On one side is the **Palazzo San Giorgio**, which has housed various government departments for several centuries and has two rooms that are open to the public. **Piazza Bianci** was the heart of the old city and is now the commercial centre. From it, *Via San Luca* leads to the **Galleria Nazionale di Palazzo Spinola** (*Piazza Superiore di Pellicceria 1)*, which displays some excellent paintings.

To the north is **Via Garibaldi**, home to several Renaissance palaces. Two of these, **Palazzo Bianco** (no.11) and **Palazzo Rosso** (no.18) are now galleries with excellent collections, including Flemish and Dutch masterpieces. Both palaces are worth a visit to see the incredible decor.

If you fancy a swim, the suburb of Albaro (take bus no.41 from Principe) has a beach with showers and other washing facilities.

OSLO

Home to Munch, Ibsen, the Vikings, dynamite, the Nobel prizes and more recently the Middle East peace talks, Oslo still takes a back seat to its better-known, younger Scandinavian counterparts when it comes to tourism. The Viking capital, hemmed in by water, mountains and trees, was consecrated in 1050. It became a province of Denmark in the 15th century and, during reconstruction after a terrible fire, was renamed Christiania after the Danish King Christian. Oslo retrieved its name only in 1925, although the linguistic similarities between Danish and Norwegian live on and the city of today is laid-back and refreshing. Spend at least two days here if you want to visit the museums at Bygdøy.

Tourist Information

Vestbaneplassen 1; tel: 22 83 00 50, open Oct–Apr, Mon–Fri 0900–1600; May, Mon–Fri 0900–1800, Sat–Sun 0900–1600; Jun–Sep, Mon–Fri 0900–2000, Sat–Sun 0900–1600; and Sept, Mon–Fri 0900–1800, Sat–Sun 0900–1600. A smaller kiosk, at the **main station** *(tel: 22 17 11 24)* opens daily 0800–2300 (out of season 1500–1630). Both issue copies of *The Official Guide for Oslo* (free), a monthly listings guide, *What's On In Oslo*, and maps. An Inter-Rail centre at the station, Jun–Sept, Mon–Sun 0700–2300, has showers and information. **Youth information**: *Møllergata 3; tel: 22 41 51 32.*

Arriving and Departing

Airport

Fornebu Airport (7km west) is 20 mins away by bus. The **Flybussen** (airport bus; Nkr.30) picks up from the main station, bus terminal and some hotels. Telephone enquiries are answered by individual airlines only, but try SAS; *tel: 67 59 67 16.*

Buses

Long-distance buses leave from *Bussterminalen, Schweigaards gt. 10; tel: 22 17 01 66.*

Stations

Oslo has two central stations. **Oslo Sentral-stasjon** (known locally as Oslo S), *Jernbanetorget; tel: 22 36 80 00*, lies in the city hub. It is well-equipped and all international, and most domestic trains, stop here. It connects with the T-bane (turn right out of station) and many bus lines. The other station is **Nationaltheateret**.

Getting Around

Most big attractions are some distance from the centre but excellent transport connections make them easily accessible. An easy-to-use service of underground, tram, bus and ferry operates within the SL (Stor–Oslo Lokaltrafik) network. There are 8 **underground** lines (final destination indicates direction), 5 **tram** routes running east–west and 20 **bus** services which converge on Oslo Central Station. **Ferry** connections to Bygdøy, *Rådhusbrygge 3*, (in front of City Hall) operate Apr–Sept only. There are all-year sailings to Hovedoya and some islands in the Fjord from *Vippetangen* (bus no.29).

The **Trafikanten** (modern tower-like construction outside Sentralstasjon), *Jernbanetorget; tel: 22 17 70 30*, handles transport queries, provides maps and sells tickets. Open 0700–2300; *tel: 22 38 80 90*. **Night trams** and **buses** run 2400–0600. Taxis are available only from a rank or by phone. Credit-card payment is widely accepted.

Tickets

Buy tickets for 1, 10 or 24 hours (a **flexikort**) at the Trafikanten, Nationaltheatret station, or at Narvesen kiosks.

The **Oslo Card**, valid for 24 hours, allows free public transport (including a mini-cruise on the fjord), free admission to most sights and museums and discounts on cinema tickets and car hire. With a 3-day card, you also get 30% off NSB tickets anywhere in Norway. Available from tourist offices, post offices, hotels, camping sights and petrol stations.

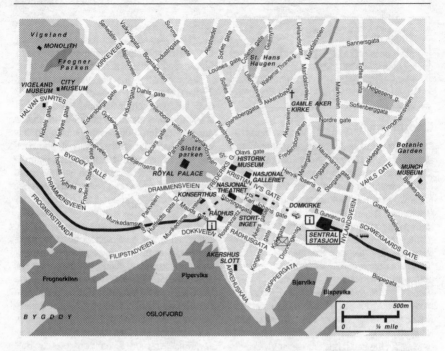

Living in Oslo

Accommodation

Bookings can be made from either tourist office. Hotels start at about Nkr.300 per person, in a double, although prices are cheaper in the summer (to encourage tourism). International chains with property in the city include: *Hn, SA, SC.*

The more central of the two **hostels, Haraldsheim**, *Boks 41, Grefsen; tel: 22 15 50 43* is often full in summer. July–Aug, some beds are available for Nkr.75 at *Inter-Rail Point Møllergata.1; tel: 22 42 10 66.*

The tourist office at Sentralstasjon can also arrange private accomodation (min. two nights) on arrival (Nkr.260 double room; Nkr.155 single). **Ellingsen Pensjonat,** *Holtegata 25*, is usually full on account of its extremely cheap rooms (Nkr.180 single; Nkr.280 double). **Bogstad campsite** is open all year but a long way out. **Ekeberg**, summer only, is half the journey (10 mins on buses no.22/45/46).

The **Oslo Package**, available summer (Jun 24–Aug 16), Easter, Christmas and weekends, offers rooms in 20 hotels from Nkr.295 including breakfast and, more importantly, the Oslo Card. (Free for children sharing adult rooms).

Food and Drink

Eating out in Oslo can be very expensive. Cheapish options include sandwiches from the baker, fast-food, Chinese, or self-catering from cheap supermarkets. Hotel rooms often include a large buffet-style breakfast, which can help to save on lunch. Feasts of the help-yourself-all-evening variety are available from many big hotels. The most expensive food, in general, tends to be Norwegian, French or Japanese. For restaurant listings look in *The Official Guide for Oslo.*

Embassies

Australia and New Zealand: Not represented – contact the UK embassy.
Canada: *Oscarsgate 20; tel: 22 46 69 55*
UK: Thomas Heftyesgate 8; tel: 22 55 24 00
US: *Drammensveien 18; tel: 22 44 85 50*

Communications

The main **post office,** *13–15 Dronningensgate,* opens Mon–Fri 0800–1730, Sat 0900–1500. The Poste Restante office is open until 2000.

Oslo phone numbers have eight digits; there is no area code.

Entertainment

Most of Oslo's nightlife stretches from the *Aker Brygge* to the *Historik Museum,* taking in Chinatown and the City Hall. Look in *What's On In Oslo* for up-to-date events listings. Well-known operas are performed at **Den Norske Opera** (Norwegian Opera House), and the **Oslo Konserthus** (concert house) stages 'folklore events' (Mon and Thurs, July–Aug). English-language films are undubbed and Oslo Card holders get discounts (May–July).

Sightseeing

Many sights lie on the grid of streets that nestle behind the waterside hill fortress, **Akershus.** However, expect to make the odd journey out of town for the better ones such as the Vigeland Park and the Munch Museum. Most attractions open only in summer.

Oslo's main artery, **Karl Johans gate,** stretches out from the station for over a kilometre to the 19th-century Royal Palace, lined by shops and cafés. Historic buildings along the way include **Oslo Domkirke,** *Stortovet 1.* Of the original cathedral, (1697), only the pulpit, altarpiece and organ front remain. The stained-glass window is by the ubiquitous Vigeland. Further down on the left is the rounded, yellow brick **Stortinget** (Parliament building) built in 1866, overlooking *Eidsvollsplass,* a green city square, and the **National Theatre.**

To the north, *Universitetsgata* leads to the **Nasjonalgalleriet** (National Gallery), *Universitetsgata 13,* with Norway's biggest collection of art (includes a room dedicated to Edvard Munch (1863–1944) and works by Gauguin, Monet, and Picasso). The **Royal Palace** (not open to public), is half-way between the station and the statue park, **Vigelandsparken.** Gustav Vigeland's 175 statues in bronze and granite line the park's central avenue and bridge. These large,

earthy, animated statues are a sensual celebration of life, leading towards the phallic *monolith of life,* a compression of tumbling bodies. (On sunny days the fountains cast a rainbow in front of the monolith.) For the **Vigelandsmuseet** (Vigeland Museum), *Nobels gate 32,* head south, past **Oslo City Museum.**

Still spurning the city-centre, a visitor to the **Munch Museum,** *Tøyengata 53* (close to the Botanical Gardens and the Zoo), will encounter a myriad collection of drawings and paintings. This is also, usually, home of the painter's most famous work, *The Scream,* which was stolen in early 1994. At a similar distance, services are still held in the **Gamle Aker Kirke,** *Akersveien 25,* Oslo's oldest building (1080).

Perched in the hills overlooking Oslo is the famous ski-jump **Holmenkollbakken,** *Kongenveien 5,* (reached by T-bane). Nearby are the **Ski Museum,** featuring pre-historic skis, the *ski-simulator* and the **Tryvannstarnet,** a 588m ski-tower offering views of Sweden, Mount Gausta and the Oslo fjords. If you arrive by boat it should be visible 20 mins before you land.

Bygdøy

The **Bygdøy** peninsula, on the far side of the bay, is home to several fine museums and one of Oslo's biggest tourist attractions. There are regular ferries in summer from the Rådhus (City Hall), pier 3, or take buses no.30/30X all year.

The **Norsk Folkemuseum** (Norwegian Folk Museum), *Museumsveien,* a collection of 150 buildings dating from the Middle Ages to the 19th century, is Norway's largest museum of cultural history. The centre-piece is a stave church built around 1200. Indoor exhibitions include jewellery, furnishing and ecclesiastical art. The **Vikingskiphuset** (Viking Ship Museum), *Huk aveny 35,* houses three superb examples of Viking craftmanship, resurrected from the Oslo fjord. The chief exhibit at the **Kon Tiki Museum,** *Bygdøynesvn. 36,* is Thor Heyer-dahl's balsa raft, the *Kon Tiki,* used in 1947 to prove the possibility that the Polynesians came originally from South America. Opposite, the tent-shaped **Fram-museet** is home to the polar exploration ship, *Fram,* used during Amundsen's epic journey to the South Pole in 1911.

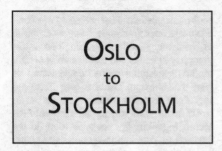

OSLO
to
STOCKHOLM

This route follows what was part of the historic King's Road from Oslo to St Petersburg, and stretches across the quiet, undulating hills and expansive lakes of southern Sweden.

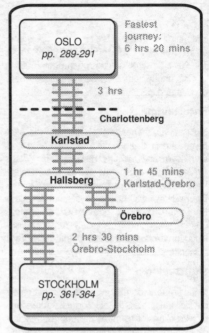

OSLO
pp. 289-291

Fastest journey:
6 hrs 20 mins

3 hrs

Charlottenberg

Karlstad

Hallsberg

1 hr 45 mins
Karlstad-Örebro

Örebro

2 hrs 30 mins
Örebro-Stockholm

STOCKHOLM
pp. 361-364

TRAINS

ETT tables: 470, 469.

→| Fast Track

Three trains run daily (only one on Saturdays), taking 6 hrs 20 mins (dining-car; reservations required), and 8 hrs by night (first- and second-class sleepers and couchettes; no dining-car).

⁓ On Track

Oslo–Border–Karlstad

Three trains run daily, taking about 3 hrs.

Karlstad–Örebro

Six trains run daily, taking about 1 hr 45 mins, (change at Hallsberg).

Örebro–Stockholm

Trains every two hours, taking 2 hrs 30 mins (change at Hallsberg).

KARLSTAD

Station: *tel: (054) 14 33 50*. Behind main shopping street.
Tourist Office: Bibliotekshuset, *V. Torggatan 26; tel: (054) 19 59 01*, (moves to conference centre July 94). Pick up *A Walk around Central Karlstad.*

Karlstad, by Lake Vänern (Sweden's largest), is a popular holiday destination for Scandinavian families who come here to water-ski, fish, sail, and sun-bathe. It is also home to Sweden's longest stone bridge, *Östra Bron.* **Mariebergs-skogen**, *Långövägen*, is a leisure park with an open-air museum, amusements and animals. Good for children.

ÖREBRO

Station: *tel: (0) 19 17 22 08*.
Tourist Office: in castle, *tel: (0) 19 21 21 21*. June 13–Aug 21, Mon–Fri 1000–1900, Sat–Sun 1000–1700. Otherwise, Mon–Fri 0900–1700.

This is a quiet, leafy residential town. The pretty **Örebro Slott** (Castle) flanked by four round towers, stands on a small island in the Black River. There is a charming walk along the river towards **Wadköping** (*Skytteparken*), past neatly painted summer houses tucked into the trees. When you get there, **Wadköping** is a 'timber-built town' with a few weather-boarded houses selling postcards and teas. Climb the **water tower** for a view of the town.

PARIS

With probably the most romantic image in the world, Paris is an enchanting city, a place of elegance and gaiety, chic and shock, but it is also a busy, pragmatic capital. There is an enormous amount to see and do, so allow at least three days. Try to avoid Mondays and Tuesdays, as many museums are shut then.

Tourist Information

Paris Convention and Visitors' Bureau, 127 av. des Champs-Elysées; tel: 49 52 53 54 (metro: Etoile/George V). Open 0900–2100 daily except 25 Dec, 1 Jan and 1 May. It has vast amounts of useful information on everything in Paris and the surrounding Île de France, a booking service for excursions, a France-wide hotel reservation desk, Euro Disney booking desk, a bureau de change (except Sundays) and an SNCF (rail) information and booking desk.

Further offices are at: **Gare du Nord** (tel: 45 26 94 82), May–Oct, Mon–Sat 0800–2100 and Sun 1300–2000; Nov–Apr, Mon–Sat 0800–2000. **Gare d'Austerlitz** (tel: 45 84 91 70), Mon–Sat 0800–1500. **Gare de l'Est** (tel: 46 07 17 73), May–Oct, Mon–Sat 0800–2100; Nov–Apr, Mon–Sat 0800–2000. **Gare de Lyon** (tel: 43 43 33 24) and **Gare Montparnasse** (tel: 43 22 19 19) are both open May–Oct, Mon–Sat 0800–2100; Nov–Apr, Mon–Sat 0800–2000.

For **youth information**, try C.I.D.J., 101 Quay Branly, 75740 Paris; tel: 44 49 12 00. Open Mon–Sat 0930–1830.

Arriving and Departing

Airports

Charles de Gaulle (Roissy) Airport is 26 km/16 miles north-east of Paris on autoroute A1. The information phone line (tel: 48 62 22 80) operates 24 hrs daily. Facilities including a tourist information (tel: 48 62 22 80) and hotel reservation office (tel: 48 62 27 29), open 0700–1900. **Air France** (tel: 48 64 14 24) run coaches every 15–20 minutes from the airport to pl. Charles de Gaulle/Etoile and Porte Maillot. The **RATP Roissybus** (tel: 48 04 18 24) leaves every 15 mins from Opéra Garnier. There are also RATP buses to Gare de l'Est, Gare Montparnasse and Nation. Journey time: 40 mins–1 hr. **Rail** services run every 15 mins from the Gare du Nord to Charles de Gaulle RER rail station (calling at several stations throughout the city centre en route), with a shuttle service on to the terminals (journey time about 35 mins). A taxi to the centre costs about FFr.170.

Orly Airport (14 km south of Paris on autoroute A6) also has a 24-hr information line (tel: 49 75 15 15). **Air France** (tel: 41 75 44 40) operates buses every 12 mins between the airport, Les Invalides and Gare Montparnasse (journey time: 30 mins). The **RATP Orlybus** runs every 13 mins from pl. Denfert-Rochereau and the **RER Line B** goes to Gare Antony, where it connects with the Orlyval shuttle service to the airport. RATP information (tel: 43 46 14 14), open 0600–2100.

Stations

There are six main SNCF stations in Paris, all with a wide range of services, from tourist information and left luggage offices to bookstalls, newsstands and cafés. Each has its own metro stop and is also served by RER lines. For information about fares and timetables tel: 30 64 50 50; to make telephone reservations for SNCF trains tel: 45 65 60 60 (0700–2200); for other SNCF enquiries tel: 45 82 50 50.

Paris-Est (tel: 40 18 20 00) for trains to Champagne, north-east France, Luxembourg, southern Germany, Austria and northern Switzerland. **Paris-Nord** (tel: 49 95 10 00) for trains to north-west France, Scandinavia, UK, Belgium, Holland and northern Germany. **Paris-Saint-Lazare** (tel: 42 85 88 00) for Normandy and the UK via Dieppe. **Paris-Montparnasse** (tel: 40 48 10 00) for trains to Brittany, the Loire Valley and south-west France. **Paris-Austerlitz** (tel: 45 84 14 18) for trains to the Loire Valley, south and south-west France, Spain and Portugal. **Paris-Lyon** (tel: 40 19 60 00) for trains to eastern France, the Auvergne, Provence, the French Riviera, Switzerland and Italy.

Getting Around

One of the greatest joys of Paris is to stroll through its charming streets and squares, or along the peaceful banks of the River Seine. The city centre is compact, and main sights are clustered in accessible groups, but you will still need to use the excellent public transport network, consisting of the metro, buses, the RER (three suburban rail lines crossing through central Paris) and other suburban SNCF rail services.

A good transport map covering metro, buses and RER services (called *Le Petit Plan de Paris*), and a good, free street map of the centre, sponsored by *Printemps*, are available from all tourist information centres, most hotels, and some metro stations. If you need more detail, there are various map books on sale at newsagents and bookshops for about FFr.50.00.

Tickets

Although Paris is divided into eight concentric zones, the same, single-price tickets are used on all the various transport networks, and you simply use more tickets the more zones you travel through. If you are planning to use relatively little public transport, the best way to buy these is as a book of ten tickets (a *carnet*). Single tickets are currently FFr.6.90, but a carnet is only FFr.39.00. If you want the freedom to jump on and off transport as often as you like, ask for a one day **Formule 1** pass. The cost varies from FFr.27.00 for the inner city zones to FFr.90.00 for five zones (which will get you out to Versailles). For longer visits, buy a **Paris Visite** card (three zones for three days at FFr.90.00, to five zones for five days at FFr.275). The cheapest form of pass, if you are to be in town for some length of time, however, is the weekly **Carte Orange**, (two zones for FFr.59.00, valid from Monday to Sunday). For this, you will need some identification and passport photos.

All tickets are available at main metro, RER and SNCF stations and *carnets* and Formule 1 passes are also sold at some newsagents (*tabacs*). In addition, Paris Visite and Formule 1 cards can be bought at the main tourist office

(see p. 293) and the airports. RATP have two tourist offices at *53bis, quai des Grands Augustins, 75006; tel: 40 46 42 17* (metro: *Saint-Michel*), and *pl. de la Madeleine, 75001; tel: 40 06 71 45* (metro: *Madeleine*). For general RATP information *tel: 43 46 14 14*.

The Metro

The metro (subway) system is excellent, often quoted as the finest in the world, running 0530–0100, with numerous stops and trains every few minutes. The lines are numbered and colour-coded on the maps, but the platforms are labelled according to the last stop on the line (for example, if heading west on the red line, the last stop is *La Défense*, so the line is labelled thus). To change trains, look for the *Correspondance* sign. You put your ticket through an automatic barrier to get in.

Buses

There is a good bus service across the city during the day, but services are much less frequent (dependent on the route) after about 2030 and on Sundays. Buses are also zoned, but the zones are smaller and you may have to use more than one ticket. They are marked at bus stops and on the sides of buses. Put single tickets through the punch machine beside the driver as you board. *Do not* put your pass through the machine, but just show it to the driver. To get off, press the request-stop button (*arrêt demandé*) and press the button beside the door to open it.

From 0100 to 0500, there is a restricted night bus service (*Noctambus*), with ten lines fanning out from Châtelet (*av. Victoria* or *rue Saint-Martin*) to the surburbs. There is one bus an hour each way on each route. From 1230 to 2000 on Sundays and public holidays, between 11 April and 26 September, the **Balabus** follows a special route designed to travel between all Paris's top tourist attractions.

Several companies run guided sightseeing bus tours. Among them are: **Paris Vision**, *214 rue de Rivoli, 75001; tel: 42 60 31 25* (metro: *Tuileries*); **Cityrama**, *4 pl. des Pyramides, 75001; tel: 42 60 30 14* (metro: *Palais Royal*); and **Paris Bus**, with departures from the Eiffel Tower; *tel: 42 30 55 50* (metro: *Trocadéro*).

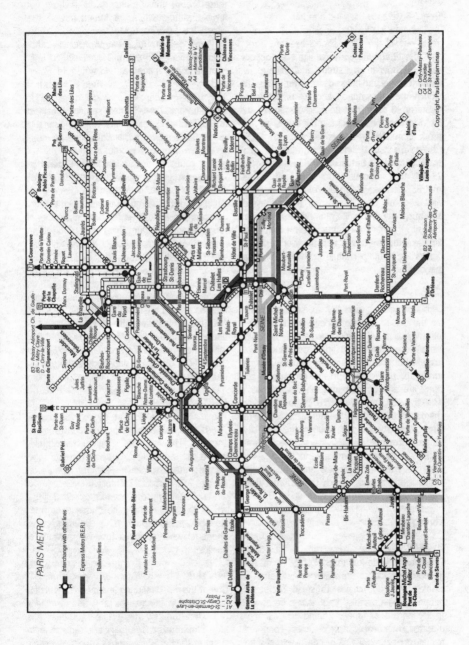

River journeys

The Seine, its islands and *quais* (quays) together create one of the world's most beautiful stretches of river and the Parisians take every opportunity to show it off to tourists. Of the many boat trips, the most famous are the **Bâteaux Mouches** (metro: *Alma Marceau*), which operate every 30 mins from Pont de l'Alma (*tel: 42 25 96 10* for bookings; *tel: 40 76 99 99* for information). The **Vedettes de Paris** (*tel: 47 05 71 29*; Paris Visite ticket holders are entitled to a discount), and the **Bâteaux Parisiens** (*tel: 44 11 33 44*) both operate from the Pont d'Iéna (metro: *Bir Hakeim/Trocadéro*). The cheapest and most useful trips are on the unguided **Batobus**, operated by RATP during the summer (*tel: 44 11 33 44*). This is effectively a water bus service, with five stops at main tourist sights. Tickets FFr.12.00 per stage or FFr.60.00 for a day pass.

Taxis

Taxis are plentiful, with 487 taxi ranks throughout the city. Flagging one down in the street is allowed, but is rarely successful. Officially licensed taxis have two lights on the roof, a large white one if the taxi is free for hire, a smaller orange one if it is already occupied. There are three price bands which apply from 0700 to 1900, from 1900 to 0700, and a higher charge for night trips to the surburbs. Prices rarely exceed about FFr.70.00 within the city centre, but you will have to pay supplements at stations, at Air France terminals, for luggage, for more than three passengers and for animals. Avoid unofficial taxis, which charge what they like (which is a lot).

Living in Paris

Accommodation

Paris has a wide range of hotels, from the glamorous, such as the George V, through a whole variety of chains to small backstreet pensions. It is advisable, if not always necessary, to try and book ahead during the summer months. For cheaper hotels, expect to pay a minimum of FFr.250 a night per room. Look for these around the stations, in the lively, if not always salubrious, area of *Montmartre/Pigalle*, and in the *Marais* and *Montparnasse*.

Paris Sejour Réservation, 90 av. des *Champs-Elysees 75008; tel: 47 53 80 81* (metro: *George V*) is a reservation system for hotels and self-catering apartments. **Bed & Breakfast 1**, *7 rue Campagne Première 75014; tel: 43 35 11 26* (metro: *Raspail*) offers bed and breakfast and self-catering apartments at very reasonable rates. The main tourist office has a hotel reservation desk (see p. 293).

For youth hostels, contact the **Fédération Unie des Auberges de Jeunesse**, *27 rue Pajol, 75018; tel: 46 07 00 01* (metro: *Porte de la Chapelle*) or the **Acceuil des Jeunes en France**, which runs over 5,000 cheap beds in a variety of locations and has four offices at: *119 rue Saint-Martin, 75004; tel: 42 77 87 80* (metro: *Châtelet-les-Halles*); *139 boul. Saint-Michel, 75006; tel: 43 54 95 86* (metro: *Port-Royal*); *16 rue du Pont Louis-Philippe, 75004; tel: 42 72 72 09* (metro: *Hotel-de-Ville*); and, during summer months only, the Gare du Nord (*tel: 49 95 10 00*). There are no **campsites** in central Paris. The nearest are in the *Bois de Boulogne* (*tel: 45 24 30 00*), Le Tremblay (*tel: 43 97 43 97*), Torcy (*tel: 60 05 42 32*) and *Montigny-le-Bretonneux* (*tel: 30 58 56 20*).

Communications

The main **post office**, at *52 rue du Louvre, 75001; tel: 40 28 20 00* (metro: *Louvre-Rivoli/Les Halles*) is open 24 hrs a day for making telephone calls and collecting poste restante mail. Address letters to: *Poste Restante, 52 rue du Louvre, 75001 Paris RP, France*.

To phone Paris from abroad: *tel: 33 (France) + 1 (Paris) + number*; to phone Paris from elsewhere in France: *tel: 16 + 1 + number*; to phone elsewhere in France from Paris: *tel: 16 + number*.

Eating and Drinking

One of the most enduring images of Paris is of a lazy day spent idling at the table of a pavement café. Unfortunately, this will cost you dear. It is always more expensive to sit at a table than to stand at the bar, while drinks in bars and cafés can be extortionately expensive anyway. Moreover, a quick snack or salad in that same café can be as expensive as a full three-course set meal. If you are on a budget and are tired of hamburgers, buy a sandwich and a can from a pavement stall, or, even more cheaply, head for the nearest bakery (*boulangerie*), and buy some bread. Then find a supermarket or delicatessen (*charcuterie*) for your cheese, salami, pâté and fruit and choose yourself a shady, free garden square in which to rest your aching feet.

This should leave you with enough money to enjoy a full meal in the evening, when you can make the most of the two- or three-course set meals (*le menu*), many of which also include wine and coffee. Almost every restaurant serves at least one, with two or three choices per course, and prices upwards from FFr.60.00.

There are literally thousands of restaurants in Paris, catering for all possible tastes, with every version of French cuisine as well as a host of others, from Indian and Chinese to Greek. Choose your area (*Montparnasse, Montmartre/ Pigalle* and the *Marais* are good places to start), remembering to keep away from obviously touristy areas such as the *pl. du Tertre* or the *Île de la Cité*, where prices rise and quality falls. The side streets a few yards away will have a good selection. Then wander and read menus until you find one to suit your taste and pocket.

Embassies and Consulates

Australia: *4 rue Jean Rey, 75015; tel: 40 59 33 00* (metro: *Bir Hakeim*).
Canada: *35 av. Montaigne, 75008; tel: 47 23 01 01* (metro: *Franklin D. Roosevelt*).
New Zealand: *7ter rue Léonard-da-Vinci, 75016; tel: 45 00 24 11* (metro: *Victor Hugo*).
UK: *9 av. Hoche, 75008; tel: 42 66 91 42* (metro: *Charles-de-Gaulle/Étoile*).
USA: *2 rue Saint Florentin, 75001; tel: 42 96 14 88* (metro: *Concorde*).

Money

All banks and the plentiful bureaux de change, will change money for you. **Thomas Cook** travellers' cheques can be cashed free of commission charges in the bureaux listed on p. 300, and if denominated in French francs are

accepted as cash in hotels, larger restaurants and stores. (Due to a recent spate of forgeries and 'runners' however, an increasing number of shops and restaurants are becoming reluctant to accept either travellers' cheques or Eurocheques, so check before you purchase anything.) Major credit cards are all widely accepted throughout Paris.

Entertainment

There are variations according to the time of year, but there is almost always plenty to do in Paris, as long as you can pay for it. Throughout the summer, a host of festivals brings music of all sorts into the halls, churches and even onto the streets. For good street entertainment, go to the square near the *Centre Georges Pompidou*, which is always alive with performers.

There are two excellent, cheap, weekly guides to entertainment, available from newsagents – *l'Officiel des Spectacles* and *Pariscope*, which has an eight-page English-language supplement. The tourist office runs an English-language telephone hotline on 49 52 53 56. For late bookings, there is a half-price ticket kiosk (credit cards not accepted) at *15 pl. de la Madeleine, 75008* (metro: *Madeleine*); open Tues–Sat 1230–2000, Sun 1230–1800, closed Mon.

Nightlife

Paris is most famous for its cabaret, from huge revues like the *Moulin Rouge* to acid stand-up of the sort delivered in *café-théâtres* such as the *Lapin Agile*. If you want it, head towards Montmartre. The problem is that the big shows are exorbitantly expensive these days, while you need very good French to understand the rather wordy comedy. There are several good venues offering live jazz or rock, and the number of discos and dance clubs you would expect in any major European city.

Theatres, Cinemas and Concerts

For those who can speak French, there are several **theatres**, from the famed *Comédie Française* to small experimental performance spaces. More importantly, Paris has two superb **opera** houses, with regular seasons of both ballet and opera, with the cheapest seats at

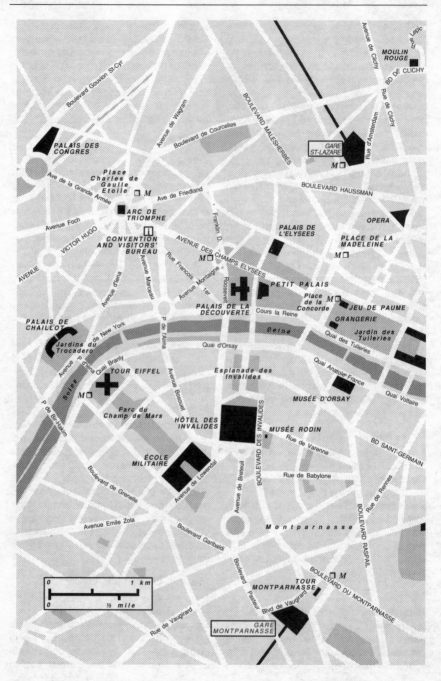

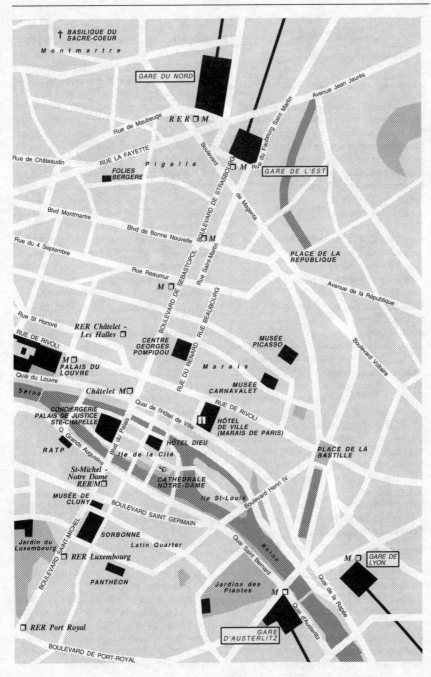

Thomas Cook

Thomas Cook travellers' cheque emergency refund number:
tel: 47 55 52 52 (toll-free)

The following Thomas Cook locations can offer: commission-free encashment of Thomas Cook travellers' cheques; emergency assistance in the case of lost or stolen Thomas Cook travellers' cheques (locations marked *) and MasterCard cards (locations marked **); extended opening outside banking hours.
Gare de Montparnasse, pl. Raoul Dautry *
Gare Neuilly/Porte Maillot, 82 av. de la Grande Armée *
Gare du Nord, rue Dunkerque
Tour Eiffel, Champs de Mars
Gare St Lazare, Salle des Pas Perdus *
Gare de l'Est, rue du 8 Mai 1945
8 pl. de l'Opera * **
2 rue Lepic *

---

fairly moderate prices. There are also numerous **concerts**, held everywhere from purpose-built concert halls to museums and churches. On Sundays, at 1730, there is always a free organ recital at Notre Dâme. Ask about other free concerts at the tourist office.

There are huge numbers of **cinemas** throughout the city, with everything from Hollywood blockbusters to retrospectives and art films on offer VO (*Version Originale*) means the film has subtitles; VF (*Version Française*) means it's been dubbed. There are discounts at most cinemas for students, senior citizens and for everyone on Wednesdays.

Shopping

People cross the world to shop in Paris – if they are rich enough. You can get everything here, but don't expect to find bargains. For really upmarket window shopping, try the *rue St Honoré* and *rue de Rivoli*, where there is also a good English-language bookshop (metro: *Palais Royal/Tuileries*), and streets near the *Champs Elysées*, such as the *av. Montaigne* and *rue*

Francois 1er (metro: *Franklin D. Roosevelt/ Champs Elysées Clemenceau*), where the haut couture houses congregate. For the large department stores, such as Galeries Lafayette and Printemps, head towards *Boulevard Haussman* (metro: *Havre-Caumartin/Chaussée d'Antin*). For small, trendy boutiques, try the refurbished market at *Les Halles* (metro: *Les Halles*) or the streets around the church of St Germain-des-Prés (metro: *St Germain des Prés*).

Paris also still has a lively selection of excellent **markets**, from colourful streets such as the *rue Mouffetard* (metro: *Censier-Daubenton*), *rue Lepic* (metro: *Blanche*), and *rue Cler* (metro: *École Militaire*) to the flower markets on the *rue Lepine* (which turns into a bird market on Sundays, metro: *Cité*) and in the *pl. de la Madeleine* (metro: *Madeleine*). Probably the most famous of all however, is the Flea Market of *Saint Ouen*, open from Saturday to Monday (metro: *Saint-Ouen/Clignancourt*).

Sightseeing

Almost everything in Paris has an entrance fee, and this can be quite steep. Some places give you up to 50% discount if you have an ISIC card (see p. 15), but otherwise, buy a *Carte Inter-Musée*. This is a pass for 65 different sights, including the most famous in and around Paris. Not only is it almost guaranteed to save you money, but it allows you to queue jump. Prices are: one day/FFr.60; three days/FFr.120; five days/FFr.170 (on sale at all participating museums and monuments, tourist offices and main metro stations).

The sights in Paris tend to be clustered in well-contained groups. The following suggestions include only the best and most famous.

The Islands

The oldest area in the city is on the islands in the Seine: the **Île de la Cité** and **Île St Louis** (metro: *Cité*). Take the time to wander the side streets and look at sights such as the **Palais de Justice** and the **Conciergerie**, but don't miss the two superb churches: the great **Cathedral of Nôtre Dame**, built between 1163 and 1345, one of the finest Gothic churches in the world, and the tiny **Sainte-Chapelle**, in the courtyard of the

Palais de Justice, with acres of stunningly beautiful stained glass. On a sunny day, it's like standing in a kaleidoscope.

The Right Bank

Just over the bridge, the **Hôtel de Ville** marks the start of the **Marais**, a district filled with charming small streets and squares, as well as several fine museums. Of them all, the greatest is the unmissable **Centre Georges Pompidou** (otherwise known as the Beaubourg), *19 rue Beaubourg* (metro: *Hotel de Ville/Chatelet-Les Halles*), a controversial building, filled with wonderful modern art. Other nearby museums include the **Musée Carnavalet**, *23 rue de Sevigne*, dedicated to the history of Paris, and the **Musée Picasso**, *5 rue de Thorigny* (metro for both: *Saint-Paul/Chemin Vert*).

Back beside the river, the **Louvre** (metro: *Palais-Royal*) is one of the greatest art galleries in the world and a sightseeing marathon with 18 km/11 miles of corridors. Its most famous exhibits, the *Mona Lisa* (La *Joconde* in French) and the *Venus de Milo*, are always surrounded by vast crowds. Other equally stunning exhibits have half the number of people. From here, the formal **Jardins des Tuileries** lead along the river to the **pl. de la Concorde**. At the far end are two small but enchanting galleries, the **Jeu de Paume**, *20 rue Royale* (metro: *Concorde/Tuileries*), dedicated to the Impressionists, and the **Orangerie**, *pl. de la Concorde* (metro: *Concorde*), devoted entirely to eight of Monet's waterlily paintings. From *Concorde*, the **Champs-Elysées** lead up towards the **Arc de Triomphe**, *pl. Charles-de-Gaulle Etoile*, while the river continues on towards the **Palais de Chaillot**, *pl. du Trocadéro* (metro: *Trocadéro*) directly opposite the Eiffel Tower. This is the home of the **Musée du Cinema Henri Langlois**.

The Left Bank

Having craned upwards at or stood in the queue for the **Eiffel Tower** (metro: *Champs-de-Mars*), head over to **Les Invalides** *av. de Tourville* (metro: *Latour-Maubourg/Varenne*) to see Napoleon's tomb and the **Musée de l'Armée**. Behind this you will find the **Musée Rodin**, *77 rue de Varenne* (metro: *Varenne*).

Continuing along the river, the **Musée d'Orsay**, *1 rue de Bellechasse* (metro: *Solférino*), is a converted railway station that now houses a truly spectacular collection of 19th- and early 20th-century art, including works by the great Impressionists, from Monet and Manet to Van Gogh. Not to be missed at any cost.

Beyond this is the **Latin Quarter**, home of the **Sorbonne** and the traditional student district. For the tourist, its main attractions are the wonderful medieval **Musée de Cluny**, *6 pl. Paul-Painlevé* (metro: *Cluny-La Sorbonne/St Michel/Odeon*) and the two great parks: the **Jardin de Luxembourg**, *boul. St Michel* (metro: *Luxembourg*) and the **Jardin des Plantes**, *quai St Bernard* (metro: *Austerlitz*), which also houses the **Museum of Natural History**.

Views of Paris

From the top of the hill (or even better, from the dome of Sacré-Coeur) on **Montmartre** (metro: *Abbesses* or *Anvers* for the funicular to the top); from the top of the **Eiffel Tower**; from the top of the 59-storey high **Tour Montparnasse** (metro: *Montparnasse-Bienvenue*); from the top of the **Grande-Arche de la Défense** (RER: *La Défense*); from the tower of the **Cathédrale de Nôtre Dame** (metro: *Cité*).

Side Tracks from Paris

Allow time for trips into the suburbs and a little way out of town as well, for some of the sights here equal the best in the centre, such as the great châteaux of **Versailles** and **Fontainebleau**, the modern suburbs of **La Défense** and **La Villette** (home to the massive **Cité des Sciences**) and, of course, **Euro Disney**.

Connection: Paris to Brussels

From Paris you can connect with **Brussels** and join the **Brussels–Amsterdam** (see pp. 94–95), **Brussels–London** (see pp. 230–232), or **Brussels–Frankfurt** (see pp. 136–140) route. There are frequent trains daily from Paris (Nord) to Brussels (Midi/Nord). Journey time ranges from 2 hrs 30 mins to 3 hrs, depending on the type of train.

PARIS
to
BARCELONA

Straight through central France to the Catalan coast, this route serves Toulouse sausages on Limoges porcelain and joins two of Europe's cultural capitals.

TRAINS

ETT tables: 47, 133, 141, 138, 139.

→ Fast Track

One night train (sleepers; dining-car), taking 11 hrs, runs Paris (Austerlitz)–Barcelona (França) direct. A day train runs Paris (Austerlitz)–Barcelona (Sants), taking 13–14 hrs (change at the Cerbère/Port Bou border).

⤳ On Track

Paris–Orléans

Several trains run daily Paris (Austerlitz)–Les Aubrais (2 km from Orléans, which has a connecting service), taking about 1 hr.

From Orléans, you can travel across to Tours to join the Paris–Madrid route (see p. 315) or to Angers, to join the Paris–Brest route (p. 306).

Orléans–Châteauroux

Several trains run daily, taking 1 hr 30 mins.

Châteauroux–Limoges

About 12 trains run daily, taking 1 hr.

From Limoges, you can reach Tours, Poitiers, Angoulême or Bordeaux, on the Paris–Madrid route (see p. 315), and Lyon, on the Paris–Marseille (p. 322) and Zurich–Lyon (p. 400) routes.

Limoges–Cahors

Several trains daily, taking 2 hrs–2 hrs 30 mins.

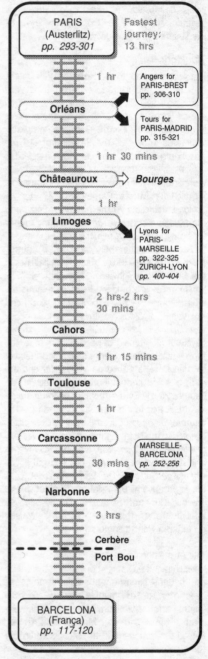

PARIS (Austerlitz) pp. 293-301 — Fastest journey: 13 hrs

1 hr — Angers for PARIS-BREST pp. 306-310

Orléans

Tours for PARIS-MADRID pp. 315-321

1 hr 30 mins

Châteauroux ⇨ Bourges

1 hr

Limoges — Lyons for PARIS-MARSEILLE pp. 322-325 ZURICH-LYON pp. 400-404

2 hrs-2 hrs 30 mins

Cahors

1 hr 15 mins

Toulouse

1 hr

Carcassonne

MARSEILLE-BARCELONA pp. 252-256

30 mins

Narbonne

3 hrs

Cerbère
Port Bou

BARCELONA (França) pp. 117-120

Cahors–Toulouse

Six to seven trains run daily, taking 1 hr 15 mins.

Toulouse–Carcassonne

Eight to nine trains run daily, taking 50 mins.

Carcassonne–Narbonne

Eleven trains run daily, taking 30–35 mins.

From here, the route joins the Marseille–Barcelona route (see p. 252).

ORLÉANS

Station: *tel: 38 53 50 50.*
Tourist Office: *pl. Albert 1er; tel: 38 53 05 95* (by station). Jun–Sept Mon–Sat, 0900–1900, Sun 0930–1230, 1500–1830; closed Sun, rest of year. Youth information and discount tickets from the **Centre Régional d'Information Jeunesse (CRIJ)**, *5 blvd de Verdun, tel: 38 54 37 70.* Mon and Thurs, 1300–1800, Tues and Wed, 1000–1800, Fri 1000–1900, Sat 1400–1900.

Accommodation and Food

A good base for visiting châteaux in the Loire Valley, Orléans is always crowded, so it is worth booking ahead. For hotels: ask the tourist office, or look around *rue du Faubourg Bannier* and *pl. Gambetta.* **IYHF**: *14 rue du Faubourg Madeleine; tel: 38 62 45 75* (central). Nearest **campsite**: St-Jean-de-Ruelle, *rue de la Roche; tel: 38 88 39 39* (3 km west on river). For restaurants, try around *rue de Bourgogne* pedestrian zone.

Sightseeing

Besieged by everyone from the Huns to the Germans, Orléans' most famous hour was in 1428–9, when Joan of Arc raised the English siege, and went on to become one of France's most beloved and enduring heroines. It is now full of memorials and mementos of the saintly peasant.

The most important monument in the city is the **Cathédrale de Sainte-Croix**, *pl. Ste-Croix.* There have been churches on this site since the Roman era, but the Huguenots destroyed the last in 1568, and work on the current one began only in 1601. The dazzling 19th-century stained-glass windows tell the story of Joan of Arc. In the 15th–16th-century Hotel des Créneaux (also in the square), the **Musée des Beaux-Arts** has some 18th–19th-century French art, with works by Watteau, Boucher and Gaugin.

Nearby, the 16th-century **Hotel Groslot** (also the Town Hall), *pl. de l'Etape*, is open to the public, with richly decorated rooms and fine gardens. The **Musée Archéologique et Historique de l'Orléannais**, Hôtel Cabu, *pl. Abbé Desnoyers*, has an excellent archaeological collection, including some Gallo-Roman bronzes.

In *pl. Martroi* is a statue of Joan of Arc, and round the corner, at *3 pl. de Gaulle*, the **Maison de Jeanne d'Arc** (rebuilt on the site of a house in which she once stayed) has a memorial museum.

Side Tracks from Orléans

From Orléans (Les Aubrais) there are four services daily to **Bourges** (change at Vierzón on two of these), taking 1 hr–1 hr 30 mins.

Sixty km east, Bourges is today the quiet capital of Berry, but was once one of the most powerful cities in France and a centre of artistic achievement. Its current relative obscurity has helped to preserve the medieval hill town, centred on the vast **Cathédrale de St-Étienne**, (see the superb early 13th-century stained glass). There are also several other museums, plus the 15th-century **Palais de Jacques Coeur**, commissioned by Jacques Coeur, a commoner who became treasurer of France.

CHÂTEAUROUX

Station: *tel: 54 27 50 50.*
Tourist Office: *pl. de la Gare; tel: 54 34 10 74.*

Sightseeing

Seemingly a dull industrial town, this has a small but delightful core of old houses and narrow streets. The **Couvent des Cordeliers** (13th-century) stands beside some lush public gardens. Next door is the larger and very attractive **Jardin Public des Belles-Isles**. On *rue St-Martial*, are the 13th-century **Église St-Martial**, named after the 5th-century evangelist who converted this area of France, and the **Musée Bertrand** (in the 18th-century mansion of Maréchal Bertrand, a leading Napoleonic general), devoted to fine art, Napoleonic history and the Berry region. On *rue Amiral*, is the huge, 19th-century Byzantine **Église de Notre-Dame**. The 15th-century **Château Raoul**, after which the city was named, is now the Préfecture. Nearby, the 15th-century **Porte St-Martin** began life as a city gate but later became the local jail. In **Déols** (suburb), a magnificent Romanesque tower and some fragments of arcading are the remains of the once powerful 10th-century **Abbaye de Déols**.

LIMOGES

Station: *tel: 55 01 50 50* (near tourist office). **Tourist Office**: *blvd de Fleurus; tel: 55 34 46 87*.

Accommodation and Food

There are many hotels at reasonable prices, Limoges is rarely overcrowded and the tourist office has a booking service. Try the **Foyer des Jeunes Travailleuses**, *20 rue Encombe Vineuse; tel: 55 77 63 97*. **Campsite**: *La Vallée de l'Aurence; tel: 55 38 49 43* (5 km: bus no. 20). For the best restaurants, try the old town.

Sightseeing

Capital of the Limousin region, this is a large, industrial city with a delightful centre, famous for producing magnificent porcelain. On the eastern edge of the old town, surrounded by well-maintained botanical gardens and overlooking the River Vienne, is the imposing Gothic **Cathédrale de Saint-Étienne**, *pl. Saint-Étienne*. Built from the 13th century onwards, this is a flamboyant building, which has suffered from ugly repairs and reinforcements. Next door, in the 18th-century Episcopal Palace, the **Musée Municipale**, *pl. de l'Evêché*, has a fascinating collection of Limoges enamels. **Musée de la Résistance** is behind the cathedral.

The centre of the old town is a web of dark, narrow streets, filled with half-timbered houses, small boutiques, antique and china shops. On *rue de la Boucherie* is the tiny **Chapelle de**

Saint-Aurelien, built by the Butchers' Guild in the 15th century. On *rue Saint-Martial*, the **Crypte de Saint-Martial** (open summer only) is the only remains of a once-powerful abbey.

The city's greatest highlight, on *pl. Winston-Churchill*, is the magnificent **Musée Adrien-Dubouche**, home to the national collection of porcelain and faïence, with over 12,000 pieces.

CAHORS

Station: *tel: 65 22 50 50* (central). **Tourist Office**: *pl. Aristide Briand; tel: 65 35 09 56*. Mon–Sat, 1000–1230, 1330–1900, and Sun 1000–1200; Oct–May, Mon–Sat, 1000–1200, 1400–1800.

Important in the Roman and medieval periods, Cahors became famous for wine considered for a while to be finer than that of Bordeaux. It is still capital of Quercy. Its most famous monument is the 14th-century **Pont Valentré**, a fortified bridge with three towers. The **Cathédrale de Saint-Étienne**, inland from *quai Champollion*, was built in the late 11th and early 12th centuries, although the heavily fortified façade was only added in the 14th century, and the cloister is 16th century. It has a remarkable nave roof, fine sculptures on the West Front and beautiful 14th-century wall paintings inside.

TOULOUSE

Station: *tel: 61 62 50 50*, 2 km north of the *pl. Capitôle* and by bus station (*tel: 61 48 71 84*). **Tourist Office**: Donjon du Capitôle, *rue Lafayette; tel: 61 11 02 22*. Mon–Sat 0900–1900, Sun 0900–1300; Oct–Apr, Mon–Fri 0900–1800, Sat 0900–1230, 1400–1800. Régional office (CRT), *12 rue Salambo; tel: 61 47 11 12*.

Getting Around

The bus service, run by **SEMVAT** (information office, *7, pl. Esquirol; tel: 61 41 70 70*), is good, and the first section of a new metro has recently opened, which serves the station and the city centre. The tourist office and ticket booths issue transport and other maps. Tickets are zoned (a two-zone ticket is far cheaper than two one-zone fares). Buy a *carnet* (strip) of ten for best value. The tourist office runs regular guided coach and walking tours of the city.

Accommodation and Food

A variety of hotels is available. Look in the centre, around *pl. Wilson*; otherwise, try *blvd Bonrepos* (near station and less pleasant). **IYHF**: Villa des Rosiers, *125, rue Jean Rieux; tel: 61 80 49 93* (bus no.14: *pl. Dupuy*, then no.22: *Leygues*). Many **campsites** are close by. Ask the tourist office for details and hotel bookings.

There are many restaurants, including several for gourmets with gold cards. For less expensive options, try around *rue St-Rome*, and *rue du Taur*. For market food stalls and picnic ingredients, try *Les Halles, Parking Victor Hugo*, or daily morning markets on *blvd Victor Hugo, pl. des Carmes* or *blvd de Strasbourg*. Specialities include cassoulet, foie gras and Armagnac.

Sightseeing

Capital of the Midi region, Toulouse has an ancient history, beginning life as a minor Roman settlement before becoming a Visigothic and Frankish capital. It was the centre of an important County from the 10th century onwards, and the site of two horrendous Huguenot massacres in the mid-16th century. Many of the grandiose town houses are built of a pinky-red brick, earning the city the epithet of *Ville Rose*. Toulouse is also a lively university town, a great cultural and artistic centre and a pioneer of the future, home to Aerospatiale, the main European centre for aeronautic research.

The most famous landmark, the superb Romanesque **Basilique de Saint-Sernin**, is all that remains of an 11th-century Benedictine monastery, set up to assist pilgrims en route to Santiago de Compostela. It is dedicated to and holds the remains of the first local bishop, St Saturninus, martyred in 257 AD. One of the largest Romanesque churches ever built, it has a five-tier tower and an extra-long nave, built to allow pilgrims room to sleep, eat and worship in the church. The 12th-century *Porte Miègeville* has Romanesque wall paintings and fine capitals in the left transept. **Notre Dame du Taur** (14th-century), *rue du Taur*, marks the spot where St Sernin is said to have met his grisly end.

The official centre of the city is *pl. du Capitôle*. The 18th-century Town Hall is named after the democratic *capitulari* (magistrates) who used to govern the city. The fortified **Église des Jacobins**, *rue Lakanal*, a short walk away, is a Flamboyant Gothic church, burial place of the philosopher and theologian, Thomas Aquinas.

Musée des Augustins (*rue de Metz/rue d'Alsace-Lorraine*) has a collection of Romanesque and Gothic sculpture as well as fine paintings by such luminaries as Delacroix, Corot and Toulouse-Lautrec. The **Musée Saint-Raymond**, *pl. St-Sernin*, is an excellent local archaeology museum. There are many other interesting museums. The tourist office issues passes for entry to any six. There are also numerous fine houses, visible only from the outside.

CARCASSONNE

Station: *tel: 68 47 50 50* (1 km from the river). **Tourist Office**: *15, blvd Camille-Pelletan; tel: 68 25 07 04.*

Sightseeing

There are two distinct towns: seemingly modern and grid-like **Ville Basse** (dating to the 13th century) on one side of the River Aude, and almost too fairy-tale perfect **Bastide** town perched on a crag on the other. Carcassone has been used as a stronghold by the Romans, Visigoths, Moors, and Cathars for nearly 1,500 years, until the border of France shifted southwards to Perpignan in the 17th century. The fortified walls then fell into disrepair until 1855 when the town was rebuilt by the enthusiastic historical 'restorer', Viollet le Duc.

Allow plenty of time to walk the streets and ramparts of the town. If you are walking up, look for the footpath beside the church of **St Gimer**, leading to the 12th-century **Château Comtal**, now housing the **Musée Lapidaire**. Besides the château, is the beautiful, mainly Romanesque **Église de St-Nazaire**. In the **Ville Basse** is the **Musée de Beaux Arts**, *rue Verdun*, with 17th–18th-century Flem-ish paintings and a good porcelain collection. The 13th-century **Cathédrale de Saint-Michel** has a rich treasure and fine rose window.

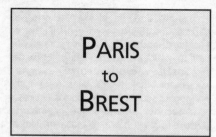

PARIS
to
BREST

This circular route through Brittany covers an area of spectacular coastal cliffs, fine beaches, charming villages of timber-framed houses, megaliths, and châteaux. If you don't want to do it all, take the Fast Track to Brest and meander back along whichever route you choose.

TRAINS

ETT tables: 125, 121, 130, 126, 123.

→ Fast Track

Paris–Brest

The journey between Paris (Montparnasse) and

Brest takes 4 hrs–4 hrs 30 mins by TGV (supplement payable) and approx. 7 hrs 30 mins on ordinary (overnight) trains (most have buffet service). First- and second-class couchettes are usually available.

On Track

Paris–Chartres

Trains depart every 60–90 mins from Paris (Montparnasse); journey time is around 1 hr 10 mins.

Chartres–Le Mans

At least seven trains run on weekdays (fewer at weekends); journey time is 1 hr–1 hr 30 mins.

Le Mans–Rennes

A route served by TGV (at least eight daily), but not by other trains. Journey time 1 hr 15 mins–2 hrs.

Rennes–Brest

About eight trains run daily (half are TGVs); the

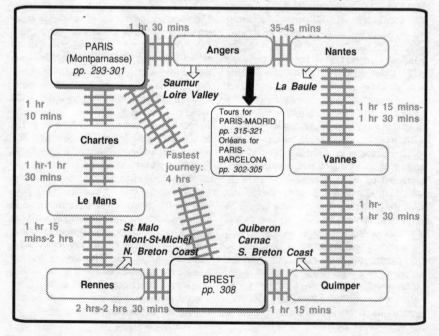

journey takes about 2 hrs 30 mins (2 hrs on TGVs).

Brest–Quimper

There are six trains a day (less at weekends); journey time about 1 hr 15 mins.

Quimper–Vannes

There are at least six trains a day (usually more); journey time: around 1 hr–1 hr 30 mins.

Vannes–Nantes

At least five trains run daily, taking about 1 hr 15 mins–1 hr 30 mins.

Nantes–Angers

There are at least three ordinary trains and ten TGVs a day between Nantes and Angers (St-Laud), the journey taking 35–45 mins.

Angers–Paris

At least ten TGV trains run daily between Angers (St-Laud) and Paris (Montparnasse); journey time approx. 1 hr 30 mins. There are few ordinary trains. These usually take twice as long except on Friday evenings out of Paris and Sunday evenings out of Angers.

CHARTRES

Station: *tel: 37 36 25 40*. Five to ten-mins walk from the centre (by cathedral) or take a bus. **Tourist Office**: *pl. de la Cathédrale, tel: 37 21 50 00*.

An attractive town pre-dating the Romans, its pulling-power lies in one building: the stunning 12th–13th-century **Notre-Dame Cathedral**, almost unchanged since first built and arguably the world's finest Gothic structure. The façade provides perfect examples of Romanesque sculpture and the interior is lit by superlative medieval stained-glass windows that include a much-envied deep blue, for which the secret ingredient has been lost.

LE MANS

Station: *tel: 43 24 50 50*; in the centre of town.
Tourist Office: *Hôtel des Ursulines, rue Étoile; tel: 43 28 17 22*.

There are many historic buildings in this old town, most notably the lovely **Cathédrale de St-Julien**, *pl. des Jacobins*, a mixture of Gothic, Romanesque and Renaissance styles. **Notre-Dame de la Couture**, *pl. Aristide-Briand*, is another building which spans the years, dating from the 10th–18th centuries. The town's main claim to fame, however, lies in the 24-hour motor race which takes place here annually (in mid-June) and is a test of endurance as much as driving ability. There's also a 24-hour motorcycle race every April.

RENNES

Station: *tel: 99 65 50 50*. This is fairly central; bus nos.1/20/21/22 run to *pl. de la République*. **Tourist Office**: *pont de Nemours; tel: 99 79 01 98*. Mon–Sat 0900–1900, Sun 1000–1300 and 1500–1700 (shorter in winter). They distribute *Spectacles, Informations* – a guide to what's on.

Accommodation

There are many hotels in the area of the station. The **IYHF**, *canal Saint-Martin 10; tel: 99 33 22 33* is 3 km out of town. Bus nos.20/22 (no.2 at weekends). **Campsite**: *rue du Professeur Maurice Audin; tel: 99 36 91 22*, open Apr–Sept.

Getting Around

There's a comprehensive bus service and the tourist office provide colour-coded maps of the network. However, most places of interest are within walking distance of each other.

Sightseeing

Brittany's administrative capital was once a junction of Roman roads, but only became really important in the 10th century. The town that grew was built largely of wood and was almost completely destroyed by a fire in 1720. The place was rebuilt (mostly of reddish granite) in the formally elegant style typical of the 18th century. Today it is a university town, an agricultural centre and of industrial importance. In the first 9/10 days of July, the whole town is taken over by the *Festival des Tombées de la Nuit*, a joyous street celebration of the Breton culture.

The 17th-century **Palais de Justice**, *pl. du Palais*, was one of few structures to survive the fire. Ironically, it was mostly destroyed by another fire in February 1994 as this book went to press. Nearby is the 18th-century **Town Hall**, containing some fine Flemish tapestries.

The stucco decorations in the 18th–19th-cen-tury **Cathédrale St-Pierre**, *rue St-Sauveur*, are admirable; there's also a 16th-century Flemish retable. There are many lovely old houses in the surrounding district. The **Musée de Bretagne**, *quai Emile-Zola 20*, has various well-presented exhibits about the region; the **Musée des Beaux Arts** (up-stairs) houses a collection of French art from the 14th century onwards.

There are several different sections (including a rose garden) and many sculptures in the 19th-century **Jardin du Thabor**, *pl. Ste-Melaine*, on the site of a former abbey of which little remains. Marking the position of the abbey is a much rebuilt church, **Notre-Dame**, in which traces of 14th–17th-century styles are seen.

The **Ecomusée du Pays de Rennes**, *Chatillon-sur-Seiche* (8 km south of the centre, on the outskirts of town), gives you an excellent idea of how the region developed, by showing the changing lifestyle of farmers over five centuries.

Side Tracks from Rennes

There are regular buses from Rennes to St-Malo and other towns in Brittany. The long-distance bus station is at *boul. Magenta* (off *pl. de la Gare*); *tel: 99 30 87 80*.

The romantically-named **Côte d'Emeraude** and **Côte de Granit Rose**, along the **north Breton coast**, are lined by wild and rugged cliffs, interspersed with old, sheltered fishing ports, many of which have now become resorts.

St-Malo, with a fine white sand beach and valuable harbour (used by ferries), was almost completely flattened in World War II, but has been carefully restored. It has a castle, and is the best place from which to visit the unmissable monastery of **Mont-St-Michel**, perched on a craggy island that is joined to the mainland by a causeway at low tide. Nearby **Dinard** also has fine beaches, but a very different atmosphere, having grown in Edwardian times.

A little way inland, **Dol-de-Bretagne** was

built mainly in the 13th century and has a fine cathedral and streets lined by typically Breton medieval timber-framed houses. At **Champdolent** stands one of the finest menhirs on the north coast. Not far away is **Dinan**, with a feudal castle, Romanesque church and cobbled streets of well-preserved 15th-century houses.

Heading west, there are numerous small fishing villages, such as **Guingamp** and **Landerneau** (with an inhabited medieval bridge).

BREST

Station: *tel: 98 80 50 50* (about 4 km from Oceanopolis).
Tourist Office: *pl. de la Liberté*; *tel: 98 44 24 96*. Mon–Sat 0900–1900.

Brest, on the Finistère peninsula, is noted for its perfect natural harbour. It became France's prime port in the 17th century and in World War II the Germans used it as a U-boat base. It was the target of bombing raids by the Allies and the Germans blew up most of what remained when they withdrew. Today it is a pleasant university town with wide avenues, spacious squares, green spaces and a still-important harbour. **Oceanopolis** is a 'sea centre' with huge aquariums and at Ste-Anne-du-Portzic is a **Marine Research Centre**. The **Castle**, dating mainly from the 15th century, houses the **Musée de la Marine** (naval museum). Across the river is the **Tour Tanguy**, now a museum about the town.

QUIMPER

Station: *tel: 98 90 26 21*. This is a short walk along the river from the central *pl. du Buerre*.
Tourist Office: *rue Déesse 7*; *tel: 98 53 04 05*.

This is the oldest town in Brittany, a peaceful place, with many half-timbered houses and a fine Gothic cathedral, **St-Corentin**. The **Musée des Beaux Arts**, *Hôtel de Ville*, contains a diverse collection of works from the 16th century to the present day and the **Musée Breton** houses varied exhibits connected with the area. Also of interest are the **Musée de Faïence**, several working potteries producing the famous *faïence de Quimper* and the **Musée de la Crêpe** (pancake museum), 3km out of town.

🌀 Side Tracks from Quimper

The **south Breton coast** is less exciting scenically than the north, but has better beaches and is warmer and more sheltered, so it takes the lion's share of the package-tourist trade.

Quiberon, once an island, is now a pretty holiday destination attached to the mainland by a narrow sandbank. From here, take a boat to **Belle-Île**, the largest of the islands off the Breton coast. It has almost everything, from fortifications and a citadel to wonderful scenery and beaches, good walking and picturesque villages.

Back on the mainland, in and around **Carnac**, are some 5,000 menhirs. The most famous formation is the *Alignements du Ménec*, probably dating from the 3rd century BC and consisting of over 1,000 megaliths stretching for more than 1 km. If you have the money, take a helicopter trip over them. Carnac is also a major resort, with numerous campsites and caravan parks and a long beach packed in summer.

VANNES

Station: *tel: 97 42 50 50*. 10–15 mins walk along *rue Favrel Lincy* to *pl. de la République*.
Tourist Office: *rue Thiers 1*; *tel: 97 47 24 34*.

Once the home of Breton kings, Vannes looks out over the Golfe du Morbihan, a stretch of water dotted with small islands, one of which has the best Neolithic carvings in France (boat tours available). The town is known for its medieval ramparts, gardens and gabled houses. **La Cohue** was originally a covered market and, after a gap of eight centuries, is one again. It houses the **Musée de Beaux Arts** and the **Musée du Golfe et de la Mer**. Across the street is **St-Pierre**, a mainly 16th-century cathedral with a 13th-century wooden spire and a 15th-century nave. Nearby, in *rue Noc*, are the **Musée d'Histoire Naturelle** and the **Musée Archéologique**.

NANTES

Station: *tel: 40 08 50 50*. About 1 km from the *pl. du Commerce*. Frequent trams link the station with the town centre.

Tourist Office: *pl. du Commerce*; *tel: 40 47 04 51*. Mon–Fri 0900–1900 and Sat 1000–1800.

Accommodation

There are three **IYHF** hostels: *pl. de la Manufacture 2*; *tel: 40 20 57 25* (the most accessible, but open only July and August); *pl. Ste-Elizabeth 1*; *tel: 40 20 00 80* and *boul. Vincent-Gache 9*; *tel: 40 47 91 64*. **Campsite**: Camping du Val de Cens, *boul. du Petit Port 21*; *tel: 40 74 47 94* (3 km from town). Bus nos.51/53 from *pl. du Commerce* to the *Marhonnière* stop.

Sightseeing

Both buses and trams serve the town efficiently, but the main sights are easily reached on foot.

The ancient university town, once capital of Brittany, is a lively cultural centre. It was important in Roman times, then went into decline, gaining prominence again in the 15th century.

The imposing **Château des Ducs** was home to the Dukes of Brittany and has had countless famous residents over the centuries, including

---

Menhirs, Lace and Pardons

Brittany has a distinct cultural heritage not only as a Celtic country within a Gallic state, but stretching back to the early Bronze Age. Throughout the area are thousands of gigantic standing stones (known as menhirs – literally 'tall men'), often carefully lined up over many miles. Still impressive, there are almost as many theories about their origins as there are stones. The most popular claim is that they are a type of calendar/clock, used for sun or moon worship, or to calculate dates for sowing and harvesting.

The Celtic tradition lives on in the Breton language, but these days the distinctive Celtic national costume, with its black dress and white lace coif (headdress), is only worn for the many festivals or 'pardons' held throughout Brittany. These are colourful events, with a high mass, religious procession and traditional music and dance. Catch one if you can.

---

such legendary figures as Bonnie Prince Charlie and the pirate Bluebeard (executed here). It is largely 15th century, but traces of a 13th-century structure remain. The once-dry moat is full again, crossed by a stone bridge linked to the 15th-century drawbridge. There are three very different museums within the grounds. The **Musée Regionale des Arts Populaires** depicts Breton folklore and history, using murals, costumes, furniture and handicrafts. The **Musée des Salorges** is a museum of the town's naval history since the 18th century and includes items connected with the slave trade. The **Musée des Arts Decoratifs** is devoted to local textiles.

The Gothic **Cathédrale de St-Pierre et St-Paul**, *pl. St-Pierre*, was started in the 15th century, but has needed restoration several times. The interior is of white Vendée stone, with vaults soaring 37m into the air.

The **Musée des Beaux Arts**, *rue Georges Clemenceau*, has 13th–20th-century paintings, including two large works by Rubens. The excellent art collection in **Palais Dobrée** was amassed by a wealthy ship-owning family. The **Musée d'Histoire Naturelle**, *rue Voltaire 12*, houses thousands of stuffed specimens, from mammals to insects, while the **Musée Jules Verne**, *rue de l'Hermitage 3, Ile Feydeau*, re-creates the author's fictional worlds. Nearby is a **Planetarium**, *rue des Acadiens 8*.

The **Ste-Croix district** (west of château) is the oldest part of town. *Rue de la Juiverie, rue Bossuet* and *pl. du Change*, in particular, are lined with 18th-century timber-framed houses. **Église Ste-Croix** (17th-century) has a bell-tower where trumpet-bearing angels sound the hours. **Cité Radieuse** is a must for fans of Le Corbusier (no.31 bus). In July, **les Fêtes de l'Été** is a huge dance, music and theatre festival.

Side Track from Nantes

Trains run frequently (take about an hour) to **La Baule** (very popular and very expensive), which claims to have Europe's most beautiful beach.

ANGERS

Station: *tel: 40 08 50 50* or *41 88 43 18* is near the Mairie, about 10 mins walk (past the *Jardin des Plantes*) to the château – or bus no.22.
Tourist Office: *pl. du President Kennedy; tel: 41 23 51 11*. Mon–Sat 0900–1900 and Sun 1030–1830. In winter there's a lunch-break (1230–1400) and no Sunday opening.

Once capital of the Counts of Anjou (Plantagenets), this is a large, attractive town dominated by the massive stone walls of the 13th-century **Château**, but the 17 towers are no longer intact and the moat has been converted into formal gardens and a deer park. Inside the château are fantastic medieval tapestries, including the wonderful 14th-century *Apocalypse* (based on the Book of Revelations) – do not miss this. Across the river the **Hôpital St-Jean**, contains another spectacular tapestry, the 20th-century *Chant du Monde*. The **Cathédrale de St-Maurice** has a medieval façade and Gothic vaulting over an unusually wide nave, lit by stained glass dating from several different eras.

Side Tracks from Angers

The châteaux of the 225-mile long **Loire Valley** were mostly medieval fortresses converted into luxurious country residences by 16th-century nobles. Trains run along the valley every two hours and connecting buses go to many of the châteaux, but independent travel (car or bicycle) is a more satisfactory way to explore.

There are frequent trains from Angers (taking 20–25 minutes) to **Saumur**, a delightful town, with a famous riding school and a white château containing museums devoted to equine matters and to the decorative arts. Saumur is surrounded by vineyards and mushroom caves.

Connection: Angers to Tours

Several trains run daily between Angers and Tours, from where you can connect with the Paris–Madrid route, p. 315. The journey takes from approx. 1 hr to 1 hr 15 mins.

PARIS
to
FRANKFURT

This route between France and Germany crosses the Champagne, Alsace and Moselle regions. The superlative Rheims Cathedral should not be missed, Nancy has a relatively untouched 18th-century centre, and Trier is crammed with Roman remains.

TRAINS

ETT tables: 30, 173, 177, 170, 172, 173, 725.

➡ Fast Track

There are four trains daily between Paris (Gare de l'Est) and Frankfurt (Hbf). The three day trains take just over 6 hrs, have dining-cars and charge a supplement. The overnight trains average 8 hrs, carry no supplement and have couchettes or sleeping-cars, but no refreshment service.

∿∿ On Track

Paris–Épernay

At least six trains a day depart from Paris (Est); the journey takes a little over 1 hr.

Épernay–Rheims (Reims)

The five daily trains take 20–30 mins.

Rheims–Châlons-sur-Marne

There are at least three services a day, taking about 40 mins.

Châlons-sur-Marne–Nancy

At least six trains run daily, taking 1 hr 15 mins.

Nancy–Metz

The service is approximately hourly. The journey time varies, but should be less than an hour.

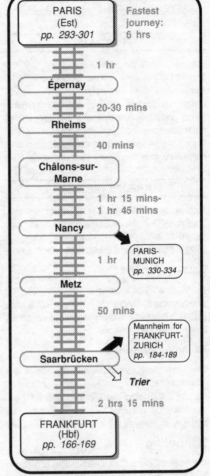

Metz–(Border)–Saarbrücken

At least six trains run daily. Supplements are payable on most weekend services and the journey time is around 50 mins. Border formalities are minimal and no change of train is necessary.

Saarbrücken–Frankfurt

Eight through trains run daily, taking 2 hrs 15 mins; there are many other services if you are prepared to change (good connections) at Mannheim, adding an extra 10 mins to the journey.

From Mannheim it is possible to make side

Route

trips to Heidelberg (see p. 185) and Heilbronn (see p. 186), on the Frankfurt–Zurich route.

ÉPERNAY

Station: *tel: 26 88 50 50.*
Tourist Office: *7 av. de Champagne; tel: 26 55 33 00.*

Épernay and Rheims are the major champagne-producing towns and home to most of the well-known houses (which can be visited). The biggest here is **Moët et Chandon**. Épernay's museum is largely devoted to champagne.

RHEIMS (REIMS)

Station: *tel: 26 88 50 50* (north-west of centre). **Tourist Office**: *2 rue Guillaume de Machault; tel: 26 47 25 69* (left of the cathedral). Mon–Sat 0900–1830/1930 and Sun 0930–1730/1830.

Getting Around

The main area of interest is between *Hôtel de Ville* and the Cathedral. St-Rémi is 1 km southeast, not far from the champagne caves. There's an extensive bus network.

Accommodation

There are some reasonable places: ask at the tourist office. **IYHF**, *parc Léo-Lagrange; tel: 26 40 52 60.* **Camping** (Apr–Sept) *av. Hoche (Châlons road); tel: 26 85 41 22.* International hotel chains with property in the area include: *Me, Nv.*

Sightseeing

The Remes were a Gaulish tribe who prospered by allying themselves with the Romans. Their town later became a stronghold of Christianity, but was reduced to little more than rubble during World War I. Much has been reconstructed and it is now a mixture of ancient and contemporary styles. The two main attractions are happily united: some profits from champagne going towards restoration, while some of the cathedral's stained glass depicts wine production.

The unmissable **Cathédrale de Notre-Dame**, *pl. du Cardinal Luçon*, is a 13th-century masterpiece where 25 French kings were crowned and it is still a place of worship. The magnificent western façade features three ornate portals, a rose window and enormous statues, topped by 15th-century twin towers. The interior is less ornate, but still impressive. The neighbouring **Palais du Tau** was the bishops' residence. Its treasures include medieval sculptures that once adorned the cathedral, 15th-century Arras tapestries and the bejewelled gold coronation cup.

The **Musée des Beaux-Arts**, *8 rue Chanzy*, is housed in the 18th-century Abbaye St-Denis. It contains mainly French art, including many Corot landscapes, but there are also a few notable Cranach portraits. The three-arched tri-umphal **Porte de Mars**, *pl. de la République*, is 33m long and was the largest in the Roman Empire, while the **Crypto-porticos**, *pl. du Forum*, formed part of a Roman Forum circa 200 AD.

Basilique St-Rémi, *rue Simon*, is an enormous 11th-century Benedictine abbey-church built to honour St-Rémigius. It has been excellently restored and is a happy blend of various styles of church architecture. The long thin nave and high windows create a superb effect and there's a notable 12th-century choir with five chapels. The adjoining monastic quarters (much altered in the 17th and 18th centuries) house the treasury.

Visits to the superb **Champagne caves** include the chance to sample the products. Ask the tourist office for details. Among the great names based in Rheims are **Veuve Cliquot**, **Pommery**, **Mumm** and **Taittinger**.

CHÂLONS-SUR-MARNE

Station: *tel: 26 88 50 50.* Buses to the centre leave from outside.
Tourist Office: *quai des Arts 3; tel: 26 65 17 89.*
Thomas Cook: *Via Voyages, 5 pl. Foch; tel: 26 68 36 57* (provide helpful services to visitors).

This small town is a pleasant place of canals spanned by ancient bridges, pretty parks, well-restored old mansions and several interesting churches and museums, but there's no disputing the two chief attractions. **Cathédrale St-Étienne** is famed for the deep green in its stained-glass windows and also has an interesting treasury. **Église-Notre-Dame-en-Vaux** is a fine 12th-century church with 16th-century rose windows and elegant lead spires.

NANCY

Station: *tel: 83 56 50 50.* 5 mins walk southwest of *pl. Stanislas.*
Tourist Office: *pl. Stanislas 14; tel: 83 35 22 41.* Mon–Sat 0900–1900 and Sun 1000–1300.

Getting Around

It's possible to walk round the main sights (there's a leaflet detailing the old buildings) but, unless you're a keen walker, you'll probably prefer to take some buses. The tourist office can supply a colour-coded map of the network.

Accommodation

The town has many small budget hotels.

Sightseeing

Noticeable in the central **pl. Stanislas** are two monumental Guibal fountains framed by Lamour railings. Stanislas was a deposed Polish king who came to Nancy in the middle of the 18th century and employed local artists in a happy collaboration that has resulted in a town which combines artistry and practicality. On the south side, the **Hôtel de Ville** bears his coat-of-arms. On the west, the **Musée des Beaux-Arts** contains European paintings from the 14th century onwards.

A little to the north, **Musée Historique Lorrain**, *Grande Rue 64*, is housed in the old ducal palace and has a very grand entrance. It is devoted to the artistic history of the area and contains everything from Gallo-Roman artefacts to 15th- and 16th-century tapestries. The early 18th-century **Cathédrale**, to the south of *pl. Stanislas*, is impressive in itself and the treasury has some magnificent 10th-century silverware.

METZ

Station: *tel: 87 63 50 50.* To the south-east of the centre, with minibuses every few minutes.
Tourist Office: *pl. d'Armes; tel: 87 75 65 21.* There's a branch in the station. Ask them for the listing *Calendrier des Manifestations.*

Getting Around

The centre is easily explored on foot. Elsewhere there are two minibus lines (blue and green) which operate frequently Mon–Sat 0730–1930. Ask the tourist office for *Transports Par Minibus*, which details the routes (stops are named; buy tickets on board).

Accommodation

The best way to find cheap lodgings is to ask the tourist office. **IYHF**: *Carrefour, rue Marchant 6; tel: 87 75 07 26*, near the Cathedral.

Sightseeing

Metz, at the confluence of the Moselle and Seille rivers, is a 3,000-year-old town. There is still a quarter of narrow, winding streets around the cathedral and the 14th-century *pl. St-Louis* is surrounded by Italian-influenced medieval mansions of golden-hued limestone.

The Gothic **Cathédrale St-Etienne**, *pl. d'Armes*, began life as two churches sharing a vault. The unified building, enhanced over the centuries, gives an overall impression of harmony and has a vast area of stained glass from different periods: the light streaming through them gives the high vaulted interior a glow that has been called the 'Lantern of God'. The **Musée d'Art et d'Histoire**, *rue du Haut-Poirier 2*, consists of several sections.

On the edge of town, the Romanesque-Gothic **St-Eucaire** and **Port des Allemands**, the restored gate of a medieval fortification, are worth a visit. Another remnant of the old defences is **Tour Camoufle**, a 15th-century slate-roofed structure.

SAARBRÜCKEN

Station: Hbf, *tel: (10681) 19419*, 10 mins walk from the centre.
Tourist Office: *Info-Pavilion, Triererstr.2; tel: (0681) 309 8222.* Mon–Fri 0730–2000 and Sat 0730–1600.

Saarbrücken is basically a coal town with a few historic buildings in the old centre. The **Altes Rathaus** houses the **Abenteuer Museum**, which is a rather bizarre collection about 'primitive' peoples visited by Abenteuer during his globetrotting. The **Modern Gallerie** is also worth seeing: a collection of 19th–20th-century art, including works by Dufy, Monet and Rodin. The same ticket gets you into **Alte Sammlung**, which covers the Middle Ages to the 19th century.

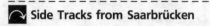 **Side Tracks from Saarbrücken**

TRIER

Station: Hbf, *tel: (0651) 19419*, is 10 mins walk south of *Porta Nigra*. At least six trains run daily (far more on weekdays); the journey takes 1 hr. **Tourist Office**: behind *Porta Nigra; tel: (0651) 97 80 80*. Mon–Sat 0900–1800/1845 and Sun 0800/0900–1300/1530. You can get a city map and a hotel list from automatic machines.

Getting Around

The *Altstadt* is well preserved and most of the sights are in the centre, more-or-less in a line from *Porta Nigra* to the Imperial Baths.

Accommodation and Food

There are a few budget hotels in town and it is worth asking the tourist office for something across the Moselle. **IYHF**: *Am Moselufer 4; tel: (0651) 29292* (on the other side of *Porta Nigra* from Hbf, 30 mins walk – or bus nos.2/8 most of the way). **Campsites**: One is in the schloss, *Monaiserstr.; tel: (0651) 86210* (bus no.40: *Zewenerstr.*). The other is on the west bank of the Moselle, *Luxembourgerstr.81; tel: (0651) 86921*. Hotel chains with property in the area: *Ra, SC*.

Sightseeing

Germany's oldest city was probably settled around 400 BC and has a traceable history dating back to Augustus Caesar in 16 BC. It was later (306–337) ruled by Constantine the Great and became a religious centre equal to Rome. It houses some really impressive Roman/early Christian remains, the best group being north of the Alps.

Trier is a place that breathes history and one street by the cathedral is called *Sieh am Dich* (Look Around You), where, it is claimed, you can see 2,000 years of history in as many steps.

The enormous, well-preserved **Porta Nigra** ('Black Gate' – named centuries ago for the dark patina that had already formed over the lime-stone façade) is the focal point of the town and has become its symbol. To the north-east, the Rococo **St Paulinus** was designed by Neumann and is one of the town's finest churches, with amazingly detailed ceiling paintings.

Hauptmarkt is a large pedestrian zone and popular meeting place lined with old houses and open-air restaurants and full of market stalls. In the centre are a Celtic cross (circa 958) and a fountain with ornate Renaissance sculptures. The colourful **Dreikönigshaus** was a merchant's home with its front door on the first floor.

Parts of the original 4th-century walls (the earliest Christian church north of the Alps) were incorporated into the **Dom** when it was started in 1030. The **Schatzkammer** (Treasury) has some unique items, including the seldom-displayed robe said to have been worn by Christ during the Crucifixion. The **Liebfrauenkirche** (1235) is a pure Gothic church in the form of a Greek cross that occupies the other part of Constantine's original double-church.

The superb **Bischöfliches Museum**, *Windstr.*, has medieval statuary, sacred art, models of the Roman cathedral and panels of remarkably fresh Roman frescos. The huge **Konstantinbasilika**, *Konstantinplatz*, part of Constantine's palace, is the largest surviving single-hall structure of the ancient world. Having been badly damaged, it is no longer the gloriously decorated place it once was, but the dimensions are still impressive.

Rheinisches Landesmuseum, *Ostallee 44* (at the southern end of the pleasant and well-tended **Palastgarten**), contains a truly impressive collection of Roman remains. Close by are **Kaiserthermen**, the fairly well-preserved Imperial Baths, and the 20,000-seat **Amphitheatre** (c. AD 100). **Karl-Marx-Haus**, *Bruckenstr. 10*, is where Karl Marx was born and is now a well-arranged museum about him.

There's a unique restaurant in the Roman cellars of the cathedral, *Hauptmarkt 5*. It's decorated with Roman pottery and serves Roman recipes from a 1st-century AD book written by Apicius, an epicure who spent a fortune on food and committed suicide when funds were running so low that he had to contemplate a normal diet.

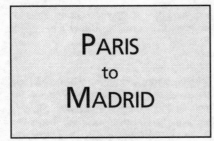

PARIS
to
MADRID

The main rail thoroughfare from France to Spain, this is also a route that takes you past the châteaux of the Loire Valley; the great wine lands of Cognac and Bordeaux; the elegant Belle Époque coastal resorts of Biarritz and San Sebastián (Donostia); through the heart of the Spanish Basque Country; and to the great cathedral city of Burgos.

TRAINS

ETT tables: 46, 135, 136, 137, 430.

 Fast Track

There are two overnight trains, which depart in the early evening each day, between Paris (Austerlitz) and Madrid (Chamartín):

The *Francisco de Goya* takes about 13 hrs. Rail passes are *not* valid on this train and fares are high. It has first- and second-class sleeping-cars and a restaurant car. The *Puerta del Sol* takes about 16 hrs. Rail passes *are* valid on this train. Light refreshments are available during the French part of the journey, but not once you cross into Spain (about half the journey). The train is all second-class, with couchettes. The frontier is crossed at Irún, but you can sleep through this part of the journey, as there are no real border formalities.

On Track

Paris–Tours

Over a dozen TGV services run daily from Paris (Montparnasse), the journey taking a little over an hour. The indirect journey changing at Orléans doubles the time, but allows stops at the château towns of Blois and Amboise.

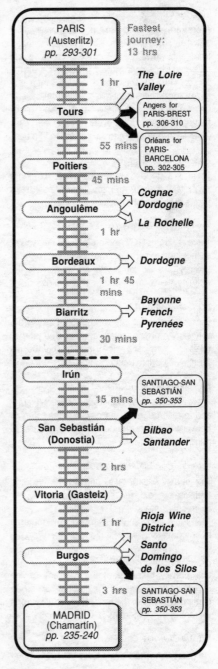

PARIS (Austerlitz) pp. 293-301 — Fastest journey: 13 hrs

1 hr — The Loire Valley

Tours

Angers for PARIS-BREST pp. 306-310

Orléans for PARIS-BARCELONA pp. 302-305

55 mins

Poitiers

45 mins

Angoulême — Cognac / Dordogne / La Rochelle

1 hr

Bordeaux — Dordogne

1 hr 45 mins

Biarritz — Bayonne / French Pyrenées

30 mins

Irún

SANTIAGO-SAN SEBASTIÁN pp. 350-353

15 mins

San Sebastián (Donostia) — Bilbao / Santander

2 hrs

Vitoria (Gasteiz)

1 hr — Rioja Wine District

Burgos — Santo Domingo de los Silos

SANTIAGO-SAN SEBASTIÁN pp. 350-353

3 hrs

MADRID (Chamartín) pp. 235-240

Route

Tours–Poitiers

There are about a dozen trains every day between Tours and Poitiers. They actually depart from and arrive at St-Pierre-des-Corps, 3 km away, which is connected to Tours by a shuttle service. The TGV trains take about 55 mins, the fastest local trains generally take a little over an hour. If you are not interested in seeing Tours, there are several trains every day between Paris (both Montparnasse and Austerlitz) and Poitiers.

Poitiers–Angoulême

There is a good daily service; most trains are TGVs, taking about 45 mins. The ordinary trains take a little over an hour.

Angoulême–Bordeaux

There are trains (TGV and ordinary) at intervals of an hour or two throughout the day. The TGV services take almost exactly an hour, while the ordinary trains take about 1 hr 20 mins.

Bordeaux–Biarritz

Services operate at intervals of about 2 hrs from very early morning to late evening. The journey takes anything from 1 hr 45 mins by TGV to 2 hrs 30 mins by other trains.

Biarritz–(Border)–Irún

There approximately eight trains between Biarritz and Irún throughout the day, but the intervals between them are irregular. The journey takes 30 mins.

Irún–San Sebastián (Donostia)

The journey usually takes only 15–30 mins and there are over a dozen direct trains every day, but at irregular intervals.

There is also a service every 30 mins operated by the private railway FV (Ferrocarriles Vascos).

San Sebastián–Vitoria (Gasteiz)

The journey takes about 2 hrs. Many of the RENFE trains between Irún and San Sebastián continue to Vitoria, the total journey Irún–Vitoria averaging 2 hrs 45 mins (2 hrs by express).

Vitoria–Burgos

There are six express trains a day between Vitoria and Burgos, not counting night trains at inconvenient hours. The journey time is 1 hr 20 mins.

Burgos–Madrid

Between Burgos and Madrid (Chamartín) there are at least six trains each day (some in the morning and some in the late afternoon/early evening), plus two at around 2300. The number of stops varies considerably, so the journey time also varies – from approx. 3 to 5 hrs.

TOURS

Station: *tel: 47 20 50 50*. Near the Mairie in the city centre.
Tourist Office: *pl. Jean-Jaurès; tel: 47 05 58 08*.

Accommodation

Many people like to stay in the small villages and towns around Tours, rather than in the city itself. However, you can find a reasonable range of cheap hotels in the area around the station and the old town, near the river. There is a **Youth Hostel** at *Parc de Grandmont; tel: 47 25 14 45*, 4 km from the station.

Sightseeing

Founded by the Romans on the banks of the Loire River, by the 4th century Tours was at the centre of five major trade routes. By the 8th century, it had become an important cultural centre and place of pilgrimage. Home to one of the oldest and most influential universities in France, the city also thrived during the 16th and 17th centuries when the French court and nobility streamed into the region. Today, it is the largest city along the Loire, with widespread and very ugly suburbs hiding a golden heart, much of which has been sensitively restored after serious damage during World War II.

The city's two main sights stand next to each other, just off *rue Jules Simon*. The elaborately ornate **Cathédrale de St Gatien** was built between the 13th and 16th centuries and contains fine examples of almost every sort of medieval architecture, from the Romanesque through Gothic to the Renaissance. There are some wonderful 13th-century stained-glass windows, while the **Cloître de la Psalette** to one side has some beautiful 15th- and 16th-century frescoes. Next door, in the 18th-century Episcopal Palace, is the **Musée des Beaux-Arts**, with a wide and fascinating art collection including works by Rembrandt, Delacroix and Degas, as well as several carefully reconstructed 18th-century rooms.

The heart of the **old town**, around the *pl. Plumereau* and *pl. Floire-le-Roi* on the south bank, is a maze of narrow streets, mostly pedestrianised, and half-timbered houses, many of which have been carefully restored and turned into trendy boutiques. The houses themselves are worthy of attention, but you can also visit the 13th-century **Église de Saint-Julien**, *rue Nationale*, with some fine 20th-century stained glass and museum of Touraine wine. Next door, the **Musée de Compagnonnage** housed in the old monks' dormitory has a fascinating collection on the old guild trades, while the nearby renaissance **Hôtel Gouin**, *rue de Commerce*, is home to a small archaeology museum.

- - - - - - - - - - - - - - - - - -

⌒ Side Tracks

Right in the centre of the most château-laden part of France, Tours is an excellent place from which to explore the adjoining valleys of the **Loire**, Loir, Cher and Indre, all strewn with such famous castles as Amboise, Azay-le-Rideau, Chambord, Chenonçeaux, Chinon, Langeais, Loches and Villandry. Most are some distance from the city, and each other, so you will need transport – car, moped or bicycle – and a regional map (available from the tourist office) unless you stick to coach tours.

From Tours, there are also good connecting train services to **Nantes** and **Angers** on the Breton route (see p. 306) and to **Orléans** on the Paris–Barcelona route (see p. 302).

- - - - - - - - - - - - - - - - - -

POITIERS

Station: *tel: 49 58 50 50.* About 10-mins walk from the centre: up a hill and a flight of stairs. **Tourist Offices:** *8 rue Grandes Écoles; tel: 49 41*

21 24. 15 rue Carnot; tel: 49 41 58 22.

Sightseeing

Poitiers is one of the earliest Christian centres of France, with the result that today, as well as several beautiful secular buildings, it boasts an impressive array of wonderful churches. The oldest, first built in 356, is the **Baptistère de Saint-Jean**, *rue Jean-Jaurès*. Almost next door is the 12th–13th-century **Cathédrale de Saint-Pierre**, *rue de la Cathédrale*. Squat from the outside, once inside the nave soars high, crowned by some lovely 13th-century stained glass and choir stalls. Behind the cathedral is the **Église de Ste-Radegonde**, *rue de la Mauvinière*, first built in the 6th century with fine Romanesque and Gothic additions and alterations. Some distance away, the flamboyantly decorated **Église de Notre-Dame-la-Grande**, *rue de Regatterie*, is a triumph of Romanesque art, while on the western edge of the old city is possibly the best of them all, the **Église de Saint-Hilaire-le-Grand**, an elegant, domed and arcaded Romanesque church, built mainly in the 11th century and still containing several frescoes from that period.

- - - - - - - - - - - - - - - - - -

⌒ Side Track

Clearly signposted from the autoroute, 7 km north of the city, is the massive, exciting **Futuroscope** museum and theme park. Dedicated to the photographic image, from early history to experimental cinema, it has something for everyone including a vast dome showing virtually spherical films, Imax screens, a 3D cinema and simulator.

Every Sat, Apr–Oct, and every evening, July–end Aug, the spectacular sound and light show, the *Water Symphony*, has water jets synchronised with music, images projected onto walls of water, laser and fireworks. Free to daytime visitors.

There are reduced-rate taxis (about FFr40.00 return) just outside Poiters station, or buses from the town centre.

In the forest of hotels nearby are several offering ultra-cheap rates.

- - - - - - - - - - - - - - - - - -

ANGOULÊME

Station: *tel: 45 69 61 45*. This is north of the centre, on the road to Limoges, but there are a number of buses into town.
Tourist Office: *pl. St-Pierre; tel: 45 95 16 84*. Closed Monday.

Angoulême has an attractive old district, but it pales beside the other great historic centres on this route. The main reason for stopping here is so that you can head off into the depths of the surrounding countryside.

⌒ Side Tracks

Head west and you are into the **Cognac** region, famous for its brandy. Reach the coast and you come to the famous historic port of **La Rochelle**. A little way south-east is the northern section of the **Dordogne**, the ancient territory of Perigord. Home of *foie gras*, this is one of the great gastronomic centres of France. It is also an enchantingly pretty region, highly popular with the British, of whom some 25,000 own holiday homes in the area. There are some local trains, but the bus service is feeble and you really need to hire a car.

BORDEAUX

Airport: Bordeaux-Mérignac, 12 km from the city, *tel: 56 34 84 84*.
Stations: St Jean, *tel: 56 92 50 50*. About 2 km from the south of the centre; you can walk it in 20–30 minutes, or there are numerous buses. Two other stations, the **Gare St Louis** and the **Gare d' Orléans**, serve local trains.
Tourist Office: *12 cours du 30 Juillet; tel: 56 44 28 41*.
Thomas Cook bureau de change: at Gare St Jean, *Parvis Louis Armand*.

Getting Around

Most of the greatest sights of interest are within a 1 square km block in the city centre, so you should be able to get around on foot. There is a good bus network however and you can buy a one- or three-day pass, the *Carte Bordeaux*

Découverte, from the station or tourist office.

Accommodation

The city has a wide range of accommodation, suitable for all pockets. Major hotel groups represented in the city include *Me, Nv, Pu* and *Sf*.

As this is a port, many of the cheapest hotels, scattered around the docks, can be fairly basic. There is a **Youth Hostel** (the **Foyer des Jeunes**) at *22 cours Barbey; tel: 56 91 59 51*, just under 1 km from the St Jean station.

Sightseeing

Set on the Garonne River just before it joins the Dordogne and Gironde to travel out to sea, Bordeaux is the sixth largest port in France, a busy, working city with an elegant 18th-century centre surrounded by large amounts of industrial gloom. Most of all, however, the city has given its name to one of the greatest groups of wines in the world, including such great marks as Châteaux Lafite and Mouton-Rothschild, Médoc, Sauternes and St Emilion. The area's vintners were also responsible in part for creating a tradition of great wine in those other increasingly famous areas – the Spanish Rioja and California.

The 18th-century heart of Bordeaux stretches out behind a line of docks and wine warehouses on the left bank of the river. Head across the **Pont de Pierre** to get the best possible view, or take a boat tour on the **Embarcadère Vedettes**, which leave regularly from the Esplanade de Quinconces.

To see the best of the city's great buildings, walk from the Esplanade down the *cours du 30 Juillet* to the *pl. de la Comédie* on which stands the wonderful neo-classical **Grand Théâtre**, stopping off en route at the **Maison de Vin**, *1 cours du 30 Juillet; tel: 56 52 82 82*, to arrange a wine tour and tasting.

From the *pl. de la Comédie*, the beautiful **cours du Chapeau Rouge** leads to the **pl. de la Bourse**, a lovely square on which stand the **Musée Maritime**, housed in the 18th-century Customs House, and the elegant **Hôtel de la Bourse**. Just to the south of this begins the **quartier Saint-Pierre**, the bustling old town filled with small boutiques and cafés.

About 1 km from here, along the *rue des Trois-Canils*, you come to the city's richest gathering of fine buildings and museums, including, amongst others, the 11th–15th century **Cathédrale de St-André** and the superb 18th-century **Hôtel de Ville**, (both on *pl. Rohan*), the **Musée des Beaux-Arts**, *rue Montbazon*, and the **Musée des Arts Decoratifs**, *rue Bouffard*.

Other museums worth a visit include the archaeological **Musée d'Aquitaine**, *cours Victor Hugo/cours Pasteur*, and the **Musée d'Histoire Naturelle**, tucked into the south-west corner of the grand **Jardin Public**, *rue Duplessey*.

Side Tracks

Probably the main reason for coming to Bordeaux is to visit the great wineries spread out through the surrounding countryside. There are bus tours (ask at the Tourist Office), but if you prefer your independence, you will need to provide yourself with transport – and remember there are strict drink-driving laws!

This is also the best place from which to visit the southern Dordogne, with such dramatic sights as the prehistoric cave paintings of **Les Eyzies** and the superbly preserved medieval towns of **Sarlat** and **Rocamadour**. Again, public transport is limited.

BIARRITZ

Station: Biarritz la Négresse, *tel: 59 55 50 50*. About 3 km outside town: take blue bus nos. 2/9.
Tourist Office: *1 pl. Ixelles; tel: 59 24 20 24*

Sightseeing

Biarritz came into its own in the mid-19th century, one of many resorts along the Atlantic coast which grew rapidly and elegantly into playgrounds for the rich and famous. Here, it was the Empress Eugénie and her retinue who came to bathe and play. So, over the years, did everybody else from Queen Victoria to Winston Churchill. With the start of World War I, the city's heyday was at an end and today many of its great buildings are decaying atmospherically.

There are two distinct and very different areas worth a wander, the old fishing village around the **Port des Pêcheurs**, and the grander Belle Epoque development along the coastal sweep of the **Grande Plage**.

Side Tracks

There are several other charming coastal towns near Biarritz, including **Bayonne** (on the line from Bordeax to Biarritz), with a fine **cathedral**, and **Musée des Basques**, **St Jean Pied-de-Port** and **St Jean de Luz**.

This is also the best place from which to branch inwards and upwards into the remote Basque territory of the **French Pyrenées**. The trains run along the coast – you will need to hire a car for the mountains.

IRÚN

Station: (RENFE) *Estación del Norte; tel: (43) 61 22 36*. This is central.
Tourist Offices: *Behobia, Complejo Aduanero, 20300 Irún; tel: (43) 62 26 27;* and at the *Estación del Norte; tel: (43) 61 15 24.*

Irún is a bustling border town, largely 20th-century since it was almost totally destroyed in the Spanish Civil War. You may need to change trains here, but go straight on to San Sebastián as there is little of any interest to see in Irún.

SAN SEBASTIÁN (DONOSTIA)

Stations: (RENFE) **Estación del Norte**; *tel: (43) 27 92 56*. Central: opposite the Maria Christina Bridge; cross the bridge and it is a few minutes walk through the 19th-century area to the old town. (FV) **Estación Amara**, *Calle Easo; tel: (43) 45 01 31*. About 15-mins walk from the old town.
Tourist Office: *Calle Reina Regente s/n, 20003; tel: (43) 42 10 02.*

Getting Around

You should be able to reach everywhere on foot. There is a good bus service along the main roads.

Accommodation and Food

Sadly and unusually, the great mass of cheap hotels and private lodgings are not in the old town, but in the modern extension beyond Amara station. This can be a fairly rough area, so women should be careful. The hotels in the centre tend to cater for families on beach holidays. **IYHF**, *Parque Villa s/n; tel: 45 29 70/29 37 51.* There is a **campsite** on the fringes of the city.

For the best small restaurants, try the old town and the fishing harbour at the north end of the Playa de la Concha.

Sightseeing

Known as San Sebastián to the Spanish and as Donostia to the Basques, this is one of the largest cities in the individualist Basque province, with a language and culture very different to that of Castilian Spain. Once a confined old town, dedicated to whaling, deep-sea fishing and the tourist trade developed by the pilgrim route to Santiago de Compostela (see p. 350), San Sebastián has had extraordinarily bad luck over the centuries, and has been destroyed several times by fire or invading armies, so there are few pre-19th century remnants. The city really came into its own in the mid-19th century, when someone recommended sea-bathing as a cure for Queen Isabella II's herpes! She arrived, along with a great retinue, and San Sebastián became the in-place to be. It is still one of the more fashionable of the Spanish resorts.

The city has three distinct areas with completely different characters. The 'old' town, nestled at the foot of Monte Urgull, is mainly 19th century, but was rebuilt along the old lines, with a maze of small streets, tiny darkened shops and bars, arcaded plazas and churches. Behind this, is an area of monumental 19th-century elegance. Across the river, and further inland, are some remarkably ugly modern developments.

Most people who come here are ready to join the multi–coloured throng along the magnificent curved beach, but also take the time to wander the streets of the city centre, which have few real architectural gems, but are

nevertheless pleasing. Near the foot of Monte Urgull are the arcaded **Plaza de la Constitución,** the Gothic **Church of San Vicente**, the beautiful baroque **Basilica of Santa María del Coro** and the **Museum of San Telmo**. At the far end of the quay is the **Aquarium and Oceanographic Museum**, and you should also climb **Monte Urgull** itself, both to see the much-rebuilt fort, and for the superb views.

◠ Side Tracks

From San Sebastián, the narrow gauge coastal railways lead west, through a series of charming, if increasingly touristy, villages, to **Bilbao** and **Santander**. Both cities are seen primarily as port towns, partly because of the ferry links with the UK, but they are also well worth a visit, Bilbao for its old centre and museums, Santander as an attractive resort town with a good beach.

VITORIA (GASTEIZ)

Station: (RENFE); *tel: (45) 14 12 07.* Off the *Calle Eduardo Dato*, about two blocks from the cathedral and tourist office.
Tourist Office: *Parque de la Florida, s/n; tel: (45) 13 13 21.*

Sightseeing

Known by the Spanish as Vitoria and by the Basques as Gasteiz, this is probably the least–visited city in the Basque region, despite the fact that it is the capital of the whole Basque Autonomous Community. Known for making playing cards and chocolate truffles, it is also a charming and beautiful city, an almost perfectly preserved medieval hill town surrounded by elegant, arcaded plazas and gardens, dating from the 17th, 18th and 19th centuries.

El Campillo, the old hill town, is a tangled web of narrow dark streets, filled with cheap hotels as well as several fine churches and museums. Look out particularly for the **Church of San Miguel**, beside the steps at the top of the monumental **Plaza de la Virgen Blanca** and the old **Cathedral of Santa María**. The huge neo-Gothic **Cathedral of María Immaculada** is surrounded by parkland in the flat new town, and from here a tree-lined **promenade**, housing the **Museums of Arabic Art**, **Arms** and **Playing Cards**, runs for 3km to the village of **Armentia**.

BURGOS

Station: Conde de Guadalhorce; tel: 20 95 20. For train enquiries tel: (47) 20 35 60. About 1km south-west of the cathedral, on the far side of the Arlanzon River.
Tourist Office: Plaza Alonso Martinez 7, 09003 Burgos; tel: (47) 20 31 25.

Getting Around

Although Burgos is spread out, the vast majority of tourist entertainment is contained within the tiny old town around the cathedral. Everything here is within walking distance, and here too, you will find most of the small hotels, bars and restaurants.

Sightseeing

Burgos is both a large and busy modern city and one of Spain's great historic centres. Named after the bourgeois traders who settled around the foot of the 9th-century castle, for over 500 years Burgos was a trading crossroads. In the 11th century it became the capital of Christian Spain and the home of Rodrigo Diaz de Vivar, better known as El Cid.

During the Civil War in the 1930s, Burgos again rose to fame, as the Nationalist Headquarters. It was here that Franco formed his

El Cid

Rodrigo Diaz (1043–1099) was a brilliant Spanish mercenary who won several battles against the Moors before embarrassing the King of Castile and being exiled. He then signed on with the Muslim Emir of Zaragoza and spent the rest of his life fighting for either side, winning every time. Admired by all, he became known as *El Campeador* ('the Champion') by the Christians and *El Cid* ('The Lord') by the Muslims.

Falangist government and (18 months later) declared a ceasefire that ended the war.

Today, the city is still deeply Catholic with an enormous number of interesting old churches.

The **Cathedral**, undoubtedly the biggest attraction, was consecrated in 1260 but work continued until the 17th century and it's now the third largest cathedral in Spain (after Toledo and Seville) and possibly also the richest. Have a good look at the exterior before you start exploring the 19 chapels and 38 altars, all dripping in gold leaf. Amidst the splendour, look out for the 15th-century Flycatcher Clock, El Cid's tomb, and a grotesquely realistic crucifix, with a body of buffalo hide, human hair and finger nails.

If you have any time left after exploring the cathedral, the sights most worth seeing include: The small **Church of San Nicolas**, with a magnificent 16th-century retable; the Gothic **Church of San Estaban**; and the **Arch of Santa María**, a fortified 14th-century gateway, altered and decorated in 1536 as a tribute to Charles V. The figures depicted are people important in the town's history. They include the founder (Diego Porcelos), El Cid and Charles himself. Little remains of the **old castle** and the climb is steep, but the view from the top is worth it.

Outside the old city, but within walking distance, the **Provincial Museum** (in the 16th-century Casa de Miranda) is one of Spain's best museums. On the outskirts of town, (take a bus or taxi) are two final sights worthy of a trek: the superb **Convent of Las Huelgas Reales**, a convent with royal patronage and inmates who became not only very rich, but a powerful political force in Spain; and the **Cartuja de Miraflores**, a Carthusian monastery which became the royal pantheon.

⌁ Side Tracks

From Burgos, you can reach several sections of the pilgrim route to Santiago de Compostela and connect with the Santiago–San Sebastián route (see p. 350). Just to the east is the **Rioja wine district**, while a short way south is the wonderful Benedictine monastery of **Santo Domingo de los Silos**.

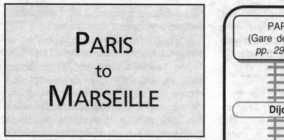

PARIS
to
MARSEILLE

This is the main route heading south from Paris to the French Riviera and Provence. It is also a fascinating voyage of discovery through the great vineyards of Burgundy, the Rhône valley, and the heart of Roman France.

TRAINS

ETT tables: 149, 155, 161, 163.

→ Fast Track

At least eight trains run daily. Through day trains are TGVs, taking 5 hrs (supplement payable). Night trains, with couchettes, take 8–9 hrs. Some have sleeping cars and refreshments.

⤳ On track

Paris–Dijon

Many trains run from Paris (Gare de Lyon). TGVs take about 1 hr 30 mins; others take 3 hrs.

Dijon–Mâcon

Some ten trains run daily to Mâcon (Ville). The journey takes 1 hr–1 hr 30 mins.

Mâcon–Lyon

Ten daily trains run Mâcon (Ville)–Lyon (usually Perrache, although a few use Port Dieu or stop at both). Most (but not all) take just under 1 hr, while the fastest take 40 mins.

Lyon–Avignon

About 12 trains depart daily, taking 2 hrs to 2 hrs 30 mins. Most services depart from Lyon Part-Dieu, although there are some which leave from Perrache, so check locally.

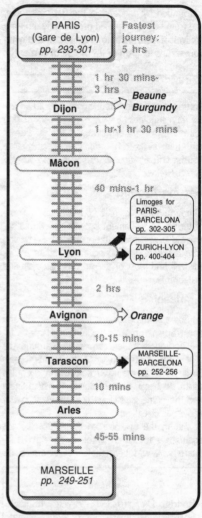

PARIS
(Gare de Lyon)
pp. 293-301

Fastest journey: 5 hrs

1 hr 30 mins–3 hrs

Dijon ➪ *Beaune Burgundy*

1 hr–1 hr 30 mins

Mâcon

40 mins–1 hr

Limoges for PARIS-BARCELONA pp. 302-305

Lyon ➜ ZURICH-LYON pp. 400-404

2 hrs

Avignon ➪ *Orange*

10-15 mins

Tarascon ➜ MARSEILLE-BARCELONA pp. 252-256

10 mins

Arles

45-55 mins

MARSEILLE
pp. 249-251

Avignon–Tarascon

About seven trains run daily, taking 10–15 mins.

Tarascon–Arles

Around four trains run daily, but departures are uneven. The journey takes about 10 mins.

Arles–Marseille

At least ten trains a day, arriving at Marseille (St Charles). The journey time averages 45–55 mins.

DIJON

Stations: **Ville** (major services) and **Porte-Neuve**. *Tel: 80 41 50 50* for information.
Tourist Office: *34 rue des Forges; tel: 80 30 35 39*. Open Mon–Fri 0800–1200 and 1400–1800 (1700 Fri). Also at *29 pl. Darcy; tel: 80 43 42 12*. Open daily 0900–1200 and 1400–1900/2100.

Getting Around

The tourist offices offer guided tours of the old town. If you want to do your own thing, ask for the leaflet which suggests a walking circuit. There's an efficient **bus** service in the new town, but most services stop around 2030.

Accommodation and Food

There aren't many cheap hotels in the centre; try the **Hostellerie Sauvage**, *64 rue Monge; 80 41 31 21* (near *pl. Darcy*). The **IYHF**, *Centre de Rencontres Internationales/A J, 1 blvd Champollion; tel: 80 71 32 12*, is about 4 km from the centre (bus no.6 from *pl. Darcy*; change to no.5 (to *Épirey*) at *République*). Students could try the **Foyer International d'Étudiants**, *av. Maréchal-Leclerc; tel: 80 71 51 01* (bus no.4 to *St Appollinaire*; stop at the Velodrome). **Campsite**: *Camping du Lac*, off *blvd Kir; tel: 80 43 54 72*. By a lake about 1 km from Ville station (bus no.18).

Dijon is a gastronomic centre and home of cassis. Kir (cassis with white wine) was also invented here. **Grey-Poupon**, *32 rue de la Liberté*, is *the* place to buy mustard. Another local speciality is spiced bread (*pain d'épice*). The *patisseries* (bakeries) are good, as are the cheese shops. There is a food market on Tuesday and Friday mornings on **rue Françoise-Rude**.

Sightseeing

Under the Dukes of Burgundy, Dijon became a centre for the arts and sciences, with wealth and influence to rival the French Crown. The rows of *hôtels particuliers* (elegant 17th-century mansions) in the old town have been carefully restored. The large student population in Dijon keeps things lively. In summer, the town hosts a series of music festivals and there's a Festival of Folklore in September, culminating in the *Fête de la Vigne*, a celebration of the grape harvest.

The **Palais des Ducs** should not be missed. The medieval kitchens are worth seeing and the *Salle des Gardes* contains marvellously carved tombs. The main attraction however is the wing containing **Musée des Beaux Arts,** which has one of the finest collections in France. The paintings range from Titian and Rubens to the Impressionists and there are also superb sculptures, tapestries, furniture and silverwork.

The palace faces the **place de la Libération**, a crescent of *hôtel particuliers*. Behind the palace is an area full of these lovely old houses, notably **rue des Forges** (wander down the side alleys to get a glimpse of the courtyards). In the parallel *rue de la Chouette*, the **Église de Notre Dame** has numerous gargoyles, 13th-century stained-glass windows and an owl which you should touch for luck. Among the contents are a Virgin carved from black wood and a Gobelins tapestry. The **Église St-Michel** has a Renaissance façade and a Gothic interior with an unusual vault. The **Cathédrale de St-Benigne**, *rue Docteur Maret*, has a patterned roof of glazed tiles (characteristic of Burgundy), a timber spire and a circular crypt. The neighbouring **Musée Archéologique** covers the Côte d'Or, while the **Musée de la Vie Bourguignonne**, *rue Ste-Ann*, is devoted to 19th-century Burgundian life. The **Musée Magnin** houses original 17th-century furnishings.

West is the **Jardin de l'Arquebus** (botanical garden), on the edge of which are the ornate **Chartreuse de Champmol** gateway, a **natural history museum** and the **Puits de Moise**, which is carved with strangely lifelike statues.

◣ Side Tracks from Dijon

The **Musée du Vin de Bourgogne** is in the charming town of **Beaune**, about 45 kms south of Dijon. Local tourist offices have details of wine tours and tastings.

MÂCON

Station: *tel: 80 93 50 50*, reservations *tel: 80 43 52 56*.
Tourist Office: *187 rue Carnot; tel: 85 39 71 37*.
On the banks of the Saône, Mâcon deserves a

brief glimpse, with an **old town** filled with impressive Renaissance architecture. Pause at the **Musée des Ursulines** for an eclectic mix of archaeology and 17th-century art. **Place des Herbes** is seductive, hosting a daily market.

LYON

Stations: **Perrache** (on *Presqu'Île*) and **Part-Dieu** (on modern east bank). For information *tel: 78 92 50 50*.

Tourist Information: *pl. Bellecour; tel: 78 42 25 75* opens 15th Jun–15th Sept, Mon–Fri 0900–1900, Sat 0900–1800, Sun 1000–1800. For the rest of the year, opening times are Mon–Fri, 0900–1800; Sat 0900–1700; Sun 1000–1700. There are also offices at *Gare Perrache, Fourvière*, and **Villeurbanne**, *3 av. Aristide-Briand; tel: 78 68 13 20*. Pick up a map and the excellent multilingual sightseeing brochure *Lyon Vous Aimerez*. Youth information: **Centre Régional d'information Jeunesse** (CRIJ), *9 quai des Célestins; tel: 78 37 15 28*. Open Mon-Sat, 1000-1900, (closed lunchtime Sat). Rhône Valley **Regional tourist office**: *5 pl. de la Baleine; tel: 78 42 50 04*.

Thomas Cook: bureaux de change are at Port Dieu and Perrache stations. Via Voyages, *27/29 rue Ferrandière*, offers services for visitors.

Getting Around

A well-connected transport system (run by TCL) and consisting of **buses, metro** and a **funicular** up Fourvière, covers all the main area of interest. Tickets are interchangeable and you can buy a book (*carnet*) of six. A one-day pass, the **Ticket Liberté** (FFr.20) is available from the tourist office or TCL agencies (*tel: 78 71 70 00*).

For **guided tours** organised by the tourist office contact the **Bureau des Guides,** *5 pl. St-Jean; tel: 78 42 25 75*. There are also numerous **boat** trips both around the city and through outlying villages. For details, ask the Tourist Office, or contact the **Société Naviginter,** *13 bis quai Rambaud; tel: 78 42 96 81*. The **bâteaux mouches** depart from *quai des Célestins*.

Accommodation and Food

There are many hotels at all levels in Lyon. There is also a widely based 'two nights for one' dis-

count scheme: *Bon Weekend à Lyon*. The tourist office has details and a booking service. **IYHF:** *51 rue Roger Salengro; tel: 78 76 39 23*.

You can eat exceptionally well here but you won't always find good food cheaply. Smaller places offering good regional cuisine are known locally as *bouchons*. For the best options, head up into the **Vieille Ville**. Good food **markets** take place at *quai St-Antoine, blvd de Croix-Rousee*, and, under cover, *Les Halles, 102 cours Lafayette*.

Sightseeing

Lyon, the third largest city in France, is built over the confluence of the Saône and Rhône Rivers and has three distinct areas. The *Presqu'île* (the peninsula between the two rivers) is home to the huge *pl. Bellecour*, and the main, elegant shopping centre. On the west bank stands the core of the medieval city, while Fourvière Hill behind it houses the Roman remains. On the east bank are the modern town and the university. 'Modern' Lyon was founded as the Roman colony of Lugdunum in 43 BC, and has been rich and powerful almost ever since, gaining wealth and influence as a trading centre in the silk and printing trades.

The West Bank

Fourvière Hill, reached by funicular, is the original city centre, and home to a large collection of **Roman** remains. Nearby, the **Musée de la Civilisation Gallo-Romain**, *17 rue Cléberg*, has a fabulous collection of prehistoric, Gallic and Roman artefacts and art, including an Iron Age chariot and some superb mosaics. The most obvious landmark however is the flamboyant 19th-century **Basilique de Notre-Dame de Fourvière**, built in a Byzantine-Romanesque style with lots of gold and marble. In an old chapel at *5 pl. de Fourvière*, the **Musée de Fourvière** houses religious art and manuscripts.

Beside the Saône, at the foot of the hill, is the **Vieille Ville**, a mainly 15th–17th-century Renaissance quarter of charming squares and narrow streets. The **Cathédrale de Saint-Jean**, dating from the 12th–15th centuries, has lovely 13th-century stained glass. Next door is a **treasury**. On *pl. du Petit Collège* are two museums, the **Musée Historique de Lyon**, with displays about the city's 2,000 years of history, and the little **Musée** de la Marionette, about puppets. Above all, however, this is a place for walking and admiring the ancient, elegant buildings. Ask the Tourist Office for their leaflet on walking tours of the *traboules*, a network of covered passages and alleys snaking across the district.

The Presqu'île

At the heart of this narrow peninsular is the **place de Bellecour**. The surrounding grid of streets constitutes the modern city centre. The **Musée des Tissus**, *34 rue de la Charité*, has a collection of 14th–18th-century textiles, including numerous oriental carpets, and a display on the Lyonnais silk trade from the 17th century onwards. Next door, the **Musée des Arts Décoratifs** has 17th–18th-century furniture, art and tapestries, while nearby, on *rue des Remparts-d'Ainay*, an attractive 10th–12th-century church is all that remains of the **Abbaye de Saint-Martin-d'Ainay**.

Further north, the **Musée de l'Imprimerie et de la Banque**, *13 rue de la Poulaillerie*, offers a surprisingly compelling history of printing. The 17th-century Palais St-Pierre is home to the wonderful **Musée des Beaux Arts**, *pl. des Terreaux*, which has a superb fine art collection, second only in size to the Louvre. The **Musée Saint-Pierre d'Art Contemporain**, *16 rue Président Edouard Herriot*, hosts temporary exhibitions by modern artists. For other museums and attractions, ask at the tourist office.

AVIGNON

Station: *tel: 90 82 56 29* (reservations). For centre-ville, head through *Porte de la République* and straight up (north) *cours Jean-Jaurès*.
Tourist Office: *41 Cours Jean-Jaurès; tel: 90 82 65 11*. Open summer 0900–2000, winter 0900–1800. Closed Sunday. Hotel reservations. Also in the station; *tel: 90 82 05 81*.

Accommodation and Food

In summer reservations are essential. The nearest IYHF hostel is at Villeneuve-les-Avignon (*7, chemin de la Justice*, bus no.10 from opposite the station). In Avignon try *rue Joseph-Vernet* (left off Jean-Jaurès) and *rue Perdiguier* (right off Jean Jaurès) for reasonable hotels. **Campsites**: on Île

de la Barthelasse (bus no.10 from the station).
Rue des Teinturiers is good for restaurants, *cours Jean-Jaurès* for fast food. *Pl. de l'Horloge* by the Palais des Papes has many bars and cafés. In July and August the **festival** takes over town.

Sightseeing

Avignon is a curious cultural centre on the banks of the Rhône. Although founded by the Romans, it is most famed for its lengthy stint as the alternative Vatican. Seven popes lived here, from 1309–1377, when they returned to Rome. A year later, the church divided and the 'anti-pope' returned to Avignon, splitting Europe for 40 years. The Great Schism finally ended in 1417, but the town remained under Papal government until the French Revolution. The fortified 14th-century **Palais des Papes**, *pl. de l'Horloge*, is impressive, with a 50m-long banqueting hall, the **Grand Tinel**. Next door, the **Petit Palais** has an excellent collection of Gothic and Renaissance art. Tumbling into the Rhône is the **Pont St Bénézet** of song fame – pay to walk to the end and dance back (the real dancing is said to have happened in the various inns under the bridge).

Bordering the river is the park of **Le Rocher des Doms**. Back in town, **Musée Calver,** *rue Joseph Vernet*, houses impressionist art, Egyptian mummies and other artistic curios. There's a vegetable and fruit market at **Les Halles**, *pl. Pie* (daily except Monday), and a flower market, *pl. des Carmes*, (Saturday).

Side Tracks from Avignon

Orange, with its impressive Roman theatre, is the gateway to Provence. Try around *pl. aux Herbes* for hotels and *pl. Sylvian* for restaurants. Some train services from Lyon call at Orange (the journey takes 1 hr 45 mins from Lyon); from Avignon, the journey takes 15 mins. **Station**: *tel: 90 34 17 82*. **Tourist Office**: *Cours Aristide Briand* (off *rue St Martin); tel: 90 34 70 88*. Open 0900–1900.

TARASCON, ARLES AND MARSEILLE

For information on Tarascon and Arles, see pp. 253–254; for Marseille, see p. 249.

PARIS to MILAN

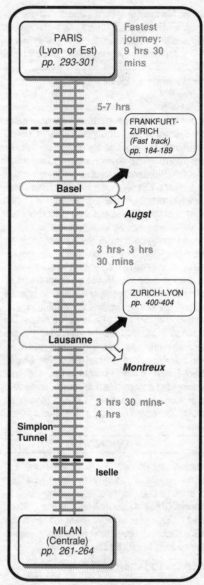

This route between France and Italy is mainly in Switzerland, through breathtaking Alpine scenery. Basel is crammed with fine museums and Lausanne is an excellent base for exploring Lake Geneva.

TRAINS

ETT tables: 44, 171, 260, 82.

→ Fast Track

There are two EN trains daily between Paris (Gare de Lyon) and Milan (Centrale), which travel via Lyon and do not pass through Basel. They both carry sleeping-cars and couchettes. The frontier posts vary according to line, but you are not woken up. Journey time averages about 9 hrs 30 mins.

⤳ On Track

Paris–(Border)–Basel (Bâle)

Daily services between Paris (Est) and Basel (SBB) include: EC trains (supplement payable), taking just under 5 hrs and carrying dining-cars; other day-trains, taking 5 hrs 30 mins and offering a buffet service; and overnight trains with sleeping-cars and couchettes that take 6–7 hrs. Border formalities take place at Basel station.

Basel–Lausanne

IC and ordinary trains alternate hourly between Basel (SBB) and Lausanne, the journey taking a little under 3 hrs on IC, nearer 3 hrs 30 mins on the others. All have a buffet service.

At Lausanne, this route intersects the Zurich–Lyon route, see p. 400.

Lausanne–(Border)–Milan (Milano)

At least five IC trains run daily between Lausanne and Milan (Centrale), plus one EC train (supplement payable), all with refreshment services. Journey time varies from 3 hrs 30 mins to over 4 hrs. Border formalities are barely noticeable.

BASEL (BÂLE)

Stations: Basel occupies a corner between France and Germany and is a frontier town for both. The main station, **SBB (Schweizerische Bundesbahnen)**, *tel: (061) 272 67 67*, 15 mins walk south of the centre (tram nos.1/8) handles Swiss and principal German services. The French part of the station, **Bahnhof SNCF**, *tel: (061) 271 50 33*, handles French services. **Badischer Bahnhof DB (Deutsche Bahn)**, *tel: (061) 691 55 11* (in Kleinbasel, but linked to SBB by rail) handles German local services.

Tourist Office: *Blumenrain 2, Schifflande; tel: (061) 261 50 50*, near the Mittlere Bridge. Mon–Fri 0830–1800 and Sat 0830–1300. *At the SBB station; tel: (061) 271 36 84*, Mon–Fri 0830–1900 and Sat 1830–1230 (longer hours in summer).

Getting Around

Most of the old centre is pedestrianised. Elsewhere there's a frequent tram service, supplemented by buses. Information and tickets are available from machines at every stop.

Accommodation

Hotels are expensive, but anyone under 26 can get reductions. **IYHF:** *St Alban-Kirchrain 10; tel: (061) 272 05 72*, 15 mins walk from the SBB station (tram no.2).

Sightseeing

Mittlere Rheinbrücke is the most picturesque of the six bridges across the River Rhine. The medieval centre is on the south-west bank, in **Grossbasel**, while **Kleinbasel** is a small area on the north-east bank. Basel has been sponsoring artists since the mid-17th century and now has 27 museums and galleries, containing Switzerland's best collection of art treasures.

Just south of the Rhine, *Münsterplatz* is dominated by the 12th-century red sandstone **Münster**, which has a lovely Romanesque portal surrounded by elegant carvings, a rose window

featuring the wheel of fortune and decorative twin towers. Inside are the sarcophagi of various nobles and the simple marble tomb of Erasmus, who spent the last years of his life here. His dissatisfaction with the religious practices of his time paved the way for the Lutherans.

The **Historisches Museum** has been housed in the Gothic **Barfüsserkirche**, *Barfüsserplatz*, since the 19th century. It contains 15th- and 16th-century *objets d'art*, including Luther's chalice, locally made tapestries, wood sculptures and furniture. The 18th–19th-century sections of the collection are on display in the 18th-century **Haus zum Kirschgarten**, *Elizabethenstr.27*, about 300m north of SBB.

The world-class **Kunstmuseum**, *St-Alban-Graben 16* (tram no.2), is in a suitably imposing building that was constructed 1932–36 especially to house the art treasures the town had been accumulating since the 17th century. These include works by Picasso, Braque, Dali, Witz, the world's largest collection of Hans Holbein the Younger, Van Gogh's *Daubigney's Garden* and Holbein's *Portrait of Erasmus.*

The **Antikenmuseum**, *St-Alban-Graben 5*, goes back somewhat further, with some very fine vases as one highlight of a comprehensive collection of ancient Greek artefacts. The **Museum für Gegenwartskunst**, *St-Alban-Rheinweg 60*, concentrates on contemporary work with a permanent collection including pieces by Stella, Warhol and Beuys.

The **Basler Papiermühle**, *St-Alban-Tal 35–37*, on the waterfront in a restored medieval mill, offers a history of paper-making, with demonstrations of processes such as book-binding.

Of the two main surviving medieval city gates, **St-Alban-Tor**, *St-Alban-Graben*, takes second place to the splendid 14th-century **Spalentor**, *Spalengraben.*

At *Augustinergasse 2* are the **Naturhistorisches Museum**, which displays natural history exhibits ranging from dinosaur skeletons to minerals, and the **Museum für Völkerkunde**. This ethnographical collection is global and far too large to be shown in one go, so what you see varies, but is invariably excellent.

The recently restored 16th-century **Rathaus**, has an ornate red façade that includes an enormous clock. It towers over *Marktplatz*, the historic and modern heart of Basel. For a taste of the past, take the steep steps on *Totengasslein*, between *Marktplatz* and the 13th-century **Peterskirche**, *Petersgraben*, which contains late medieval frescos.

The **Zoologischer Garten**, *Binningerstr.40*, west of SBB, has gained a reputation for breeding armoured rhinos, but is also known for its collections of pygmy hippos, gorillas and penguins. Elephants provide rides for children.

The **Fasnacht-Brunnen/Tinguely-Brunnen**, *Theaterplatz*, is an extraordinary fountain that was built in 1977 and resembles a watery scrapyard. The town's older fountains include the tall **Holbeinbrunnen**, *Spalenvorstadt*, based partly on a Holbein drawing and a Dürer engraving.

Fasnacht is a crazy three-day carnival that takes over the town promptly at 0400 on the Monday after Ash Wednesday. A noisy and colourful fancy dress extravaganza, its great fun.

🌊 Side Track from Basel

Augst is 20 mins by train from SBB or (more fun) 1 hr 30 mins by ferry from the dock at Schifflände (**Basler Personenschiffahrts-Gesell-schaft**; *tel: (061) 261 24 00)*. The extensive ruins of an old Roman settlement, **Augusta Raurica**, have been completely rebuilt and the site takes some time to explore fully. A magnificent and varied collection of mostly 4th-century objects (discovered in 1962) can now be seen in the **Römermuseum**, a reconstruction of an ordinary home. The 2nd-century AD theatre is used for diverse summer performances.

LAUSANNE

Station: *tel: (021) 20 80 71*, between the centre and Ouchy, joined to both by the Metro. The tourist office here is limited.

Main Tourist Office: *ave de Rhodanie 2, Ouchy; tel: (021) 617 14 27*. Easter–mid-Oct, Mon–Sat 0800–1900, Sun 0900–1200 and 1300–1800. Mid-Oct–Easter, Mon–Fri 0800–1800, Sat 0830–1200 and 1300–1700. Get the free and comprehensive *Lausanne Official Guide*.

Getting Around

The old town is at around 500m and the lake at 370m; moving between them is hard work, a problem the **Metro** was designed to solve. The very few stops include the old town, the station (below it) and Ouchy (the waterfront). The old town is small and, despite the hills, best explored on foot (much of it is pedestrianised). Elsewhere, there is an excellent network of buses and trams.

Accommodation

There's plenty of budget accommodation. **IYHF:** *chemin de Muguet 1; tel: (021) 616 57 82*, near Ouchy. **Campsite:** *Camping de Vidy, chemin du Camping 3; tel: (021) 24 20 31*, by the lakeside. International hotels in the city include: *Nv*.

Sightseeing

The French-speaking city is in a beautiful location, with **Lake Geneva (Lac Léman)** to the south and the Alps to the north. It has been a cultural centre for centuries and the medieval town surrounding the cathedral has been carefully restored. Ouchy is a mecca for watersports.

The Centre

The upper Metro terminal is at 'Sainfe', *pl. St-Francois*, just south of the main area of interest and dominated by the 15th-century steeple of the mostly 13th–14th-century **Église St-François**.

The magnificent **Cathédrale de Notre-Dame** was consecrated in 1215. Italian, Flemish and French craftsmen all had a hand along the way and it is commonly accepted as a perfect example of Burgundian-Gothic. Unfortunately most of the interior decorations were removed when the town became Protestant in 1536, but the basic structure was unchanged and there are glorious 13th-century rose windows in the south transept, some intricately carved 16th-century choir stalls and a few 15th-century frescos. Following a tradition that has died out elsewhere, the watch is still called from the steeple every hour from 2000 to 0200.

The **Musée Historique de Lausanne**, *pl. de la Cathédrale 4*, is housed in the **Ancien-Evêché**, the bishops' palace until the early 15th century. Among the exhibits is a remarkable large-scale model of 17th-century Lausanne. At the northern end of the centre, **Château St-Maire**, now the seat of the cantonal government, was another bishops' residence (15th–16th centuries), also with fortified towers.

Escaliers-du-Marché, a wooden-roofed medieval staircase, links the cathedral square to *pl. de la Palud*, an ancient square surrounded by old houses and featuring the 18th-century monumental **Fontaine de la Justice** and a clock with moving figures that spring to life every hour. Also on the square are the arcades of the restored 15th–17th-century **Hôtel de Ville**. West of the cathedral, the splendid Florentine-style **Palais de Rumine**, *pl. de la Riponne 6*, was built by a Russian family at the turn of the century. It now houses the modern university, as well as several museums. The **Musée Cantonale d'Histoire Naturelle**, is a wide-ranging zoological and geological collection that includes the bones of a whole mammoth and a colony of (living) ants. The **Musée Cantonale des Beaux-Arts** has a permanent display of mainly 18th–20th-century French-Swiss art alongside temporary exhibits. The **Musée Cantonale d'Archéologie et d'Histoire** contains relics from ancient times, notably a gold bust of Marcus Aurelius.

About 10-mins walk north-west (bus no.2), the fascinating **Collection de l'Art Brut**, *av. des Bergières 11*, should not be missed. This is housed in the **Château de Beaulieu** and is a bizarre post-war collection founded by Jean Dubuffet, who rebelled against the culture vultures of his time and assembled the works of almost anyone who was not a 'real' painter, from amateur dabblers to the criminally insane.

North of the centre

The **Fondation de l'Hermitage**, *route du Signal 2*, is an early 19th-century villa full of period fixtures and fittings, which hosts touring exhibitions of contemporary art.

For great views across the lake, take bus no.16 further north to the **Forêt de Sauvabelin** (650m), a 140-acre beech forest with a choice of walking paths. It encompasses a deer reserve

around a small lake (a natural skating rink in winter). Paths lead to the **Vivarium**, *chemin de Boissonnet 82*, a zoo specialising in reptiles.

Ouchy

The *quai de Belgique* is a shady, flower-lined, waterside promenade, with great views across Lake Geneva to the Savoy Alps. The 13th-century keep of **Château d'Ouchy** survives, incorporated into a lakeside hotel.

Baron Pierre de Coubertin, founder of the modern Olympics in 1915, chose Lausanne as the headquarters of the International Olympic Committee. It has never hosted the Games but the town remains the heart of the movement. The unique **Musée Olympique**, *quai d'Ouchy 1*, (opened June 1993) is a large complex designed to retain the natural beauty of its surrounding park, so trees frame marble pillars featuring the Olympic rings and only one storey of the building is visible at a time. Symbolism is strong, but 20th-century technology has created audio-visual displays and interactive machines allowing you to focus on 'your' sport.

Side Tracks from Lausanne

Frequent trains link the waterfront towns and **CGN**, *ave de Rhodanie 17; tel: (021) 617 06 66*, operate several ferries from Ouchy, including services to **Geneva** (at the western end of the lake), **Evian** (in France, on the southern shore) and Montreux.

Montreux (eastern end of the lake; 1 hr 30 mins by ferry), became popular when a casino was opened in 1883. **Tourist Office:** *pl. du Débarcadère; tel: (021) 963 12 12*. The famous **Jazz Festival** occupies two and a half weeks in mid-July (book well ahead). The town has a flower-packed 10-km-long waterside promenade and several mountain railways climb into the surrounding mountains, but the major sight is the remarkably well-preserved 13th-century **Château de Chillon** (at *Veytaux*, 3 km south). Below the finely decorated 16th-century rooms is a prison complete with a torture chamber and pillar on which Byron carved his name.

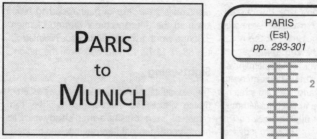

PARIS
to
MUNICH

This route between France and Germany offers a good mixture of attractions, from exceptional buildings and museums to the ritzy spa of Baden-Baden, and the Black Forest.

TRAINS

ETT tables: 32, 173, 727, 730, 760.

➡ Fast Track

There are two EC trains daily (one in the morning, the other in the afternoon) and one overnight train, between Paris (Est) and Munich. Day trains take about 8 hrs 30 mins, have dining-cars and charge a supplement. The overnight train, which carries no supplement, takes about 10 hrs and offers a buffet service, as well as couchettes and sleeping-cars. The border is crossed at Kehl, but formalities are minimal.

∿ On Track

Paris (Est)–Nancy
See the Paris–Frankfurt route, p. 311.

Nancy–Strasbourg

There are 8–12 services daily. A supplement is payable on the faster trains. The journey time varies from 1 hr 10 mins to 1 hr 25 mins.

Strasbourg–(Border)–Baden-Baden

There are at least three trains a day, taking about 35 mins. The border (at Kehl) is a mere formality. More services are available if you are prepared to change at Appenweier or Offenburg.

Baden-Baden–Karlsruhe

Trains are frequent (roughly half an hour apart

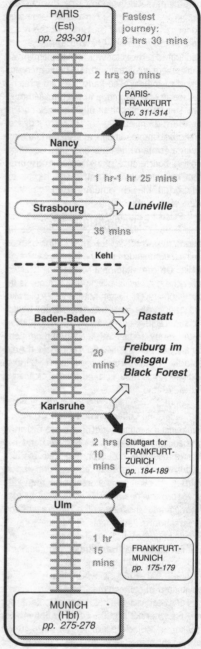

PARIS
(Est)
pp. 293-301

Fastest journey:
8 hrs 30 mins

2 hrs 30 mins

PARIS-
FRANKFURT
pp. 311-314

Nancy

1 hr-1 hr 25 mins

Strasbourg ⇨ *Lunéville*

35 mins

Kehl

Baden-Baden ⇨ *Rastatt*

20 mins

Freiburg im Breisgau Black Forest

Karlsruhe

2 hrs 10 mins

Stuttgart for
FRANKFURT-
ZURICH
pp. 184-189

Ulm

1 hr 15 mins

FRANKFURT-
MUNICH
pp. 175-179

MUNICH
(Hbf)
pp. 275-278

during the day) and the journey takes about 20 mins.

Karlsruhe–Ulm–Munich (München)

In addition to services for which a supplement is payable, there are IR trains at two-hour intervals for most of the day. The Karlsruhe–Ulm stretch takes about 2 hrs 10 mins and the Ulm–Munich about 1 hr 15 mins, the through journey being about 3 hrs 25 mins.

You could also disembark at **Stuttgart** (about halfway between Karlsruhe and Ulm, see the Frankfurt–Zurich route, p. 184), or at **Augsburg** (about halfway between Ulm and Munich, see the Frankfurt–Munich route, p. 175).

STRASBOURG

Station: tel: 88 22 50 50. This is east of the island, straight along rue du Maire Kuss.
Tourist Offices: **Regional office:** pl. de la Cathédrale 17; tel: 88 52 28 22. June–Sept daily 0800–1900. Easter–May and Oct daily 0900–1800. Nov–Easter, Mon–Sat 0900–1800, and Sun 0930–1230 and 1400–1700. **Branches:** pl. de la Gare; tel: 88 32 51 49 and pont de l'Europe; tel: 88 61 39 23. Both open June–Sept daily 0800–1900. Nov–Easter Mon–Fri 0900–1230 and 1345–1800. Easter–May and Oct daily 0900–1230 and 1345–1800.

Getting Around

Most things of interest are on (or just off) the island and easily walkable. A good bus network covers the suburbs, but services are sparse on Sundays. Boat trips operate on the Ill and Rhine Mar–Oct. Details from **Port Autonome de Strasbourg**, rue de Nantes 15; tel: 88 84 13 13.

If you are staying for a while, consider getting the **Strasbourg Pass** (details from the tourist office and hotels), which is a 3-day pass covering a number of different activities and attractions.

Accommodation

Hotels in Strasbourg are not cheap. Investigate areas just outside town if you are on a budget. There are two **IYHF** hostels: rue de l'Auberge de Jeunesse 9, Montagne Verte; tel: 88 30 26 46, 2 km from the station (bus nos.3/13/23), and rue des Cavaliers, Parc du Rhin; tel: 88 60 10 20, 1 km from the German border (bus no.11, then 32). Also worth trying is CIARUS, rue Finkmatt 7; tel: 88 32 12 12, 15 mins walk from the station.

Sightseeing

The old capital of Alsace began life as a Celtic fishing village and is an attractive place, the centre of interest being a river island which is home to half-timbered houses, covered bridges, flower-lined canals, historical buildings and some good museums. The European Parliament is housed in **Palais de l'Europe**, an imposing modern building on the River Ill, some way north of the island.

The outstanding **Cathédrale de Notre-Dame** took three centuries to build and provides an excellent example of Gothic architecture, with three ornate portals and a delicate 142m spire. In the south transept are the 13th-century Pilier des Anges and an enormously complex 19th-century Astronomical Clock, which strikes noon at 1231 each day (but begins to swing into action at 1215). The perfectly proportioned high nave is highlighted by lovely stained-glass windows, the late 15th-century stone pulpit is intricately carved and there are some superb statues.

Just south is pl. du Château, named for the 18th-century bishops' residence, the **Château des Rohan**, which now houses three museums. Also in the square is the more interesting **Musée de l'Oeuvre Notre-Dame**, with a huge collection of local art, notably medieval and Renaissance. In 1997 the **Musée d'Art Moderne** (currently at pl. du Château 5) will move to larger premises.

Musée Alsacien, quai St-Nicolas 23 (south across the river), covers the popular arts and traditions of rural Alsace and includes whole rooms in period style.

To the west of the island are **Ponts Couverts**, three bridges with square towers that are remnants of the 14th-century fortifications. The adjoining area of **La Petite France** is full of winding streets and picturesque 16th–17th-century houses.

◣ Side Track from Strasbourg

Lunéville (just over an hour by reasonably

frequent trains) has a superb 18th-century *Château* that was home to the Dukes of Lorraine. Modelled on Versailles, it contains some fine Rococo furnishings and is surrounded by magnificent gardens. *St Jacques* is also interesting, with a striking façade where two decorative towers flank a huge ornate clock.

- - - - - - - - - - - - - - - - - - -

BADEN-BADEN

Station: Hbf, *tel: (07221) 19419*. This is a long way north-west of town, but there is a good bus service.
Tourist Office: *Haus des Kurgastes, Augustaplatz 8; tel: (07221) 21 27 50.* Mon–Sat 0900–2200 and Sun 1000–2200.

Sightseeing

Very fashionable in the 19th century, Baden-Baden is still frequented by the sort of people who can afford to go anywhere, the mineral springs and casino being as much of a draw as ever. The Romans built the first thermal baths here and remnants can still be seen under *Römerplatz*, where the main baths are situated. **Friedrichsbad** combines the old-world charm of a beautifully renovated Renaissance building with the best in modern technology – and charges accordingly. It is renowned for its 2-hour therapeutic Roman-Irish bath, which consists of 14 different stages of treatment. Nudity is mandatory. Neighbouring, ultra-modern **Caracalla-Therme**, *Römerplatz 11*, is less fashionable, but has the same basic facilities for about half the price – and permits bathing suits. The pump room, **Trinkhalle**, *Kaiserallee 3*, has murals of local legends connected with the town's waters.

The **Casino**, *Kurhaus, Kaiserallee 1*, was redecorated in French style in 1853 and is promoted as the world's most beautiful casino.

- - - - - - - - - - - - - - - - - - -

↻ Side Track from Baden-Baden

Five mins from Baden-Baden by frequent train (on the Baden-Baden–Karlsruhe line), **Rastatt** has an enormous reddish sandstone *Schloss*, an 18th-century structure. Some of the lovely reception rooms are open, you can visit the

richly ornamented church and the complex includes an excellent military museum.

FREIBURG IM BREISGAU

Freiburg is 55 mins from Baden-Baden by frequent trains, worth visiting in its own right and the best base for the Black Forest. Get the *Freiburg Official Guide*, which covers both the forest and the town. **Hbf** *(tel: (0761) 19419)* is 15 mins walk west of the centre. The **tourist office** *(Rotteckring 14; tel: (0761) 368 9090)* is two blocks from Hbf. Open Mon–Sat 0900–2130 and Sun 1000–1200 (shorter hours in winter).

Getting Around

Most sights are in *Altstadt* and walkable but, if you are not staying in the centre, a multi-ride ticket (several types exist) is probably worthwhile.

Accommodation

It's probably worth paying the tourist office booking fee, because most budget accommodation is suburban. You can only get a private room if you are staying for at least three nights. Hotel chains with property in the town: *Nv*.

IYHF: *Kartauserstr.151; tel: (0761) 67656*, at the extreme east of town (tram no.1: *Hasemannstr.*). **Campsites**: *Hirzberg, Kartauserstr.99; tel: (0761) 35054*, near the IYHF. Out of season, *St Georg, Basler Landstr.62; tel: (0761) 43183*, south-west of the centre, is open all year.

Sightseeing

Some of the old streets have narrow streams running through them. These were part of the old drainage system (*Bächle*) and also used for watering livestock. They are still useful, as they help to keep temperatures down in summer, but you need to watch your step.

Altstadt was accidentally bombed by the Luftwaffe in 1940 and deliberately by the Allies in 1944, but has been very well restored. **Schwabentor** and **Martinstor** are parts of the medieval fortifications in the south-east of *Altstadt*, with the most interesting section of town between them and the red sandstone **Münster**, *Münsterplatz* – a very fine example of Gothic architecture, with a tapering 116m spire that is a city landmark. The exterior sculptures portray a range of biblical characters (including Satan). The mixed Romanesque-Gothic interior is illuminated by 13th–16th-century stained glass, many sections depicting the guilds who paid for them.

There's a daily market in **Münsterplatz**. The **Historisches Kaufhaus**, an arcaded merchants' hall, has statues and spires on the façade. It is flanked by handsome Baroque palaces, **Erzbischofliches Palais** and **Wenzingerhaus**. The latter contains a Rococo staircase and frescoed ceiling.

The **Neues Rathaus** consists of two Renaissance mansions linked by a bridge. On *Rathausplatz* are the Gothic monastery-church of **Martinskirche** and the elegant **Haus zum Walfisch**: a recreation of the house where Erasmus lived for two years.

Augustiner, *Salzstr.*, is the town's best museum, housed in a former monastery and containing a superb display of 13th–15th-century religious and folkloric art from the Upper Rhine area, as well as old masters.

KARLSRUHE

Station: Hbf, *tel: (0721) 19419*, 25 mins walk south of the centre (tram nos.3/4).

Tourist Office: *Bahnhofplatz 6; tel: (0721) 35530* and *35 53 11*. Mon–Fri 0800–1900 and Sat 0800–1300. Opposite Hbf. They have good maps and provide a free room-booking service. The local listing is *Karlsruhe Programme*.

Getting Around

The 24-hour ticket is worthwhile, if you venture away from the centre. **Rhine cruises** operate Easter–Nov from the western edge of town. The tourist office can provide details.

Accommodation

Hotel chains with property in the area: *Ra, SC*. The tourist office can supply a list of reasonable accommodation in nearby villages. **IYHF**: *Moltkestr.2b; tel: (0721) 28248*, west of *Schlossgarten* (tram nos.3/4: *Europaplatz*).

Campsite: *Turmbergblick, Tiengererstr.40; tel: (0721) 44060*, 5 km east of the centre, by the River Pfinz in *Durlach* (tram nos.1/2).

The Black Forest (Schwarzwald)

Easily Germany's largest, loveliest and most-visited woodland, the Black Forest covers an area of 170 km north–south and 60 km east–west. The name is thought to have resulted from the dark conifers that blanket the upper slopes, oaks and beeches being more common lower down.

Despite mass tourism and the unattractive establishments that spring up to profit from it, this remains a friendly region, still extensively forested and home to some excellent wines. Many farmers wear traditional dress, thatched houses are common and such local crafts as wood-carving and clock-making are still very much in evidence (the cuckoo-clock was invented here).

From Freiburg, which is surrounded by the forest, there are frequent public transport links with the smaller settlements. Once there, it's easy to find accommodation at reasonable prices and the best way to explore is on foot: there are hundreds of well-marked trails that are used for hiking in summer and skiing in winter.

The local tourist authority, **Fremdenverkehrsverband**, *Bertoldstr.45, 7800 Freiburg; tel: (0761) 31317*, suggest scenic motoring routes with stops at interesting small towns, most of which can be reached by local trains and used as a base for local walks. Bus services are infrequent (many privately owned) so, if you decide to spend a day in the remoter central regions, make sure you know the time of the last bus back. Alternatively, there are organised coach tours and private railways with scenic routes – the tourist office can provide full information.

Sightseeing

A major industrial and university city, with some outstanding museums, Karlsruhe was designed around a **Schloss** established in 1715 by Margrave Karl Wilhelm as a place where he could get away from his wife (Karlsruhe, 'Karl's rest'). It is an enormous neo-classical building occupying three sides of a hexagon and facing a semi-circle of buildings, the inter-vening space consisting of a formal garden. Nine streets radiate from the semi-circle, creating a fan shape – with the schloss and garden as the handle. This now contains the not-to-be-missed **Landesmuseum**, which has a superb collection of artefacts from diverse ancient cultures,. and some first-rate art nouveau. Of particular interest is *Türkenbeute*, an eclectic display of items that a nobleman brought back from Turkey in the late 17th century.

Behind the palace is the large **Schlossgarten**, to the west of which is the **Orangerie**, *Hans Thoma-Str. 6*, with a fine selection of 19th and 20th-century European art, while the **Kunsthalle**, *Hans-Thoma-Str. 2*, contains wide-ranging 15th–19th-century European works, from German primitives to Impressionists.

Marktplatz, the enormous central square, is a short distance south of the schloss, dominated by a pyramid of red sandstone that serves as a gravestone for Karl Wilhelm.

The pink **Rathaus** is on the western side and the Corinthian-col-umned **Stadtkirche** on the east. In **Prinz-Max-Palais**, *Karlstr.10*, south-west of the schloss, is an interesting array of objects, including what is claimed to be the world's first bicycle.

ULM

Station: Hbf, *tel: (0731) 19419*.
Tourist Office: *Münsterplatz; tel: (0731) 64161*. Mon–Fri 0900–1800 and Sat 0900–1230.

Getting Around

Most things of interest are easily walkable, on the north bank of the Danube.

Accommodation

There are some reasonable central hotels; ask the tourist office to find you one. For cheap pensions, look in the suburb of *Pfuhl* (to the east). **IYHF**: *Grimmelfingerweg 45; tel: (0731) 38 44 55*, 4 km south-west of the centre (bus no.9 from Hbf or bus no.4 from Rathaus, both to *Schulzentrum*, then walk round the stadium).

Sightseeing

Ulm was the birthplace of Albert Einstein (1879) and the scene of man's first serious attempt to fly. Most of the historic centre was wiped out in 1944, but the streets that escaped major damage have been lovingly restored.

Fortunately the magnificent late-Gothic **Münster** sustained only minor damage. It has five impressive portals and the Gothic west spire is the tallest in the world (161m). The foundations were laid in 1377, but the spire was designed in the 15th century and completed only in 1890. If you climb a 768-step spiral staircase to 143 m, you'll have a view that encompasses the Danube, the Black Forest and (on a clear day) the Swiss Alps. The basic interior design is simple, which emphasises its dimensions, but the 15th-century choir stalls are covered with striking wood-carvings and there's a lovely delicate tabernacle and an enormous fresco of the *Last Judgment*.

The graceful Gothic/Renaissance **Rathaus** (south, across *Neue Str.*, from the Münster) is a photogenic collection of buildings restored in 16th-century style. The exterior is covered by religious frescos and statues and there's an intricate astronomical clock on the west front. Behind it is a Renaissance mansion housing **Ulmer Museum**, which covers art and culture from pre-history to modern times and is noted for works by early Ulm masters.

A little further south is **Metzgerturm** (1345), the former prison, known as the 'leaning tower of Ulm' because it is about 2m off the vertical. From here you can walk along the 15th-century ramparts beside the Danube. To the east is **Fischerviertel**, the 16th-century fishermen's quarter, a picturesque area of half-timbered houses. One of the most interesting buildings is the **Schiefe Haus** (c.1500), which leans precariously over the small River Blau.

The unique **Deutsches Brotmuseum**, *Salzstadelstr.10*, is concerned with the history of bread since the beginning of time.

The suburb of **Wiblingen**, about 5 km south of Ulm (bus nos.3/8), has a Benedictine monastery-church, an extensive Baroque complex with amazing *trompe l'oeil* frescos and a lavishly adorned library.

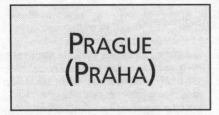

PRAGUE (PRAHA)

Prague is one of the loveliest cities in the world, particularly famous for its Baroque architecture, most of which has been preserved intact since the last building boom in the 17th century. It has a fascinating history, very lively music scene, a vast number of museums and churches and delightful green spaces. Allow yourself several days to do it justice.

Tourist Information

The main office of the **Prăzská informačni služba** (Prague Information Service, known as PIS) is at *Na príkopě 20*, near *Václavske náměsti* (Wenceslas Square); *tel: (02) 54 44 44*. Open Mon–Fri 0800–1900, weekends 0800–1530 (later in summer). They are also at *Staroměstské náměsti 22*, in the heart of the old town, and at the Central Railway Station (Hlavní Nádraži).

Arriving and Departing

Airport

Ruzyně Airport is 16 km west of the city (flight enquiries, *tel: (02) 36 78 14/36 77 60*).. There are a 24-hour currency exchange booth, an accommodation bureau, post and telephone facilities at the airport. Czech Airlines (ČSA) run a bus service every 30 mins from 0530 to 1900 to their terminal in Staré Město (*Revoluční 25*). Czech Airhandling's excellent mini-bus service runs door-to-door, but costs more.

Trains

Praha Hlavní Nádraži, (Central Railway Station), *Wilsonova; tel: (02) 26 49 30*, is the city's main station, although some long-distance and international services also operate into **Nádraži Praha-Holešovice**, *tel: (02) 80 75 05*, in the 7th district (a little way out). Both stations are on Metro Line C, which connects to the city centre.

Hlavní Nádraži has information and accommodation offices.

Getting Around

Visiting the main attractions is easy, as they are confined to small areas. Nevertheless, you will need to use some public transport. PIS offices issue free street plans. The most reliable and up-to-date map, by Kartografie Praha (1:20,000), includes routes of public transport.

Single tickets (*jízdenky*) allow you 1 hr on the metro, or 1 leg of a bus or tram journey. A better buy is the inexpensive 5-day **tourist ticket** (*denní jízdenka*), which is valid on all forms of public transport. Tickets are on sale at *tabák* (tobacconists/newsagents) or from main metro stations. Alternatively, a **Prague card**, available from, Čedok, (travel agency) *Na přikopě 18*, or American Express, *Václavské náměsti 56*, combines a 3-day transport ticket with free entry to major sights. Children under 12 travel free. All public transport runs from about 0500 to 2400.

Wenceslas Square (*Václavské náměsti*) is very lively by day, with all manner of shops, hotels, and fast-food places. However, parts of it also double as the red light district at night (extending into the surrounding streets).

Metro, Trams and Buses

A wonderfully efficient and modern **metro** (3 lines) covers most areas you are likely to visit, except the Hradčany (Castle Hill) itself. There is also a good network of **trams** running on main arteries and across the river. Be careful, as pickpockets are rife on popular tourist routes (eg no. 22). The infrequent **night trams** all stop at *Lazarská*, just off *Václavské náměsti* (*Wenceslas Square*). You will rarely need to use **buses** unless you are staying out in the suburbs. The **Central Bus Station** is at *Křižíkova 4; tel: (02) 2421 1060* (metro: *Florenc*).

Taxis

Avoid taxis, if at all possible – aggressive overcharging of foreigners is endemic and there have even been cases of violence. If a taxi ride is unavoidable, get one called rather than hailing one in the street (*tel: (02) 35 03 20/34 24 10/ 2491 1559/2344*).

Living in Prague

Accommodation

Although Prague is gradually bringing its high-class accommodation up to Western standards, many hotels are still over-priced for what they offer. A shortage of beds has done nothing to diminish the problem. If you prefer to stick to a well-known chain, the following have hotels in Prague: *Fo, Ic, Ih* and *Pe*.

Accommodation Bureaux: *Hlavní nádraží (AVE); tel: (02) 2422 3226/3521*. Open daily 0600–2300. **Čedok**, *Panská 5; tel: (02) 2421 3495* (open Mon–Fri 0900–2145, weekends 0830–1630) can make a computer check on hotels with vacant rooms. For **youth-orientated information**, try CKM-SSM, *Žitna 2 ; tel: (02) 2491 0251*, (open daily 0900–1800), or the Youth Hostel Reservation Office, *Žitna 10; tel: (02) 29 29 84*, (open Mon–Sat 0700–1900). In July and August, CKM also lets cheap rooms in student hostels and a similar service is provided by Uniset, *Spálená 5 (tel: (02) 2491 0113)*.

There are six **campsites**. For information, contact UAMK, *Mánesova 20 (tel: (02) 74 74 00* or *2422 1635)*. Closed at weekends.

Communications

The **Central Post Office** and **Poste Restante** are at *Jindřišska 14*, off *Václavské náměsti, tel: (02) 2422 8856/8588*. (24-hr service for parcels, telegrams and telephones). Stamps and phone-cards can be purchased here or from *tabák*.

The telephone system is erratic. The modern phone booths accept phone cards. Local calls (coins only) are made on the yellow and black telephones; long-distance calls on the grey ones. Most have instructions in English. For an English-speaking operator, *tel: (02) 0135*; to make collect calls, *tel: (02) 0132*. The Prague area code is *02*.

Eating and Drinking

There are three main categories of eating house: **restaurace** (restaurant), **vinárna** (wine-bar/restaurant) and **pivnice** (beer cellar). Prices range from expensive in fashionable inner-city locations to great value in hiss'n'spit dives serving locally brewed beer. To avoid unpleasant surprises, study the prices on the menu posted on the door.

Although touristy, the classic **U Flekú** beer garden and cellar, *Křemencova 11; tel: (02) 2491 5119*, is worth a visit for its black ale. Several Prague breweries have their own 'pubs', while others serve the legendary Pilsner Urquell or Budweiser. Enjoy!

Fast food is available at **U Bindrú**, *Staroměstské náměsti*, opposite the Old Town Hall, and from **McDonalds**, *Václavské náměsti*.

Embassies

Australia: *Činska 4, Praha 6; tel: (02) 311 0641/ 2431 0070*.

Canada: *Mickiewiczova 6, Hradčany, Praha 6; tel: (02) 2431 1108*.

UK: *Thunovska 10, Malá Strana; tel: (02) 2451 0439*. (The UK embassy acts for New Zealand and Irish citizens.)

USA: *Tržiště 15, Malá Strana; tel: (02) 2451 0848*.

Money

Banking hours are usually Mon–Fri 0800–1400. For fair dealing, go to **Thomas Cook** *Václavské náměsti 47; tel: (02) 2422 9537* or the **Živnostenská Banka**, *Na příkopě 20*. The many exchange kiosks give poor rates. Travellers cheques and Eurocheques are widely accepted; credit cards are only useful in luxury shops, hotels and restaurants.

Entertainment

Consult the two English-language newspapers, *Prognosis* and *The Prague Post*, for weekly listings of events. The Czech publications, *Program* (weekly) and *Prehled* (monthly) also give details of what's on.

There is an excellent array of classical music and theatre (in Czech), but there are also many delightful and easily understood puppet and mime shows.

The rock and disco scene has exploded into life since the end of Communist rule, with cult discos like **Bunkr**, *Lodecká 2, Staré Město; tel: (02) 2481 0475* – originally a bomb shelter for Party bigwigs.

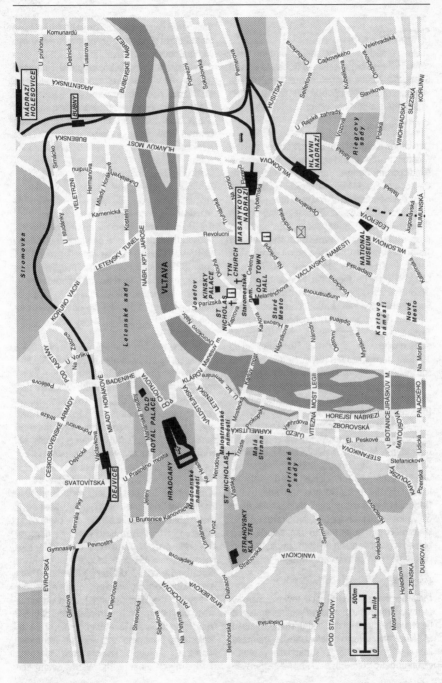

Shopping

The main speciality of Bohemia is beautiful crystal glass. There is a big selection at **Bohemia Crystal Shop-Jafa**, *Maiselova, 15; tel: (02) 2481 0009.* Bohemia-Moser, *Na příkopě, 12; tel: (02) 2421 1293*, offers a mailing service.

Sightseeing

Old Prague is divided into **Staré Město** and **Nové Město** to the east, and **Malá Strana** and **Hradčany** to the west of the River Vltava. At the heart of *Staré Město* is the picturesque **Staroměstské náměsti** (*Old Town Square*), (metro/tram nos. 17/18: *Staroměstská*), a time capsule ringed by medieval and Baroque structures. Find time to visit the **Staroměstská radnice** (Old Town Hall), with its astrological clock, the Baroque **Kostel Sv Mikuláše** (St Nicholas Church), built by the great Prague architects, Christoph and Kilian Ignác Dientzenhofer, the Baroque **Kinsky Palace**, the somewhat forbidding but very ancient **Kostel panny Marie před Týnem** (Tyn Church), and the Gothic **U Kamenného** (House of the Stone Bell). The 1915 **Monument to Jan Hus** in the middle of the square is a traditional rallying point for Czechs – Hus was a 15th-century religious reformer who fought against a corrupt Catholic church and foreign domination of Bohemia.

Nové Město is a less compact area with fewer sights, but all visitors to Prague will spend some time in the famous, lively **Václavské náměsti** (*Wenceslas Square*) (metro: *Můstek* or *Muzeum*), which witnessed the climax of the 'Velvet Revolution' in 1989. At the top end is the **National Museum** (see under Museums) in front of which stand an equestrian **statue of St Wenceslas** and a **shrine to Jan Palach**, who burned himself to death on 16th January 1969 in protest at the Warsaw Pact invasion.

West Bank

Malá Strana is a picturesque town of narrow cobbled streets and diminutive squares squeezed between the river and the wedge-shaped plateau of Hradčany. Here, **Malostranské náměsti** (Lesser Quarter Square) is particularly worth visiting (metro/tram nos. 12/22: *Malostranská*),

dominated by the Dientzenhofer's other **Kostel Sv Mikuláše** (Church of St Nicholas), and ringed with Baroque palaces. Not far away are the even more delightful **Velkopřevorské náměsti** (*Grand Prior's Square*) and the adjoining **Maltézské náměsti** (*Square of the Knights of Malta*), which contain some interesting churches and palaces, together with the celebrated **John Lennon Wall**, a pop-art folly (tram nos. 12/22: *Hellichova*).

Hradčany

This huge hilltop castle is the focal point of Prague (tram no. 22: *Malostranské náměsti/ Pražský hrad*). Dominating the whole complex is the magnificent **Katedrála Svatého Vita** (St Vitus Cathedral), the core of which was built by Matthew of Arras and Peter Parler between 1344 and 1385. Highlights include the Wenceslas Chapel, with walls studded by precious stones, the late-Gothic Royal Oratory, the fabulous *Baroque Tomb of St John Nepomuk* by Fischer von Erlach and the oak panel reliefs in the ambulatory.

Nearby, much of the **Starý Královský Palác** (Old Royal Palace) was built by Benedikt Ried for King Vladislav Jagiello in the 15th century. Don't miss the magnificent late-Gothic Vladislav Hall, the so-called Riders' Stairway (which really was used by mounted knights who jousted in the hall) and the Bohemian Chancellery, where the most famous of Prague's four defenestrations occurred, when Protestant nobles threw Frederick II's ambassadors from the window in 1618.

To the north-east are the **Klášter Sv Jiří** (Convent of St George) and the Romanesque **Bazilika Sv Jiří** (Basilica of St George). Near this is the **Lobkowicz Palace**, which contains a museum of Bohemian history. At the north of the castle plateau, **Zlatá Ulička** (Golden Lane) is lined by diminutive Renaissance houses. Franz Kafka lived at no. 22, between 1916 and 1917 (it is now a bookshop owned by the Kafka Society).

Beyond the Hradčany itself is an attractive area beginning with **Hradčanske náměsti** (*Hradčany Square*). Take tram nos. 12/22 to *Malostranské náměsti* and walk up *Nerudova*. Note the graffitoed **Schwarzenberg Palace** on the south side (housing the War Museum), the

Tuscany Palace to the west and the noble **Archbishop's Palace** to the north. If you walk up *Loretánská*, you come to the imposing **Cernín Palace**, from whose window Foreign Minister Jan Masaryk plunged (or was pushed) to his death in 1948. Nearby is the **Loreta shrine**, an imitation of the famous Loreto near Ancona that claims to possess the house of the Virgin Mary. The Baroque bell-tower has a much-admired carillon and the cloisters, the Santa Casa and the Treasury are all worth a visit. Beyond the Loreta is the **Strahovský Klášter**, (Strahov Monastery), take tram no. 22: *Památník písemnictiví*, whose star attraction is the Philosophical Hall with marvellous frescos by Franz Anton Maulpertsch.

Charles Bridge

This beautiful, medieval sandstone bridge, commissioned by Charles VI in 1357, remained the city's only permanent river crossing until 1836. It has now become the standard image of Prague. At each end are high towers, and the parapet is lined by Baroque statues (mainly 1683–1714, with a few copies and later works). Note especially Jan Brockuff's *St John Nepomuk* (1683), a vivid depiction of Wenceslas IV's Vicar-General who, according to legend, was flung from the bridge for refusing to reveal the secrets of the Queen's confession to the King.

Galleries and Museums

The rich **National Gallery** collection is scattered round four venues: the **Šternberský Palác** (Sternberg Palace), *Hradčany náměsti 15* (tram no. 22: *Pražský hrad*), with major works by European masters, including Breughel, El Greco, Dürer, Rembrandt, Klimt, Cézanne, Manet, Dégas and Picasso. The **Klášter sv Jiří na Pražském** (St George's Convent), *Jirské náměste 33*, houses old Bohemian art. The **Anežsky Klášt-er** (St Agnes Convent), *U milisrdných 17* (tram nos. 5/14/26: *Revoluční*) is devoted to 19th-century artists of the Czech national revival and the **Zámek Zbraslav** (Zbraslav Castle), *Zbraslav nad Vltavou* (metro: *Smíchovské nádraži*, then bus nos. 129/241) has a remarkable display of 19th- and 20th-century Czech sculpture.

The **Národní Museum** (National Museum), *Václavské náměsti 68* (metro: *Muzeum*), is chiefly interesting for its architecture and pantheon. More stimulating is the **Museum hlavniho města Prahy** (Museum of the City of Prague), *Na pořici 52*, (metro/tram nos. 3/8/24: *Florenc*), which has Antonin Langweil's model of the city (1826) featuring 2,228 buildings. Of the many other museums, give priority to the fine collection of furniture and glass at the **Umělec-koprůmyslové Museum** (Museum of Decorative Arts), *Ulice 17 listopadu 2*; the Franz Kafka Permanent Exhibition, *U Radnice 5* (Metro/tram nos. 17/18: *Staroměstská*, for both of these); and **Bertramka**, *Mozartova 169*, (tram nos. 4/6/7/9: *Bertramka*), a 17th-century villa which houses an exhibition of Mozart's life and work.

Other sights

Prague has a superb array of church architecture, from Romanesque rotundas to Josip Plečnik's stunning, 1933 **Kostel nejsvětějšího srdce páné** (Church of the Sacred Heart), *Náměsti Jiriho z Poděbrad* (metro: same name). Also find time to visit the fine Baroque **Kostel Svatého Jakuba** (St James), *Malá Štupartská* (metro: *Náměsti Republiky*) and the remarkable **Kostel nanebevzetí panny Marie a Karla velikého** (Church of the Assumption of Our Lady and Charlemagne), *Ke Karlovu*, (metro: *IP Pavlova*), with lovely Gothic star vaulting.

The old Jewish ghetto of **Josefov** (metro/tram no. 17: *Staroměstská*) was swept away in 1893, leaving behind the only preserved and functioning medieval **synagogue** in Central Europe and a haunting **Old Jewish Cemetery**. The surrounding buildings (which include the **Old-New Synagogue**, the Rococo **Town Hall** with a Hebraic clock and the **Pinkas Synagogue** with a holocaust memorial) constitute a **National Jewish Museum** (one ticket for access to all sights).

At **Vyšehrad** (metro: *Vyšehrad*), south of Nové Město, the ancient citadel where the Slavic tribes first settled, sights include the **Slavin Pantheon** of leading Czechs in the cemetery next to the **Church of St Peter and St Paul** and breathtaking views over the Vltava from the bastions.

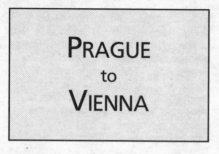

PRAGUE to VIENNA

This route connects two of the great cities of the old Austro-Hungarian empire, via the historic capital of Moravia.

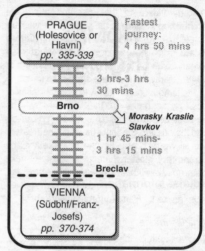

PRAGUE (Holesovice or Hlavní) pp. 335-339

Fastest journey: 4 hrs 50 mins

3 hrs-3 hrs 30 mins

Brno

Morasky Kraslie Slavkov

1 hr 45 mins- 3 hrs 15 mins

Breclav

VIENNA (Südbhf/Franz-Josefs) pp. 370-374

TRAINS

ETT tables: 96a, 880, 878.

→ Fast Track

Four services daily (two EC). Three run Prague (Holešovice)–Vienna (Südbhf), taking 4 hrs 50 mins. The other follows a different route, avoiding Brno, and runs Prague (Hlavní)–Vienna (Franz-Josefs), taking 5 hrs 30 mins. A dining-car is usually available.

~ On Track

Prague–Brno

Several trains daily, taking 3 hrs–3 hrs 30 mins.

Brno–Vienna

Six trains daily, arriving Vienna Nord/Südbhf. Journey takes 1 hr 45 mins–3 hrs 15 mins.

BRNO

Station: (*tel: (05) 422 14 803* or *275 62*). For town centre head up *Masarykova*.
Tourist Office: In station, 23 hours daily, and **Old Town Hall** *Radnicka 4–10; tel: (05) 239 25.*

Sightseeing

Once capital of Moravia, Brno has historic buildings, but marks of the 19th-century industrial boom remain. Chief sights (most close on Mon) are within 1 km of the station. Nearby, **Dóm Na Petrove** (18th–19th-century neo-

Gothic Cathedral of Sts Peter and Paul), crowns **Petrov Hill.** The 13th-century **Špilberk Castle,** was rebuilt in the 19th century due to damage by Napoleon's assault. A little way south-west of the castle is the abbey where in the 19th century the monk Gregor Mendel worked out the fundamentals of genetics by studying the breeding of pea plants in the abbey garden. Garden and pea plants are still there, along with a small museum.

Old City Hall, *Radnická ul.,* has Gothic-, Renaissance- and Baroque-style buildings. The Gothic portal is by the renowned Brno artist, Anton Pilgram. In the entrance is a wheel made in 1636 as part of a bet to fell a tree, make a wheel and roll it 50km to Brno in one day. In the crypt of the **Kapucínské Klaster** (the Capuchin Monastery) are over 100 mummified bodies, airdried in 1650, amongst which is the now headless Baron Trenck (1711–1749), commander of Austria's feared pandour troops.

~ Side Tracks from Brno

The limestone caves of **Moracský Kráslie** form a series of dramatic underground rivers, stalagmites and stalactites in the middle of a forest. Two buses run daily to nearby Blansko (taking 1 hr). At **Slavkov**, 20 km east by bus, is the site of Napoleon's famous victory of Austerlitz..

ROME (ROMA)

The 'Eternal City', filled with museums and galleries, churches and ruins, redolent of the Caesars and the creative genius of Michelangelo, Rome needs no introduction.

Tourist Information

Main tourist information office, **EPT** (Rome Provincial Tourist Board): *Via Parigi 5 (near Via XX Settembre); tel: (06) 48 83 748* (metro: *Repubblica*). Hotel reservations, listings, maps and itineraries. Other tourist and hotel information desks: **Leonardo da Vinci Air-port**; *tel: (06) 65 01 02 55*; **Stazione Termini**; *tel: (06) 48 71 270*. All open 0800–1900 daily.

Arriving and Departing

Airports

Leonardo da Vinci (Fiumicino) is 36 km southwest of Rome; *tel: (06) 65 951*. Taxis into the centre are hassle-free, but expensive (L.60,000–70,000). Less expensive is the 45-mins train service, every 20 mins, 0600–0100, to **Tiburtina** station (for further information, *tel: (06) 65 951*). At time of going to press, a new express rail link to **Termini** had just opened.

Aeroporto Ciampino (*tel: (06) 794 921*) is closer to town, 16 km to the south-east. A bus service (ACOTRAL or ATAC) runs every 10–20 mins to **Anagnina Metro Station** (services to Termini every 30 mins between 0530 and 2230). Expect to pay at least L.50,000 by metered taxi.

Trains

There are four main railway stations: **Termini**, *Piazza dei Cinquecento; tel: (06) 4775*; seat reservations: *tel: (06) 48 84 069*, is Rome's largest, handling all the main national and international lines. A wide range of services includes bureaux de change, tourist and hotel information. It is also well served by taxis, buses and night buses, and is the focus of the metro system.

Ostiense, *tel: (06) 57 58 748*, serves some long distance north-south trains.

Roma-Nord, *tel: (06) 36 10 441*, serves Viterbo (2 hrs); Bracciano (90 mins) and other parts of northern Lazio.

Tiburtina, *tel: (06) 43 42 39 72*, serves some long distance north-south trains. Trains arriving after midnight stop here.

Getting Around

The *centro storico* (historic centre) is fairly compact, traffic-free and easy to see on foot. However, many of the most important sights lie outside this area. The main arteries are well served by buses, but stick to those and you miss Rome's ebullient streetlife, medieval alleys and Baroque squares. Most hotels supply a basic street map. For more detail, and bus and metro maps, ask at news-stands, tobacconists and tourist information offices. Failing that, Romans positively glow with enthusiasm when you ask for help with directions.

Tickets

You must purchase your ticket before travelling. Tickets are on sale at all metro stops, bus termini with green **ACOTRAL** kiosks, and at news-stands and tobacconists displaying **ATAC** (bus and tram) and **ACOTRAL** (metro) signs. You can also get tickets from the **ATAC Information Booth**, *Piazza dei Cinquecento* (metro: *Termini*).

Metro, Buses and Trams

The **Metropolitana** has only two lines – A and B – and is not much use in the centre. Line A (red) is open 0530–2400; Line B (blue) is open 0530–2100, Mon–Fri. Tickets are for a single journey, but there are also monthly passes, a ticket valid for 90 mins (L.800), and a 24-hr BIG ticket (L.2,000), which are valid on all forms of public transport.

Rome's excellent **bus** service is centred on *Piazza dei Cinquecento*, with major stops (*fermate*) in *Piazza Venezia*, *Largo Argentina* and *Piazza del Risorgimento*. Buses are orange, the number is at the front and they generally stop

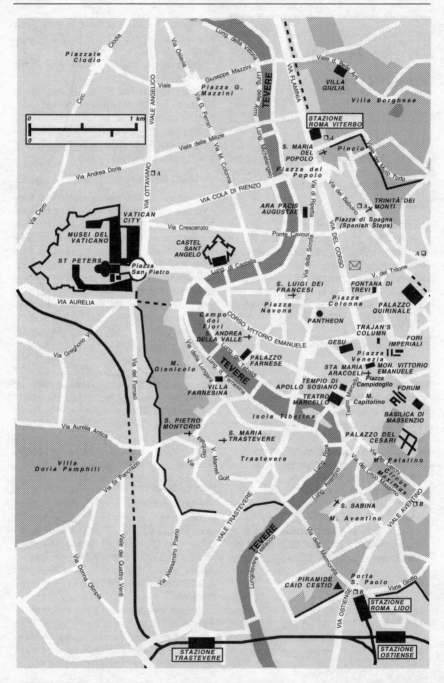

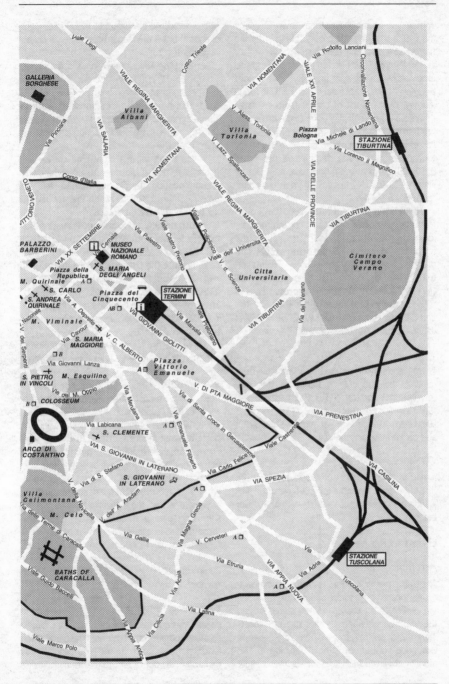

without you having to flag them down. Only one (no.119, a small electric bus) is able to enter the narrow streets of the *centro storico*.

Time-stamp your ticket in the machine as you enter (heavy on-the-spot fines if you are caught ticketless). The basic ticket is valid for one journey, but a block of ten (red) tickets saves money, as does a half-day ticket (*biglietto orario*), valid from either 0600–1400 or 1400–2400. Passes include a one-day pass; an eight-day tourist pass, the *Carta Settimanale per Turisti* (L.10,000); and a one-month pass valid for all lines (L.22,000). For bus and tram information: *tel: (06) 46 95 44*.

Night buses run from 2400–0800. Buy tickets from the conductor on board. For information, look in the *Tuttocittà* supplement of the telephone directory. **Sightseeing tours** are provided by **ATAC** (tickets and information from ATAC in *Piazza dei Cinquecento*), **CIT** (*tel: (06) 479 11*); **American Express** (*tel: (06) 67 641*); **Green Line Tours** (*tel: (06) 482 74 80*); and **Carrani Tours** (*tel: (06) 47 42 501*). Expect to pay about L.100,000 for a full day's tour.

Taxis

There are plenty of metered taxis, available from ranks or by phone (call: **Radiotaxi** (*tel: (06) 3570*); **Roma Sud** (*tel: (06) 3875*); **Capitale** (*tel: (06) 4994*); or **Cosmos** (*tel: (06) 8433*). There are surcharges for luggage, at night (2200–0700) and on Sundays and holidays.

Carriages

A ride in an open carriage (*carrozzella*) can be fun, but expensive (about L.80,000 per hour). For anything longer, agree a price with the driver beforehand.

Living in Rome

Accommodation

There are plenty of hotels, from the opulent, mainly located close to the *Spanish Steps* and the *Via Veneto*, to the basic, largely clustered around the *Via Nazionale* and Termini station. Moderately priced, centrally located hotels are generally very popular, and you should book up to two months ahead in high season. For the cheaper

hotels, expect to pay around L.62,000 per night, even without a private bathroom. Some do not take credit cards.

Among the major hotel groups in the city are *Ch, Ex, Fo, Hl, Hn, Ic, Pu* and *Sh*.

The tourist offices will provide lists of residential hotels and make bookings. **International Services**, *Via del Babuino, 79; tel: (06) 36 00 18*, has a list of self-catering studios and apartments.

If you don't mind a night-time curfew and pilgrims, several religious institutions offer cheap accommodation; try **Domus Mariae**, *tel: (06) 662 31 38*; and **Istituto Madri Pie**, *tel: (06) 63 19 67* – both near the Vatican.

Youth hostels: **Associazione Italiana Alberghi per la Gioventù** (IYHF), *Via Cavour 44–47, tel: (06) 48 71 152*. Only holders of AIG or IYHF cards can use the **Ostello del Foro Italico**, *Viale delle Olimpiadi, 61, tel: (06) 32 36 279*. The **YWCA** is at *Via C. Balbo, 4, tel: (06) 48 83 917*. The **Protezione della Giovane**, *Via Urbana 158; tel: (06) 48 81 489*, will locate accommodation for women under 25.

There are no campsites in central Rome; although there are ten within a bus ride away.

Communications

Post: the main post office, *Piazza San Silvestro; tel: (06) 6771* (open Mon – Fri, 0800–2100; Sat 0800–1200) has 24-hr phones, fax and telex, and poste restante (address letters c/o *Palazzo delle Poste, Roma, Fermo Posta* – put the surname first, underlined). Stamps are available from post offices and tobacconists displaying a black-and-white **T**. Letters posted at the main post office, or anywhere within the Vatican City (use Vatican stamps in blue post boxes) arrive faster than those posted in the red pavement boxes.

Telephones: to phone Rome from abroad: *tel: 39 (Italy) + 6 (Rome) + number*. To phone Rome from elsewhere in Italy: *tel: 06 (Rome) + number*.

Eating and Drinking

Italian cafés and bars have hefty seating charges, so most Romans have their breakfast, and often lunch, standing up at the bar. You generally pay first and take your receipt to the counter. Picnics are a good alternative. Some delicatessens will fill a roll with the ingredients of your choice (try the delicatessen in the *Campo dei Fiori* vegetable market).

Restaurants are more expensive than *trattorie*, which offer substantial amounts of simple, robust Roman-style food, washed down with local wine. Some – go to *Trastevere* – have no name, their purpose defined only by cooking smells, loud chatter and paper table cloths. Some don't even have menus, so just point to whatever seems delicious on the next table. Expect to pay around L.20,000 for three courses, bread (*coperta*) and wine. *Pizzerie* are a cheap alternative, while you can taste different wines and have delicious tiny snacks at an *enoteca*. Vegetarian restaurants are rare but most Italian menus are adaptable.

The **Campo dei Fiori** neighbourhood is best for *al fresco* (open-air) dining, while the streets off the nearby *Piazza Farnese* have stylish, but reasonably cheap venues. **Trastevere** has boisterous, crowded, rough-and-ready eateries, which may involve queuing, but are worth the wait. Other popular places are around *Piazza Navona* and the *Pantheon*, while the *Ghetto* and the old slaughterhouse area of **Testaccio** offer some of the best traditional Roman cooking. Read the menu in the window to gauge price.

Embassies and Consulates

Australia: *Via Alessandra, 215; tel: (06) 85 42 721.*
Canada: *Via G.B. De Rossi, 27; tel: (06) 841 53 41.*
New Zealand: *Via Zara, 28; tel: (06) 440 29 28.*
UK: *Via XX Settembre, 80A; tel: (06) 482 54 41.*
USA: *Via Veneto, 119A/121; tel: (06) 467 41.*

Money

Banks (open 0830–1330; 1500–1600), hotels and bureaux de change (open 0830/0900–1300; 1530/1600–1930/2000) will change money. Major credit cards and Eurocheques are widely accepted (check before entering *trattorie* and *pensioni*).

Thomas Cook Italia have bureaux de change at *Via della Conciliazione 23/25* and *Piazza Barberini 21A/21D*.

Entertainment

Trovaroma (published with *La Repubblica* on Thursdays) and *Metropolitan*, (published fortnightly in English) are very comprehensive 'what's on' guides, available from newsstands. Rome is a busy cultural city, so also read listings sections of the daily papers like *Il Messagero*, *Il Manifesto* and *Paese Sera*.

Nightlife is not great in comparison to, say, London. Most Italians like nothing better than to while away the evening in a restaurant. However, there are good venues for dancing, vibrant clubs (jazz, salsa, African, Latin) and overflowing, noisy bars. There is also a thriving gay scene.

The summer is Rome's liveliest season for **theatres** and **concerts**, with many performances set beneath the stars, or possibly within some ancient ruin or Renaissance garden. The **Teatro dell'Opera** moves out to the ruins of the *Baths of Caracalla* in July and August. As a rule, tickets for these events (apart from opera) cannot be booked in advance. There are also many choral concerts in the churches – watch the billboards outside for details.

Shopping

Rome is a busy shopping centre. Best buys are from the delicatessens and grocery stores – olive oil, dried *funghi* (mushrooms) – in and around *Via della Croce* and the *Campo dei Fiori*. *Via del Corso* sells cheaper versions of the designer clothing on sale in the *Via dei Condotti* (big names like Gucci) and its parallel streets, while cheaper still are the clothes stalls of the *Porta Portese* and *Via Sannio* markets (metro: *San Giovanni*). There is a strong artisan goldsmith and silversmith tradition here (*Ghetto, Via dei Coronari, Via dell'Orso*), and Rome is fairly well served by antique shops (*Via dei Coronari, Via Giulia, Via del Babuino*).

Sightseeing

Most places charge an entrance fee; some are free on Sundays. A **museum entry card** (two-, four- or seven-day) gives access to a wide variety of museums and galleries (L.15,000–L.50,000). Opening times can vary, so check before you set out. The EPT publishes *Musei e Monumenti di*

Roma giving details of current changes and closures as well as information about exhibitions.

Rome, dominated by its seven hills (Aventine, Capitoline, Celian, Esquiline, Palatine, Quirinal and Viminal), is cut by the fast-flowing Tiber. The **Aventine**, with magnificent views over the river, is topped by ancient **Santa Sabina**, evocative of early Christian Rome. At its foot are the **Circus Maximus**, scene of ancient chariot races, and the **Temples of Hercules** and **Portinus**.

The **Capitoline**, once the sacred heart of the Roman Empire, is today dominated by Michelangelo's **Piazza del Campidoglio**, with its magnificent **Capitoline Museums**, with their collections of classical sculpture, and the early **Church of Santa Maria in Aracoeli**.

The great basilica of **Santa Maria Maggiore** dominates the **Esquiline**. Nearby, **San Pietro in Vincoli** houses the chains with which St Peter was imprisoned, and Michelangelo's superb statue of *Moses*. Beyond it, **Trajan's Market** (the world's first shopping mall) and **Trajan's Column** face the **Forum**, site of the temples and basilicas of Imperial Rome.

The **Celian Hill** is quiet, covered mainly by the gardens of the **Villa Celimontana**. In front of it, the formal **Farnese Gardens** on the **Palatine** are filled with the ruins of Imperial Palaces. Below lies Rome's most famous landmark, the **Colosseum**, where early Christians were fed to the lions. Beyond it are **San Giovanni in Laterano** and a section of the ancient **Aurelian Walls**. At the base of the **Quirinal** is the **Fontana di Trevi** – into which, to ensure your return, you must throw a coin, while on its summit sits the President of Italy's residence.

On the **Quirinal** is the **Palazzo Barberini** art gallery and **Santa Maria della Vittoria**, which contains Bernini's strangely beautiful statue, *The Ecstasy of St Theresa*. Here too Borromini's **San Carlo** and Bernini's **Sant'Andrea Quirinale** are the best of the Roman Baroque style. Nearby, Michelangelo's **Santa Maria degli Angeli** and the **Museo Nazionale Romano** were fashioned from the ancient **Baths of Diocletian**.

The **Vatican City**, state within a city and home of the Pope and the Catholic Church, houses numerous treasures - amongst them **St Peter's Cathedral**, the **Vatican Museums**, and the **Sistine Chapel**, with Michelangelo's stunning frescos. Nearby is the **Castel Sant' Angelo**, built as a Roman tomb, converted into a fortress, used as a palace, and now a museum.

The **Campo dei Fiori**'s vegetable market adds life and colour to the district near **Palazzo Farnese** and **Santa Andrea della Valle**. Nearby, the old Jewish **Ghetto** is one of Rome's quaintest neighbourhoods. Across the Tiber, on the Janiculum, **San Pietro in Montorio** is adjacent to Bramante's **Tempietto** – one of the greatest buildings of the High Renaissance. Below it are the **Church of Santa Maria in Trastevere**, containing early Christian mosaics, and the riverside **Villa Farnesina**, which was decorated in part by Raphael. The **Porta Portese** is Trastevere's Sunday flea market.

The **Piazza Navona** takes its shape from the ancient **Circus of Domitian**, which it replaces. At its centre is Bernini's **Fountain of the Four Rivers** and, nearby, the **Piazza della Rotonda** provides the setting for the **Pantheon** – a Classical building still in use, once a temple, now a church.

The **Spanish Steps** link the *Piazza di Spagna* with the **Pincio** hill and the **Villa Borghese gardens**, which contain the **Villa Giulia Etruscan Museum** and the **Museo Borghese** – unmissable if you like Bernini. **Santa Maria del Popolo** contains important Caravaggio paintings.

◠ Side Tracks from Rome

Although Rome itself would exhaust months of sightseeing, here is a selection of the best-known places just outside the city. **Via Appia Antica**, including the ancient catacombs, can be reached by bus. The **EUR district** (monumental architecture of the Fascist era, but also a funfair and a good Museum of Roman Civilisation) is on metro line B, as is **Ostia Antica** with the ruins of the ancient Roman port. Trains from Termini run to the Alban Hills, which include the wine areas of **Frascati** and **Castelli Romani** and the papal residence of **Castel Gandolfo**, as well as to **Tivoli**, site of **Hadrian's Villa** and the charmingly eccentric **Villa d'Este**, its garden flowing with fountains.

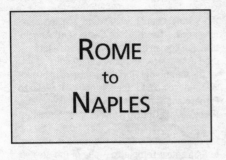

ROME
to
NAPLES

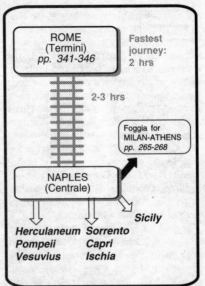

This route between Rome and Naples uses the main rail artery of central and southern Italy.

TRAINS

ETT tables: 405.

→ Fast Track

There is a very frequent service between Rome and Naples consisting of a mixture of IC (buffet facilities) and more local services. Trains depart from and arrive at different stations, so check details carefully before travelling. The journey takes anything from 2 hrs to just under 3 hrs, so it's worth selecting your train with care.

NAPLES (NAPOLI)

Stations: Most long-distance trains use **Stazione Centrale**, *tel: (081) 553 4188*. *Stazione Piazza Garibaldi* is the metro station directly beneath Centrale. **Mergellina** and **Campi Flegrei**, also terminals for some trains, are further west. The metro links all three stations. **Stazione Circumvesuviana**, *tel: (081) 779 2444*, handles trains to Pompeii and Sorrento. It is adjacent to Centrale and is well signposted.
Tourist Office: The City Tourist Board is at *Palazzo Reale, Piazza Plebiscito; tel: (081) 418 744*, with branches in *Piazza del Gesù; tel: (081) 552 3328*, Mon–Sat 0900–1900 and Sun 0900–1500, and at *Via Partenope*, by *Castell dell'Ovo; tel: (081) 764 5688*. Pick up a town map and a copy of the monthly listing *Qui Napoli*. Ente Provinciale per il Turismo (EPT) maintains a spartan but helpful office in the Stazione Centrale; *tel: (081) 268 779*. They also have an office in Stazione di Mergellina; *tel: (081)*

761 2102. **Youth information**: *Via Mezzocannone 25; tel: (081) 5527960.* Open Mon–Fri 0930–1330 and 1500–1830, and Sat 0930–1230.

Getting Around

The **metro** runs west to *Pozzuoli* and *Solfatara*. Trains can be infrequent and stations quiet out of peak hours. Buy tickets at kiosks and cancel them in the machines by the entrances. **Buses** are more frequent and more extensive. Buy tickets from street kiosks. Day passes are available.

Frequent **hydrofoils** and **ferries** ply across the bay and out to the islands. Most leave from Molo Beverello (by *Castel Nuovo*) but some go from Mergellina.

Accommodation

The tourist office has a list of hotels and can occasionally help in finding a place to stay, but confirm prices with the hotel before committing yourself. International hotel chains with property in the city include: *HI, Ex*.

Cheap hotels cluster in and around the noisy, and not particularly salubrious, *Piazza Garibaldi*. Better areas to look are near the waterfront in *Mergellina* and *Santa Lucia*, where there are

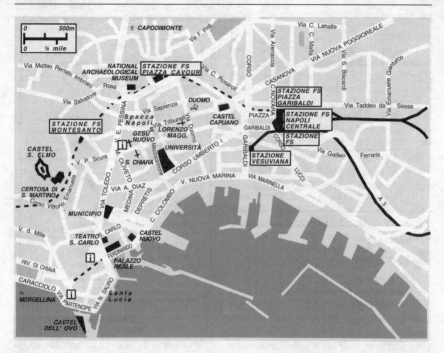

some cheapish options amongst the expensive hotels, and around *Piazza Dante* in the centre of town. The **IYHF**, *23 Salita della Grotta a Piedigrotta; tel: (081) 761 2346,* is located close to Stazione Mergellina. **Campsites** are mainly in *Pozzuoli* (on the metro), west of Naples. **Volcana Solfatara**, *16 Via Solfataral; tel: (081) 526 7413,* is the nearest to the city.

Sightseeing

Naples is clearly in 'the south'. There is more dust, noise and shabbiness than in Rome or Milan and in some ways the town seems more evocative of North Africa than northern Italy. Modern Naples is hectic and crowded. Petty crime is rife, notably pickpocketing and bag-snatching, so be very careful, especially after dark.

Originally the Greek colony of Neapolis, Naples became a desirable winter resort for wealthy Romans, including the likes of Virgil and Nero. Of the many families that ruled Naples, the Anjou and Aragon dynasties of the 13th–16th centuries were amongst the most influen-

tial and many remnants from that era dot the city. The archaeological museum is truly outstanding and Naples Bay, overlooked by Vesuvius and scattered with gorgeous island resorts, provides a succession of magnificent views.

Do not miss the world-class **National Archaeological Museum**, *Piazza Museo* (metro: *Piazza Cavour*), which contains an unparalleled collection from Pompeii and Herculaneum: bronzes, sculptures, mosaics, silver, glass objects and a huge, intricate model of Pompeii.

South of the museum is the heart of medieval Naples, **Spacca Napoli**, centred around *Via Benedetto Croce* and *Piazza Gesù Nuovo*, where you'll find the **Church of Gesù Nuovo**, a 16th-century construction with fine frescos and sculptures. The church of **Santa Chiara**, *Via B Croce*, was where Neapolitan royalty worshipped (the 14th-century tomb of Robert of Anjou is worth a look). Further east is the **Duomo San Gennaro**, *Via Duomo*, with a flask containing some of the saint's blood which, allegedly, liquefies miraculously twice every year.

Down by the waterfront, the massive **Castel Nuovo** (or **Maschio Angoino**) guards the port. The castle is a composite of construction and restoration from the 13th century onwards, with a fine Triumphal Arch. The nearby **Palazzo Reale** was the seat of the 18th-century kings. The adjacent **Teatro di San Carlo** ranks second only to La Scala (Milan) in the Italian opera league. **Santa Lucia**, the waterfront district to the south, is where **Castel dell'Ovo** sticks out into the bay.

The third major castle in Naples, **Castel Sant' Elmo**, shares a raised spur with **San Martino Monastery**, which dates from the Angevin period. Inside the monastery is the **National Museum of San Martino**, with exhibits on Neapolitan history and a collection of Neapolitan paintings.

Further inland, the **Capodimonte Museum and Gallery**, *Capodimonte Park, Vomero Hill*, contains salons decorated entirely in local ceramics. The gallery has a diverse, and exceptionally good, collection of European art. The **Tomb of Virgil** is at *Salita della Grotta*.

Side Tracks from Naples

In some ways, the glorious Bay of Naples offers more than the city itself and **Sorrento** is one of the finest resorts. There are regular train services daily from Napoli Circumvesuviana to Sorrento, the journey taking 55–65 minutes. Alternatively, catch a ferry from Beverello (some services depart from Mergellina). There are about 8 sailings daily, journey time is approx. 25 mins.

The Circumvesuviana railway has stops at **Herculaneum** (station: *Ercolano*) and **Pompeii**, the Roman cities buried in AD 79 by the eruption of Vesuvius. Most of the objects discovered during excavations are in the museum in Naples, but the ruins are mesmeric and eerie. Herculaneum is only partially excavated, and reasonably uncrowded, but what can be seen is very well preserved. The larger Pompeii is far more impressive and features all Roman town planning can be identified. **Vesuvius** itself can be scaled by chair-lift or by

---

Pompeii

Pompeii was inhabited in the 8th century BC and was a prosperous trading centre for the Greeks and Etruscans, but what remains today is a perfect record of ordinary Roman life, preserved almost in its entirety by being buried for centuries under 10m of volcanic ash.

In AD 79 Mount Vesuvius began rumbling so ominously that most of the population of around 20,000 fled the town. About 2000 remained, however, and either choked to death on the toxic fumes or were buried alive – some trying to escape, their terror horrifyingly evident, others caught unawares in the middle of everyday activities.

---

car and foot. From the top you can look inwards to the crater or outwards, for probably the best view of the bay area.

The island of **Capri** is renowned for its wonderful setting, mild climate, Greek and Roman remains and incomparable *Blue Grotto*. **Ischia**, less well known than Capri, also has a remarkable setting.

There are about nine sailings daily to Capri and Ischia departing from Molo Beverello (journey time 40 mins: Capri; 80 mins: Ischia). Hydrofoils depart hourly from Mergellina (journey time 35 mins for both Capri and Ischia).

There are also regular trains from Naples to **Sicily** (trains are carried by train ferry from Villa San Giovanni to Messina Marittima). Services depart about eight times daily (from either Centrale or Campi Flegrei, journey time is approx. 10 hrs to 10 hrs 30 mins.

Connection: Naples to Athens

From Naples you can take the train via Foggia to **Brindisi**, to connect with the Milan–Athens route (see p. 265) towards Greece. A change of train will be necessary in either Caserta or Bari unless the overnight service is used. Journey time approx. 5 hrs 40 mins–8 hrs 35 mins.

SANTIAGO DE COMPOSTELA
to
SAN SEBASTIÁN

This rail journey follows the line of the old pilgrim route, using the narrow-gauge FEVE trains for most of its length. It winds across the relatively little-known north-west of Spain, joining two very different cities, the ancient pilgrimage centre of Santiago and the chic coastal resort of San Sebastián. It offers sights of great mountain peaks and seas of wheat and vines, tiny, perfect Romanesque chapels and magnificent cathedrals dripping in gold.

TRAINS

ETT tables: 441, 440, 431, 430.

→ Fast Track

With no through trains, there is no fast way to do this route. The whole purpose of including it is to allow you to dawdle along the line of the pilgrim route to Santiago, a journey with magnificent scenery, and some of the finest Romanesque and medieval architecture in the world.

⤳ On Track

Santiago–Orense (Ourense)

There are six stopping trains a day between Santiago and Orense, the journey taking about 2 hrs.

Orense–Ponferrada

There are 7 trains a day and the journey takes about 3 hrs.

Ponferrada–Astorga

There are six non-stop trains a day, but they leave

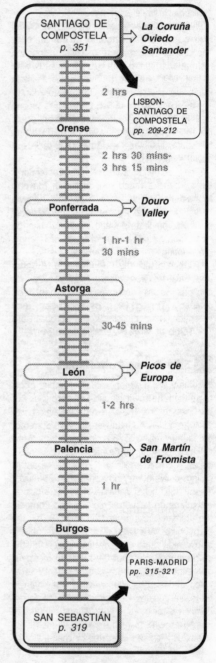

SANTIAGO DE COMPOSTELA
p. 351

⇨ La Coruña
Oviedo
Santander

2 hrs

LISBON-SANTIAGO DE COMPOSTELA
pp. 209-212

Orense

2 hrs 30 mins-
3 hrs 15 mins

Ponferrada ⇨ Douro Valley

1 hr-1 hr 30 mins

Astorga

30-45 mins

León ⇨ Picos de Europa

1-2 hrs

Palencia ⇨ San Martín de Fromista

1 hr

Burgos

PARIS-MADRID
pp. 315-321

SAN SEBASTIÁN
p. 319

at very irregular intervals and one is after midnight. The journey usually takes 1 hr 20 mins.

Astorga–León

The Ponferrada–Astorga trains all continue to León: allow another 45 mins for the journey.

León–Palencia

There are about a dozen non-stop trains daily, scattered throughout the day from around 0700 to the early hours of the next morning. The journey takes 1–2 hrs.

Palencia–Burgos

Although there are six trains each day, they go in clusters, often at awkward hours of the night. The journey takes about 1 hr.

This route joins the Paris–Madrid line in Burgos. For a description of Burgos and the route onwards to San Sebastián, see p. 315.

SANTIAGO DE COMPOSTELA

Airport: Santiago has an international airport at *Labacolla*, 12 km east of the city on the N-544 to Lugo; *tel: (981) 59 74 00*.
Station: 1 km south of the old city. *tel: (981) 59 60 50*.
Tourist Office, *Rúa del Villar 43*; *tel: (981) 58 40 81* (about two blocks from the cathedral) has excellent maps, sightseeing information and hotel and camping lists.

Getting Around

The old city is tiny and everything of interest to the tourist is easily accessible on foot.

Accommodation

There is a wide range of accommodation, from the five-star de luxe *Hostal de los Reyes Católicos*, a magnificent 16th-century pilgrim hostel built by Ferdinand and Isabella and now one of Spain's best hotels, to a wide array of small, relatively inexpensive guest houses in both the old and new parts of the city. There are three large campsites just outside the city. During the city's main fiesta, in the three weeks leading up to the feast of St James on 25 July, the town is

---

The Camino de Santiago

St James the Apostle was thought to be responsible for introducing Christianity to Spain. He was martyred in Palestine in AD 44 and his body was said to have been placed in a boat and wafted by angels to Galicia. His tomb became an immediate focus for pilgrims when rediscovered in the 9th century. In the same century, the saint supposedly appeared on the battlefield and fought with the victorious Christian troops against the Moors. In honour of this, he became the patron saint of Spain. Millions made the arduous trek across Europe to his tomb, bearing the badge of the scallop shell. As churches, monasteries and hostels were built along the route, it became the inspiration behind the development of Romanesque architecture. Today, the devout still believe that a trip to Santiago will ensure that their sins are forgiven and their stay in purgatory will be halved.

---

absolutely packed and it is necessary to book accommodation well in advance.

Sightseeing

One of the holiest places in the world to Roman Catholics, Santiago de Compostela has, for the last thousand years, been a magnet for millions of pilgrims. The newer sections of the city do not have a great deal of charm, but the old town (contained within the medieval walls) is arguably the most beautiful city in Europe. You could probably rush round everything in a day, but it would be a shame not to allow yourself longer.

There were Celtic, Roman and Suebian towns on the site, but the present city was founded only when the tomb of St James was discovered in AD 813, supposedly by a shepherd who was guided to the site by a star. Destroyed in AD 997 by the Moors, the town was rebuilt during the 11th century and began its golden age. In the 12th century the pope declared it a Holy City: for the Catholics, only Jerusalem and Rome share this honour.

The **Cathedral** (started in 1075) is superb and should not be missed. The existing 18th-century Baroque façade covers the original 12th-century façade, the *Pórtico de la Gloria*, which is probably the greatest single surviving work of Romanesque art in the world, with 200 exceptionally imaginative and detailed sculptures. A Jesse tree on the central column is known as the 'Pilgrim Pillar', as it is traditional for pilgrims to kiss the base to celebrate their arrival in the Holy City. Centuries of this have worn deep finger-holes in the column. The interior is dominated by a Mexican silver altar, dazzling 17th-century Baroque altarpiece and a fine statue of St James.

There are four plazas surrounding the cathedral, the largest of them being the **Plaza del Obradoiro**. All four are architectural gems and there are also many other fine churches and monasteries as well as a host of charming secular buildings tucked down the narrow side streets.

〰 Side Track from Santiago

In Santiago, the route across northern Spain meets up with the coastal route south to Lisbon (see p. 209). It is also possible to head north on the coastal route to **San Sebastián** via **La Coruña**, **Oviedo** and **Santander**. You need to allow at least 2 days for this, though.

ORENSE (OURENSE)

Station: *tel: (988) 21 10 64*. North of the Mino River, about 1.5 km from the city centre.
Tourist Offices: **City** *Edificio Torre, Curros Enriquez 1; tel: (988) 23 47 17*. **Provincial** *Avenida de la Habana 105; tel: (988) 22 08 39*.

In ancient times the Romans established a settlement near three thermal springs. In the 6th–7th centuries, the town became the seat of Suebian kings, but was ravaged by the Moors in AD 716 and not rebuilt until the 10th century. The modern town is a bustling commercial centre but the old section is attractive. The old bishop's palace now houses the **Archaeological and Fine Arts Museum**, while the **Cathedral** itself dates from the 12th–13th centuries but was heavily renovated in the 16th–17th centuries. The 13th-

century Romanesque **Iglesia de la Trinidad** and **Puente Viejo** (old bridge) are also impressive.

PONFERRADA

Station: *tel: 41 00 67*, a few minutes walk from the town centre.
Tourist Office: *Gil y Carrasco 4; tel: 41 22 50*, beside the river.

Founded in the 11th century on the site of a Roman settlement, this was a pilgrim base, named after a long-gone iron bridge across the River Sil. The largely intact old town is dominated by a huge 12th-century pentagonal **Templar Castle**, which was enlarged in the 14th century and heavily restored. The 16th-century **Basilica** and 17th-century Baroque **Town Hall** are worth seeing and there are numerous attractive old buildings of humbler origin. In recent times, the town has grown into a centre of mining and heavy industry, which tends to detract from its charm.

ASTORGA

Station: *tel: (987) 61 50 63*, about 1 km east of the town centre.
Tourist Office: *Avenida Jose Antonio 23; tel: (987) 61 52 05*.

Described by Pliny in the 1st century AD as a 'magnificent city', this is now a small country town, capital of the bleak moorland region of La Maragatería. Sections of the 6-metre **Roman walls** survive around the old town. The 15th–17th-century- Cathedral has a bizarre mixture of styles, from late Gothic to Renaissance, Baroque and Plateresque, while next-door is a flamboyant **Episcopal Palace** designed by Gaudi in 1889, which now houses the **Museum of the Pilgrim Way**. Smaller buildings of interest centre on the Plaza Mayor.

LEÓN

Stations: RENFE: **El Norte**, *Avenida de Astorga; tel: 22 37 04*, on the west bank of the river. FEVE: *Avenida Padre Isla 48; tel: 22 59 19*, near the Basilica de San Isidoro.
Tourist Office: *Plaza de la Regla 4*, next to the

cathedral; *tel: (987) 29 21 00.*

Getting Around

The outstanding monuments are all within easy walking distance of each other in the old city.

Accommodation

The city has a wide range of hotels and guest houses, ranging downwards from the ultra-luxurious **San Marcos** (see below). Ask for details at the tourist office.

Sightseeing

Nestling between the Bernsega and Torio rivers and surrounded by rolling *meseta* (plains), León was founded by the Romans in AD 68 as a base for the Iberian 7th Legion. Over the years, it changed hands several times and was ruled by Visigoths, Moors and Christians. In 1188 Alfonso IX summoned his first Cortés (parliament) here – one of the earliest democratic governments in Europe – but the court moved away permanently in the 13th century and León became little more than a trading centre until 1978, when it was made the capital of the province of León. Today it is, once again, a thriving city; an attractive place of wide streets and shady plazas.

Of all the city's buildings, the most spectacular from the outside is the 16th-century, Plateresque **Hospital de San Marcos** (now one of Spain's finest hotels), founded by Ferdinand and Isabella as a pilgrim hostel. What is left of the old city is still bounded by fragments of the 14th-century **city walls**, which followed the line of the original Roman (and medieval) fortifications. Thirty-one of the original 80 bastions are still standing.

The **Royal Basilica of San Isidoro**, amidst the charming streets and plazas of the old town, has a not-to-be-missed pantheon, where marble pillars with superbly carved capitals support a barrel-vaulted roof covered by magnificent 12th-century frescos. The neighbouring treasury contains a rich collection of religious art.

Not far away is the **Cathedral of Santa Maria de Regla**, a graceful 13th–14th-century building with some of the finest stained glass in Europe – with 125 windows, containing some 1,800 square metres of glass, dappling the entire cathedral with a kaleidoscope of light.

- - - - - - - - - - - - - - - - - - - -

Side Track from León

This is the best place from which to head north into the high mountains of the **Picos de Europa**, a truly stunning and relatively remote range which still shelters a few wolves and bears. Said to have been the first sign of European land seen by sailors returning from the New World, they rise almost vertically from the Bay of Blscay and offer magnificent views and walking.

- - - - - - - - - - - - - - - - - - - -

PALENCIA

Station: *tel: 74 30 19*, off the *Avenida de los Vacceos*, a few minutes walk from the heart of the old city.
Tourist Office: *Calle Mayor, 149; tel: 74 00 68*, halfway between the station and the cathedral.

A long, narrow town with the Río Carrion to the west and the railway to the east, Palencia's prosperity comes from coal mining in the Cantabrián Mountains to the north and grain farming on the Tierra del Campos to the south. The earliest settlement was in Celtic times and Palencia was the seat of Spain's first university, founded by Alfonso VIII in the early 13th century. The main place of interest is the 14th–16th-century **Cathedral**, which has an intriguing interior, rich in both paintings and sculptures. There's also an interesting **Archaeological Museum**.

- - - - - - - - - - - - - - - - - - - -

Side Tracks from Palencia

There are several of the finest small Romanesque churches on the pilgrim route near Palencia, most notably at **San Martín de Fromista**. It is also possible to take a train north through the Picos de Europa to **Santander**, a fine coastal resort and the main ferry port to the UK.

- - - - - - - - - - - - - - - - - - - -

SAN SEBASTIÁN

For details of San Sebastián, see the Paris–Madrid route, p. 319.

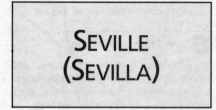

SEVILLE (SEVILLA)

Seville is a romantic, theatrical place which sparks the imagination. Its attractions include historic buildings (the Giralda, Cathedral and Alcázar), fictional connections (Don Juan, Carmen and Figaro were all set here) and fiestas.

Tourist Information

Tourist Offices: Regional: *Avda. de la Constitución 21; tel: (54) 422 14 04 and 421 81 57.* **Municipal**: *Paseo de las Delicias 9; tel: (54) 423 44 65.* Viajes TIVE, *Avda. Reina Mercedes 53; tel: (54) 461 59 16.*

Thomas Cook network member: Viajes Internacional Expreso, *Virgen de Lujan 26; tel: (54) 45 56 06 and Alemanes 3; tel: (54) 21 38 28.*

Arriving and Departing

Airport

San Pablo Airport, 12 km east of town, has one terminal (*tel: (54) 451 61 11*) and a tourist information desk (*tel: (54) 425 50 46*).

There is an hourly EA (*Especial Aeropuerto*) bus from Puerta de Jerez which takes 30 mins.

Trains

The main station is **Santa Justa** (*tel: (54) 441 08 55*). This is centrally located.

Buses

The main bus Station is at *Plaza de San Sebastián, Calle José Maria Osborne 11; tel: (54) 441 71 11.*

Getting Around

Travel Information

The station is 40-mins walk from the centre, but it is on the airport road and the EA bus (see above) stops outside the station. Bus no 70 links the rail and bus stations and the bus terminal is a 10-min walk from the centre.

You should get a city map and plan your sightseeing route because, although the prime sights are in a very small area, the secondary ones are quite widespread. Unless you are a very keen walker you'll probably want to get a few buses along the way.

Buses

The city bus service is efficient and route maps are often included on street maps.

Taxis

White with green lights on top, taxis in Seville are reasonably plentiful and cheap. They can be hailed in the street.

Living in Seville

Accommodation

A busy tourist and business city, Seville has a wide range of hotels, including *Ml* and *Ra*. Accommodation is very difficult to obtain, unless pre-booked, during Holy Week (see p. 356).

For the least expensive lodgings, try north of Santa Cruz and around Plaza Nueva, towards the river and around the old Córdoba rail station. **IYHF:** at *Isaac Peral 2; tel: (54) 461 31 50* .

All three **campsites** are about 12 km out of town. The main one is *Camping Sevilla, Ctra. N-IV km 534; tel: (54) 451 43 79.* This is near the airport and the airport bus will get you there. Alternatively, you can take the Empresa Casal bus towards Carmona (hourly) or the no 70 to Parque Alcosa (800 m away). The other two sites are at Dos Hermanas (*Club de Campo, Avda. Libertad 13; tel: (54) 472 02 50* and *Camping Villson, Ctra. N-Iv km 554.8; tel: (54) 472 08 28*) and served by buses (from the bus station) every 30–45 minutes.

Communications

The main **post office** is at *Avda. de la Constitución 32*, open Mon–Fri 0800–2100, Sat 0900–1900. The facilities for poste restante (*lista de correos*) close Sat. p.m.

International **phone calls** can be made from

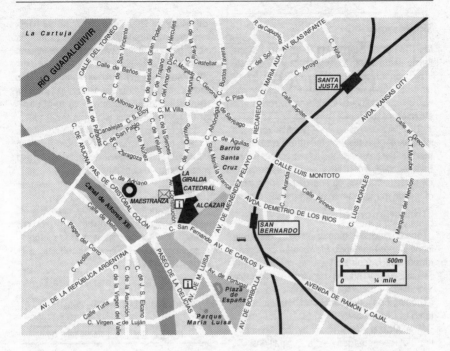

Plaza. Gavidia 7, open Mon–Sat 1000–1400 and 1730–2200.

Eating and Drinking

Seville is probably the best place to sample such typical Andalucian dishes as *gazpacho* (chilled tomato and pepper soup) and *pescaíto frito* (deep-fried fish). The liveliest bars and restaurants, frequented by students, are in the central **Barrio Santa Cruz** area.

Embassies and Consulates

Canada: *2nd Floor, Avda. de la Constitución 30; tel: (54) 422 94 13.*
UK: *Plaza Nueva 8; tel: (54) 422 88 73.*
USA: *Paseo de las Delicias 7; tel: (54) 423 18 83.*

Security

Seville is noted for its high level of petty crime and you must be on the alert for bag-snatchers and pickpockets: on no account leave anything of value in either your hotel room or your car.

Entertainment

Seville is the home of **flamenco** and it's easy to find, but you should be selective because it is often staged especially for tourists. If you ask around, you should be able to find more genuine (and cheaper) performances.

Semana Santa (Holy Week) is a world-famous festival lasting from Palm Sunday to Good Friday, one feature of which is hooded penitents guiding candle-lit floats through the streets. The **April Feria** (April Fair) is a week-long festival which includes folklore displays, circuses and bullfighting.

Nightlife

Seville is full of extremely lively bars, clubs and discos. notably in the Los Remedios district in the south of the city, but little will seem to be happening until close to midnight. Bear in mind that dining out in Spain happens later in the evening than in Northern Europe and North America, and nightlife happens after dining hours. The Spanish stay up *very* late.

Sightseeing

Most places of interest are to be found in the **Barrio Santa Cruz**. A pleasant place for a stroll, it lives up to one's idealised image of Spain; white and yellow houses with wrought iron window grilles, flower-bedecked balconies and attractive patios.

The focal point is the **Giralda** tower, a minaret that has towered over the old city since the 12th century. It is in excellent condition and the staircase is worth climbing: it was designed for horsemen to ride up and consists of a series of gentle ramps, although the walk can be exhausting. The upper storeys were mid-16th century additions.

The **Cathedral** is the largest Gothic structure in the world. The *Capilla Mayor* has a vast gilded retable which took 82 years to complete. The *Sacristía Mayor* houses the treasury and the *Sacristía de los Calices* contains Murillos and a Goya. Among other things of interest is the tomb of Christopher Columbus.

The **Alcázar** was inspired by the Alhambra, but has been marred by later additions. Of particular note are the *Salon de Embajadores*, the *Patio de las Muñecas*, the Salon of Charles V and the series of ivy-clad patios separated by arched Moorish walls.

The neighbouring **Casa Lonja** on *Plaza del Triunfo* contains a collection of documents relating to the discovery of the Americas.

The **Hospital de la Caridad** on *Calle Temprano* (2 blocks west of the Lonja) was commissioned by a reformed rake, the real-life inspiration for Don Juan. It contains several works by Murillo and Valdes Leal.

Nowadays the 18th-century **Fabrica de Tabacos** (on *Calle de San Fernando* south of the Alcázar) houses parts of the university, but it was once a tobacco factory: a place which employed over 10,000 women (supposedly including Carmen).

South-east of the factory is **María Luisa Park**, a delightful mixture of wilderness areas and formal gardens laid out for a trade fair in 1929. It contains **Plaza de España**, which was the central pavilion, and **Plaza de América**, a peaceful place where the excellent **Archaeolo-** **gical Museum** is situated. Each of the Latin American countries which exhibited at the fair built a pavilion in its own national style, and most of them survive.

The **Museo de Bellas Artes**, *Plaza del Museo* (between Santa Cruz and Cartuja), has a collection of 13th–20th-century Spanish paintings that is second only to that in the Prado.

The decorative **Maestranza** (Bullring), *Paseo de Colon* (near the river), dates from the 18th century and is the oldest in Spain. If you have a strong stomach, you may like to know that fights are held every Sunday from April to October.

Cartuja Park (across the river from the old town) was the site of Expo '92 and has reopened as a theme park with many interesting pavilions: some 65% of the original ones remain.

🏔 Side Tracks from Seville

JEREZ DE LA FRONTERA

Station: *Plaza de la Estación; tel: (56) 34 23 19.* This is a 10-minute walk from the centre of town.

Tourist Office: *Calle Alameda Cristina 7; tel: (56) 33 11 50.*

From Seville there are several trains daily. Journey time is approximately 1 hr on AVE and Talgo services (Inter-Rail/Eurail cards not valid; all passengers must pay a supplement), and 1 hr 20 mins via any other service.

The town has given its name to its main product, sherry, and the *bodegas* are the town's main attraction. In August they are usually closed but the town is very lively for the harvest festival in September.

Jerez is also known for its Equestrian School and the old town (to the west) is an attraction in itself, with many palms and orange-trees and a number of attractive old mansions with flower-filled patios.

Among the **bodegas** you will find such familiar names as Harvey and Sandeman. Most offer tours that finish with a tasting and most (not all) charge a fee. The **Real Escuela de**

Andaluza de Arte Equestre (School of Equestrian Art), *Avda. Duque de Abrantes*, stage a show every Thursday (at other times you can watch the horses being exercised and visit the stables).

Other places of interest are: the **Fundación Andaluza de Flamenco** (a centre of flamenco), the **Alcázar** and the **Plaza de la Asunción**. At the beginning of May, there is a week-long horse fair.

CADÍZ

Station: *Plaza de Sevilla; tel: (56) 26 33 57*. This is centrally located, close to Plaza San Juan de Díos.

Tourist Office: *Calle Calderón de la Barca 1; tel: (56) 21 13 13*.

Regular services operate daily from Jerez de la Frontera to Cadíz: journey time approximately 40 mins by Talgo and 45 mins by any other service. If you want to go direct from Seville to Cadíz, there are approximately 14 services daily, the journey taking about 1 hr 30 mins by Talgo and 2 hrs by other services.

Cádiz is one of the oldest settlements in Spain (founded in 1100 BC by the Phoenicians), and was a vitally important port at the time of the conquest of the Americas (which was why Sir Francis Drake attacked and burnt it). It was at the height of its power and prosperity in the 18th century.

The old city is on a promontory and full of winding streets and blind alleys; a marvellously evocative place for a stroll. The places of specific interest are on the mainland, to which the old town is connected by a causeway. There's a huge carnival every February.

The **Catedral Nueva** is a perfectly proportioned place with a dome of glazed yellow tiles. The **Museo Histórico Municipal** contains an 18th-century ivory and mahogany scale model of Cádiz. The chapel of **Hospital de Mujeres** houses El Greco's *St Francis in Ecstasy* and **Santa Ceuvca** has three Goya frescos.

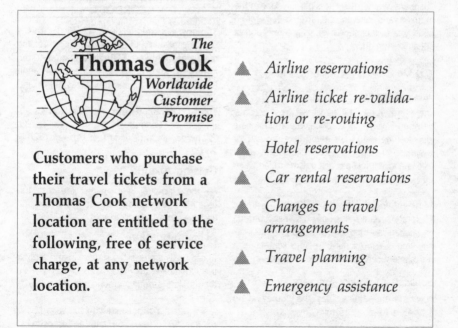

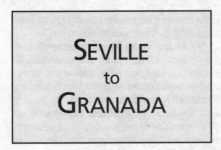

SEVILLE
to
GRANADA

This journey takes you through the marvellous old Andalusian cities of Seville, Córdoba, and Granada. What it lacks in convenience it makes up for in the sights it offers. In particular, the (literally) wonderful Moorish complexes of the Alhambra and the Mezquita should not be missed.

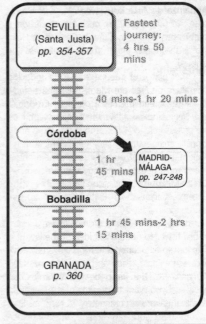

SEVILLE (Santa Justa) pp. 354-357 — Fastest journey: 4 hrs 50 mins

40 mins-1 hr 20 mins

Córdoba

1 hr 45 mins — MADRID-MÁLAGA pp. 247-248

Bobadilla

1 hr 45 mins-2 hrs 15 mins

GRANADA p. 360

TRAINS

ETT tables: 425, 426.

 Fast Track

There are two direct services per day, one in the morning and one in the afternoon. Around midday, a further service offers a connection at Bobadilla-Antequera.

 On Track

Seville–Córdoba

There are about 17 direct services per day between Seville and Cordóba; the approximate journey time is 40 mins if you take the AVE or Talgo services (Inter-Rail/Eurail cards not valid; all passengers must pay a supplement), and 1 hr 20 mins if you take any other train.

Córdoba–Bobadilla-Antequera

There are several trains daily between Córdoba and Bobadilla Antequera. The approximate journey time is 1 hr 45 mins. There is sometimes a refreshment service, so it's worth checking.

Bobadilla-Antequera–Granada

There are three trains a day, the journey taking 1 hr 45 mins–2 hrs 15 mins.

CÓRDOBA

Stations: Central; *tel: (57) 47 76 65*. This is centrally located and around 1 km north of the main area of interest. **El Brillante** station, to the north-west and connected to the main station by bus (*tel: (57) 48 74 46*), serves Seville and Granada.

Tourist Offices: (Provincial) *Calle Torrijos 10 (Palacio de Congresos); tel: (57) 47 12 35.* (Municipal) *Plaza de Juda Levi s/n; tel: (57) 47 20 00.*

Getting Around

All the places of real interest are clustered together in a small area near the river and the best way to explore is on foot.

Accommodation

Cheap areas are near the station, in and around the *Judería* and off *Plaza de las Tendillas*. Also, though less savoury, around the *Plaza de la Corredera*.

There is a **Youth Hostel** at *Plaza Juda Levi s/ n; tel: (57) 29 01 66* and a **Campsite** at

Campamento Municipal, Avda. Brillante; tel: (57) 47 20 00 (about 2 km north of the station; take bus nos.10/11 from *Avda. Cervantes*). Hotel chains with property in the town: *Ml, Pr.*

Sightseeing

Once the capital of the Moorish caliphate and one of the greatest cities in Europe, Córdoba today is a pleasant town filled with a harmonious blend of Catholic, Jewish and Moorish architecture. The main attraction is undoubtedly the Mezquita: arguably the grandest and most beautiful mosque ever erected.

The **Mezquita** was founded in the 8th century by Caliph Abd ar-Rahman I. This superb mosque took nearly 200 years to build and once housed the original copy of the Koran. Climb the bell-tower to get a good idea of the layout. At its foot, the **Puerta del Perdón** (covered with delicate carvings) leads through the massive outer walls to the **Patio de los Naranjos**, a classic courtyard with fountains for ritual cleansing, palms and orange-trees.

From here you can admire the fantastic **forest of 850 pillars**, joined by two-tiered Moorish arches in stripes of red brick and white stone. The overall effect is of unity, but they are not identical: materials used include alabaster, marble, jasper, onyx, granite and wood; some pillars are smooth, others have ribs or spirals. Most are Roman in origin and were shipped in from places as far apart as France and North Africa, then cut to size. The capitals are equally varied.

The Christian 'improvements' after the Moors departed included building a cathedral within the complex and blocking out the light that was an integral part of the design.

The **Third Mihrab** was the heart of the mosque and (unlike the other two) survived the Christian vandalism. Its walls are covered in mosaics of varied colours and friezes from the Koran: a place where appreciation grows as each examination reveals something new.

The **Puente Romano** is a bridge of mainly Moorish construction, but the arches have Roman foundations. Downstream are the remains of **Arab water-wheels**. The **Torre de la Calahorra** (on the other side) is a high-tech museum with a model of the Mezquita as it was before the Christians got to work on it.

The **Alcázar de los Reyes Catolicos**, on the north bank, retains the original Moorish terraced gardens and pools. Less gloriously, it was the headquarters of the Spanish Inquisition for over three centuries.

The **Judería** is the old Jewish quarter, a maze of lanes with flowers in every conceivable corner surrounding a tiny **Synagogue** on *Calle Judios*. The grisly **Museo de Arte Taurino** on *Plaza de Maimonides* is devoted to bullfighting. The **Museo Arqueologico**, *Plaza Paez*, is in a 16th-century mansion with visible Roman foundations.

Plaza del Potro features an attractive fountain topped by a rearing colt (*potro*), an inn (*posada*) where Cervantes is thought to have stayed (it gets a mention in *Don Quixote*) and the **Museo de Bellas Artes**.

BOBADILLA

Bobadilla Antequera is the main rail junction for this part of Spain. The **station** (*tel: (58) 272 00 22*) is centrally located.

At Bobadilla you can join the Madrid–Malaga route (p. 247) either before or after visiting Granada, to reach the Costa del Sol, inland Andalusia and Gibralter.

GRANADA

Station: *tel: (58) 20 41 00* (centrally located). **Tourist Offices:** *Calle Libreros 2* (by the cathedral); *tel: (58) 22 59 90* and *22 10 22*. There are other branches at *Plaza Mariana Pineda 10; tel: 22 66 88* and *Calle Martínez Campo 21* (Viajes TIVE); *tel: (58) 25 02 11*.

Getting Around

The station is some way from the centre, so take a bus (no.11), then head straight for the hill on which the Alhambra is perched. It's a steep climb, or take bus no.2 from *Plaza Nueva*.

The authorities are planning to ban traffic from the historic centre but will provide some kind of special ride to carry visitors to places of major interest.

Accommodation

There are many budget hotels off *Plaza Nueva, Plaza Real, Plaza de la Trinidad* and *Gran Vía*. Hotel chains with property in the town: *MI, Pr*.

Youth Hostel: *Camino de Ronda 171; tel: (58) 27 26 38*. The nearest **campsite** is at *Sierra Nevada, Avda. Madrid 107; tel: (58) 15 09 54* (bus no.3). Not much further out (and with a pool) is *Camping El Ultimo, Camino Huetor Vega 22; tel: (58) 12 30 69*.

Sightseeing

Granada was the last of the great Moorish cities to succumb to Ferdinand and Isabella's ferocious Christian Reconquista in 1492. The main reason for visiting the city is to see the superb hilltop fortress-palace, the Alhambra.

The **Alhambra** was a citadel in the 11th century, but most of the exterior dates from rebuilding in the 13th–14th centuries and is reasonably simple, belying the wealth of decoration inside. There are three sets of buildings: the Alcazaba (Fortress), the Alcázar (Palace) and the Generalife (Summer Palace and Gardens). The number of visitors to some areas of the Alhambra is now being limited and tickets specify the times of day for which they are valid.

You can book in advance (*tel: (58) 22 09 12*).

The main entrance to the **Alcazaba** (from which there is a splendid view) is through the *Puerta de la Justicia*. The **Alcázar** was the main palace, richly decorated and stunningly beautiful, with brilliant use of light and space. Of particular note are the *Mexuar* (council chamber), the *Diwan*, the *Sala de Embajadores* (the largest room, where ambassadors and other dignitaries were received), the *Sala de las Dos Hermanas* (possibly the most beautiful) and the *Court of Lions* (so-named for its famous fountain). The main Christian edifice in the complex is the 16th-century *Palace of Charles V* (never finished). The **Generalife** is a comparatively simple building, noted primarily for its superb patios and gardens. The Moors, coming from desert areas, really appreciated water and the River Darro was diverted to supply the many pools and fountains.

In the city below, the **Cathedral** and the **Capilla Real** (regal mausoleum) are worth seeing: they are just off the *Gran Vía de Colón*. The **Albaicin quarter**, north of the city centre, retains some Moorish atmosphere and is a rewarding place for a stroll. The gypsy cave-dwellings of **Sacromonte**, just outside the town, are also worth a visit.

The Conquistadores

During the early years of their joint reign, in the late 15th century, the 'Catholic Monarchs', Ferdinand and Isabella were not only fighting a major war against the Moors, but also a civil war to establish Ferdinand's claim to the throne. In doing so, they reorganised the military orders, the 'Santa Hermandad' (Holy Brotherhood), and from these grew the dreaded Inquisition. By 1492, they had won everything and both they and their followers were growing restless. Filled with religious fervour and anxious to replenish the coffers, eager minds stretched out towards new conquests. In August that year, Christopher Columbus (or Cristobal Colón, as he is known in Spain) was finally given a fleet of ships and set sail to discover the Caribbean islands. He made two more voyages and on the third, in 1498, he finally found the South American mainland and paved the way for the great Spanish conquest.

The early 16th-century conquistadores (literally conquerors or adventurers) were an unruly lot, who spent as much time fighting each other as they did subduing the peoples they had set out to conquer. The most famous are probably Cortés, who was of noble birth and (by the standards of the time) behaved like a gentleman, and Francisco Pizarro, who was of low birth and (by anyone's standards) a nasty piece of work. Between them, they completely wiped out the great Aztec and Inca civilizations.

STOCKHOLM

Aesthetic and somewhat anaesthetised, Stockholm, hyped as Beauty On Water, stretches over 14 islands, a floating city of classical buildings, 60s blocks, medieval cobbled streets and grand boulevards.

Tourist Information

The Tourist Centre, *Svelteness, Kungsträdgården; tel: (08) 789 24 90* opens Jun–Aug, Mon–Fri 0900–1900 and Sat–Sun 0900–1700; Sept–May, Mon–Fri 0900–1800 and Sat–Sun 0900–1500. **Hotellcentralen** (accommodation booking office), at the main station, is a smaller outlet but adequate for most queries (*tel: 24 08 80*). Other offices: **Kaknäs Tower,** *Djurgården; tel: (08) 791 86 66*; **City Hall,** *Hantverkargartan, 1; tel: (08) 651 21 12* (summer only)

Arriving and Departing

Airport

Arlanda Airport, *tel: 797 60 00* is 45 km north. The **Flygbussarna,** *tel: 600 10 10,* leave every 10–15 mins 0630–2300 and connect with overnight flights. Journey time about 40 minutes. The **City Terminalen** (City Terminal), *Klarabergsviadukten,* is beside the main railway station.

Ferries

For passengers to Turku and Helsinki, bus no.53 leaves for the port every 15 mins from outside the central station. **Silja Line**: *Kungsgatan 2; tel: 22 21 40.* A shuttle bus operates between the port and the nearest metro, *Ropsten.* **Viking Line**: *Stureplan 8; tel; 714 56 00.* Boats depart from *Tegelvikshamnen.*

Buses

The domestic bus line, **Swebus,** *tel: 020 640 640,* has an extensive network. The main station is at *Cityterminalen, Klarabergsviadukten 72.*

Stations

There are two main stations. **Stockholm Central** (Central Station) is an almost obligatory destination as you will find it has the longest opening hours for postal services and currency exchange. There are connections here with local commuter trains and the **Tunnelbanan** (underground). The newly opened **Stockholm Syd** in Flemmingsberg is for commuters. For train information, *tel: 020 75 75 75, 0700–2300.*

Getting Around

Free maps are available from the tourist offices and on board the boat if your inward journey is by sea. Better than these, *Stockholm and the Surrounding Areas* (Skr.10) includes a map of the underground. Get this, and a useful guide, *Discover Stockholm,* from the tourist office.

Public Transport

Storstockholms Lokaltrafik (SL) run buses and trains (underground and commuter) in a five-zone network. The **SL information office,** *Sergels Torg (opposite Kultur Huset); tel: 23 60 00,* is open Mon–Thur 0830–1830, Fri 0830–1730 and has maps and timetable details.

The underground **Tunnelbanan** (T-banan) has 99 stations, but with only three lines, red, green or blue, is easy to use. Stops are distinguished by a blue 'T' on a white background. Many **buses** depart from *Sergels Torg, Odenplan, Fridhemsplan* and *Slussen.* A **Nattbus** (night service) runs 2400–0500. In summer *Turistlinjen,* a special service around most big sights, allows you to hop on and off throughout the day. The tourist office provides a combined map and guide in English for the route. Sightseeing **riverboat** tours run all day May–September. The best deal here is to buy a **Stockholm Card** (see below) which includes a free two-hour tour of Stockholm from the water.

Enthusiasts have resurrected a private **tram** line from *Norrmalstorg* to *Djurgården.* Ticketing for this is separate.

Tickets

A single (Skr.9) is valid for one hour on all SL transport. Tickets valid for 24 hours (Skr.60) are economical if you plan to make several journeys,

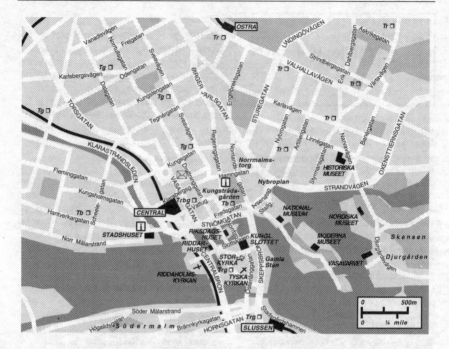

but tickets for the **Turistlinjen** are cheaper still, at Skr.40. Tickets valid for 72 hours (Skr.115) are also available. The *Rabattkuponger* offers 15 journeys for Skr.85 (punch for the requisite number of zones each time you make a journey), which can be more suited to a less intensive use of the network. The combination **Stockholm Card** *Stockholmskort* which costs Skr.150 (per 24 hours) offers free transport on all SL services (except airport bus), free Touristlinjen travel, boat trips, entrance to 66 attractions and discounts on shopping and eating.

Tickets are on sale at *Pressbyrån* kiosks, tourist offices, stations and on buses. The Stockholm Card can also be bought at the Viking and Silja line terminals, hotels and camping grounds. For travel information, *tel: 600 10 10.*

Living in Stockholm

Accommodation

The **Hotellcentralen** (Central Hotel Booking Service), *Central Station; tel: 24 08 80* is open throughout May 0800–1900, Jun–Aug 0800–

2100, Sept 0800–1900 and Oct–May 0800–1700. Only advance bookings are free but you can pick up a copy of *Stockholm Hotels* (free), which lists telephone numbers and prices. Advance booking is recommended. Hotel chains with property in the city include: *SA, SC, Sh.*

Hostels are quite central. For a novel experience, try **AF Chapman**, *tel: 679 5015*, a tall ship moored in the harbour. Hotels are much cheaper at the weekends and during summer when they start at about Skr.250 for a single, but there are few for this price. The **Stockholm Package** offers a reduced rate hotel room with a Stockholm Card thrown in.

Communications

The pink **main post office**, at the junction of *Vasagatan* and *Mäster Samuelsgatan; tel: 781 2055,* opens Mon–Fri 0800–1830, Sat 1000–1400. Central Station branch opens Mon–Fri 0700–2200, Sat–Sun 1000–1900. The **Telecentre** next door opens daily 0800–2100 for faxing and phoning. Buy phone cards here or from the vending machines in the station.

Eating and Drinking

Restaurants are more affordable at lunch time when many serve the *Dogens rått* (menu of the day) for about Skr.50. Chinese and Italian food is usually less expensive, hot-dog stands are convenient and ice-cream is abundant. **Gamla Stan** (old town), the city's main tourist attraction, has a wide range of restaurants. *Stockholm This Week* carries listings. If you can afford the slightly higher prices, there is a good selection of places serving Swedish food. In **Södermalm**, the many restaurants and bars are slightly cheaper.

Embassies and Consulates

Australia: *Block 5, Sergels Torg 12; tel:(08) 613 2900.*
Canada: *Tegelbacken 4; tel: 23 79 20*
New Zealand: *Consulate General, Arsenalsgatan 8C; tel: (08) 611 6824.*
UK: *Skarpogatan 6-8; tel: (08) 667 0140.*
USA: *Secretariat, Strandvagen 101; tel: (08) 783 5300.*

Entertainment

For events listings, look in *Discover Stockholm*. The tourist office will book tickets for concerts, sporting events and theatre. Last-minute theatre tickets are available with a 25% discount from the **Palmhouse,** *Norrmalstorg*, Mon 1200–1700, Tues–Sat 1200–1900.

The **Kulturhuset**, *Sergels Torg 3; tel: 7 000 100*, is an arts complex built as an antithesis to the 1960s commercial architecture hogging the centre of town. It is filled with international music, theatre, exhibitions, cafés and English-language journals.

Much of the nightlife con-centrates around **Stureplan** and **Birger Jarls-gatan**. Some clubs stay open until 0500.

Shopping

Most of the shops are found around *Hamngatan, Drottninggatan, Sergels Torg,* the old town, and the pedestrian street *Sergelgatan*. **NK** and **Åhléns** are two large and well-stocked department stores.

The markets at **Östermalmstorg** (indoor) and **Hötorget**, (off *Vasagatan)*, sell fruit and vegetables, herrings and cheeses.

Sightseeing

Stockholm has over 50 museums, making the Stockholm Card particularly attractive. For a DIY walking tour look in *Stockholm This Week*. Museums are usually closed on Mondays.

Gamla Stan

The city received its foundation charter in 1252 and the first fortifications were erected a few years later. **Gamla Stan** (the Old City) is today the most charming area of Stockholm, with narrow medieval streets dividing the centuries-old, often brightly coloured buildings.

The **Kungliga Slottet** (Royal Palace) is a 600-roomed mix of Rococo and Baroque, built 1690–1754. There are separate entrance fees for the royal apartments, the treasury, armoury and palace museum. Start with the apartments and the treasury. The guards change at noon.

Stortorget

The **Stortorget**, scene of a political bloodbath in 1520, is shaped by tall medieval buildings with colourful façades and gabled roofs. Royal marriages and burials take place in the **Storkyrkan** (Stockholm's parish church, later upgraded to cathedral), with a fine medieval (1489) wooden sculpture of St. George and the Dragon.

Stockholm's German heritage, a leftover from its years as a Hanseatic trading town, is evident in the **Tyska Kyrkan** (German church), off *Västerlånggatan*. **Riddarholmskyrkan**, *Riddarholmen*, has been the resting place of monarchs for six of its 700 years.

The **Riddarhuset** (House of Nobles), *Riddarhustorget 10*, is a masterpiece of Dutch Baroque architecture. The **Stadshuset** (City Hall), *Norr Mälarstrand*, hosts the annual Noble Banquet and is a fine example of modern architecture (see the mosaics).

The Djurgården

The **Djurgården** is a charming mix of parkland and history. One pocket, **Skansen**, houses the city's original open-air museum with 150 historical buildings, a zoo and an aquarium. The nearby **Vasamuseet** holds the resurrected royal ship, *Vasa*, which became posthumously famous

---

after sinking within minutes of its maiden voyage. The park itself, the old royal hunting ground, is divided in two by the **Djurgårdsbrunnsviken River**, north of which stands the **Kaknäs Tower**, Scandinavia's tallest building with a viewing platform 128m up. Bus nos.44/47 make the journey across the *Djurdgårdsbron*.

In the southern half of the park, both the **Rosendals Slott** and the **Prins Eugens Waldemarsudde** are open to the public. A full list of the many other museums in the city is included in *Stockholm This Week*. These cover diverse topics from *Jewish History* to *Swedish Tobacco* and *Puppets*. The **Nationalmuseum**, *Blasieholmskajen*, and **Moderna Museet**, *Skeppensholmen*, have the best art collections, while the **Nordiska Museet**, *Djurgårdsbron*, chronicles life in Scandinavia from the 16th century.

⌒ Side Tracks from Stockholm

Home of the Swedish royals, the Baroque **Drottningholm Palace** is surrounded by water and sculptured gardens. The 18th-century theatre sometimes stages opera, ballet and plays. 11km west from the capital, on Lövön, it can be reached by boat (embark opposite the Town Hall), or by S-bahn (*Brommaplan*) and bus.

THE SKÄRGÅRDEN ARCHIPELAGO

Stockholm's mottled coastline is part of a 40-mile stretch of islands and skerries. Of the total 24,000 only 150 are inhabited all year but a few more sprout holidaymakers in the summer. The larger islands near the mainland can be reached by bridge or ferry. **Vaxholm** is 1 hr away by boat. Some islands have a Youth Hostel or campsite (**Finnhamn** has both), and a selection of chalets, hotels and guest houses. According to the ancient *Altemansråtten* everyone has free access to the countryside but if you want to camp for more than one night near someone's home you must seek their permission.

The main ferry operator is **Waxholmsbolaget**, *Stromkajen*, (opposite the Grand Hotel); *tel: (08) 679 5830*. The **Inter-Skerries Card** allows 16 days of free ferry transport and pays for itself after only two trips.

UPPSALA

Tourist Office: Uppsala Turistbyra, *Fyris Torg 8; tel: (018) 27 48 00*
Station: main railway and bus stations are 15 mins walk from the old town and Fyrisån River. Trains from Stockholm run hourly and take 45–50 mins.

Sightseeing

Much of Sweden's history focuses on Uppsala. In **Gamla Uppsala** (Old Uppsala), 5 km north of the new city, are the burial mounds of Sweden's 6th-century kings, Aun, Egil, and Adils. The geographic importance shifted in the 13th century to what is now the new Uppsala, with the building of the **Domkyrkan** (cathedral). The original cathedral took 150 years to build and was consecrated in 1485. What you see today however is mainly 18th- and 19th-century. Important historical figures buried inside include St. Erik (Sweden's patron saint), Gustavus Vasa (the 16th-century Reformation leader) and the 18th-century botanist Linnaeus (who invented the standard classification system for plants). There is a museum in the north tower.

In 1477 Scandinavia's first university was built here. Nine hundred years older is the Silver Bible on display in the **Carolina Rediviva library**, a rare example of the extinct Gothic language. Overlooking the town are the remains of the **red castle** (1540) whose blood-stained dungeons are open to the public in summer. There are also several other museums, of **Egyptology, archaeology, natural history, art** and one dedicated to **Linnaeus**.

STOCKHOLM
to
HELSINKI

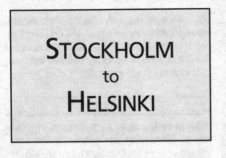

A breathtaking ferry route past the plunging fjords of the Gulf of Bothnia and the chance to cross the forests and lakes of southern Finland by train.

TRAINS

ETT tables: 1250, 1255, 1257, 490.

→ Fast Track

Two ferry lines, **Silja** and **Viking** (see Stockholm, p. 361) run daily overnight services, taking about 15 hrs. Ferries are luxurious, with a wide range of shops and entertainment, restaurants and cabins (reserve). The crossing is free for Eurailers; 30% discount for Inter-Railers. Details below show the fastest train route.

∿ On Track

Stockholm–Border–Turku (Åbo)

Silja and Viking Lines (see Fast Track) sail twice daily (one overnight), taking 11–12 hrs. Eurailers travel free; Inter-Railers get 50% discount.

Turku–Helsinki

Eight trains daily, taking 2 hrs 15 mins.

TURKU (ÅBO)

Station: *tel: (921) 632 2272*. For the harbour, get off at the end of the line.
Tourist Office: **City Tourist Office**, *Kasityolais-katu 3; tel: (921) 9700 5515* (short walk – right, then straight ahead – from station). Mon–Fri 0830–1600 (0800 summer). **Tourist Information Centre**, *Aurakatu 4; tel; (921) 9700 5515* (head towards river): June 1–Sept 15, Mon–Fri

0830–1930, Sat–Sun 1000–1700; Sept 16–May 31, Mon–Fri 0830–1800, Sat–Sun 1000–1700.

Sightseeing

Turku, billed as Finland's first town, was the capital of Finland until 1812 when the power base was moved to Helsinki. Today much of its passing traffic consists of holidaymakers going to or from Stockholm.

Turku's 13th-century **Cathedral** and **Castle** are both outwardly modest and unelaborate in style. The **castle**, a defensive building at the mouth of the River Aura, has been bombed, burnt and rebuilt in piecemeal style. There is a **museum** in the banqueting hall and special children's events are organised in summer.

Along the banks of the river are a smattering of (average) museums, the **Sibelius Museum** (musical instruments), the **Waïnö Aaltonen Museum**, the **Pharmacy Museum**, and the City Theatre. Between the station and the tourist information centre are the **Art Museum**, with Finnish painting from the early 19th-century, and the **Orthodox Church** which faces onto the market square.

There is an **IYHF** hostel on *Linnankatu 39; tel: (921) 316 578.*

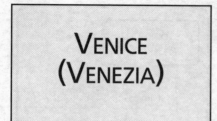

VENICE (VENEZIA)

The island city of Venice with its chequered history and magnificent works of art and architecture has captured the imagination of travellers for centuries. Its tourism magnets include splendid secular and sacred buildings, art galleries, its unique spider-web of canals and some of the finest food in Italy. Venice is a compact city and many of its highlights can be absorbed in two or three days, but it will certainly reward a longer stay.

Tourist Information

The **Azienda Promozione Turistica** (**APT**), *Calle dell'Ascensione 71C, tel: (041) 522 6356* (off *Piazza San Marco*) is open daily except Sunday, Apr–Oct, 0830–1930; Nov–Mar, 0830–1330. APT also has offices at **Santa Lucia station**, *tel: (041) 719 078*, and at the Lido, *Gran Viale Santa Maria Elisabetta 6A, tel: (041) 526 5721*.

For youth information, contact the **Comune di Venezia Assessorato al Gioventù**, *San Marco 1529; tel: (041) 270 7650*. Rolling Venice, a new year-round scheme for 14–30 year olds, offers cheap entry to museums, art galleries, theatres, cinemas and cultural events, maps, cut-price shopping guide and reductions on public transport. In 1993 it cost L.5000. Available from APT offices. The Rolling Venice office, *Santa Lucia Station; tel (041) 720 161*, is open 15 Jun–30 Sept, 0800–2000.

Arriving and Departing

Airport

Marco Polo International Airport is 13 km north-east of Venice; flight information (*tel: (041) 661 262*). The ATVO bus no.5 operates half-hourly (hourly in winter) between the airport and *Piazzale Romana*, where those travelling on

into Venice must transfer to the city's water-borne public transport system (ACTV). The Co-operative San Marco ferry service operates from the airport (daylight hours, summer) via the Lido to the *Piazza San Marco* in the heart of Venice.

Stations

To get to Venice proper, take a train terminating at **Santa Lucia** station; some trains will deposit you at **Mestre**, on the mainland. The two stations are ten minutes apart by rail, and all Santa Lucia trains call at Mestre. A frequent local service operates between Mestre and Santa Lucia

Santa Lucia has its own *vaporetto* (water-bus) stop, right outside the station, at the north-east end of the Grand Canal. Santa Lucia enquiries, *tel: (041) 715555*

Getting Around

Europe's only roadless city is a joy to explore, with its great public buildings and magnificent palaces overlooking the grand canal or un-expectedly tucked away on the maze of smaller canals called *rii* which separate the city's 100-plus islands. Prepare yourself for plenty of walking, and don't be surprised when you get lost. A good map, with *vaporetto* routes and street names, is available from the tourist office and at Venice's many news-stands.

Tickets

A three-day **turisticche** (tourist ticket), cost L18000, enables you to use all vaporetto routes except the Line 2 express, and is ideal for those planning to explore some of Venice's outlying islands. Tickets are sold singly or in booklets of ten from kiosks at main stops, open 0600–2100, and must be validated in the machine provided at each pier before boarding. The line 2 express costs approximately 50% more than normal services. The **ACTV Rolling Venice Rover Ticket**, (see Tourist Information), is valid on most boats for 72 hrs.

Vaporetto (water-bus)

Other cities have the bus, the train, the tram or the metro. Venice has the *vaporetto*. These water-buses, operated by the ACTV transport authority, run at 10–20 minute intervals in

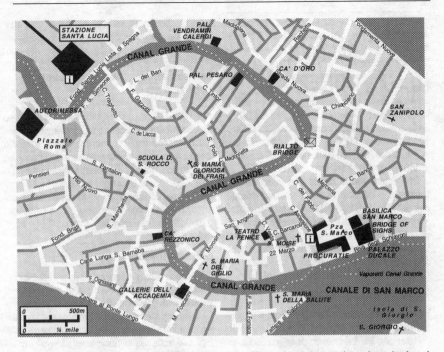

daytime and approximately hourly from midnight to 0600. The most useful lines are Line 1, which runs the length of the Grand Canal, stopping frequently, and Line 2, the express service connecting Santa Lucia station, the Rialto, *piazza San Marco* and the Lido. *Vaporetto* piers bear the line number, but make sure you are heading the right way – it is easy to lose your bearings. Other lines connect central Venice with its island suburbs in the lagoon. Line 5 is a round-the-islands service taking in Murano and handy if you are staying at the youth hostel on Isola del Giudecca, which has its own stop. ACTV, *Piazzale Roma, tel: (041) 520 7555.*

Rolling Venice, a new year-round scheme for 14 to 29-year-olds, offers cheap entry to museums, art galleries, theatres, cinemas and cultural events, maps, cut-price shopping guide and reductions on public transport. In 1993 it cost L.5000. Available from APT offices.

Traghetto (gondola ferry)

The cheapest gondola ride in Venice is the *traghetto*. These two-gondolier boats cross the

Grand Canal at many points along its length (signposted *Traghetto*) and cost less than half the price of a single water-bus ticket.

Water Taxi

Water taxis are very expensive. You could take 40 trips on the Line 2 express for the cost of one taxi ride along the Grand Canal. The fare system is extremely complicated.

Gondola

Gondola rides are costly, but if you decide to treat yourself to a once-in-a-lifetime experience you should go in the evening, when the canals and the buildings overlooking them are at their most magical. Official rates, which are set according to time, not distance, are available from the APT, but make sure you agree a price with your gondolier before setting out.

Living in Venice

Accommodation

Don't come to Venice looking for cheap and

cheerful accommodation. Space is at a premium, and although the city has some of Europe's grandest luxury hotels (such as the legendary Cipriani) there are slim pickings for those on a tight budget, especially in summer, when booking ahead is strongly advisable.

AVA (Venetian Hotel Association) has reservation desks at Santa Lucia station, *tel: (041) 715 016* or *(041) 715 288*, open daily Apr–Oct 0800–2200; Nov–Mar, 0800–2130, and at Marco Polo International Airport. Hotel chains with property in the city include: *Ch, BW, Ra, Ex, Pu.*

The main **youth hostel** (Albergho per la Gioventù) is on Isola del Giudecca (*vaporetto*: line 5), *tel: (041) 523 8211.* For further hostel information, contact the **Associazone Alberghi per la Gioventù**, *Palazzo della Civilta del Lavoro, Quadrato della Concordia, 00144 Roma, tel: (06) 593 1702.* The nearest campsite is on the Lido, *Camping San Nicolò; tel: (041) 526 7415.*

Communications

Main post office: Poste Centrali, *Rialto, Fontego dei Tedeschi, tel: (041) 522 0606.*

To phone Venice from abroad: *tel: 39 (Italy) + 41 (Venice) + number*; to phone Venice from elsewhere in Italy: *tel: (041) + number.*

Eating and drinking

Like all Italian cities, Venice takes pride in its distinctive regional cuisine, and eating and drinking is a central part of the local way of life. As you would expect of a race of lagoon-dwellers and mariners, Venetian cooking leans heavily toward seafood.

In an expensive country for travellers, Venice is one of the more expensive cities and the price of a meal or even a drink in one of the restaurants and cafés catering to tourists around the *Piazza San Marco* or *Rialto* will take your breath away. Drinks at a table cost up to three times as much as those taken at the bar.

Good news for budget travellers is the array of eat-as-you-go snacks available; buy a slice of pizza from a snack-bar, absorb an espresso standing at the bar of a back-street café, and you will save enough money to eat well in the evening at a small *trattoria* – look for places catering to ordinary Venetians rather than

tourists, though these are not always easy to find in a city so thoroughly devoted to tourism.

Embassies and Consulates

UK: *Campo Santa Maria della Carità 1051, Dorsoduro, tel: (041) 522 7207.*

Money

All central banks will change your money, as will bureaux de change in the city centre, at the station and at the airport. Ask for a supply of small-denomination bills – every shop and café in Italy is perennially short of change.

Thomas Cook bureaux de change are located at *5126 Riva del Ferro (Rialto); tel: (041) 5287358* and *Piazza San Marco, 142; tel: (041) 5224751.*

Entertainment

The entertainment calendar is busier in summer than in winter, with events like the annual **Venice film festival** (late August to early September). Music – opera, classical and choral – is prominent. The free *Guest in Venice* guide, available from the APT and at most hotel front desks, will tell you what's on. The big event of the year is **Carnival**, ten days of masked balls, fancy dress parties and colourful street celebrations around Shrove Tuesday each year.

Nightlife

Venice has numerous bars and clubs offering live music, dancing and late-night drinking. As everywhere in Italy, nightlife only begins to warm up at midnight. The best guide to nightlife venues and events is *Notturno Veneziana*, available at APT offices.

Theatres, Cinemas and Concerts

Venice is not a great theatrical city and Italian drama is a closed book to non-natives. **Opera**, with its gorgeous costumes and magnificent arias is, on the other hand, accessible to everybody and the works of Verdi, Puccini and others are in performance virtually year-round. The main venue, the **Teatro La Fenice**, is closed in August.

Free concerts are often held in the city's churches, especially in tandem with other summer cultural events; enquire at APT offices for details of these. Venice has fewer city centre cinemas than any other Italian city, but the **Palazzo del Cinema** on the Lido is the venue for the annual film festival and for frequent showings of international movies year-round.

Shopping

The Venetians' aptitude for commerce has been sharpened by more than 11 centuries of international trade and 200 years of tourism. Bargain buys are thin on the ground, and many people touring the neighbouring islands of the lagoon, such as Murano, are disappointed to find prices are much the same as in the city centre. **Venetian glass** is the big shopping deal, but much of what is sold is as overrated as it is overpriced; try major vendors such as Cenedese or Salviati, both on *Piazza San Marco*. More affordable, and uniquely Venetian, are the painted papier-mâché masks sold in many small stores. The best time to visit the Rialto open-air market is early morning; it's closed on Sunday and quiet on Monday.

Sightseeing

The beauty of sightseeing in Venice is that the city is a living museum with (as yet) no admission charge, although there is talk of introducing one. There is, however, a steep entrance fee for almost all Venice's major sights. The biggest concentration of these is around the **Piazza San Marco**, making it the logical starting point for exploring the city. Almost all the rest – including the palaces of medieval Venice's great magnates – are strung out along the length of the S-shaped Grand Canal.

Piazza San Marco

Close to the mouth of the Grand Canal and overlooking the Canale di San Marco, the *Piazza* is Venice at its most striking – and, in summer, at its most crowded. Highlights are the **Basilica di San Marco**, consecrated in 1094, with its sumptuous façade, elaborate mosaics, and

museum containing sculpture and carvings from all over the medieval Venetian empire. Next to it stand the **Palazzo Ducale** (Doge's Palace), rebuilt in 1577, and the **Bridge of Sighs**. Opposite, the **Campanile di San Marco** (see below) completes the quartet of the square's most important buildings.

Canale Grande (Grand Canal): East Bank

Following the canal in its serpentine northwestward trend from *San Marco* you can stop off at the baroque church of **San Moise** and its neighbour **Santa Maria del Giglio** and pass beneath the **Ponte di Rialto** before stopping at the **Ca' d'Oro**, the most lavish of all the Venetian aristocratic palaces. Last call is the Renaissance **Palazzo Vendramin Calergi**.

Canale Grande: West Bank

On the west bank of the canal, heading northwest from its junction with the Canale di San Marco, stand the **Galleria dell'Accademia**, the **Ca' Rezzonico** and the **Ca' Foscari**, two more splendid palaces.

A short walk west of the canal, between the Rio della Frescada and the Campo di San Paolo, are the **Scuola di San Rocco** with its collection of canvases by Tintoretto and the **Frari**, principal church of the Franciscan order.

View of Venice

The **Campanile di San Marco** on *Piazza di San Marco* is a 20th-century reconstruction of a thousand-year-old bell-tower which fell down in 1912. Take the lift to the top for a panoramic view of Venice and its lagoon.

The Islands

Organised sightseeing tours of the outlying island **Murano** and its neighbours **Burano** and **Torcello** are little more than showcase trips for the glass factories. You can visit these and other islands just as easily – and much more cheaply – on an ordinary *vaporetto*. Worth it for the view, but the big sights are all in Venice itself.

VIENNA
(WIEN)

Of Central Europe's three greatest cities – Vienna, Prague and Budapest – the Austrian capital is the most modern and culturally the most lively. Vienna's chief attractions are a rich store of architecture from the Gothic period to the present, a great number of dramatic, musical and artistic events all year round and hundreds of atmospheric places to eat and drink.

Tourist Information

The **Town Information Office**, *Kärntner Str. 38; tel: (01) 513 88 92*, is open daily 0900–1900. There are also information and accommodation bureaux at **Westbahnhof**, open daily 0615–2300; **Südbahnhof**, open daily 0630–2200; and **Schwechat Airport**, open daily Jun–Sept 0830–2300; Oct–May 0830–2200.
Thomas Cook network member Reisen + Freizeit, *Mariahilferstr. 20; tel: (0222) 526 58 02*, offer a range of services to incoming tourists.

Arriving and Departing

Airport

Schwechat International Airport is 19 km east of Vienna; flight information, *tel: (01) 711 10-2233*; tourist information, *tel: (01) 711 10-0*. Bus transfers run to the **City Air Terminal** (Hilton; *tel: (01) 5800-35404*) every 30 mins 0500–2300, and to **Westbahnhof**, via Südbahnhof, every hour 0730–2030. Journey time about 30 mins. There is also a cheap train service to **Wien Mitte Station**, *Landstr. Hauptstr.*, (adjacent to City Air Terminal), hourly 0730–2030 (journey time: 20–25 mins). The airport has tourist and accommodation offices, telephone and postal facilities.

Stations

Vienna has three main stations. **Westbahnhof**,

Mariahilferstr./Europaplatz; tel: (01) 58 00-310 60, serves destinations in Germany, Switzerland and Hungary. **Südbahnhof**, *Wiener Gurtel/Arsenalstr.; tel: (01) 5800-310 50*, serves the south, Italy, former Yugoslavia, the Czech Republic and Hungary. **Franz-Josefs-Bahnhof**, *Julius-Tandler-Platz; tel: (01) 5800-310 20*, serves the north and trains to Berlin and the Czech Republic. All three are 3–4 km outside the *Ringstr.*, and are connected to the centre by metro or tram.

Travellers should check carefully to see which station their train uses. For general rail information, *tel: (01) 1717*; for taped information on routes to the west and Central Europe, *tel: (01) 1552*; for the south and South-East Europe, *tel: (01) 1553*.

Getting Around

The old city (*Innenstadt*) was enclosed by bastions until 1857 and is now encircled by the famous *Ringstrasse*. This makes sightseeing on foot relatively painless.

The best (and cheapest) street plans, '*24 Stünden für Wien*', are published by the Wiener Stadtwerke in the form of a separate sheet for each *Bezirk* (District). For a short visit, the *Innere Stadt* (District 1) would probably suffice. (It may be necessary to go to **Freytag Berndt und Artaria**, *Kohlmarkt 9*, to obtain these.) Otherwise, there is little to choose between the usual offerings covering the whole city.

Tickets

Public transport is efficient but relatively expensive, with U-Bahn, trams and buses all using the same tickets, on sale from all **Tabak/Trafik** (tobacconists and newsagents). Single tickets, sold in blocks of 5, and valid for one journey, are the most expensive option.

Far better value are the 24-hr **Tageskarte Wien** and the 72-hr **excursion ticket**. Alternatively, the **Umwelt Streifnetzkarete** gives you eight separate units, each one valid for 24 hrs, to use when required (simply validate the tickets in the automatic puncher on the bus or tram or at the entrance to the U-Bahn). Always buy tickets ahead, as they are more expensive on board and fines are heavy if you are caught without one.

U-Bahn, Trams and Buses

The marvellously clean and modern **U-Bahn**, or underground railway, of Vienna was built in the 1960s and has been continuously extended since then. It replaced, but in some areas still runs in tandem with, the turn-of-the-century **Stadtbahn** (City Transit Railway). There are currently five lines, operating between 0500 and 2400. Vienna's **trams** run on 33 radial routes and in both directions round the *Ringstr.*, between 0500 and 2400. **Buses** fill the gaps not covered by trams and function during roughly the same hours, although there are some special all-night buses on main routes (supplement payable), which leave from *Schwedenplatz* in the centre.

Taxis

Not cheap, but extremely efficient. You may well have to use taxis to get home late at night (*tel: (01) 40 100*, and they should arrive within 5 mins, almost anywhere in the city). Hailing cabs is not allowed, but there are plenty of strategically placed ranks.

Living in Vienna

Accommodation

The Vienna Tourist Board issues lists of both hotels and pensions (obtainable from Tourist Information Offices and Accommodation Bureaux) categorised according to quality. Don't expect to find much below AS.500 per night, except for seasonal hotels, youth hostels and campsites. Major hotel groups represented in Vienna include *Ch, Hn, Ib, Ic, Ma, Me, Nv, Pe, Pu, Ra, SA* and *SC*.

There are **accommodation offices** in the *Opernpassage* U-Bahn concourse, in front of the Opera House, *tel: (01) 56 23 46*, at all major railway stations and the airport. **IYHF** information is available from the Tourist Information Bureaux. There are nine youth hostels, but the only central one is the **City Hostel**, *Seilerstatte 30, tel: (01) 512 8463/512 7923*.

There are **campsites** at *Huttelbergstr. 40, tel: (01) 94 14 49*, (open all year) and *Breitenfurter Str. 269, tel: (01) 86 92 18* (open mid-March–mid-November), both some distance from town.

Communications

The **Central Post Office** and **Poste Restante** is at *Barbaragasse 2, tel: (01) 512 76 81-0* (open 24 hrs) and there are also 24-hr post offices at the Westbahnhof and Südbahnhof. Telephone cards can be purchased at Trafik/Tabak and post offices. Some phone booths in the centre (e.g. in *Wallner Str.* and *Goldschmiedgasse*) accept standard credit cards and have instructions in English. The Vienna area code is 01.

To phone Vienna from abroad: *tel: 43 (Austria) + 01 (Vienna) + number*; to phone Vienna from elsewhere in Austria: *tel: 01 + number*.

Eating and Drinking

Vienna not only gave the world the *Wiener Schnitzel* and *Sachertorte*, but is well endowed with restaurants of all types and prices, throughout the inner city. There are several typically Viennese institutions such as the moderately priced **Beisl**, specialising in Viennese food, **Kellern**, atmospheric wine-bar/restaurants in Baroque cellars, and **Konditoreien**, coffee houses, both serving simple hot food at reasonable prices. **Demel's Coffee House**, *Kohlmarkt 14*, has achieved legendary status.

Just outside town, in delightful villages such as Grinzing, Heiligenstadt and Neustift am Walde, on the edge of the picturesque Vienna Woods (*Wienerwald*), are the famous taverns known as **Heurigen**, where local wine is served with traditional food, usually from mid-afternoon until midnight. For cheap eating and fast food, try the counters in butchers' shops, *Würstelstände* (hot dog stalls), sandwich bars (the cognoscenti go to **Trzesniewski**, *Dorotheergasse 1*) and the **Naschmarkt** self-service chain (*Schwarzenbergplatz, Schottentor*).

Embassies and Consulates

Australia: *Mattiellistr. 2-4; tel: (01) 512 85 80*
Canada: *Dr-Karl-Lueger-Ring 10; tel: (01) 533 36 91*
New Zealand: *Lugeck 1; tel: (01) 512 66 36*
UK: *Jauresgasse 12; tel: (01) 75 61 17* (Consulate)
USA: *Gartenbaupromenade 2; tel: (01) 31 55 11* (Consulate)

Money

Banks open Mon–Fri, 0800–1500 (–1730 Thurs); branch offices close for lunch, 1230–1330. There are exchange bureaux at main stations, the airport and the city air terminal. Credit cards, Eurocheques and travellers' cheques are all widely accepted.

Entertainment

Programm, an indispensable monthly listing of all entertainment but cinemas, is free from Tourist Information Offices. Cinemas (including those showing films in English) are listed in newspapers. Night life and the 'in scene' focuses on the 'Bermuda Triangle', an area of lively bars, discos and pubs close to *Schwedenplatz*, but Vienna is mostly famed as one of the world's great centres of classical music, with everything from chamber concerts to grand opera on offer. Ticket prices can be high, but the **Staatsoper** sells cheap standing-room tickets on the day (prepare to queue). The **Vienna Boys' Choir** performs at the Hofburg Chapel on Sundays at 0915, Sept–Jun. **Youth events** and discount information from **Jugend-info**, *Bellaria Passage*, near *Dr-Karl-Renner-Ring, tel: (01) 526 4637*.

Shopping

Kärntner Str. is Vienna's most exclusive shopping area; **Mariahilferstr.** is home to the large department stores. Ornamental objects with an Austrian flavour are found at **Österreichische Werkstätten**, *Karntner Str. 26; tel: (01) 512 24 18*. A local speciality is **Augarten** porcelain, on sale at the manufactory in *Obere Augartenstr.; tel: (01) 211 24*.

Sightseeing

Focal point of Vienna is the Romanesque and Gothic **Stephansdom** (St Stephen's Cathedral; U-Bahn: *Stephansplatz*), with its jazzy green and gold roof. The loveliest parts are the Gothic Albertine Choir (1340) and the magnificent 14th-century, 136.7m South Tower (the 'Steffl' to locals), with 343 steps. Inside the cathedral, highlights include the pulpit (1510) and organ loft by Anton Pilgram; a Gothic wing altar in the North Apse and the fabulous Renaissance tomb of Friedrich III in the South Apse. The embalmed entrails of Habsburg rulers repose in the Ducal Crypt (in the catacombs).

Hofburg

The great Habsburg residence occupies a vast area of central Vienna and has 18 wings, 54 stairways and 2,600 rooms. The main sights are the **Burgkapelle** (chapel), home of the famous Vienna Boys' Choir; the **Schatzkammer** (Treasury), containing the crown of the Holy Roman Empire; the **Imperial Apartments**, preserved as the penultimate emperor, Franz Josef, had them; the **Winter Riding School**, where the famous Lippizaner horses perform (if you cannot get tickets for the main performance, queue at the door of the Redoute, *Josefsplatz*, to be admitted to 'morning training'); and the **National Library** commissioned by Charles VI, and built by Fischer von Erlach, father and son.

Galleries and Museums

Vienna's major museum and gallery is the **Kunsthistorisches Museum** (Museum of Art History), *Burgring 5* (tram nos.1/2: *Burgring*), based on the collection of the Habsburgs. The main museum contains classical and Egyptian antiquities, Palaeo-Christian art, decorative art and, above all, a world-famous picture gallery with a superb collection of Breughels as well as masterpieces by Rembrandt and Velázquez. There are three other branches – in the Neue Burg (part of the Hofburg) where Musical Instruments and Armour are displayed; in the Burg itself (Crown Jewels, Ecclesiastical Treasures) and at the Palace of Schönbrunn (Coaches and Carriages). The superb 18th-century Baroque **Belvedere Palace**, *Prinz-Eugen-Str. 27* (tram D), built for Prince Eugene of Savoy, has two galleries and delightful **gardens**. The **Österreichische Galerie** (Austrian Gallery), *Oberes (Upper) Belvedere*, has important works by artists of the Biedermeier period (1814–1848), the Vienna Secession and Austrian Expressionism. The **Baroque Museum**, *Unteres (Lower) Belvedere*, at the Rennweg end of the park, containing works by many leading Baroque artists who worked in Austria, including Georg Raphael Donner.

The **Museum für angewandte Kunst**

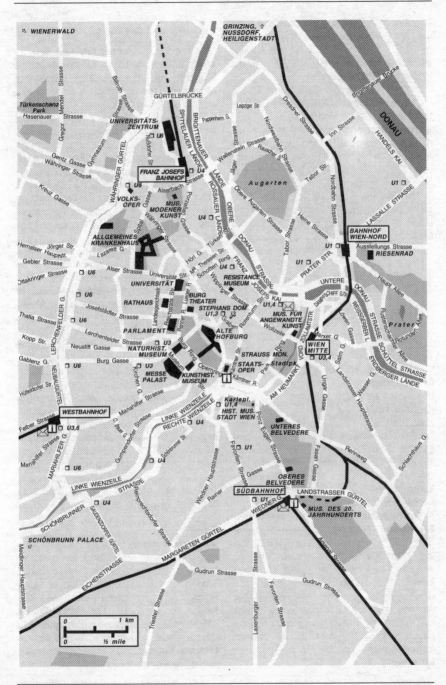

(Museum of Applied Art), *Stubenring 5* (tram nos.1/2: *Dr-Karl-Lueger-Platz*), is a marvellous cornucopia of Oriental, European and Austrian artefacts. Modern art enthusiasts will enjoy the **Museum des 20 Jahrhunderts** (Museum of the 20th Century), *Schweizer Garten* (tram D) and the **Museum Moderner Kunst im Palais Liechtenstein** (Museum of Modern Art in the Liechtenstein Palace), *Fürstengasse 1* (tram D), housed in a fine Baroque building, with works by Austrian Expressionists and other leading European 20th-century artists such as Léger, Max Ernst, and Magritte.

The **Albertina**, *Augustinerstr.* (U-Bahn: *Karlsplatz/Oper*), houses the world's greatest collection of drawings and prints. The **Theatre Museum**, *Lobkowitzplatz 2*, and *Hanuschgasse 3* (U-Bahn: *Karlsplatz/Oper*) charts the history of Vienna's world famous theatre (photographs, costumes, stage-sets and memorabilia); and the delightful **Uhrenmuseum** (Clock Museum), *Schulhof 2* (U-Bahn: *Schottentor*) features 900 clocks of every conceivable type.

Churches

Vienna abounds with intriguing churches. In the Gothic **Augustinerkirche**, *Augustinerstr.3* (U-Bahn: *Karlsplatz/Oper*), the hearts of the Habsburgs are kept in silver urns. The **Kapuzinerkirche**, *Neuer Markt* (U-Bahn: *Karlsplatz/Oper*), is above the Capuchin crypt where Habsburg bodies were laid to rest in impressive Baroque tombs. Examples of Viennese Gothic include the **Church of Maria am Gestade**, *Am Gestade* (trams nos.1/2: *Börse*), the **Minoritenkirche**, *Minoritenplatz* and the **Michaelerkirche**, *Michaelerplatz* (both U-Bahn: *Herrengasse*).

There are also two superb Baroque churches: **Peterskirche**, *Petersplatz* (U-Bahn: *Stephansplatz*), built by Lukas von Hildebrandt (1708); and the 1713 **Karlskirche**, *Karlsplatz* (U-Bahn: *Karlsplatz/Oper*), the masterpiece of Johan Bernard and Joseph Emanuel Fischer von Erlach. Fronted by two vast Roman-style columns, with a great copper dome, it was built by Charles VI in thanksgiving for the end of a plague epidemic. The frieze on the columns features scenes from the life of St Charles Borromeo.

Minor Sights and Musicians

The fine Baroque **former City Hall**, *Wipplingerstr. 8* (tram nos.1/2: *Börse*) now holds the **Museum of the Austrian Resistance Movement** (against Nazism). On the curious art nouveau **Anker Clock**, *Hoher Markt* (U-Bahn: *Schwedenplatz*), 12 figures or pairs of figures from Austrian history move across the clock-face and parade together at 1200. For an idea of the architectural splendours of the Ringstrassen era, take tram nos.1/2 around the ring, which pass the neo-Gothic **Rathaus** (City Hall) by Friedrich Schmidt, the **Burgtheater**, the **Parliament** by Theophil Hansen (he also built the Academy of Fine Arts), and the **Opera** by Van der Null and Siccardsburg.

Near to the **Academy of Fine Arts** is Joseph Olbrich's extraordinary exhibition hall for the painters of the Viennese Secession. And close to that, on *Karlsplatz*, is the **Historical Museum of the City of Vienna**, opposite the famous **Musikverein** concert hall. (All the above are within walking distance of U-Bahn *Karlsplatz/Oper*.) A few minutes walk across the Ring past the **Hotel Sacher**, brings you to fashionable **Kärntner Str.**, which leads to the even more fashionable **Graben**, the place in Vienna to see and be seen.

The **Pasqualati House**, *Molker Bastei* (tram nos.1/2: *Schottentor*) is one of innumerable lodgings used by Beethoven, who also has a museum at the **Beethoven House**, *Probusgasse 6* (bus nos.37A/38A) in Heiligenstadt. Mozart's lodging, the so-called **Figaro House**, *Domgasse 5* (U-Bahn: *Stephansplatz*) has memorial rooms. The **Schubert Museum** is at the composer's birthplace, *Nussdorfer Str. 54* (tram nos.37/38).

Further out

Schloss Schönbrunn (tram no. 58 from *Burgring*, U-Bahn 4 to *Schönbrunn*), is a grandiose Rococo palace (tours of the richly decorated interiors, and a superb park). The legendary **Prater** (U-Bahn: *Praterstern*) is a vast park with a fun-fair and big wheel. The **Vienna Woods** (*Wienerwald*), the picturesque hilly country to the north-west, and *heurigen* villages such as **Grinzing**, **Nußdorf** and **Heiligenstadt**, can be reached by easy tram-rides from the city centre.

VIENNA to BUDAPEST

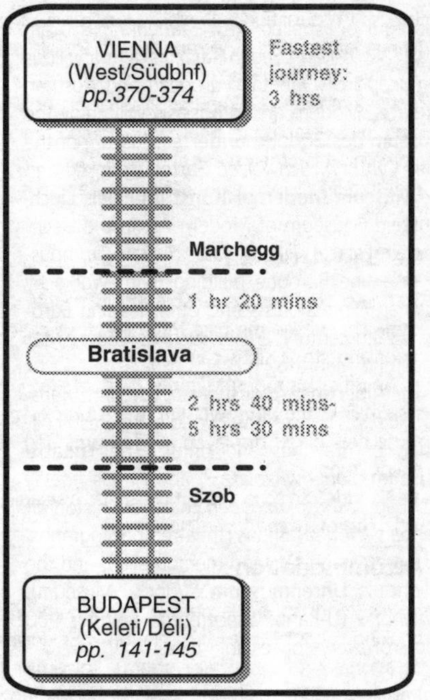
VIENNA
(West/Südbhf)
pp.370-374
Fastest journey: 3 hrs
Marchegg
1 hr 20 mins
Bratislava
2 hrs 40 mins–
5 hrs 30 mins
Szob
BUDAPEST
(Keleti/Déli)
pp. 141-145

A short route which nevertheless manages to cross three countries, Austria, Slovakia and Hungary, connecting the ancient and modern capitals of Hungary.

TRAINS

ETT tables: 890, 888, 889.

Fast Track

There are several direct services daily between Vienna and Budapest (a supplement is payable on some services). Journey time ranges from 3 hrs to 3 hrs 20 mins (approximately). Trains depart from either Westbahnhof or Südbahnhof in Vienna, and arrive at either Keleti or Déli in Budapest, so check details carefully before you travel. There is a dining-car/buffet service on most trains.

This is an entirely different route from that taken by the On Track trains. The border is crossed at Hegyeshalom with little formality.

On Track

Vienna (Wien)–Bratislava

There are four direct services daily from Vienna (Süd) to Bratislava (Hlavní); journey time ranges from 1 hr 10 mins to 1 hr 20 mins. The border is crossed at Marchegg.

Bratislava–Budapest

Seven services daily operate between Bratislava (Hlavní) and Budapest (Nyugati/Keleti), but one of these is summer only and two others arrive or depart during the early hours. The one EC service takes about 2 hrs 40 mins. Other trains take from around 3 hrs to 5 hrs 30 mins to complete the journey. The border is crossed at Rajka, Štúrovo/Szob, or Komárom, depending on which train you have caught.

BRATISLAVA

Station: Most trains serve main station, Hlavna Stanica, *tel: 204 44 84* or *498 275*, 1.5 km north of old town centre. There are exchange facilities at Hlavna Stanica, but no tourist office and few English speakers. Go downstairs to reach the trams (no. 1 to old town). Nové Město station (*tel: 60 702*) is about 3 km north-east of the centre (accessible by tram).

Tourist Office: Bratislava Information Service (BIS), *18 Panska; tel: 333 715* or 334 325. Staff speak English and recent maps of the town are available. Slovakotourist, *13 Panska; tel: 333 466*, speak some German.

For four centuries Bratislava lay on the *Limes Romanus*, the frontier between the Roman Empire and Barbarian lands. In the 16th century, when much of Hungary lay under

Turkish occupation, Bratislava became the Hungarian capital, a position it held for almost 250 years. Now, as capital of the newly independent Slovak Republic, the city is beginning to re-establish its international importance. However, it is largely bleak and industrial, lacking the stateliness of neighbouring Budapest and Vienna.

Getting Around

Bratislava's streets have suffered two sets of name changes in the past three years, so check maps and street signs carefully.

An efficient, though slightly antiquated, tram system links the old town with the suburbs. The route network is displayed inside trams and at major stops.

A wide selection of tickets is available, including one- and two-day passes.

Accommodation

Hotels tend to be expensive. There are no booking agencies in the station but locals occasionally offer private rooms to arriving travellers. BIS can book private rooms and hotels, but focus more on information. **CKM-Slovakia**, *16 Hviezdoslavovo Nam; tel: 334 114* or *331 607*, has a wider variety of accommodation, including university dorms in the summer and a student hotel open all year round. Try also **CEDOK-Slovakia**, *5–9 Jesenskeho; tel: 367 624*. In addition, some companies set aside some of their employee accommodation for visitors.

There are two **YHA** hostels: *Bernolákova 3; tel: 42612* and *Drienuová 14; tel: 238 000*.

Embassies

Australia, **Canada** and **New Zealand** have no diplomatic establishments in Bratislava, the nearest being in Vienna, but their citizens can contact the British Embassy in case of emergency.

UK: Currently at *17 Panska; tel: 335 922*, the British Embassy plans to move to *35 Grosslingova* some time in 1994. The new phone number is not available at the time of going to press, but you will be able to get it from the British Council (*tel: 331 074*), who will be remaining at *17 Panska*.

USA: *4 Hviezdoslavove Nam; tel: 330 861* or *333 338*.

Sightseeing

Bratislava has a regional, rather than a capital, air. Even the Danube loses some of its majesty as it passes through the town, the ranks of tower blocks and striped factory chimneys dominating the riverscape. In an attempt to recreate some sense of grandeur, many of the older and more distinguished squares and buildings are being refurbished.

The **Castle** is the most distinctive sight in town. Evidence has been found of fortifications dating back to at least the 9th century, but the main castle was burnt down in 1811 during the Napoleonic wars. The present structure is 1960s vintage and displays some of the exhibits from the **Slovak National Museum**'s collection. There's a good view of the unusual design of the SNP bridge across the Danube.

During Bratislava's period as Hungarian capital, 11 kings were crowned in **St Martin's Cathedral**, across *Staromětska* from the castle.

The old town conservation area, largely pedestrianised, also contains the **Mirbach Palace**, *Radicna St*, and the **Franciscan Church**, one of Bratislava's oldest surviving structures, dating back to 1290.

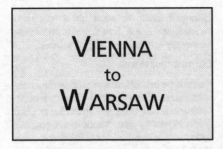

VIENNA
to
WARSAW

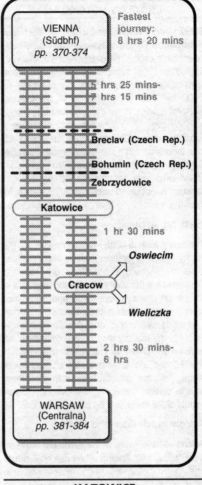

VIENNA
(Südbhf)
pp. 370-374

Fastest
journey:
8 hrs 20 mins

5 hrs 25 mins–
7 hrs 15 mins

Breclav (Czech Rep.)

Bohumin (Czech Rep.)

Zebrzydowice

Katowice

1 hr 30 mins

Oswiecim

Cracow

Wieliczka

2 hrs 30 mins–
6 hrs

WARSAW
(Centralna)
pp. 381-384

The countryside on this route is pleasant if not particularly inspiring, but in Cracow, you will find one of the last undiscovered pearls of medieval Europe, the cultural capital of Poland and the former diocese of Pope Joh Paul II. By contrast, the route also passes one of Europe's darkest monuments, the former concentration camp of Auschwitz.

TRAINS

ETT tables: 95a, 860, 865.

Fast Track

Two named trains run daily, departing Vienna Südbahnhof. The morning Sobieski (EC) takes 8 hrs 20 mins (restaurant car); the overnight Chopin (reservations required) has couchettes and sleepers and takes about 10 hrs 30 mins.

On Track

Vienna (Wien)–Katowice

Both the Sobieski (journey time about 5 hrs 25 mins) and the Chopin (taking 7 hrs 15 mins) call at Katowice (see details above). Other services are slower and involve changes.

One direct overnight (second-class couchettes) service runs Vienna to Cracow. Journey time: 8 hrs 15 mins.

Katowice–Cracow (Kraków)

Several trains run daily, taking 1 hr 30 mins.

Cracow–Warsaw (Warszawa)

About a dozen trains run daily (with dining-car), most requiring reservations and taking 2 hrs 30 mins–2 hrs 45 mins (5–6 hrs at night).

KATOWICE

Tourist Office: (COIT), *11 ul. Mlynska; tel: 53 8834.* Open Mon–Fri 0900–1700, Sat 0900–1300.

As the largest city in Poland's industrial heartland, Katowice is less than inspiring, but it does have social interest. The **Muzeum Słaskie** (Silesian Museum), *ul. Wojciecha Korfantego 3* has some Polish paintings, and the **Wojewodzki Park**, has a cable car and big wheel, but the city also boasts proudly of its 30 magnetic-card telephones.

CRACOW (KRAKÓW)

Tourist Information: the useful **Central Tourist Information Office**, *ul.Pawia 8; tel: 22 04 71*, near the station, opens Mon–Fri 0800–2100, Sat 0900–1500. Information also from **Orbis**, *Rynek Główny 41*; tel: 22 40 35, open Mon–Fri 0800–1900, Sat 0800–1400 and at the **Cracovia Hotel**. Look out for the free monthly magazine *Welcome to Cracow* for practical details.
Station: **Cracow Główny** (main), *tel: 22 22 48*, is a short walk from the town centre. **Płaszów Station**, which serves trains to Oświecim (Auschwitz), the salt mines and some night services, is about 30 mins from the centre by Tram no.13.

Getting Around

The **Stary Miasto** (Old Town), encircled by the *Planty*, a belt of greenery where the defensive walls once stood, is pedestrian only. Beyond this, there is a network of buses and trams. Tickets are on sale at kiosks, Orbis and sometimes from the driver. Punch *both* ends of the ticket on board (once only is for concessions). *Kraków Plan Miasta*, the city map with a distinctive red and yellow cover, has bus and tram routes marked and is sold at news-stands and bookshops. Taxis are still relatively cheap. Find them at the station (expect to be swamped), taxi stands or, cheaper still, by phoning for one.

Accommodation and Eating

Fo and *HI* have hotels in the town. For those on a limited budget, finding a bed can be difficult. The tourist office will make reservations and arrange private accommodation. It is also quite common to be approached by individuals at the station. Remember to check the location and price before agreeing. The two **hostels** are at *ul. Kościuszki 88; tel: 22 19 51*, and *ul. Oleander 4; tel: 33 88 22*, both about 15-mins walk from town. There are three **campsites**; try *Krak, ul. Radzikowskiego 99; tel: 37 21 22*.

Rynek Główny and surrounding streets are dotted with comparatively cheap restaurants. For good Polish food, try **Staropolska**, *ul. Sienna 4*, or **Wierzynek**, *Rynek Główny 15*. **Bella Italia** does delicious pizzas. Cafés such as

Zielony Balonik are good for sampling the excellent cakes. For picnics, go to the delicatessen-style grocers (east side of square).

Communications

The main **post office** (with Poste Restante), *ul.Wielopole 1*, opens 0730–2100, Sat 0800–1400 and Sun 0900–1100. The telephone section, efficient by past standards, is open 24 hours (queues are common). Telephone cards, needed for international calls, and the increasingly out-moded telephone coins are on sale.

Entertainment

Evening activities are quite thin on the ground considering the student population and the city's artistic traditions. However, there are some cinemas, concerts and clubs that go on until late. Films are usually undubbed, and the 18 cinemas are a popular source of entertainment.

Money

Central Cracow is full of *Kantors* (exchanges). Change travellers cheques in bank *Pekao* on the square, open Mon–Fri 0730–1900, Sat 0730–1735. Credit cards are rapidly gaining sway.

Sightseeing

Capital of Poland for 500 years, and one of a handful of places to survive World War II, Cracow's symbolic significance and beauty are immense. Poles regard it as the spiritual heart of their country; UNESCO lists it as one of the world's 12 most precious cultural relics. In spite of this, years of desperate pollution under Communism left the city swathed in a pall of soot. Today, it is belatedly being cleaned up, and shops full of designer goods and antiques have added a new chic. Cracow's two million works of art are now rivalled in number only by the number of visitors that come here each year.

Museums have fairly erratic opening hours, but the best of Cracow can be appreciated from the street.

Stare Rynek

One of the largest and most beautiful market places in medieval Europe, **Rynek Główny** is never swamped by the crowds, flower stalls and

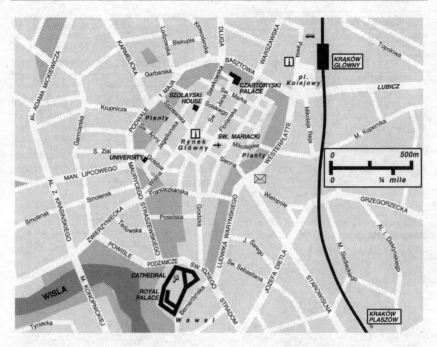

cafés, but try visiting late at night or early in the morning for full impact. The size of the **Sukiennice** (Cloth Hall) that stands centre-stage, and the surrounding aristocratic houses make for a harmonious and beautiful setting, ideal for postcard writing and drinking coffee.

The long, dark Gothic Cloth Hall started as a roof over the trading stalls. It was enlarged during the reign of Casimir the Great and reconstructed in the Renaissance style following a fire in 1555. It is still commercial, filled with stalls selling amber, silver and thick woollen jumpers to tourists. A branch of the **National Museum**, on the first floor, houses Polish paintings on historical themes and from the Enlightenment period, including works by Jan Matejko.

The **City Hall Tower** (good view from top), is all that remains from the Gothic Town Hall, destroyed in the 1820s as part of a civic rebuilding programme. Inside are some historical exhibits and a basement café. In the opposite corner of the square, **St. Adalbert's Church** is the oldest in Cracow. Further north, **Mariacki** (St Mary's Church) has a hugely impressive wooden Gothic altar, adorned by 200 figures, the work of Veit Stoss. Legend has it that a watchman was shot down from the tower by Tartar invaders. The *hejnat*, the melody he trumpeted to sound the alarm is broadcast daily nationwide at noon.

The University district

The **university**, *ul. Jagiellonska 15*, the second oldest in Central Europe, received its royal charter in 1364. It was renamed *Jagiellonian University* during a revival in fortunes in the early 15th century. Famous students include Copernicus and Pope John Paul II.

Numerous gifts on display in the **University Museum** include 35 globes, one of which, from 1510, features the earliest illustration of America, marked 'a newly discovered land'. Tours of the university take in the alchemy rooms (supposedly Dr. Faustus's laboratory) lecture rooms, assembly hall and professors' apartments.

Museums

There are over two dozen museums (get a guide

---

book from the tourist office). Exhibits in the 18th-century **Czartoryski Palace**, *19 Sw. Jana Street*, include a large collection of ancient art and works by Rembrandt and Leonardo da Vinci. **Szołayski House**, *9 Szczepaanski Square*, has 14th–18th-century art and sculpture. Modern art, from the late 19th century, is housed at *al. 3 Maja* and **Muzeum Historii Fotografii** a photographic museum, is at *Rynek Główny 17*.

Wawel

Wawel Hill, surrounded by the Wisla River, is a site of patriotism and pride for Poles who flock to visit the Cathedral and the fortified Royal Castle (both built by King Casimir the Great).

Forty-one of Poland's 45 kings are buried in the **Cathedral**, along with national heroes and poets. The last coronation took place in 1734. The present Gothic construction was built 1320–1364 but the first church was erected here in the 11th century. Relics of the earliest building are on display in the castle's west wing. The most famous of the 19 side chapels is the golden-domed Renaissance **Zygmuntowskar** (Sigismund's Chapel), built 1519–31 by Bartolomeo Berecci. Climb the **cathedral tower** for a good view and see the 2.5 m diameter *Zygmunt bell*, rung to celebrate church or national holidays. Some Gothic fragments such as the Danish tower, and the *Kurza Stopa* (Hen's Foot) still ex-ist, but the majority of the **Castle** was rebuilt in 1502–36 after a fire, in the Italian style, with three-storey arcades surrounding a cobbled courtyard. Brocade, leather and tapestries cover the walls; ceilings are beamed and coffered. Displayed in the **Royal Chambers** are 136 exquisite Arras tapestries, while the *Treasury* houses what's left of the crown jewels.

- - - - - - - - - - - - - - - - - - -

〰 Side Tracks from Cracow

OŚWIECIM (AUSCHWITZ)

Auschwitz, the German name for Oświecim, is synonomous with the atrocities of the Holocaust. In this, the largest of the concentration camps, between 1.5 and 2 million people, mainly Jewish, met brutality and death at the hands of the SS. Men, women and children from across occupied Europe were transported here in cattle trucks, often surviving up to 10 days. They were promised jobs, some bought ficticious land. Anyone deemed unfit upon arrival was ostensibly allowed a bath. Cyanide gas pouring from the shower heads poisoned up to 2000 at a time. The rest met hard physical labour and passed daily through gates bearing the inscription *Arbeit Macht Frei* (Freedom through Work).

When Soviet liberation forces arrived in May 1945 they found emaciated survivors, the machinery of death and 7000 kg of women's hair, due to be made into cloth or used to stuff mattresses. The piles of spectacle frames, shoe-polish tins, baby clothes and monogrammed suit-cases are on display. Regular screenings of the liberators' films are shown in several languages.

Nearby **Birkenau** was, for the Nazis, a better designed death factory. This is even more hard-hitting. Trains (1 hr 45 mins) leave from Cracow, mostly from Płaszów station.

WIELICZKA (MAGNUM SAL)

Wieliczka's salt mine features, along with Cracow, on the UNESCO heritage list. Mined for 700 years, it has 350 miles of tunnelling, with 2040 chambers, and used to provide 40% of the area's wealth.

Underground, the mine is a dazzling feat of salt sculpture, with 40 chapels carved entirely from salt in memory of the many who lost their lives here. Larger than life salt statues of, amongst others, Copernicus and St. Anthony animate the tunnels. Most magnificent of all is the largest chapel with salt chandeliers and even salt relief pictures on the walls. Guided tours in English. Trains leave from Cracow Płaszów.

- - - - - - - - - - - - - - - - - - -

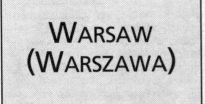

WARSAW (WARSZAWA)

Two-thirds of Warsaw's population, 99% of its Jewish population, and 80% of buildings were destroyed during the Nazi occupation. The city today has a drab image, founded on the post-war scramble to rehouse and rebuild, which resulted in many pockets of concrete jungle. The monumental significance of the town should not be underestimated however. What is left is a tribute to the enduring tenacity of the Varsovians, who have recreated their city from the rubble, often with the help of old paintings and photographs. A political football, bounced between Germany and Russia, with devastating effects on its citizens, Warsaw may not be the prettiest of towns, but it is historically compelling. Spend at least two days here.

Tourist Information

The **Informator Turystyczny** (IT), pl. Zamkowy 1/13; tel: 635 18 81, opens daily 0800–1800. Free handouts are thin on the ground and the staff are not always conversant but the service here is infinitely better than at the nominal information desks in the airport and station. Orbis Travel (**Thomas Cook** network member) on Marszalkowka Str. 142; tel: 276 766 offers services for visitors.

Larger hotels, such as the Marriott, opposite the station, often have the free Welcome to Warsaw and What, Where, When, with a city map, practical information, articles, and listings. The Warsaw Voice (English-language newspaper), is also worth getting.

Arriving and Departing

Airport

Okęcie Airport, 1A ul. Zwirki Wigury; tel: 650 42 20 or 46 17 00, lies 6 km south of the city.

MZK's Airport Citybus runs every 20–30 minutes from 0600–2300 (journey time about 30 mins). Take bus no.175 to the central railway station and the new town, or no.188 to **Olszynka Grochóowska** station.

Stations

Warszawa Centralna, (Central Railway Station), 54 Jerozolimskie av; tel: 25 50 10 (for international information); tel: 20 45 12 (for national information); and tel: 20 03 61 to 9 (for local details). Notorious for crime and best avoided at night, this sometimes confusing multi-level station lies about 30 mins walk from the old town or 10 mins by taxi.

Other large stations are **Warszawa Wschodnia**, tel: 022 18 34 97, on the east bank of the Vistula (Wista) River, and the western suburban station, **Warszawa Zachodnia**, tel; 022 18 34 97 (3 km west of Centralna, opposite bus station; tel: 23 63 94.).

Getting Around

The River Vistula divides Warsaw with most sights on the west bank, in and around the old town square, and along the lengthy Royal Way. Most sights are walkable but public transport will probably be necessary at some stage.

Tickets

Bus and tram tickets are sold at kiosks marked Bilety MZK and also sometimes by street hawkers, in restaurants, and at the post office. (The newsagent at the station is handy if you've just arrived.) On board, punch both ends of the ticket (once is for a concession fare). Spot checks lead to fines of Zł. 200,000 or more.

Public Transport

The 26 **tram** lines and 150 **bus** lines operate on a grid system. Buses, which are generally crowded, run from 0430–2300 on weekdays. Night buses run every 45 minutes and cost three times the normal fare. **Taxis** should all have a meter. Pick one up from the taxi stands, or, more cheaply, order one by phone. (Radio taxi; tel: 919.)They currently use a multiplier on the meter reading, such as x600, to calculate the fare, as they cannot keep up with inflation.

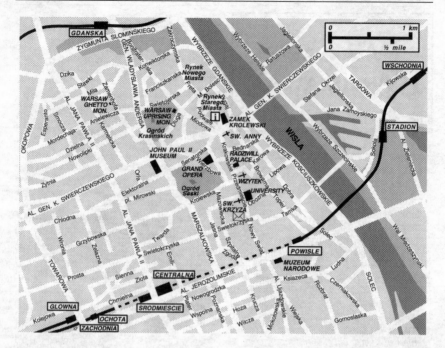

There are plans to open a new metro route from *Ursynów Natolin* to *Polna Str.*

Living in Warsaw

Accommodation

The tourist office leaflet, *Hotels, Warsaw and the environs*, gives details of all accommodation. The more expensive business hotels often charge in dollars. Next step down are Tourist Class Hotels, and there are also some pensions and budget hotels along *Krakówskie Przedmiéscie* and *Nowy Swiąt*. For private rooms, try any of several accommodation bureaux near the station. There are five **hostels**, two belonging to IYHF, at *ul. Smolna 30; tel: 278 952* (central) and *ul. Karolkowa 53a; tel: 328 829* (in Wola suburb, take tram nos.1/13/20 or 24 to *al. Solidarnosci*). There are six **campsites**, although only one is open all year. Hotel chains with property in the city include: *Fo, Hl, Ma, Nv, Ic.*

Eating

Westernisation has resulted in an array of well-known hamburger joints, hot-dog stands, ethnic restaurants and pizzerias. Good Polish food is also increasingly available in the new restaurants, almost all of them exclusively for tourists at prices completely unaffordable to Poles. Look around the Old Square and adjacent streets. During the day outdoor tables and chairs can make this a good place to take a break. The tendency still seems to be towards early closing (about 2100). Booking is advisable if you want to eat much later. Most good restaurants take credit cards.

Communications

The main **post office**, *ul. Swiętokrzyska, 31–33*, is open 0800–2000, for counter facilities and poste restante. Coin phones are being phased out, but the more reliable card-operated phones are still quite thin on the ground.

To phone Warsaw from abroad: *tel: 48 (Poland) + 22 (6 digit nos. in Warsaw) or 2 (7 digit nos. in Warsaw)*; to phone Warsaw from elsewhere in Poland: *tel: 22 (6 digit nos. in Warsaw) or 2 (7 digit nos. in Warsaw)*.

Embassies

Australia: *ul. Estonska 3/5; tel: 17 60 81*
Canada: *ul. Matejki 1/5* (door on *ul. Pieknej*);
tel: 29 80 51
New Zealand: if necessary, contact the UK
embassy.
UK: *Al. Roz 1; tel: 628 10 01-5*
USA: *Al. Ujazdówskie 29/31; tel: 628 30 41-9*

Money

This is still very much a cash economy and many
of the bureaux de change (*kantor*) will not cash
travellers' cheques. Try Orbis Travel (**Thomas
Cook** network member), *Marszalkówka Str.
142*, one of the large hotels, or the branch of
NBP, *pl. Powstancow Warszawy*. Inflation is
rampant and there is talk of a devaluation soon.
If it doesn't happen, keep a careful track of your
zeros. It is illegal for foreigners to receive dollars.
Credit cards are accepted at big hotels, restaurants, and shops catering specifically to tourists. You can get cash advances on credit cards
at Orbis Travel.

Entertainment

There is a good range of entertainment, from
the spit'n'sawdust dives to the chic Irish pub,
and usually dingy discos. There is plenty of live
music, including Polish rock and roll, jazz, and
above all, classical. (See Tourist Information for
entertainment listings).

There are Chopin concerts every Sunday
throughout the summer under Chopin's monument (*Lazienki Park*). There are also several other
venues for concerts, opera and ballet, and a
strong selection of theatres. Cinemas are increasingly showing foreign (i.e. American) films,
usually subtitled not dubbed.

The Soviet **Palac Kultury i Nauki** (Palace of
Culture and Science), a present from Stalin, has
been transformed, now housing a casino,
theatres, cinemas, and a nightclub.

Shopping

Look out for local specialities such as silver,
leather, crystal and, above all, amber, which can
still be a good buy. The best shopping and
window-shopping is amongst the mass of street
vendors around the **Old Market Square**, in
front of the **Palace of Culture** and in the
Russian Market, *10th Anniversary Stadium,
Praga*, where Russian vendors sell off anything
from furs to clothes pegs and war-time
memorabilia. The other really good visit is the
Wola antique market (Sunday only) for clothes,
furniture, and books. Take bus B, K or no.159.
Both the Russian and **Wola** markets are very
crowded by 10am.

Sightseeing

Rynek Starego Miasta

Very much a focal point, this seemingly old
square lined with colourful burghers' houses is
in fact a thoughtful post-war reconstruction.
Any artistic licence used doesn't diminish its
charm. Antique shops and restaurants watch
the daytime bustle but by nightfall it's pretty
quiet. On the north side the **Muzeum Histor-
yczne M. St. Warszawy** (Warsaw Historical
Museum) chronicles the city's turbulent history.
There is a short film, *Warsaw After All*, soon to
be updated with a post-communist chapter. The
Mickiewicz Muzeum (East side) is a shrine to
Polish literature and in particular the romantic
poet of the same name whose national
importance is testified by his burial in Cracow
Cathedral.

South-east, behind the square, the **Archika-
tedra sw. Jana**, another war casualty flattened
by German tanks, has been rebuilt in the original Gothic style. Continue along *Swietojansk* to
pl. Zamkowy, overshadowed by the castle,
Zamek Krolewski. Both royal residence and
Polish parliament, this site was chosen in the
14th century for strategic reasons; today its
importance is largely symbolic. Burnt and
bombed in 1939 and completely demolished
five years later, Nazi damage was only erased in
the 1980s when rebuilding work was completed. Tours of the castle reveal the majestic
interiors and a cellar full of silver.

North

The 16th-century **Barbakan** fortress was once
part of the city walls, but is now flanked by
artists-come-entrepreneurs. Nearby is the 1855

statue of the **Warsaw Mermaid**, which has become the symbol of the city. From here *ul. Freta* leads to **Rynek Nowego Miasta** (New Market Square) past **sw. Jacka** (St. Jacek's Church) and the **Marie Curie Museum** (no.16). The 18th-century New Square is the quieter and less decorative of the two. On it stands the **Church of the Blessed Sacrament**, founded in 1688 by Queen Maria in memory of her husband's (King Sobieski) victory against the Turks at Vienna.

From the New Square, *ul. Dluga* leads to *pl. Krasinskich*, site of a **Monument and Museum** to the 63-day long **Warsaw Uprising**. They are flanked by the **Raczynski Palace** (south-east) and **Krasinski Palace**, fronting the park.

The Royal Way

The **Krakówskie Przedmiescie** (Royal Way) starts in the **Stare Miasto** (Old Town Square) and heads south for 10 kms, under various names, all the way to **Wilanów**, the royal summer palace. It is the city's main thoroughfare, dotted with historical buildings and noble houses.

The 15th-century **Kościol Sw. Anny** (St Anne's Church), *Krakówskie Przedmiescie 68*, is a stylistic hotch-potch. Inside the walls drip with Baroque and Rococo extravagance. The tower is open for roof-top views.

Passing the **Adam Mickiewicz Monument**, you come to the **Radziwill Palace** (1643) where the Warsaw Pact was signed in May 1955. In the **Saski Gardens** opposite, the **Tomb of the Unknown Soldier** is guarded round the clock.

Commanding *Pl. Teatralny*, the intimidating neo-classical **Grand Opera and Ballet Theatre** (1825–33) faces the **Monument to the Heroes of Warsaw**. Chopin played the organ in the **Kościol Wizytek** (Nuns of the Visitation Church) *Kościol Sw. Krzyza 34*, considered a masterpiece of the Baroque. **Warsaw University**, closed first by the Czar (1831–1915) and then the Nazis,

stands in front of the 17th-century **Kazimierz Palace**. **Kościol Swiętego Krzyza** (Holy Cross Church) has local affection as the resting place of Chopin's heart (in an urn on the left column by the nave). The **Copernicus Monument** by the great Dane Thorvaldsen marks the **Staszic Palace**, now the Polish Academy of sciences.

Museums

Pride of place amongst the many museums goes to the **Muzeum Narodowe** (National Museum), *al. Jerozolimskie 3*, home to an excellent collection of paintings successfully hidden during the war. The **Ethnographic Museum**, *ul. Kredytowa 1*, didn't fare so well and lost its collection, but has been restocking with worldwide tribal items and Polish folk art. The new **John Paul II Museum**, *pl. Bankowy*, has a huge collection of thematically arranged religious art and great European works, from Titian and Tintoretto to Breughel, Rembrandt and Rodin. It is also possible to tour the royal palaces, the neo-Classical **Lazienski Palace**, *Lazienski Park*, and the grand **Wilanów Palace**, on the outskirts of town (bus nos.122, 130, 180, 193 and 422).

Jewish Warsaw

Before the war, Warsaw had one of Europe's largest Jewish communities, living mainly in the **Muranów** and **Mirów** districts. Under Nazi occupation, numbers fell from 380,000 to only 300. There are two great monuments – to the **Heroes of the Warsaw Ghetto**, *ul. Zamenhofa*, and the white marble monument to **Concentration Camp Victims**, *Umschlarplatz*, at the spot where hundreds of thousands of Jews were herded onto trains bound for the nearby camps.

The **Jewish Historical Institute**, *ul. Thomackie 3/5*, has a museum detailing the story of the desperate and brave Jewish resistance. **Nozyk**, *ul. Twarda*, is the only remaining synagogue.

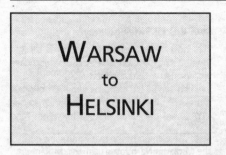

WARSAW to HELSINKI

This route takes you through a rolling and sparse wilderness of solitary houses tucked amidst silver birch trees, to the capital cities of the three newly independent Baltic states. A few years ago this journey would have been webbed in bureaucracy and virtually impossible for any Westerner, although the area was popular with Soviet holidaymakers.

TRAINS

ETT tables: 93, 900, 919, 914, 1295, 1296.

→ Fast Track

There is no really fast track. The fastest possible route will be Warsaw–Tallinn, and Tallinn–Helsinki by boat (see On Track), taking over 24 hours.

Warsaw (Warszawa)–Tallinn

The Balti Ekspress (one daily; reservation needed) is the fastest service; it currently takes 22 hrs 30 mins, but improvements to the service in 1994 may take as much as 5 hrs off this time. It has first- and second-class sleepers, and a dining-car. Unfortunately, due to different track gauges, you cannot avoid having to change trains at the Lithuanian border station of Šeštokai.

For ferries to Helsinki, *see On Track.*

∿ On Track

Warsaw (Warszawa)–(Border)–(Belarus)–(Border)–Vilnius

The easiest and recommended way to make this approx. 13-hr journey is by overnight sleeper. The change of trains at Šeštokai (see above) will prevent unbroken sleep, however.

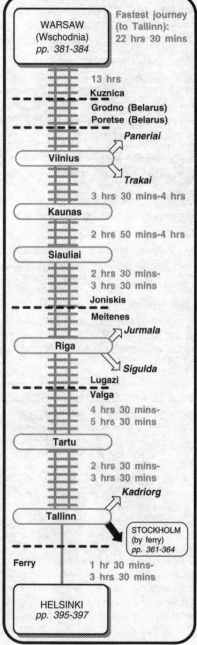

WARSAW (Wschodnia) pp. 381-384

Fastest journey (to Tallinn): 22 hrs 30 mins

13 hrs
Kuznica
Grodno (Belarus)
Poretse (Belarus)

Paneriai

Vilnius

Trakai

3 hrs 30 mins-4 hrs

Kaunas

2 hrs 50 mins-4 hrs

Siauliai

2 hrs 30 mins-
3 hrs 30 mins
Joniskis
Meitenes

Jurmala

Riga

Sigulda
Lugazi
Valga

4 hrs 30 mins-
5 hrs 30 mins

Tartu

2 hrs 30 mins-
3 hrs 30 mins

Kadriorg

Tallinn

STOCKHOLM (by ferry) pp. 361-364

Ferry

1 hr 30 mins-
3 hrs 30 mins

HELSINKI pp. 395-397

Vilnius–Kaunas

Six fast trains, running mostly overnight, take about 2 hrs. Frequent but slower day trains take 3 hrs 30 mins–4 hrs.

Kaunas–Šiauliai

This service runs about every two hours 0900–1700, taking 2 hrs 50 mins–3 hrs 50 mins. Six trains run daily, but three are overnight (taking 3–4 hrs).

Šiauliai–(Border)–Riga

Five trains run daily, taking 2 hrs–2 hrs 30 mins.

Riga–(Border)–Tartu

Three trains run daily, taking 4hrs 30 mins–5 hrs 30 mins.

Tartu–Tallinn

There are seven trains a day. The journey takes between 2 hrs 30 mins and 3 hrs 30 mins.

Tallinn–Helsinki

The crossing by ferry takes about 3 hrs 30 mins, and 1 hr 30 mins by hydrofoil. You can also sail direct to Stockholm (sailings are every other day, overnight).

VILNIUS

Station: the **Stotis** (station), *tel: (8) 63 00 88*, is a hang-out for local hobos and not a good place to linger although you can buy cheap bananas here – a fact surprisingly worth knowing. Buying tickets can be confusing, complicated and frustrating so make sure you have time to spare.
Buses: the main **bus station**, *tel: 26 24 82*, is next door to the station.
Tourist Office: Vilnius has no tourist information office, so you should pick up the candid and essential *Vilnius in your pocket* (*VIYP*), on sale in the station and all over town. A joint venture by Lithuanian, Belgian and American writers, it gives hotel, restaurant and bar reviews and some sightseeing information in a style far livelier than that of the city.

Getting Around

The most attractive part of the city is the old town. Public transport isn't essential if you have well-located accommodation.

There are 50 bus lines and some 20 trolleybus routes. For the only public transport map see *VIYP*. Use the same tickets for buses and

Travelling by train in the Baltics

Many of the trains (read 'benches on wheels') are still Russian-run, with large Babushkas supervising the coal buckets and listening to the radio in their relative havens of comfort at the end of each carriage. Once the speakers in the carriage are switched on, only a Walkman could save you in the battle of volume control. But while your journey might not always be this melodious it will certainly be slow. Counting the blades of grass outside is one way to pass the time. Or you could try communicating with said Babushka on the topic of why you can't find a toilet. (They are sometimes locked, but if need be write WC on a piece of paper and wave it around.) You will also get some entertainment when the ticket inspector comes around. Just as you were congratulating yourself on your nice, cheap, uncomplicated pass, you realise that he has no idea what it is (check on the back for an explanation in all the Baltic languages).

Chances are you will cross a border at some point. The train will stop and teenagers with uniform and attitude sneer at passports as their team mates search your rucksack for stowaways. On night journeys this is done by torchlight but in an equally gruff manner. Forget all you've ever read about the Citizens Charter, these boys are second in command to the President – one assumes. Go well prepared, be laid-back about the whole affair and you will be spell-bound by the countryside and those around you.

trolleybuses, on sale in kiosks and from buses displaying the words *parduodami bilietai* (here you must buy at least five). Validate tickets on board. Buses and trolleybuses run 0500–0030.

Living in Vilnius

Accommodation

VIYP lists details of various hotels, pensions and hostels from £100 a night to £2 or less. There is a **youth hostel information office** 300m straight ahead from the station. To stay at one of the three youth hostels you need to buy a Lithuanian Hostel Association Card, available from the hostels for 20 litas. To **camp**, you will have to go to *Trakai*, 25km out of town.

Communications

The central **post office**, *Gedimino pr 7; tel: 61 66 14*, opens Mon–Fri 0800–2000, and Sat and Sun 1100–1900. Phoning abroad can still be a problem, but a trip to the modern **exchange**, *Gedimino 7* (better than the 24-hour exchange at *Vilniaus 33*) will probably get you through.

Eating

The cheapest food is from street stalls selling sausage rolls, bananas and small pizzas. Vilnius has a remarkable selection of good restaurants (mostly non-smoking), which are increasingly out of the price range of locals. Prices can (but rarely do) reach parity with Western restaurants but the quality is then correspondingly better. Generally speaking, what's for sale in the shops is far less tempting and certainly less varied. Restaurants can close early. For watered-down beer and atmosphere on tap, visit Vilnius's beer bars (see *VIYP* for details).

Embassies

Australia: none, nearest are Moscow or Warsaw
Canada: none, nearest is Riga, see p 389.
New Zealand: none, nearest is Moscow
UK: *2 Antakalnio Gatve; tel: (2) 22 20 70*
US: *Akemnu 6; tel: 22 30 31*

Shopping

Vilnius has yet to be flooded with Western imports but a trip to one of the hard currency stores will serve as a reminder of brand names you left behind and the cheap fashions of yesteryear. In many other stores, the solitary dangling garments point to the Soviet past and current dire economic straits. Gift shops selling handicrafts and amber proliferate behind unmarked doors in the old town. The main shopping street is *Pilies.*

Security

Streets empty at about 2000. Areas to avoid on your own at night are *Uzupio* and *Kalvariju* and the station.

Sightseeing

Vilnius is serene, green and dilapidated, with churches on almost every street corner, the occasional empty window pane framing houses full of rubble and a pastoral quality absent in either Tallinn or Riga.

The old town is easily explored on foot. Make time to wander in the tucked-away, quiet and crumbling side streets. Museums close on Mondays, Tuesdays or weekends.

Castle Hill, overlooking the city, is a good place to get your bearings, but for an even better view climb the sole surviving tower of **Gedimino Castle**. Built in the 14th century and 48 m high, the Lithuanian tricolour was hoisted here in October 1988, as a deeply symbolic act of independence. Archaeological finds from the 13th–16th-century castle are on display in the small tower museum **Vilniaus pilies muziejus**.

Katedos aikste (*Cathedral Square*) is the focal point for the town and the site of anti-Soviet mass-demonstrations in the run-up to independence. The **Arkikatedra Bazilika** (Cathedral), was originally dedicated to the god of thunder. Reconstructed 11 times, the latest in 1777–1801, in the classical style, it spent 30 years under Communism as an art gallery. The Baroque **Kazimieras Chapel** inside is worth a visit. Behind the Cathedral, the popular **Kalnu Park** is a shady, stream-side sanctuary, which leads to the church of Sts Peter and Paul.

Churches

Sŷ. Petro ir Povilo Baznycias (Sts Peter and Paul), *Antakalnio 1*, is the supreme example of

Baroque church architecture in Lithuania. The interior is decorated with over 2000 lively stucco figures.

Sŷ. Onos (St Anne's), *Maironio 8*, is an equally eminent example of Gothic church architecture, with an intricate and delicate construction using 33 different types of brick. The oldest Baroque church **Sŷ. Kazimiero** (St Casimir's), *Didzioji 34*, takes its name from Lithuania's patron saint. It was, ironically, used as a *Museum of Atheism* under the Soviets.

Museums

The **Lietuvos nacionalinis muziejus** (Museum of National Culture and History), *Arsenalo 1*, traces Lithuania's fascinating story from the Stone Age to the inter-war period of independence.

Lietuvos valstybinis žydu muziejus, *Pamenkalnio 12*, (the State Jewish Museum) follows chronologically. Pre-war Vilnius was one of Europe's greatest centres of Jewry (in 1914 30% of the population was Jewish) with a strong publishing and intellectual tradition. During World War II, 95% of Vilnius's Jewish population was killed and 96 synagogues were destroyed.

A reminder of Soviet occupation, the **KGB museum**, *Gedimino 40*, is guided by former inmates of the prison, spared the fate of thousands in Siberia.

There are two museums displaying Lithuanian art, **Lietuvos dailes muziejus** (the Lithuanian Art Museum), *Didžioji 31*, and the folk art **National Gallery**, *Studentu 8*.

The 12-courtyard **university** is one of Vilnius's most elegant classical complexes. Its history begins in the 17th century but it was closed down for nearly a century (1832–1919) by the Tsarist regime. **St John's Courtyard** is dominated by its church, organ-like with its multi-storeyed pillars. In an adjoining courtyard, look out for the observatory tower (1569).

◠ Side Tracks from Vilnius

One hundred thouand people, 70% of them Jews, were murdered by the Nazis at **Paneriai**, 10km from Vilnius. This is now the site of the **Paneriu muziejus** (the Museum of Genocide), *Agrastu 17*. Set in the forest, the grassed-over death pits serve as a chilling reminder.

32km from Vilnius, Lithuania's former capital, **Trakai**, is distinguished by its red-brick 14th-century fortress, which stands on an island surrounded by five lakes. Local trains run to Trakai from Vilnius.

KAUNAS

Station: the city stretches out north-west from the station, *tel: 22 10 93*, parallel with the banks of the river Nemunas.

Tourist Office: none, but fresh from the people that brought you *Vilnius in Your Pocket* comes *Kaunas in Your Pocket*, available at kiosks, bookshops and hotels.

Getting Around

Kaunas has two distinct centres of gravity: **Senamiestis** (the old town), a peninsula bordered by the converging Neris and Nemunas Rivers; and **Naujamiestis** (the new town).

Trolleybuses and more numerous buses both exist but aren't strictly necessary. The distance across town is only 3–4 kms. Buy tickets from kiosks and validate them on board.

Accommodation and Food

With only two hotels that promise constant hot water and only six in total, deciding where to stay should be relatively easy. There are also a few hostels.

Restaurants are more numerous: check *Kaunas in Your Pocket* for listings and reviews.

Sightseeing

Lithuania's second largest city and the interim capital under Polish Occupation (1920–40), Kaunas is described as more typically Lithuanian than Vilnius. It has also succumbed relatively little to the ravages of a war-riddled history. All museums are free on Wednesdays.

From the remains of the 14th-century **castle**, wander down to the much better preserved **Rotušes aikste** (Town Hall Square). Over 25% of the 16th-century houses that edge the square, of which Gildija (no.3) is the oldest, have been restored. In the middle of the square, a 53m-high, white-tiered Baroque spire marks the **Town Hall**. On the south side of the square is a **Jesuit monastery**, used as a school under the Soviets, but now returned to its rightful owners.

South, on the banks of the River Nemunas, stands **St Vytautas Church**, Lithuania's biggest, dating to the 1400s. The single-towered **cathedral**, now a basilica, marks the junction of *Vilniaus gatve* which leads into the new town.

The central pedestrianised avenue, *Laisves aleja* (Freedom Avenue) leads up to the beautiful blue and white **orthodox church** on *Independence Square*. Along the avenue, a slab in front of the Music Theatre marks the spot where the 19-year-old Romas Kalanta immolated himself in protest against the Soviet regime. The monument obliquely opposite represents Vytautas the Great slaying his enemies – Russian, Pole, Tartar and German soldiers lie vanquished beneath him.

At 64 *Putvinskio gatve*, the **Žmuidzinavičius Collection** (Devils Museum), houses 1700 devil statues, including Hitler and Stalin, collected from 1876 onwards. By *Unity Square*, take the **funicular** up to *Aleksopo* and *Žaliakalnif*, very near to **Christ's Resurrection Church**, for a great view.

On the northern perimeter of Kaunas, *Žemaičiu plentas 73*, a museum and powerful memorial sculptures mark the **Ninth Fort**, where the Nazis massacred tens of thousands. Lithuania's main open-air museum, **Rumšiškes**, lies 12 km east of town.

ŠIAULIAI

Station: the **station**, *tel: 30652*, is a short walk from the pedestrianised town centre.
Tourist Office: the office at *Vapori 22A; tel: 34509*, can help with accommodation, guides, and maps. Open Mon–Fri 0900–1800.

Sightseeing

Founded in 1236, Šiauliai is Lithuania's fourth-largest town, named after the battle of Saule, where Lithuanians defeated the German Livonian Knights.

Most visitors to Šiauliai come to witness the extraordinary **Hill of Crosses**, some 10 km north of the town. The Pope's visit caused much publicity but the importance of these 80,000 crosses lies more as a symbol of resistance, hope and suffering, than as an overt sign of Catholic worship. The origins are obscure although the highly decorative crosses show strong Pagan accents. But it is the Soviet failure to extinguish this spiritual torch that is most remarkable. Each time the crosses were bulldozed, they would slowly reappear again, planted mostly under the cover of darkness. Guards took note of visiting cars and the hill was surrounded by polluted water, but these, and other measures were equally ineffective. What is equally staggering, considering the number of crosses, is that those standing today have all been planted since 1975.

Šiauliai itself is somewhat devoid of historical sights, although it does have a Renaissance **Church of Sts Peter and Paul**, at the junction of *Tilzes* and *Ausros Aleja*, with one of the tallest spires in Lithuania (70m). In **Sun Clock Square**, at the bottom of *S. Salkausko*, a tall fluted column supporting a golden eagle, functions as a huge sundial. The **Photography Museum**, *Vilniaus gatve 140*, verges on the unexciting but accompanying local exhibitions might make the stop pay off. Finally, head towards the charmingly eccentric **Cat Museum**, *Zuvininku gatve*, which features such humble exhibits as a tin of cat food.

RIGA

Station: Riga has one main station, **Stacijas laukums**, *tel: (2) 007*, a few minutes walk from the old town.
Buses: buses are a better form of transport than trains in Latvia. The **Autosta** (main bus station), *tel: (2) 213 611*, is a good centre for both long-distance and city buses. Turn left as you leave the railway station.
Tourist Office: the **Latvian Tourist Board** *4 Pils sq; tel: (2) 22 99 45*, open Mon–Fri 0900–1800, is opposite the unremarkable Castle. To get there from the station, follow the Daugava River north as far as **Vansu Tilts** (the old bridge). **Latvian Youth Tourism:** *2 kr., Barona str; tel: (2) 22 53 07*. Don't be misled by the blue signs with a white letter 'i' (for information) at the station and around town. These will lead you to a travel

agent. Other sources of infor-mation include the post office near the Freedom Monument, and the Hotel Riga, Hôtel de Rome and the gifts section of the bookshop (no.24), all on *Aspazijas Bulv.*

Riga This Week is a big disappointment to anyone familiar with *Tallinn This Week* or *Vilnius in Your Pocket*, but it's still probably worth the extortionate US$1 charge. For sightseeing, get hold of *A Day in Riga*.

Getting Around

The very crowded red **buses**, black **trams** and blue **trolleybuses** operate 0530–0100. Tickets are on sale in kiosks and should be punched on board. Fares are calculated by zone, (tickets with a red line for zone 1, a green line for zone 2 and a yellow line for zone 3). Most tourist destinations are in zone 1; the airport is in zone 3.

There are many **taxi** ranks, but those outside the big hotels tend to be more expensive. State taxis (white with a green sign) have fixed fares. Private taxis do not always have meters and are open to negotiation. Agree a price before travelling. Journeys after 2200 are 50% more expensive.

Living in Riga

Accommodation

Riga's pockets of wealth include several three- and four-star hotels that make up the backbone of the city's accommodation. Most are cheaper than in the West, but some still cost more than US$100 a night.

For cheaper options, try the **private accommodation agency**, *Elizabetes 4; tel: (2) 331 473* (only one of the two women who run this speaks English). **IYHF:** *Laiudotas iela 2A; tel: (2) 55 12*

Communications

The main **Post Office**, *Brivibas bulv. 21*, near the Freedom Monument, is open 24 hours and has plenty of telephone cabins (pay after the call). To use other public phones, buy tokens from the kiosks or post office.

Eating

For local colour and authenticity, the 1930s

Central Market, *Negu iela 7*, (behind the station) looks like an aircraft hangar and is unmissable. Avoid gawping and taking photos and breathe in the heady mix of cheeses and smoked meats. Eating outside is easy, Riga is relatively green. Try the area around the Freedom Monument, or the Kronvalda Parks and Esplanade.

Meat is still in short supply but money talks and delicious food is surprisingly easy to come by in the hotel restaurants (which do offer some regional dishes, specially for tourists). New restaurants are opening weekly. The area around St Mary's Cathedral is a good place to look both for these and for the numerous cafés dotted all over the old town.

As elsewhere in the Baltics, avoid expensive imported produce. Most internationally recognised chocolate bars are on sale, as are things like orange juice. However, as one example, you can get ten local apple juices for the price of a glass of orange. Riga's *Black Balsam* isn't a hair conditioner but a mix of cognac, ginger and oak bark, drunk with vodka or coffee. Another local speciality is a particular brown bread, sometimes used with cream to make soup.

Embassies

Australia: none, the nearest are Warsaw or Moscow
Canada: *Elizabetes iela 45/47; tel: 883 0141*
New Zealand: none, the nearest is Moscow
UK: *Elizabetes iela 2; tel: 320 737*; changing to *Alunana 5* in Aug 94
USA: *Raina bulv. 7; tel: 210005*

Sightseeing

A silhouette of spires behind the Dauga River, a gabled, recently renovated Old Town, and Europe's largest collection of Art Nouveau buildings – Riga is physically the most cosmopolitan of the Baltic capitals. It all suggests a wealth which eludes the people of today, as they struggle with the fall-out of independence.

A wander through the old streets in central Riga takes in most of the city's architectural beauties. Museums are often closed on Mondays and sometimes Tuesdays.

The **Vecriga** (old town) lies sandwiched

between the old moat and the Pilsetas canals. For a view over the rooftops head for **Petera Baznica** (St Peter's Church), *Skarnu iela 19*, named after Riga's patron saint. Although first built here in 1209, the prototype of its elegant steeple was only completed in 1694. It has since been twice destroyed and rebuilt, in the wake of lightning (in the 18th century) and by German bombs (in 1941). The 120m steeple is crowned by a weather rooster the size of a pig.

The striking skyline is dominated by the **Doma Baznica** (St Mary's Cathedral), *Doma laukums 1*, on the city's central square, and the green spire of **St Jekabs** (St Jacob's Church). The organ (1883) and the stained glass are St Mary's most impressive features, best enjoyed while listening to one of the many organ concerts. The cathedral is flanked by the light brown **Latvia Radio House** and the **Stock Exchange**. It was to the Cathedral Square that Latvians came to protest for freedom in 1990.

Immured in the walls of **Jana Baznica** (the Church of St John), *24 Skarnu iela*, are the bodies of two 13th-century monks, buried alive to fulfill a local superstition and ensure the church would stand forever. From the churchyard you can see part of the city wall.

The **'Three Brothers'**, *17, 19,* and *21 M Pils iela* are the most famous of Riga's old houses. The earliest, with the small windows, is from the 15th century.

The rather run-down **Riga Castle**, *Pils laukums 3*, is worth visiting mainly for its Museums of **Latvian History, Foreign Art** and **Latvian Literature**. Plans are afoot for the building to resume a role in government.

The **Pulvertornis** (Gun Powder Tower), *Torna iela*, was initially part of the city wall. It earned its name in the 16th century, when it was used to store huge quantities of the lethal powder, turning it into a potentially monumental bomb. Today it houses the **Latvian War Museum**.

The **Brivibas Piemnieklis** (Freedom Monument), *Brivibas Bulv.*, is a highly symbolic, 42 m obelisk, commissioned in 1922 during a brief gasp of freedom. (Latvia has lived for centuries in an almost perpetual state of occupation from Germans, Swedes and more recently Nazis and Russians.) During the years of Soviet occupation the area was prohibited, but the monument itself was, surprisingly, never dismantled.

The **Motormuzejas** (Riga Motor Museum), *S Eizenšteina iela 6*, shows the history of motor-car engineering and numbers in its collection the personal cars of Stalin and Brezhnev.

Side Tracks from Riga

Jurmala, Latvia's seaside resort, 20km west of Riga, has been a popular holiday destination since the early 19th century. The name, meaning sea-shore, applies to a string of towns and resorts that hug the beach, sand dunes and pine woods beside a heavily polluted sea. Swimming unfortunately (or perhaps luckily) is prohibited. Nevertheless this is a hugely popular destination. Jurmala is reached by train (1–3 every hour), or by boat along the Lielupe and Daugava Rivers.

Sigulda is an equally popular antithesis to city life. Thick with greenery, and dotted with caves and castles, Sigulda overlooks the Gauja River valley and is known as the Latvian Switz-erland. In winter people come here to ski and in summer for walking and boating.

Sigulda Castle (1207) stands in tatters. Behind it, the 19th-century **New Castle** is now a sanatorium. From the town, a bridge and cable cars, 40 m above the river, cross to the north bank. A short walk east from here are **Krimulda Castle**, **Turaida Castle** (whose red-brick tower offers an excellent view), and **Gutmanis Cave**, daubed with 300-year-old graffitti. Bob-sleighing and skiing are also available. Reached by bus or train from Riga.

TARTU

Station: *tel: 30967*, a short walk from Toomemagi Hill.
Tourist Office: *Küütri 3; tel: 321 41*. This is open Mon–Fri 1000–1800.. It stocks pocket guides to the town, an erratic collection of literature, dictionaries and glossy Western magazines.

Sightseeing

Estonia's second-largest town is surprisingly small, but richly packed with a cultural heritage that, for some, makes it the *real* capital. The town's fame stems largely from its university, first founded by the Swedes in 1632. It was closed between 1700 and 1832 but today 8,000 students attend its courses. The yellow, white and pillared main university building, **Ulikooli**, *Ulikooli 18*, is considered Estonia's best neo-Classical piece.

Round the corner, the sloping, cobbled **Raeckoja Plats** (*Town Hall Square*) is supervised by the pink and white Dutch-style **Town Hall** (1782–89) and flanked by low, brightly coloured classical houses.

Overlooking the square, **Toomemagi Park** covers an area larger than the old town. Statues of famous Estonians, monuments and the roofless, windowless Gothic cathedral punctuate the English-style park. **Inglisild** (Angel's bridge) and **Kuradisild** (Devil's Bridge) earn their names from linguistic confusion. The word 'Angel' was confused with 'English' and 'Devil's Bridge' is the unfortunate translation of the name of the man who pioneered the use of rubber gloves in surgery.

For some local history visit the **Museum of the University** in the Cathedral's former choir or **Estonian National Museum** at *Veski 32*.

TALLINN

Station: Balti jaam, *tel: (2) 624 058, is a 10-min walk from the centre, and can also be reached by tram no. 1 and bus no. 22. The station is currently being modernised.*

Ferries: there are ferries to Helsinki and Stockholm from the **Tallinna Reisisadam** (harbour), a 15-min walk from the city centre (also accessible by tram nos.1/2 or bus no.65). For ferries to Helsinki, contact **Tallink**, *tel: (2) 442 440.* For the hydrofoil to Helsinki, contact **Estonian New Line**, *tel: (2) 428 382 (reservations); (2) 493 095 (information). Departures from Tallinn Linnahall.*

Buses: there is a good network of local and long-distance buses in Estonia, often faster than the train but more expensive. The main bus station, **Maaliinide Autobussijaam**, *is at Lastekodu 46; tel: (2) 42 25 49.*

Tourist Office: there is a helpful **City Tourist Office** at *Raeckoja Square 18; tel: (2) 44 88 86,* (due to move to no.8 sometime in 1994). Open Mon–Fri 0900–1700, and Sat and Sun 1000–1500 (often 1 hr later in summer). Here you can get maps, books, guides, travel information and a free sheet listing cheap accommodation. The **Ageba travel agency** in the station sells the amazingly useful *Tallinn This Week* and will help find accommodation.

Getting Around

Getting around on foot is no problem, although the climb through the cobbled streets of the old town can be quite steep. Maps are easy to find (see tourist information).

Buses, trams and **trolleybuses** skirt around the old town. Tickets can be bought in advance from kiosks (at the station, look for the one with tickets stuck in the window) and should be punched on board. Single tickets are valid for one journey, on one form of transport. The only available passes are monthly, with a student discount on production of an ISIC Card.

Living in Tallinn

Accommodation

The suitably named Palace Hotel is certainly not typical of what's currently on offer, although there is a building boom underway and most hotels are in the process of making much needed renovations. For the moment, those seeking modest accommodation will find more choice, and it is always advisable to book ahead. Check you have hot water and that your room is satisfactory before moving in. The further out of town you go, the cheaper it gets.

For **hostel**-style accommodation, **Hotel Agnes**, *Narva mnt. 7; tel: (2) 438 870,* is clean, if spartan, and well located. For Youth Hostels, contact **Estonian Youth Hostels**, *Liivalaia 2; tel: (2) 44 10 96.* Student accommodation is available in the summer months from **Kloostrimetsa Camp**, *Kloostrimetsa 56A; tel: (2) 23 86 86.* The **Family Hotel Association**, *Mere puiestee 6; tel: (2) 441 187,* will find 'upper-middle-class' families with spare rooms to rent and sometimes whole apartments.

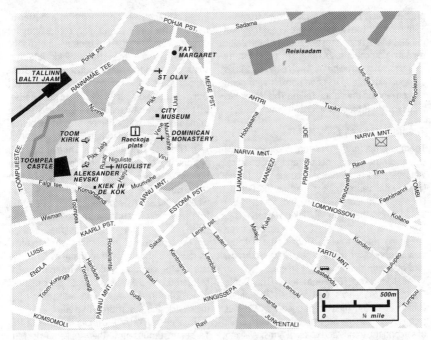

Communications

The central **post office**, *Narva maantee 1; tel: 442 347*, is open Mon–Fri 0800–2000, and Sat 0800–1700. You can also get stamps at big hotels and the tourist office.

Pay phones in the street are being abandoned and will eventually be replaced with card phones. International calls are still quite difficult but try the ground floor of the post office; open daily 0700–2200.

Eating and Drinking

The old town is full of cafés and restaurants and the best thing to do is browse until one takes your fancy. There are still some fairly grim old-style Soviet establishments, but a new generation of more user-friendly places is rising rapidly. Tea-time could well be the best part of the day if you go to **Maiasmokk**, *16 Pikk*.

Embassies

Australia, **New Zealand:** none; if necessary apply to the British Embassy
Canada: *13 Toom-Kooli, Tompea; tel: 44 90 56*

UK: *20 Kentimanni; tel: 455 328*
USA: *20 Kentmanni; tel: 31 20 20 or 45 50 05*

Entertainment

Art exhibitions and concert performances are prolific. For listings, look in *Tallinn This Week*. Theatre and cinema trips for foreigners are more than likely to involve language difficulties, as films are usually Russian, with Estonian sub-titles.

Instead, try a sauna, an integral part of Estonian culture. The more expensive hotels usually have one (the Olympia has large windows and a fantastic view). Public saunas are probably cheaper and a good way to meet and mix with the locals. Ask at the tourist office.

Sightseeing

Independent since August 1991, Estonia stands face to face with Finland, and of everywhere in the Baltic, the gallop towards capitalism seems most obvious in Tallinn. (Nowhere else will you find a guidebook to shopping.) Though it has suffered in the interim, with only 22 years of independence in nearly seven centuries, Tallinn prospered as a Hanseatic trading town from the 13th century. Today, its well-preserved medieval remains make it the most beautiful of the Baltic capitals. You could rush around in a day, but try to spend longer. *Tallinn, A Travel Guide* (21 kr) is a useful, illustrated, 70-page booklet with good background on the sights. **Tallinn This Week** has an adequate if much briefer run-down.

Toompea (The Upper Town)

Toompea, the fortified hill-top, was traditionally home of the rulers, gentry and ecclesiastics. Whoever had most recently conquered Tallinn (Estonia has variously been part of the Danish, Livonian (German), Swedish and Soviet orbit) would hoist their flag on **Pikk Herman** (Tall Herman), at 50m the tallest of the castle's three remaining round towers. From Castle Hill, the view of the lower town is of yellows and reds, roof tiles, and slender church steeples.

At *Toom kooli 6*, **Toom kirik** (The Dome Church or St Mary's Cathedral) is the oldest church in Tallinn (first mentioned in 1233 but reconstructed after a fire in 1684). Inside, it is full of sarcophagi, tombs and coats of arms. Walking south onto *Lossi plats* reveals the stylistically maverick **Aleksander Nevski** (Russian Orthodox Church), crowned by fig-like domes.

Downhill, **Kiek in de Kök** (literally 'peep in the kitchen'), *1 Komandandi*, is a round tower with walls four metres thick. It gained its joke-name because the watchmen could supposedly see from here into the homes below. There is a branch of the **City Museum** inside, which includes regular photographic displays.

Vanalinn (The Lower Town)

Pikk jalg leads into the lower town, the heart of which is the **Raeckoja plats** (*Town Hall Square*). Whippings and market stalls once animated this spacious square dominated by the **Raeckoja**. This is Europe's oldest town hall (1371–1404), arcaded, with narrow windows and crowned by an awkwardly thin 17th-century steeple. The attached weather vane is of Vana Toomas (Old Thomas), the patron saint of Tallinn. The **Raeapteek** pharmacy at no.11 was in the hands of the Burchart family for over 350 years and the adjacent passageway **Saia kang** (White-bread passage) was once home to a cluster of bakeries. The lower town's glory comes from the ornate 15th- and 16th-century merchants' houses that line the streets. **Pikk jalg** has some of the best. **Ajaloomuuseum** (the State History Museum) is at no.17 (once the Great Guild House). Number 24 was also a guild house, that of the Brotherhood of Blackheads, the unmarried merchants named after their patron saint, the African St Mauritius. Further down *Pikk jalg*, **Oleviste kirik** (St Olaf's Church) has two patrons: the Norwegian king, Olaf, and Olev the builder, who braved contemporary superstition to construct the steeple and fell to his death when doing so. As prophesied, a snake and a frog were seen emerging from the mouth of the fallen Olev. Tallinn is still equipped with a surprising number of the bastions which fortified its town wall (there were as many as 60 in the late 16th century. **Paks Margareeta** (Fat Margaret), *70 Pikk*, is a stout, pock-marked tower 24m in diameter, with walls nearly 5m thick enclosing a **maritime museum**.

Parallel to *Pikk jalg*, *Lai jalg* is home to the **Tarbekunstimuuseum** (the Applied Arts Museum), at no.17, while the group of burghers' houses at nos.38–40 are nicknamed 'The Three Brothers' on account of their masculine appearance. The **Tallinna linnamuuseum** (City Museum), *Vene 17*, houses an exhibition of 18th–19th-century Tallinn and 14th–18th-century crafts, in a 15th-century merchant's house.

Amongst Tallinn's best churches are the **Dominiiklaste Klooster** (Dominican Monastery), *Vene 16*, housing a collection of stone carvings; the essentially 15th-century **Niguliste kirik** (Church of St. Nicholas), *Niguliste 13*, with sacred art exhibits; and the **Puhavaimu kirik** (Holy Ghost Church) at *Puhavaimu 2*.

- - - - - - - - - - - - - - - - - - - -
Side Tracks from Tallinn

Kadriorg, 2 km from Tallinn, was the royal seaside summer residence built by the Russian Tsar Peter the Great for his Estonian wife Catherine. The palace, a mixture of French and Italian influences, set in **Kadriorg Park**, houses a collection of 50,000 works of Estonian art.

- - - - - - - - - - - - - - - - - - - -

HELSINKI

Station: the well-equipped Art Deco station, *tel: 1010 115*, links up with the labyrinthian metro stop at **Rautatientori** (*Railway Square*).
Ferries: there are many sailings each day to Tallinn and several to Stockholm. **Silja Line:** *Mannerheimintie 2; tel: (90) 18041.* **Viking Line:** *Mannerheimintie 14; tel: (90) 12351.* If you arrive at the Olympia terminal, tram nos.3T or 3B run into town frequently. From **Katajan-okka** passenger terminal, take tram no.4. Viking Line run a courtesy bus from the harbour to the station.
Airport: Vantaa Airport, *tel: 9700 8100*, is 20 km north. The Finnair bus departs every 15–20 mins from the station (in front of the post office) from 0500–2400. It takes 30 mins and costs FMk 20. Bus no.615 (also from the station, platform 12) costs FMk 15, takes slightly longer, and operates a shorter day.
Tourist Office: the **City Tourist Office**, *Pohjoisesplanadi 19; tel: 169 3757*, opens May 17– Sept 15, Mon–Fri 0830–1800 and Sat 0830– 1300; Sept 16–May 15, Mon 0830–1630 and Tue–Fri 0830–1600. Collect a copy of the useful, free, English-language brochure *Helsinki This Week*. Nearby, at *Eteläesplanadi 4*, is the **Finnish Tourist Board**, *tel: 4030 1300*. The **Youth information centre**, *Stationstunneln, Kompass; tel: 90 626 846*, opens Mon 0900–1100 and 1400–1600, Tues–Thu 1200–1900, and Fri 1200–1700.

Getting Around

The centre is compact and walkable, but there is a good network of buses and trams, useful for serious sightseeing, and a metro, designed for commuters. Maps are easy to come by; ask at the tourist office, on the ferry, or at the Ageba office (0800–2000) in the port.

Trams

The 3T/3B tram is the same service running on a circular route – the different letters denote whether it is taking the clockwise or anti-clockwise direction. It runs every few minutes, passing all the sightseeing highlights. (Pick up a short commentary from the tourist office).

Tickets

The **Helsinki Card** gives unlimited use of public transport (including boat trips to **Korkeasaari** and **Suomenlinna**); free museum entrance (normally expensive); sightseeing trips; and discounts in shops and restaurants.

The one- (FMk 85), two- (FMk 110) or three- (FMk 130) day card is available from the tourist office, hotel booking office, Stockmann's, the station, airport, some hotels and hostels, and the Silja Line Terminal. Single tickets cost FMk 9 and a ten-trip ticket FMk 75. *Tourist Tickets* are valid on all public transport within the city boundaries for one, three, or five days and cost about a third the price of the Helsinki card. For more information, *tel: 1010 111*.

Living in Helsinki

Accommodation

Accommodation is wide-ranging and varied. There is a **Hotel Booking Centre** at the station, *tel: 171 133*, outside the main concourse by the platforms. Open: June 1–Aug 31, Mon–Sat 0900–1900, Sun 1000–1800; otherwise, Mon– Fri 0900–1700. Only advance bookings are free. The tourist office won't make bookings but has computerised listings, phone cards and a phone box. There are six **youth hostels**. **Camping:** *Rastila; tel: 316 551* from mid-May to mid-Sept (a metro and bus ride 13 km out of town).

Communications

The main **post office**, a paradigm of modern efficiency, is by the station, *Mannerheimintie 11; tel: 1955 117*. Open Mon–Fri 0900–1700; or, for poste restante, Mon–Fri 0800–2100, Sat 0900–1800 and Sun 1100–2100.

Eating

Picnics are a good option (in summer). For supplies visit the markets and the bakeries.
Restaurant recipes come from all over the world but while in Helsinki try Finnish or Russian. Be warned, however, these aren't cheap. Fresh fish is in abundance around the port; for fast food try the *Mannerheimintie* area. Restaurants usually close by 2400–0200.

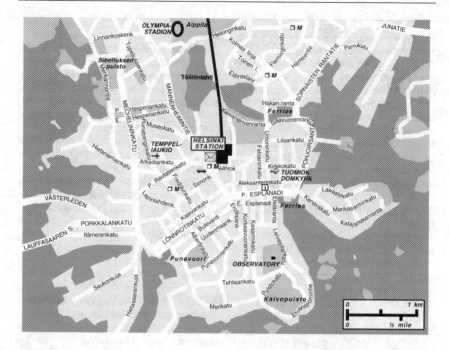

Embassies

Australia: no embassy, but try the Australian Government Information Office, *Museokatu 25A; tel: 447 233*

Canada: *Pohjoisesplanadi 25; tel: 171 141*

New Zealand: none; if necessary, apply to the British Embassy.

UK: *Itainen Puistotie 17; tel: 661 293*

USA: *Itainen Puistotie 14A; tel: 171 931*

Entertainment

Helsinki This Week has two months of listings which include exhibitions, opera, ballet and cinema (all 30 cinemas show films in their original language). In the summer, look out for concerts in the park. Clubs generally close at 0300 or 0400.

Saunas come as an added extra at most public swimming pools.

Shopping

There are two main axes. *Mannerheimintie*, Helsinki's main artery, named after the former head of state Gustaf Mannerheim, is graced by **Stockmann** (the smartest department store in town), other shops, places to eat, lots of people and a few important buildings (see 'Sightseeing'). The tree-lined *Esplanadi* is almost as busy, but the park separating the north, *Pohjoisesplanadi*, from the south, *Eteläesplanadi*, makes it more strollable. The northern section is particularly good for window shopping with a few shops specialising in Finnish design. *Korkeavuorenkatu* is popular with denizens of coffee shops, galleries and second-hand clothes' shops. Amongst the best buys are the beautiful hand-crafted fabrics, silver, and items for the home.

Sightseeing

As part of Sweden from 1155 to 1809, after which Finland fell into the Russian orbit, Helsinki is now a bilingual capital with street names in both Swedish and Finnish. Tsarist rule produced a flurry of building in the neo-Classical style (largely by the architect Engel, and inspired by St

Petersburg). But don't expect a mini-Russia, Finland has been independent for over 75 years and Helsinki is today more Scandinavian in feel.

Museums usually close Mondays, and sometimes Tuesdays.

Markets

Many of the sights are north and west of *Kauppatori* market, a colourful waterside display of fruit, vegetables and flowers. Look out for the semi-clad **Havis Amanda** statue, considered very risqué when she first appeared at the turn of the century. The Victorian indoor market, **Kauppahalli**, *Etelaranta*, is also worth a visit.

Churches

Senaatintori (*Senate Square*) is surrounded by some of Helsinki's best architecture. Above all, the neo-Classical, green-domed *Tuomiokirkko* (Lutheran Cathedral), cuts an imposing figure against the skyline. Largely the work of Engel, his conception was single-domed, but plans were revised after his death and alterations (such as the pediment-gracing statues and copies of Thorvaldsen's work in the Copenhagen *Church of our Lady*) were made. Inside are several figures of great Lutherans, (including the man himself). The cathedral is flanked on the west by the Ionic pillars of the **Yliopisto** (University building) and, to the east, the Corinthian **Valtioneuvosto** (Council of State Building).

The **Temppeliaukiokirkko** (Church in the Rock), *Lutherinkatu 3*, was hewn out of granite rock in 1969, in the middle of a residential square, and capped with a copper-wire dome. It has become one of Helsinki's top sights, but for a more serene experience ask about English-language services.

The Byzantine **Uspensky Cathedral**, *Kanavakatu 1*, red, blue, gold and onion-domed, is a reminder of Finland's Russian past and now serves the Finnish orthodox community.

The chief glory of **Rautatientori** (*Railway Square*) is the station itself, an award-winning piece of art deco architecture. On the north-side

the **Kansallisteatteri** (National Theatre) is an example of the National Romantic style.

Museums

The **Suomen Kansallismuseo** (National Museum), *Mannerheimintie 34*, (another building in the National Romantic style) is an excellent guide to Finnish history and culture with sections on prehistory, history and ethnography. Much of the history of independent Finland coincides with the period of office of Marshal Mannerheim (1917–46), the military commander whose home is now the **Mannerheim Museo**, *Kallionnantie 14*. At no.8, the **Cygnaeuksen taidegalleria** (Cygnaeus Art Collection) is a collection of influential 19th-century national artists.

South of *Railway Square*, the **Valtion taidemuseo** (Finnish National Gallery), *Kaivokatu 2-4*, has the largest collection of paintings, sculpture and drawings in Finland from the late 19th century to the 1960s, with emphasis on the *National awakening*. Cross over the road for the **Helsingin kaupungin taidemuseo** (Helsinki City Art Museum), *Tamminiementie 6*. The **Sinebrychoffin taidemuseo** (Sinebrychoff Museum of Foreign Art), *Bulevardi 40*, has a good Swedish and Russian collection. Further afield, in **Sibeliuksen puisto** (Sibelius Park) is a dignified monument (made of hundreds of steel pipes, resembling an elaborate mouth organ) to the Finnish composer, Jean Sibelius (1865–1957). The 1952 **Olympic Stadium** has a tower (opening 1994) offering a good view of the city.

The Islands

Four main islands hug the Helsinki peninsula. All are connected by ferry or bridge and are popular for walking and sunbathing. **Suomenlinna** has a fine old fortress and several small museums. **Korkeasaari** has a zoo with over 1,000 animals, including snow leopards and Siberian tigers. **Seurasaari** houses Finland's largest open-air museum, with 80 historic buildings (Lapp, Middle Ages, 17th century). **Pihlajasaari** has the area's best beaches.

ZURICH
(ZÜRICH)

Zurich, Switzerland's largest city and one of its most expensive, is an important rail hub, so you may well find you have some time to spend here. If you do, allow a few hours to look round the old town.

Tourist Information

Tourist Office: *Bahnhofplatz 15; tel: (01) 211 40 00.* Daily 0800/0900–2000/2200 (closes 1800 in winter). They issue good street maps and the weekly listing, *Zurich News.*

Arriving and Departing

Stations

Zurich Hauptbahnhof (HB) (*tel: (01) 211 50 10*) is north of the centre, on the west side of the River Limmat. All bus services call here. **Bahnhofstr.** (runs south from HB) is the main area for shops and cafés.

Getting Around

Although it is Switzerland's largest city, Zurich is quite small by European standards and easy to explore on foot. The public transport company is **VBZ Zuri-Line.** Buses and trams leave the terminal by HB every 12 mins (6 mins in peak time) 0530–2400 on all routes. VBZ issue free route plans and tickets are available from machines at every stop. Various **lake cruises** leave from *Burkliplatz.* Information from the counter there (*tel: (01) 482 10 33*), or from the tourist office.

Living in Zurich

Accommodation

There's a wide choice of hotels, so you have a chance of finding something affordable: ask the tourist office for suggestions. Hotel chains with property in the city include: *Ch, Hn, Ra.* **IYHF:**

Mutschellenstr.114; tel: (01) 482 35 44, south of Zurich in Wollishofen (tram nos.7/10: *Morgental,* then 15-mins walk). **Marthahaus,** *Zahringerstr.36; tel: (01) 251 45 50,* is a more convenient private hostel in *Niederdorf* (main nightlife area), which stretches along the eastern bank for about 1 km north of *Münsterbrücke.* **Campsite:** *Seestr.559, Wollishofen; tel: (01) 482 16 12* (bus nos.61/65 from *Burkliplatz*).

Communications

To phone Zurich from abroad: *tel: 41* (Switzerland) + *1* (Zurich); to phone Zurich from elsewhere in Switzerland: *tel: (01).*

Eating and drinking

Eating out in Zurich can be very expensive. The tourist office produce a guide called *Preiswert Essen in Zurich* – Cheap Eats in Zurich. If you are, or look as though you could be, a student, use one of the university mensas (refectories) on *Rämistr.* (71 and 101). Take tram no. 6 from *Bahnhofsplatz* to ETH Zentrum.

Entertainment

There's no shortage of bars and cabarets, and street performers are common. E/d,f against the title of a film indicates that it is in English with German/French subtitles.

Sightseeing

Zurich is a prosperous city, scenically located at the northern tip of Lake Zurich (Zürichsee). The River Limmat runs north/south through the centre, with *Altstadt* (old town) on the east bank and *Bahnhofstr.* on the west. The scenery, open-air cafés, variety of shopping and medieval squares make it a place to enjoy life. The **Uetliberg Railway** from HB goes up to Uto-Kulm (871m), the city's best-known vantage point and one with an excellent view of the Alps. Uetliberg is a good place for a mountain walk: an hour would take you to Albisguetli, from where tram no.13 runs back to the city. **The Swiss National Museum** is just north of HB, in a strange 19th-century building resembling a castle and devoted to Swiss history. Am-ong the exhibits are some fascinating examples of religious art, an impressive display of ancient weaponry and

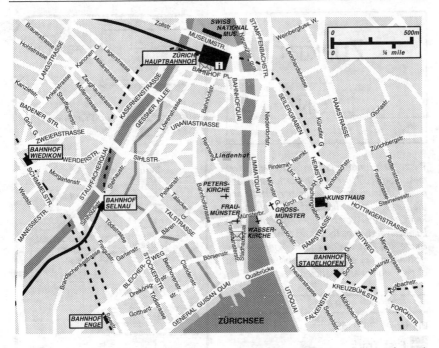

reconstructed rooms from all periods. **Lindenhof**, the highest point of the old city, is a square where remnants of the Roman fortress can still be seen. The 13th-century **Peterskirche**, a little to the south, has a beautifully simple interior and a medieval tower dominated by an enormous 16th-century clock. Further south, at the western end of *Münsterbrücke*, the 13th-century **Fraumünster** is noted for its wonderful Chagall stained glass. Across Münsterbrücke stands **Grossmünster**, *Zwingliplatz*, an old cathedral with modern stained glass, twin towers, octagonal domes and a statue of Charlemagne. Nearby **Wasserkirche (Water Church)**, *Limmatquai 31*, is a lovely late Gothic structure attached to **Helmhaus** (18th-century cloth market). *Limmatquai* (along the eastern river bank) is also the place to see the very ornate **Zunfthäuser**, old guild halls. The **Kunsthaus** (Fine Arts Museum), *Heimplatz* (east of Grossmünster), has a marvellous selection ranging from late Gothic to the 20th century, and including a definitive collection of Giacometti sculptures. **Graphiksammlung**, *Rämistr.101*,

contains superb changing displays of woodcuts, etchings and engravings by such masters as Dürer, Rembrandt, Goya and Picasso. **Museum Rietberg**, *Villa Wesendonck, Gabler-str.15*, just south-west of the centre (tram no.6), contains an outstanding collection of Asian and African art, housed in a building where Wagner once lived.

Side Track from Zurich

The **Principality of Liechtenstein**, independent since 1719, is 80 km south-east of Zurich, on the Austrian border. Trains don't call there, so get off at Sargans or Buchs and take a bus over the border to the capital, **Vaduz**. The full journey takes about 1 hr 30 mins. It's a green and mountainous country covering only 158 sq km, with a comprehensive bus system. Liechtenstein's main claim to fame is that it produces its own stamps, and so attracts philatelists from all over the world. The **Tourist Office**, *Stadtle 37*, opens Mon–Fri 0800–1200 and 1330–1700.

Sightseeing

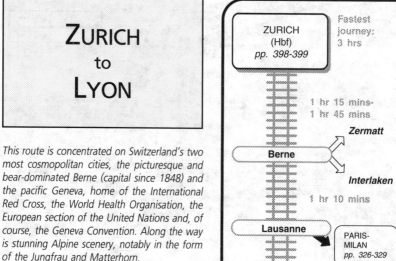

ZURICH
to
LYON

This route is concentrated on Switzerland's two most cosmopolitan cities, the picturesque and bear-dominated Berne (capital since 1848) and the pacific Geneva, home of the International Red Cross, the World Health Organisation, the European section of the United Nations and, of course, the Geneva Convention. Along the way is stunning Alpine scenery, notably in the form of the Jungfrau and Matterhorn.

TRAINS

ETT tables: 260, 159.

 Fast Track

There are no direct services between Zurich and Lyon, but trains run hourly between Zurich (HB) and Geneva (Cornavin), taking 3 hrs, and some have good connections with those for Lyon (Part-Dieu), which take about 1 hr 50 mins from Geneva. Border formalities are almost non-existent.

 On Track

Zurich–Berne (Bern)

Day trains run hourly between Zurich (HB) and Berne (Hbf), taking 1 hr 15 mins – 1 hr 45 mins.

Berne–Geneva (Genève)

Trains run hourly by day from Berne (Hbf) to Geneva (Cornavin), taking just over an hour.

Trains call at Lausanne (roughly half-way), where you can connect with the Paris–Milan route (see p. 326).

Geneva–(Border)–Lyon

At least six trains daily run between Geneva

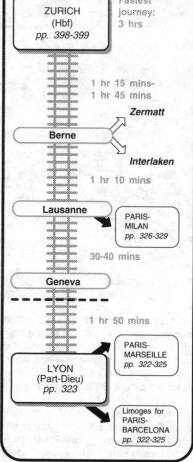

(Cornavin) and Lyon (Part-Dieu), taking about 1 hr 50 mins. Most also serve Lyon Perrache, which lengthens the journey by about 10 mins. You probably won't even notice the border.

BERNE (BERN)

Station: **Hbf**, *tel: (031) 21 11 11*, is at the western end of the old centre.

Tourist Office: Verkehrbüro, in the station complex; *tel: (031) 311 66 11*. Open June–Sept, daily 0900–2030; Oct–May, Mon–Sat

0900–1830 and Sun 1000–1700. Information on the whole country and a board outside with details of accommodation. *This Week in Berne* lists events.

Getting Around

A single east–west road with several names (*Spitalgasse, Marktgasse, Kramgasse, Gerectig-keitsgasse*) cuts through the centre, linking Hbf and Nydeggbrücke. Other than the museums, almost everything of interest is on (or just off) this. There's an excellent tram and bus network.

Accommodation

Accommodation is not cheap. Best value is the **IYHF** hostel: *Weihergasse 4; tel: (031) 22 63 16*, 10 mins from Hbf, just below Bundeshaus. Alternatively, ask the tourist office.

Campsites: *Eichholz, Strandweg 49; tel: (031) 54 26 02*, 3.5 km south-east of the centre (tram no.9 to Wabern terminal); *Eymatt, Hinterkappelen; tel: (031) 36 10 07*, 5 km north-west of the centre (Postbus from Hbf).

Embassies and Consulates

Australia: *Alpenstr. 29; tel: (031) 43 01 43*
Canada: *Kirchenfeldstr. 88; tel: (031) 352 63 81*
UK: *Thunstr. 50; tel: (031) 352 50 21*
USA: *Jubilaumsstr. 93; tel: (031) 351 70 11*

Sightseeing

Berne was founded by Berchtold V, Duke of Zahringen, in 1191. While out hunting, he said he would name it after the first creature he killed. This was a bear, now the town's ubiquitous mascot.

A fire in 1405 virtually destroyed the original wooden settlement and subsequent building was in sandstone. The reconstruction was un-usually harmonious, with 6 km of arcades and deliberately uneven roofs.

The overall impression is strikingly medieval and the old town was listed as a UNESCO World Landmark in 1983.

The Centre

The first of many monumental fountains you pass is **Pfeiferbrunnen**, *Spitalgasse*, a typical 16th-century creation with technicolour carvings and flowers around the base.

Bundeshaus, *Bundesplatz* (to the right), is the parliament building. A lookout provides fine views over the river and, on clear days, you can see the Alps. A diagram identifies the peaks.

The 13th-century **Kafigturm**, *Marktgasse*, marks what was then the western boundary of the town. The earlier **Zytgloggeturm**, *Theaterplatz*, was the original western gate and remained so until 1256. In the 16th century the astronomical clock was added. At four minutes to the hour a mechanical jester summons the main procession of puppets – mostly bears in various guises.

In *Kornhausplatz* (to the left), the city's most famous fountain, **Kindlifresserbrunnen**, depicts a child-eating ogre.

On the right is *Münsterplatz*, home of the Gothic **Münster**. Construction started in 1421, continuing through the Reformation, although many decorative touches were removed. A magnificent depiction of the *Last Judgment* above the main entrance, elaborate carvings on the pews and choir stalls and some superb 15th-century stained glass remain unscathed. The 100m steeple (Switzerland's highest) was topped off only in 1893.

Back on *Gerechtigkeitsgasse*, you pass **Gerectigkeitsbrunnen**, where the Goddess of Justice stands over the severed heads of historical figures. Cross the river by the 15th-century **Untertorbrücke** or by **Nydeggbrücke**.

To the right are the 500-year-old **Bärengraben** (bear pits), the home of Berne's mascots. The plump brown beasts are always eager to accept carrots from you (on sale there) and frequently perform tricks. They breed happily and the cubs make their first public appearance at Easter.

The Museums

Kunstmuseum Bern, *Hodlerstr.8–12* (near **Lorrainebrücke**, north of Hbf), is worth a detour. It has an exceptional display of Ferd-inand Hodler and the world's largest collection of Paul Klee, but also exhibits works by such diverse artists as Fra Angelico, Matisse, Kan-dinsky, Cézanne and Picasso.

Route–Berne   **401**

The other major museums are around Helvetiaplatz, south of the River Aare, across **Kirchenfeldbrücke** (tram nos.3/5). **Kunsthalle,** *Helvetiaplatz 1,* hosts temporary exhibitions of contemporary art. Across the 'square', **Schweizerisches Alpines Museum** contains an interesting assemblage of items connected with the history of mountaineering, including a model of the Bernese Oberland. **Bernisches Historisches Museum,** on the south side, has many exhibits captured during 15th-century wars, including superb Flemish tapestries and priceless church treasures.

The **Schweizerisches Schützenmuseum,** *Bernastr.5,* is devoted to the evolution of firearms, with examples of every type and a section on marksmanship – a Swiss hobby since William Tell. The **Naturhistorisches Museum** *(no.15)* concentrates on African animals (apart from the inevitable bears) and has a slide-show about taxidermy.

Philatelists should not miss one of the world's largest collections of postage stamps, in the nearby **Schweizerisches PTT Museum,** *Helvetiastr.16.*

– – – – – – – – – – – – – – – – – – –

◈ Side Tracks from Berne

ZERMATT

The rail journey to Zermatt involves a change in Brig, so allow around 3 hrs 30 mins. The **tourist office** is by the station, *tel: (028) 66 11 81.* Although it is only a small place, Zermatt is a major ski resort and a centre for mountain walking, its popularity resting on its proximity to the 4,477m **Matterhorn,** which is best appreciated by walking a little out of town. It's madly touristy, but nothing (except the frequent clouds) can detract from the glory of the magnificent jagged peak. A network of cable-cars provides superb views of the whole area.

INTERLAKEN

Stations: Ostbahnhof, *tel: (036) 22 30 24,* on Lake Brienz, is the terminal for most trains; **Westbahnhof,** *tel: (036) 22 35 25,* is central, by Lake Thun. The two stations are 15 mins apart on foot, 5 mins by rail, with most trains stopping at both. From Berne, Westbahnhof is the first stop, the journey averaging 50 mins by hourly trains.

Tourist Office: *Höheweg 7; tel: (036) 22 21 21.* Mon–Fri 0800–1200 and 1400–1800/1830; Sat 0800–1200. In July–Aug it's also open Sat 1400–1700; Sun 1700–1900. There are machines on the platforms that dispense print-outs for tourists (in English).

Getting Around

You don't need transport, but it's fun to have a ride in a horse-drawn carriage.

Accommodation

There's no shortage of hotels, but private rooms are better value. Register early in the height of both the summer and winter seasons.

IYHF: *Aareweg 21; tel: (036) 22 43 53,* 20 mins walk east from Ostbahnhof, in the village of Böningen on Lake Brienz (bus no.1). There's also an excellent **private hostel: Balmer's Herberge,** *Hauptstr.23; tel: (036) 22 19 61,* 15-mins walk from both stations, in the suburb of Matten (bus nos.5/15). Seven **campsites** are close by, so ask the tourist office for details.

Sightseeing

Interlaken's main attraction is as a pleasant base for exploring the spectacular mountains. The town began life in 1130, as a village surrounding an Augustinian monastery between Lakes Thun and Brienz, hence the name. There is one main street, *Höheweg,* which runs between the stations and is home to the **Casino** (the ceiling for bets is SFr.5).

The 19th-century **Kursaal** was renovated in 1968 and is now the centre of the town's social life. It stands in a landscaped park, the **Höhematte,** which gives superb views of the Jungfrau massif. You can watch Swiss cheese being made at **Chas-Dorfli,** *Centralstr.3.*

Across the River Aare is **Unterseen,** with the oldest buildings in the region. Cross the pedestrian bridge and walk along the river (past some fine Victorian and Edwardian houses) to *Marktplatz,* with its 17th-century town hall and palace, 14th-century church and museum about alpine tourism.

Interlaken is dominated by the **Jungfrau** (4,158m), 18 km to the south. There are trains to the base from Ostbahnhof, then a private rack railway ascends to **Jungfraujoch** (at 3,454m, the highest rail terminal in Europe). If you don't mind queuing for the lift, you can go up a further 111m. This trip is undeniably breathtaking, but also very expensive (currently SFr.160), although you can save about a third by taking the (very early) first train.

There are less spectacular, but far cheaper, funicular rides up the relatively small **Harderkulm** (1,320m) and **Heimwehfluh** (669m), both close to town.

GENEVA (GENÈVE)

Stations: Gare de Cornavin, *tel: (022) 731 64 50*, is the main terminal, 10-mins walk north of the centre (bus nos.5/6/9). **Gare Genève Eaux-Vives**, *tel: (022) 736 16 20*, on the eastern edge of the city, is the terminal for SNCF services from Annecy and St Gervais (bus no.12).

Tourist Office: In Cornavin; *tel: (022) 738 52 00*. From mid-June to mid-Sept, Mon–Fri 0800–2000, Sat–Sun 0800–1800; from mid-Sept to mid-June, Mon–Sat 0900–1800. *What's On in Geneva* is an entertainment guide. **Thomas Cook Suisse S.A.**, *9 chemin des Anémones, Châtelaine; tel: (022) 7969000* offers services for visitors.

Getting Around

Geneva's sights are fairly scattered and a bit of route-planning is worthwhile, with a good network of buses to get you between the areas of interest. From May to September **Compagnie Generale de Navigation (CGN)** operate regular **lake ferries** from *quai du Mont-Blanc; tel: (022) 722 39 16*.

Accommodation

Most hotels are expensive, but there are plenty of hostels and private rooms. Hotel chains with property in the city include: *Ch, Pe, Fo, Ic, Hn,*

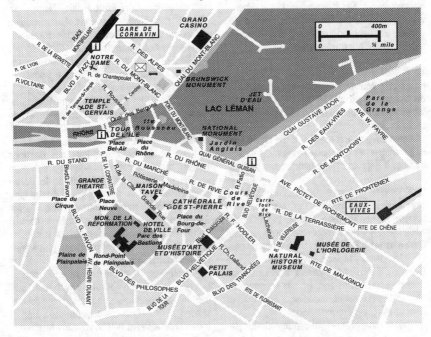

Ra, Ex, Pu. **IYHF**: *30 rue Rothschild; tel: (022) 732 62 60*, 15 mins from Cornavin (bus no.1). **Campsite:** *chemin de Conches 10; tel: (022) 347 06 03*, 4 km east of town (bus no.8).

Sightseeing

Geneva is at the western tip of **Lake Geneva (Lac Léman)**, and split by the River Rhône into two distinct sections. The international area is on the **Rive Droite** (north side) and the old town on the **Rive Gauche** (south side).

Rive Droite

Well to the north of the centre (bus nos.5/8/14/ F/Z) is *pl. des Nations*, near which most of the international organisations are grouped.

The **Musée International de la Croix-Rouge**, *av. de la Paix 17*, is a stern building with high-tech exhibits tracing the history of the Red Cross and its Islamic offshoot, the Red Crescent. Profoundly moving, it covers man's inhumanity to man as well as natural disasters.

The **Palais des Nations**, *av. de la Paix 14*, was built 1929–37 to house the League of Nations, which was dissolved in 1940. When it was replaced by the **UN** in 1945, Geneva was chosen as the headquarters of the European section. There are guided tours.

The **Musée Ariana** (recently reopened), *av. de la Paix 10*, next to the UN building, now houses the **Musée Suisse de la Céramique et du Verre**, with some 18,000 objects covering seven centuries of international glassware and ceramics.

Between here and the lake is the lovely **Jardin Botanique**, a perfect place for a quiet stroll. It includes a deer and llama park and an aviary.

Rive Gauche

The **Jardin Anglais**, on the waterfront, is famous for its **Horloge Fleurie** (floral clock), while the city's trade mark, the 140m fountain known as **Jet d'Eau**, spouts from a nearby pier. The 12th-century **Maison Tavel**, *rue du Puits St-Pierre 6*, is now an excellent museum, with several period rooms and exhibits covering the 14th to 19th centuries, including a relief map of Geneva as it was around 1850.

The original 12th–13th-century Gothic fa-çade of the **Cathédrale-St-Pierre** was not improved by 18th-century additions. Most interior decorations were stripped out in the Reformation, but there are some frescos in the neo-Gothic *Chapelle des Maccabées*. Calvin preached here, his chair having been saved for posterity. The north tower, reached by a 157-step spiral staircase, offers a great view of the old town.

In the fascinating **Site Archéologique**, catwalks allow you to see the result of extensive 1980s excavations beneath the cathedral. The layers include a 4th-century baptistery and 5th-century mosaic floor. Sculptures found during the digs are also on display.

Two blocks south, the vast marble **Musée d'Art et d'Histoire**, *rue Charles Galland 2*, has several rooms in period style, a whole room devoted to Hodler landscapes and some woodcuts by the local artist Valloton, as well as large sections on such diverse subjects as arms and porcelain. The extraordinary painting *The Fishing Miracle*, by Witz, portrays Christ walking on the water – of Lake Geneva!

The 19th-century **Petit Palais**, *Terrasse St-Victor 2*, has an impressive array of art, including works by Cézanne, Renoir and the Surrealists. The nearby **Collection Baur**, *rue Munier-Romilly 8*, contains some lovely Japanese and Chinese *objets d'art*, ranging from Samurai swords to jade and delicate porcelain.

Don't miss the amazing assortment of timepieces in the **Musée de l'Horlogerie et de l'Emaillerie**, *route de Malagnou 15*. It's an experience to be there when they sound the hour.

West of the cathedral, **Parc des Bastions** houses the university (founded by Calvin in 1599) and the vast **Monument de la Réformation**, erected in 1917. This is a 90m-long wall with four central characters (Farel, Calvin, Bèze and Knox), each over 4.5m high, flanked by the comparatively modest 2.75m statues of lesser figures of the Reformation, plus varied bas-reliefs and inscriptions.

Carouge, south of the River Arve (20 mins by bus no.12), is a Baroque suburb with fine 18th-century architecture. Centred on the plane-shaded *pl. du Marché* is a picturesque area of Italian-style arcaded buildings, many restored.

ZURICH
to
MILAN

From Switzerland's largest city, this route leads south, calling at Lake Lucerne and Lake Lugano, from where you can access the northern Italian lakes before terminating in Milan, and possibly heading on into the heart of Italy. This is a spectacularly scenic journey, which will take you through the rugged, snow-capped heart of the Alps, to some of Switzerland's prettiest towns, and through the St. Gotthard Pass.

TRAINS

ETT tables: 84, 295, 290.

→ Fast Track

There are services about every two hours, the journey taking approximately 4 hrs 30 mins. Most trains have a dining-car or buffet service. Border formalities are minimal.

ᰔ On Track

Zurich–Lucerne (Luzern)

The service is hourly, taking just under an hour.

Lucerne–Lugano

There are at least six ordinary trains a day, with an average journey time of 3 hrs. There are also about five EC trains (no supplement payable in Switzerland), which take about 2 hrs 45 mins. All the trains have a refreshment service.

Lugano–(Border)–Milan (Milano)

There are frequent trains (seldom more than an hour apart) during the day, taking 1 hr 30 mins, with a supplement payable on some. The border is crossed at Chiasso, but formalities are minimal.

ZURICH
pp. 398-399

Fastest journey:
4 hrs 30 mins

1 hr

Lucerne

Lake Lucerne
Altdorf
Vitznau
Mt Rigi
Mt Pilatus

3 hrs

Como
Italian Lakes

Lugano

Chiasso

1 hr 30 mins

MILAN
pp. 261-264

LUCERNE (LUZERN)

Station: *tel: (041) 23 66 77.* On the south bank of the River Reuss, where it meets the lake.
Tourist Office: *Frankenstr.1; tel: (041) 51 71 71* (by station). Open Mon–Fri 0830–1800; Sat 0900–1300/1700. In winter it closes 1200–1400.

Route–Lucerne

Getting Around

The yellow-orange City-Bus is free, connecting the pedestrian area to public transport.

Accommodation

Lucerne has a few pension-type places, so it is worth asking the tourist office if they have anything economical.

IYHF: Sedelstr. 12, Am Rotsee; tel: (041) 36 88 00, by the lake north-west of town (bus no. 18 to Goplismoos; after 1930, tram no.1: Schlossberg plus 15 mins-walk).

Campsite: Lidostr. 8; tel: (041) 31 21 46 (bus no. 2: Verkehrshaus), on the north river bank, east of town.

Sightseeing

Until one of them (Kapellbrücke) burnt down in 1993, Lucerne was characterised by two wooden-roofed bridges that straggled crookedly across the River Reuss, both with a series of triangular paintings suspended from the beams. The ones on **Spreuerbrücke** (to the western end of the centre) are macabre, depicting the Dance of Death.

Fortunately, about half the 17th-century paintings on the 14th-century **Kapellbrücke** were saved from the fire, but it is likely to be some time before restoration of the bridge is complete and, until then, it will not be possible to reach the 13th-century **Water Tower** which became the city's symbol after several changes of function over the centuries.

Am Rhyn Haus, Furrengasse 21, just off one of the charming old squares (**Kornmarkt**), contains a small collection of works executed by Picasso towards the end of his life.

On the riverbank not far from the northern end of Spreuerbrücke is **Nolliturm**, a fortified gate that marks one end of a well-preserved stretch of **Musegg Wall**, the old fortifications. You can follow this all the way (and climb three of the nine surviving towers) as it curves eastwards to end just off Löwenplatz.

Across the square, the **Bourbaki Panorama**, Löwenstr.18, is a 19th-century mural depicting a Franco-German battle and covering 1,300 sq m of canvas. Just north is the city's mascot, **Löw-endenkmal**, a touching portrayal of a dying lion carved out of a cliff, commemorating the Swiss Guards massacred at the Tuileries in Paris during the French Revolution. Above it is the **Glacier Garden**, Denkmalstr.4, a fascinating natural museum created by movements of the Reuss glacier millions of years ago.

Returning south, towards the river, the graceful twin-spired **Hofkirche** has an organ with 4,950 pipes and a 10-ton bell.

The **Richard Wagner Museum**, Tribschen, Wagnerweg 27, is by the lake 1.5 km south-east of the centre (bus nos.6/8, or walk east along the lake from the station). The composer lived here for several years, while composing both Siegfried and the Meistersinger, and the house contains memorabilia connected with him.

Verkehrshaus, Lidostr.5, 2 km east of town (near the campsite), can be reached by a pleasant lakeside walk (or bus no.2). It is the country's main transport museum, with wide-ranging exhibits, including a section on space travel.

The town has a number of other worthwhile museums covering different subjects.

Side Tracks from Lucerne

Lucerne is in the heart of Switzerland and a good base for excursions all over the country. There's a vast range of possibilities (from panning for gold to bungee jumping), so it really is worth examining all the options.

Lake Lucerne covers 114 sq km and has many small settlements to which there are frequent cruises in summer. You could visit **Altdorf** (where William Tell shot the apple from his son's head); or **Vitznau**, to travel on Europe's oldest rack-and-pinion railway up **Mt Rigi** (1,800m); or take a rack (cogwheel) railway and cable-car up **Mt Pilatus** (2,132m), from where the view is downwards in every direction. On a clear day, you can see seven cantons (counties).

A little further from town, 35 km away, (an hour by train) is **Engelberg**, from where there's a Rotair (rotating cable-car) that gives an unparalleled view of the permanently snow-capped **Mt Titlis** (3,020m).

LUGANO

Station: *tel: (091) 22 65 02.* Overlooks the town, with a funicular descending to the tourist office.

Tourist Office: *Riva Albertolli 5; tel: (091) 21 46 64.* Open Mon–Sat 0800/0900–1200 and 1400–1600/1830. As well as information about Lugano and cruises on the lake, they can suggest itineraries for mountain walks and tell you about hiking tours.

Sightseeing

The attraction of Lugano lies primarily in its natural setting, on a lakeside surrounded by mountains, an ideal base for mountain walking and watersports. It is the largest town in the Italian-speaking canton of **Ticino** and its atmosphere is more Italian than Swiss, with a pleasant, laid-back lifestyle. **Funiculars** climb the two mountains guarding the bay: **Monte Bre** (930m: from Cassarate) and **San Salvatore** (912m: from Paradiso), providing magnificent views of the Alps.

The 16th-century **Cattedrale San Lorenzo** is just below the station, 5 mins south of the centre. The other notable religious building is **Santa Maria Degli Angioli**, with its marvellous Renaissance mural of the *Passion and Crucifixion*. **Villa Ciani**, once an aristocrat's residence, is being restored to its former magnificence and is due to reopen (as an art gallery) in 1994. In the meantime, the **Cantonal Art Gallery** has many interesting 20th-century works.

Side Tracks from Lugano

If you wish to visit the lovely **Italian Lakes**, there are frequent trains from both Lugano and Milan to **Como**, from where you can get a ferry or bus to your chosen destination.

ZURICH
to
VIENNA

This route between Zurich and Vienna runs through spectacular Alpine scenery and includes Salzburg, the epitome of a desirable picture-postcard – and a must for lovers of Mozart.

TRAINS

ETT tables: 86, 810, 800.

→ Fast Track

Two trains run daily between Zurich (Hbf) and Vienna (Westbahnhof), plus one overnight. Day trains take about 9 hrs and have a dining-car. The night train (supplement payable) takes slightly longer, and is an EN service which continues to Budapest; it conveys sleeping cars, couchettes and reclining seats. The border is crossed at Buchs and formalities are minimal.

∾ On Track

Zurich–(Border)–Innsbruck

There are four air-conditioned EC trains a day between Zurich (Hbf) and Innsbruck (Hbf), each taking about 3 hrs 50 mins. (EC trains do not carry a supplement in Switzerland; in Austria they do so only in first class.) Border formalities (at Buchs) are minimal.

Innsbruck–Kitzbühel

Trains run every two hours between Innsbruck (Hbf) and Kitzbühel, taking a little over an hour.

Kitzbühel–Salzburg

Services run every two hours and most have a refreshment service. The journey usually takes around 2 hrs 20 mins.

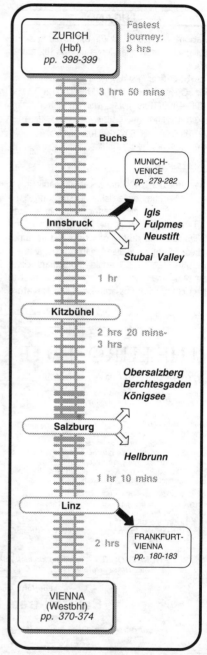

Salzburg–Vienna (Wien)

Trains between Salzburg and Vienna (West-bahnhof) are frequent (at least hourly) and many have dining-cars. The journey time varies considerably, however. EC trains take just over 3 hrs, IC trains about 3 hrs 20 mins and stopping trains almost 4 hrs.

Many IC trains stop at Linz (about 1 hr 20 mins from Salzburg and about 2 hrs from Vienna), where you could join the Frankfurt–Vienna route (see p. 180).

INNSBRUCK

Station: Hauptbahnhof (Hbf), *tel: (0512) 17 17.* Tram (nos.1/3) and various buses connect Hbf with Altstadt; otherwise it's a 10 mins walk. **Tourist Office**: Innsbruck Information, *Burggraben 3; tel: (0512) 53 56,* on the edge of Altstadt, offers all tourist services but charges to book accommodation. Open daily 0800–1900. Hbf: *tel: (0512) 58 37 60.* Daily 0900–2200. **Fremdenverkehrsverband Innsbruck-Igls** is above Innsbruck-Information, *Burggraben 3; tel: (0512) 598 50.* Daily 0800–1900. They dispense free brochures and maps, and a list of private rooms in Innsbruck and Igls. **Jugend-warteraum** (youth waiting room) is in Hbf; *tel: (0512) 58 63 62.* Staff speak English, offer a free booking service and supply leaflets and maps.

All these offices can provide the invaluable *Innsbruck Information,* which includes maps and lists of budget accommodation. For entertainment, get the *Innsbrucker Summer/Winter* (as applicable). See **Tirol-Info,** *Wilhelm-Greil-Str.17; tel: (0512) 53 20* (Mon–Fri 0830–1800 and Sat 0900–1200), for information about the region. If staying for at least three nights, book for all of them and ask your pension/hotel about joining *Club Innsbruck.* Membership is free and entitles you to free bike tours, discounts on cable-cars and museums and the chance to participate in a hiking programme.

Reisen and Freizeit Gmbh & Co KG, *Brixner-str.3; tel: (512) 59926* (**Thomas Cook** network member) offers services for visitors.

Getting Around

Innsbruck is a compact city and most things are easily walkable from Altstadt, but there is an excellent tram and bus system. Eurail passes offer a 20% reduction on the Seegrube, Hafelekar, Patscherkofel and Mutterer Alm cable-cars.

Accommodation and Food

Budget rooms are scarce in June, when only three hostels are open, but rooms are usually available at the university from July. There are several hostels, three of them in the same area (take bus R). Two are **IYHF:** *Reichenauerstr.147; tel: (0512) 461 79* or *461 80* and *Volkshaus, Radetzkystr.47; tel: (0512) 46 66 82,* just around the corner. The independent hostel is: **Jugendzentrum St Paulus,** *Reichenauerstr.72; tel: (0512) 442 91.* **Campsite:** *Kranebitter Allee 214; tel: (0512) 28 41 80,* west of town. Hotel chains with property in the city include: *Ib, SC.*

If you feel like splashing out on a good meal (with Tyrolean music in the evening), the 14th-century **Goldener Adler** tavern, *Herzog-Friedrichstr.,* is famous, as it has been frequented by such luminaries as Goethe, Heine and Sartre.

Sightseeing

Surrounded by snow-capped peaks and straddling the River Inn, it's difficult to imagine a more scenic setting for the Tyrolean capital and Innsbruck is a perfect base for Alpine walking, as well as skiing. There are over 150 cable-cars and chair-lifts and an extensive network of trails. **Altstadt** is the old town, centred on the city's emblem, the 15th-century **Goldenes Dachl** ('Golden Roof' – with 2,657 gilded copper tiles). Inside is the **Olympiamuseum,** which celebrates the two occasions on which Innsbruck was chosen to host the Winter Olympics (1964 and 1976). The old town has a number of splendid 15th- and 16th-century buildings. The 15th-century **Helblinghaus** has extremely elaborate 18th-century stucco decorations. The nearby city tower, **Stadtturm,** offers an excellent view. Behind Goldenes Dachl is the Baroque **Domkirche St Jakob,** with an amazing *trompe l'oeil* ceiling (depicting St James) and an altar featuring Cranach's *Intercession of the Virgin.*

Hofburg, *Rennweg,* has an enormous ballroom and is filled with portraits of the royals who were residents in its days as a palace, while the

16th-century **Hofkirche**, the imperial church, is crammed with enormous bronze statues of them. The neighbouring **Tiroler Volkskunst-museum**, *Universitätsstr.*, concentrates on Tyrolean culture, featuring wood-panelled rooms in period styles, traditional costumes and the like. The **Tiroler Landesmuseum Ferdinandeum**, *Museumstr.15*, is more diverse; exhibits including beautiful old stained glass, medieval altars and works by Cranach and Rembrandt, as well as Tyrolean paintings.

Triumphbogen, *Leopoldstr.*, is an 18th-century triumphal arch. Nearby are the beautiful Rococo **Basilika Wilten** and the Baroque **Stiftskirche Wilten**. On *Maria-Theresien-Str.* are the **Palais Troyer-Spaur**, the **Palais-Trapp-Wolkenstein** (bearing the von Trapp family's coat of arms) and the neo-Classical **Alteslandhaus**.

Alpenzoo has a comprehensive collection of Alpine fauna: 800 animals of 140 species, kept in their natural habitats. To get there, cross the River Inn by the covered bridge and follow the signs (or take bus Z). Alternatively, you can take the **Hungerburgbahn funicular** (free if you buy a zoo ticket before boarding). After stopping at the zoo, it continues to climb to a plateau, from where a succession of cable-cars take you almost to the summit of **Nordkette**, the peak which dominates Innsbruck.

Just out of town (tram nos.3/6) is **Schloss Ambras**, a medieval castle rebuilt in Renaissance style which contains many paintings and weapons belonging to Archduke Ferdinand, displayed much as they were in his day.

◠ Side Tracks from Innsbruck

Igls is a pretty ski-resort village on the outskirts of town (bus J or tram no.6). It's a good base for summer hiking, as are the mountain villages of **Fulpmes** and **Neustift**, both in the glacier-carved **Stubai Valley**. There are buses to both, plus STB trains to Fulpmes.

KITZBÜHEL

Stations: *tel: (05356) 40 55 31*. The railway loops around the town and there are stations at both ends. **Hbf** (about 15 mins walk from the centre) is used by all trains from Salzburg. **Hahnenkamm**, the first stop on services towards Innsbruck, is a little more convenient, but only half the trains stop here.

Tourist Office: *Hinterstadt 18; tel: (05356) 22 72 or 21 55*. July–Sept, Mon–Sat 0830–1930 and Sun 0900/1000–1700; Oct–June, Mon–Fri 0830–1200 and 1500–1830, and Sat–Sun 0830/0900–1200.

Getting Around

The centre of town is small but its suburbs extend into the valley. The whole area is honey-combed with cable-cars (and other lifts), between which there are shuttle buses. Regular bus services run to the suburbs and connect all the towns in the area. For information contact **Postautodienst**, *tel: (05356) 27 15*.

Accommodation

Except in the skiing season, there are plenty of pensions and rooms at reasonable prices. In the season, you would do better to stay in one of the surrounding villages. **IYHF:** *Oberndorf 64, Niederstrasseerhof; tel: (05352) 3651*.

Sightseeing

Kitzbühel began life in the 16th century, as a centre for mining copper and silver. Mementoes of these early days can be seen in a **Mining Museum** on the corner of *Hinterstadt*, one of the main squares. The other, *Vorderstadt*, is lined with attractively painted houses. The medieval centre is very picturesque and has a couple of interesting churches with ancient frescos: the 15th-century Gothic **Pfarrkirche** and **Liebfrauenkirche** (which has a monumental tower).

Kitzbühel is one of the best skiing areas in the world and every January for over 50 years it has hosted one of the most famous downhill races, the **Hahnenkamm Downhill Ski Competition**. The town's facilities for winter sports are superb, but the prices reflect this fact and, in season, it is a very upmarket resort.

The town has excellent nightlife year-round and offers plenty of facilities for summer visitors. These include three golf courses, two lake beaches, thirty tennis courts, two stables (and two indoor arenas, so riding is not restricted to the summer months), squash courts, **Kinderland** (a children's playground) and a casino. Another attraction is **Aquarena**, a huge complex that includes an indoor landscaped swimming pool, sauna, solarium and peat bath.

The **Kitzbüheler Hornbahn** cable-car can take you up to 1,800m, site of the **Alpen Blumengarten** (open mid-Oct–Apr), in which there are 120 different types of Alpine flowers.

There are over 120 km of well-tended footpaths and trails, covering both the valley and the mountains, so hikers are spoiled for choice. You can get a map, the *Panoramakarte*, from the tourist office or join a guided walk. Most trails can be reached by postbus from Hbf, but you may need to take a cable-car for some of them. It is worth noting that, although you have to pay to ride up, many descents are free.

SALZBURG

Station: Hbf, *tel: (0662) 17 17*, on the northern edge of the new town, 15–20 mins walk from the old centre (bus nos.1/5/6/51 to Staatsbrücke, the main bridge).
Tourist Office: *Mozartplatz 5, Altstadt; tel: 84 75 68 or 80 72 34 62. July–Aug daily 0800–2200. Apr–June and Sept–Oct daily 0900–1900. Nov–Mar Mon–Sat 0900–1800. At Hbf, by platform 10: tel: (0662) 87 17 12 Mon–Sat 0845–1930/2130.*

Getting Around

Most of the centre is pedestrianised. The low curve of Mönchsberg shelters the old town in the south and west, while the River Salzach runs along the south-east. Across the river, the east bank is dominated by Kapuzinerberg, to the north of which, along the river-bank, clusters the new town's area of interest. The bus and trolley-bus network is excellent and routes are indicated on all maps. Horse-drawn carriages are also available (in *Residenzplatz*). If you want to relive the von Trapp story, there's a good choice of English-language *Sound of Music* tours.

Accommodation

There are hotels in every category, pensions,

private rooms, seven IYHF hostels, private hostels and several campsites, but you should still book ahead during the *Salzburger Festspiele* (late-July and Aug). If you can't find space, try **Hallein** (20 mins by train) or cross into Germany and stay at **Berchtesgaden** (see Side Tracks below). Hotel chains with property in the area include: *HI, Me, Nv, Rd, Sh*.

Most convenient **IYHF** branches are: *Glockengasse 8; tel: (0662) 876241*, on the northern edge of *Kapuzinerberg*, open Apr–Oct; *Haunspergstr.27; tel: (0662) 75030*, two blocks west of Hbf, but only open July–Aug; and *Josef-Preis-Allee 18; tel: (0662) 84 26 70*, open year-round and a little south-east of *Altstadt* (trolley nos.5/55). **Campsites:** *Bayerhamerstr.14; tel: (0662) 87 11 69* is closest, north-east of the new town and walkable from Hbf; *Stadtblick, Rauchenbichlerstr.21; tel: (0662) 50652* (bus no.51); and *Samstr.22; tel: (0662) 66 04 94* (bus no.33).

Sightseeing

The city's wealth was founded on a salt industry dating back to the Iron Age, but tourism is now the main source of income. Salzburg is a real chocolate-box place, where soaring snow-capped peaks provide a backdrop for medieval turrets and spires. Much of the city's present appearance is due to the influence of the 16th century Prince-Archbishop Wolf Dietrich, while its heart belongs to Mozart. Reminders of him are ubiquitous, not least during the January **Mozart Festival**. More recently, the phenomenal success of *The Sound of Music* brought the town a fresh surge of fame.

Above Altstadt looms the formidable **Festung Hohensalzburg**, on the south-west end of **Mönchsberg**. Construction of the castle began in 1077 and continued until the 17th century. The complex is almost perfectly preserved and has everything from medieval torture chambers to state rooms, including Austria's only barrel organ, a 200-pipe affair that booms out after the 7th-century 35-bell carillon of the **Glockenspiel**, *Mozartsplatz*, has pealed (at 0700, 1100 and 1800). The castle can be approached from two directions. From *Festungsgasse*, behind the Dom, you can walk or take the cable-railway straight up. Alternatively, the **Mönchsberglift** operates

Kitzbühel–Salzburg

from *Gstattengasse* (by Museumsplatz) and takes you to the *Café Winkler lookout*, whence there are trails east to the castle.

Narrow *Getreidegasse* is bordered by 17th–18th-century houses with decorative wrought-iron signs. At no.9 is **Mozart's Geburtshaus**, where the composer was born and spent most of his first 17 years. It's now a museum, the exhibits including stage sets for his operas and an undersized violin he used when a boy.

The elegant *Residenzplatz* is dominated by the **Residenz**, Dietrich's palace, where Mozart conducted. Hourly tours include living quarters, grandiose Baroque state rooms and **Rezidenz-galerie**, an art gallery with a superb collection featuring works by Titian, Rembrandt, Breughel, Caravaggio and Rubens, among others.

The **Dom**, in the adjacent *Domplatz*, is a magnificent Baroque building that, at Dietrich's behest, replaced a Romanesque structure. Mozart worked here as *konzertmeister* and court organist. The connecting **Dommuseum** has an odd selection of items treasured by the Renaissance rulers, such as conch shells and a whale's tooth.

The **Franziskanerkirche**, *Hofstallgasse*, is a reconstruction of an 8th-century edifice and a mishmash of architectural styles. It has a fine Baroque altar built around an earlier Gothic sculpture and nine stucco-ornamented chapels.

The enormous **Festspielhaus**, *Hofstallgasse*, built into the side of the mountain on the western side of Altstadt, is the principal venue for the festival. North-east is **Pferdeschwemme**, a 17th-century Baroque horse trough with an equine motif.

The stunning **Stiftskirche St Peter**, *St-Peter-Bezirk*, a mass of pastel-coloured ceiling mouldings and plump cherubim, almost pales into insignificance beside the incredibly decorative organ. There is an ancient, atmospheric cemetery and **Catacombs (Katakomben)** that date back to 250 AD.

Near Altstadt, **Kapuzinerberg** is named for the simple Capuchin monastery on its summit. It offers a good view of the city from the top.

Walk east along *Linzergasse*, an enchanting medieval street, to **Sebastiankirche**, where the graveyard contains the tiled mausoleum of Dietrich and the tomb of Paracelsus.

Makartplatz is home to **Dreifaltigkeitskirche** (the Church of the Holy Trinity), designed by Fischer von Erlach and noted for its elegant curving exterior as well as the rather dark Rottmayr frescos it contains.

The **Mozarts Wohnhaus**, *Makartplatz 8* (his home 1773–1787) was badly damaged in World War Two. It now houses objects relating to him and period instruments, while the **Mozarteum**, *Schwarzstr.26*, incorporates the summer house where he composed *The Magic Flute*.

Schloss Mirabell, *Mirabellplatz*, was built for Dietrich's mistress in the 17th century, rebuilt in the early 18th century and further reconstructed after a fire in the 19th century. It now houses public offices and the *Marmorsaal*, an extraordinarily ornate venue for chamber music concerts. You do not need to attend one of these to appreciate the Baroque excesses of the interior, however, since they are shown to perfection in the incredible *Angel Staircase*, with its mass of marble cherubs.

Side Tracks from Salzburg

Just south of town (5 km) is the unique 17th-century **Lustschloss Hellbrunn**, reached by half-hourly bus. This Italian-designed pleasure-palace is noted for elaborate water-based booby-traps which catch the unwary in a succession of concealed fountains. The adjacent zoo *(Tiergarten)*, keeps animals in natural surroundings, and there's a small folklore museum.

Hourly buses (taking 45 mins) run to the villages of **Obersalzberg** and **Berchtesgaden** (in Germany), which achieved fame as Hitler's country retreat. The ascent to his **Kehlsteinhaus (Eagle's Nest)** is a nail-biting experience rewarded by breathtaking views. Also in the area are **Salt Mines**, tours of which are great fun and should not be missed by anyone with an adventurous nature, and Germany's highest and most scenic lake, **Königsee**. The beautiful mountain scenery, lush valleys and network of trails make for superb mountain walking. The **tourist office** is by the station; *tel: (08652) 50 11.*

SPECIAL TRAINS

STEAM TRAINS AND LITTLE RAILWAYS

The following is a selection of minor lines, sometimes operated by steam train, which head off the beaten track into areas of spectacular scenery, adding spice to your itinerary. There are many more such lines in Europe, and specialist operators, and enthusiasts' clubs and literature can suggest other worthwhile trips.

Austria

South from St Pölten (near Vienna) a narrow-gauge line heads over farming country, then up the gorge of the River Pielach to Laubenbach-mühle. Here a steep, half-spiral climb takes you to **Winterbach** (stunning views from hotel); a further climb over the mountains leads to **Mariazell**, a religious pilgrimage centre (station about 2 km away).

A minor line from Unzmarkt to Murau in Kärnten (Carinthia) winds up the valley of the River Mur to Tamsweg; this branches off the main line from Vienna to Venice. Murau-Stolzalpe is the largest town along the line, before the train heads up into the mountains of the Tauern Range. Midweek steam trains run from Murau in summer.

France

The narrow-gauge line from **La Tour de Carol** to **Villefranche** is one of the highlights of train travel in France, with excellent mountain views and a rustic charm of its own. In summer there are special open carriages. Connecting trains run from Villefranche to the coast at **Perpignan**.

Also narrow-gauge, but privately operated, is the line from **Nice**, which follows the Var valley before striking through the mountains to reach the small town of **Digne**.

Germany

A narrow-gauge line runs from Wernigerode through the Harz Mountains National Park and small, unspoilt villages like **Sorge** and **Elend** to Nordhausen. Many trains are operated by steam locomotives.

The Aalen–Nördlingen–Donauwörth line, close to Stuttgart, crosses the foothills of the Swabian Alps (*Schwäbische Alb*). **Nördlingen** (a small, almost completely walled town) and **Donauwörth**, on the Danube, are both on the **Romantic Road** – see p. 177.

Norway

The spectacular **Flåm** railway with 20 tunnels in as many kilometres leaves the Oslo–Bergen line (see p. 150) at **Myrdal**. Connection can be made at Flåm with the fast ferries along the fjord.

Poland

Steam trains still operate some services on the **Poznań** to **Wolsztyn** line. The line passes through typical Polish countryside where old farming methods are still much in evidence. In May, look out for the storks' nests on tall structures.

Portugal

Take a train along the Douro Valley from **Oporto** to **Pocinho**, just for the ride. There are three a day, but the journey takes about 5 hrs 30 mins, and so needs to be planned. There is accommodation in **Regua** and **Pinao** (both en route). From Regua onwards you are in wine country and spectacular scenery.

Spain

The coastal line from San Sebastián to Ferrol has varied scenery (mountains, rivers, sea etc.) along its length – allow several days for the journey, for there are not many trains.

Try the Strawberry Line from **Madrid** (Atocha) to **Aranjuez** and back, on a Victorian steam train which used to carry the town's famous fruit and vegetables to the capital, and now provides a fun day trip. The fare includes guided tours and admission fees in Aranjuez.

Switzerland/Italy

One of the lesser-known lines is the Centovalli route from **Domodossola** (Italy) to **Locarno** (Switzerland). There is a very steep climb from Domodossola to **Santa Maria Maggiore** which affords stunning views; the line then clings to the hillside, soars across deep valleys (Centovalli = '100 valleys') and goes through numerous tunnels before crossing into Switzerland at Camedo. Locarno is an upmarket holiday resort on the northern edge of Lago Maggiore.

CRUISE AND LUXURY TRAINS

These aristocrats of the railway world provide a taste of luxury and an atmosphere of the 1920s and '30s. They are far from cheap, of course, but they are the nearest equivalent on land to the world of the cruise liner. For full details of booking any of these, consult a good travel agent or the sources suggested below.

Al-Andaluz Express (Spain)

Seven days of luxury, cruising around the great cities of Andalucia on board a luxury vintage train, made up from 1920s carriages, all carefully restored for maximum comfort. Departs every Mon from Seville for Córdoba, Granada, Ronda, Jerez de la Frontera. Occasionally runs to Barcelona, Burgos, Segovia and Santiago de Compostela.
Cost: £1774 per person in high season (only slightly less at other times).
Information: Spanish National Tourist Offices.
Booking (UK): Mundicolor, *276 Vauxhall Bridge Road, London SW1V 1BE; tel: 071-828 6021.* Cox & King, *St James Court, Buckingham Gate, London SW1E 6AF; tel: 071-834 7472.*

Cantabrian Express (Spain)

Less luxurious than the Al-Andaluz, but still very comfortable, this is a week-long sightseeing journey leaving every Sat from either Santiago de Compostela or San Sebastián, taking you 1000 km along the north Spanish coast and through the foothills of the Picos de Europa.
Cost: Ptas 161,000 per person (sharing).

Information and booking: Emilia Gonzalez, Transcantabrico-Feve, *Avda Santander s/n, 33001 Oviedo, Asturias, Spain; tel: (Spain +) 985 529 0104.*

Venice–Simplon Orient Express

The original Orient Express began on its long journey across Europe, from London to Istanbul, in 1883 and achieved an almost legendary status, inspiring 19 books, six films and a piece of music (a foxtrot). However, World War II nearly killed it off, and the advent of cheap air travel, and the descent of the Iron Curtain, finished it. It came to a standstill in 1977. Almost immediately, a phoenix rose from the ashes in the form of the Venice–Simplon Orient Express, a privately run cruise train that has become a byword of opulence. All the carefully restored carriages, in both the British and the continental sections, were used on the original train in the '20s and '30s.

There are two strands. From London Victoria, the train runs to Folkestone, and passengers take the SeaCat to Boulogne to join the main train to Paris. A second route heads south from Düsseldorf to Frankfurt and on to Basel, where the two trains link up. It then goes on to Zurich, Innsbruck, Verona and Venice. There are also services beyond Venice to Vienna and Budapest. It is possible to travel on any of the legs, in either direction. There is one departure each week, leaving London on Thurs and Venice on Wed.
Cost: £895 per person one-way London–Venice. There are also several packages which include return flight and hotel accommodation.
Information and booking (UK): Venice–Simplon Orient Express, *Sea Containers House, 20 Upper Ground, London SE1 9PF; tel: 071-928 6000.*

Swiss Expresses

There are several luxury trains running short journeys through the Swiss Alps, and into the Italian lake district in some instances. Best-known are the **Glacier Express** (7 hrs 30 mins, Zermatt–Davos/St Moritz); **Zermatt Express** (3 hrs 17 mins, Zermatt–Brig–Interlaken); **Bernina Express** (approx. 4 hrs, Chur–St Moritz–Tirano).

CONVERSION TABLES

INCHES AND CENTIMETRES

Unit	Inches	Feet	Yards
1mm	0.039	0.003	0.001
1cm	0.39	0.03	0.01
1metre	39.40	3.28	1.09

Unit	mm	cm	metres
1 inch	25.4	2.54	0.025
1 foot	304.8	30.48	0.304
1 yard	914.4	91.44	0.914

To convert cms to inches, multiply by 0.3937
To convert inches to cms, multiply by 2.54

24 HOUR CLOCK

Midnight = 0000 12 noon = 1200 6 pm = 1800
6 am = 0600 1 pm = 1300 Midnight = 2400

WEIGHT

Unit	Kg	Pounds
1	0.45	2.205
2	0.90	4.405
3	1.35	6.614
4	1.80	8.818
5	2.25	11.023
10	4.50	22.045
15	6.75	33.068
20	9.00	44.889
25	11.25	55.113
50	22.50	110.225
75	33.75	165.338
100	45.00	220.450

1 kg = 1000 g
100 g = 3.5 oz
1 oz = 28.35 g
1 lb = 453.60 g

FLUID MEASURES

Litres	Imp. gal.	US gal.
5	1.1	1.3
10	2.2	2.6
15	3.3	3.9
20	4.4	5.2
25	5.5	6.5
30	6.6	7.8
35	7.7	9.1
40	8.8	10.4
45	9.9	11.7
50	11.0	13.0

1 litre (l) = 0.88 imp.quarts
1 litre (l) = 1.06 US quarts
1 imp. quart = 1.14 l
1 imp. gallon = 4.55 l
1 US quart = 0.95 l
1 US gallon = 3.81 l

DISTANCE

km	miles	km	miles
1	0.62	30	21.75
2	1.24	40	24.85
3	1.86	45	27.96
4	2.49	50	31.07
5	3.11	55	34.18
6	3.73	60	37.28
7	4.35	65	40.39
8	4.97	70	43.50
9	5.59	75	46.60
10	6.21	80	49.71
15	9.32	90	55.92
20	12.43	100	62.14
25	15.53	125	77.67

1 km = 0.6214miles
1 mile = 1.609 km

METRES AND FEET

Unit	Metres	Feet
1	0.30	3.281
2	0.61	6.563
3	0.91	9.843
4	1.22	13.124
5	1.52	16.403
6	1.83	19.686
7	2.13	22.967
8	2.44	26.248
9	2.74	29.529
10	3.05	32.810
14	4.27	45.934
18	5.49	59.058
20	6.10	65.520
50	15.24	164.046
75	22.86	246.069
100	30.48	328.092

LADIES' SHOES

UK	Europe	USA
3	36	4.5
4	37	5.5
5	38	6.5
6	39	7.5
7	40	8.5
8	41	9.5

MENS' SHOES

UK	Europe	USA
6	40	7
7	41	8
8	42	9
9	43	10
10	44	11
11	45	12

LADIES' CLOTHES

UK	France	Italy	Rest of Europe	USA
10	36	38	34	8
12	38	40	36	10
14	40	42	38	12
16	42	44	40	14
18	44	46	42	16
20	46	48	44	18

MENS' CLOTHES

UK	Europe	USA
36	46	36
38	48	38
40	50	40
42	52	42
44	54	44
46	56	46

MENS' SHIRTS

UK	Europe	USA
14	36	14
15	38	15
15.5	39	15.5
16	41	16
16.5	42	16.5
17	43	17

TEMPERATURE

°C	°F	°C	°F	Conversion Formula
-20	-4	10	50	$°C \times 9 \div 5 + 32 = °F$
-15	5	15	59	1 Deg. °C = 1.8 Deg. °F
-10	14	20	68	1 Deg. °F = 0.55 Deg. °C
-5	23	25	77	
0	32	30	86	
5	41	35	95	

This index lists place names and topics in one alphabetical sequence. All references are to page numbers. **Bold** numbers refer to map pages. To find routes between cities, see pp 8–9.

A

Aachen 139
Aalborg 152
Aalsmeer 91
Aarhus 151–152
Abrantes 246
Accommodation 10–11
Aix-en-Provence 251
Al-Andaluz Express 414
Albufeira 214
Alexandropolis 116
Algarve 215
Alkmaar 91
Allowances, customs 13–14
Amsterdam 84–91, **86**
Angers 310
Angoulême 318
Antibes 260
Antwerp (Antwerpen) 94–95
Apeldoorn 93
Aranjuez 241–242
Arezzo 162
Århus see Aarhus
Arles 253
Arnhem 103–104
Assisi 163–164
Astorga 352
Athens (Athinai) 108–112, **111**
Augsburg 178–179
Auschwitz see Oświecim
Austria 30–32
AVE 70
Avignon 325
Avila 239–240

B

Babies, travelling with 11–12
Bad Wimpfen 186
Baden-Baden 332
Balearic Islands 243
Baltic Pass 25
Bamberg 178
Bandol 251
Banks, opening hours 17
Barcelona 117–120, **119**
Basel (Bâle) 327–328
Bavarian Forest 182
Bayonne 319
Bayreuth 178
Beaune 323
Belgium 32–34
Berchtesgaden 412
Bergen 153–154
Berlin 121–125, **123,** transport map **122**
Berne (Bern) 400–402
Béziers 255
Biarritz 319
Bicycles 11
Bilbao 320
Black Forest 333
Bobadilla 247, 359
Bodensee see Constance, Lake
Bologna 266–267
Bonn 105–106
Bordeaux 318–319
Border crossings 11
Boulogne 233
Bourges 303
Braga 211
Bran Castle 203
Brasov 202–203
Bratislava 375–376
Braunschweig see Brunswick
Bremen 97–98

Brest 308
Brindisi 268
Britain see United Kingdom
Brno 340
Bruges (Brugge) 231–232
Brunswick 93
Brussels (Bruxelles) 130–134, **133**
Bucharest (Bucuresti) 199–202, **201**
Budapest 141–145, **143**
Bulgaria 34–35
Burgas 197
Burgos 321

C

Cáceres 245
Cadíz 357
Cagnes-sur-Mer 284–285
Cahors 304
Calais 233
Camargue 253
Camping 11
Cannes 259–260
Cantabrian Express 414
Capri 349
Carcassonne 305
Carnac 309
Cascais 208
Cassis 251
Castel Gandolfo 346
Châlons-sur-Marne 312
Channel ferries 234
Channel Tunnel 29
Chartres 307
Châteauroux 303–304
Children, travelling with 11–12
Cinque Terre 271
Classes on trains 27
Climate 12
Clothing 12–13
Coimbra 210
Colditz 174
Collioure 256
Cologne 139–140, **140**
Como 407
Constance, Lake 188–189
Consulates see individual cities and countries
Copenhagen 146–149, **147**
Córdoba 358–359
Corfu 268
Corinth 268

Corsica 271
Costa Brava 256
Costa del Azahar 243
Costa del Sol 248
Couchettes 28
Cracow 378–380, **379**
Crime 18–20
Cruise trains 414
Cuenca 242
Currency 13
Customs allowances 13–14
Cycling 11
Czech Republic 36–37

D

Delft 227
Delphi 114–115
Den Haag see Hague
Denmark 37–38
Dijon 323
Dinan 308
Dinant 137–138
Dining cars 28
Disabled travellers 14–15
Dol-de-Bretagne 308
Donostia see San Sebastián
Dordogne 318, 319
Douro Valley 413
Dresden 126
Driving 15
Düsseldorf 104–105

E

Efteling 91
Eisenach 171
El Escorial 239
Electricity 15
Embassies see individual cities and countries
Emergencies see individual cities and countries for emergency numbers
Empoli 273
Épernay 312
Erfurt 171–172
Essen 104
Estonia 38–40
Estoril 208
ETT see Thomas Cook European Timetable
Eurail Pass 23–24
Euro Disney 301
Euro-Domino pass 24
EuroCity (EC) 26

EuroNight (EN) 26
Europass 24
European East Pass 25
Eurostar trains 26, 29
Eze 285

F

Faro 214–215
Fatima 208
Ferries see Channel ferries
Figueres 256
Finding your train 27
Finland 40–41
Firenze see Florence
Florence 157–160, **159**
Foggia 349
Fontainebleau 301
France 41–44
Frankfurt am Main 166–169, **168**
Freiburg im Breisgau 332–333
Fréjus 259
Fulda 171
Füssen 179

G

Garmisch-Partenkirchen 280
Gasteiz see Vitoria
Geneva (Genève) 403–404, **403**
Genoa (Genova) 288
Germany 44–47
Gerona (Girona) 256
Ghent 232
Gibraltar 248
Gniezno 128–129
Göteborg see Gothenburg
Gotha 171
Gothenburg 156
Gouda 226–227
Granada 359–360
Greece 47–48
Gubbio 163
Guidebooks 21

H

Haarlem 229
Hague, The 227–228
Hamburg 98–100, **99**
Hamelin (Hameln) 100
Hanover (Hannover) 93
Health 15–16

Heidelberg 185–186
Heilbronn 186
Hellbrunn 412
Helsingborg 156
Helsinki 395–397, **396**
Hitchhiking 16
Holidays, public 18
Holland see Netherlands
Hook of Holland 226
Hoorn 91
Hotels 10
Huelva 215
Hungary 48–50

I

Igoumenitsa 268
Innsbruck 409–410
Insurance 16
Inter-Rail Pass 22–23
InterCity (IC) 26
Interlaken 402–403
International Student Identity Card (ISIC) 15
International Youth Hostel Federation (IYHF) 10–11
Irún 319
Ischia 349
ISIC 15
Istanbul 190–194, **191**
Italy 50–53
IYHF 10–11

J

Jerez de la Frontera 356–357
Juan-Les-Pins 260
Jurmala 391

K

Kadriorg 394
Kalambaka 115
Karlsruhe 333–334
Karlstad 292
Katowice 377
Kaunas 388–389
Keukenhof Gardens 229
Kitzbühel 410–411
Koblenz 106–107
København see Copenhagen
Köln see Cologne
Königstein 169
Konstanz 188–189
Korinthos see Corinth

Kraków see Cracow
Kristiansand 152–153
Kronberg 169

L

La Baule 310
La Ciotat 251
La Rochelle 318
La Spézia 271
Language 16–17
Larissa 115
Latvia 53–55
Lausanne 328–329
Le Mans 307
Legoland 152
Leiden 228–229
Leipzig 173–174
Léon 352–353
Leuven 134
Levadia 114
Levanto 271
Liechtenstein 399
Liège 138–139
Limoges 304
Linz 183
Lisbon (Lisboa) 204–208, **205**
Lithuania 55–56
Litohoro 115
Loire Valley 310, 317
London 216–224, **220–221**, transport map **217**
Lone travellers 19
Louvain see Leuven
Lübeck 100–101
Lucca 272–273
Lucerne (Luzern) 405–406
Lugano 407
Luggage 17, 21
Lunéville 331–332
Luxembourg 135
Luxury trains 414
Lyon 324–325

M

Mâcon 323–324
Madrid 235–239, **237**
Mainz 107
Málaga 248
Malmö 155–156
Mannheim 185
Marseille 249–251, **250**
Marvão 246
Mechelen 134

Meissen 126
Menton 287
Mestre 366
Meteora 115
Metz 313
Milan (Milano) 261–264, **263**
Monaco 286–287
Mönchengladbach 105
Mont-St-Michel 308
Montpellier 254–255
Montreux 329
Motor-rail 15
Munich (München) 275–278, **276**
Museums:
    discounts 15
    opening hours 17

N

Namur 137
Nancy 313
Nantes 309–310
Naples (Napoli) 347–349, **348**
Narbonne 255
Netherlands 56–59
Neuschwanstein 179
Nice 283–285, **285**
Nîmes 254
Norway 59–61
Nuremberg (Nürnberg) 177–178

O

Obidos 208
Ochsenfurt 176
Odense 151
Odenwald 186
Olhao 215
Olympia 268
Oostende see Ostend
Oporto 210–211
Orange 325
Örebro 292
Orense (Ourense) 352
Orient Express 414
Orléans 303
Oslo 289–291, **290**
Osnabrück 93
Ostend (Oostende) 230–231
Ostia 346
Oświecim 380

Overnight trains 27–28

P

Padua (Padova) 282
Palencia 353
Palmela 214
Paris 293–301, **298-299,**
  transport map **295**
Passau 182–183
Passes and tickets 22–26;
  see also under individual
  countries
Passport regulations 17
Patras 268
Pavia 270
Pendolino 53
Perpignan 255–256
Perugia 162–163
Pisa 271–272
Plovdiv 196–197
Poitiers 317
Poland 61–62
Police 19–20
Polrail Pass (Poland) 62
Pompeii 348–349
Ponferrada 352
Pontevedra 212
Portofino 270–271
Portugal 62–65
Potsdam 125
Poznań 127–128
Prague (Praha) 335–339,
  337
Private railways 413–414
Public holidays 18

Q

Queluz 208
Quiberon 309
Quimper 308

R

Rail Europe–Senior Card 24
Rail passes *see* Passes and
  tickets
Rapallo 271
Ravenna 267
Refreshments on trains 28
Regensburg 181–182
Rennes 307–308
Reservations 26
Rheims (Reims) 312
Rhine Gorge 106
Riga 389–391

Rimini 267
Rioja wine district 321
Rocamadour 319
Romania 65–66
Romantic Road 177
Rome 341–346, **342–343**
Ronda 247–248
Roskilde 101
Rothenburg ob der Tauber
  177
Rotterdam 226

S

Saarbrücken 313–314
Safety 18–20
Sagunto 243
St-Jean-Cap-Ferrat 285
St-Malo 308
St-Paul-de-Vence 285
St-Raphaël 259
St-Tropez 258–259
Sales taxes 18
Salzburg 411–412
San Gimignano 274
San Marino 267–268
San Remo 287–288
San Sebastián 319–320
Santa Margherita Ligure
  270
Santander 320
Santiago de Compostela
  351–352
Saumur 310
Scanrail pass 25
Scheveningen 228
Schwangau 179
Schwetzingen 186
Security 18–20
Segovia 239–240
Senior citizen discounts 15,
  24, 44
Sétubal 214
Seville (Sevilla) 354–356,
  355
Shops, opening hours 17
Šiauliai 389
Sicily 349
Siena 273–274
Sighisoara 203
Sigulda 391
Sintra 208
Skärgården 364
Sleeping cars 28
Slovak Republic 66–67

Smoking 20
Sofia (Sofija) 197–199, **198**
Solo travellers 19
Sorrento 348
Spain 67–71
Spello 165
Spoleto 165
Stavanger 153
Steam trains 413–414
Stockholm 361–364, **362**
Strasbourg 331
Straubing 182
Student discounts 15, 25,
  46
Stuttgart 186–188, **187**
Supplements 26
Sweden 71–72
Switzerland 72–74

T

Talavera de la Reina 245
Talgo 70
Tallinn 392–394, **393**
Tarascon 254
Tarragona 243
Tartu 391–392
Tavira 215
Tax refunds 18
Telephones 20
TGV 43
Thebes 114
Theft 18–20
Thessaloniki 115–116
Thivai *see* Thebes
Thomas Cook European
  Timetable 4, 21
Thuringian Forest 171
Tickets *see* Passes and
  tickets
Time zones 20
Tivoli 346
Toilets 20–21
Toledo 240
Toruń 129
Toulon 258
Toulouse 304–305
Tours (French city) 316–317
Trains, types 26–27
Trakai 388
Travellers' cheques 13
Trier 314
Troia Peninsula 214
Trujillo 246
Turkey 74–76

Turku 365
Tuy (Tui) 212

U

Ulm 334
United Kingdom 76–78
Uppsala 364
Utrecht 103

V

Valença do Minho 212
Valencia 242–243
Valencia de Alcantara 246
Vannes 309
VAT (Value Added Tax) 18
Venice (Venezia) 366–369,
  367
Ventimiglia 287
Verona 280–281
Versailles 301
Viana do Castelo 211–212
Vicenza 281–282
Vienna 370–374, **373**
Vigo 212
Vila Real de Santo António
  215
Villefranche-sur-Mer 285
Vilnius 386–388
Visas 17
Vitoria 320
Volendam 91
Volos 115
Volterra 274

W

Warsaw 381–384, **382**
Washing facilities, trains 28
Waterloo (Belgium) 134
WCs 20–21
Weimar 172–173
Wieliczka 380
Wien *see* Vienna
Wiesbaden 107
Women travellers 19
Würzburg 176

Y

Youth hostels 10–11
Youth passes 25

Z

Zandvoort 229
Zermatt 402
Zurich 398–399, **399**

READER SURVEY
Fill in this form and you can win a set of full-colour guidebooks!

If you enjoyed using this book – or if you didn't – please help us to improve future editions, by taking part in our reader survey. Every returned form will be acknowledged, and to show our appreciation for your help we will give you the chance to win a set of Thomas Cook illustrated guidebooks for your travel bookshelf. Just take a few minutes to complete and return this form to us.

When did you buy this book?

Where did you buy it? (Please give town/city and if possible name of retailer)

Did you/do you intend to travel in Europe by train this year?
☐ Have travelled ☐ Will travel this year ☐ Not this year
If so, which countries did you/do you intend to visit?

In which month did you/do you intend to travel?

For how long (approx.)?
Did you/will you travel on: ☐ An Inter-Rail pass? ☐ A Eurail pass?
☐ Other passes or ticket(s)? Please specify:

Did you/do you intend to use this book:
☐ For planning your trip? ☐ During the trip itself? ☐ Both?

Did you/do you intend to also purchase any of the following travel publications for your trip?
☐ Thomas Cook European Timetable
☐ Thomas Cook New Rail Map of Europe
☐ Thomas Cook European Rail Travellers' Phrasebook
☐ Other guidebooks/maps. Please specify:

Please rate the following features of On the Rails around Europe for their value to you
(Circle the 1 for "little or no use," 2 for "useful," 3 for "very useful"):

The themed itineraries on pages 79–83	1	2	3
The "Travel Essentials" section on pages 10–21	1	2	3
The "Travelling by Train" section on pages 22–29	1	2	3
The "Country by Country" section on pages 30–78	1	2	3
Information on rail routes and trains	1	2	3
The rail route diagrams	1	2	3
Information on towns and cities	1	2	3
The city maps	1	2	3

Please use this space to tell us about any features that in your opinion could be changed, improved, or added in future editions of the book, or any other comments you would like to make concerning the book:

Your age category:

☐ Under 26　　　　　　　☐ 26–50　　　　　　　☐ over 50

Your name: Mr/Mrs/Ms　　　(First name or initials)
(Last name)

Your full address (please include postal code or zip code):

Your daytime telephone number:

Please detach this page and send it to: The Project Editor, On the Rails around Europe, Thomas Cook Publishing, PO Box 227, Peterborough PE3 6SB, United Kingdom.

North American readers: Please mail replies to: E. Taylor, On the Rails around Europe, Passport Books, 4255 West Touhy Avenue, Lincolnwood (Chicago), Illinois 60646-1975, USA.

Over £200/$300* worth of guidebooks to be won!

*All surveys returned to us before the closing date of 31 October 1994 will be entered for a prize draw on that date. The senders of the first **five** replies drawn will each be invited to make their personal selection of any six books from the Thomas Cook Travellers* range of guidebooks, worth over £40/$75*, to be sent to them free of charge. With 24 cities and countries to choose from, this new, full colour series of guides covers the major tourist destinations of the world. Each book, retail price £6.99/$12.95*, offers 192 pages of sightseeing, background information, and travel tips.*

*North American readers please note: in the United States this range is published by Passport Books under the name ''Passport's Illustrated Guides from Thomas Cook''. North American winners will receive the US editions of their selected books.

Prizewinners will be notified as soon as possible after the closing date and asked to select from the list of titles. Offer is subject to availability of titles at 1 November 1994. A list of winners will be available on receipt of a stamped self-addressed envelope.

ORDER FORM

BRITISH AND EUROPEAN RAIL PASSES
(Effective Jan. 1, 1994)

EURAIL PASS (17 Countries)

☐ 15 Days $498   ☐ 21 Days $648
☐ 1 Month $798   ☐ 2 Months $1,098
☐ 3 Months $1,398

EURAIL FLEXIPASS – 1st Class

☐ 5 days in 2 Months $348
☐ 10 Days in 2 Months $560
☐ 15 Days in 2 Months $740

EURAIL SAVERPASS – 1st Class

☐ 15 Days $430   ☐ 21 Days $550
☐ 1 Month $678

Price is per person/3 people must travel together at all times. (Two people may travel between Oct 1st and March 31st)

EURAIL YOUTHPASS* – 2nd Class

☐ 15 Days $398   ☐ 1 Month $578
☐ 2 months $768

EURAIL YOUTH FLEXIPASS* – 2nd Class

☐ 5 Days in 2 Months $255
☐ 10 Days in 2 Months $398
☐ 15 Days in 2 Months $540

* Pass holder must be under age 26 on first day of use.

EURAIL DRIVE PASS

There is an excellent Rail/Drive program that combines a Eurail Pass with Hertz or Avis Rent-a-Car. Call us for a comprehensive brochure.

EUROPASS (5 Countries)
France/Germany/Italy/Switzerland/Spain

3 COUNTRIES EUROPASS

☐ 5 Days in 2 Months $280
☐ 6 Days in 2 Months $318
☐ 7 Days in 2 Months $356

4 COUNTRIES EUROPASS

☐ 8 Days in 2 Months $394
☐ 9 Days in 2 Months $432
☐ 10 Days in 2 Months $470

5 COUNTRIES EUROPASS

☐ 11 Days in 2 Months $508
☐ 12 Days in 2 Months $546
☐ 13 Days in 2 Months $584
☐ 14 Days in 2 Months $622
☐ 15 Days in 2 Months $660

Note: You must specify the countries when ordering and the countries must border each other, e.g. Spain/France/Italy.

EUROPASS
ASSOCIATE COUNTRIES

These countries may be added to any EuroPass for a flat charge per country. They expand the geographic scope of the pass, not the length.

☐ Austria $35   ☐ Portugal $22
☐ Belgium & Luxembourg $22

Youth rates – All EuroPasses are available for persons under age 26 at substantial discounts.

For Travelers from North America

CALL TOLL FREE
1-800-367-7984
(Charge to Visa, Discover or MasterCard)

Forsyth Travel Library, Inc.
9154 W. 57th, P. O. Box 2975
Shawnee Mission, KS 66201-1375

Forsyth Travel Library, Inc., is the leading agent in North America for the European and British Railroads and distributor of the famous Thomas Cook European Timetable. We are international rail travel specialists. Members: ASTA, Better Business Bureau of Kansas City, MO and International Map Trades Association. Free catalogs upon request listing all rail passes, timetables, accessories and maps. Official membership agency for American Youth Hostels/International Hostelling.

All prices shown are US Dollars – prices in effect March 1, 1994

BRITRAIL PASSES
Unlimited travel in England, Scotland & Wales

Validity Period	Adult		Senior (60+)		Youth (16–25)
	First	Standard	First	Standard	Standard
BRITRAIL PASS – Unlimited travel every day					
8 Days	☐ $299	☐ $219	☐ $279	☐ $199	☐ $179
15 Days	☐ $489	☐ $339	☐ $455	☐ $305	☐ $269
21 Days	☐ $615	☐ $425	☐ $555	☐ $379	☐ $339
1 Month	☐ $715	☐ $495	☐ $645	☐ $445	☐ $395
BRITRAIL FLEXIPASS – Travel any days within 1 Month					
4 Days/1 Month	☐ $249	☐ $189	☐ $229	☐ $169	☐ $155
8 Days/1 Month	☐ $389	☐ $269	☐ $350	☐ $245	☐ $219
15 Days/1 Month	☐ $575	☐ $395	☐ $520	☐ $355	☐ $309*

* Youth pass valid for 2 months

FREEDOM OF SCOTLAND TRAVEL PASS

☐ 8 Days $145 ☐ 15 Days $205
☐ 22 Days $259

FREEDOM OF SCOTLAND FLEXIPASS
☐ Any 8 Days of Travel in 15 Days $185

ENGLAND/WALES PASS
Any 4 Days ☐ $219 First
in 1 Month ☐ $149 Standard

BRITIRELAND PASS
– Includes round-trip ticket on Stena Line Ferry between Britain and Ireland. Includes Northern Ireland.

Validity	First	Standard
Any 5 Days in 1 Month	☐ $389	☐ $269
Any 10 Days in 1 Month	☐ $599	☐ $419

BRITFRANCE PASS
– Includes free one-way Hoverspeed crossing between Britain and France

Validity	First	Standard
Any 5 Days in 1 Month	☐ $359	☐ $259
Any 10 Days in 1 Month	☐ $539	☐ $399

BRITGERMAN PASS
– Does not include travel between countries

Validity	First class only
Any 5 Days in 1 Month	☐ $359
Any 10 Days in 1 Month	☐ $539

SEAT RESERVATIONS, GROUP RATES, CROSS-CHANNEL SERVICES, IRISH SEA SERVICES – call for rates.

LONDON EXTRA – Combines a BritRail pass good in S. E. England and a London Visitor Travel Card

Validity Period	Adult		Child	
	First	Standard	First	Standard
3 Days	☐ $109	☐ $85	☐ $35	☐ $26
4 Days	☐ $129	☐ $105	☐ $36	☐ $27
7 Days	☐ $189	☐ $155	☐ $46	☐ $37

LONDON SERVICES
LONDON VISITOR TRAVEL CARD
Unlimited Inner Zone on Underground and red buses

Duration	Adult	Child
3 Days	☐ $25	☐ $11
4 Days	☐ $32	☐ $13
7 Days	☐ $49	☐ $21

GATWICK EXPRESS
– Non-stop from Gatwick Airport to Victoria Station every 15 minutes. Takes only 30 minutes. Fastest way to London! Round trip – buy two one-ways.

☐ First Class $22 One-way
☐ Standard $15 One-way

SLEEPERS – We can confirm overnight sleepers on Anglo-Scottish and West Country routes. Accommodation supplement is $57 per person First Class and $48 per person Second Class.
CHILDREN'S RATES (5-15) are half fare for most passes. Call for rates.

EUROPEAN COUNTRY & AREA PASS\

AUSTRIA RABBIT CARD

| Any 4 Days in 10 Days | $153 | First |
| | $103 | Second |

BENELUX TOURRAIL PASS

| Any 5 Days in 1 Month | $205 | First |
| | $137 | Second |

CENTRAL EUROPE PASS ■
Travel in Germany, Poland, Czech Republic and Slovakia

| Any 8 days in 1 Month | $348 | First |

CZECH FLEXIPASS

| Any 5 Days in 15 | $69 | First |

EUROPEAN EAST PASS
Travel in Austria, Hungary, Poland, Czech Republic and Slovakia

| Any 5 Days in 15 | $185 | First |
| Any 10 Days in 1 Month | $299 | First |

FINNRAIL PASS

	First	Second
3 Days in 1 Month	$125	$85
5 Days in 1 Month	$169	$115
10 Days in 1 Month	$239	$159

FRANCE RAILPASS

	First	Second
3 Days in 1 Month	$180	$125
Addl Rail Days (6 max)	$ 39	$ 29

*France offers a comprehensive series of Rail 'n' Drive, Rail 'n' Fly * Fly Rail 'n' Drive passes. Ask for our free catalog.*

GERMAN RAIL PASS – Adult

Validity	First/Twin*	Second/Twin*
5 Days in 1 Month	$260/$234	$178/$160
10 Days in 1 Month	$410/$369	$286/$257
15 Days in 1 Month	$530/$477	$386/$331

* Twin: Price valid when 2 people traveling together.

GREEK RAILPASS

| Any 3 Days in 15 | $80 First Class |

HUNGARIAN RAILPASS

| Any 5 Days in 15 | $55 First Class |

ITALIAN RAILPASS
Please add a $10 admin. fee to the cost of each Italian pass/ non-refundable

	First	Second
8 Days	$226	$152
15 Days	$284	$190
21 Days	$330	$220
1 Month	$396	$264

ITALIAN FLE\

Any 4 Days in 9		
Any 8 Days in 21		
Any 12 Days in 30		

ITALIAN KILOMETRIC TICKE\
Up to 20 trips by 5 people in 60 days – limit 3000 km

| $264 First | $156 Second |

NETHERLANDS DOMINO PASS ■

	First	Second
3 Days in 1 Month	$81	$53
5 Days in 1 Month	$135	$88
10 Days in 1 Month	$243	$159

POLRAIL PASS
Unlimited travel in Poland (prices increase 5/29/94)

| 8 Days | $50 First | $35 Second |

PORTUGUESE RAILPASS

| Any 4 Days in 15 | $99 First |

PRAGUE EXCURSION PASS ■
From any Czech Republic border crossing to Prague and return First Class

| $49 Adult | $39 Youth | $25 Child |

SCANRAIL PASS

	First	Second
Any 4 Days in 15	$199	$159
Any 9 Days in 21	$339	$275
1 Month	$499	$399

Call for Youth and ScanRail 55+ Senior rates

SPAIN FLEXIPASS

	First	Second
Any 3 Days in 1 Month	$185	$145
Any 5 Days in 1 Month	$265	$225
Any 10 Days in 1 Month	$470	$345

SWISS PASS
Good on Swiss National Railroads, most private railroads, lake steamers, city transport, buses and aerial tramways. A complete system!

8 Days	$266	$186
15 Days	$312	$214
1 Month	$430	$296

SWISS FLEXIPASS

| Any 3 Days in 15 | $222 First |
| | $148 Second |

SWISS CARD
1 round trip within Switzerland from any airport or border crossing plus 50% reduction on all travel purchased for one month

| $118 First | $96 Second |

SHIPPING There is a $7.50 shipping charge for all orders. We ship by 2nd Day/AIR UPS. Rush service with overnight delivery is available at a charge of $25. ■ ADMINISTRATIVE FEE $10 for your total order (one pass or several) is assessed by the European Railroads. RAIL/DRIVE Programs are available for most countries. Call for rates and free brochures. POINT-TO-POINT TICKETS, SLEEPERS, RESERVATIONS, GROUP RATES (10 or more, 25 or more) – we can help you with all of these. Call for rates.